ST Public

GW01238030

Major UK HGV Fleets (inc Trailers)

2024

(5th edition)

Researched & Updated by: Jonathan Gallagher

Printed & Distributed by: ST Publications.
51 Kendal Street, Wigan, WN6 7DJ

Front Cover: WS Transport, Scania, 6 x 1154 PF73 KVB, photographed on the M6 at Knutsford (Jon Gallagher)

Rear Cover: Culina / Stobart, Scania's, PN24 DFP & DGO, H1154 & H1164 photographed at Appleton (Mark Woodgate)

Contents

Introduction

Welcome to the 5th Edition of this publication.

Once again there has been a mountain of changes to the fleets contained within this book, which will continue to be published twice annually and will include as many fleets as possible.

Apart from the Maritime fleet which is an official listing all the other fleets are produced by amalgamating many spotters sightings and so are unofficial.

Due to popular demand we have reverted back to listing the Culina fleet in fleet number order and then the vehicles without fleet numbers listed in year of registration order.

Acknowledgements

ST Publications would like to place on record our thanks to Lucy Robinson and all at Maritime, Felixstowe, Jonathan Gallagher, Jonathan Gwendella and Lucy-Emma Sames, also to the staff at GreenTrucks for giving permission to use some of the information contained on their marvellous website. For up to date information and chat see http://greentrucks.proboards.com/ where everyone is always happy to help.

ST Publications
51 Kendal Street
Wigan
WN6 7DJ
07760284494

Barry Jones
March 2024

Allelys

#	Reg	Make	Livery	#	Reg	Make	Livery
1	PO58 NCF	Daf	Allelys White	37	T900 AHH (22)	Man	Allelys HH
1	MX65 DPO	Daf	Allelys White	38	T444 AHH (66)	Man	Allelys HH
2	DE10 HZU	Daf	Allelys White	39	T222 AHH (65)	Mercedes	Allelys HH
3	YX16 NUA	Daf	Allelys White	40	T333 AHH (66)	Mercedes	Allelys HH
4	YX65 NVV	Daf	Allelys White	41	T500 AHH (02)	Daf	Allelys HH
6	PL64 ELJ	Daf	Allelys White	42	T888 AHH (69)	Man	Allelys HH
7	FE10 BWG	Daf	Allelys White	43	T700 AHH (71)	Man	Allelys HH
8	BV65 LXZ	Daf	Allelys White	44	T111 AHH (64)	Man	Allelys HH
10	GD65 OTX	Daf	Allelys White	45	T800 AHH (19)	Man	Allelys HH
11	VX20 YWM	Daf	Allelys White	46	T666 AHH (19)	Daf	Allelys HH
12	DG17 KKU	Daf	Allelys White	47	FJ64 VKZ	Daf	Allelys HH
13	FN68 HYB	Daf	Allelys White	48	T555 AHH (19)	Daf	Allelys HH
14	FN68 HYF	Daf	Allelys White	49	W948 RWP	Daf	Allelys HH
15	VX68 WNR	Daf	Allelys White		E575 FLD	Krupp	Crane Hire
16	VX72 ZBC	Daf	Allelys White		Y593 NJO	Franna	Crane Hire
17	PC06 DAF (64)	Daf	Allelys White		VA56 XHV	Liebherr	Crane Hire
19	VX19 YKJ	Daf	Allelys White		VF12 KRE	Liebherr	Crane Hire
20	AY18 VFL	Daf	Allelys White		LL10 OFE	Mercedes	Abnormal Load
21	FJ64 VNZ	Daf	Allelys White		CV11 EAC	Volkswagon	Abnormal Load
22	VX12 GVT	Daf	Allelys White		KV61 KUA	Mercedes	Abnormal Load
23	FG66 EDJ	Daf	Allelys White		HV62 KFE	Ford	Abnormal Load
24	NX64 TXP	Daf	Allelys White		LM62 ZYR	Mercedes	Abnormal Load
25	PL15 KLP	Daf	Allelys White		NK13 WZH	Ford	Abnormal Load
26	BM04 ZNZ (14)	Daf	Allelys White		VX14 XGG	Mercedes	Abnormal Load
27	VN64 FUW	Daf	Allelys White		DU15 GUF	Volkswagon	Crane Hire
28	DK64 UMY	Daf	Allelys White		BN17 CVB	Mercedes	Abnormal Load
29	YY16 CCN	Daf	Allelys White		EN17 EKC	Mercedes	Abnormal Load
30	DY16 TYC	Daf	Allelys White		WX67 YYL	Mercedes	Abnormal Load
31	YW14 DJO	Daf	Allelys White		KX19 TZL	Mercedes	Abnormal Load
32	YK15 BTM	Daf	Allelys White		MX11 BZV	Daf	Allelys White
33	FN14 XAZ	Daf	Allelys White		MF63 AOM	Daf	Allelys White
34	SV15 NNB	Daf	Allelys White		YX64 TVU	Daf	Allelys White
35	DA63 MHL	Daf	Allelys White		MX16 HGL	Daf	Allelys White
36	YY64 PXK	Daf	Allelys White		WU73 FHD	Man	Allelys HH

A.W. Jenkinson

Livery Codes

A&A	A & A Recycling			AWJ	AW Jenkinson			SYL	Sylvagen		
400 AWJ (12)	Scania	AWJ		PX68 KHF	Scania	AWJ		PV19 EHS	Scania	AWJ	
P100 AWJ (63)	Scania	AWJ		PX68 KHK	Scania	AWJ		PV19 EHT	Scania	SYL	
X554 SHH	Volvo	AWJ		PX68 ZHB	Scania	AWJ		PV19 EHW	Scania	AWJ	
EY59 OGP	Scania	AWJ		PX68 ZHE	Scania	AWJ		PV19 EHX	Scania	AWJ	
PK63 ZFN	Scania	White		PX68 ZHO	Scania	AWJ		PV19 EHY	Scania	AWJ	
MX64 GRK	Scania	AWJ		PX68 ZHV	Scania	AWJ		PV19 EHZ	Scania	AWJ	
PX15 ENF	Volvo	A&A		PY68 SSV	Scania	AWJ		PV19 EJA	Scania	AWJ	
SN15 L7H	Scania	Blue		PY68 SSZ	Scania	AWJ		PV19 EJC	Scania	AWJ	
PX65 JJU	Scania	AWJ		PY68 STX	Scania	AWJ		PV19 EJD	Scania	AWJ	
PX65 JJV	Scania	AWJ		PY68 STZ	Scania	AWJ		PV19 EJE	Scania	AWJ	
PX65 JNV	Scania	AWJ		PY68 SUA	Scania	AWJ		PV19 EJF	Scania	AWJ	
PX65 JPV	Scania	A&A		PY68 SUH	Scania	AWJ		PV19 EJO	Scania	AWJ	
PX66 ACO	Volvo	A&A		PY68 SUV	Scania	AWJ		PV19 EJU	Scania	AWJ	
PX66 AEP	Volvo	A&A		PY68 SVA	Scania	AWJ		PV19 EJX	Scania	AWJ	
PX17 JXK	Scania	AWJ		BM19 XLR	Scania	AWJ		PV19 EJY	Scania	AWJ	
PX18 JXA	Scania	A&A		PV19 EHM	Scania	AWJ		PV19 EKH	Scania	AWJ	
PX18 JXB	Scania	A&A		PV19 EHN	Scania	AWJ		PV19 EKL	Scania	AWJ	
PX68 KGK	Scania	AWJ		PV19 EHO	Scania	AWJ		PV19 EKM	Scania	AWJ	
PX68 KGO	Scania	AWJ		PV19 EHP	Scania	AWJ		PV19 EKN	Scania	AWJ	

Reg	Make	Fleet	Reg	Make	Fleet	Reg	Make	Fleet
PV19 EKO	Scania	AWJ	PX69 KYO	Scania	AWJ	PY69 KHX	Scania	AWJ
PV19 EKP	Scania	AWJ	PX69 KYP	Scania	AWJ	PY69 KHZ	Scania	AWJ
PV19 EKU	Scania	AWJ	PX69 KYR	Scania	AWJ	PY69 KJA	Scania	AWJ
PV19 EKZ	Scania	AWJ	PX69 KYS	Scania	AWJ	PY69 KJF	Scania	AWJ
PV19 ENC	Scania	AWJ	PX69 KYT	Scania	AWJ	PY69 KJJ	Scania	AWJ
PV19 ENF	Scania	AWJ	PX69 KYU	Scania	AWJ	PY69 KJK	Scania	AWJ
PV19 KRJ	Scania	AWJ	PX69 KYV	Scania	AWJ	PY69 KJN	Scania	AWJ
PV19 KSE	Scania	AWJ	PX69 KYW	Scania	AWJ	PY69 KJO	Scania	AWJ
PV19 KSJ	Scania	AWJ	PX69 KYY	Scania	AWJ	PY69 KJU	Scania	AWJ
PV19 KSN	Scania	AWJ	PX69 KYZ	Scania	AWJ	PY69 KKA	Scania	AWJ
PV19 KSX	Scania	AWJ	PX69 KZB	Scania	AWJ	PY69 KKB	Scania	AWJ
PV19 KSZ	Scania	AWJ	PX69 KZC	Scania	AWJ	PY69 KKD	Scania	AWJ
PV19 UTA	Scania	AWJ	PX69 KZD	Scania	AWJ	PY69 KKE	Scania	AWJ
PV19 UTE	Scania	AWJ	PX69 KZF	Scania	AWJ	PY69 KKG	Scania	AWJ
PV19 UTF	Scania	AWJ	PX69 KZG	Scania	AWJ	PY69 KKH	Scania	AWJ
PV19 UTG	Scania	AWJ	PX69 KZK	Scania	AWJ	PY69 KKJ	Scania	AWJ
PX19 KWH	Scania	AWJ	PX69 KZL	Scania	AWJ	PY69 KKL	Scania	AWJ
PX19 KWJ	Scania	AWJ	PX69 KZM	Scania	AWJ	PK20 HWO	Scania	AWJ
PX19 KWK	Scania	AWJ	PX69 KZN	Scania	AWJ	PK20 HWP	Scania	AWJ
PX19 KWL	Scania	AWJ	PX69 KZO	Scania	AWJ	PK20 HWW	Scania	AWJ
PX19 KWM	Scania	AWJ	PX69 KZP	Scania	AWJ	PX20 LTO	Scania	AWJ
PX19 KWN	Scania	AWJ	PX69 KZR	Scania	AWJ	PX20 LTT	Scania	AWJ
PX19 KWR	Scania	AWJ	PX69 KZS	Scania	AWJ	PX20 LTU	Scania	AWJ
PX19 KWU	Scania	AWJ	PX69 KZT	Scania	AWJ	PX20 LTY	Scania	AWJ
PX19 KWV	Scania	AWJ	PX69 KZV	Scania	AWJ	PX20 LTZ	Scania	AWJ
PX19 KWW	Scania	AWJ	PX69 KZW	Scania	AWJ	PX20 LUA	Scania	AWJ
PX19 KXM	Scania	A&A	PX69 KZY	Scania	AWJ	PX20 LUB	Scania	AWJ
PX19 KXN	Scania	A&A	PX69 KZZ	Scania	AWJ	PX20 LUD	Scania	AWJ
PX19 KXO	Scania	SYL	PX69 LAA	Scania	AWJ	PX20 LUE	Scania	AWJ
PX19 KXP	Scania	AWJ	PX69 LAO	Scania	AWJ	PX20 LUF	Scania	AWJ
PX19 KXR	Scania	AWJ	PX69 LBF	Scania	AWJ	PX20 LVH	Scania	AWJ
PX19 KXU	Scania	AWJ	PX69 LBG	Scania	AWJ	PX20 LVM	Scania	AWJ
PX19 KXV	Scania	AWJ	PX69 LBJ	Scania	AWJ	PX20 LVR	Scania	AWJ
PX19 KXW	Scania	AWJ	PX69 LBK	Scania	AWJ	PX20 LVT	Scania	AWJ
PX19 KYA	Scania	AWJ	PX69 LBN	Scania	AWJ	PX20 LVU	Scania	AWJ
PX19 KYC	Scania	AWJ	PX69 LBP	Scania	AWJ	PX20 LVV	Scania	AWJ
PX19 KYE	Scania	AWJ	PX69 LBU	Scania	AWJ	PX20 LVW	Scania	AWJ
PX19 KYH	Scania	AWJ	PX69 LBV	Scania	AWJ	PX20 LVY	Scania	AWJ
PX19 KYJ	Scania	AWJ	PY69 AOK	Scania	AWJ	PX20 LVZ	Scania	AWJ
PX19 KYN	Scania	AWJ	PY69 AOL	Scania	AWJ	PX20 LWF	Scania	AWJ
PX19 KYO	Scania	AWJ	PY69 AOM	Scania	AWJ	PX20 LWG	Scania	AWJ
PX19 KYP	Scania	AWJ	PY69 AON	Scania	AWJ	PX20 LWH	Scania	AWJ
PX19 KYS	Scania	AWJ	PY69 AOO	Scania	AWJ	PX20 LWJ	Scania	AWJ
PX19 KYT	Scania	AWJ	PY69 AOP	Scania	AWJ	PX20 LWK	Scania	AWJ
PX19 KYU	Scania	AWJ	PY69 AOR	Scania	AWJ	PX20 LWL	Scania	AWJ
PX19 KYZ	Scania	AWJ	PY69 AOS	Scania	AWJ	PO70 ZKR	Scania	AWJ
PX19 KZA	Scania	AWJ	PY69 AOT	Scania	AWJ	PO70 ZKV	Scania	AWJ
PX19 KZB	Scania	AWJ	PY69 AOU	Scania	AWJ	PO70 ZKX	Scania	AWJ
PX19 KZL	Scania	AWJ	PY69 AOV	Scania	AWJ	PO70 ZKZ	Scania	AWJ
PX19 KZN	Scania	AWJ	PY69 AOW	Scania	AWJ	PO70 ZLE	Scania	AWJ
PX19 KZP	Scania	AWJ	PY69 KHD	Scania	AWJ	PO70 ZLN	Scania	AWJ
PX19 KZR	Scania	AWJ	PY69 KHE	Scania	AWJ	PO70 ZMZ	Scania	AWJ
PX19 KZS	Scania	AWJ	PY69 KHH	Scania	AWJ	PY70 AYV	Volvo	AWJ
PX19 KZT	Scania	AWJ	PY69 KHK	Scania	AWJ	PY70 AYW	Volvo	AWJ
PX19 LBO	Scania	AWJ	PY69 KHL	Scania	AWJ	PY70 AYX	Volvo	AWJ
PE69 FSA	Scania	A&A	PY69 KHO	Scania	AWJ	PY70 AYZ	Volvo	AWJ
PE69 FSC	Scania	A&A	PY69 KHP	Scania	AWJ	PY70 AZC	Volvo	AWJ
PE69 FSD	Scania	A&A	PY69 KHT	Scania	AWJ	PY70 AZN	Volvo	AWJ
PX69 KVJ	Scania	AWJ	PY69 KHU	Scania	AWJ	PY70 AZT	Volvo	AWJ
PX69 KVL	Scania	AWJ	PY69 KHV	Scania	AWJ	PY70 AZV	Volvo	AWJ

Reg	Make	Op	Reg	Make	Op	Reg	Make	Op
PY70 AZW	Volvo	AWJ	PK21 OZM	Scania	AWJ	PF71 DZS	Scania	AWJ
PY70 AZX	Volvo	AWJ	PK21 OZO	Scania	AWJ	PF71 DZT	Scania	AWJ
PY70 AZZ	Volvo	AWJ	PK21 OZP	Scania	AWJ	PF71 DZU	Scania	AWJ
PY70 BAA	Volvo	AWJ	PK21 OZR	Scania	AWJ	PF71 DZV	Scania	AWJ
PY70 BAO	Volvo	AWJ	PK21 OZT	Scania	AWJ	PF71 DZW	Scania	AWJ
PY70 BAU	Volvo	AWJ	PK21 OZU	Scania	AWJ	PF71 DZX	Scania	AWJ
PY70 BBE	Volvo	AWJ	PK21 RFJ	Scania	AWJ	PF71 DZY	Scania	AWJ
PY70 BBF	Volvo	AWJ	PK21 RFL	Scania	AWJ	PJ71 MXX	Scania	AWJ
PY70 BBJ	Volvo	AWJ	PK21 RFN	Scania	AWJ	PJ71 MXY	Scania	AWJ
PY70 BBK	Volvo	AWJ	PK21 RFO	Scania	AWJ	PJ71 MXZ	Scania	AWJ
PY70 BBN	Volvo	AWJ	PK21 RFX	Scania	AWJ	PJ71 MYA	Scania	AWJ
PY70 GZC	Volvo	AWJ	PK21 RFZ	Scania	AWJ	PJ71 VCZ	Scania	AWJ
PY70 GZD	Volvo	AWJ	PK21 RGO	Scania	AWJ	PJ71 VDA	Scania	AWJ
PY70 GZE	Volvo	AWJ	PK21 RGU	Scania	AWJ	PJ71 VDC	Scania	AWJ
PY70 GZF	Volvo	AWJ	PK21 RGV	Scania	AWJ	PJ71 VDD	Scania	AWJ
PY70 GZG	Volvo	AWJ	PK21 RGX	Scania	AWJ	PJ71 VDL	Scania	AWJ
PY70 GZH	Volvo	AWJ	PK21 RGZ	Scania	AWJ	PJ71 VDM	Scania	AWJ
PY70 GZJ	Volvo	AWJ	PK21 RHA	Scania	AWJ	PJ71 VDO	Scania	AWJ
PY70 GZK	Volvo	AWJ	PK21 RHE	Scania	AWJ	PJ71 VDP	Scania	AWJ
PY70 GZL	Volvo	AWJ	PK21 RHF	Scania	AWJ	PJ71 VDR	Scania	AWJ
PY70 GZN	Volvo	AWJ	PK21 RHJ	Scania	AWJ	PJ71 VDT	Scania	AWJ
PY70 GZO	Volvo	AWJ	PK21 RHO	Scania	AWJ	PJ71 VDV	Scania	AWJ
PY70 GZP	Volvo	AWJ	PK21 RHU	Scania	AWJ	PJ71 VDX	Scania	AWJ
PY70 GZR	Volvo	AWJ	PK21 RHV	Scania	AWJ	PJ71 VDY	Scania	AWJ
PY70 GZV	Volvo	AWJ	PK21 RHX	Scania	AWJ	PJ71 VDZ	Scania	AWJ
PY70 GZX	Volvo	AWJ	PK21 RHZ	Scania	AWJ	PJ71 VEA	Scania	AWJ
PY70 GZZ	Volvo	AWJ	PK21 RJJ	Scania	AWJ	PJ71 VEB	Scania	AWJ
DX21 WNN	Volvo	A&A	PK21 RJO	Scania	AWJ	PJ71 VEF	Scania	AWJ
DX21 WNO	Volvo	A&A	PK21 RJU	Scania	AWJ	PJ71 VEH	Scania	AWJ
PJ21 YLT	Scania	AWJ	PK21 RJV	Scania	AWJ	PJ71 VFF	Scania	AWJ
PJ21 YLU	Scania	AWJ	PK21 RJZ	Scania	AWJ	PK71 FVE	Scania	AWJ
PJ21 YLV	Scania	AWJ	PK21 RKA	Scania	AWJ	PK71 FVF	Scania	AWJ
PJ21 YLW	Scania	AWJ	PK21 RKE	Scania	AWJ	PK71 FVG	Scania	A&A
PJ21 YLX	Scania	AWJ	PK21 RKF	Scania	AWJ	PN71 DSE	Scania	AWJ
PJ21 YLZ	Scania	AWJ	PN21 FFP	Scania	AWJ	PN71 DSO	Scania	AWJ
PJ21 YMA	Scania	AWJ	PN21 FFR	Scania	AWJ	PN71 DSU	Scania	AWJ
PJ21 YMC	Scania	AWJ	PN21 FLL	Scania	AWJ	PN71 DSV	Scania	AWJ
PJ21 YMD	Scania	AWJ	PN21 FLM	Scania	AWJ	PN71 DTF	Scania	AWJ
PJ21 YMH	Scania	AWJ	PN21 FLP	Scania	AWJ	PN71 DTO	Scania	AWJ
PJ21 YMK	Scania	AWJ	PN21 FLR	Scania	AWJ	PN71 DTU	Scania	AWJ
PJ21 YML	Scania	AWJ	PN21 FLV	Scania	AWJ	PN71 DTV	Scania	AWJ
PJ21 YMM	Scania	AWJ	PN21 FLW	Scania	AWJ	PN71 DTX	Scania	AWJ
PJ21 YMO	Scania	AWJ	PN21 FLX	Scania	AWJ	PN71 DTZ	Scania	AWJ
PJ21 YMP	Scania	AWJ	PN21 FLZ	Scania	AWJ	PN71 DUH	Scania	AWJ
PJ21 YMR	Scania	AWJ	PN21 FMD	Scania	AWJ	PN71 DUJ	Scania	AWJ
PJ21 YMT	Scania	AWJ	PN21 FMF	Scania	AWJ	PN71 DUU	Scania	AWJ
PJ21 YMU	Scania	AWJ	PN21 FMG	Scania	AWJ	PN71 DUV	Scania	AWJ
PJ21 YMV	Scania	AWJ	PN21 FMJ	Scania	AWJ	PN71 DUY	Scania	AWJ
PJ21 YMW	Scania	AWJ	PN21 FMK	Scania	AWJ	PN71 DVA	Scania	AWJ
PK21 OYW	Scania	AWJ	PN21 FML	Scania	AWJ	PN71 DVB	Scania	AWJ
PK21 OYX	Scania	AWJ	PN21 FMO	Scania	AWJ	PN71 DVC	Scania	AWJ
PK21 OYZ	Scania	AWJ	PN21 FMX	Scania	AWJ	PN71 DVF	Scania	AWJ
PK21 OZC	Scania	AWJ	PN21 FMZ	Scania	AWJ	PN71 DVJ	Scania	AWJ
PK21 OZD	Scania	AWJ	PN21 FNO	Scania	AWJ	PN71 DVL	Scania	AWJ
PK21 OZE	Scania	AWJ	PN21 FNP	Scania	AWJ	PN71 DVM	Scania	AWJ
PK21 OZF	Scania	AWJ	PN21 FNR	Scania	AWJ	PN71 DVR	Scania	AWJ
PK21 OZG	Scania	AWJ	PX21 WZL	Volvo	A&A	PN71 DVT	Scania	AWJ
PK21 OZH	Scania	AWJ	PX21 WZM	Volvo	A&A	PN71 DVU	Scania	AWJ
PK21 OZJ	Scania	AWJ	PE71 WJX	Scania	AWJ	PN71 DVV	Scania	AWJ
PK21 OZL	Scania	AWJ	PF71 DZR	Scania	AWJ	PN71 DVX	Scania	AWJ

Reg	Make	Fleet	Reg	Make	Fleet	Reg	Make	Fleet
PN71 DWA	Scania	AWJ	PN22 DZJ	Scania	AWJ	PJ72 OSF	Scania	AWJ
PJ22 GYX	Scania	AWJ	PN22 DZK	Scania	AWJ	PJ72 OSG	Scania	AWJ
PJ22 GYY	Scania	AWJ	PN22 DZL	Scania	AWJ	PJ72 UCA	Scania	AWJ
PJ22 GYZ	Scania	AWJ	PN22 EBO	Scania	AWJ	PJ72 UCB	Scania	AWJ
PJ22 GZA	Scania	AWJ	PN22 EBP	Scania	AWJ	PJ72 UCC	Scania	AWJ
PJ22 GZB	Scania	AWJ	PN22 EBU	Scania	AWJ	PJ72 UCD	Scania	AWJ
PJ22 GZC	Scania	AWJ	PN22 EBV	Scania	AWJ	PJ72 UCU	Scania	AWJ
PJ22 GZD	Scania	AWJ	PN22 EBX	Scania	AWJ	PJ72 UCV	Scania	AWJ
PJ22 GZE	Scania	AWJ	PN22 EBZ	Scania	AWJ	PN72 DYS	Scania	AWJ
PJ22 GZF	Scania	AWJ	PN22 ECA	Scania	AWJ	PN72 DYU	Scania	AWJ
PJ22 GZG	Scania	AWJ	PN22 ECE	Scania	AWJ	PN72 DYV	Scania	A&A
PJ22 GZH	Scania	AWJ	PN22 ECF	Scania	AWJ	PN72 DYX	Scania	AWJ
PJ22 GZK	Scania	AWJ	PN22 ECJ	Scania	AWJ	PN72 DYY	Scania	AWJ
PJ22 GZL	Scania	AWJ	PN22 ECT	Scania	AWJ	PN72 DZA	Scania	AWJ
PJ22 GZM	Scania	AWJ	PN22 ECV	Scania	AWJ	PN72 DZC	Scania	AWJ
PJ22 GZN	Scania	AWJ	PN22 ECW	Scania	AWJ	PN72 DZD	Scania	A&A
PJ22 GZO	Scania	AWJ	PN22 ECX	Scania	AWJ	PN72 DZE	Scania	AWJ
PJ22 GZP	Scania	AWJ	PN22 ECY	Scania	AWJ	PN72 DZH	Scania	AWJ
PJ22 GZR	Scania	AWJ	PN22 ECZ	Scania	AWJ	PN72 ECT	Scania	AWJ
PJ22 GZS	Scania	AWJ	PN22 EDC	Scania	AWJ	PN72 ECW	Scania	AWJ
PJ22 GZT	Scania	AWJ	PN22 EDF	Scania	AWJ	PN72 ECX	Scania	AWJ
PJ22 GZU	Scania	AWJ	PN22 EDJ	Scania	AWJ	PN72 ECY	Scania	AWJ
PJ22 GZW	Scania	AWJ	PN22 EDK	Scania	AWJ	PN72 EDC	Scania	AWJ
PJ22 GZX	Scania	AWJ	PN22 EDL	Scania	AWJ	PN72 EDF	Scania	AWJ
PJ22 GZY	Scania	AWJ	PN22 EDO	Scania	AWJ	PN72 EDJ	Scania	AWJ
PJ22 GZZ	Scania	AWJ	PN22 EDR	Scania	AWJ	PN72 EDL	Scania	AWJ
PJ22 HAA	Scania	AWJ	PJ72 FFX	Scania	AWJ	PN72 EDO	Scania	AWJ
PJ22 HAE	Scania	AWJ	PJ72 FFY	Scania	AWJ	PN72 EDP	Scania	AWJ
PJ22 HAO	Scania	AWJ	PJ72 FFZ	Scania	AWJ	PN72 EDU	Scania	AWJ
PJ22 HAU	Scania	AWJ	PJ72 FGA	Scania	AWJ	PN72 EDX	Scania	AWJ
PJ22 HAX	Scania	AWJ	PJ72 FGC	Scania	AWJ	PN72 EEA	Scania	AWJ
PJ22 HBA	Scania	AWJ	PJ72 FGD	Scania	AWJ	PN72 EEB	Scania	AWJ
PJ22 HBB	Scania	AWJ	PJ72 FGE	Scania	AWJ	PN72 EEF	Scania	AWJ
PJ22 HBC	Scania	AWJ	PJ72 FGF	Scania	AWJ	PN72 EEG	Scania	AWJ
PJ22 HBD	Scania	AWJ	PJ72 FGG	Scania	AWJ	PN72 EEH	Scania	AWJ
PJ22 HBH	Scania	AWJ	PJ72 FGK	Scania	AWJ	PN72 EEJ	Scania	AWJ
PJ22 HBK	Scania	AWJ	PJ72 FGM	Scania	AWJ	PN72 EEM	Scania	AWJ
PJ22 HBL	Scania	AWJ	PJ72 FGN	Scania	AWJ	PN72 EEO	Scania	AWJ
PJ22 HBN	Scania	AWJ	PJ72 FGV	Scania	AWJ	PN72 EER	Scania	AWJ
PJ22 HBO	Scania	AWJ	PJ72 FGX	Scania	AWJ	PN72 EES	Scania	AWJ
PJ22 HBP	Scania	AWJ	PJ72 FGZ	Scania	AWJ	PN72 EET	Scania	AWJ
PJ22 HBX	Scania	AWJ	PJ72 FHA	Scania	AWJ	PN72 EEV	Scania	AWJ
PJ22 HBY	Scania	AWJ	PJ72 FHB	Scania	AWJ	PN72 EEX	Scania	AWJ
PJ22 HCC	Scania	AWJ	PJ72 FHC	Scania	AWJ	PN72 EEY	Scania	AWJ
PJ22 HCD	Scania	AWJ	PJ72 FHD	Scania	AWJ	PN72 FHG	Scania	AWJ
PJ22 HCE	Scania	AWJ	PJ72 FHE	Scania	AWJ	PX72 VEA	Volvo	AWJ
PJ22 HCH	Scania	AWJ	PJ72 FHF	Scania	AWJ	PX72 VEB	Volvo	AWJ
PN22 DXA	Scania	AWJ	PJ72 FHG	Scania	AWJ	PX72 VEF	Volvo	AWJ
PN22 DXB	Scania	AWJ	PJ72 OOG	Scania	AWJ	PX72 VEH	Volvo	AWJ
PN22 DXC	Scania	AWJ	PJ72 OOH	Scania	AWJ	PX72 VEK	Volvo	AWJ
PN22 DXD	Scania	AWJ	PJ72 OOU	Scania	AWJ	PX72 VEL	Volvo	AWJ
PN22 DXE	Scania	AWJ	PJ72 OPA	Scania	AWJ	PX72 VEM	Volvo	AWJ
PN22 DXH	Scania	AWJ	PJ72 OPB	Scania	AWJ	PX72 VEO	Volvo	AWJ
PN22 DXJ	Scania	AWJ	PJ72 OPC	Scania	AWJ	PF23 EKM	Scania	AWJ
PN22 DXK	Scania	AWJ	PJ72 OPD	Scania	AWJ	PF23 EKN	Scania	AWJ
PN22 DXL	Scania	AWJ	PJ72 OPE	Scania	AWJ	PF23 EKR	Scania	AWJ
PN22 DZE	Scania	AWJ	PJ72 OSB	Scania	AWJ	PF23 EKT	Scania	AWJ
PN22 DZF	Scania	AWJ	PJ72 OSC	Scania	AWJ	PF23 EKU	Scania	AWJ
PN22 DZG	Scania	AWJ	PJ72 OSD	Scania	AWJ	PF23 EKX	Scania	AWJ
PN22 DZH	Scania	AWJ	PJ72 OSE	Scania	AWJ	PF23 EKY	Scania	AWJ

A.W. Jenkinson (cont)

Reg	Make	Fleet	Reg	Make	Fleet	Reg	Make	Fleet
PF23 ELU	Scania	AWJ	PK23 LRY	Scania	AWJ	PN23 EXS	Scania	AWJ
PF23 ELV	Scania	AWJ	PK23 LRZ	Scania	AWJ	PN23 EXW	Scania	AWJ
PF23 ELW	Scania	AWJ	PK23 LSD	Scania	AWJ	PN23 EXX	Scania	AWJ
PF23 ELX	Scania	AWJ	PK23 LSE	Scania	AWJ	PN23 EXZ	Scania	AWJ
PF23 EMJ	Scania	AWJ	PK23 LSJ	Scania	AWJ	PN23 EYC	Scania	AWJ
PF23 EMK	Scania	AWJ	PK23 LSL	Scania	AWJ	PF73 CEU	Scania	AWJ
PF23 EMV	Scania	AWJ	PK23 LSN	Scania	AWJ	PF73 CEV	Scania	AWJ
PF23 EMX	Scania	AWJ	PK23 LSO	Scania	AWJ	PF73 CEX	Scania	AWJ
PF23 ENC	Scania	AWJ	PK23 LSU	Scania	AWJ	PF73 CFA	Scania	AWJ
PF23 ENH	Scania	AWJ	PK23 LSV	Scania	AWJ	PF73 CFD	Scania	AWJ
PF23 ENJ	Scania	AWJ	PK23 LSX	Scania	AWJ	PF73 CFE	Scania	AWJ
PF23 ENL	Scania	AWJ	PK23 LSY	Scania	AWJ	PF73 CFG	Scania	AWJ
PF23 ENM	Scania	AWJ	PK23 LSZ	Scania	AWJ	PF73 CFJ	Scania	AWJ
PF23 ENO	Scania	AWJ	PK23 LTA	Scania	AWJ	PF73 CFK	Scania	AWJ
PF23 ENP	Scania	AWJ	PK23 LTE	Scania	AWJ	PF73 CFL	Scania	AWJ
PF23 ENR	Scania	AWJ	PK23 LTF	Scania	AWJ	PF73 CFN	Scania	AWJ
PF23 ENV	Scania	AWJ	PK23 LTJ	Scania	AWJ	PF73 CFO	Scania	AWJ
PF23 ENW	Scania	AWJ	PK23 LTN	Scania	AWJ	PF73 CFU	Scania	AWJ
PF23 ENX	Scania	AWJ	PK23 LTO	Scania	AWJ	PF73 CFV	Scania	AWJ
PF23 ENY	Scania	AWJ	PK23 LTT	Scania	AWJ	PF73 KWL	Scania	AWJ
PF23 EOB	Scania	AWJ	PK23 LTU	Scania	AWJ	PF73 KWM	Scania	AWJ
PF23 EOC	Scania	AWJ	PK23 LTV	Scania	AWJ	PF73 KWP	Scania	AWJ
PF23 EOD	Scania	AWJ	PK23 LTX	Scania	AWJ	PF73 KWR	Scania	AWJ
PF23 EOE	Scania	AWJ	PK23 LTY	Scania	AWJ	PF73 KWS	Scania	AWJ
PF23 EOH	Scania	AWJ	PK23 LUA	Scania	AWJ	PF73 KWT	Scania	AWJ
PF23 EOJ	Scania	AWJ	PK23 LUD	Scania	AWJ	PF73 KWU	Scania	AWJ
PF23 EOK	Scania	AWJ	PK23 LUE	Scania	AWJ	PF73 KWW	Scania	AWJ
PF23 EOO	Scania	AWJ	PK23 LUF	Scania	AWJ	PF73 KWX	Scania	AWJ
PF23 EOT	Scania	AWJ	PK23 LUH	Scania	AWJ	PF73 KWZ	Scania	AWJ
PF23 EOU	Scania	AWJ	PK23 LUJ	Scania	AWJ	PF73 LAE	Scania	AWJ
PF23 EOW	Scania	AWJ	PK23 LUL	Scania	AWJ	PF73 LAO	Scania	AWJ
PF23 EPE	Scania	AWJ	PK23 LUO	Scania	AWJ	PF73 LBA	Scania	AWJ
PF23 EPJ	Scania	AWJ	PK23 LUP	Scania	AWJ	PF73 LBE	Scania	AWJ
PF23 EPL	Scania	AWJ	PK23 LUR	Scania	AWJ	PF73 LBG	Scania	AWJ
PF23 EPP	Scania	AWJ	PK23 LUT	Scania	AWJ	PF73 LBJ	Scania	AWJ
PF23 EPU	Scania	AWJ	PK23 LUY	Scania	AWJ	PF73 LBK	Scania	AWJ
PF23 EPZ	Scania	AWJ	PK23 LVA	Scania	AWJ	PF73 LBL	Scania	AWJ
PF23 VNO	Scania	AWJ	PK23 LVB	Scania	AWJ	PF73 LBN	Scania	AWJ
PF23 VNP	Scania	AWJ	PK23 LVC	Scania	AWJ	PF73 LBO	Scania	AWJ
PF23 VNR	Scania	AWJ	PK23 LVD	Scania	AWJ	PF73 LBP	Scania	AWJ
PF23 VNS	Scania	AWJ	PK23 LVE	Scania	AWJ	PF73 LCA	Scania	AWJ
PF23 VNT	Scania	AWJ	PK23 LVF	Scania	AWJ	PF73 LCC	Scania	AWJ
PF23 VNU	Scania	AWJ	PK23 LVG	Scania	AWJ	PF73 LCL	Scania	AWJ
PF23 VNV	Scania	AWJ	PK23 LVH	Scania	AWJ	PF73 LCM	Scania	AWJ
PF23 VNX	Scania	AWJ	PK23 LVJ	Scania	AWJ	PF73 LCT	Scania	AWJ
PJ23 NBZ	Scania	AWJ	PK23 LVM	Scania	AWJ	PF73 LCU	Scania	AWJ
PJ23 NCC	Scania	A&A	PL23 JVO	Scania	AWJ	PF73 RHV	Scania	AWJ
PK23 EBC	Scania	AWJ	PL23 JVP	Scania	AWJ	PF73 RHX	Scania	AWJ
PK23 EBD	Scania	AWJ	PL23 JVR	Scania	AWJ	PF73 RHY	Scania	AWJ
PK23 EBF	Scania	AWJ	PL23 JVT	Scania	AWJ	PF73 RHZ	Scania	AWJ
PK23 EBG	Scania	AWJ	PL23 JVU	Scania	AWJ	PF73 RJJ	Scania	AWJ
PK23 EBJ	Scania	AWJ	PL23 JVV	Scania	AWJ	PF73 RJU	Scania	AWJ
PK23 EBL	Scania	AWJ	PL23 JVW	Scania	AWJ	PF73 RJZ	Scania	AWJ
PK23 EBM	Scania	AWJ	PL23 JVX	Scania	AWJ	PF73 RKA	Scania	AWJ
PK23 EBN	Scania	AWJ	PN23 EXB	Scania	AWJ	PF73 RKE	Scania	AWJ
PK23 EBO	Scania	AWJ	PN23 EXC	Scania	AWJ	PF73 RKK	Scania	AWJ
PK23 EBX	Scania	AWJ	PN23 EXH	Scania	AWJ	PF73 RKO	Scania	AWJ
PK23 EBZ	Scania	AWJ	PN23 EXJ	Scania	AWJ	PF73 RKU	Scania	AWJ
PK23 ECF	Scania	AWJ	PN23 EXK	Scania	AWJ	PF73 RLO	Scania	AWJ
PK23 ECJ	Scania	AWJ	PN23 EXO	Scania	AWJ	PF73 RLY	Scania	AWJ

A.W. Jenkinson (cont)

Reg	Make	Op		Reg	Make	Op
PF73 RMU	Scania	AWJ		PJ73 XTC	Scania	AWJ
PF73 RMV	Scania	AWJ		PJ73 XTD	Scania	AWJ
PF73 RMX	Scania	AWJ		PJ73 XTE	Scania	AWJ
PF73 RMY	Scania	AWJ		PJ73 XTF	Scania	AWJ
PF73 RMZ	Scania	AWJ		PJ73 XTG	Scania	AWJ
PF73 RNA	Scania	AWJ		PJ73 XTH	Scania	AWJ
PJ73 JUH	Scania	AWJ		PJ73 XTL	Scania	AWJ
PJ73 JUK	Scania	AWJ		PJ73 XTM	Scania	AWJ
PJ73 JUO	Scania	AWJ		PJ73 XTN	Scania	AWJ
PJ73 JUT	Scania	AWJ		PJ73 XTO	Scania	AWJ
PJ73 JUU	Scania	AWJ		PJ73 XTP	Scania	AWJ
PJ73 JUW	Scania	AWJ		PJ73 XTR	Scania	AWJ
PJ73 JUX	Scania	AWJ		PJ73 XTS	Scania	AWJ
PJ73 JVA	Scania	AWJ		PJ73 XTT	Scania	AWJ
PJ73 JVC	Scania	AWJ		PJ73 XTU	Scania	AWJ
PJ73 JVD	Scania	AWJ		PJ73 XTW	Scania	AWJ
PJ73 JVE	Scania	AWJ		PJ73 XTY	Scania	AWJ
PJ73 JVF	Scania	AWJ		PJ73 XUA	Scania	AWJ
PJ73 JVG	Scania	AWJ		PL73 HFW	Scania	AWJ
PJ73 JVH	Scania	AWJ		PL73 YBP	Scania	AWJ
PJ73 JVK	Scania	AWJ		PN73 EOX	Scania	A&A
PJ73 JVL	Scania	AWJ		PN73 EWT	Scania	AWJ
PJ73 JVM	Scania	AWJ		PN73 EWU	Scania	AWJ
PJ73 JVN	Scania	AWJ		PN73 EWV	Scania	AWJ
PJ73 JVO	Scania	AWJ		PN73 EWW	Scania	AWJ
PJ73 JVP	Scania	AWJ		PN73 EWX	Scania	AWJ
PJ73 JVR	Scania	SYL		PN73 EXA	Scania	AWJ
PJ73 JVT	Scania	AWJ		PN73 EXB	Scania	AWJ
PJ73 JVU	Scania	AWJ		PN73 EXC	Scania	AWJ
PJ73 JVW	Scania	AWJ		PN73 EXD	Scania	AWJ
PJ73 JVX	Scania	AWJ		PN73 EXE	Scania	AWJ
PJ73 JVY	Scania	AWJ		PN73 EXG	Scania	AWJ
PJ73 JVZ	Scania	AWJ		PN73 EXK	Scania	AWJ
PJ73 JWA	Scania	AWJ		PN73 EXL	Scania	AWJ
PJ73 TJU	Scania	AWJ		PN73 EXM	Scania	AWJ
PJ73 TJV	Scania	AWJ		PN73 EXO	Scania	AWJ
PJ73 TKD	Scania	AWJ		PN73 EXP	Scania	AWJ
PJ73 TKO	Scania	AWJ		PX73 VJN	Volvo	AWJ
PJ73 TKT	Scania	AWJ		PX73 VJO	Volvo	AWJ
PJ73 TKU	Scania	AWJ		PX73 VJP	Volvo	AWJ
PJ73 TKX	Scania	AWJ		PX73 VJU	Volvo	AWJ
PJ73 TKZ	Scania	AWJ		PX73 VJV	Volvo	AWJ
PJ73 TLF	Scania	AWJ		PX73 VJY	Volvo	AWJ
PJ73 TLK	Scania	AWJ		PX73 VJZ	Volvo	AWJ
PJ73 TLN	Scania	AWJ		PX73 VKA	Volvo	AWJ
PJ73 TLO	Scania	AWJ		PX73 VKB	Volvo	AWJ
PJ73 XSO	Scania	AWJ		PX73 VKC	Volvo	AWJ
PJ73 XSP	Scania	AWJ		PX73 VKD	Volvo	AWJ
PJ73 XSR	Scania	AWJ		PX73 VKE	Volvo	AWJ
PJ73 XST	Scania	AWJ		PX73 VKF	Volvo	AWJ
PJ73 XSU	Scania	AWJ		PX73 VKG	Volvo	AWJ
PJ73 XSV	Scania	AWJ		PX73 VKH	Volvo	AWJ
PJ73 XSW	Scania	AWJ		PX73 VKJ	Volvo	AWJ
PJ73 XSX	Scania	AWJ		PX73 VKK	Volvo	AWJ
PJ73 XSY	Scania	AWJ		PX73 VKL	Volvo	AWJ
PJ73 XSZ	Scania	AWJ		PX73 VKM	Volvo	AWJ
PJ73 XTA	Scania	AWJ		PX73 VKN		

BM Transport

Reg	Make	Reg	Make	Reg	Make	Reg	Make
KCZ 543 (19)	Volvo	182 MN 313	Scania	241 MN 98	Scania	V55 BMT (22)	Volvo
MXZ 3696 (18)	Volvo	191 MN 356	Scania	F10 RHL	Volvo	V60 BMT (22)	Volvo
MXZ 3697 (18)	Volvo	191 MN 357	Scania	J300 BMT (22)	Volvo	V66 BMT (22)	Volvo
MXZ 3698 (18)	Volvo	191 MN 360	Scania	J500 BMT (22)	Volvo	V88 BMT (65)	Scania
MXZ 4524 (18)	Volvo	191 MN 363	Scania	J600 BMT (69)	Scania	V100 BMT (21)	Volvo
MXZ 4525 (18)	Volvo	191 MN 364	Scania	J800 BMT (69)	Scania	V200 BMT (71)	Volvo
MXZ 4706 (18)	Volvo	191 MN 743	Scania	J900 BMT (68)	Scania	V222 BMT (71)	Volvo
OXZ 3255 (20)	Renault	191 MN 837	Scania	K200 BMT (68)	Scania	V300 BMT (71)	Volvo
OXZ 3256 (20)	Renault	191 MN 841	Volvo	K300 BMT (19)	Scania	V333 BMT (71)	Volvo
OXZ 3259 (20)	Renault	192 MN 331	Scania	K400 BMT (20)	Scania	V400 BMT (22)	Volvo
OXZ 3261 (20)	Renault	192 MN 332	Scania	K500 BMT (20)	Scania	V444 BMT (71)	Volvo
OXZ 3304 (20)	Renault	192 MN 333	Scania	K600 BMT (20)	Scania	V500 BMT (71)	Volvo
OXZ 5748 (20)	Scania	201 MN 471	Scania	K700 BMT (20)	Scania	V555 BMT (22)	Volvo
OXZ 5749 (20)	Scania	201 MN 472	Scania	K800 BMT (20)	Scania	V600 BMT (22)	Volvo
TXZ 2504 (72)	Scania	211 D 4348	Scania	K900 BMT (69)	Scania	V666 BMT (22)	Volvo
03 MN 2780	Volvo	211 MN 617	Iveco	L100 BMT (72)	Renault	V700 BMT (71)	Volvo
03 MH 8981	Scania	211 MN 94	Scania	L300 BMT (72)	Iveco	V777 BMT (71)	Volvo
05 MN 1651	Volvo	211 MN 949	Scania	L400 BMT (72)	Iveco	V888 BMT (72)	Scania
05 DL 343	Volvo	211 MN 950	Scania	L500 BMT (72)	Iveco	V900 BMT (71)	Volvo
05 MN 6386	Scania	211 MN 951	Scania	L600 BMT (72)	Renault	V999 BMT (71)	Volvo
08 MH 8805	Scania	211 MN 952	Scania	M300 BMT (70)	Scania	YN13 JPU	Volvo
08 MN 6709	Volvo	221 MN 671	Volvo	M400 BMT (70)	Scania	YN13 JRV	Volvo
09 MN 431	Scania	221 MN 800	Scania	M555 BMT (70)	Scania	GF63 HBA	Volvo
131 MN 1317	Scania	222 MN 388	Scania	M700 BMT (70)	Scania	GJ63 UOF	Volvo
132 MN 1008	Scania	222 MN 289	Scania	M777 BMT (20)	Scania	GK63 DGE	Volvo
132 MN 1029	Volvo	222 MN 390	Scania	M999 BMT (20)	Scania	KR63 YVX	Volvo
132 MN 1030	Volvo	222 MN 391	Scania	R15 BMT (23)	Renault	KR63 YWW	Volvo
132 MN 1034	Volvo	222 MN 392	Scania	R23 BMT (23)	Renault	KR63 YXN	Volvo
132 MN 1036	Volvo	222 MN 397	Scania	R24 BMT (23)	Renault	KS63 VLV	Volvo
132 MN 225	Volvo	222 MN 398	Scania	R29 BMT (23)	Renault	DN15 NLE	Volvo
141 MN 1946	Volvo	222 MN 399	Scania	R200 BMT (22)	Renault	DN15 NLF	Volvo
141 MN 1952	Volvo	222 MN 400	Scania	R222 BMT (23)	Renault	TH15 BMT (22)	Volvo
142 CN 470	Scania	222 MN 66	Scania	R300 BMT (22)	Renault	KY65 OLH	Volvo
142 MN 266	Volvo	231 MN 127	Iveco	R400 BMT (22)	Renault	KY65 OLJ	Volvo
142 MN 267	Volvo	231 MN 128	Iveco	R500 BMT (22)	Renault	KY65 OLK	Volvo
142 MN 964	Volvo	231 MN 129	Iveco	R600 BMT (22)	Renault	KY65 OLM	Volvo
142 MN 970	Volvo	231 MN 727	Renault	R700 BMT (22)	Renault	KY65 OLN	Volvo
151 MH 2529	Scania	231 MN 736	Scania	S19 BMT (72)	Scania	KY65 OML	Volvo
152 MN 270	Volvo	231 MN 737	Scania	S26 BMT (69)	Scania	KY65 OMM	Volvo
152 MN 271	Volvo	231 MN 739	Scania	S70 BMT (71)	Scania	KU65 OMO	Volvo
152 MN 408	Volvo	231 MN 770	Scania	S77 BMT (21)	Scania	KY65 OMP	Volvo
152 MN 485	Volvo	231 MN 855	Volvo	S90 BMT (71)	Scania	KY65 OMR	Volvo
161 G 4739	Scania	231 MN 856	Volvo	S100 BMT (21)	Scania	BW66 EHO	Iveco
162 MN 953	Iveco	231 MN 872	Renault	S222 BMT (71)	Scania	BW66 EHT	Iveco
162 MN 954	Iveco	231 MN 874	Renault	S300 BMT (21)	Scania	KU68 BZA	Volvo
172 MN 26	Volvo	231 MN 915	Scania	S321 BMT (19)	Scania	KU68 BZB	Volvo
181 MN 1009	Iveco	231 MN 916	Scania	S333 BMT (21)	Scania	KU68 BZC	Volvo
181 MN 816	Volvo	231 MN 917	Scania	S400 BMT (21)	Scania	KU68 BZD	Volvo
181 MN 817	Volvo	232 MN 315	Volvo	S444 BMT (21)	Scania	KU68 BZE	Volvo
181 MN 818	Volvo	232 MN 316	Volvo	S500 BMT (21)	Scania	KU68 BZF	Volvo
181 MN 858	Volvo	232 MN 317	Volvo	S600 BMT (21)	Scania	KU69 YCD	Volvo
181 MN 859	Volvo	232 MN 318	Volvo	S666 BMT (19)	Scania	KU60 YCF	Volvo
181 MN 880	Volvo	232 MN 325	Scania	S700 BMT (21)	Scania	KU69 YCG	Volvo
181 MN 881	Volvo	232 MN 326	Scania	S777 BMT (21)	Scania	KU69 YCH	Volvo
181 MN 899	Volvo	232 MN 327	Scania	S800 BMT (21)	Scania	KU69 YSB	Volvo
181 MN 900	Volvo	232 MN 36	Scania	S900 BMT (71)	Scania	KU69 YSC	Volvo
181 MN 901	Volvo	232 MN 37	Scania	T100 BMT (52)	Scania	KU69 YSD	Volvo
181 MN 902	Volvo	232 MN 38	Scania	T400 BMT (21)	Volvo	KU69 YSE	Volvo
182 MN 312	Scania	241 MN 97	Scania	V13 BMT (23)	Volvo		

Brian Yeardley

Registration	Make	Livery	Name	Allocation
1948 BV (68)	Renault	02 CargoBY	Star of the Stage	Featherstone
B15 BYC (15)	Mercedes	Brian Yeardley	Star Appeal	Featherstone
E6 BYC (64)	Volvo	Brian Yeardley	No Name	Featherstone
H17 BYC (13)	Volvo	Brian Yeardley	Sky Lantern	Featherstone
H19 BYC (13)	Volvo	Brian Yeardley	Estimate	Featherstone
L66 BYC (14)	Mercedes	CargoBY	Farhh	Featherstone
M16 BYC (13)	Scania	Brian Yeardley	Ruler of the World	Featherstone
M18 BYC (16)	Volvo	Brian Yeardley	Night Music	Featherstone
R12 BYC (67)	Volvo	Brian Yeardley	Manic Monday	Featherstone
S10 BYC (16)	Volvo	Stokholm BY	No Name	Featherstone
T26 BYC (16)	Mercedes	Brian Yeardley	Rhythm of Sound	Featherstone
V18 BYC (18)	Scania	Brian Yeardley	Swedish Eagle	Featherstone
Y40 BYC (65)	Scania	Brian Yeardley	Gothenburg	Featherstone
VL07 HJJ	Renault	Brian Yeardley	No Name	Romania
CA11 BYC (67)	Volvo	Brian Yeardley		Featherstone
HE11 BYC (16)	Scania	Brian Yeardley	Arrogate	Featherstone
GF63 XDE	Daf	Brian Yeardley	No Name	Featherstone
HT14 CBF	Daf	Brian Yeardley	No Name	Featherstone
HT14 DAO	Daf	Brian Yeardley	No Name	Featherstone
YJ14 MXB	Daf	Brian Yeardley	Leading Light	Featherstone
BC15 BYC (15)	Volvo	Brian Yeardley	Gleneagles	Featherstone
DC65 BYC (65)	Mercedes	Brian Yeardley	Shared Belief	Featherstone
EC65 BYC (65)	Mercedes	Brian Yeardley	Golden Horn	Featherstone
FC65 BYC (65)	Mercedes	Brian Yeardley	Solow	Featherstone
AB16 BYC (18)	Scania	Brian Yeardley	Perfectly in Tune	Featherstone
MX66 FGK	Daf	Brian Yeardley	No Name	Featherstone
AC67 BYC (67)	Daf	Brian Yeardley	Oriental Fox	Featherstone
BC67 BYC (67)	Daf	Brian Yeardley	Ulysses	Featherstone
CC67 BYC (67)	Daf	Brian Yeardley	Churchill	Featherstone
GN67 UMU	Daf	Brian Yeardley	No Name	Featherstone
DC18 BYC (18)	Daf	Brian Yeardley	Hit the Beat	Featherstone
FC68 BYC (68)	Daf	Brian Yeardley	Tokyo Joe	Featherstone
GC68 BYC (68)	Daf	Brian Yeardley	Hillbilly Rock	Featherstone
HC68 BYC (68)	Daf	Brian Yeardley	Mr Bojangles	Featherstone
JC68 BYC (19)	Daf	Brian Yeardley	Uptown Funk	Featherstone
KC68 BYC (68)	Daf	Brian Yeardley	That's Entertainment	Featherstone
KU68 GUG	Scania	Brian Yeardley	No Name	Featherstone
MC68 BYC (68)	Daf	Brian Yeardley	Abbey Road	Featherstone
NC68 BYC (68)	Daf	Brian Yeardley	Hotel California	Featherstone
OC68 BYC (68)	Daf	Brian Yeardley	London Calling	Featherstone
AC19 BYC (19)	Daf	Brian Yeardley	One More Night	Featherstone
BC19 BYC (19)	Daf	Brian Yeardley	Radio Ga Ga	Featherstone
CC19 BYC (19)	Daf	Brian Yeardley	Hammer to Fall	Featherstone
EC19 BYC (19)	Daf	Brian Yeardley	We Will Rock You	Featherstone
FC19 BYC (69)	Daf	Brian Yeardley	Against all Odds	Featherstone
GC19 BYC (19)	Daf	Brian Yeardley	Invisible Touch	Featherstone
GF19 LYW	Volvo	Brian Yeardley	Kingman	Featherstone
HC69 BYC (69)	Daf	Brian Yeardley	Bring the Noise	Featherstone
JC69 BYC (69)	Daf	Brian Yeardley	Slave to the Rhythm	Featherstone
KC69 BYC (69)	Daf	Brian Yeardley	Night Moves	Featherstone
LC69 BYC (69)	Daf	White	No Name	Featherstone
MC69 BYC (69)	Daf	Brian Yeardley	Moves like Jagger	Featherstone
BL23 NKE	Daf	Brian Yeardley		Featherstone
BV23 FLK	Daf	Brian Yeardley		Featherstone
BV23 FLM	Daf	Brian Yeardley		Featherstone
BC 01 LBY	Mercedes	Lazar	No Name	Romania
BC 10 LBY	Mercedes	Lazar	No Name	Romania
BC 12 LBY	Mercedes	Lazar	No Name	Romania
BC 13 LBY	Mercedes	Brian Yeardley	Lethal Force	Featherstone
BC 14 LBY	Mercedes	Lazar	No Name	Romania
BC 15 LBY	Mercedes	CargoBY	No Name	Romania

Reg		Make	Operator		Country
BC 16 LBY		Mercedes	Brian Yeardley	No Name	Romania
BC 22 LBY		Mercedes	Lazar	No Name	Romania
BC 45 LAZ		Mercedes	Brian Yeardley	No Name	Romania
BC 84 LAZ		Volvo	TruckingBY	No Name	Romania
BP 57 517		Scania	Stokholm BY	No Name	Denmark
CV 83 187		Volvo	Stokholm BY	No Name	Denmark
BWE 23 J		Volvo	Stokholm BY	No Name	Poland
BZ 13 334		Volvo	Stokholm BY	No Name	Denmark
CV 83 186	253	Volvo	Stokholm BY	No Name	Denmark
CV 83 187	254	Volvo	Stokholm BY	No Name	Denmark
DF 67 408		Volvo	Stokholm BY	No Name	Denmark
DF 67 740		Volvo	Stokholm BY	No Name	Denmark
DF 67 741		Volvo	Stokholm BY	No Name	Denmark
DF 67 743		Volvo	Stokholm BY	No Name	Denmark
DF 67 744		Volvo	Stokholm BY	No Name	Denmark
DJ 58 308		Scania	Stokholm BY	No Name	Denmark
DL 28 231	255	Volvo	Stokholm BY	No Name	Denmark
DL 52 351		Volvo	Stokholm BY	No Name	Denmark
DM 92 331		Scania	Stokholm BY	No Name	Denmark
DM 92 332		Scania	Stokholm BY	No Name	Denmark
DM 92 343	256	Scania	Stokholm BY	No Name	Denmark
DN 22 250		Scania	Stokholm BY	No Name	Denmark
DN 22 531		Daf	Stokholm BY	No Name	Denmark
DN 86 786		Scania	Stokholm BY	No Name	Denmark
DN 86 787		Scania	Stokholm BY	No Name	Denmark
DP 19 988		Volvo	Stokholm BY	No Name	Denmark
DP 19 990		Volvo	Stokholm BY	No Name	Denmark
DP 80 688		Volvo	Stokholm BY	No Name	Denmark
DP 80 689		Volvo	Stokholm BY	No Name	Denmark
DS 11 303	257	Volvo	Stokholm BY	No Name	Denmark
DS 11 304		Volvo	Stokholm BY	No Name	Denmark
PKP 05 A		Volvo	Stokholm BY	No Name	Poland

Bulmans / M Woodhouse (Penrith / Lancaster)

Reg	Make	Operator	Reg	Make	Operator
YE 16 CHH	Mercedes	M. Woodhouse	PX 70 LYH	Daf	Bulmans
YJ 16 YWD	Mercedes	M. Woodhouse	PX 70 LYJ	Daf	Bulmans
YJ 16 YXC	Mercedes	M. Woodhouse	PX 70 LYK	Daf	Bulmans
YC 17 OCJ	Mercedes	M. Woodhouse	PX 70 LYO	Daf	Bulmans
YK 17 LHM	Mercedes	M. Woodhouse	PX 70 LYR	Daf	Bulmans
YK 17 LYW	Mercedes	M. Woodhouse	PX 70 LYS	Daf	Bulmans
PN 67 PBV	Daf	M. Woodhouse	PX 70 LYT	Daf	Bulmans
PN 67 PBX	Daf	M. Woodhouse	PX 70 LYU	Daf	Bulmans
YB 67 WPJ	Mercedes	M. Woodhouse	PX 70 LYV	Daf	Bulmans
YD 67 JBO	Mercedes	M. Woodhouse	PY 70 EGC	Daf	Bulmans
YD 67 JJY	Mercedes	M. Woodhouse	PY 70 EGD	Daf	Bulmans
YD 67 KMZ	Mercedes	M. Woodhouse	ND 21 RVK	Mercedes	M. Woodhouse
YB 18 WMT	Mercedes	M. Woodhouse	ND 21 RVM	Mercedes	M. Woodhouse
YJ 18 RFX	Mercedes	M. Woodhouse	NJ 21 FBE	Mercedes	M. Woodhouse
YJ 18 RFY	Mercedes	M. Woodhouse	PX 21 NWB	Daf	Bulmans
YJ 18 RHA	Mercedes	M. Woodhouse	PX 21 NWC	Daf	Bulmans
YJ 18 RHE	Mercedes	M. Woodhouse	PX 21 NWD	Daf	Bulmans
YB68 VMW	Mercedes	M. Woodhouse	PX 21 NWE	Daf	Bulmans
PX 19 LCO	Daf	Bulmans	PX 21 NWF	Daf	Bulmans
YJ 19 RNF	Mercedes	M. Woodhouse	PX 21 NWG	Daf	Bulmans
NK 69 ZZJ	Volvo	M. Woodhouse	PX 21 NWH	Daf	Bulmans
PX 70 LXZ	Daf	Bulmans	PX 21 NWJ	Daf	Bulmans
PX 70 LYA	Daf	Bulmans	PX 21 NWK	Daf	Bulmans
PX 70 LYC	Daf	Bulmans	PX 21 NWL	Daf	Bulmans
PX 70 LYD	Daf	Bulmans	PX 21 NYK	Daf	Bulmans
PX 70 LYF	Daf	Bulmans	PX 21 NYL	Daf	Bulmans
PX 70 LYG	Daf	Bulmans	PX 21 NYM	Daf	Bulmans

Bulmans / M Woodhouse (cont)

Reg	Make	Operator	Reg	Make	Operator
ND 71 RHY	Mercedes	M. Woodhouse	NJ23 BYL	Mercedes	M. Woodhouse
NJ 71 BFE	Mercedes	M. Woodhouse	PN23 CEO	Mercedes	M. Woodhouse
NJ 71 BXP	Mercedes	M. Woodhouse	PN23 CEU	Mercedes	M. Woodhouse
NJ 71 CDZ	Mercedes	M. Woodhouse	PX23 MBF	Daf	Bulmans
PX 71 LYG	Daf	Bulmans	PX23 MBO	Daf	Bulmans
PX 71 LYH	Daf	Bulmans	PX23 XFN	Daf	Bulmans
PX 71 LYJ	Daf	Bulmans	PX23 XFO	Daf	Bulmans
PX 71 LYK	Daf	Bulmans	PX23 XFP	Daf	Bulmans
PX 71 LYO	Daf	Bulmans	PX23 XFR	Daf	Bulmans
PX 71 LZW	Daf	Bulmans	PX23 XFS	Daf	Bulmans
PX 71 MEV	Daf	Bulmans	NJ73 BSY	Mercedes	M. Woodhouse
PY 71 FNZ	Daf	Bulmans	PX73 MKA	Daf	Bulmans
NJ 22 AEB	Mercedes	M. Woodhouse	PX73 MKC	Daf	Bulmans
PF 22 OLT	Daf	M. Woodhouse	PX73 MKE	Daf	Bulmans
PJ 22 AOG	Daf	M. Woodhouse	PX73 MKF	Daf	Bulmans
PX 22 MBO	Daf	Bulmans	PX73 MKG	Daf	Bulmans
PX 22 MBU	Daf	Bulmans	PX73 MKJ	Daf	Bulmans
PN 72 FXW	Daf	M. Woodhouse	PX73 MKK	Daf	Bulmans
PX 72 LZJ	Daf	Bulmans	PX73 MKL	Daf	Bulmans
PX 72 LZK	Daf	Bulmans	PX73 MKM	Daf	Bulmans
PX 72 LZL	Daf	Bulmans	PX73 MKN	Daf	Bulmans
PX 72 LZM	Daf	Bulmans	PX73 MKO	Daf	Bulmans
PX 72 LZO	Daf	Bulmans	PX73 MKP	Daf	Bulmans
PX 72 LZP	Daf	Bulmans	PX73 MKU	Daf	Bulmans
PX72 LZR	Daf	Bulmans	PX73 MKV	Daf	Bulmans
NJ23 BYK	Mercedes	M. Woodhouse			

Campeys of Selby

Reg	Make	Reg	Make	Reg	Make	Reg	Make
YC63 URD	Scania	YT19 EHH	Scania	YK71 XRE	Scania	FN23 BNE	Daf
WN65 CDY	Scania	YN69 YDS	Scania	YN71 ZZG	Scania	FN23 BNF	Daf
WN65 CFM	Scania	YN69 YDT	Scania	YT71 AAE	Scania	FN23 BNJ	Daf
WN65 PYV	Scania	YN69 YDU	Scania	YT71 AAF	Scania	FN23 BNK	Daf
YN16 MWJ	Scania	YN69 YFX	Scania	YT71 AAJ	Scania	FN23 BNL	Daf
YN16 MWK	Scania	YN69 YFY	Scania	YT71 AAK	Scania	YK23 WNF	Volvo
YN16 MWL	Scania	YN69 YFZ	Scania	FN72 BWJ	Daf	YK23 WNG	Volvo
BV66 VXF	Scania	YN20 YVA	Scania	FP72 PZW	Daf	YK23 WNJ	Volvo
SN66 NLV	Scania	YN20 YVB	Scania	FP72 PZX	Daf	YL23 HWS	Volvo
WU66 BBV	Scania	YN20 YVC	Scania	FP72 PZY	Daf	YL23 HWT	Volvo
YD66 BXL	Scania	YN20 YVD	Scania	NU72 VUC	Iveco	YL23 HWU	Volvo
YD66 BXM	Scania	YN20 YVE	Scania	NU72 VWJ	Iveco	YT23 BWA	Scania
DK67 UWL	Daf	YN20 YVF	Scania	NV72 BGK	Iveco	YT23 BWB	Scania
PN67 OSB	Daf	YN70 YUA	Scania	NV72 BGO	Iveco	YT23 BWC	Scania
YN18 XVC	Scania	YN70 YUB	Scania	NV72 BGU	Iveco	YT23 BWD	Scania
YN18 XVD	Scania	YN70 YUC	Scania	NV72 BGX	Iveco	YK73 WOH	Volvo
YN18 XVE	Scania	YN70 YUD	Scania	YN72 ZYV	Scania	YK73 WOJ	Volvo
YN18 XYA	Scania	YN70 YUE	Scania	YT72 AOA	Daf	YK73 WOM	Volvo
YN18 XYB	Scania	YN70 YUF	Scania	YT72 AOB	Daf	YK73 WOR	Volvo
YN18 XYC	Scania	NX21 UNF	Man	YT72 AOC	Daf	YT73 CDE	Daf
BF68 DCZ	Scania	YD21 FCC	Scania	YT72 AOD	Daf	YT73 CDF	Daf
BF68 DDO	Scania	YD21 FCE	Scania	YT72 AOE	Daf	YT73 CDK	Daf
BJ68 EPL	Scania	YD21 FCF	Scania	YT72 AOF	Daf	YT73 CDN	Daf
MK68 LUJ	Scania	YD21 FCG	Scania	YT72 AOG	Daf	YT73 CDO	Daf
MK68 LUO	Scania	YD21 FCJ	Scania	BL23 YPU	Scania	YT73 CDU	Daf
YN68 YCV	Scania	YT21 ENP	Daf	EV23 COS	Daf	YT73 CDV	Daf
YN68 YCW	Scania	YK71 XRA	Scania	FN23 BNA	Daf	YT73 CDX	Daf
YN68 YCX	Scania	YK71 XRB	Scania	FN23 BNB	Daf	YT73 CDY	Daf
YT19 EHF	Scania	YK71 XRC	Scania	FN23 BND	Daf	YT73 CDZ	Daf
YT19 EHG	Scania	YK71 XRD	Scania				

Collett (Halifax)

Reg	Make	Reg	Make	Reg	Make	Reg	Make
09 D 129214	Daf	YC13 CXN	Daf	CN66 YML	Man	WK18 LVN	Man
131 D 32106	Man	YH63 KUE	Mercedes	CN66 YMM	Man	WK18 LVO	Man
152 D 24861	Daf	YW14 DJV	Daf	CN66 YMO	Man	EJ68 DFG	Scania
V547 LYS	Man	YW14 DJX	Daf	CN66 YMP	Man	RV68 YDC	Man
YJ57 TXN	Man	YB64 WPM	Daf	DK66 KRZ	Man	WU68 OLA	Man
MX09 CFJ	Man	YB64 WPO	Daf	DK66 KTE	Man	WU19 JZA	Man
YJ09 WSU	Volvo	YE64 RPU	Daf	DK66 KTF	Man	WU19 JZP	Man
BX59 GCF	Man	YE64 RPV	Daf	DK66 KTL	Man	YK20 RXM	Volvo
DE12 NJJ	Man	YJ64 EWT	Mercedes	SJ66 NMA	Mercedes	YK70 UYO	Volvo
YK12 FRA	Man	PO15 MKV	Daf	SJ66 NME	Mercedes	YM21 CSZ	Mercedes
EJ13 NPN	Man	YJ15 DZC	Daf	SF17 AOC	Mercedes	YK71 POV	Daf
NU13 ZTB	Man	YJ15 DZK	Daf	SF17 AOD	Mercedes	MV22 WOR	Man
NU13 ZTC	Man	YK15 VAF	Daf	CN18 ZMO	Man	MW22 KVC	Man
NX13 TBO	Man	YK15 VAH	Daf	CN18 ZMU	Man	WU22 CVH	Man
NX13 TBU	Man	CN16 GDF	Man	MV18 UEU	Man	WU22 CYO	Man
WX13 RVP	Man	CN16 GHJ	Man	MV18 UEW	Man	WU23 FHR	Man
WX13 RVR	Man	NX16 KKA	Man	MV18 UEX	Man	DA73 XTU	Man
WX13 RVT	Man	NX16 KKB	Man	SN18 OWK	Man	KY73 GZF	Daf
WX13 RVU	Man	NX16 KKC	Man	SN18 OWM	Man	MV73 YSJ	Man
WX13 RVW	Man	NX16 KKD	Man				

Cranage (Holmes Chapel / Tarleton)

Reg	Make	Operator	Reg	Make	Operator
MW 62 YJA	Scania	Cranage	AT 21 CAT	Scania	Ascroft Transport
PN 14 HLM	Volvo	Cranage	CH 21 CAT	Scania	Cranage
PO 14 VHH	Scania	CAT	MX 21 EGC	Scania	CAT
PO 65 VJJ	Scania	Cranage	MX 21 EGD	Scania	CAT
PO 65 VLL	Scania	CAT	AT 71 CAT	Scania	Ascroft Transport
RA 16 BHO	Daf	White	AT 22 CAT	Scania	Ascroft Transport
PO 66 UUA	Scania	TXM Plant	PJ 22 HDZ	Scania	Cranage
PO 66 UUB	Scania	Cranage	PJ 22 HEU	Scania	Cranage
PO 66 UUC	Scania	Cranage	PJ 22 HFD	Scania	Ascroft Transport
PO 66 UUD	Scania	Cranage	PN 22 CAT	Scania	CAT
PO 18 MXC	Scania	Cranage	PN 22 EOB	Scania	Cranage
RY 18 CAL	Scania	Cranage	PN 22 EOC	Scania	Cranage
PO 68 XXD	Scania	CAT	PN 22 EOD	Scania	Cranage
PO 68 XXE	Scania	Cranage	PO 22 CAT	Scania	CAT
PJ 19 FRK	Scania	Cranage	MX 72 AZU	Scania	CAT
PV 19 ELC	Scania	Cranage	MX 72 AZV	Scania	CAT
PO 69 YHH	Scania	Cranage	AT 23 CAT	Scania	Ascroft Transport
PN 20 BBV	Scania	Cranage	MX73 DFF	Scania	Cranage
PN 20 BBX	Scania	Cranage	PN73 ECC	Scania	Cranage
RY 20 CAL	Scania	Cranage	PN73 EHH	Scania	Cranage
RY 70 CAL	Scania	Cranage			

Crouch (Kibworth)

Reg	Make	Model
460 UXF	Ward LA	6w Recovery LHD
RSJ 505	AEC	Metador 4w Recovery
TOW 575	Foden	Alpha 3000 6w Recovery
TOW 2 X	Oshkosh	M1070 8w Recovery LHD
TOW 3 X	Scania	R500 6w (NG) Recovery
A4 TOW	Volvo	FMX 540 8w Recovery
A17 TOW	Daf	FAS 530 6w XF Recovery
A21 TOW	Volvo	FL 280 4w Flatbed
B251 KNV	Mercedes	Unimog 4w Recovery
D22 TOW	Renault	D280 4w Flatbed
E477 MPV	Foden	6w Recovery
E1 TOW	Daf	FASXF 530 Recovery
E7 TOW	Volvo	FMX 540 8w Recovery
H123 BMH	Daf	400 8w Recovery
J21 TOW	Daf	FACF 530 SC 4w Recovery
J25 TOW	Daf	FTCF 510 4w SC Recovery
J26 TOW	Man	TGE 6.180 Panel Van
J29 TOW	Daf	FANCF 450 6w SC Flatbed
J999 TOW	Mercedes	Actros 2551 6w Flatbed
K21 TOW	Mercedes	Atego 1530 4w Flatbed
K28 TOW	Man	TGS 26.360 6w L Flatbed
K29 TOW	Daf	FASCF 330 6w Flatbed
K31 TOW	Renault	D240 4w Flatbed
K121 TOW	Renault	D240 4w Flatbed
K123 TOW	Renault	D280 4w Flatbed
K321 TOW	Renault	D240 4w Flatbed
K951 EEP	Oshkosh	M1070 8w Recovery LHD
L111 UNT	Daf	3600 6w Recovery
M1 SOS	Mercedes	Atego 1323 4w Flatbed
M24 TOW	Scania	R520 6x2 V8 Top
M25 SOS	Daf	FASXF 530 Recovery
M40 TOW	Scania	R620 8w HL Recovery
N2 TOW	Man	TGX 26.640 Recovery
N5 TMD	Volvo	FH 4x2 GXL
N25 TOW	Mercedes	Actros 2535 6w Flatbed
N26 TOW	Volvo	FL 280 4w Flatbed
N29 TOW	Renault	D240 4w Flatbed
N293 CRP	Daf	FT85.360 Ati 4w Flatbed
P21 TOW	Ford	Transit Custom 300
P24 TOW	Volvo	FL 4w Flatbed
P200 OGN	Daf	FAS75.270 Ati 6w Flatbed
Q362 BAL	Scammell	S24 6w Recovery LHD
Q962 RRP	Scammell	S26 6w Recovery
R5 CUE	Scania	R114G 460 8w Recovery
R7 TOW	Daf	FAS 530 6w XG Recovery
R17 DFR	Foden	6x6 Recovery
R17 TOW	Scania	G450 8w Flatbed
R19 TOW	Daf	FTSXF 510 6x2 SSC
R21 TOW	Daf	XF95 6w Recovery
R23 TOW	Volvo	FMX 500 4w G Recovery
R25 TOW	Volvo	FMX 500 4w G Recovery
R27 TOW	Iveco	Eurocargo 150E25 Flatbed
R29 TOW	Volvo	FL 280 4w Flatbed
R31 TOW	Iveco	Daily 70C17
S66 TOW	Iveco	Eurocargo 150E25 Flatbed
S666 TOW	Mercedes	Axor 1824 4w Flatbed
V8 TOW	Scania	S730 6x2 (NG) HL
V22 TOW	Mercedes	Atego 1523 4w Flatbed
V29 TOW	Volvo	FMX 540 6w G Recovery
V31 TOW	Volvo	FMX 540 6w G Recovery
V66 TOW	Scania	P94D 230 4w Flatbed
V88 TOW	Daf	FTSXF105 510 6x2 SC Tag
V121 TOW	Volvo	FM 480 6w G Recovery Tag
W8 TOW	Volvo	FL 280 4w Flatbed
W31 TOW	Mercedes	Axor 4w Recovery
X23 TOW	Mercedes	Axor 1823 4w Flatbed
X26 TOW	Mercedes	Atego 1523 4w Flatbed
X29 TOW	Volvo	FL 280 4w Flatbed
X31 TOW	Iveco	EuroCargo 150E25 Flatbed
X60 TOW	Mercedes	Atego 1523 4w Flatbed
X66 TOW	Volvo	FH 520 6x2 GXL Tag
X70 TOW	Volvo	FL 210 4w Flatbed
X200 TOW	Mercedes	Sprinter 516 Cdi Panel Van
Y5 TOW	Mercedes	Actros 2543 Recovery
Y8 TOW	Volvo	FE 320 6w Flatbed
Y25 USA	Peterbuilt	357 6w Recovery Truck
Y26 USA	Ford	Unknown Breakdown Truck
Y300 TOW	Ford	Transit Custom 300
Y555 TOW	Volvo	FM 6w G Recovery
Y777 TOW	Iveco	EuroCargo 150E25 Flatbed
Y888 TOW	Ford	Transit Custom
CR06 CHY	Mercedes	Arocs 3336 6w Recovery
CR56 TOW	Daf	FALF45 180 4w Flatbed
MJ56 BVR	Volkswagon	Crafter CR35 136 LWB
KX57 CME	Liebherr	4 Axle Crane 100t
AJ58 OVR	Man	TGX 26.440 6x2 XLX
CR10 TOW	Scania	R620 8w Top Recovery
ML60 HZM	Peugeot	Partner 625 Professional Hdi
DC12 TOW	Land Rover	Discovery XS Auto 4x4
DC62 TOW	Scania	P360 4w Recovery
ER63 TOW	Daf	FACF85 460 Recovery
BF64 VCY	Fiat	Doblo 16v Multijet
CN64 TCV	Ford	C-Max Titanium Tdci Auto
FH16 REC	Volvo	FH16 750 6x4 GXL
FH16 TOW	Volvo	FH16 750 6x2 GXL
FH16 TUG	Volvo	FH16 750 8x4 GXL
SR65 TOW	Mercedes	Atego 1323 4w Flatbed
SR18 REC	Daf	FASXF 530 Recovery
CR21 TOW	Daf	FALF 210 4w Flatbed
MA21 HYZ	Ford	Transit
AY71 TYO	Daf	FASXF 530 Recovery
SL71 OFS	Daf	FACF 6w Flatbed

Culina Group

Vehicle Make Codes

ELE	Electra	IVE	Iveco	MIT	Mitsubishi	SCA	Scania	VOL	Volvo
ISU	Isuzu	MER	Mercedes	REN	Renault	TER	Terberg		

Fleet No	Registration	Make	Owner	Name	Allocation
E 1	GN71 BUA	ELE	Great Bear		
F 1613	PN66 KOU	MER	Tesco		Doncaster
EVML3403	N16 STA (19)	Daf	Stardes	Dame Vera Lynn	
EVML3408	R50 STA (23)	Daf	Blue		
F 1620	PN66 KPY	MER	Tesco		Doncaster
F 1663	FN04 CDV	IVE	White		
F 1669	PK18 XRL	MER	Tesco		Doncaster
F 1678	PF68 JZE	MER	Tesco		Doncaster
F 1680	PF68 JZK	MER	Tesco		Doncaster
F 1688	BC19 TGX	REN	TPN		Teesside
F 1696	BV70 CXA	REN	TPN		Teesside
F 1697	BV70 CXB	REN	TPN		Dagenham
F 1698	BV70 CXC	REN	TPN		Teesside
F 1699	BV70 CXD	REN	TPN		Teesside
F 1700	BV70 CXE	REN	TPN		Teesside
F 1701	LN70 ZCA	ISU	TPN		Teesside
F 1702	LN70 ZCE	ISU	TPN		Dagenham
F 1703	LN70 ZCF	ISU	TPN		Dagenham
F 1705	KX70 ZYS	MER	Tesco		Goole Tesco
F 1706	KX70 ZWY	MER	Tesco		Goole Tesco
F 1707	BV70 CXF	REN	TPN		Dagenham
F 1708	BV70 CXM	REN	TPN		Dagenham
F 1709	BV70 CXL	REN	TPN		Dagenham
F 1710	KX70 ZZB	MER	Tesco		Goole Tesco
F 1711	KX70 ZYY	MER	Tesco		Goole Tesco
F 1713	KX70 ZYU	MER	Tesco		Goole Tesco
F 1714	BV70 CXG	REN	TPN		Dagenham
F 1715	BV70 CXK	REN	TPN		Dagenham
F 1716	BV70 CXN	REN	TPN		Dagenham
F 1717	BV70 CXO	REN	TPN		Dagenham
F 1718	KX70 ZZE	MER	Tesco		Goole Tesco
F 1719	KX70 ZZF	MER	Tesco		Goole Tesco
F 1720	KX70 ZZH	MER	Tesco		Goole Tesco
F 1721	KN70 CZO	MER	Tesco		Goole Tesco
F 1933	PF68 SGY	MER	Tesco		Doncaster
F 1937	BN17 CFD	REN	TPN		Teesside
F 1943	JU57 TPN (18)	REN	TPN		Dagenham
F 1953	PO69 XEM	MER	Tesco		Doncaster
F 1954	PO69 XES	MER	Tesco		Doncaster
F 1955	PO69 XET	MER	Tesco		Doncaster
F 1962	BD69 DPN	REN	TPN		Widnes
F 1972	BU20 VGN	REN	TPN		Dagenham
F 1975	BU20 VJC	REN	TPN		Dagenham
F 1978	BF18 UDV	REN	TPN		Dagenham
F 1982	BV70 CZD	REN	TPN		Dagenham
F 1983	BV70 C7F	REN	TPN		Dagenham
F 1985	BU69 XGJ	REN	TPN		Dagenham
F	BV21 NRE	REN	TPN		Stockton
F	PN23 CGO	MER	Tesco		Doncaster
F 7435	NX17 JFF	Man	MMiD		
H 003	PY70 AUA	REN	White		Goole
H 005	PY21 CHJ	REN	White		Goole
H 006	PY21 CHK	REN	White		Goole
H 007	PX71 LNU	REN	White		Goole

Culina Group (cont)

H 024	PO70 ZKE	SCA	Stobart	Paige Madison	Owner Driver
H 101	PN73 FUB	Daf	Stobart		
H 102	PN73 FUH	Daf	Stobart		
H 103	PN73 FUJ	Daf	Stobart		
H 116	PO68 YOD	SCA	Stobart	Kathrine Bridget	Owner Driver
H 117	PX71 MHF	Man	Stobart		
H 122	PN21 FFG	SCA	Stobart	Kayleigh Jade	Owner Driver
H 123	PJ22 HBE	SCA	Stobart		Owner Driver
H 124	MV22 VEB	SCA	Stobart		Owner Driver
H 125	MV22 VEA	SCA	Stobart		Owner Driver
H 126	PN21 FFH	SCA	Stobart	Trudi Jayne	Owner Driver
H 128	PN21 FFJ	SCA	Stobart	Violet Pauline	Owner Driver
H 130	PY18 NSE	SCA	Ed Brewer		Owner Driver
H 131	PX19 OEV	SCA	Ed Brewer	Fee	Owner Driver
H 133	PJ22 HBF	SCA	Ed Brewer	Olivia Macie	Owner Driver
H 134	PJ22 HBG	SCA	Ed Brewer	Dinah Marian	Owner Driver
H 135	MV22 VDY	SCA	Ed Brewer		Owner Driver
H 136	MV22 VDX	SCA	Ed Brewer		Owner Driver
H 185	PJ73 SYU	SCA	Stobart		Owner Driver
H 186	PJ73 SYZ	SCA	Stobart		Owner Driver
H 187	PJ73 SZC	SCA	Stobart		Owner Driver
H 188	PK73 XSZ	SCA	Stobart		Owner Driver
H 189	PK73 XTL	SCA	Stobart		Owner Driver
H 190	DX73 VTF	Volvo	Stobart		Owner Driver
H 191	DX73 VTG	Volvo	Stobart		Owner Driver
H 192	DX73 VTJ	Volvo	Stobart		Owner Driver
H 193	PN24 DMY	SCA	Stobart		Owner Driver
H 210	PN24 DFL	SCA	Stobart		Owner Driver
H 211	PN24 DFV	SCA	Stobart		Owner Driver
H 212	PN24 DKE	SCA	Stobart		Owner Driver
H 213	PN24 DKD	SCA	Stobart		Owner Driver
H 214	PN24 DOJ	SCA	Stobart		Owner Driver
H 215	PK24 AHA	SCA	Stobart		Owner Driver
H 218	PO68 YDD	SCA	Stobart	Beth Alana	Owner Driver
H 220	PN19 FJP	SCA	Stobart	Belinda	Owner Driver
H 221	PO68 YFZ	SCA	Stobart	Joy	Owner Driver
H 223	PN19 FCZ	SCA	Stobart	Heidi Jane	Owner Driver
H 224	PN19 FDA	SCA	Stobart	Ivy Alice	Owner Driver
H 225	PN19 FDD	SCA	Culina		
H 226	PN19 FDJ	SCA	Stobart	Gerry Teresa	Owner Driver
H 227	PN19 FDP	SCA	Stobart	Helen Yvonne	Owner Driver
H 228	PN19 FDM	SCA	Stobart	Brenda	Owner Driver
H 229	PN19 FDV	SCA	Stobart	Tanya Jane	Owner Driver
H 230	PN19 FDX	SCA	Stobart	Cassandra Jan	Owner Driver
H 231	PN19 FDY	SCA	Great Bear		
H 232	PN19 FEG	SCA	Culina		
H 233	PN19 FKF	SCA	Culina		
H 234	PN19 FDZ	SCA	Culina		
H 235	PN19 FEF	SCA	Stobart	Hailie Reegan	Owner Driver
H 236	PN19 FEJ	SCA	Stobart	Lily Jane	Owner Driver
H 270	PN24 DLV	SCA	Stobart		Owner Driver
H 271	PN24 DMO	SCA	Stobart		Owner Driver
H 272	PN24 DNU	SCA	Stobart		Owner Driver
H 273	PK24 AGX	SCA	Stobart		Owner Driver
H 274	PN24 DOA	SCA	Stobart		Owner Driver
H 1000	PF73 OZD	SCA	Culina		Market Drayton
H 1001	PF73 OYY	SCA	Culina		
H 1002	PF73 OYZ	SCA	Stobart		Wakefield
H 1003	PF73 OZA	SCA	Culina		
H 1004	PF73 OZB	SCA	Culina		

H 1005	PF73 OZE	SCA	Culina	Telford
H 1006	PF73 OZC	SCA	Culina	
H 1007	PF73 OZG	SCA	Culina	
H 1008	PF73 OZH	SCA	Stobart	Wakefield
H 1009	PF73 OZJ	SCA	Culina	
H 1010	PF73 OZK	SCA	Culina	
H 1011	PF73 OZM	SCA	Culina	Telford
H 1012	PF73 OZN	SCA	Culina	
H 1013	PF73 OZR	SCA	Stobart	Morrisons, Wakefield
H 1014	PF73 OZS	SCA	Stobart	Morrisons, Wakefield
H 1015	PF73 OZT	SCA	Culina	
H 1016	PF73 OZP	SCA	Culina	
H 1017	PF73 OZU	SCA	Warrens	
H 1018	PF73 RAU	SCA	Stobart	
H 1019	PF73 RAX	SCA	Stobart	
H 1020	PF73 RBO	SCA	Stobart	
H 1021	PF73 OZV	SCA	Warrens	Bolton
H 1022	PF73 RBY	SCA	Warrens	
H 1023	PF73 RBU	SCA	Warrens	
H 1024	PF73 OZW	SCA	Warrens	Bolton
H 1025	PF73 RBZ	SCA	Warrens	Bolton
H 1026	PF73 RBV	SCA	Stobart	Wakefield
H 1027	PF73 RBX	SCA	Stobart	
H 1028	PF73 RCO	SCA	Great Bear	Rugby
H 1029	PN24 DJK	SCA	Great Bear	
H 1030	PF73 RNJ	SCA	Stobart	
H 1031	PF73 RCV	SCA	Stobart	Rugby
H 1032	PF73 OZL	SCA	Culina	
H 1033	PF73 OZX	SCA	Stobart	Wakefield
H 1034	PF73 OZO	SCA	Stobart	Rugby
H 1035	PF73 RNE	SCA	Stobart	
H 1036	PF73 RNN	SCA	Stobart	
H 1037	PF73 RNO	SCA	Stobart	
H 1038	PF73 RNU	SCA	Stobart	
H 1039	PF73 RNV	SCA	Stobart	
H 1040	PF73 RNX	SCA	Stobart	
H 1041	PF73 RNY	SCA	Stobart	
H 1042	PF73 RNZ	SCA	Culina	
H 1043	PF73 ROH	SCA	Culina	
H 1044	PF73 ROU	SCA	Stobart	
H 1045	PF73 RPO	SCA	Stobart	
H 1046	PF73 RPU	SCA	Stobart	Rugby
H 1047	PF73 RPV	SCA	Stobart	Rugby
H 1048				
H 1049	PN24 DJD	SCA	Warrens	Rugby
H 1050	PF73 RCU	SCA	Culina	
H 1051				
H 1052				
H 1053	PN24 DHV	SCA	Warrens	Rugby
H 1054				
H 1055	PN24 DHY	SCA	Warrens	Rugby
H 1056	PN24 DHO	SCA	Warrens	Rugby
H 1057				
H 1058				
H 1059				
H 1060	PF73 KUW	SCA	Stobart	
H 1061	PF73 KYY	SCA	Stobart	
H 1063	PN24 DJU	SCA	Culina	
H 1095	PN24 DMU	SCA	Culina	
H 1098	PN24 DHL	SCA	Culina	Lutterworth

H 1129	PN24 DNX	SCA	Culina	
H 1140	PN24 DFK	SCA	Stobart	Coventry
H 1144	PN24 DFJ	SCA	Stobart	Coventry
H 1147	PN24 DHK	SCA	Stobart	Coventry
H 1148	PN24 DFO	SCA	Stobart	Coventry
H 1154	PN24 DFP	SCA	Stobart	Rugby
H 1157	PN24 DFU	SCA	Stobart	Rugby
H 1159	PN24 DHD	SCA	Fowler Welch	
H 1161	PN24 DFY	SCA	Warrens	Rugby
H 1163	PN24 DFZ	SCA	Stobart	Daventry
H 1164	PN24 DGO	SCA	Stobart	Coventry
H 1165	PN24 DFX	SCA	Warrens	Swift Point
H 1167	PN24 DGW	SCA	Warrens	Rugby
H 1168	PN24 DHJ	SCA	Warrens	Rugby
H 1169	PN24 DGH	SCA	Great Bear	Lutterworth
H 1170	PN24 DGV	SCA	Great Bear	Salford
H 1171	PN24 DHC	SCA	Great Bear	Salford
H 1172	PN24 DHE	SCA	Great Bear	Salford
H 1173	PN24 DGX	SCA	Stobart	Bellshill
H 1174	PN24 DGZ	SCA	Stobart	
H 1175	PN24 DHF	SCA	Stobart	Rugby
H 1176	PN24 DGY	SCA	Stobart	
H 1178	PN24 DHG	SCA	Great Bear	Desborough
H 2000	KX22 DKF	SCA	Stobart	Appleton
H 2001	PJ72 OPX	SCA	Great Bear	
H 2002	PJ72 OPY	SCA	Great Bear	
H 2004	PJ72 OPT	SCA	Stobart	Bridgwater Morrisons
H 2005	PJ72 OPZ	SCA	Stobart	
H 2006	PJ72 ORC	SCA	Great Bear	
H 2007	PJ72 ORF	SCA	Great Bear	
H 2008	PN23 DZE	SCA	Stobart	
H 2014	PJ72 ORG	SCA	Great Bear	
H 2015	PJ72 ORH	SCA	Great Bear	
H 2016	PJ72 ORL	SCA	Great Bear	
H 2017	PJ72 ORN	SCA	Stobart	
H 2018	PJ72 ORO	SCA	Stobart	Morrisons, Burton L
H 2019	PJ72 ORP	SCA	Stobart	Morrisons, Burton L
H 2020	PJ72 ORK	SCA	Stobart	Morrisons, Burton L
H 2021	PJ72 ORS	SCA	Stobart	Morrisons, Burton L
H 2025	PJ73 ORV	SCA	Stobart	
H 2026	PN23 DZD	SCA	Culina	
H 2027	PJ72 ORW	SCA	Fowler Welch	Spalding
H 2028	PJ72 ORT	SCA	Stobart	
H 2029	PJ72 ORU	SCA	Stobart	
H 2030	PN23 DZF	SCA	Culina	
H 2032	PJ72 OPK	SCA	Stobart	Bridgwater Morri
H 2034	PJ72 UCT	SCA	Great Bear	
H 2035	PJ72 UCH	SCA	Great Bear	
H 2036	PN23 DZG	SCA	Great Bear	
H 2037	PN23 DZH	SCA	Culina	Avonmouth
H 2038	PJ72 ORY	SCA	Great Bear	
H 2039	PJ72 UCN	SCA	Great Bear	
H 2043	PJ72 UCS	SCA	Great Bear	
H 2044	PJ72 UCO	SCA	Fowler Welch	Washington
H 2048	PN23 EVK	SCA	Culina	
H 2049	PJ72 OSA	SCA	Stobart	
H 2050	PJ72 UCP	SCA	Stobart	
H 2051	PN23 EVH	SCA	Culina	
H 2052	PN23 EVL	SCA	Culina	
H 2053	PN23 EVJ	SCA	Culina	

H 2054	PN23 DZJ	SCA	Culina	
H 2055	PN23 DXG	SCA	Culina	
H 2056	PN23 DXE	SCA	Culina	
H 2057	PN23 DWY	SCA	Culina	
H 2058	PN23 DXP	SCA	Great Bear	Markham Vale
H 2059	PN23 DXD	SCA	Culina	Avonmouth
H 2060	PN23 DXH	SCA	Culina	
H 2061	PN23 DXM	SCA	Culina	
H 2062	PN23 DWZ	SCA	Great Bear	
H 2063	PN23 DXF	SCA	Culina	Avonmouth
H 2064	PN23 DXY	SCA	Culina	
H 2065	PN23 DXK	SCA	Culina	
H 2066	PN23 DXW	SCA	Culina	
H 2067	PN23 DXA	SCA	Culina	Avonmouth
H 2068	PN23 DXO	SCA	Culina	
H 2069	PN23 DXJ	SCA	Culina	
H 2070	PN23 DXT	SCA	Culina	
H 2071	PN23 DXB	SCA	Culina	
H 2072	PN23 DXC	SCA	Culina	
H 2073	PN23 DXU	SCA	Culina	
H 2074	PN23 DXS	SCA	Culina	
H 2075	PN23 DXR	SCA	Great Bear	
H 2076	PN23 DYY	SCA	Culina	
H 2077	PN23 DXL	SCA	Culina	
H 2078	PN23 DXV	SCA	Culina	Avonmouth
H 2079	PN23 DXX	SCA	Culina	
H 2080	PN23 DXZ	SCA	Great Bear	
H 2081	PN23 DYH	SCA	Culina	
H 2082	PN23 DYM	SCA	Culina	
H 2083	PN23 DYG	SCA	Great Bear	
H 2084	PN23 DYX	SCA	Great Bear	
H 2085	PN23 DYO	SCA	Great Bear	
H 2086	PN23 DYP	SCA	Great Bear	
H 2087	PN23 DYD	SCA	Great Bear	
H 2088	PN23 DYV	SCA	Great Bear	
H 2089	PN23 DYC	SCA	Great Bear	
H 2090	PN23 DYF	SCA	Great Bear	
H 2091	PN23 DYA	SCA	Great Bear	
H 2092	PN23 DYJ	SCA	Great Bear	
H 2093	PN23 DYW	SCA	Great Bear	
H 2094	PN23 DYS	SCA	Great Bear	
H 2095	PN23 DYT	SCA	Great Bear	
H 2096	PN23 DYB	SCA	Great Bear	
H 2097	PN23 DZC	SCA	Great Bear	
H 2098	PN23 DYU	SCA	Great Bear	
H 2099	PN23 DZA	SCA	Great Bear	
H 2100	PN23 DZB	SCA	Great Bear	
H 2101	PN23 DZK	SCA	Great Bear	
H 2102	PN23 ECJ	SCA	Great Bear	
H 2103	PN23 ECT	SCA	Great Bear	
H 2104	PN23 ETA	SCA	Great Bear	
H 2105	PN23 ETD	SCA	Great Bear	
H 2100	PN23 ETE	SCA	Great Bear	
H 2107	PN23 ETF	SCA	Great Bear	
H 2108	PN23 ETJ	SCA	Great Bear	
H 2109	PN23 ETK	SCA	Great Bear	
H 2110	PN23 ETL	SCA	Great Bear	
H 2111	PN23 ETO	SCA	Great Bear	
H 2112	PN23 ETR	SCA	Great Bear	
H 2113	PN23 ETU	SCA	Great Bear	

H 2114	PN23 ETV	SCA	Great Bear	
H 2115	PN23 ETX	SCA	Great Bear	
H 2116	PN23 ETY	SCA	Great Bear	
H 2117	PN23 ETZ	SCA	Great Bear	
H 2118	PN23 EUA	SCA	Great Bear	
H 2119	PN23 EUB	SCA	Great Bear	
H 2120	PN23 EUC	SCA	Great Bear	
H 2121	PN23 EUD	SCA	Great Bear	
H 2122	PN23 EUE	SCA	Great Bear	
H 2123	PN23 EUF	SCA	Great Bear	
H 2124	PN23 EUH	SCA	Great Bear	
H 2125	PN23 EUJ	SCA	Great Bear	
H 2126	PN23 EUK	SCA	Great Bear	
H 2127	PN23 EUL	SCA	Great Bear	
H 2128	PN23 EUM	SCA	Great Bear	
H 2129	PN23 EUO	SCA	Great Bear	
H 2130	PN23 EUP	SCA	Great Bear	
H 2131	PN23 EUR	SCA	Great Bear	
H 2132	PN23 EUT	SCA	Culina	
H 2133	PN23 EUU	SCA	Great Bear	
H 2134	PN23 EUV	SCA	Great Bear	
H 2135	PN23 EUW	SCA	Great Bear	
H 2136	PN23 EUX	SCA	Great Bear	
H 2137	PN23 EUY	SCA	Fowler Welch	
H 2138	PN23 EUZ	SCA	Great Bear	
H 2139	PN23 EVB	SCA	Great Bear	
H 2140	PN23 EVC	SCA	Great Bear	
H 2141	PN23 EVD	SCA	Culina	
H 2142	PN23 EVF	SCA	Stobart	
H 2143	PN23 EVG	SCA	Great Bear	
H 2144	PK23 DXP	SCA	Stobart	
H 2145	PK23 DXX	SCA	Stobart	
H 2146	PK23 DXR	SCA	Stobart	
H 2147	PK23 DXS	SCA	Stobart	
H 2148	PK23 DYA	SCA	Stobart	
H 2149	PK23 DXY	SCA	Great Bear	
H 2150	PK23 DYB	SCA	Stobart	
H 2151	PK23 DXV	SCA	Fowler Welch	
H 2152	PK23 DXW	SCA	Stobart	
H 2153	PK23 DXZ	SCA	Stobart	
H 2154	PK23 DYC	SCA	Stobart	
H 2155	PK23 DYN	SCA	Stobart	
H 2156	PK23 DXU	SCA	Stobart	
H 2157	PK23 DYD	SCA	Fowler Welch	
H 2158	PK23 DYJ	SCA	Fowler Welch	
H 2159	PK23 DYF	SCA	Stobart	
H 2160	PK23 DYM	SCA	Stobart	
H 2161	PK23 DYG	SCA	Great Bear	
H 2162	PK23 DXT	SCA	Stobart	
H 2163	PK23 DYO	SCA	Fowler Welch	Lutterworth
H 2164	PK23 DYH	SCA	Great Bear	
H 2165	PK23 DZC	SCA	Great Bear	
H 2166	PK23 DYS	SCA	Great Bear	
H 2167	PK23 DZD	SCA	Great Bear	
H 2168	PK23 DYU	SCA	Culina	
H 2169	PK23 DYP	SCA	Great Bear	
H 2170	PK23 DZB	SCA	Great Bear	
H 2171	PK23 DZG	SCA	Fowler Welch	Washington
H 2172	PK23 DZJ	SCA	Culina	
H 2173	PK23 DZA	SCA	Fowler Welch	

H 2174	PK23 DYT	SCA	Fowler Welch	
H 2175	PK23 DYV	SCA	Great Bear	
H 2176	PK23 DZE	SCA	Fowler Welch	Lutterworth
H 2177	PK23 DZF	SCA	Fowler Welch	
H 2178	PK23 DYW	SCA	Culina	
H 2179	PK23 DYX	SCA	Culina	
H 2180	PK23 DYY	SCA	Fowler Welch	
H 2181	PK23 DZP	SCA	Fowler Welch	
H 2182	PK23 DZO	SCA	Culina	
H 2183	PK23 DZH	SCA	Fowler Welch	
H 2184	PK23 DZL	SCA	Fowler Welch	
H 2185	PK23 DZN	SCA	Culina	
H 2186	PK23 DZR	SCA	Warrens	Spalding
H 2187	PK23 DZW	SCA	Warrens	Spalding
H 2188	PK23 DZX	SCA	Culina	
H 2189	PK23 DZZ	SCA	Culina	
H 2190	PK23 EAA	SCA	Culina	
H 2191	PK23 EAE	SCA	Culina	
H 2192	PK23 EAF	SCA	Culina	
H 2193	PK23 EAC	SCA	Fowler Welch	
H 2194	PK23 EAJ	SCA	Culina	
H 2195	PK23 EAO	SCA	Fowler Welch	
H 2196	PK23 EAW	SCA	Culina	
H 2197	PK23 EAX	SCA	Culina	
H 2198	PK23 EAY	SCA	Warrens	
H 2199	PK23 LKC	SCA	Culina	
H 2200	PK23 EBA	SCA	Fowler Welch	
H 2201	PK23 LKE	SCA	Culina	
H 2202	PK23 LKD	SCA	Culina	
H 2203	PK23 LKF	SCA	Culina	
H 2204	PK23 LKG	SCA	Culina	
H 2205	PK23 LKJ	SCA	Great Bear	
H 2206	PK23 LKN	SCA	Culina	
H 2207	PK23 LKL	SCA	Culina	
H 2208	PK23 LKM	SCA	Great Bear	
H 2209	PK23 LKO	SCA	Culina	
H 2210	PK23 LKP	SCA	Culina	
H 2211	PK23 LKU	SCA	Culina	
H 2212	PK23 LKV	SCA	Culina	
H 2213	PK23 LKX	SCA	Culina	
H 2214	PK23 LKY	SCA	Culina	
H 2215	PK23 LKZ	SCA	Culina	
H 2216	PK23 LLC	SCA	Culina	
H 2217	PK23 LLD	SCA	Culina	
H 2218	PK23 LLF	SCA	Culina	
H 2219	PK23 LLG	SCA	Culina	
H 2220	PK23 LLJ	SCA	Culina	Telford
H 2221	PK23 LLM	SCA	Culina	Telford
H 2222	PK23 LLN	SCA	Culina	
H 2223	PK23 LLO	SCA	Great Bear	
H 2224	PK23 LLP	SCA	Culina	
H 2225	PK23 LLR	SCA	Culina	
II 2226	PK23 LLT	SCA	Culina	Telford
H 2227	PK23 LLU	SCA	Culina	
H 2228	PK23 LLV	SCA	Culina	
H 2229	PK23 LLW	SCA	Great Bear	
H 2230	PK23 LLX	SCA	Culina	
H 2231	PK23 LLZ	SCA	Culina	Telford
H 2232	PK23 LME	SCA	Culina	
H 2233	PK23 LMF	SCA	Great Bear	

H 2234	PK23 LMJ	SCA	Ball Trucking	
H 2235	PK23 LML	SCA	Great Bear	
H 2236	PK23 LMM	SCA	Culina	
H 2237	PK23 LMO	SCA	Culina	
H 2238	PK23 LMU	SCA	Culina	
H 2239	PK23 LMV	SCA	Culina	
H 2240	PK23 LMX	SCA	Culina	
H 2241	PK23 LMY	SCA	Great Bear	
H 2242	PK23 LNA	SCA	Great Bear	
H 2243	PK23 LNC	SCA	Great Bear	
H 2244	PK23 LND	SCA	Great Bear	
H 2245	PK23 LNE	SCA	Ball Trucking	
H 2246	PK23 LNF	SCA	Great Bear	
H 2247	PJ23 MSU	SCA	Stobart	
H 2248	PJ23 MRY	SCA	Stobart	Rugby
H 2249	PJ23 MSV	SCA	Stobart	Rugby
H 2250	PJ23 MTK	SCA	Stobart	
H 2251	PJ23 MUA	SCA	Stobart	Rugby
H 2252	PJ23 MSX	SCA	Stobart	Rugby
H 2253	PJ23 MSY	SCA	Stobart	Rugby
H 2254	PJ23 MTE	SCA	Stobart	
H 2255	PJ23 MSO	SCA	Stobart	
H 2256	PJ23 MTF	SCA	Stobart	Dagenham
H 2257	PJ23 MTO	SCA	Stobart	
H 2258	PJ23 MTU	SCA	Stobart	Rugby
H 2259	PJ23 MTV	SCA	Stobart	Rugby
H 2260	PJ23 MTX	SCA	Stobart	
H 2261	PJ23 MUB	SCA	Stobart	Rugby
H 2262	PJ23 MUC	SCA	Stobart	Rugby
H 2263	PJ23 MUY	SCA	Stobart	
H 2264	PJ23 MVZ	SCA	Stobart	
H 2265	PJ23 MTY	SCA	Stobart	Rugby
H 2266	PJ23 MVN	SCA	Stobart	Rugby
H 2267	PJ23 MTZ	SCA	Stobart	Rugby
H 2268	PJ23 MUE	SCA	Stobart	Rugby
H 2269	PJ23 MVA	SCA	Stobart	Rugby
H 2270	PJ23 MUO	SCA	Stobart	Rugby
H 2271	PJ23 MVC	SCA	Stobart	
H 2272	PJ23 MVD	SCA	Stobart	
H 2273	PJ23 MUP	SCA	Stobart	
H 2274	PJ23 MUU	SCA	Stobart	Rugby
H 2275	PJ23 MUV	SCA	Great Bear	
H 2276	PJ23 MVE	SCA	Stobart	
H 2277	PJ22 MUW	SCA	Stobart	
H 2278	PJ23 MVF	SCA	Stobart	Rugby
H 2279	PJ23 MVG	SCA	Stobart	
H 2280	PJ23 MVO	SCA	Stobart	
H 2281	PJ23 MVP	SCA	Stobart	
H 2282	PJ23 MVR	SCA	Stobart	Rugby
H 2283	PJ23 MVH	SCA	Stobart	
H 2284	PJ23 MVK	SCA	Great Bear	
H 2285	PJ23 MVL	SCA	Great Bear	
H 2286	PJ23 MVS	SCA	Stobart	Rugby
H 2287	PJ23 MVM	SCA	Stobart	Rugby
H 2288	PJ23 MVT	SCA	Stobart	Rugby
H 2289	PJ23 MVU	SCA	Stobart	
H 2290	PJ23 MWA	SCA	Stobart	
H 2291	PJ23 MWC	SCA	Stobart	
H 2292	PJ23 MVV	SCA	Stobart	Rugby
H 2293	PJ23 MWD	SCA	Stobart	

H 2294	PJ23 MWE	SCA	Stobart	Rugby
H 2295	PJ23 MWF	SCA	Stobart	Rugby
H 2296	PJ23 MWG	SCA	Culina	
H 2297	PJ23 MWK	SCA	Stobart	Rugby
H 2298	PJ23 MWL	SCA	Stobart	
H 2299	PJ23 MWM	SCA	Stobart	Rugby
H 2300	PJ23 MVW	SCA	Great Bear	
H 2301	PJ23 MVX	SCA	Culina	
H 2302	PJ23 MVY	SCA	Culina	
H 2303	PJ23 MWN	SCA	Culina	
H 2304	PJ23 MWO	SCA	Stobart	Rugby
H 2305	PJ23 MWP	SCA	Stobart	
H 2306	PJ23 MWU	SCA	Stobart	
H 2307	PJ23 MWV	SCA	Stobart	
H 2308	PJ23 MWW	SCA	Stobart	Walkers, Leicester
H 2309	PJ23 MWX	SCA	Culina	
H 2310	PJ23 MYA	SCA	Culina	
H 2311	PJ23 MYB	SCA	Stobart	Walkers, Leicester
H 2312	PJ23 MYT	SCA	Culina	
H 2313	PJ23 MYG	SCA	Great Bear	
H 2314	PJ23 MYC	SCA	Culina	
H 2315	PJ23 MYO	SCA	Stobart	Walkers, Leicester
H 2316	PJ23 MYP	SCA	Stobart	
H 2317	PJ23 MYD	SCA	Great Bear	
H 2318	PJ23 MZG	SCA	Stobart	Walkers, Leicester
H 2319	PJ23 MYU	SCA	Stobart	
H 2320	PJ23 MZL	SCA	Great Bear	
H 2321	PJ23 MYF	SCA	Great Bear	
H 2322	PJ23 MZN	SCA	Great Bear	
H 2323	PJ23 MYR	SCA	Great Bear	
H 2324	PJ23 MYV	SCA	Culina	Walkers, Leicester
H 2325	PJ23 MZO	SCA	Great Bear	
H 2326	PJ23 MYW	SCA	Great Bear	
H 2327	PJ23 MYH	SCA	Great Bear	
H 2328	PJ23 MYK	SCA	Stobart	
H 2329	PJ23 MYX	SCA	Stobart	Walkers, Leicester.
H 2330	PJ23 MYN	SCA	Culina	Walkers, Leicester
H 2331	PJ23 MYY	SCA	Culina	
H 2332	PJ23 MYS	SCA	Culina	
H 2333	PJ23 MYZ	SCA	Stobart	Walkers, Leicester
H 2334	PJ23 MZD	SCA	Stobart	Walkers, Leicester
H 2335	PJ23 MZE	SCA	Stobart	Walkers, Leicester
H 2336	PJ23 MZF	SCA	Culina	
H 2337	PJ23 MZP	SCA	Great Bear	
H 2338	PJ23 MZT	SCA	Great Bear	
H 2339	PJ23 MZU	SCA	Culina	
H 2340	PJ23 MZV	SCA	Culina	
H 2341	PJ23 MZW	SCA	Great Bear	
H 2342	PJ23 MZX	SCA	Great Bear	
H 2343	PJ23 MZY	SCA	Stobart	Walkers, Leicester
H 2344	PJ23 MZZ	SCA	Culina	
H 2345	PJ23 NAE	SCA	Culina	
H 2346	PJ23 NAO	SCA	Stobart	Walkers, Leicester
H 2347	PJ23 NAU	SCA	Culina	
H 2348	PJ23 NBA	SCA	Stobart	Walkers, Leicester
H 2349	PJ23 NBB	SCA	Culina	
H 2350	PJ23 NBD	SCA	Great Bear	
H 2351	PJ23 NBE	SCA	Great Bear	
H 2352	PJ23 NBF	SCA	Culina	
H 2353	PJ23 NBG	SCA	Culina	

H 2354	PJ23 NBK	SCA	Great Bear	
H 2355	PJ23 NBL	SCA	Stobart	
H 2356	PJ23 NBM	SCA	Great Bear	
H 2357	PJ23 NBN	SCA	Great Bear	
H 2358	PJ23 NBO	SCA	Culina	
H 2359	PJ23 NBX	SCA	Great Bear	
H 2360	PJ23 NBY	SCA	Stobart	Walkers, Leicester
H 2361	PF23 OFE	SCA	Great Bear	Markham Vale
H 2362	PF23 OGC	SCA	Great Bear	
H 2363	PF23 OGD	SCA	Culina	
H 2364	PF23 OGE	SCA	Culina	
H 2365	PF23 OFG	SCA	Great Bear	
H 2366	PF23 OGG	SCA	Culina	
H 2367	PF23 OGH	SCA	Great Bear	
H 2368	PF23 OFH	SCA	Culina	
H 2369	PF23 OFJ	SCA	Great Bear	
H 2370	PF23 OFK	SCA	Culina	
H 2371	PF23 OFL	SCA	Warrens	
H 2372	PF23 OFM	SCA	Culina	
H 2373	PF23 OFN	SCA	Great Bear	
H 2374	PF23 OFO	SCA	Culina	Hereford
H 2375	PF23 OFP	SCA	Great Bear	
H 2376	PF23 OFR	SCA	Culina	
H 2377	PF23 OFS	SCA	Great Bear	
H 2378	PF23 OFT	SCA	Culina	
H 2379	PF23 OFU	SCA	Warrens	
H 2380	PF23 OFV	SCA	Culina	
H 2381	PF23 OFW	SCA	Warrens	
H 2382	PF23 OFX	SCA	Culina	
H 2383	PF23 OFY	SCA	Culina	
H 2384	PF23 OFZ	SCA	Culina	
H 2385	PF23 OGA	SCA	Culina	
H 2386	PF23 OGB	SCA	Culina	
H 2387	PF23 OGJ	SCA	Culina	
H 2388	PF23 OGK	SCA	Culina	
H 2389	PF23 OGL	SCA	Great Bear	
H 2390	PF23 OGM	SCA	Warrens	
H 2391	PF23 OGN	SCA	Culina	
H 2392	PF23 OGO	SCA	Warrens	
H 2393	PF23 OGP	SCA	Culina	
H 2394	PF23 OGR	SCA	Great Bear	
H 2395	PF23 OGS	SCA	Culina	
H 2396	PF23 OGT	SCA	Culina	Hereford
H 2397	PF23 OGU	SCA	Great Bear	
H 2398	PF23 OGV	SCA	Great Bear	
H 2399	PF23 OGW	SCA	Culina	Hereford
H 2400	PF23 OGX	SCA	Culina	
H 2401	PF23 OGY	SCA	Warrens	
H 2402	PF23 OGZ	SCA	Warrens	
H 2403	PF23 OHA	SCA	Culina	
H 2404	PF23 OHB	SCA	Culina	
H 2405	PF23 OHC	SCA	Great Bear	
H 2406	PF23 OHD	SCA	Culina	Hereford
H 2407	PF23 OHE	SCA	Culina	
H 2408	PF23 OHG	SCA	Culina	
H 2409	PF23 OHH	SCA	Great Bear	
H 2410	PF23 OHJ	SCA	Culina	Hereford
H 2411	PF23 OHK	SCA	Culina	
H 2412	PF23 OHL	SCA	Warrens	
H 2413	PF23 OHN	SCA	Warrens	

H 2414	PF23 OHO	SCA	Culina	
H 2415	PF23 OHP	SCA	Great Bear	
H 2416	PF23 OHR	SCA	Culina	Hereford
H 2417	PF23 OHS	SCA	Culina	
H 2418	PF23 OHT	SCA	Warrens	
H 2419	PF23 OHU	SCA	Stobart	Bridgwater
H 2420	PF23 OHV	SCA	Warrens	
H 2421	PF23 OHW	SCA	Great Bear	
H 2422	PF23 OHX	SCA	Culina	
H 2423	PF23 OHY	SCA	Culina	
H 2424	PF23 OHZ	SCA	Culina	
H 2425	PF23 OJA	SCA	Great Bear	Markham Vale
H 2426	PF23 OJB	SCA	Culina	
H 2427	PF23 OJC	SCA	Warrens	
H 2428	PF23 OJD	SCA	Stobart	Rugby
H 2429	PF23 OJE	SCA	Warrens	
H 2430	PF23 OJG	SCA	Great Bear	
H 2431	PF23 OJH	SCA	Great Bear	
H 2432	PF23 OJJ	SCA	Warrens	
H 2433	PF23 OJK	SCA	Warrens	Rugby
H 2434	PF23 OJL	SCA	Culina	
H 2435	PF23 OJM	SCA	Warrens	
H 2436	PF23 OJN	SCA	Culina	
H 2437	PF23 OJO	SCA	Warrens	
H 2438	PL23 JXO	SCA	Warrens	Warrens, Rugby
H 2439	PL23 JZM	SCA	Warrens	
H 2440	PL23 JXN	SCA	Warrens	
H 2441	PL23 JXS	SCA	Warrens	
H 2442	PL23 JXU	SCA	Stobart	Bridgwater
H 2443	PL23 JXX	SCA	Great Bear	
H 2444	PL23 JXP	SCA	Warrens	
H 2445	PN73 ELH	SCA	Stobart	
H 2446	PL23 JXV	SCA	Warrens	Rugby
H 2447	PL23 JYB	SCA	Great Bear	
H 2448	PL23 JXZ	SCA	Warrens	Warrens, Rugby
H 2449	PL23 JXR	SCA	Warrens	
H 2450	PL23 JXT	SCA	Warrens	
H 2451	PL23 JXW	SCA	Great Bear	
H 2452	PL23 JYC	SCA	Culina	
H 2453	PL23 JYJ	SCA	Culina	Warrens, Rugby
H 2454	PL23 JXY	SCA	Stobart	Bridgwater
H 2455	PL23 JYG	SCA	Great Bear	
H 2456	PL23 JYE	SCA	Culina	
H 2457	PN73 ELX	SCA	Culina	
H 2458	PL23 JYK	SCA	Culina	Warrens, Rugby
H 2459	PL23 JYD	SCA	Great Bear	
H 2460	PL23 JYP	SCA	Warrens	
H 2461	PL23 JYR	SCA	Stobart	Bridgwater
H 2462	PN23 EMF	SCA	Culina	
H 2463	PL23 JYT	SCA	Culina	
H 2464	PL23 JYU	SCA	Fowler Welch	
H 2465	PF23 VOY	SCA	Culina	
H 2466	PL23 JZV	SCA	Stobart	Bridgwater
H 2467	PN73 ELV	SCA	Culina	
H 2468	PL23 JYZ	SCA	Warrens	Warrens, Rugby
H 2469	PN73 ELW	SCA	Culina	
H 2470	PL23 JZA	SCA	Stobart	Bridgwater
H 2471	PL23 JYN	SCA	Stobart	Bridgwater
H 2472	PL23 JYH	SCA	Stobart	Bridgwater
H 2473	PF23 VOH	SCA	Stobart	Bridgwater

H 2474	PN73 ELJ	SCA	Culina	
H 2475	PL23 JYY	SCA	Warrens	
H 2476	PL23 JYF	SCA	Great Bear	
H 2477	PL23 JZC	SCA	Warrens	
H 2478	PN73 EMJ	SCA	Culina	
H 2479	PL23 JZD	SCA	Warrens	
H 2480	PL23 JZO	SCA	Stobart	Bridgwater
H 2481	PL23 JZP	SCA	Stobart	Bridgwater
H 2482	PL23 JZE	SCA	Stobart	Bridgwater
H 2483	PL23 JZF	SCA	Stobart	Bridgwater
H 2484	PL23 JZR	SCA	Stobart	Bridgwater
H 2485	PL23 JZG	SCA	Culina	
H 2486	PL23 JZJ	SCA	Warrens	
H 2487	PL23 JZK	SCA	Warrens	
H 2488	PL23 JZT	SCA	Culina	
H 2489	PF23 VOJ	SCA	Stobart	Bridgwater
H 2490	PN73 ELO	SCA	Culina	
H 2491	PN73 ELU	SCA	Stobart	Hawleys Lane
H 2492	PN73 ESV	SCA	Stobart	Hawleys Lane
H 2493	PN73 ESY	SCA	Stobart	
H 2494	PN73 EOZ	SCA	Stobart	
H 2495	PN73 ESU	SCA	Stobart	Morrisons, Bridgwater
H 2496	PN73 ETA	SCA	Stobart	
H 2497	PN73 ETD	SCA	Stobart	Hawleys Lane
H 2498	PF23 VOG	SCA	Culina	
H 2499	PN73 ENK	SCA	Stobart	
H 2500	PN73 EMK	SCA	Great Bear	
H 2501	PN73 EPO	SCA	Great Bear	
H 2502	PN73 ENJ	SCA	Culina	
H 2503	PN73 EMV	SCA	Culina	
H 2504	PN73 EMX	SCA	Culina	
H 2505	PN73 ENC	SCA	Culina	
H 2506	PN73 ENF	SCA	Culina	Market Drayton
H 2507	PN73 ENH	SCA	Great Bear	
H 2508	PN73 ENY	SCA	Stobart	Morrisons, Bridgwater
H 2509	PN73 ELH	SCA	Culina	
H 2510	PN73 EOA	SCA	Great Bear	
H 2511	PN73 ENM	SCA	Great Bear	
H 2512	PN73 ENW	SCA	Great Bear	Desborough
H 2513	PN73 ETE	SCA	Stobart	
H 2514	PN73 ENO	SCA	Great Bear	
H 2515	PN73 ENX	SCA	Great Bear	
H 2516	PN73 ETF	SCA	Great Bear	
H 2517	PN73 EOY	SCA	Great Bear	
H 2518	PN73 EPA	SCA	Great Bear	
H 2519	PN73 EPD	SCA	Stobart	
H 2520	PN73 EPE	SCA	Stobart	
H 2521	PN73 EPJ	SCA	Stobart	
H 2522	PN73 EPK	SCA	Stobart	
H 2523	PN73 EPL	SCA	Culina	
H 2524	PN73 EPU	SCA	Stobart	Rugby
H 2525	PN73 EPV	SCA	Stobart	Rugby
H 2526	PN73 EPX	SCA	Stobart	
H 2527	PN73 EPY	SCA	Stobart	
H 2528	PN73 EPZ	SCA	Stobart	
H 2529	PN73 ERJ	SCA	Stobart	Bridgwater
H 2530	PN73 ERK	SCA	Stobart	Morrisons, Bridgwater
H 2531	PN73 ERO	SCA	Warrens	
H 2532	PN73 ERU	SCA	Stobart	
H 2533	PN73 ERV	SCA	Culina	

H 2534	PN73 ERX	SCA	Fowler Welch	Washington
H 2535	PN73 ERZ	SCA	Stobart	COOP Coventry
H 2536	PN73 ESF	SCA	Stobart	
H 2537	PN73 ESG	SCA	Stobart	
H 2538	PN73 ESO	SCA	Stobart	
H 2539	PN73 ETJ	SCA	Fowler Welch	Washington
H 2540	PN73 ETK	SCA	Great Bear	
H 2541	PN73 ETL	SCA	Great Bear	
H 2542	PN73 ETO	SCA	Stobart	Daventry
H 2543	PN73 ETR	SCA	Stobart	Appleton
H 2544	PN73 ETU	SCA	Fowler Welch	Washington
H 2545	PN73 EUB	SCA	Fowler Welch	
H 2546	PN73 ETX	SCA	Stobart	
H 2547	PN73 ETY	SCA	Stobart	
H 2548	PN73 EUC	SCA	Stobart	Appleton
H 2549	PN73 EUD	SCA	Fowler Welch	
H 2550	PN73 EUE	SCA	Culina	Milton Keynes
H 2551	PN73 EUF	SCA	Fowler Welch	Fowler Welch
H 2552	PN73 EXS	SCA	Culina	Milton Keynes
H 2553	PN73 ETZ	SCA	Culina	Milton Keynes
H 2554	PN73 EXZ	SCA	Culina	
H 2555	PN73 EXT	SCA	Culina	Milton Keynes
H 2556	PN73 EYB	SCA	Culina	
H 2557	PN73 EXU	SCA	Culina	
H 2558	PN73 EXV	SCA	Culina	Milton Keynes
H 2559	PN73 EXW	SCA	Culina	Milton Keynes
H 2560	PN73 EXX	SCA	Fowler Welch	Washington
H 2561	PN73 EYD	SCA	Fowler Welch	
H 2562	PN73 EYF	SCA	Culina	
H 2563	PN73 EYG	SCA	Culina	
H 2564	PN73 EYH	SCA	Stobart	COOP Coventry
H 2565	PN73 EYJ	SCA	Great Bear	
H 2566	PN73 EYK	SCA	Great Bear	
H 2567	PN73 EYL	SCA	Stobart	Appleton
H 2568	PN73 EYM	SCA	Stobart	
H 2569	PK73 XSX	SCA	Culina	Milton Keynes
H 2570	PK73 XSY	SCA	Culina	Burton Latimer
H 2572	PK73 XTA	SCA	Culina	Milton Keynes
H 2573	PK73 XTB	SCA	Stobart	Burton Latimer
H 2574	PK73 XTC	SCA	Stobart	
H 2575	PK73 XTD	SCA	Stobart	Rugby
H 2576	PK73 XTE	SCA	Culina	Milton Keynes
H 2577	PK73 XTF	SCA	Stobart	
H 2578	PK73 XTG	SCA	Culina	Milton Keynes
H 2579	PK73 XTH	SCA	Culina	Rugby
H 2580	PK73 XTJ	SCA	Stobart	Rugby
H 2582	PK73 XTM	SCA	Great Bear	
H 2583	PK73 XTN	SCA	Culina	
H 2584	PK73 XTO	SCA	Stobart	Morrisons, Bridgwater
H 2585	PK73 XTP	SCA	Fowler Welch	Washington
H 2586	PK73 XTR	SCA	Fowler Welch	
H 2587	PK73 XTS	SCA	Stobart	Morrisons, Bridgwater
H 2500	PK73 XTT	SCA	Great Bear	
H 2589	PK73 XTU	SCA	Great Bear	
H 2590	PK73 XTV	SCA	Great Bear	
H 2591	PK73 XTW	SCA	Stobart	Morrisons, Bridgwater
H 2592	PK73 XTX	SCA	Stobart	
H 2593	PK73 XTY	SCA	Great Bear	
H 2594	PK73 XTZ	SCA	Great Bear	Lutterworth
H 2595	PK73 XUA	SCA	Stobart	

H 2596	PK73 XUB	SCA	Stobart		Northampton
H 2597	PK73 XUC	SCA	Stobart		Morrisons, Bridgwater
H 2598	PK73 XUD	SCA	Great Bear		
H 2599	PK73 XUE	SCA	Culina		
H 2600	PK73 XUF	SCA	Stobart		Morrisons, Bridgwater
H 2601	PK73 XUG	SCA	Stobart		Morrisons, Bridgwater
H 2602	PK73 XUH	SCA	Warrens		Rugby
H 2603	PK73 XUJ	SCA	Stobart		Morrisons, Bridgwater
H 2604	PK73 XUL	SCA	Stobart		Morrisons, Bridgwater
H 2605	PK73 XUM	SCA	Stobart		Morrisons, Bridgwater
H 2606	PK73 XUN	SCA	Fowler Welch		Lutterworth
H 2607	PK73 XUO	SCA	Stobart		Morrisons, Bridgwater
H 2608	PK73 XUP	SCA	Warrens		
H 2609	PK73 XUR	SCA	Stobart		Morrisons, Bridgwater
H 2610	PK73 XUS	SCA	Stobart		
H 2611	PK73 XUT	SCA	Stobart		Morrisons, Bridgwater
H 2612	PK73 XUU	SCA	Culina		Rugby
H 2613	PJ73 JOA	SCA	Warrens		Rugby
H 2614	PJ73 JOV	SCA	Warrens		Rugby
H 2615	PJ73 JPF	SCA	Fowler Welch		Lutterworth
H 2616	PJ73 JNN	SCA	Fowler Welch		Lutterworth
H 2617	PJ73 JPO	SCA	Fowler Welch		Lutterworth
H 2618	PJ73 JOH	SCA	Fowler Welch		Lutterworth
H 2619	PJ73 JOU	SCA	Fowler Welch		Lutterworth
H 2620	PJ73 JNO	SCA	Culina		Lutterworth
H 2621	PJ73 JPU	SCA	Stobart		
H 2622	PJ73 JPV	SCA	Stobart		
H 2623	PJ73 JPX	SCA	Culina		Lutterworth
H 2624	PJ73 JPY	SCA	Great Bear		Lutterworth
H 2625	PJ73 JNU	SCA	Culina		
H 2626	PJ73 JNV	SCA	Stobart		
H 2627	PJ73 JNX	SCA	CulinaPN		Minworth
H 2628	PJ73 JNZ	SCA	Stobart		
H 2629	PJ73 JTU	SCA	Stobart		Daventry 1
H 2630					
H 2631	PJ73 JSU	SCA	Stobart		
H 2632	PJ73 JTV	SCA	Stobart		Daventry 1
H 2633	PJ73 JTX	SCA	Stobart		Daventry 1
H 2634	Pj73 JTY	SCA	Stobart		Daventry 1
H 2635	PJ73 JWP	SCA	Stobart		Morrisons, Wakefield
H 2636	PJ73 JTZ	SCA	Warrens		Rugby
H 2637	PJ73 JUA	SCA	Stobart		Morrisons, Wakefield
H 2638	PJ73 JWU	SCA	Stobart		
H 2639	PJ73 JUC	SCA	Stobart		Morrisons, Wakefield
H 2640	PJ73 JUE	SCA	Stobart		Morrisons, Wakefield
H 2641	PJ73 JWV	SCA	Stobart		Morrisons, Wakefield
H 2642	PJ73 JSV	SCA	Stobart		
H 2643	PJ73 JSX	SCA	Fowler Welch		Washington
H 2644	PJ73 JSY	SCA	Stobart		
H 2645	PJ73 JRO	SCA	Culina		Lutterworth
H 2646	PJ73 JRU	SCA	Stobart		
H 2647	PJ73 JSZ	SCA	Stobart		Morrisons, Wakefield
H 2648	PJ73 JTO	SCA	Stobart		
H 2649	PJ73 JRV	SCA	Stobart		Morrisons, Bridgwater
H 2650	PJ73 JRX	SCA	Stobart		
H 2651	PJ73 JRZ	SCA	Stobart		
H 2652	PJ73 JWW	SCA	Stobart		Morrisons, Bridgwater
H 2653	PJ73 JWX	SCA	Stobart		Morrisons, Wakefield
H 2654	PJ73 JWY	SCA	Stobart		
H 2655	PJ73 SXR	SCA	Stobart		Morrisons, Wakefield

H 2656	PJ73 SXU	SCA	Stobart	Rugby
H 2657	PJ73 SXT	SCA	Stobart	
H 2658	PJ73 SXY	SCA	Stobart	
H 2659	PJ73 TBY	SCA	Stobart	
H 2660	PJ73 SXV	SCA	Stobart	
H 2661	PJ73 SXZ	SCA	Stobart	
H 2662	PJ73 TDO	SCA	Stobart	Morrisons, Wakefield
H 2663	PJ73 SYC	SCA	Stobart	Daventry 1
H 2664	PJ73 SYF	SCA	Stobart	
H 2665	PJ73 SXS	SCA	Stobart	Appleton
H 2666	PJ73 SYW	SCA	Stobart	Morrisons, Wakefield
H 2667	PJ73 TDU	SCA	Stobart	Morrisons, Wakefield
H 2668	PJ73 SYA	SCA	Stobart	
H 2669	PJ73 SXW	SCA	Stobart	
H 2670	PJ73 SXX	SCA	Stobart	
H 2671	PJ73 SYH	SCA	Stobart	
H 2672	PJ73 XUP	SCA	Stobart	Morrisons, Wakefield
H 2673	PJ73 SYS	SCA	Stobart	
H 2674	PJ73 SYE	SCA	Stobart	Appleton
H 2675	PJ73 SYG	SCA	Stobart	
H 2676	PJ73 SYT	SCA	Stobart	Morrisons, Wakefield
H 2677	PJ73 XUR	SCA	Stobart	Morrisons, Wakefield
H 2678	171 D 3945	SCA	Topaz	Dublin
H 2679				
H 2680	171 D 3951	SCA	Topaz	Dublin
H 2681	171 D 3949	SCA	Topaz	Dublin
H 2682	171 D 6524	SCA	Topaz	Dublin
H 2683	171 D 3939	SCA	Topaz	Dublin
H 2684	171 D 6519	SCA	Topaz	Dublin
H 2685	EGZ 7175	SCA	Topaz	Belfast
H 2686	171 D 7677	SCA	Topaz	Dublin
H 2687	171 D 11713	SCA	Topaz	Dublin
H 2688	171 D 11745	SCA	Topaz	Dublin
H 2689	171 D 11715	SCA	Topaz	Dublin
H 2690				
H 2691	PN19 FJE	SCA	Culina	
H 2692	EGZ 7176	SCA	Topaz	Belfast
H 2693	171 D 9175	SCA	Topaz	Dublin
H 2694	171 D 9174	SCA	Topaz	Dublin
H 2695	171 D 8823	SCA	Topaz	Dublin
H 2696	171 D 9590	SCA	Topaz	Dublin
H 2697	171 D 9593	SCA	Topaz	Dublin
H 2698	171 D 9585	SCA	Topaz	Dublin
H 2699	171 D 9581	SCA	Topaz	Dublin
H 2700	171 D 9583	SCA	Topaz	Dublin
H 2701	171 D 9588	SCA	Topaz	Dublin
H 2702				
H 2703	PJ73 SYR	SCA	Warrens	Rugby
H 2704	PJ73 SYO	SCA	Stobart	Bridgwater
H 2705	PJ73 SYX	SCA	Warrens	Rugby
H 2706	PJ73 SYP	SCA	Stobart	Morrisons, Wakefield
H 2707	PJ73 SYY	SCA	Stobart	Morrisons, Bridgwater
H 2708	PJ73 SYV	SCA	Stobart	Wakefield
H 2709				
H 2710				
H 2711	PJ73 SZD	SCA	Stobart	Wakefield
H 2712	PJ73 SZE	SCA	Stobart	Burton Latimer
H 2713	PJ73 SZF	SCA	Stobart	Burton Latimer
H 2714	PJ73 TAV	SCA	Stobart	Wakefield
H 2715	PJ73 TBO	SCA	Stobart	Morrisons, Wakefield

H 2716	PJ73 TBU	SCA	Stobart	Morrisons, Wakefield
H 2717				
H 2718	PJ73 TCX	SCA	Stobart	Wakefield
H 2719	PJ73 SZG	SCA	Stobart	Wakefield
H 2720	PJ73 SZK	SCA	Stobart	Wakefield
H 2721	PJ73 SZL	SCA	Stobart	
H 2722	PJ73 SZN	SCA	Stobart	Bridgwater
H 2723	PJ73 SZO	SCA	Stobart	Burton Latimer
H 2724	PJ73 SZP	SCA	Stobart	Bridgwater
H 2725	PJ73 SZR	SCA	Stobart	
H 2726	PJ73 SZT	SCA	Stobart	
H 2727				
H 2728	PJ73 SZV	SCA	Stobart	
H 2729	PJ73 SZW	SCA	Stobart	
H 2730	PJ73 SZX	SCA	Stobart	Burton Latimer
H 2731	PJ73 SZY	SCA	Stobart	Burton Latimer
H 2732	PJ73 SZZ	SCA	Stobart	
H 2733	PJ73 TAU	SCA	Great Bear	Markham Vale
H 2734	PJ73 TBV	SCA	Stobart	Wakefield
H 2735	PJ73 TBX	SCA	Stobart	Wakefield
H 2736	PJ73 TBZ	SCA	Stobart	Wakefield
H 2737	PJ73 TCK	SCA	Stobart	Wakefield
H 2738	PJ73 TCO	SCA	Stobart	Burton Latimer
H 2739	PJ73 TCU	SCA	Stobart	Wakefield
H 2740	PJ73 TCV	SCA	Fowler Welch	Washington
H 2741	PJ73 TCY	SCA	Stobart	Wakefield
H 2742	PJ73 TCZ	SCA	Stobart	Burton Latimer
H 2743	PJ73 TDV	SCA	Stobart	Wakefield
H 2744	PJ73 TDX	SCA	Culina	Washington
H 2745	PJ73 XUS	SCA	Fowler Welch	Washington
H 2746				
H 2747	PJ73 XUT	SCA	Stobart	Morrisons, Bridgwater
H 2748				
H 2749	PJ73 XUU	SCA	Fowler Welch	Washington
H 2750	PJ73 XUV	SCA	Stobart	Wakefield
H 2751	PJ73 XUX	SCA	Stobart	Wakefield
H 2752	PJ73 XUY	SCA	Fowler Welch	Wakefield
H 2753	PJ73 XUZ	SCA	Stobart	Wakefield
H 2754	PJ73 XVA	SCA	Stobart	Wakefield
H 2755	PJ73 XVB	SCA	Fowler Welch	Bridgwater
H 2756	PJ73 XVC	SCA	Stobart	Bridgwater
H 2757	PJ73 XUW	SCA	Stobart	Wakefield
H 2758	PJ73 XVD	SCA	Stobart	Wakefield
H 2759	PJ73 XVE	SCA	Stobart	Wakefield
H 2760	PJ73 XVF	SCA	Stobart	Wakefield
H 2761	PJ73 XVG	SCA	Great Bear	Markham Vale
H 2762	PJ73 XVH	SCA	Stobart	Wakefield
H 2763	PJ73 XVK	SCA	Stobart	Wakefield
H 2764				
H 2765	PJ73 XVL	SCA	Stobart	Wakefield
H 2766	PJ73 XVM	SCA	Stobart	Wakefield
H 2767	PJ73 XVN	SCA	Stobart	Wakefield
H 2768	PJ73 XVO	SCA	Stobart	Wakefield
H 2769	PJ73 XVP	SCA	Great Bear	Markham Vale
H 2770	PJ73 XVR	SCA	Stobart	Wakefield
H 2771	PJ73 XVS	SCA	Stobart	Rugby
H 2772	PJ73 XVT	SCA	Stobart	Wakefield
H 2773	PJ73 XVU	SCA	Stobart	Wakefield
H 2774	PF73 KXD	SCA	Stobart	Rugby
H 2775	PF73 KXG	SCA	Stobart	Rugby

H 2776	PF73 KYG	SCA	Stobart	Rugby
H 2777	PF73 KXH	SCA	Stobart	Wakefield
H 2778	PF73 KXM	SCA	Stobart	Wakefield
H 2779	PF73 KXK	SCA	Stobart	Wakefield
H 2780	PF73 KXJ	SCA	Stobart	Wakefield
H 2781	PF73 KXL	SCA	Stobart	Morrisons, Wakefield
H 2782	PF73 KXR	SCA	Stobart	Wakefield
H 2783	PF73 KXV	SCA	Stobart	Wakefield
H 2784	PF73 KXC	SCA	Stobart	Wakefield
H 2785	Pf73 KXN	SCA	Stobart	Wakefield
H 2786	PF73 KXO	SCA	Stobart	Wakefield
H 2787	PF73 KXY	SCA	Stobart	Wakefield
H 2788	PF73 KXP	SCA	Stobart	Bridgwater
H 2789	PF73 KXT	SCA	Stobart	Bridgwater
H 2790	PF73 KXU	SCA	Stobart	Bridgwater
H 2791	PF73 KXW	SCA	Stobart	Bridgwater
H 2792	PF73 KXX	SCA	Stobart	
H 2793				
H 2794	PF73 KXS	SCA	Warrens	
H 2795				
H 2796	PF73 KXZ	SCA	Stobart	Bridgwater
H 2797				
H 2798	PF73 KYA	SCA	Stobart	Bridgwater
H 2799	PF73 KYH	SCA	Stobart	Morrisons, Bridgwater
H 2800	PF73 KYJ	SCA	Warrens	Rugby
H 2801	PF73 KYK	SCA	Stobart	COOP Coventry
H 2802	PF73 KYS	SCA	Stobart	
H 2803	PF73 KYN	SCA	Stobart	
H 2804	PF73 KYO	SCA	Stobart	Wakefield
H 2805	PF73 KYP	SCA	Stobart	Wakefield
H 2806	PF73 KYT	SCA	Warrens	
H 2807	PF73 KYR	SCA	Culina	
H 2808	PF73 KZC	SCA	Culina	
H 2809	PF73 KZD	SCA	Culina	
H 2810	PF73 KYU	SCA	Culina	
H 2811	PF73 KYV	SCA	Warrens	Rugby
H 2812				
H 2813				
H 2814				
H 2815	PF73 KYW	SCA	Culina	
H 2816				
H 2817	PF73 KZE	SCA	Culina	
H 2818	PF73 KYX	SCA	Stobart	Wakefield
H 2819				
H 2820				
H 2821	PN24 DJO	SCA	Culina	
H 2822	PF73 KZG	SCA	Stobart	Morrisons, Wakefield
H 2823	PF73 KYZ	SCA	Stobart	Burton Latimer
H 2824	PF73 KZA	SCA	Stobart	Daventry 1
H 2825	PF73 KZB	SCA	Stobart	Wakefield
H 2826	PF73 KZO	SCA	Stobart	
H 2827	PF73 KZH	SCA	Stobart	Morrisons, Wakefield
H 2828	PF73 KZJ	SCA	Stobart	Wakefield
H 2829	PF73 KZK	SCA	Stobart	
H 2830	PF73 KZP	SCA	Stobart	
H 2831	PF73 KZL	SCA	Stobart	Wakefield
H 2832	PF73 KZM	SCA	Stobart	Morrisons, Wakefield
H 2833				
H 2834				
H 2835				

H 2836					
H 2837					
H 2838					
H 2839					
H 2840	PF73 KZN	SCA	Stobart		
H 2841	PF73 KZR	SCA	Stobart		
H 2842	PF73 KZS	SCA	Stobart		
H 2843	PF73 KZT	SCA	Stobart		Wakefield
H 2844	PF73 KZU	SCA	Stobart		
H 2845	PF73 KZV	SCA	Stobart		Wakefield
H 2846	PF73 KZW	SCA	Stobart		
H 2847	PF73 KZX	SCA	Stobart		Wakefield
H 2848	PF73 KZY	SCA	Stobart		
H 2849	PF73 KZZ	SCA	Stobart		Wakefield
H 2850	PF73 LAA	SCA	Stobart		
H 2746	PO67 VLU	SCA	Stobart	Phillipa Emily	Widnes
H 2795	PO67 VLL	SCA	Stobart	Clare Judith	Widnes
H 2797	PO67 VLR	SCA	Stobart	Hollie Sylvia	Rugby
H 2812	PO67 VLS	SCA	Stobart		
H 2813	PO67 VLZ	SCA	Stobart		
H 2814	PO67 VMA	SCA	Stobart		
H 2816	PO67 VMD	SCA	Stobart		
H 2820	PO67 VMH	SCA	Stobart		
H 2835	PO67 XRS	SCA	Stobart		
H 2836	PO67 VLX	SCA	Stobart	Karen	Carlisle
H 2838	PO67 XSK	SCA	Stobart	Sophie Heather	Sherburn
H 2839	PO67 XRT	SCA	Stobart	Meg Emily	Goresbrook
H 2851	PO67 XMC	SCA	Stobart	Diane Jane	Wakefield
H 2853	PO67 XRZ	SCA	Stobart		Bellshill Morrisons
H 2855	PO67 XSB	SCA	Stobart		Bellshill Morrisons
H 2857	PO67 XSD	SCA	Stobart	Pauline Tracey	Braunstone
H 2858	PO67 XSE	SCA	Stobart		Bellshill
H 2859	PO67 XSF	SCA	Stobart	Abigail Lynn	
H 2860	PO67 XSG	SCA	Stobart	Jenni	Cannock
H 2889	PO67 XSX	SCA	Stobart		Bellshill Morrisons
H 2893	PO67 XTB	SCA	Stobart	Glenda Margaret	Carlisle
H 2897	PO67 XTF	SCA	Stobart	Deborah Jean	Newport
H 2907	PO67 XTR	SCA	Stobart		
H 2912	PO67 VKV	SCA	Stobart	Jessica Melanie	Leicester
H 2913	PO67 VKE	SCA	White - MMiD		
H 2914	PO67 VKF	SCA	Stobart	Cheryl Lynn	Goresbrook
H 2915	PO67 VKG	SCA	Stobart	Florance	Doncaster
H 2916	PO67 VKH	SCA	Stobart		
H 2917	PO67 VKJ	SCA	Stobart		
H 2922	PO67 VKN	SCA	Stobart		
H 2923	PO67 XTX	SCA	Stobart	Debbie Julie	Stoke
H 2924	PO67 XTY	SCA	Stobart	Glenda Isabel	Cannock
H 2926	PO67 XUA	SCA	Stobart	Sally Ann	Leicester
H 2928	PO67 XUC	SCA	Culina		
H 2929	PO67 XMG	SCA	Stobart		
H 2933	PO67 VKP	SCA	Stobart	Isabel Nancy	Rugby
H 2938	PO67 VNB	SCA	Stobart	Valerie June	Stoke
H 2942	PO67 VNF	SCA	Stobart	Sandra Anne	Stoke
H 2950	PO67 XUP	SCA	Stobart		
H 2954	PO67 VNH	SCA	Stobart		Bellshill
H 2957	PO67 VNL	SCA	Stobart	Alison Corinne	Trafford Park
H 2963	PO67 XUW	SCA	Stobart	Brenda Eileen	Lillyhall
H 2965	PO67 XVM	SCA	Stobart	Maisy Jayne	Trafford Park
H 2969	PO67 XVS	SCA	Stobart	Susan Patricia	Wakefield
H 2970	PO67 XVT	SCA	White - MMiD		

H 2973	PK67 URX	SCA	Stobart	Charlotte Becky	Rugby
H 2974	PK67 URY	SCA	Stobart	Amelia Ruby	Rugby
H 2977	PO67 VNV	SCA	Stobart		
H 2981	PO67 XVY	SCA	White - MMiD		
H 2988	PO67 XXJ	SCA	Stobart	Louise Barbara	Trafford Park
H 2992	PO67 XWJ	SCA	White - MMiD		
H 2993	PO67 XWK	SCA	Stobart	Molly Sasha	Rugby
H 2995	PO67 XWN	SCA	Stobart		
H 2999	PO67 XWT	SCA	Stobart		Bellshill
H 3001	GN22 XXL	MER	Fowler Welch		Teynham, Kent
H 3002	GN22 XXT	MER	Fowler Welch		Teynham, Kent
H 3003	GN22 XXJ	MER	Fowler Welch		Teynham, Kent
H 3004	GN22 XXP	MER	Fowler Welch		Teynham, Kent
H 3005	GN22 XXO	MER	Fowler Welch		Teynham, Kent
H 3006	GN22 XXR	MER	Fowler Welch		Teynham, Kent
H 3007	GN22 XXM	MER	Fowler Welch		Teynham, Kent
H 3008	GN22 XXK	MER	Fowler Welch		Teynham, Kent
H 3009	GN22 XVY	MER	Culina		Rugby T-Stop
H 3010	GN72 YMM	MER	Stobart		Morrisons S-bourne
H 3011	GN72 YMP	MER	Stobart		Morrisons S-bourne
H 3012	GN72 YML	MER	Stobart		Burton Latimer
H 3013	GN72 YMR	MER	Fowler Welch		Taynham, Kent
H 3014	GN72 YMJ	MER	Stobart		
H 3015	GN72 YMS	MER	Stobart		Morrisons S-bourne
H 3016	GN72 YMW	MER	Stobart		
H 3017	GN72 YMK	MER	Stobart		
H 3018	GN72 YMO	MER	Stobart		Morrisons S-bourne
H 3019	GN72 YMG	MER	Stobart		
H 3020	GN72 YMD	MER	Stobart		
H 3021	GN72 YMH	MER	Stobart		
H 3022	GN72 YMF	MER	Stobart		
H 3023	GN72 YMA	MER	Stobart		Morrisons S-bourne
H 3024	GN72 YMC	MER	Stobart		
H 3025	GN72 YME	MER	Stobart		Morrisons S-bourne
H 3026	GN72 YMT	MER	Stobart		Morrisons S-bourne
H 3027	GN72 YPH	MER	Stobart		
H 3028	GN72 YPA	MER	Stobart		
H 3029	GN72 YPC	MER	Stobart		
H 3030	GN72 YMU	MER	Stobart		Morrisons S-bourne
H 3031	GN72 YPE	MER	Stobart		Morrisons S-bourne
H 3032	GN72 YMX	MER	Stobart		
H 3033	GN72 YPF	MER	Stobart		
H 3034	GN72 YPG	MER	Stobart		Morrisons S-bourne
H 3035	GN72 YMY	MER	Stobart		
H 3036	GN72 YMZ	MER	Stobart		
H 3037	GN72 YPJ	MER	Culina		
H 3038	GN72 YPK	MER	Stobart		
H 3039	GN72 YMV	MER	Stobart		
H 3040	GN72 YPD	MER	Stobart		
H 3041	GF72 NCV	MER	Stobart		Walkers Leicester
H 3042	GF72 NGV	MER	Stobart		Walkers Birchwood
H 3043	GF72 NGX	MER	Warrens		Walkers Birchwood
H 3044	GF72 UJO	MER	Culina		
H 3045	GF72 NGY	MER	Great Bear		
H 3046	GN72 YRR	MER	Stobart		Walkers Leicester
H 3047	GN72 YRW	MER	Warrens		
H 3048	GF72 UJP	MER	Stobart		Walkers Leicester
H 3049	GN72 YRV	MER	Fowler Welch		Portsmouth
H 3050	GF72 URC	MER	Stobart		
H 3051	GF72 KMJ	MER	Stobart		Walkers Birchwood

H 3052	GF72 KMO	MER	Stobart	Walkers Birchwood
H 3053	GF72 KMU	MER	Stobart	Walkers Birchwood
H 3054	GF72 KOH	MER	Stobart	Morrisons S-bourne
H 3055	GF72 KOJ	MER	Stobart	
H 3056	GF72 LMU	MER	Stobart	
H 3057	GF72 LNY	MER	Stobart	Morrisons S-bourne
H 3058	GF72 UJB	MER	Stobart	Morrisons S-bourne
H 3059	GF72 LOH	MER	Stobart	Walkers Birchwood
H 3060	GF72 LPA	MER	Stobart	Walkers Birchwood
H 3061	GF72 MEU	MER	Stobart	Walkers Birchwood
H 3062	GF72 MVV	MER	Stobart	Morrisons S-bourne
H 3063	GF72 POU	MER	Stobart	Walkers Birchwood
H 3064	GF72 ROH	MER	Stobart	Morrisons S-bourne
H 3065	GN72 YRM	MER	Stobart	Walkers Leicester
H 3066	GN72 YRJ	MER	Stobart	Walkers Birchwood
H 3067	GF72 RXP	MER	Stobart	Walkers Birchwood
H 3068	GF72 UJG	MER	Stobart	Morrisons S-bourne
H 3069	GF72 SFJ	MER	Great Bear	
H 3070	GF72 NGZ	MER	Stobart	Walkers Leicester
H 3071	GN72 YPT	MER	Stobart	
H 3072	GN72 YRG	MER	Stobart	Walkers Leicester
H 3073	GN72 YPM	MER	Stobart	
H 3074	GN72 YRC	MER	Stobart	
H 3075	GN72 YRF	MER	Stobart	Walkers Birchwood
H 3076	GN72 YPZ	MER	Stobart	Morrisons S-bourne
H 3077	GN72 YRL	MER	Warrens	
H 3078	GN72 YPY	MER	Stobart	Walkers Birchwood
H 3079	GN72 YPL	MER	Stobart	
H 3080	GN72 YPU	MER	Stobart	
H 3081	GN72 YRA	MER	Fowler Welch	
H 3082	GN72 YRK	MER	Fowler Welch	Portsmouth
H 3083	GN72 YRS	MER	Stobart	Walkers Birchwood
H 3084	GN72 YRE	MER	Fowler Welch	
H 3085	GN72 YRT	MER	Stobart	Walkers Birchwood
H 3086	GN72 YRO	MER	Stobart	Walkers Leicester
H 3087	GF72 NCC	MER	Great Bear	Michellin, Stoke
H 3088	GN72 YRU	MER	Culina	Bristol
H 3089	GN72 YPO	MER	Stobart	Morrisons S-bourne
H 3090	GN72 YPP	MER	Stobart	
H 3091	GN72 YPV	MER	Stobart	Morrisons S-bourne
H 3092	GF72 NCJ	MER	Fowler Welch	
H 3093	GF72 NCU	MER	Fowler Welch	
H 3094	GN72 YRP	MER	Stobart	Walkers Birchwood
H 3095	GN72 NGU	MER	Stobart	Walkers Leicester
H 3096	GF72 NCD	MER	Fowler Welch	
H 3097	GF72 NBY	MER	Fowler Welch	
H 3098	GN72 YRD	MER	Stobart	
H 3099	GN72 YPR	MER	Stobart	
H 3100	GN72 YPX	MER	Stobart	
H 3101	GN72 YPW	MER	Stobart	
HG 3179	WV23 BFX	IVE	Morrisons	Gadbrook
HG 3180	WV23 BFY	IVE	Morrisons	Gadbrook
HG 3181	WV23 BFZ	IVE	Morrisons	Gadbrook
HG 3182	WV23 BGE	IVE	Morrisons	Gadbrook
HG 3183	WV23 BGF	IVE	Morrisons	Gadbrook
HG 3184	WV23 BGK	IVE	Morrisons	Gadbrook
HG 3185	WV23 BGO	IVE	Morrisons	Gadbrook
HG 3186	WV23 BGU	IVE	Morrisons	Gadbrook
HG 3187	WV23 BGX	IVE	Morrisons	Gadbrook
HG 3188	WV23 BGY	IVE	Morrisons	Gadbrook

HG 3189	WV23 BGZ	IVE	Morrisons		Gadbrook
HG 3190	WV23 BHA	IVE	Morrisons		Gadbrook
HG 3191	WV23 BHD	IVE	Morrisons		Gadbrook
HG 3192	WV23 BHE	IVE	Morrisons		Gadbrook
HG 3193	WV23 BHF	IVE	Morrisons		Gadbrook
HG 3194	WV23 BHJ	IVE	Morrisons		Gadbrook
HG 3195	WV23 BHK	IVE	Morrisons		Gadbrook
HG 3196	WV23 BHL	IVE	Morrisons		Gadbrook
HG 3197	WV23 BHN	IVE	Morrisons		Gadbrook
HG 3198	WV23 BHO	IVE	Morrisons		Gadbrook
HG 3199	WV23 BHP	IVE	Morrisons		Gadbrook
HG 3200	WV23 BHU	IVE	Morrisons		Gadbrook
HG 3201	WV23 BHW	IVE	Morrisons		Gadbrook
HG 3202	WV23 BHX	IVE	Morrisons		Gadbrook
HG 3203	WV23 BHY	IVE	Morrisons		Gadbrook
HG 3204	WV23 BHZ	IVE	Morrisons		Gadbrook
HG 3205	WV23 BJE	IVE	Morrisons		Gadbrook
HG 3206	WV23 BJF	IVE	Morrisons		Gadbrook
HG 3207	WV23 BJJ	IVE	Morrisons		Gadbrook
HG 3208	WV23 BJK	IVE	Morrisons		Gadbrook
HG 3209	WV23 BJO	IVE	Morrisons		Gadbrook
HG 3210	WV23 BJU	IVE	Morrisons		Gadbrook
HG 3211	WV23 BJX	IVE	Morrisons		Gadbrook
HG 3212	WV23 BJY	IVE	Morrisons		Gadbrook
HG 3213	WV23 BJZ	IVE	Morrisons		Gadbrook
HG 3214	WV23 BKA	IVE	Morrisons		Gadbrook
HG 3215	WV23 BKD	IVE	Morrisons		Gadbrook
HG 3216	WV23 BKE	IVE	Morrisons		Gadbrook
HG 3217	WV23 BKF	IVE	Morrisons		Gadbrook
HG 3218	WV23 BKG	IVE	Morrisons		Gadbrook
HG 3219	WV23 BKJ	IVE	Morrisons		Gadbrook
HG 3220	WV23 BKK	IVE	Morrisons		Gadbrook
HG 3221	WV23 BKL	IVE	Morrisons		Gadbrook
H 3404	PN19 FJO	SCA	Culinaventor		
H 3405	PN19 FJK	SCA	Culinaventor		
H 3427	PN20 AXM	SCA	Williams Racing		Hawleys Lane
H 3428	PN20 AXO	SCA	Williams Racing		Hawleys Lane
H 3429	PN20 ABZ	SCA	Williams Racing		Carlisle
H 3430 (R5)	PO20 ZZW	SCA	Williams Racing		Hawleys Lane
H 3447	GK21 AOJ	MER	Silver		Hawleys Lane
H 3448	GK21 AOL	MER	White		Hawleys Lane
H 3449	GK21 AOM	MER	White		Hawleys Lane
H 3450	GK21 AON	MER	White		Hawleys Lane
H 3451	GK21 AOO	MER	White		Hawleys Lane
H 3452	GK21 AOP	MER	White		Hawleys Lane
H 3453	GK21 AOR	MER	White		Hawleys Lane
H 3508	GN18 VPJ	MER	Stobart	Elizabeth Ann	Carlisle
H 3511	GN23 ZBE	MER	Stobart		Carlisle
H 3512	GN23 ZBF	MER	Stobart		
H 3513	GN23 ZBG	MER	Stobart		
H 3514	GN23 ZBJ	MER	Stobart		
H 3515	GN23 ZBL	MER	Stobart		
H 3516	GN23 ZBO	MER	Stobart		
H 3517	GN23 ZBP	MER	Stobart		Daventry
H 3518	GN23 ZBR	MER	Stobart		Daventry
H 3519	GN23 ZBT	MER	Stobart		Carlisle
H 3520	GN23 ZBU	MER	Stobart		Teesport
H 3521	GN23 ZBV	MER	Stobart		Teesport
H 3522	GN23 ZDE	MER	Fowler Welch		
H 3523	GN23 ZDD	MER	Fowler Welch		

H 3524	GN23 ZDC	MER	Fowler Welch	
H 3525	GN23 ZDA	MER	Fowler Welch	
H 3526	GN23 ZDK	MER	Fowler Welch	
H 3527	GN23 ZDG	MER	Fowler Welch	
H 3528	GN23 ZDH	MER	Great Bear	
H 3529	GN23 ZDJ	MER	Great Bear	
H 3530	GN23 ZDL	MER	Great Bear	
H 3531	GN23 ZDM	MER	Fowler Welch	
H 3532	GN23 ZDO	MER	Fowler Welch	
H 3533	GN23 ZDP	MER	Fowler Welch	
H 3534	GN23 ZDR	MER	Great Bear	
H 3535	GN23 ZDS	MER	Fowler Welch	
H 3536	GN23 ZDT	MER	Fowler Welch	
H 3537	GN23 ZDU	MER	Fowler Welch	
H 3538	GN23 ZDV	MER	Fowler Welch	
H 3539	GN23 ZDW	MER	Great Bear	
H 3540	GN23 ZDX	MER	Great Bear	
H 3541	GN23 ZDY	MER	Fowler Welch	
H 3542	GD23 KNP	MER	Great Bear	
H 3543	GF23 AEU	MER	Great Bear	
H 3544	GN23 ZDF	MER	Great Bear	
H 3545	GD23 NZE	MER	Great Bear	
H 3546	GF23 ELX	MER	Great Bear	
H 3547	GD23 MFU	MER	Culina	
H 3548	GD23 MFP	MER	Great Bear	
H 3549	GF23 EWX	MER	Great Bear	
H 3550	GF23 HFH	MER	Culina	
H 3551	GF23 JNJ	MER	Stobart	Morrisons Stockton
H 3552	GF23 JNU	MER	Stobart	Morrisons Stockton
H 3553	GF23 EWZ	MER	Great Bear	
H 3554	GD23 NZF	MER	Great Bear	Sheffield
H 3555	GF23 EWY	MER	Great Bear	
H 3556	GN73 YVP	MER	Great Bear	
H 3557	GF23 HMH	MER	Culina	
H 3558	GF23 HLZ	MER	Great Bear	Sheffield
H 3559	GN73 YVA	MER	Stobart	Morrisons Stockton
H 3560	GN73 YVG	MER	Stobart	
H 3561	GN73 YVB	MER	Stobart	Morrisons Stockton
H 3562	GF23 PZE	MER	Stobart	Morrisons Stockton
H 3563	GN73 YVF	MER	Stobart	
H 3564	GF23 KFU	MER	Stobart	Morrisons Stockton
H 3565	GF23 RKE	MER	Culina	
H 3566	GN73 YVU	MER	Stobart	Morrisons Stockton
H 3567	GN73 YVC	MER	Stobart	
H 3568	GN73 YVT	MER	Stobart	
H 3569	GN73 YVR	MER	Stobart	Morrisons Stockton
H 3570	GF23 KFV	MER	Stobart	Morrisons Stockton
H 3571	GN73 YVV	MER	Stobart	Morrisons Stockton
H 3572	GN73 YVX	MER	Stobart	Morrisons Stockton
H 3573	GN73 YVM	MER	Stobart	Morrisons Stockton
H 3574	GN73 YVS	MER	Stobart	
H 3575	GN73 YVL	MER	Stobart	Morrisons Stockton
H 3576	GN73 YVW	MER	Stobart	Morrisons Stockton
H 3577	GN73 YVK	MER	Stobart	Morrisons Stockton
H 3578	GN73 YVH	MER	Stobart	
H 3579	GN73 YVJ	MER	Stobart	Morrisons Stockton
H 3580	GN73 YVD	MER	Stobart	Morrisons Stockton
H 3581	GN73 YVO	MER	Stobart	Morrisons Stockton
H 3582	GN73 YVE	MER	Stobart	
H 3583	GN73 YVY	MER	Stobart	Morrisons Stockton

Culina Group (cont)

H 3584	GN73 YYA	MER	Great Bear		
H 3585	GN73 YVZ	MER	Great Bear		Morrisons Stockton
H 3586	GN73 YWE	MER	Stobart		Morrisons Stockton
H 3587	GN73 YWK	MER	Great Bear		Sutton-in-Ashfield
H 3588	GN73 YWF	MER	Great Bear		Morrisons Stockton
H 3589	GN73 YWL	MER	Stobart		Morrisons Stockton
H 3590	GN73 YXL	MER	Great Bear		Sutton-in-Ashfield
H 3591	GN73 YWA	MER	Stobart		Morrisons Stockton
H 3592	GN73 YWJ	MER	Stobart		Morrisons Stockton
H 3593	GN73 YWD	MER	Stobart		Morrisons Stockton
H 3594	GN73 YXH	MER	Great Bear		
H 3595	GN73 YXG	MER	Great Bear		
H 3596	GN73 YXP	MER	Great Bear		
H 3597	GN73 YXM	MER	Great Bear		
H 3598	GN73 YXK	MER	Great Bear		Sutton-in-Ashfield
H 3599	GN73 YWB	MER	Stobart		Morrisons Stockton
H 3600	GN73 YXU	MER	Great Bear		
H 3601	GN73 YXS	MER	Great Bear		Sutton-in-Ashfield
H 3602	GN73 YXT	MER	Stobart		Morrisons Stockton
H 3603	GN73 YXV	MER	Great Bear		Sutton-in-Ashfield
H 3604	GN73 YXJ	MER	Great Bear		
H 3605	GN73 YXR	MER	Great Bear		
H 3606	GN73 YXO	MER	Culina		
H 3607	GN73 YXY	MER	Great Bear		
H 3608	GN73 YXW	MER	Great Bear		
H 3609	GN73 YXZ	MER	Great Bear		Sutton-in-Ashfield
H 3610	GN73 YZJ	MER	Culina		
H 4000	PX21 WZO	Volvo	Fowler Welch		Evesham
H 4001	PX21 WZP	Volvo	Fowler Welch		Evesham
H 4002	PX21 WZR	Volvo	Fowler Welch		Evesham
H 4003	PX21 WZT	Volvo	Fowler Welch		Evesham
H 4004	PX21 WZU	Volvo	Fowler Welch		Evesham
H 4005	PX21 WZV	Volvo	Fowler Welch		Evesham
H 4006	PX21 WZW	Volvo	Fowler Welch		Evesham
H 4007	PX21 WZN	Volvo	Fowler Welch		Evesham
H 4008	PX21 WZZ	Volvo	Fowler Welch		Evesham
H 4009	PX21 XBB	Volvo	Fowler Welch		Evesham
H 4010	PX21 XBC	Volvo	Fowler Welch		Evesham
H 4011	PX21 XBD	Volvo	Fowler Welch		Evesham
H 4012	PX21 XBE	Volvo	Fowler Welch		Evesham
H 4013	PX21 XBF	Volvo	Fowler Welch		Evesham
H 4014	PY21 HMA	Volvo	Fowler Welch		Evesham
H 4015	PX21 XBG	Volvo	Fowler Welch		Evesham
H 4016	PX21 XBH	Volvo	Fowler Welch		Evesham
H 4017	PX21 XBJ	Volvo	Warrens		Rugby
H 4018	PX21 XBK	Volvo	Fowler Welch		Evesham
H 4019	PX21 XBM	Volvo	Fowler Welch		Evesham
H 4020	PX21 XBN	Volvo	Fowler Welch		Evesham
H 4021	PX21 XBO	Volvo	Fowler Welch		Evesham
H 4022	PY21 HMC	Volvo	Fowler Welch		Evesham
H 4023	PY21 HLZ	Volvo	Fowler Welch		Evesham
H 4024	PX21 XBR	Volvo	Fowler Welch		Evesham
H 4025	PX21 XBT	Volvo	Stobart	Debbie Keita	Stoke
H 4026	PY21 HNJ	Volvo	Stobart	Bethany Grace	
H 4027	PY21 HNK	Volvo	Stobart	Joan Audrey	Lillyhall
H 4028	PY21 GXC	Volvo	Stobart	Scarlett Aine	Stoke
H 4029	PY21 GXD	Volvo	Stobart	Betheny Elise	
H 4030	PY21 HMD	Volvo	Stobart	Millie Molly	Stoke
H 4031	PY21 HME	Volvo	Stobart	Shelby Riise	
H 4032	PY21 HMF	Volvo	Stobart	Alex Jane	

H 4033	PY21 HMG	Volvo	Stobart	Susan Irene	Trafford Park
H 4034	PY21 HMH	Volvo	Stobart	Abigail Leona	
H 4035	PY21 HMJ	Volvo	Stobart	Sharon Gail	Newport
H 4036	PY21 HMK	Volvo	Stobart	Naomi Victoria	Stoke
H 4037	PY21 HMO	Volvo	Stobart	Jessica Isabelle	
H 4038	PY21 HMU	Volvo	Stobart	Elaine	Stoke
H 4039	PY21 HMV	Volvo	Stobart	Farron Julie	Stoke
H 4040	PY21 HMX	Volvo	Stobart	Tiree	Stoke
H 4041	PY21 HMZ	Volvo	Stobart	Gillian	Trafford Park
H 4042	PY21 HNA	Volvo	Stobart	Catherine Elizabeth	Stoke
H 4043	PY21 HNC	Volvo	Stobart	Gillian Lesley	Trafford Park
H 4044	PY21 HNB	Volvo	Stobart	Kaye Christina	Trafford Park
H 4045	PY21 HND	Volvo	Stobart	Mina Ruby	Trafford Park
H 4046	PY21 HNE	Volvo	Stobart	Lorna Victoria	Trafford Park
H 4047	PY21 HNF	Volvo	Stobart	Alice May	Trafford Park
H 4048	PY21 HNG	Volvo	Stobart	Kathleen Mary	
H 4049	PY21 HNH	Volvo	Stobart	Lacy Rae	Trafford Park
H 4050	PX71 VEF	Volvo	Great Bear		Wolverhampton
H 4051	PX71 VEH	Volvo	Great Bear		Wolverhampton
H 4052	PX71 VEK	Volvo	Great Bear		Wolverhampton
H 4053	PX71 VEL	Volvo	Great Bear		Wolverhampton
H 4054	PX71 VEM	Volvo	Stobart		Carlisle
H 4055	PX71 VEO	Volvo	Stobart		Carlisle
H 4056	PX71 VEP	Volvo	Stobart		Penrith
H 4057	PX71 VEU	Volvo	Stobart		Carlisle
H 4058	PX71 VEV	Volvo	Stobart		Trafford Park
H 4059	PX71 VEW	Volvo	Stobart		Carlisle
H 4060	PX71 VEY	Volvo	Stobart		Newport
H 4061	PX71 VFA	Volvo	Morgan McLernon		
H 4062	PX71 VFB	Volvo	Stobart		
H 4063	PX71 VFC	Volvo	Stobart		
H 4064	PX71 VFD	Volvo	Stobart		Carlisle
H 4065	PX71 VFE	Volvo	Culina		Hereford
H 4066	PX71 VFF	Volvo	Culina		Hereford
H 4067	PX71 VFG	Volvo	Stobart		Newport
H 4068	PX71 VFH	Volvo	Stobart		Carlisle
H 4069	PX71 VFJ	Volvo	Stobart		Carlisle
H 4070	PX71 VFK	Volvo	Stobart		Carlisle
H 4071	PX71 VFL	Volvo	Stobart		Lillyhall
H 4072	PX71 VFM	Volvo	Stobart		Lillyhall
H 4073	PX71 VFN	Volvo	Stobart		Carlisle
H 4074	PX71 VFO	Volvo	Stobart		Carlisle
H 4075	PX71 VCU	Volvo	Great Bear		Wolverhampton
H 4076	PX71 VCV	Volvo	Great Bear		Wolverhampton
H 4077	PX71 VCW	Volvo	Great Bear		Wolverhampton
H 4078	PX71 VCY	Volvo	Great Bear		Wolverhampton
H 4079	PX71 VCZ	Volvo	Fowler Welch		Evesham
H 4080	PX71 VDA	Volvo	Fowler Welch		Evesham
H 4081	PX71 VDC	Volvo	Fowler Welch		Evesham
H 4082	PX71 VDD	Volvo	Fowler Welch		Evesham
H 4083	PX71 VDE	Volvo	Fowler Welch		Evesham
H 4084	PX71 VDF	Volvo	Fowler Welch		Evesham
H 4085	PX71 VDG	Volvo	Great Bear		
H 4086	PX71 VDJ	Volvo	Great Bear		Wolverhampton
H 4087	PX71 VDK	Volvo	Fowler Welch		Evesham
H 4088	PX71 VDL	Volvo	Fowler Welch		Evesham
H 4089	PX71 VDM	Volvo	Stobart		Carlisle
H 4090	PX71 VDN	Volvo	Fowler Welch		Evesham
H 4091	PX71 VDO	Volvo	Fowler Welch		Evesham
H 4092	PX71 VDP	Volvo	Culina		Hereford

H 4093	PX71 VDR	Volvo	Fowler Welch	Evesham
H 4094	PX71 VDT	Volvo	Fowler Welch	Evesham
H 4095	PX71 VDV	Volvo	Fowler Welch	Evesham
H 4096	PX71 VDY	Volvo	Fowler Welch	Evesham
H 4097	PX71 VDZ	Volvo	Fowler Welch	Evesham
H 4098	PX71 VEA	Volvo	Culina	Hereford
H 4099	PX71 VEB	Volvo	Fowler Welch	Evesham
H 4100	DX22 VPR	Volvo	Stobart	Trafford Park
H 4101	DX22 VPD	Volvo	Stobart	
H 4102	DX22 VPF	Volvo	Stobart	Trafford Park
H 4103	DX22 VPG	Volvo	Stobart	Trafford Park
H 4104	DX22 VPK	Volvo	Stobart	Stoke
H 4105	DX22 VPM	Volvo	Stobart	Stoke
H 4106	DX22 VPN	Volvo	Stobart	Stoke
H 4107	DX22 VPP	Volvo	Stobart	Stoke
H 4108	DX22 VPT	Volvo	Stobart	Stoke
H 4109	DX22 VPU	Volvo	Stobart	Felixstowe
H 4110	DX22 VPV	Volvo	Stobart	Rugby
H 4111	DX22 VPW	Volvo	Stobart	Rugby
H 4112	DX22 VPY	Volvo	Stobart	
H 4113	DX22 VPZ	Volvo	Stobart	
H 4114	DX22 VPA	Volvo	Stobart	
H 4115	DX22 VPC	Volvo	Stobart	Trafford Park
H 4116	DX22 VPE	Volvo	Stobart	Felixstowe
H 4117	DX22 VPJ	Volvo	Stobart	
H 4118	DX22 VPL	Volvo	Stobart	
H 4119	DX22 VPO	Volvo	Stobart	
H 4120	DX73 VPY	Volvo	Stobart	
H 4121	DX23 VTF	Volvo	Culina	
H 4122	DX23 VTG	Volvo	Culina	
H 4123	DX73 VPZ	Volvo	Stobart	
H 4124	DX73 VRC	Volvo	Stobart	
H 4125	DX23 VTL	Volvo	Culina	
H 4126	DX23 VTM	Volvo	Culina	
H 4127	DX23 VTN	Volvo	Culina	
H 4128	DX73 VRD	Volvo	Stobart	
H 4129	DX73 VSG	Volvo	Stobart	
H 4130	DX23 VTT	Volvo	Culina	
H 4131	DX73 VSJ	Volvo	Stobart	
H 4132	DX23 VTV	Volvo	Culina	
H 4133	DX23 VTW	Volvo	Culina	
H 4134	DX23 VTY	Volvo	Culina	
H 4135	DX23 VTZ	Volvo	Culina	
H 4136	DX23 VUA	Volvo	Culina	Haverhill
H 4137	DX73 VSU	Volvo	Fowler Welch	Evesham
H 4138	DX73 VSV	Volvo	Fowler Welch	Evesham
H 4139	DX73 VSY	Volvo	Culina	Haverhill
H 4140	DX73 VSZ	Volvo	Fowler Welch	
H 4141	DX73 VTA	Volvo	Fowler Welch	
H 4142	DX73 VSP	Volvo	Stobart	
H 4143	DX73 VTC	Volvo	Fowler Welch	Evesham
H 4144	DX73 VTE	Volvo	Culina	Haverhill
H 4145				
H 4146	DX73 VSM	Volvo	Fowler Welch	
H 4147	DX73 VRE	Volvo	Stobart	
H 4148	DX73 VRF	Volvo	Culina	
H 4149	DX73 VSN	Volvo	Stobart	
H 4150	DX73 VRG	Volvo	Culina	
H 4151	DX73 VRJ	Volvo	Culina	
H 4152	DX73 VRK	Volvo	Culina	

H 4153	DX73 VRL	Volvo	Fowler Welch	Broxburn
H 4154	DX73 VRM	Volvo	Fowler Welch	
H 4155	DX73 VST	Volvo	Stobart	
H 4156				
H 4157				
H 4158				
H 4159	DX73 VTL	Volvo	Stobart	
H 4160	DX73 VTM	Volvo	Stobart	
H 4161	DX73 VTD	Volvo	Stobart	
H 4162	DX73 VSL	Volvo	Great Bear	
H 4163				
H 4164	DX73 VTN	Volvo	Stobart	
H 4165	DX73 VTW	Volvo	Culina	Haverhill
H 4166	DX73 VTY	Volvo	Culina	Haverhill
H 4167	DX73 VTZ	Volvo	Culina	
H 4168	DX73 VTP	Volvo	Warrens	Haverhill
H 4169	DX73 VTT	Volvo	Warrens	Haverhill
H 4170	DX73 VTV	Volvo	Warrens	
H 4171	DX73 VUA	Volvo	Stobart	
H 4172	DX73 VUB	Volvo	Stobart	
H 4173	DX73 VUC	Volvo	Stobart	
H 4174	DX73 VUD	Volvo	Stobart	
H 4175	DX73 VUE	Volvo	Culina	
H 4176	DX73 VUF	Volvo	Stobart	
H 4177	DX73 VUG	Volvo	Culina	
H 4178	DX73 VUH	Volvo	Culina	
H 4179	DX73 VUJ	Volvo	Stobart	
H 4180	DX73 VUK	Volvo	Culina	
H 4181	DX73 VUL	Volvo	Stobart	
H 4182	DX73 VUM	Volvo	Culina	
H 4183	DX73 VUN	Volvo	Stobart	
H 4184				
H 4185	DX73 VRN	Volvo	Fowler Welch	
H 4186	DX73 VSO	Volvo	Fowler Welch	
H 4187	DX23 VUE	Volvo	Culina	
H 4188	DX23 VUF	Volvo	Culina	Haverhill
H 4189	DX73 VRO	Volvo	Fowler Welch	
H 4190	DX73 VRP	Volvo	Fowler Welch	
H 4191	DX73 VRR	Volvo	Fowler Welch	
H 4192	DX73 VRU	Volvo	Fowler Welch	
H 4193	DX73 VRV	Volvo	Stobart	
H 4194	DX73 VRW	Volvo	Stobart	
H 4195	DX73 VRY	Volvo	Fowler Welch	Broxburn
H 4196	DX23 VUP	Volvo	Culina	
H 4197	DX73 VRZ	Volvo	Fowler Welch	
H 4198	DX73 VSF	Volvo	Stobart	
H 4199	DX73 VSA	Volvo	Fowler Welch	
H 4200	DX72 VPA	Volvo	Great Bear	
H 4201	DX72 VPC	Volvo	Great Bear	
H 4202	DX72 VPD	Volvo	Culina	
H 4203	DX72 VPE	Volvo	Great Bear	
H 4204	DX72 VPF	Volvo	Great Bear	Michelin Tyres, Stoke
H 4205	DX72 VPG	Volvo	Great Bear	
H 4206	DX72 VPJ	Volvo	Great Bear	
H 4207	DX72 VPK	Volvo	Great Bear	
H 4208	DX72 VPL	Volvo	Great Bear	
H 4209	DX72 VPM	Volvo	Great Bear	
H 4210	DX73 VSC	Volvo	Stobart	
H 4211	DX73 VSK	Volvo	Fowler Welch	
H 4212	DX73 VSD	Volvo	Stobart	

H 4213	DX73 VSE	Volvo	Stobart	
H 4300	PN23 FOD	Daf	Stobart	
H 4301	PN23 FOF	Daf	Fowler Welch	
H 4302	PN23 FOH	Daf	Stobart	
H 4303	PN23 FOJ	Daf	Stobart	
H 4304	PN23 FOK	Daf	Stobart	
H 4305	PN23 FOM	Daf	Stobart	Carlisle
H 4306	PN23 FOP	Daf	Stobart	
H 4307	PN23 FOT	Daf	Stobart	Sherburn in Elmet
H 4308	PN23 FOU	Daf	Stobart	
H 4309	PN23 FOV	Daf	Stobart	Sherburn in Elmet
H 4310	PN23 FPA	Daf	Stobart	Sherburn in Elmet
H 4311	PN23 FPG	Daf	Stobart	
H 4312	PN23 FPJ	Daf	Fowler Welch	Stafford
H 4313	PN23 FPK	Daf	Fowler Welch	
H 4314	PN23 FPU	Daf	Stobart	Sherburn in Elmet
H 4315	PN23 FPV	Daf	Stobart	
H 4316	PN23 FPX	Daf	Stobart	
H 4317	PN23 FPY	Daf	Stobart	Sherburn in Elmet
H 4318	PN23 FPZ	Daf	Stobart	
H 4319	PN23 FRP	Daf	Fowler Welch	
H 4320	PN23 FSC	Daf	Culina	Stafford
H 4321	PN23 FSD	Daf	Fowler Welch	Stafford
H 4322	PN23 FSE	Daf	Culina	
H 4323	PN23 FSF	Daf	Great Bear	
H 4324	PN23 FSG	Daf	Stobart	
H 4325	PN23 FSJ	Daf	Culina	
H 4326	PN23 FSK	Daf	Culina	Stafford
H 4327	PN23 FSL	Daf	Fowler Welch	Stafford
H 4328	PN23 FSO	Daf	Culina	Stafford
H 4329	PN23 FTA	Daf	Culina	Stafford
H 4330	PN23 FTJ	Daf	Stobart	Carlisle
H 4331	PN23 FTK	Daf	Stobart	Lillyhall
H 4332	PN23 FTO	Daf	Stobart	
H 4333	PN23 FTP	Daf	Stobart	Carlisle
H 4334	PN23 FTU	Daf	Stobart	Lillyhall
H 4335	PN23 FUT	Daf	Culina	Stafford
H 4336	PN23 FUU	Daf	Stobart	
H 4337	PN23 FUV	Daf	Culina	Stafford
H 4338	PN23 FUW	Daf	Culina	
H 4339	PN23 FUY	Daf	Stobart	
H 4340	PN23 FVC	Daf	Great Bear	
H 4341	PN23 FVD	Daf	Stobart	
H 4342	PN23 FVE	Daf	Fowler Welch	Portsmouth
H 4343	PN23 FLM	Daf	Great Bear	
H 4344	PN23 FLZ	Daf	Culina	
H 4345	PN23 FMA	Daf	Culina	
H 4346	PN23 FMC	Daf	Culina	
H 4347	PN23 FMD	Daf	Culina	
H 4348	PN23 FME	Daf	Great Bear	
H 4349	PN23 FMF	Daf	Great Bear	
H 4350	PN23 FMJ	Daf	Great Bear	
H 4351	PN23 FMK	Daf	Culina	
H 4352	PN23 FML	Daf	Fowler Welch	Portsmouth
H 4353	PJ23 FMM	Daf	Great Bear	
H 4354	PN23 FNO	Daf	Great Bear	
H 4355	PN23 FNP	Daf	Fowler Welch	Portsmouth
H 4356	PN23 FNR	Daf	Culina	
H 4357	PN23 FNS	Daf	Great Bear	
H 4358	PN23 FNt	Daf	Great Bear	

H 4359	PJ23 KUX	Daf	Fowler Welch	
H 4360	PJ23 KUY	Daf	Stobart	
H 4361	PJ23 KVC	Daf	Culina	
H 4362	PJ23 KVE	Daf	Stobart	
H 4363	PJ23 KVH	Daf	Stobart	
H 4364	PJ23 KWB	Daf	Stobart	
H 4365	PJ23 KVU	Daf	Stobart	
H 4366	PJ23 KVW	Daf	Fowler Welch	
H 4367	PJ23 KVV	Daf	Culina	
H 4368	PJ23 KVX	Daf	Stobart	
H 4369	PJ23 KWC	Daf	Fowler Welch	
H 4370	PJ23 KWY	Daf	Stobart	
H 4371	PJ23 KWZ	Daf	Stobart	Walkers Leicester
H 4372	PJ23 KWP	Daf	Great Bear	
H 4373	PJ23 KWS	Daf	Stobart	
H 4374	PJ23 KWX	Daf	Stobart	
H 4375	PJ23 KXC	Daf	Stobart	
H 4376	PJ23 KXD	Daf	Stobart	
H 4377	PJ23 KXE	Daf	Stobart	
H 4378	PJ23 KXH	Daf	Stobart	
H 4379	PJ23 KXB	Daf	Stobart	
H 4380	PJ23 KXU	Daf	Stobart	
H 4381	PJ23 KXR	Daf	Stobart	
H 4382	PJ23 KXT	Daf	Culina	
H 4383	PJ23 KXS	Daf	Great Bear	
H 4384	PJ23 KXY	Daf	Culina	
H 4385	PJ23 KXZ	Daf	Stobart	Walkers Leicester
H 4386	PJ23 KYN	Daf	Culina	
H 4387	PJ23 KYE	Daf	Stobart	Walkers Leicester
H 4388	PJ23 KYF	Daf	Culina	
H 4389	PJ23 KYB	Daf	Fowler Welch	
H 4390	PJ23 KYO	Daf	Great Bear	
H 4391	PJ23 KZC	Daf	Stobart	Wakefield
H 4392	PJ23 KZF	Daf	Great Bear	Michelin Tyres, Stoke
H 4393	PJ23 KZB	Daf	Culina	
H 4394	PJ23 KZD	Daf	Stobart	
H 4395	PJ23 KZK	Daf	Great Bear	
H 4396	PJ23 KZS	Daf	Great Bear	Michelin Tyres, Stoke
H 4397	PJ23 KZU	Daf	Fowler Welch	
H 4398	PJ23 KZR	Daf	Culina	
H 4399	PJ23 KZT	Daf	Great Bear	
H 4400	PJ23 LAA	Daf	Fowler Welch	
H 4401	PJ23 KZZ	Daf	Stobart	
H 4402	PJ23 LBE	Daf	Great Bear	
H 4403	PJ23 LBN	Daf	Fowler Welch	
H 4404	PJ23 LBK	Daf	Fowler Welch	
H 4405	PJ23 LCC	Daf	Stobart	
H 4406	PJ23 LCM	Daf	Fowler Welch	Spalding
H 4407	PJ23 LCE	Daf	Great Bear	Wolverhampton
H 4408	PJ23 LCK	Daf	Great Bear	Wolverhampton
H 4409	PN73 FTA	Daf	Stobart	
H 4410	PN73 FRP	Daf	Fowler Welch	
H 4411	PN73 FSF	Daf	Great Bear	
H 4412	PN73 FSJ	Daf	Great Bear	Sheffield
H 4413	PN73 FSE	Daf	Great Bear	
H 4414	PN73 FSK	Daf	Great Bear	
H 4415	PN73 FRZ	Daf	Great Bear	
H 4416	PN73 FSG	Daf	Great Bear	
H 4417	PN73 FSO	Daf	Great Bear	
H 4418	PN73 FRV	Daf	Great Bear	Wolverhampton

H 4419	PN73 FSX	Daf	Fowler Welch	
H 4420	PN73 FVH	Daf	Stobart	
H 4421	PN73 FPF	Daf	Stobart	
H 4422	PN73 FVK	Daf	Fowler Welch	
H 4423	PN73 FPJ	Daf	Fowler Welch	
H 4424	PN73 FPL	Daf	Fowler Welch	
H 4425	PN73 FVL	Daf	Fowler Welch	Newton Abbot
H 4426	PN73 FVM	Daf	Fowler Welch	
H 4427	PN73 FPO	Daf	Fowler Welch	
H 4428	PN73 FPP	Daf	Fowler Welch	
H 4429	PN73 FVO	Daf	Fowler Welch	
H 4430	PN73 FPT	Daf	Fowler Welch	
H 4431	PN73 FVP	Daf	Fowler Welch	
H 4432	PN73 FOV	Daf	Warrens	
H 4433	PJ23 KXF	Daf	Stobart	Walkers Leicester
H 4434	PJ23 KXG	Daf	Stobart	Walkers Leicester
H 4435	PJ23 KYG	Daf	Great Bear	
H 4436	PJ23 KYH	Daf	Great Bear	
H 4437	PJ23 KYK	Daf	Fowler Welch	
H 4438	PJ23 KZO	Daf	Fowler Welch	
H 4439	PJ23 KZH	Daf	Fowler Welch	
H 4440	PJ23 KZL	Daf	Fowler Welch	
H 4441	PJ23 KZM	Daf	Great Bear	Michelin Tyres, Stoke
H 4442	PJ23 KZV	Daf	Great Bear	
H 4443	PJ23 LBP	Daf	Fowler Welch	
H 4444	PN73 FVW	Daf	Fowler Welch	
H 4445	PJ23 LBL	Daf	Fowler Welch	
H 4446	PN73 FVX	Daf	Fowler Welch	Spalding
H 4447	PN73 FVY	Daf	Fowler Welch	
H 4448	PN73 FVZ	Daf	Fowler Welch	
H 4449	PN73 FBG	Daf	Stobart	Crawley
H 4450	PN73 FPK	Daf	Stobart	Crawley
H 4451	PN73 FRO	Daf	Great Bear	Sheffield
H 4452	PN73 FRU	Daf	Great Bear	Wolverhampton
H 4453	PN73 FRX	Daf	Great Bear	
H 4454	PN73 FSS	Daf	Fowler Welch	
H 4455	PN73 FSU	Daf	Fowler Welch	
H 4456	PN73 FSV	Daf	Fowler Welch	Spalding
H 4457	PN73 FSY	Daf	Fowler Welch	
H 4458	PN73 FSZ	Daf	Stobart	
H 4459	PN73 FTC	Daf	Fowler Welch	
H 4460	PN73 FTD	Daf	Stobart	
H 4461	PN73 FTE	Daf	Great Bear	
H 4462	PN73 FTF	Daf	Fowler Welch	Newton Abbot
H 4463	PN73 FTJ	Daf	Fowler Welch	Newton Abbot
H 4464	PN73 FTK	Daf	Stobart	Crawley
H 4465	PN73 FTO	Daf	Great Bear	Sheffield
H 4466	PN73 FTP	Daf	Warrens	
H 4467	PN73 FTZ	Daf	Fowler Welch	
H 4468	PN73 FUA	Daf	Fowler Welch	
H 4469	PN73 FNV	Daf	Stobart	
H 4470	PN73 FUD	Daf	Fowler Welch	
H 4471	PN73 FPA	Daf	Warrens	
H 4472	PJ73 YXS	Daf	Warrens	
H 4473	PN73 FUO	Daf	Fowler Welch	
H 4474	PN73 FUP	Daf	Fowler Welch	
H 4475	PN73 FUT	Daf	Fowler Welch	
H 4476	PN73 FUU	Daf	Fowler Welch	
H 4477	PN73 FVJ	Daf	Fowler Welch	
H 4478	PN73 FVR	Daf	Fowler Welch	

H 4479	PN73 FVS	Daf	Fowler Welch	
H 4480	PN73 FVT	Daf	Fowler Welch	
H 4481	PN73 FVU	Daf	Fowler Welch	
H 4482	PN73 FVV	Daf	Fowler Welch	
H 4483	PN73 FWA	Daf	Fowler Welch	
H 4484	PN73 FMX	Daf	Fowler Welch	
H 4485	PN73 FMY	Daf	Fowler Welch	
H 4486	PN73 FNH	Daf	Fowler Welch	
H 4487	PN73 FNE	Daf	Fowler Welch	Spalding
H 4488	PN73 FNF	Daf	Fowler Welch	
H 4489	PN73 FNG	Daf	Fowler Welch	
H 4490	PN73 FNT	Daf	Fowler Welch	
H 4491	PN73 FNU	Daf	Warrens	
H 4492	PN73 FOA	Daf	Fowler Welch	
H 4493	PN73 FOC	Daf	Fowler Welch	
H 4494	PN73 FNK	Daf	Fowler Welch	
H 4495	PN73 FNY	Daf	Fowler Welch	
H 4496	PJ73 YNN	Daf	Warrens	
H 4497	PJ73 YXU	Daf	Fowler Welch	Spalding
H 4498	PJ73 YYM	Daf	Warrens	
H 4499	PJ73 YXR	Daf	Stobart	
H 4500	PN72 FGC	Daf	Stobart	
H 4501	PN72 FHL	Daf	Stobart	Tesco Doncaster
H 4502	PN72 FHM	Daf	Stobart	
H 4503	PN72 FHO	Daf	Stobart	Tesco Goole
H 4504	PN72 FHP	Daf	Stobart	Tesco Goole
H 4505	PN72 FHR	Daf	Stobart	
H 4506	PN72 FHS	Daf	Stobart	
H 4507	PN72 FHT	Daf	Stobart	
H 4508	PN72 FJD	Daf	Stobart	Tesco Doncaster
H 4509	PN72 FHV	Daf	Stobart	
H 4510	PN72 FJF	Daf	Stobart	Tesco Goole
H 4511	PN72 FJJ	Daf	Stobart	Tesco Goole
H 4512	PN72 FJK	Daf	Stobart	
H 4513	PN72 FJO	Daf	Stobart	Tesco Goole
H 4514	PN72 FJX	Daf	Stobart	Tesco Goole
H 4515	PN72 FJY	Daf	Stobart	
H 4516	PN72 FJZ	Daf	Stobart	
H 4517	PN72 FKA	Daf	Stobart	
H 4518	PN72 FKB	Daf	Stobart	Tesco Goole
H 4519	PN72 FKO	Daf	Stobart	
H 4520	PN72 FKP	Daf	Stobart	Tesco Goole
H 4521	PN72 FKS	Daf	White	
H 4522	PN72 FKX	Daf	Stobart	Tesco Goole
H 4523	PN72 FLM	Daf	Stobart	
H 4524	PN72 FLP	Daf	Stobart	
H 4525	PN72 FLX	Daf	Stobart	Tesco Goole
H 4526	PN72 FLZ	Daf	Stobart	
H 4527	PN72 FMA	Daf	Stobart	
H 4528	PN72 FMC	Daf	Stobart	Tesco Doncaster
H 4529	PN72 FMJ	Daf	Stobart	Tesco Goole
H 4530	PN72 FNV	Daf	Stobart	Walkers Leicester
H 4531	PN72 FNW	Daf	Stobart	Walkers Leicester
H 4532	PN72 FOC	Daf	Stobart	Walkers Leicester
H 4533	PN72 FOH	Daf	Stobart	Tesco Doncaster
H 4534	PN72 FOJ	Daf	Stobart	
H 4535	PN72 FOK	Daf	Stobart	
H 4536	PN72 FOM	Daf	Stobart	Tesco Goole
H 4537	PN72 FOU	Daf	Stobart	
H 4538	PN72 FOV	Daf	Culina	Telford

Culina Group (cont)

H 4539	PJ72 EZR	Daf	Stobart	
H 4540	PJ72 EZS	Daf	Stobart	Tesco Goole
H 4541	PJ72 EZT	Daf	Stobart	
H 4542	PJ72 EZU	Daf	Stobart	Tesco Goole
H 4543	PJ72 EZV	Daf	Stobart	
H 4544	PJ72 EZW	Daf	Stobart	
H 4545	PJ72 EZX	Daf	Stobart	
H 4546	PJ72 EZZ	Daf	Stobart	
H 4547	PJ72 FAA	Daf	Stobart	Walkers Leicester
H 4548	PJ72 FAF	Daf	Stobart	Walkers Leicester
H 4549	PJ72 FAK	Daf	Stobart	Tesco Doncaster
H 4550	PJ72 FAM	Daf	Stobart	Walkers Leicester
H 4551	PJ72 FAO	Daf	Stobart	Walkers Leicester
H 4552	PJ72 FAU	Daf	Stobart	
H 4553	PJ72 FBA	Daf	Stobart	Walkers Leicester
H 4554	PJ72 FBB	Daf	Stobart	Walkers Leicester
H 4555	PJ72 FBC	Daf	Stobart	Walkers Leicester
H 4556	PJ72 FBD	Daf	Stobart	
H 4557	PJ72 FBE	Daf	Stobart	
H 4558	PJ72 FBF	Daf	Stobart	Walkers Leicester
H 4559	PJ72 FBG	Daf	Stobart	Walkers Leicester
H 4560	PJ72 FNK	Daf	Stobart	Tesco Goole
H 4561	PJ72 FBL	Daf	Stobart	Tesco Goole
H 4562	PJ72 FBN	Daf	Stobart	Tesco Goole
H 4563	PJ72 FBO	Daf	Stobart	
H 4564	PJ72 FBU	Daf	Stobart	Walkers Leicester
H 4565	PJ72 FBV	Daf	Stobart	Tesco Doncaster
H 4566	PJ72 FBX	Daf	Stobart	Tesco Goole
H 4567	PJ72 FBY	Daf	Stobart	Tesco Goole
H 4568	PJ72 FBZ	Daf	Stobart	Walkers Leicester
H 4569	PJ72 FCA	Daf	Stobart	
H 4570	PJ72 FCC	Daf	Stobart	
H 4571	PJ72 FCD	Daf	Stobart	Tesco Goole
H 4572	PJ72 FCE	Daf	Stobart	Tesco Doncaster
H 4573	PJ72 FCF	Daf	Stobart	
H 4574	PJ72 FCG	Daf	Stobart	
H 4575	PJ72 FCL	Daf	Stobart	Tesco Goole
H 4576	PJ72 FCM	Daf	Stobart	
H 4577	PJ72 FCN	Daf	Stobart	
H 4578	PJ72 FCO	Daf	Stobart	Tesco Doncaster
H 4579	PJ72 FCP	Daf	Stobart	
H 4580	PJ72 FCU	Daf	Stobart	
H 4581	PJ72 FCV	Daf	Stobart	Tesco Doncaster
H 4582	PJ72 FCX	Daf	Stobart	Tesco Doncaster
H 4583	PJ72 FCY	Daf	Stobart	Tesco Doncaster
H 4584	PJ72 FCZ	Daf	Stobart	
H 4585	PJ72 FDA	Daf	Stobart	Tesco Doncaster
H 4586	PJ72 FDC	Daf	Stobart	Tesco Doncaster
H 4587	PJ72 FDD	Daf	Stobart	
H 4588	PJ72 FTD	Daf	Stobart	Tesco Doncaster
H 4589	PJ72 FTE	Daf	Stobart	
H 4590	PJ72 FTF	Daf	Stobart	
H 4591	PJ72 FTK	Daf	Stobart	
H 4592	PJ72 FTN	Daf	Stobart	
H 4593	PJ72 FTO	Daf	Stobart	
H 4594	PJ72 FTP	Daf	Stobart	
H 4595	PJ72 FTT	Daf	Stobart	Tesco Doncaster
H 4596	PJ72 FTU	Daf	Stobart	Tesco Goole
H 4597	PJ72 FTV	Daf	Stobart	Tesco Goole
H 4598	PJ72 FTX	Daf	Stobart	

H 4599	PJ72 FTY	Daf	Stobart	Walkers Leicester
H 4600	PN72 FGD	Daf	Warrens	
H 4601	PN72 FGE	Daf	Warrens	Wakefield
H 4602	PN72 FGF	Daf	Stobart	Carlisle
H 4603	PN72 FGG	Daf	Stobart	Penrith
H 4605	PN72 FGK	Daf	Warrens	Cannock
H 4606	PN72 FGM	Daf	Stobart	Penrith
H 4607	PN72 FGO	Daf	Stobart	
H 4608	PN72 FGP	Daf	Stobart	Cannock
H 4609	PN72 FGU	Daf	Stobart	Carlisle
H 4610	PN72 FGV	Daf	Stobart	Carlisle
H 4611	PN72 FGX	Daf	Stobart	Carlisle
H 4612	PN72 FGZ	Daf	Stobart	
H 4613	PN72 FHA	Daf	Stobart	Carlisle
H 4614	PN72 FHB	Daf	Stobart	Carlisle
H 4615	PN72 FHC	Daf	Stobart	Carlisle
H 4616	PN72 FHD	Daf	Stobart	Carlisle
H 4617	PN72 FHE	Daf	Stobart	Carlisle
H 4618	PN72 FHF	Daf	Stobart	Carlisle
H 4619	PN72 FHG	Daf	Stobart	Cannock
H 4621	PN72 FHJ	Daf	Stobart	Carlisle
H 4622	PN72 FHK	Daf	Stobart	
H 4623	PN72 FHW	Daf	Stobart	
H 4624	PN72 FHX	Daf	Stobart	Wakefield
H 4625	PN72 FHY	Daf	Stobart	Wakefield
H 4626	PN72 FHZ	Daf	Stobart	Wakefield
H 4627	PN72 FJA	Daf	Stobart	
H 4628	PN72 FJC	Daf	Stobart	Wakefield
H 4629	PN72 FHU	Daf	Stobart	Cannock
H 4630	PN72 FJE	Daf	Stobart	Wakefield
H 4631	PN72 FJP	Daf	Stobart	
H 4632	PN72 FJU	Daf	Stobart	Wakefield
H 4633	PN72 FJV	Daf	Stobart	Sherburn
H 4634	PN72 FKE	Daf	Stobart	Cannock
H 4635	PN72 FKF	Daf	Stobart	
H 4636	PN72 FKG	Daf	Stobart	
H 4637	PN72 FKH	Daf	Stobart	
H 4638	PN72 FKJ	Daf	Stobart	
H 4639	PN72 FKL	Daf	Stobart	
H 4640	PN72 FKM	Daf	Stobart	Widnes Ports
H 4641	PN72 FKT	Daf	Stobart	Sherburn
H 4642	PN72 FKU	Daf	Stobart	Rugby
H 4643	PN72 FKV	Daf	Stobart	Cannock
H 4644	PN72 FKW	Daf	Stobart	Widnes Ports
H 4645	PN72 FKY	Daf	Stobart	Wakefield
H 4646	PN72 FKZ	Daf	Stobart	
H 4647	PN72 FLA	Daf	Stobart	Cannock
H 4648	PN72 FLB	Daf	Stobart	Rugby
H 4649	PN72 FLC	Daf	Stobart	
H 4650	PN72 FLD	Daf	Stobart	Rugby
H 4651	PN72 FLE	Daf	Stobart	Wakefield
H 4652	PN72 FLF	Daf	Stobart	Stoke
H 4653	PN72 FLG	Daf	Stobart	Wakefield
H 4654	PN72 FLH	Daf	Stobart	Sherburn
H 4655	PN72 FLJ	Daf	Stobart	Sherburn
H 4656	PN72 FLK	Daf	Stobart	Cannock
H 4657	PN72 FLL	Daf	Stobart	Carlisle
H 4658	PN72 FLR	Daf	Stobart	Stoke
H 4659	PN72 FLV	Daf	Stobart	
H 4660	PN72 FLW	Daf	Stobart	

H 4661	PN72 FMD	Daf	Stobart		Stoke
H 4662	PN72 FME	Daf	Stobart		Southampton
H 4663	PN72 FMF	Daf	Stobart		Sherburn
H 4664	PN72 FMG	Daf	Stobart		
H 4665	PN72 FMK	Daf	Stobart		Stoke
H 4666	PN72 FML	Daf	Stobart	Princess Ellie	Stoke
H 4667	PN72 FMM	Daf	Stobart		Stoke
H 4668	PN72 FMO	Daf	Stobart		Tesco Goole
H 4669	PN72 FMP	Daf	Stobart		Rugby
H 4670	PN72 FMU	Daf	Stobart		Sherburn
H 4671	PN72 FMX	Daf	Stobart		Wakefield
H 4672	PN72 FMY	Daf	Stobart		Wakefield
H 4673	PN72 FMZ	Daf	Stobart		Stoke
H 4674	PN72 FMV	Daf	Stobart		Rugby
H 4675	PN72 FNA	Daf	Stobart		Stoke
H 4676	PN72 FNC	Daf	Stobart		Stoke
H 4677	PN72 FND	Daf	Stobart		
H 4678	PN72 FNE	Daf	Stobart		Wakefield
H 4679	PN72 FNF	Daf	Stobart		
H 4680	PN72 FNG	Daf	Stobart		Stoke
H 4681	PN72 FNH	Daf	Stobart		Sherburn
H 4682	PN72 FNJ	Daf	Stobart		Sherburn
H 4683	PN72 FNK	Daf	Stobart		Goresbrook
H 4684	PN72 FNL	Daf	Stobart		
H 4685	PN72 FNM	Daf	Stobart		Sherburn
H 4686	PN72 FNO	Daf	Stobart		Sherburn
H 4687	PN72 FNP	Daf	Stobart		Stoke
H 4688	PN72 FNR	Daf	Stobart		Sherburn
H 4689	PN72 FNS	Daf	Stobart		Sherburn
H 4690	PN72 FNT	Daf	Stobart		
H 4691	PN72 FNU	Daf	Stobart		
H 4692	PN72 FNX	Daf	Stobart		Sherburn
H 4693	PN72 FNY	Daf	Stobart		Widnes Ports
H 4694	PN72 FNZ	Daf	Stobart		Stoke
H 4695	PN72 FOA	Daf	Stobart		Stoke
H 4696	PN72 FOD	Daf	Stobart		Sherburn
H 4697	PN72 FOF	Daf	Stobart		Sherburn
H 4698	PN72 FOP	Daf	Stobart		Stoke
H 4699	PN72 FOT	Daf	Stobart		Stoke
H 4700	PN23 FNU	Daf	Stobart		
H 4701	PN23 FNV	Daf	Great Bear		
H 4702	PN23 FMW	Daf	Stobart		
H 4703	PN23 FNX	Daf	Stobart		
H 4704	PN23 FNY	Daf	Stobart		
H 4705	PN23 FNW	Daf	Stobart		
H 4706	PN23 FOA	Daf	Great Bear		
H 4707	PN23 FOC	Daf	Stobart		Sherburn
H 4708	PN23 FPC	Daf	Great Bear		
H 4709	PN23 FPD	Daf	Culina		Stafford
H 4710	PN23 FPE	Daf	Culina		Stafford
H 4711	PN23 FPF	Daf	Culina		Stafford
H 4712	PN23 FPL	Daf	Stobart		Sherburn
H 4713	PN23 FPO	Daf	Stobart		
H 4714	PN23 FPP	Daf	Stobart		
H 4715	PN23 FPT	Daf	Culina		Stafford
H 4716	PN23 FRC	Daf	Stobart		
H 4717	PN23 FRD	Daf	Stobart		Goresbrook
H 4718	PN23 FRF	Daf	Stobart		
H 4719	PN23 FRJ	Daf	Stobart		
H 4720	PN23 FRK	Daf	Stobart		Sherburn

H 4721	PN23 FRL	Daf	Culina	Stafford
H 4722	PN23 FRO	Daf	Culina	Stafford
H 4723	PN23 FRR	Daf	Culinaventor	Stafford
H 4724	PN23 FRU	Daf	Culina	Stafford
H 4725	PN23 FRV	Daf	Fowler Welch	Stafford
H 4726	PN23 FRX	Daf	Fowler Welch	Stafford
H 4727	PN23 FRZ	Daf	Culina	Stafford
H 4728	PN23 FSA	Daf	Culina	
H 4729	PN23 FSP	Daf	Culina	Stafford
H 4730	PN23 FSS	Daf	Culina	Stafford
H 4731	PN23 FSU	Daf	Culina	Stafford
H 4732	PN23 FSV	Daf	Fowler Welch	
H 4733	PN23 FSX	Daf	Culina	Stafford
H 4734	PN23 FSY	Daf	Culina	Stafford
H 4735	PN23 FSZ	Daf	Culina	Stafford
H 4736	PN23 FTC	Daf	Stobart	Carlisle
H 4737	PN23 FTD	Daf	Stobart	Sherburn
H 4738	PN23 FTE	Daf	Stobart	
H 4739	PN23 FTF	Daf	Culina	Stafford
H 4740	PN23 FTV	Daf	Stobart	
H 4741	PN23 FTX	Daf	Stobart	Sherburn in Elmet
H 4742	PN23 FTY	Daf	Stobart	Sherburn in Elmet
H 4743	PN23 FTX	Daf	Stobart	
H 4744	PN23 FUA	Daf	Stobart	
H 4745	PN23 FUB	Daf	Stobart	
H 4746	PN23 FUD	Daf	Stobart	
H 4747	PN23 FUE	Daf	Fowler Welch	Stafford
H 4748	PN23 FUF	Daf	Stobart	
H 4749	PN23 FUH	Daf	Stobart	
H 4750	PN23 FUJ	Daf	Stobart	
H 4751	PN23 FUM	Daf	Stobart	Stoke
H 4752	PN23 FUO	Daf	Stobart	
H 4753	PN23 FUP	Daf	Stobart	Stoke
H 4754	PN23 FVA	Daf	Stobart	Stoke
H 4755	PN23 FVB	Daf	Stobart	
H 4756	PN23 FLP	Daf	Culina	
H 4757	PN23 FLR	Daf	Great Bear	
H 4758	PN23 FLV	Daf	Culinaventor	Stafford
H 4759	PN23 FLW	Daf	Great Bear	
H 4760	PN23 FLX	Daf	Stobart	Stafford
H 4761	PN23 FMG	Daf	Culina	
H 4762	PN23 FMO	Daf	Culina	
H 4763	PN23 FMP	Daf	Culina	Haverhill
H 4764	PN23 FMU	Daf	Fowler Welch	
H 4765	PN23 FMV	Daf	Culina	
H 4766	PN23 FMX	Daf	Ball Trucking	
H 4767	PN23 FMY	Daf	Great Bear	
H 4768	PN23 FMZ	Daf	Culina	Stafford
H 4769	PN23 FNA	Daf	Fowler Welch	
H 4770	PN23 FNC	Daf	Culina	
H 4771	PN23 FND	Daf	Great Bear	
H 4772	PN23 FNE	Daf	Great Bear	
H 4773	PN23 FNF	Daf	Stobart	
H 4774	PN23 FNG	Daf	Great Bear	
H 4775	PN23 FNH	Daf	Great Bear	
H 4776	PN23 FNJ	Daf	Fowler Welch	
H 4777	PN23 FNK	Daf	Culina	
H 4778	PN23 FNL	Daf	Culina	
H 4779	PN23 FNM	Daf	Fowler Welch	
H 4780	PJ23 KVA	Daf	Fowler Welch	

H 4781	PJ23 KVO	Daf	Stobart	
H 4782	PJ23 KVD	Daf	Fowler Welch	Portsmouth
H 4783	PJ23 KVM	Daf	Stobart	
H 4784	PJ23 KVP	Daf	Culina	
H 4785	PJ23 KVB	Daf	Stobart	Walkers, Leicester
H 4786	PJ23 KVK	Daf	Great Bear	
H 4787	PJ23 KVF	Daf	Great Bear	
H 4788	PJ23 KVG	Daf	Stobart	
H 4789	PJ23 KVL	Daf	Stobart	Walkers, Leicester
H 4790	PJ23 KVT	Daf	Stobart	Walkers, Leicester
H 4791	PJ23 KVR	Daf	Stobart	
H 4792	PJ23 KVS	Daf	Great Bear	
H 4793	PJ23 KVY	Daf	Culina	
H 4794	PJ23 KVZ	Daf	Fowler Welch	Portsmouth
H 4795	PJ23 KWA	Daf	Stobart	
H 4796	PJ23 KWD	Daf	Stobart	
H 4797	PJ23 KWE	Daf	Great Bear	
H 4798	PJ23 KWF	Daf	Stobart	
H 4799	PJ23 KWO	Daf	Culina	
H 4800	PJ23 KWG	Daf	Stobart	
H 4801	PJ23 KWK	Daf	Stobart	
H 4802	PJ23 KWN	Daf	Great Bear	
H 4803	PJ23 KWL	Daf	Stobart	Walkers, Leicester
H 4804	PJ23 KWH	Daf	Stobart	
H 4805	PJ23 KWM	Daf	Great Bear	
H 4806	PJ23 KXA	Daf	Stobart	
H 4807	PJ23 KWW	Daf	Stobart	
H 4808				
H 4809	PJ23 KWR	Daf	Great Bear	
H 4810	PJ23 KWU	Daf	Culina	
H 4811	PJ23 KWV	Daf	Great Bear	
H 4812	PJ23 KXN	Daf	Stobart	
H 4813	PJ23 KXM	Daf	Culina	
H 4814	PJ23 KXL	Daf	Culina	
H 4815	PJ23 KXO	Daf	Great Bear	
H 4816	PJ23 KXP	Daf	Stobart	
H 4817	PJ23 KXW	Daf	Stobart	
H 4818	PJ23 KXX	Daf	Stobart	
H 4819	PJ23 KYA	Daf	Stobart	Walkers, Leicester
H 4820	PJ23 KYC	Daf	Stobart	Walkers, Leicester
H 4821	PJ23 KYP	Daf	Culina	
H 4822	PJ23 KYR	Daf	Great Bear	
H 4823	PJ23 KYU	Daf	Great Bear	Michelin Tyres, Stoke
H 4824	PJ23 KYT	Daf	Great Bear	
H 4825	PJ23 KYS	Daf	Stobart	
H 4826	PJ23 KYW	Daf	Stobart	
H 4827	PJ23 KYZ	Daf	Great Bear	
H 4828	PJ23 KYV	Daf	Great Bear	
H 4829	PJ23 KYX	Daf	Fowler Welch	
H 4830	PJ23 KYY	Daf	Stobart	Michelin Tyres, Stoke
H 4831	PJ23 KZG	Daf	Stobart	
H 4832	PJ23 KZA	Daf	Culina	
H 4833	PJ23 KZE	Daf	Fowler Welch	
H 4834	PJ23 KZP	Daf	Fowler Welch	
H 4835	PJ23 KZX	Daf	Fowler Welch	
H 4836	PJ23 KZW	Daf	Fowler Welch	Spalding
H 4837	PJ23 LAE	Daf	Great Bear	Sheffield
H 4838	PJ23 LBG	Daf	Fowler Welch	
H 4839	PJ23 LBA	Daf	Great Bear	Sheffield
H 4840	PJ23 LBF	Daf	Great Bear	

H 4841	PJ23 LAO	Daf	Stobart	
H 4842	PJ23 KZY	Daf	Stobart	Wakefield
H 4843	PJ23 LBU	Daf	Fowler Welch	
H 4844	PJ23 LCX	Daf	Stobart	
H 4845	PJ23 LBV	Daf	Great Bear	Sheffield
H 4846	PJ23 LBZ	Daf	Great Bear	
H 4847	PJ23 LBY	Daf	Fowler Welch	
H 4848	PJ23 LCA	Daf	Great Bear	
H 4849	PJ23 LCF	Daf	Great Bear	
H 4850	PN73 FPU	Daf	Great Bear	Sheffield
H 4851	PN73 FPV	Daf	Fowler Welch	Newton Abbot
H 4852	PN73 FPX	Daf	Fowler Welch	Spalding
H 4853	PN73 FPY	Daf	Fowler Welch	
H 4854	PN73 FPZ	Daf	Fowler Welch	
H 4855	PN73 FRC	Daf	Fowler Welch	
H 4856	PN73 FRD	Daf	Fowler Welch	Newton Abbot
H 4857	PN73 FRF	Daf	Fowler Welch	Portsmouth
H 4858	PN73 FRJ	Daf	Fowler Welch	Portsmouth
H 4859	PN73 FRK	Daf	Fowler Welch	Newton Abbot
H 4860	PN73 FRL	Daf	Fowler Welch	Newton Abbot
H 4861	PN73 FRR	Daf	Stobart	
H 4862	PN73 FSA	Daf	Stobart	Sherburn
H 4863	PN73 FSC	Daf	Stobart	
H 4864	PN73 FSD	Daf	Stobart	Carlisle
H 4865	PN73 FSP	Daf	Fowler Welch	
H 4866	PN73 FTT	Daf	Fowler Welch	Spalding
H 4867	PN73 FTU	Daf	Fowler Welch	
H 4868	PN73 FTV	Daf	Stobart	
H 4869	PN73 FTX	Daf	Stobart	
H 4870				
H 4871				
H 4872				
H 4873				
H 4874				
H 4875				
H 4876				
H 4877				
H 4878				
H 4879				
H 4880				
H 4881				
H 4882				
H 4883				
H 4884				
H 4885				
H 4886				
H 4887				
H 4888				
H 4889				
H 4890				
H 4891				
H 4892				
H 4893				
H 4894				
H 4895				
H 4896				
H 4897				
H 4898				
H 4899				
H 4900	PN73 FTY	Daf	Stobart	

H 4901	PN73 FUE	Daf	Fowler Welch	
H 4902	PN73 FUF	Daf	Fowler Welch	Spalding
H 4903	PN73 FUG	Daf	Fowler Welch	Newton Abbot
H 4904	PN73 FUM	Daf	Fowler Welch	Portsmouth
H 4905	PN73 FUV	Daf	Fowler Welch	
H 4906	PN73 FUW	Daf	Fowler Welch	Portsmouth
H 4907	PN73 FUY	Daf	Fowler Welch	Spalding
H 4908	PN73 FVA	Daf	Fowler Welch	Portsmouth
H 4909	PN73 FVB	Daf	Stobart	
H 4910	PN73 FVC	Daf	Fowler Welch	
H 4911	PN73 FMV	Daf	Fowler Welch	
H 4912	PN73 FVD	Daf	Fowler Welch	
H 4913	PN73 FVE	Daf	Stobart	Goresbrook
H 4914	PN73 FVF	Daf	Stobart	
H 4915	PN73 FVG	Daf	Stobart	Sherburn in Elmet
H 4916	Pn73 FWB	Daf	Fowler Welch	
H 4917	PN73 FMZ	Daf	Fowler Welch	
H 4918	PN73 FNC	Daf	Culina	
H 4919	PN73 FND	Daf	Fowler Welch	
H 4920	PN73 FNM	Daf	Fowler Welch	
H 4921	PN73 FNO	Daf	Fowler Welch	
H 4922	PN73 FMP	Daf	Fowler Welch	Spalding
H 4923	PN73 FNS	Daf	Fowler Welch	Spalding
H 4924	PN73 FNW	Daf	Fowler Welch	
H 4925	PN73 FNZ	Daf	Fowler Welch	
H 4926	PN73 FOM	Daf	Fowler Welch	
H 4927	PN73 FOU	Daf	Fowler Welch	
H 4928	PN73 FNA	Daf	Fowler Welch	
H 4929	PN73 FNX	Daf	Fowler Welch	
H 4930	PN73 FNR	Daf	Warrens	
H 4931	PN73 FNL	Daf	Warrens	
H 4932	PN73 FPC	Daf	Fowler Welch	Spalding
H 4933	PN73 FOT	Daf	Fowler Welch	Spalding
H 4934	PN73 FOD	Daf	Fowler Welch	Spalding
H 4935	PN73 FPD	Daf	Stobart	Goresbrook
H 4936	PN73 FOP	Daf	Stobart	
H 4937	PN73 FOH	Daf	Stobart	
H 4938	PN73 FOJ	Daf	Stobart	Goresbrook
H 4939	PN73 FOF	Daf	Stobart	
H 4940	MX24 FVV	Daf	Culina	
H 4941	PJ73 YXP	Daf	Stobart	
H 4942	PJ73 YXT	Daf	Culina	
H 4943	PJ73 YVK	Daf	Warrens	
H 4944	PJ73 YYO	Daf	Warrens	
H 4945	PJ73 YYU	Daf	Fowler Welch	
H 4946	PJ73 YYL	Daf	Warrens	
H 4947	PJ73 YYH	Daf	Warrens	
H 4948	PJ73 YYE	Daf	Fowler Welch	
H 4949	PJ73 YZC	Daf	Fowler Welch	
H 4950	PJ73 YZF	Daf	Stobart	Goresbrook
H 4951	PJ73 YZD	Daf	Warrens	
H 4952	PJ73 YZH	Daf	Culina	
H 4953	PJ73 YZE	Daf	Stobart	Stoke
H 4954	PJ73 YZG	Daf	Stobart	
H 4955	PF73 JZC	Daf	Stobart	
H 4956	PF73 JZD	Daf	Stobart	
H 4957	PF73 JZE	Daf	Stobart	
H 4958	PF73 JZA	Daf	Stobart	Goresbrook
H 4959	PF73 JYW	Daf	Stobart	Goresbrook
H 4960	PF73 JYY	Daf	Stobart	Goresbrook

H 4961	PF73 JYZ	Daf	Stobart		Goresbrook
H 4962	MX24 FWG	Daf	Culina		
H 4963	MX24 FWE	Daf	Culina		
H 4964	MX24 FWF	Daf	Culina		
H 4965		Daf	Culina		
H 4966		Daf	Culina		
H 4967	MX24 FWH	Daf	Culina		
H 5000	PO67 XWV	SCA	White - MMiD		
H 5001	PO67 XWW	SCA	Stobart	Darcy Emilia	Widnes
H 5004	PO67 XWZ	SCA	White - MMiD		
H 5007	PO67 XXC	SCA	Stobart	Chloe Rebecca	Appleton
H 5010	PO67 XXF	SCA	Stobart	Aaliyah Rose	Trafford Park
H 5035	PO67 XYT	SCA	Morgan McLernon		
H 5045	PO67 XZC	SCA	Stobart	Nichola Lucy	Cannock
H 5048	PO67 XZF	SCA	Stobart	Kira Louise	Rugby
H 5050	PO67 XZH	SCA	Stobart	Christina Jeanne	Leicester
H 5053	PO67 XUZ	SCA	Stobart	Annette Lesley	Rugby
H 5054	PO67 XUV	SCA	Stobart		
H 5056	PO67 XUX	SCA	Stobart		Bellshill Morrisons
H 5070	PK67 URB	SCA	Stobart	Elise Marie	Cannock
H 5076	PK67 URJ	SCA	Stobart	Rosalea Aurelia	Birchwood
H 5108	PO67 XZL	SCA	Stobart	Cathy Louise	Widnes
H 5112	PO67 XZR	SCA	Stobart	Laurissa Ann	Sherburn
H 5114	PO67 XVD	SCA	White - MMiD		
H 5116	PO67 XZT	SCA	Stobart		Bellshill
H 5118	PO67 XZV	SCA	Stobart	Naomi Gale	Goresbrook
H 5120	PO67 XZX	SCA	Stobart		
H 5125	PO67 YAE	SCA	Stobart	Rebekah Mary	Burton Latimer
H 5129	PO67 XVH	SCA	Stobart		Bellshill
H 5132	PO67 YAF	SCA	Stobart	Ria Jessai	Stoke
H 5147	PO18 NUK	SCA	Stobart	Marianne Joy	Stoke
H 5178	PO18 ODV	SCA	Stobart		Doncaster
H 5183	PO18 NWG	SCA	Stobart	Emma Jane	Livingston
H 5192	PO18 NWU	SCA	Stobart		
H 5199	PO18 NWA	SCA	Stobart		
H 5279	PO18 OEK	SCA	Stobart		
H 5291	PO18 OFM	SCA	Stobart	Nina Lavina	Stoke
H 5305	PO18 OKM	SCA	White - MMiD		
H 5322	PO18 NRY	SCA	Stobart	Larissa Lorena	Teesport
H 5330	PO68 YAW	SCA	White		
H 5334	PO68 YAU	SCA	Fowler Welch		
H 5341	PO68 YAG	SCA	Stobart	Nita Carole	Sherburn
H 5349	PO18 OLC	SCA	iForce		Corby
H 5374	PO18 OLN	SCA	Warrens		Warrens, Rugby
H 5384	PO18 NNA	SCA	Warrens		Warrens, Rugby
H 5385	PO18 NNB	SCA	Warrens		Warrens, Rugby
H 5392	PO18 NNK	SCA	Stobart	Glenise Joy	Rugby
H 5402	PO18 NNZ	SCA	Warrens		Warrens, Rugby
H 5424	PO68 XYC	SCA	Stobart		Wakefield Morrisons
H 5429	PO18 NTU	SCA	White - MMiD		
H 5439	PK18 YJV	SCA	Warrens		Warrens, Rugby
H 5448	PK18 YKJ	SCA	Warrens		Warrens, Rugby
H 5453	PK18 YKL	SCA	Warrens		Rugby
H 5455	PK18 YKN	SCA	Warrens		Warrens, Rugby
H 5457	PK18 YKP	SCA	Warrens		Warrens, Rugby
H 5458	PK18 YKU	SCA	Warrens		Rugby
H 5460	PO68 YBA	SCA	Great Bear		
H 5461	PO68 YCT	SCA	Warrens		Warrens, Rugby
H 5465	PO68 YCZ	SCA	Great Bear		
H 5466	PO68 YDA	SCA	Pallet Network		

H 5468	PO68 YCV	SCA	Stobart	Yasmin Paula	Carlisle
H 5469	PO68 YDB	SCA	Stobart	Valerie Elise	Carlisle
H 5472	PO68 YCH	SCA	Stobart	Cleo Theresa	Braunstone
H 5476	PO68 YCC	SCA	White		
H 5479	PO68 YCL	SCA	Culina		
H 5480	PO68 YCF	SCA	Warrens		Warrens, Rugby
H 5482	PO68 XYL	SCA	Warrens		
H 5486	PO68 YBR	SCA	Warrens		Rugby
H 5487	PO68 YCR	SCA	White	Hawleys Lane	
H 5491	PO68 YBU	SCA	Fowler Welch		
H 5497	PO68 YCS	SCA	Pallet Network		
H 5500	PO68 YBK	SCA	Stobart	Linda Lou	Northampton
H 5503	PO68 YBW	SCA	Culina		
H 5506	PO68 YCJ	SCA	Culina		
H 5512	PO68 YHC	SCA	Great Bear		
H 5514	PO68 YGF	SCA	Stobart		Wakefield Morrisons
H 5523	PO68 YHJ	SCA	Warrens		
H 5527	PO68 YHF	SCA	Warrens		Warrens, Rugby
H 5533	PO68 YGL	SCA	Warrens		Rugby
H 5537	PO68 YHD	SCA	White - MMiD		
H 5539	PO68 YGP	SCA	Stobart		
H 5543	PO68 YHX	SCA	Great Bear		
H 5550	PO68 YHU	SCA	Warrens		Rugby
H 5552	PO68 YJA	SCA	White - MMiD		
H 5553	PO68 YJX	SCA	MMiD - MMiD		
H 5555	PO68 YJG	SCA	Stobart	Fay Jayne	Carlisle
H 5557	PO68 YJB	SCA	White - MMiD		
H 5561	PO68 YJL	SCA	Stobart	Victoria Annabel	Carlisle
H 5562	PO68 YJM	SCA	White - MMiD		
H 5569	PO68 YKB	SCA	Culina		
H 5572	PO68 YJD	SCA	Warrens		Rugby
H 5573	PO68 YKC	SCA	Warrens		Warrens, Rugby
H 5577	PO68 YKD	SCA	Stobart	Karri Frances	Stoke
H 5578	PO68 YJU	SCA	Stobart	Gillian Vanessa	Rugby
H 5584	PO68 YKJ	SCA	Warrens		Warrens, Rugby
H 5585	PO68 YKK	SCA	Warrens		Rugby
H 5587	PO68 YKU	SCA	Stobart	Shelly Denise	Daventry
H 5589	PO68 YKP	SCA	Warrens		Warrens, Rugby
H 5600	PO68 YLD	SCA	Stobart	Victoria Lee	Goresbrook
H 5605	PO68 YLK	SCA	Warrens		Warrens, Rugby
H 5606	PO68 YLL	SCA	Stobart	Tessa Margaret	Daventry
H 5607	PO68 YLM	SCA	Stobart	Karen Vanessa	Daventry
H 5609	PO68 YLP	SCA	Stobart	Jade Susan	Teesport
H 5610	PO68 YLR	SCA	Warrens		Rugby
H 5613	PO68 YLU	SCA	Stobart	Gail Gaynor	Stoke
H 5616	PO68 YMA	SCA	Stobart	Natasha Elise	Crick
H 5618	PO68 YMD	SCA	Warrens		Rugby
H 5624	PO68 YLV	SCA	Morgan McLernon		
H 5632	PO68 YOF	SCA	Warrens		Warrens, Rugby
H 5633	PO68 YNR	SCA	Stobart	Honey	Daventry
H 5634	PO68 YOR	SCA	Stobart	Beatrice Emma	Daventry
H 5635	PO68 YOJ	SCA	Stobart	Reme Marie	Teesport
H 5637	PO68 YOK	SCA	iForce		Corby
H 5638	PO68 YOL	SCA	Fowler Welch		
H 5646	PO68 YNY	SCA	Warrens		Warrens, Rugby
H 5647	PO68 YOA	SCA	Warrens		Warrens, Rugby
H 5648	PO68 YON	SCA	Stobart	Katie Emily	Northampton
H 5651	PO68 YOT	SCA	Warrens		Warrens, Rugby
H 5652	PO68 YOV	SCA	Warrens		Warrens, Rugby
H 5654	PO68 YOX	SCA	Stobart	Beverley Ann	Burton Latimer

H 5656	PO68 YOY	SCA	Warrens		Warrens, Rugby
H 5659	PO68 YOC	SCA	Stobart		
H 5665	PO68 YPL	SCA	Warrens		
H 5666	PO68 YPM	SCA	MMiD - MMiD		
H 5670	PO68 YPG	SCA	White		
H 5678	PO68 YRL	SCA	Fowler Welch		
H 5681	PO68 YRR	SCA	Culina		
H 5682	PO68 YPU	SCA	Warrens		Rugby
H 5683	PO68 YPW	SCA	Stobart	Hebe Polly	Doncaster
H 5687	PO68 YRF	SCA	Stobart	Mary Ellen	Doncaster
H 5689	PO68 YRG	SCA	Warrens		Rugby
H 5694	PO68 YRW	SCA	Pallet Network		Bamber Bridge
H 5695	PO68 YRX	SCA	Pallet Network		Bamber Bridge
H 5696	PN19 FCV	SCA	White - MMiD		
H 5701	PN19 FDC	SCA	White		Bamber Bridge
H 5703	PN19 FDE	SCA	iForce		Corby
H 5704	PN19 FDF	SCA	Pallet Network		Bamber Bridge
H 5705	PN19 FDG	SCA	White		Teesside
H 5707	PN19 FDL	SCA	Pallet Network		Tyneside
H 5709	PN19 FDO	SCA	Warrens		
H 5711	PN19 FDU	SCA	iForce		Corby
H 5720	PN19 FEK	SCA	Pallet Network		Portsmouth
H 5721	PJ19 FSU	SCA	Stobart	Beverley Gail	Carlisle
H 5722	PJ19 FSS	SCA	Stobart	Rosie Lee	Carlisle
H 5723	PJ19 FSP	SCA	Stobart	Taya Jade	Bellshill
H 5729	PJ19 FSE	SCA	Stobart	Molly Joyce	Penrith
H 5730	PJ19 FSG	SCA	Stobart	Pamela Ann	Bellshill
H 5732	PN19 FEM	SCA	BCA Automotive		
H 5733	PN19 FEO	SCA	BCA Automotive		
H 5734	PN19 FEP	SCA	BCA Automotive		
H 5735	PN19 FET	SCA	BCA Automotive		
H 5736	PN19 FEU	SCA	BCA Automotive		
H 5737	PN19 FEV	SCA	BCA Automotive		
H 5738	PN19 FEX	SCA	BCA Automotive		
H 5739	PN19 FFA	SCA	BCA Automotive		
H 5740	PN19 FFB	SCA	Cinch		
H 5741	PN19 FFC	SCA	BCA Automotive		
H 5742	PN19 FFD	SCA	BCA Automotive		
H 5743	PN19 FFE	SCA	BCA Automotive		
H 5744	PN19 FFG	SCA	BCA Automotive		
H 5745	PN19 FFH	SCA	BCA Automotive		
H 5746	PN19 FFJ	SCA	BCA Automotive		
H 5747	PN19 FFK	SCA	BCA Automotive		
H 5748	PN19 FFL	SCA	BCA Automotive		
H 5749	PN19 FFM	SCA	BCA Automotive		
H 5750	PN19 FFO	SCA	BCA Automotive		
H 5751	PN19 FFP	SCA	BCA Automotive		
H 5752	PN19 FFR	SCA	BCA Automotive		
H 5753	PN19 FFS	SCA	BCA Automotive		
H 5754	PN19 FFT	SCA	BCA Automotive		
H 5755	PN19 FFU	SCA	BCA Automotive		
H 5756	PN19 FFV	SCA	BCA Automotive		
H 5757	PN19 FFW	SCA	BCA Automotive		
H 5758	PN19 FFX	SCA	BCA Automotive		
H 5759	PN19 FFY	SCA	BCA Automotive		
H 5760	PN19 FFZ	SCA	BCA Automotive		
H 5761	PN19 FGA	SCA	BCA Automotive		
H 5762	PN19 FGC	SCA	BCA Automotive		
H 5763	PN19 FGD	SCA	BCA Automotive		
H 5764	PN19 FGE	SCA	BCA Automotive		

H 5765	PN19 FGF	SCA	BCA Automotive		
H 5766	PN19 FGG	SCA	Cinch		
H 5767	PN19 FGJ	SCA	BCA Automotive		
H 5768	PN19 FGK	SCA	Cinch		
H 5769	PN19 FGM	SCA	BCA Automotive		
H 5770	PN19 FGO	SCA	BCA Automotive		
H 5771	PN19 FGP	SCA	BCA Automotive		
H 5773	PN19 FHV	SCA	Stobart	Holly Sally	
H 5774	PN19 FHW	SCA	Stobart	Clare Lucy	Stoke
H 5776	PN19 FHY	SCA	Great Bear		
H 5780	PN19 FHF	SCA	Stobart	Daisy Myrtle	Crick
H 5788	PN19 FHO	SCA	Stobart	Liberty Sofia	Rugby
H 5790	PN19 FHR	SCA	Stobart	Jayne Elizabeth	Rugby
H 5793	PN19 FJD	SCA	Stobart	Imogen Connie	Teesport
H 5795	PN19 FJF	SCA	Culina		
H 5796	PN19 FJJ	SCA	Stobart	Dympna Catherine	Teesport
H 5803	PN19 FKA	SCA	Stobart	Kacey Mae	Rugby
H 5804	PN19 FJX	SCA	Culina Group		
H 5806	PN19 FKE	SCA	Warrens		Warrens, Rugby
H 5807	PN19 FGU	SCA	BCA Automotive		
H 5808	PN19 FGV	SCA	BCA Automotive		
H 5809	PN19 FGX	SCA	BCA Automotive		
H 5810	PN19 FGZ	SCA	BCA Automotive		
H 5811	PN19 FHA	SCA	BCA Automotive		
H 5812	PN19 FHB	SCA	BCA Automotive		
H 5821	PN19 FKJ	SCA	Warrens		Rugby
H 5822	PN19 FKL	SCA	White - MMiD		Droitwich
H 5823	PJ19 FKY	SCA	BCA Automotive		
H 5824	PJ19 FKX	SCA	BCA Automotive		
H 5825	PJ19 LFU	SCA	Culina		
H 5826	PN19 FKZ	SCA	BCA Automotive		
H 5832	PJ19 FLN	SCA	Stobart	Sylvia May	Stoke
H 5833	PN19 FLA	SCA	Warrens		Warrens, Rugby
H 5836	PJ19 FKW	SCA	Warrens		Warrens, Rugby
H 5837	PJ19 FMM	SCA	White - CML		
H 5839	PN19 FKV	SCA	Stobart	Chloe Marie	Grangemouth
H 5841	PJ19 FML	SCA	Stobart	Lucy Elise	Sherburn
H 5844	PJ19 FLL	SCA	Stobart	Irene Lindsay	Sherburn
H 5846	PN19 FKX	SCA	Warrens		
H 5849	PJ19 FLD	SCA	BCA Automotive		
H 5851	PJ19 LFS	SCA	BCA Automotive		
H 5853	PJ19 FLZ	SCA	Great Bear		
H 5854	PJ19 FLA	SCA	Stobart	Simone Louise	Crick
H 5856	PJ19 LFP	SCA	Stobart	Paris	Sherburn
H 5857	PJ19 FKS	SCA	Culina		
H 5859	PJ19 FMF	SCA	Stobart	Elen Mererid	Crick
H 5864	PJ19 FLR	SCA	White - MMiD		
H 5865	PJ19 FNN	SCA	White - MMiD		
H 5868	PJ19 FLX	SCA	Culina		
H 5871	PJ19 FKZ	SCA	BCA Automotive		
H 5872	PJ19 LFR	SCA	Culina		
H 5873	PJ19 FLW	SCA	Culina		
H 5874	PJ19 FLV	SCA	Culina		
H 5878	PJ19 LDY	SCA	Stobart	Jennifer Myra	Wakefield
H 5879	PJ19 LFN	SCA	Fowler Welch		
H 5880	PJ19 LFM	SCA	Culina		
H 5881	PJ19 LDX	SCA	White - MMiD		
H 5887	PJ19 LFL	SCA	Culina		
H 5886	PJ19 LFB	SCA	BCA Automotive		
H 5888	PJ19 LEF	SCA	BCA Automotive		

H 5889	PJ19 LFA	SCA	BCA Automotive		
H 5890	PJ19 LFE	SCA	Stobart		
H 5891	PJ19 LEU	SCA	BCA Automotive		
H 5894	PJ19 LDU	SCA	BCA Automotive		
H 5895	PJ19 LDO	SCA	BCA Automotive		
H 5944	PO70 ZHB	SCA	Pallet Network		Teesside
H 5950	PO70 ZHC	SCA	Culina		
H 5951	PJ19 LCP	SCA	Stobart	Esmee Marie	Widnes
H 5952	PJ19 LCO	SCA	Stobart	Kim Leslie	Widnes
H 5953	PF19 WDK	SCA	Stobart	Kathleen Amy	Widnes
H 5954	PF19 WDJ	SCA	Stobart	Scarlett Elisabeth	Widnes
H 5955	PJ19 LCN	SCA	Stobart	Jean Christina	Widnes
H 5960	PO70 ZHF	SCA	Culina		
H 5964	PO70 ZHL	SCA	Pallet Network		Teesside
H 5967	PO70 ZHH	SCA	Pallet Network		Dagenham
H 5970	PO69 YPL	SCA	Stobart	Kate Florence	Leicester
H 5971	PO69 YSM	SCA	Stobart	Almeida	Leicester
H 5998	PO69 YOX	SCA	Stobart	Nora Elizabeth	Wakefield
H 6002	PO69 YPF	SCA	White - MMiD		
H 6008	PO70 ZHP	SCA	Stobart	Frances Julie	Rugby
H 6009	PO69 YOP	SCA	Culina		
H 6010	PO70 ZHR	SCA	Culina		
H 6023	PO70 ZHX	SCA	Stobart	Jennifer Victoria	Burton Latimer
H 6027	PO70 ZHV	SCA	Stobart	Betty Jean	Burton Latimer
H 6036	PO69 YNP	SCA	Stobart	Daisy Leigh	Leicester
H 6040	PO70 ZHY	SCA	White		
H 6042	PO70 ZJE	SCA	Culina		
H 6044	PO70 ZJJ	SCA	Stobart	Ann Georgina	Burton Latimer
H 6046	PO70 ZJN	SCA	Stobart	Jess Elizabeth	Burton Latimer
H 6048	PO70 ZJY	SCA	Great Bear		
H 6049	PO70 ZJU	SCA	Culina		
H 6050	PO70 ZJV	SCA	Stobart	Abigail Sophie	Burton Latimer
H 6051	PO69 YCN	SCA	Culina		
H 6053	PO70 ZKD	SCA	Stobart	Shan Aleen	Burton Latimer
H 6054	PO70 ZJZ	SCA	White		
H 6055	PO70 ZKA	SCA	Stobart	Kathleen Josephine	Burton Latimer
H 6056	PO70 ZKB	SCA	Stobart	Eloise Alexandra	Burton Latimer
H 6057	PO70 ZKC	SCA	Stobart	Poppi Caroline	Burton Latimer
H 6067	PO70 ZKF	SCA	White		
H 6075	PO69 XYV	SCA	Stobart	Tracy Megan	Widnes
H 6076	PO69 XYZ	SCA	Stobart	Patricia Ann	Widnes
H 6077	PO69 XYX	SCA	Stobart	Wren Mayan	Widnes
H 6078	PO69 XYY	SCA	Stobart	Samantha Lorraine	Widnes
H 6079	PO69 XYW	SCA	Stobart	Louisa Ann	Widnes
H 6080	PE69 FRU	SCA	Stobart	Miriam Ann	Rugby
H 6081	PE69 FRR	SCA	Stobart	Rebecca Charlotte	Newport
H 6082	PO69 YRP	SCA	Stobart	Maizie	Goresbrook
H 6083	PE69 FRP	SCA	Stobart	Valerie Joy	Goresbrook
H 6084	PE69 FRO	SCA	Stobart	Joyce Violet	Rugby
H 6085	PE69 FPX	SCA	Stobart	Barbara Ruth	Leicester
H 6091	PE69 FRL	SCA	Stobart		
H 6094	PE69 FRN	SCA	Stobart	Millie Charlotte	Rugby
H 6100					
H 6101	DG73 ABO	Man	Stobart		
H 6102	DG73 ABV	Man	Stobart		
H 6103	DG73 ABZ	Man	Stobart		
H 6104	DG73 ACU	Man	Stobart		
H 6105	DG73 ACX	Man	Stobart		
H 6106	DG73 AAY	Man	Stobart		
H 6107	DG73 ABN	Man	Stobart		

H 6108	DG73 ABX	Man	Stobart			
H 6109	DG73 ACJ	Man	Stobart			
H 6110	DG73 ACO	Man	Stobart		Stoke	
H 6111	DG73 ACV	Man	Stobart			
H 6112	DX73 AAV	Man	Fowler Welch			
H 6113	DG73 AAX	Man	Fowler Welch			
H 6114	DG73 ADZ	Man	Fowler Welch		Spalding	
H 6115	DK24 YVB	Man	Culina			
H 6116	DK24 YVC	Man	Culina			
H 6117	DK24 YVD	Man	Culina			
H 6118	DK24 YVE	Man	Culina			
H	DK24 YVF	Man	Culina			
H	DK24 YVG	Man	Culina			
H 6121	DK24 YVH	Man	Culina			
H	DK24 YVJ	Man	Culina			
H	DK24 YVN	Man	Culina			
H 6127	DK24 YVP	Man	Culina			
H 6128	DK24 YVR	Man	Culina			
H 6133	DK24 YVW	Man	Culina			
H 6134	DK24 YVX	Man	Culina			
H	DK24 YYW	Man	Culina			
H 6170	DE22 NLR	Man	Stobart		Carlisle	
H 6171	DA23 AMV	Man	Fowler Welch		Spalding	
H 6172	DF23 UBU	Man	Fowler Welch			
H 6173	DF23 UBW	Man	Fowler Welch			
H 6174	DF23 UBZ	Man	Fowler Welch			
H 6175	DA23 ANF	Man	Fowler Welch			
H 6176	DA23 ANR	Man	Fowler Welch			
H 6177	DF23 UCC	Man	Fowler Welch			
H 6178	DF23 UCA	Man	Fowler Welch			
H 6179	DA23 AMX	Man	Fowler Welch			
H 6180	DF23 UBY	Man	Fowler Welch			
H 6181	DF23 UBV	Man	Fowler Welch			
H 6182	DF23 UBX	Man	Fowler Welch			
H 6183	DA23 ANP	Man	Fowler Welch			
H 6184	DF23 UCB	Man	Fowler Welch			
H 6185	DF23 UDJ	Man	Fowler Welch			
H 6186	DF23 UDK	Man	Fowler Welch			
H 6187	DF23 UDL	Man	Fowler Welch			
H 6188	DF23 UDN	Man	Fowler Welch			
H 6189	DF23 UDO	Man	Fowler Welch			
H 6190	DF23 UDP	Man	Fowler Welch			
H 6191	DG73 ABU	Man	Stobart			
H 6192	DG73 ACF	Man	Stobart			
H 6193	DF23 UDM	Man	Fowler Welch			
H 6194	DF23 UDS	Man	Culina			
H 6195	DF23 UDT	Man	Stobart			
H 6196	DF23 UDU	Man	Culina			
H 6197	DG73 AAZ	Man	Stobart			
H 6198	DG73 ABF	Man	Stobart		Stoke	
H 6199	DG73 ABK	Man	Stobart			
H 6203	PE69 FMK	SCA	Stobart	Violet May	Rugby	
H 6200	PE69 FMG	SCA	Stobart	Natalie Beatrice	Goresbrook	
H 6209	PE69 FMC	SCA	Stobart	Jean Mamie	Rugby	
H 6213	PE69 FLX	SCA	Stobart	Stacey	Rugby	
H 6227	PK69 KYE	SCA	Stobart	Natasha Jayne	Goresbrook	
H 6229	PK69 KYR	SCA	Stobart	Lydia May	Goresbrook	
H 6231	PO70 ZUC	SCA	Pallet Network		Dagenham	
H 6234	PO70 ZUD	SCA	Pallet Network		Goresbrook	
H 6273	PO70 ZKG	SCA	White			

H 6284	PO70 ZKJ	SCA	Stobart		
H 6293	PO70 ZKK	SCA	Stobart	Ruby Megan	Trafford Park
H 6300	PN21 FBB	SCA	Stobart		
H 6301	PN21 FBC	SCA	Stobart	Angela Marie	Rugby
H 6302	PN21 EZM	SCA	Stobart	Melissa Jane	Rugby
H 6303	PN21 EZO	SCA	Stobart	Layla Elizabeth	
H 6304	PN21 EZP	SCA	Stobart	Anastasia Susan	Mulholland
H 6305	PN21 EZR	SCA	White		
H 6306	PN21 EZT	SCA	Stobart	Glendina Maria	Crick
H 6307	PN21 FBD	SCA	Stobart	Esther Ruth	Goresbrook
H 6308	PN21 FBE	SCA	Stobart	Emilia Rose	Carlisle
H 6309	PN21 FBF	SCA	Stobart	Eleanor Karen	Rugby
H 6310	PN21 EZU	SCA	Stobart	Melisa	Appleton
H 6311	PN21 EZV	SCA	Stobart	Macie May	Rugby
H 6312	PN21 EZW	SCA	Stobart	Lyndsey Jayne	Rugby
H 6313	PN21 EZX	SCA	Stobart	Katie Jane	Appleton
H 6314	PN21 EZZ	SCA	White		
H 6315	PN21 FBA	SCA	Stobart	Jean Cynthia	Goresbrook
H 6316	PN21 FBG	SCA	Stobart	Jayne Anne	Crick
H 6317	PN21 FBK	SCA	White - MMiD		
H 6318	PN21 FBL	SCA	White		Hawleys Lane
H 6319	PN21 FBO	SCA	White		Hawleys Lane
H 6320	PN21 EZK	SCA	Stobart	Trudie Jayne	Crick
H 6321	PN21 EZL	SCA	Stobart	Terrianne	Crick
H 6322	PN21 FBU	SCA	Stobart	Tallulah Rose	Goresbrook
H 6323	PN21 FBV	SCA	Stobart	Sybil May	Lichfield
H 6324	PN21 FBX	SCA	Stobart	Pamela Ann	Goresbrook
H 6325	PN21 FBZ	SCA	Stobart	Olivia Kirstie	Widnes
H 6326	PN21 FCA	SCA	Stobart	Nimah Harmony	Stoke
H 6327	PN21 FDF	SCA	Stobart	Menna Haf	Goresbrook
H 6328	PN21 FDG	SCA	White	Hawleys Lane	
H 6329	PN21 FDJ	SCA	Stobart	Marion Elsa	
H 6330	PN21 FCC	SCA	Stobart	Violet Pauline	Goresbrook
H 6331	PN21 FCD	SCA	Culina		
H 6332	PN21 FCE	SCA	Stobart	Kiah Amalin	Wakefield
H 6333	PN21 FCF	SCA	Stobart	Lynn Valerie	Sherburn
H 6334	PN21 FCG	SCA	Stobart	Tia Jayne	Widnes
H 6335	PN21 FCJ	SCA	Stobart	Wendy Patricia	Appleton
H 6336	PN21 FCL	SCA	Stobart	Vera Ann	Stoke
H 6337	PN21 FCM	SCA	Stobart	Valeen Denise	Wakefield
H 6338	PN21 FCO	SCA	Stobart	Tracy Millie	Wakefield
H 6339	PN21 FCP	SCA	Stobart	Thea Lara	Central
H 6340	PN21 FCU	SCA	Stobart	Morgan Alice	Dav 1
H 6341	PN21 FCV	SCA	Stobart	Suzanne Moira	Widnes
H 6342	PN21 FCX	SCA	Stobart	Dora	Sherburn
H 6343	PN21 FCZ	SCA	Stobart	Patricia Lorraine	Sherburn
H 6344	PN21 FDA	SCA	Stobart	Aria Lilley	Cannock
H 6345	PN21 FDC	SCA	Stobart	Ruby Jean	Newport
H 6346	PN21 FDD	SCA	Stobart	Anita Jane	Cannock
H 6347	PN21 FDE	SCA	Stobart	Lisa Willis	Cannock
H 6348	PN21 FDK	SCA	Stobart	Brenda Gabrielle	Cannock
H 6349	PN21 FDL	SCA	Stobart	Deborah	Wakefield
H 6350	PJ21 YLO	SCA	Stobart		
H 6351	PJ21 YLM	SCA	Stobart	Jess Francesa	
H 6352	PJ21 YLL	SCA	Stobart	Ruth Esme	
H 6353	PJ21 YLN	SCA	Stobart	Tonya Elizabeth	Appleton
H 6354	PJ21 YLP	SCA	Stobart	Nicole Ann	
H 6355	PJ21 YLR	SCA	Stobart	Elsie Edith	
H 6356	PL21 FMV	SCA	Stobart	Roxy	
H 6357	PL21 FLZ	SCA	Stobart	Rosemary Ellen	

H 6358	PL21 FLB	SCA	Stobart	Sasha Sofia	
H 6359	PL21 FKH	SCA	Stobart	Irene Margaret	Sherburn
H 6360	PL21 FMM	SCA	Stobart	Ervena Aaralin	
H 6361	PL21 FMC	SCA	Stobart	Jannine Bear	
H 6362	PL21 FMO	SCA	Stobart	Hannah Nina	Appleton
H 6363	PL21 FKP	SCA	Stobart	Abigail Isabella	
H 6364	PL21 FND	SCA	Stobart	Lauren Imogen	Widnes Ports
H 6365	PL21 FKT	SCA	Stobart	Abigail Mireya	Sherburn
H 6366	PL21 FMX	SCA	Stobart	Clara Marie	Appleton
H 6367	PL21 FLP	SCA	Stobart	Jazmine	
H 6368	PL21 FKW	SCA	Stobart	Jennifer Susan	Dav 1
H 6369	PL21 FKU	SCA	Stobart	Breeanna Isla	
H 6370	PL21 FLC	SCA	Stobart	Marisa Natalie Ena	Appleton
H 6371	PL21 FLH	SCA	Stobart	Rosemary Elaine	Rugby
H 6372	PL21 FLJ	SCA	Stobart	Tia Faye	
H 6373	PL21 FKE	SCA	Stobart	Jennifer Ruth	Sherburn
H 6374	PL21 FKF	SCA	Stobart	Elaine Amanda	Appleton
H 6375	PL21 FLV	SCA	Stobart	Joanne Madeleine	
H 6376	PL21 FKV	SCA	Stobart	Ivy Star	
H 6377	PL21 FKZ	SCA	Stobart	India Charlie	
H 6378	PL21 FMA	SCA	Stobart	Mary Dee	Appleton
H 6379	PL21 FMJ	SCA	Stobart	Eva Joyce	
H 6380	PL21 FKJ	SCA	Stobart	Siobhan Sharon	Appleton
H 6381	PL21 FLA	SCA	Stobart	Rose Blake	Appleton
H 6382	PL21 FLE	SCA	Stobart	Darcey Layla	Appleton
H 6383	PL21 FMK	SCA	Stobart	Kate Rebecca	Appleton
H 6384	PL21 FKN	SCA	Stobart	Elys Reanna	Sherburn
H 6385	PL21 FLN	SCA	Stobart	Helen	Stoke
H 6386	PL21 FKO	SCA	Stobart	Isabelle Grace	Sherburn
H 6387	PL21 FLR	SCA	Stobart	Winnifred May	
H 6388	PL21 FMD	SCA	Stobart	Pamela Lyn	
H 6389	PL21 FMU	SCA	Stobart	Stevie Kate	Sherburn
H 6390	PL21 FLF	SCA	Stobart	Stacey Leigh	Sherburn
H 6391	PL21 FLK	SCA	Stobart	Joanne Frances	Stoke
H 6392	PL21 FNE	SCA	Stobart	Joanne Frances	Lillyhall
H 6393	PL21 FLD	SCA	Stobart	Janice Charlotte	
H 6394	PL21 FNF	SCA	Stobart	Nida	
H 6395	PL21 FME	SCA	Stobart	Annie Emma	
H 6396	PL21 FNA	SCA	Stobart	Meaha Eveline	
H 6397	PL21 FLG	SCA	Stobart	Amelia May	
H 6398	PL21 FMF	SCA	Stobart	Berry Grace	Appleton
H 6399	PN71 DWD	SCA	Stobart		Appleton
H 6400	PN71 DXE	SCA	Culina		
H 6401	PN71 DXF	SCA	Stobart		Rugby
H 6402	PN71 DWX	SCA	Stobart		
H 6404	PN71 DXA	SCA	Stobart		Appleton
H 6405	PN71 DXC	SCA	Culina		
H 6406	PN71 DWC	SCA	Stobart		Morrisons Bridgwater
H 6407	PN71 DWP	SCA	Culina		
H 6409	PN71 DWY	SCA	Great Bear		Rugby
H 6410	PN71 DXB	SCA	Culina		Bridgwater Morri
H 6411	PN71 DXL	SCA	Stobart		Morrisons Bridgwater
H 6412	PN71 DXP	SCA	Warrens		Warrens, Rugby
H 6413	PN71 DXJ	SCA	Warrens		Warrens, Rugby
H 6414	PN71 DWW	SCA	Stobart		Morrisons Bridgwater
H 6415	PN71 DXO	SCA	Culina		Rugby
H 6416	PN71 DXK	SCA	Culina		
H 6417	PN71 DWK	SCA	Great Bear		Magna Park
H 6418	PN71 DWV	SCA	Stobart		Morrisons Bridgwater
H 6419	PN71 EDL	SCA	Stobart		Appleton

H 6420	PN71 DXD	SCA	Culina	
H 6421	PN71 DWG	SCA	Culina	
H 6422	PN71 EEZ	SCA	Great Bear	
H 6423	PN71 DYT	SCA	Culina	Bridgwater
H 6424	PN71 EDF	SCA	Great Bear	Magna Park
H 6425	PN71 EEH	SCA	Stobart	Appleton
H 6427	PN71 DYU	SCA	Culina	
H 6428	PN71 EDC	SCA	Stobart	
H 6429	PN71 EEJ	SCA	Great Bear	Magna Park
H 6430	PN71 DYJ	SCA	Stobart	Appleton
H 6431	PN71 ECY	SCA	Great Bear	
H 6432	PN71 DYV	SCA	Culina	
H 6433	PE71 VLW	SCA	Great Bear	Appleton
H 6434	PN71 EEU	SCA	Fowler Welch	Broxburn
H 6435	PN71 EDP	SCA	Fowler Welch	
H 6437	PN71 EDR	SCA	Stobart	Appleton
H 6438	PN71 EDU	SCA	Great Bear	
H 6439	PN71 ECT	SCA	Stobart	Appleton
H 6440	PN71 DYA	SCA	Warrens	Warrens, Rugby
H 6441	PN71 ECV	SCA	Warrens	Warrens, Rugby
H 6442	PN71 ECW	SCA	Stobart	Newport
H 6443	PN71 EEB	SCA	Great Bear	
H 6444	PN71 DXH	SCA	Warrens	
H 6445	PN71 DYM	SCA	Stobart	Rugby
H 6446	PN71 EDO	SCA	Great Bear	
H 6447	PN71 DXR	SCA	Stobart	Sherburn
H 6448	PN71 DYF	SCA	Stobart	
H 6450	PN71 DWZ	SCA	Culina	
H 6452	PN71 DXG	SCA	Stobart	
H 6453	PN71 EEG	SCA	Stobart	Newport
H 6454	PN71 DYB	SCA	Stobart	Newport
H 6455	PN71 DYC	SCA	Stobart	Appleton
H 6456	PN71 DYD	SCA	Stobart	
H 6457	PN71 DXY	SCA	Stobart	
H 6458	PN71 EEF	SCA	Great Bear	Magna Park
H 6459	PN71 DYP	SCA	Stobart	Newport
H 6460	PN71 EEV	SCA	Stobart	Newport
H 6461	PN71 DYS	SCA	Stobart	Rugby
H 6463	PN71 EDK	SCA	Fowler Welch	Portsmouth
H 6464	PN71 EEM	SCA	Stobart	Rugby
H 6465	PN71 DXT	SCA	Warrens	Appleton
H 6466	PN71 EEO	SCA	Great Bear	
H 6467	PN71 DXU	SCA	Fowler Welch	
H 6468	PN71 DYG	SCA	Stobart	Newport
H 6469	PN71 DXV	SCA	Stobart	Appleton
H 6470	PN71 EEP	SCA	Culina	
H 6471	PN71 EER	SCA	Great Bear	
H 6472	PN71 EDV	SCA	Culina	
H 6473	PN71 DXW	SCA	Culina	
H 6474	PN71 EDJ	SCA	Culina	
H 6475	PN71 EEW	SCA	Great Bear	
H 6477	PN71 EFA	SCA	Great Bear	Banbury
H 6479	PE71 VLV	SCA	Stobart	
H 6480	PN71 EDX	SCA	Fowler Welch	
H 6481	PN71 DXX	SCA	Stobart	Newport
H 6482	PN71 ECX	SCA	Stobart	Appleton
H 6483	PN71 EEA	SCA	Stobart	
H 6484	PN71 EEY	SCA	Great Bear	
H 6485	PE71 VML	SCA	Fowler Welch	Newport
H 6486	PN71 DXZ	SCA	Warrens	Warrens, Rugby

H 6487	PN71 EET	SCA	Stobart	Appleton
H 6489	PN71 EES	SCA	Culina	Newport
H 6490	PN71 EEX	SCA	Great Bear	Magna Park
H 6491	PE71 VLR	SCA	Stobart	
H 6492	PE71 VLX	SCA	Stobart	Sherburn
H 6493	PE71 VMM	SCA	Stobart	Rugby
H 6494	PE71 VMD	SCA	Stobart	Dav 1
H 6495	PE71 VMU	SCA	Stobart	Rugby
H 6496	PN71 EFB	SCA	Great Bear	
H 6497	PE71 VLN	SCA	Stobart	Newport
H 6498	PE71 VMC	SCA	Stobart	Sherburn
H 6499	PE71 VMF	SCA	Warrens	Warrens, Rugby
H 6500	PE71 VMP	SCA	Stobart	Hawleys Lane
H 6501	PE71 VMJ	SCA	Stobart	Appleton
H 6502	PE71 VLZ	SCA	Stobart	
H 6503	PE71 VLO	SCA	Stobart	Appleton
H 6504	PE71 VMV	SCA	Stobart	Rugby
H 6505	PK71 VLS	SCA	Stobart	
H 6506	PN71 EFC	SCA	Fowler Welch	Portsmouth
H 6507	PK71 VLE	SCA	Warrens	Spalding
H 6508	PE71 VLP	SCA	Culina	Sherburn
H 6509	PE71 VMG	SCA	Great Bear	
H 6510	PE71 VMH	SCA	Stobart	Newport
H 6511	PE71 VMK	SCA	Fowler Welch	Rugby
H 6512	PE71 VMR	SCA	Fowler Welch	Rugby
H 6513	PE71 VLU	SCA	Great Bear	Appleton
H 6514	PE71 VMT	SCA	Stobart	Lichfield
H 6515	PE71 VMO	SCA	Great Bear	Appleton
H 6516	PN71 EFD	SCA	Culina	Stafford
H 6517	PN71 EFE	SCA	Stobart	Sherburn
H 6518	PE71 VMA	SCA	Warrens	Warrens, Rugby
H 6520	PN71 DWE	SCA	Fowler Welch	
H 6521	PE71 VMZ	SCA	Warrens	Warrens, Rugby
H 6522	PN71 DWJ	SCA	Warrens	Warrens, Rugby
H 6523	PK71 FVY	SCA	Stobart	Rugby
H 6524	PK71 VNU	SCA	Stobart	Trafford Park
H 6528	PK71 FVO	SCA	Culina	Sherburn
H 6530	PK71 FVR	SCA	Culina	
H 6531	PK71 VNV	SCA	Fowler Welch	
H 6532	PK71 VLL	SCA	Stobart	Stoke
H 6533	PK71 VNR	SCA	Culina	
H 6534	PK71 FVT	SCA	Stobart	
H 6535	PK71 FVP	SCA	Stobart	Mossend
H 6536	PK71 FVU	SCA	Stobart	Trafford Park
H 6537	PK71 FVN	SCA	Stobart	Newport
H 6538	PK71 FVH	SCA	Stobart	Trafford Park
H 6539	PK71 VNS	SCA	Stobart	Newport
H 6540	PK71 FVM	SCA	Culina	
H 6541	PK71 FWA	SCA	Stobart	Rugby
H 6542	PK71 FVX	SCA	Warrens	Rugby
H 6543	PK71 FVL	SCA	Great Bear	
H 6544	PK71 FVZ	SCA	Stobart	Dav 1
H 6545	PK71 FWC	SCA	Stobart	Sherburn
H 6546	PK71 FVV	SCA	Stobart	Appleton
H 6547	PK71 VNT	SCA	Stobart	
H 6549	PK71 VNN	SCA	Culina	Bridgwater
H 6550	PK71 FVJ	SCA	Warrens	
H 6551	PK71 FWB	SCA	Stobart	Teesport
H 6552	PK71 FVS	SCA	Stobart	
H 6553	PK71 VLU	SCA	Culina	

H 6554	PK71 FVW	SCA	Stobart	Teesport
H 6555	PK71 VNP	SCA	Stobart	Rugby
H 6556	PK71 FVA	SCA	Warrens	Warrens, Rugby
H 6557	PE71 VMX	SCA	Warrens	Warrens, Rugby
H 6562	PK71 FVB	SCA	Stobart	Rugby
H 6563	PE71 VLT	SCA	Stobart	Trafford Park
H 6565	PK71 VLN	SCA	Fowler Welch	Appleton
H 6566	PK71 VLF	SCA	Stobart	
H 6567	PK71 VLV	SCA	Warrens	Warrens, Rugby
H 6568	PK71 VLZ	SCA	Stobart	Rugby
H 6569	PK71 VLP	SCA	Great Bear	
H 6570	PK71 VLX	SCA	Fowler Welch	
H 6572	PK71 VLO	SCA	Fowler Welch	
H 6574	PK71 VLW	SCA	Great Bear	
H 6575	PK71 VMV	SCA	Stobart	Trafford Park
H 6578	PK71 VLT	SCA	Stobart	Rugby
H 6579	PK71 VLH	SCA	Stobart	Trafford Park
H 6580	PJ71 VAA	SCA	Fowler Welch	Magna Park
H 6581	PJ71 UZX	SCA	Stobart	Sherburn
H 6582	PJ71 UZR	SCA	Fowler Welch	Portsmouth
H 6583	PK71 VLY	SCA	Stobart	Sherburn
H 6584	PK71 VLG	SCA	Fowler Welch	
H 6588	PK71 VLM	SCA	Stobart	
H 6589	PE71 VMW	SCA	Warrens	Warrens, Rugby
H 6590	PJ71 UZY	SCA	Stobart	
H 6592	PK71 VNM	SCA	Fowler Welch	
H 6593	PK71 VLR	SCA	Great Bear	
H 6594	PK71 VND	SCA	Stobart	Rugby
H 6595	PK71 VMF	SCA	Great Bear	
H 6596	PK71 VNG	SCA	Stobart	Rugby
H 6597	PK71 VNH	SCA	Stobart	Appleton
H 6598	PK71 VMD	SCA	Culina	
H 6599	PK71 VNE	SCA	Stobart	Rugby
H 6600	PK71 VME	SCA	Stobart	Teesport
H 6601	PK71 VNC	SCA	Stobart	Rugby
H 6608	PK71 VNA	SCA	Stobart	Teesport
H 6609	PK71 VNB	SCA	Great Bear	
H 6610	PK71 VMH	SCA	Fowler Welch	Broxburn
H 6611	PK71 VMJ	SCA	Fowler Welch	
H 6615	PK71 VML	SCA	Stobart	Doncaster
H 6617	PK71 VMM	SCA	Stobart	Teesport
H 6618	PK71 VMO	SCA	Great Bear	Trafford Park
H 6619	PK71 VMP	SCA	Stobart	Widnes
H 6620	PK71 VMC	SCA	Warrens	Rugby
H 6621	PK71 VMR	SCA	Stobart	Teesport
H 6622	PK71 VMW	SCA	Stobart	Rugby
H 6625	PK71 VMT	SCA	Stobart	Widnes
H 6626	PK71 VLJ	SCA	Culina	
H 6627	PK71 VMU	SCA	Stobart	
H 6628	PK71 VNJ	SCA	Stobart	Teesport
H 6629	PK71 VMZ	SCA	Stobart	Trafford Park
H 6630	PK71 VNF	SCA	Stobart	Widnes
H 6631	PK71 VNL	SCA	Stobart	Teesport
H 6632	PF71 DYX	SCA	Great Bear	
H 6637	PF71 DYP	SCA	Stobart	
H 6638	PF71 DYM	SCA	Great Bear	
H 6642	PF71 DZO	SCA	Warrens	Warrens, Rugby
H 6643	PF71 DZC	SCA	Warrens	Warrens, Rugby
H 6644	PF71 DZA	SCA	Warrens	Warrens, Rugby
H 6645	PF71 DYY	SCA	Warrens	Warrens, Rugby

H 6647	PF71 DYS	SCA	Stobart	Bridgwater Morrisons
H 6651	PF71 DZJ	SCA	Warrens	Warrens, Rugby
H 6652	PF71 DZP	SCA	Warrens	Warrens, Rugby
H 6655	PN22 DWD	SCA	Stobart	
H 6657	PK71 VPY	SCA	Culina	
H 6658	PK71 VOU	SCA	Stobart	Teesport
H 6659	PK71 VNX	SCA	Culina	Droitwich
H 6660	PK71 VPN	SCA	Great Bear	
H 6661	PK71 VNY	SCA	Stobart	Sherburn
H 6662	PK71 VOV	SCA	Stobart	Daventry
H 6663	PK71 VPO	SCA	Great Bear	
H 6664	PK71 VOY	SCA	Warrens	Warrens, Rugby
H 6665	PJ71 NAO	SCA	Culina	Bridgwater
H 6666	PJ71 MZZ	SCA	Stobart	Teesport
H 6667	PK71 VNZ	SCA	Stobart	Teesport
H 6668	PK71 VOA	SCA	Fowler Welch	
H 6669	PK71 VPA	SCA	Stobart	Teesport
H 6670	PJ71 NBD	SCA	Culina	Amesbury
H 6671	PJ71 NDF	SCA	Fowler Welch	Washington
H 6672	PJ71 NBE	SCA	Culina	
H 6673	PJ71 NDG	SCA	Culina	Bridgwater
H 6674	PJ71 NDK	SCA	Culina	Amesbury
H 6675	PK71 VOB	SCA	Stobart	
H 6676	PJ71 NBF	SCA	Stobart	Teesport
H 6677	PK71 VOC	SCA	Culina	
H 6678	PK71 VPG	SCA	Stobart	Sherburn
H 6679	PK71 VPV	SCA	Stobart	
H 6680	PK71 VOD	SCA	Culina	
H 6681	PJ71 NBG	SCA	Stobart	Doncaster
H 6682	PJ71 VAF	SCA	Fowler Welch	
H 6683	PK71 VNW	SCA	Stobart	Widnes
H 6684	PJ71 UZK	SCA	Stobart	Goresbrook
H 6685	PJ71 UZN	SCA	Stobart	
H 6686	PJ71 UZC	SCA	Fowler Welch	Washington
H 6688	PJ71 VBM	SCA	Fowler Welch	Magna Park
H 6692	PJ71 VEM	SCA	Fowler Welch	Newton Abbot
H 6700	PJ71 VBD	SCA	Fowler Welch	
H 6701	PJ71 VAK	SCA	Fowler Welch	
H 6709	PJ71 VAM	SCA	Fowler Welch	
H 6710	PJ71 VBK	SCA	Culina	Telford
H 6714	PJ71 VAO	SCA	Fowler Welch	
H 6715	PJ71 VFK	SCA	Fowler Welch	Newton Abbot
H 6719	PJ71 VFB	SCA	Fowler Welch	Washington
H 6724	PJ71 VFH	SCA	Culina	
H 6725	PJ71 VBX	SCA	Stobart	Dagenham
H 6728	PJ71 VBT	SCA	Fowler Welch	
H 6729	PJ71 VBU	SCA	Fowler Welch	
H 6731	PJ71 VBY	SCA	Fowler Welch	
H 6733	PJ71 VCA	SCA	Fowler Welch	
H 6737	PJ71 UZO	SCA	Fowler Welch	
H 6738	PE71 VNA	SCA	Fowler Welch	Washington
H 6739	PJ71 UZB	SCA	Fowler Welch	Washington
H 6740	PJ71 NJO	SCA	Fowler Welch	Washington
H 6741	PJ71 VAY	SCA	Culina	Telford
H 6742	PN22 DWC	SCA	Stobart	Bridgwater Morrisons
H 6745	PJ71 VCG	SCA	Warrens	Rugby
H 6751	PJ71 VEV	SCA	Warrens	Warrens, Rugby
H 6753	PJ71 VFP	SCA	Great Bear	
H 6754	PN22 DWK	SCA	Stobart	
H 6755	PF71 DYO	SCA	Warrens	Warrens, Rugby

H 6760	PJ71 VFU	SCA	Stobart	Bridgwater Morrisons
H 6763	PF71 DZD	SCA	Warrens	Warrens, Rugby
H 6766	PJ71 NHZ	SCA	Culina	Sherburn
H 6767	PJ71 UZL	SCA	Culina	Amesbury
H 6768	PJ71 NJF	SCA	Culina	Amesbury
H 6769	PJ71 UZG	SCA	Culina	
H 6770	PJ71 UZH	SCA	Culina	
H 6771	PJ71 NHX	SCA	Stobart	Sherburn
H 6772	PJ71 NHY	SCA	Culina	Amesbury
H 6773	PN71 DWM	SCA	Culina	Droitwich
H 6774	PJ71 UZM	SCA	Fowler Welch	
H 6775	PJ71 UZF	SCA	Stobart	Sherburn
H 6776	PJ71 NHK	SCA	Fowler Welch	Washington
H 6778	PJ71 NJK	SCA	Stobart	
H 6779	PJ71 NHH	SCA	Fowler Welch	Washington
H 6780	PJ71 NHP	SCA	Fowler Welch	
H 6783	PJ71 NHA	SCA	Fowler Welch	Washington
H 6787	PJ71 NHT	SCA	Fowler Welch	Spalding
H 6788	PJ71 NHU	SCA	Fowler Welch	
H 6789	PJ71 NHL	SCA	Culina	Amesbury
H 6790	PJ71 NJV	SCA	Fowler Welch	
H 6791	PJ71 NJE	SCA	Culina	Amesbury
H 6792	PJ71 NJN	SCA	Warrens	
H 6795	PJ71 NHN	SCA	Fowler Welch	
H 6796	PJ71 UZD	SCA	Fowler Welch	
H 6797	PJ71 NHO	SCA	Culina	Amesbury
H 6799	PJ71 UZE	SCA	Stobart	
H 6800	PJ71 NFM	SCA	Warrens	Warrens, Rugby
H 6801	PJ71 NDZ	SCA	Culina	Telford
H 6802	PJ71 NBM	SCA	Stobart	Sherburn
H 6803	PJ71 NCC	SCA	Stobart	Sherburn
H 6804	PJ71 NEF	SCA	Stobart	
H 6806	PJ71 NEO	SCA	Stobart	
H 6807	PJ71 NCY	SCA	Fowler Welch	
H 6808	PJ71 NBN	SCA	Stobart	Sherburn
H 6809	PJ71 NFN	SCA	Culina	Glasgow
H 6810	PJ71 NEU	SCA	Stobart	
H 6811	PJ71 NFA	SCA	Fowler Welch	
H 6813	PJ71 NFC	SCA	Culina	
H 6814	PJ71 NCF	SCA	Stobart	Doncaster
H 6815	PJ71 NCD	SCA	Stobart	Immingham
H 6816	PJ71 NBO	SCA	Stobart	Doncaster
H 6818	PK71 VOT	SCA	Stobart	Widnes
H 6820	PJ71 NBY	SCA	Stobart	Doncaster
H 6821	PJ71 NCZ	SCA	Stobart	Doncaster
H 6823	PJ71 NFD	SCA	Great Bear	Bellshill
H 6824	PJ71 MZX	SCA	Stobart	Sherburn
H 6845	PN22 DYX	SCA	Stobart	Bridgwater Morrisons
H 6848	PN22 DXY	SCA	Stobart	
H 6849	PN22 DYY	SCA	Stobart	Bridgwater Morrisons
H 6855	PJ71 VFW	SCA	Warrens	Rugby
H 6856	PJ71 NFU	SCA	Culina	Telford
H 6857	PK71 VPL	SCA	Warrens	Warrens, Rugby
H 6858	PJ71 NBZ	SCA	Stobart	Sherburn
H 6859	PJ71 NDC	SCA	Stobart	Sherburn
H 6861	PJ71 NBA	SCA	Stobart	Doncaster
H 6862	PJ71 NBB	SCA	Culina	Amesbury
H 6863	PK71 VPP	SCA	Stobart	Doncaster
H 6864	PK71 VOG	SCA	Stobart	Sherburn
H 6865	PK71 VPD	SCA	Stobart	Sherburn

H 6866	PK71 VPE	SCA	Fowler Welch		
H 6867	PK71 VPF	SCA	Stobart		Sherburn
H 6868	PJ71 MZY	SCA	Culina		Amesbury
H 6869	PJ71 NFK	SCA	Fowler Welch		
H 6870	PK71 VPR	SCA	Stobart		Sherburn
H 6871	PJ71 NCA	SCA	Stobart		
H 6873	PJ71 NDD	SCA	Culina		Wolverhampton
H 6874	PJ71 NFE	SCA	Culina		Carlisle
H 6875	PJ71 NGU	SCA	Stobart		Sherburn
H 6876	PJ71 NGV	SCA	Culina		Glasgow
H 6877	PJ71 NHF	SCA	Fowler Welch		
H 6878	PJ71 NGX	SCA	Stobart		Sherburn
H 6879	PJ71 NGY	SCA	Culina		Glasgow
H 6880	PJ71 NGO	SCA	Culina		Droitwich
H 6881	PJ71 NGN	SCA	Stobart		Sherburn
H 6882	PK71 VMX	SCA	Stobart		Newport
H 6883	PK71 VMG	SCA	Stobart		
H 6885	PN22 EBM	SCA	Culina		
H 6888	PK71 VMY	SCA	Stobart		
H 6892	PN22 EAX	SCA	Great Bear		Banbury
H 6895	PN22 EBL	SCA	Stobart		Bridgwater Morrisons
H 6896	PN22 EBF	SCA	Stobart		
H 6898	PN22 EBG	SCA	Stobart		
H 6899	PN22 EAO	SCA	Stobart		
H 6900	PK71 VOM	SCA	Stobart		Sherburn
H 6901	PK71 VPJ	SCA	Stobart		
H 6902	PJ71 NDU	SCA	Great Bear		Trafford Park
H 6903	PJ71 NCX	SCA	Fowler Welch		
H 6904	PJ71 NFT	SCA	Culina		Telford
H 6905	PJ71 NGE	SCA	Culina		Telford
H 6907	PJ71 NFF	SCA	Great Bear		Telford
H 6908	PJ71 NGG	SCA	Stobart		Trafford Park
H 6909	PJ71 NFZ	SCA	Warrens		Rugby
H 6910	PK71 VPT	SCA	Stobart		Sherburn
H 6911	PK71 VPU	SCA	Culina		
H 6912	PK71 VOH	SCA	Stobart		Sherburn
H 6913	PN22 DWY	SCA	Stobart		
H 6918	PN22 DXS	SCA	Stobart		Lillyhall
H 6920	PJ71 NCE	SCA	Stobart		Sherburn
H 6921	PK71 VPC	SCA	Stobart		Widnes
H 6922	PJ71 NAU	SCA	Stobart		Widnes
H 6923	PJ71 NFG	SCA	Stobart		Teesport
H 6924	PN22 DXW	SCA	Stobart	Lizzie Marie	Appleton
H 6926	PJ71 UZS	SCA	Stobart		Trafford Park
H 6932	PN22 DYU	SCA	Stobart		Bathgate
H 6945	PJ71 UZT	SCA	Stobart	Princess Ellie	
H 6946	PJ71 UZU	SCA	Stobart		
H 6947	PJ71 UZV	SCA	Stobart		
H 6948	PJ71 UZW	SCA	Stobart		Widnes
H 6949	PN22 DXZ	SCA	Stobart		Sherburn
H 6951	PN22 DZY	SCA	Stobart		
H 6955	PN22 FAK	SCA	Stobart		
H 6956	PN22 EAJ	SCA	Stobart		
H 6957	PN22 EAF	SCA	CulinaPN		
H 6958	PN22 EBK	SCA	Stobart		
H 6960	PF71 DZN	SCA	Warrens		Warrens, Rugby
H 6966	PF71 DZG	SCA	Warrens		Warrens, Rugby
H 6970	PN22 DWW	SCA	Stobart		Sherburn
H 6972	PF71 DZM	SCA	Warrens		Warrens, Rugby
H 6974	PF71 DYJ	SCA	Great Bear		

H 6975	PJ71 UZP	SCA	Stobart	Carlisle
H 6976	PJ71 VAE	SCA	Fowler Welch	
H 6977	PJ71 NFY	SCA	Fowler Welch	Broxburn
H 6978	PJ71 NCN	SCA	Stobart	Dav 1
H 6979	PJ71 NCU	SCA	Stobart	Sherburn
H 6980	PK71 VPW	SCA	Stobart	Widnes
H 6981	PK71 VOJ	SCA	Stobart	
H 6982	PK71 VOP	SCA	Stobart	
H 6983	PJ71 NFH	SCA	Culina	
H 6984	PJ71 NDE	SCA	Stobart	Widnes
H 6985	PJ71 NAA	SCA	Culina	Raunds
H 6986	PJ71 NBK	SCA	Fowler Welch	
H 6987	PK71 VOO	SCA	Stobart	Sherburn
H 6988	PJ71 NDL	SCA	Stobart	Teesport
H 6989	PJ71 NDN	SCA	Fowler Welch	
H 6990	PJ71 NCV	SCA	Stobart	Sherburn
H 6991	PJ71 NDO	SCA	Culina	Telford
H 6992	PJ71 NAE	SCA	Stobart	
H 6993	PK71 VPM	SCA	Stobart	
H 6994	PK71 VOF	SCA	Stobart	Widnes
H 6995	PK71 VPX	SCA	Stobart	Immingham
H 6996	PJ71 NFL	SCA	Fowler Welch	
H 6997	PJ71 NDV	SCA	Stobart	Appleton
H 6998	PJ71 NBL	SCA	Culina	
H 6999	PJ71 NDX	SCA	Stobart	Widnes Ports
H 7753	FT68 JXB	SCA	Stobart	Doncaster
H 7754	FT68 JXC	SCA	Culina	
H 7755	FT68 JXD	SCA	Culina	
H 7757	FT68 JXF	SCA	Culina	
H 7758	FT68 JXG	SCA	Culina	
H 7759	FT68 JXH	SCA	Morgan McLernon	
H 7760	FT68 JXJ	SCA	Stobart	
H 7761	FT68 JXK	SCA	Stobart	Wakefield Morrisons
H 7762	FT68 JXL	SCA	Stobart	Rugby T-Stop
H 7763	FT68 JXM	SCA	Stobart	Rugby T-Stop
H 7764	FT68 JXN	SCA	Morgan McLernon	
H 7765	FT68 JXO	SCA	Stobart	
H 7766	FT68 JXP	SCA	Stobart	Carlisle
H 7767	FT68 JXR	SCA	Stobart	
H 7768	FT68 JXS	SCA	Stobart	Rugby T-Stop
H 7769	FT68 JXU	SCA	Stobart	Burton Latimer
H 7770	FT68 JXV	SCA	Morgan McLernon	
H 7771	FT68 JYB	SCA	Culina	
H 7772	FT68 JYE	SCA	Stobart	Carlisle
H 7773	FT68 JYL	SCA	Stobart	
H 7774	FT68 JYP	SCA	Culina	
H 7775	FT68 JYX	SCA	Stobart	
H 7776	FT68 JZE	SCA	Culina	
H 7777	FT68 JZX	SCA	Morgan McLernon	
H 7778	FT68 KAJ	SCA	Stobart	Doncaster
H 7779	FT68 KAU	SCA	Morgan McLernon	
H 7780	FT68 KAX	SCA	Stobart	
H 7781	FT68 KBK	SCA	Stobart	Carlisle
H 7782	FT68 KCE	SCA	Morgan McLernon	
H 7783	FT68 KCF	SCA	White	
H 7784	FT68 KCX	SCA	Morgan McLernon	
H 7785	FT68 KDK	SCA	Stobart	Doncaster
H 7786	FT68 KDU	SCA	Stobart	Doncaster
H 7799	FX67 OBC	SCA	White	
H 7808	FX68 ORC	SCA	Stobart	Carlisle

H 7809	FX68 ORF	SCA	Culina	
H 7810	FX68 ORG	SCA	Stobart	
H 7811	FX68 ORH	SCA	Stobart	Wakefield Morrisons
H 7812	FX68 ORJ	SCA	Culina	Lillyhall
H 7813	FX68 ORK	SCA	Culina	Lillyhall
H 7815	FX68 ORN	SCA	Stobart	Carlisle
H 7816	FX68 ORP	SCA	Stobart	
H 7817	FX68 ORS	SCA	Stobart	
H 7818	FX68 ORW	SCA	Stobart	Carlisle
H 7819	FX68 ORY	SCA	Warrens	
H 7820	FX68 ORZ	SCA	Fowler Welch	
H 7821	FX68 OSA	SCA	Great Bear	
H 7822	FX68 OSB	SCA	Stobart	Carlisle
H 7823	FX68 OSC	SCA	Culina	
H 7824	FX68 OSD	SCA	Warrens	
H 7825	FX68 OSF	SCA	Stobart	Leicester
H 7826	FX68 OSG	SCA	Stobart	Carlisle
H 7827	FX68 OSJ	SCA	Great Bear	
H 7828	FX68 OTG	SCA	Fowler Welch	
H 7829	FX68 OTM	SCA	Stobart	Carlisle
H 7830	FX68 OTP	SCA	Stobart	Doncaster
H 7831	FX68 OTR	SCA	Stobart	
H 7981	MD19 OXS	SCA	Warrens	
H 7984	MD19 OXV	SCA	Warrens	
H 7990	MD19 OYE	SCA	Stobart	Wakefield Morrisons
H 7994	MD19 OYJ	SCA	Warrens	
H 7998	MD19 OYN	SCA	Warrens	
H 8000	MD19 OYP	SCA	Warrens	
H 8004	MD19 PCV	SCA	Stobart	Wakefield Morrisons
H 8010	MJ19 VJD	SCA	Warrens	
H 8028	ML19 FLR	SCA	Stobart	TPN Stockton
H 8029	ML19 FLV	SCA	Warrens	
H 8031	ML19 FLX	SCA	Warrens	
H 8032	ML19 FLZ	SCA	Stobart	
H 8063	ML19 FNS	SCA	Stobart	Wakefield Morrisons
H 8157	MV69 KOB	SCA	Stobart	
H 8163	MV69 KOU	SCA	Stobart	Wakefield Morrisons
H 8165	MV69 KPA	SCA	Stobart	Wakefield Morrisons
H 8167	MV69 KPF	SCA	Stobart	Wakefield Morrisons
H 8293	CN70 UXA	MER	Fowler Welch	
H 8318	PN67 HHG	MER	Culina	
H 8324	PN67 HHR	MER	Culina	
H 8701	SJ22 FMZ	Volvo	Robert Burns	Broxburn
H 8702	SJ22 FNA	Volvo	Robert Burns	Broxburn
H 8703	SJ22 FML	Volvo	Robert Burns	Broxburn
H 8704	SJ22 FMO	Volvo	Robert Burns	Broxburn
H 8705	SJ22 FMP	Volvo	Robert Burns	Broxburn
H 8706	SJ22 FMV	Volvo	Robert Burns	Broxburn
H 8707	SJ22 FMX	Volvo	Robert Burns	Broxburn
H 8708	SJ22 FMY	Volvo	Robert Burns	Broxburn
H 8709	SJ22 FMU	Volvo	Robert Burns	Broxburn
H 8710	SJ22 FMM	Volvo	Robert Burns	Broxburn
H 8711	SJ22 FMA	Volvo	Robert Burns	Broxburn
H 8712	SJ22 FMC	Volvo	Robert Burns	Broxburn
H 8713	SJ22 FMF	Volvo	Robert Burns	Broxburn
H 8714	SJ22 FMG	Volvo	Robert Burns	Broxburn
H 8715	SJ22 FMK	Volvo	Robert Burns	Broxburn
H 8716	SJ22 FLZ	Volvo	Robert Burns	Broxburn
H 8717	Y12 BTL	SCA	Warrens	
H 8718	BJ19 RYB	SCA	Warrens	

H 8746	BD72 EYA	SCA	Warrens	
H 8747	BD72 EYB	SCA	Warrens	
H 8748	BD72 EYC	SCA	Warrens	
H 8749	BD72 EYF	SCA	Warrens	
H 8750	BD72 EYG	SCA	Warrens	
H 8751	BD72 EYJ	SCA	Warrens	
H 8752	BD72 EYH	SCA	Warrens	
H 8758	BF18 HCP	SCA	Ball Trucking	
H 8760	BJ18 RMZ	SCA	Stobart	
H 8771	BV21 UCL	SCA	Ball Trucking	
H 8772	BV21 UDL	SCA	Ball Trucking	
H 8773	BV21 UDM	SCA	Ball Trucking	
H 8774	BV21 UDN	SCA	Ball Trucking	
H 8776	BV22 LHC	SCA	Ball Trucking	
H 8792	NU21 XMF	IVE	Ball Trucking	
H 8793	FX20 FMC	SCA	Ball Trucking	
H 8794	T27 BTL (70)	SCA	Ball Trucking	
H 8795	PO18 MVM	SCA	Ball Trucking	
H 9000	WV72 ALU	IVE	Morrisons	Morrisons, Gadbrook
H 9001	WV72 ANP	IVE	Morrisons	Morrisons, Gadbrook
H 9002	WV72 ANR	IVE	Morrisons	Morrisons, Gadbrook
H 9003	WV72 ANU	IVE	Morrisons	Morrisons, Gadbrook
H 9004	WV72 AOH	IVE	Morrisons	Morrisons, Gadbrook
H 9005	WV72 AOK	IVE	Morrisons	Morrisons, Gadbrook
H 9006	WV72 ASX	IVE	Morrisons	Morrisons, Gadbrook
H 9007	WV72 AOL	IVE	Morrisons	Morrisons, Gadbrook
H 9008	WV72 ATN	IVE	Morrisons	Morrisons, Gadbrook
H 9009	WV72 ATX	IVE	Morrisons	Morrisons, Gadbrook
H 9010	WV72 ATY	IVE	Morrisons	Morrisons, Gadbrook
H 9011	WV72 ATZ	IVE	Morrisons	Morrisons, Gadbrook
H 9012	WV72 AUA	IVE	Morrisons	Morrisons, Gadbrook
H 9013	WV72 AUC	IVE	Morrisons	Morrisons, Gadbrook
H 9014	WV72 AUE	IVE	Morrisons	Morrisons, Gadbrook
H 9015	WV72 AUF	IVE	Morrisons	Morrisons, Gadbrook
H 9016	WV72 AUH	IVE	Morrisons	Morrisons, Gadbrook
H 9017	WV72 AUJ	IVE	Morrisons	Morrisons, Gadbrook
H 9018	WV72 AUK	IVE	Morrisons	Morrisons, Gadbrook
H 9019	WV72 AUL	IVE	Morrisons	Morrisons, Gadbrook
H 9020	WR72 JJV	IVE	Morrisons	Morrisons, Gadbrook
H 9021	WR72 JKU	IVE	Morrisons	Morrisons, Gadbrook
H 9022	WR72 JKV	IVE	Morrisons	Morrisons, Gadbrook
H 9023	WR72 JLU	IVE	Morrisons	Morrisons, Gadbrook
H 9024	WR72 JLV	IVE	Morrisons	Morrisons, Gadbrook
H 9025	WR72 JLX	IVE	Morrisons	Morrisons, Gadbrook
H 9026	WR72 JMO	IVE	Morrisons	Morrisons, Gadbrook
H 9027	WR72 JMU	IVE	Morrisons	Morrisons, Gadbrook
H 9028	WV72 AKO	IVE	Morrisons	Morrisons, Gadbrook
H 9029	WV72 AKX	IVE	Morrisons	Morrisons, Gadbrook
H 9030	WV72 AOM	IVE	Morrisons	Morrisons, Gadbrook
L 101	PF73 KVX	SCA	Stobart	Tesco Goole
L 102	PL73 HHB	SCA	Stobart	Tesco Goole
L 103	PL73 HJX	SCA	Stobart	Tesco Goole
L 104	PL73 HJU	SCA	Stobart	
L 105	PF73 EKC	SCA	Stobart	Tesco Goole
L 106	PL73 HHE	SCA	Stobart	Tesco Goole
L 107	PL73 HGN	SCA	Stobart	Tesco Goole
L 108	PL73 HJF	SCA	Stobart	
L 109	PL73 HGC	SCA	Stobart	Tesco Goole
L 110	PL73 HHA	SCA	Stobart	Tesco Goole
L 111	PL73 HJE	SCA	Stobart	Tesco Goole

L 112	PO67 XMT	SCA	Stobart	Niamh Grace	Owner Driver
L 114	PO18 OGE	SCA	Stobart		Owner Driver
L 3364	6 AX 1061	MER	Williams	*guit vke*	Hawleys Lane
L 3365	6 AX 1060	MER	Williams	*vkf*	Hawleys Lane
L 3366	5 SL 6210	MER	Williams	*vkG*	Hawleys Lane
L 3367	6 AX 1127	MER	Williams	*vkH*	Hawleys Lane
L 3368	8 AE 8980	MER	Williams	*vkJ*	Hawleys Lane
L 3369	6 AX 1082	MER	Williams	*vkk*	Hawleys Lane
L 3410	PO20 ZZH	SCA	Williams		Appleton
L 3411	PO20 ZZJ	SCA	Williams		Appleton
L 3412	PO20 ZZK	SCA	Williams		Appleton
L 3413	PO20 ZZL	SCA	Williams		Appleton
L 3414	PO20 ZZM	SCA	Williams		Appleton
L 3415	PO20 ZZN	SCA	Williams		Appleton
L 3416	PO20 ZZP	SCA	Williams		Appleton
L 3417	PO20 ZZR	SCA	Williams		Appleton
L 3418	PO20 ZZS	SCA	Williams		Appleton
L 3419	PO20 ZZT	SCA	Williams		Appleton
L 3420	PO20 ZZU	SCA	Williams		Appleton
L 3421	PO20 ZZV	SCA	Williams		Appleton
L 3423	PO20 ZZX	SCA	Williams		Appleton
L 3424	PO20 ZZY	SCA	Williams		Appleton
L 3427	PN21 FDM	SCA	Pirelli		Hawleys Lane
L 3428	PN21 FDO	SCA	Pirelli		Hawleys Lane
L 3429	PN21 FDP	SCA	Pirelli		Hawleys Lane
L 3430	PN21 FDU	SCA	Pirelli		Hawleys Lane
L 3431	PN21 FDV	SCA	Pirelli		Hawleys Lane
L 3432	PN21 FDX	SCA	Pirelli		Hawleys Lane
L 3433	PN21 FDZ	SCA	Pirelli		Hawleys Lane
L 3434	PN21 FFA	SCA	Pirelli		Hawleys Lane
L 3435	PN21 FFB	SCA	Pirelli		Hawleys Lane
L 3436	PN21 FFC	SCA	Pirelli		Hawleys Lane
L 3437	PN21 FFD	SCA	Pirelli		Hawleys Lane
L 3438	PN21 FFE	SCA	Pirelli		Hawleys Lane
L 3439	GK21 AOA	MER	Silver		Hawleys Lane
L 3440	GK21 AOB	MER	Silver		Hawleys Lane
L 3441	GK21 AOC	MER	Silver		Hawleys Lane
L 3443	GK21 AOE	MER	Silver		Hawleys Lane
L 3444	GK21 AOF	MER	Silver		Hawleys Lane
L 3445	GK21 AOG	MER	Silver		Hawleys Lane
L 3446	GK21 AOH	MER	Silver		Hawleys Lane
L 3447	YOU 730	SCA	Silver		Hawleys Lane
L 3460	PK24 AKN	SCA	Blue		
L 3464	PK24 AKZ	SCA	Blue		
L 3470	PK24 AKP	SCA	White		
L 3472	PK24 ALY	SCA	White		
L 3481	GN24 YLL	MER	Black		
L 3483	GN24 YLO	MER	Black		
L	GN24 YLR	MER	Black		
L	GN24 YLT	MER	Black		
L 7662	PF12 JBZ	SCA	White		Rugby
L 7854	PJ17 USF	SCA	Stobart		
L 7855	PJ17 USG	SCA	Stobart		
L 7857	PJ17 USL	SCA	Stobart		Doncaster
L 7859	PJ17 USN	SCA	Stobart		
L 7862	PJ17 USS	SCA	Stobart		
L 7864	PJ17 USU	SCA	Stobart		Doncaster
L 7869	PJ17 USZ	SCA	Stobart		
L 7873	PJ17 UTE	SCA	Stobart		
L 7878	PJ17 UTL	SCA	Stobart		

L 7879	PO67 XNF	SCA	Stobart		
L 7883	PO67 XNK	SCA	Stobart		Doncaster
L 7886	PO67 XNN	SCA	Stobart	Margaret Ivy	Burton Latimer
L 7891	PO67 VPE	SCA	Stobart		
L 7897	PO67 VPG	SCA	Stobart		
L 7902	PO67 XRG	SCA	Stobart	Megan Colleen	Burton Latimer
L 7907	PO67 VOP	SCA	Stobart	Millie Florence	Burton Latimer
L 7908	PO67 VOT	SCA	Stobart	Sara Louise	Burton Latimer
L 7912	PO67 XMR	SCA	Stobart	Zoe Maria	Birchwood
L 7913	PO67 VOU	SCA	Stobart	Emily Bethan	Burton Latimer
L 7914	PO67 VOV	SCA	Stobart	Lynn Michelle	Burton Latimer
L 7923	PO67 XMY	SCA	Stobart		
L 7929	PJ17 UUD	SCA	Stobart	Lilia Frances	Widnes
L 7930	PJ17 UUE	SCA	Stobart	Penny	Widnes
L 7931	PJ17 UTM	SCA	White		
L 7932	PJ17 UUF	SCA	White		
L 7933	PJ17 UVR	SCA	White		Doncaster
L 7936	PJ17 UTV	SCA	White		
L 7937	PJ17 UTX	SCA	White		Doncaster
L 7938	PJ17 UTY	SCA	White		
L 7939	PJ17 UTZ	SCA	White		
L 7940	PJ17 UUA	SCA	White		
L 7943	PJ17 UUK	SCA	Stobart	Danielle Emma	Burton Latimer
L 7945	PJ17 UTR	SCA	White		
L 7946	PJ17 UTS	SCA	TAG		
L 7947	PJ17 UUG	SCA	Stobart		
L 7948	PJ17 UTT	SCA	White		Burton Latimer
L 7949	PJ17 UUB	SCA	White		
L 7950	PJ17 UTW	SCA	White		
L 7951	PJ17 UVS	SCA	White		
L 7952	PJ17 UTU	SCA	Stobart	Sarah Ruth	Burton Latimer
L 7953	PJ17 UUC	SCA	Stobart		
L 7960	PO18 OAC	SCA	Culina		
L 7963	PO18 OAE	SCA	Stobart		
L 7964	PO18 OAG	SCA	Culina		
L 7967	PO18 OAL	SCA	Stobart		Doncaster
L 7969	PO18 OAN	SCA	Stobart		Doncaster
L 7970	PO18 NZX	SCA	Stobart		Doncaster
L 7973	PO18 NZZ	SCA	Stobart		
L 7975	PO18 OAB	SCA	Stobart		Doncaster
L 7976	PO18 OAS	SCA	Stobart		
L 7977	PO18 OAU	SCA	Stobart		Doncaster
L 7979	PO18 NZJ	SCA	Culina		Doncaster
L 7981	PO18 NZK	SCA	Culina		Doncaster
L 7983	PO18 NZP	SCA	Stobart	Mary Philamena	Carlisle
L 7985	PO18 NZS	SCA	Stobart		Doncaster
L 7989	PO18 OAW	SCA	Stobart		Doncaster
L 7992	PO18 OAZ	SCA	Stobart		
L 7993	PO18 OBA	SCA	Stobart		
L 7994	PO18 OBC	SCA	Stobart		
L 8001	PO18 OBL	SCA	Stobart		Doncaster
L 8004	PO18 OBP	SCA	Stobart		
L 8006	PO18 OBT	SCA	Stobart		
L 8007	PO18 OBU	SCA	Stobart		Doncaster
L 8008	PO18 OBV	SCA	Culina		Doncaster
L 8009	PO18 OBW	SCA	Stobart		Doncaster
L 8010	PO18 OBX	SCA	Stobart		
L 8013	PO18 OCB	SCA	Stobart		
L 8014	PO18 OCC	SCA	Culina		Doncaster
L 8015	PO18 OCD	SCA	Culina		

L 8016	PO18 OCE	SCA	Stobart		
L 8017	PO18 OCF	SCA	Stobart		Doncaster
L 8018	PO18 OCG	SCA	Stobart		Doncaster
L 8020	PO18 OFS	SCA	Stobart		
L 8021	PO18 OFT	SCA	Stobart		
L 8022	PO18 OFU	SCA	Stobart		Doncaster
L 8023	PO18 OFV	SCA	Stobart		
L 8024	PO18 OFW	SCA	Stobart		Doncaster
L 8025	PO18 OFX	SCA	Stobart		Doncaster
L 8026	PO18 OFY	SCA	Stobart		
L 8027	PO18 OFZ	SCA	Stobart		Doncaster
L 8028	PO18 OGA	SCA	Stobart		Doncaster
L 8029	PO18 OGC	SCA	Stobart		Doncaster
L 8032	PO18 OGF	SCA	Culina		Sherburn
L 8033	PO18 OGG	SCA	Stobart		Doncaster
L 8034	PO18 OGH	SCA	Stobart		
L 8035	PO18 OGJ	SCA	Stobart		
L 8037	PO18 OGL	SCA	Stobart		
L 8038	PO18 OGM	SCA	Stobart		
L 8039	PO18 OGN	SCA	Stobart		Doncaster
L 8040	PO18 OGP	SCA	Stobart		
L 8041	PO18 OGR	SCA	Stobart		Doncaster
L 8042	PO18 OGS	SCA	Stobart		Doncaster
L 8043	PO18 OGT	SCA	Stobart		Doncaster
L 8046	PO18 OGX	SCA	Culina		
L 8048	PO18 OGZ	SCA	Culina		
L 8049	PO18 OHA	SCA	Stobart		
L 8051	PO18 OHC	SCA	Stobart		Doncaster
L 8053	PO18 OHE	SCA	Stobart		
L 8054	PO18 OHF	SCA	Stobart		
L 8058	PO18 OHK	SCA	Stobart		
L 8059	PO18 OHL	SCA	Stobart		
L 8112	GN19 GVG	MER	BCA Automotive		
L 8113	GN19 GVJ	MER	BCA Automotive		
L 8114	GN19 GVK	MER	BCA Automotive		
L 8115	GN19 GVL	MER	BCA Automotive		
L 8116	GN19 GVM	MER	BCA Automotive		
L 8117	GN19 GVO	MER	BCA Automotive		
L 8118	GN19 GVP	MER	BCA Automotive		
L 8119	GN19 GVR	MER	BCA Automotive		
L 8120	GN19 GVT	MER	BCA Automotive		
L 8121	GN19 GVU	MER	BCA Automotive		
L 8122	GN19 GVV	MER	BCA Automotive		
L 8123	GN19 GVW	MER	BCA Automotive		
L 8124	GN19 GVX	MER	BCA Automotive		
L 8125	GN19 GVY	MER	BCA Automotive		
L 8126	GN19 GVZ	MER	BCA Automotive		
L 8127	GN19 GWA	MER	Stobart	Maria Sue	Sittingbourne
L 8128	GN19 GWC	MER	Stobart	Olwen	Sittingbourne
L 8129	GN19 GWD	MER	Stobart	Pauline Jean	Sittingbourne
L 8130	GN19 GWE	MER	Stobart	Lesley Anne	Sittingbourne
L 8131	GN19 GWF	MER	Stobart	Helen Lizanca	Sittingbourne
L 8132	GN19 GWG	MER	Stobart	Simrun Rose	Sittingbourne
L 8133	GN19 GWK	MER	Stobart	Millie	Sittingbourne
L 8134	GN19 GWL	MER	Stobart	Izzie Louize	Sittingbourne
L 8135	GN19 GWM	MER	Stobart	Eleanor Grace	Sittingbourne
L 8136	GN19 GWO	MER	Stobart	Margaret Tracy	Sittingbourne
L 8137	GN19 GWP	MER	Stobart	Andrea Nerissa	Sittingbourne
L 8138	GN19 GWU	MER	Stobart	Paige Louise	Sittingbourne
L 8139	GN19 GWV	MER	Stobart	Emmie Louisa	Sittingbourne

L 8140	GN19 GWW	MER	Stobart	Heather Linden	Sittingbourne
L 8141	GN19 GWX	MER	Stobart	Jane Caroline	Sittingbourne
L 8142	GN19 GWY	MER	Stobart	Alison Helen	Sittingbourne
L 8143	GN19 GWZ	MER	Stobart	Jacqui Kelly	Sittingbourne
L 8144	GN19 GXA	MER	Stobart	Maralyn	Sittingbourne
L 8145	GN19 GXB	MER	Stobart	Amanda Liese	Sittingbourne
L 8146	GN19 GXC	MER	Stobart	Aria Jennifer	Sittingbourne
L 8147	GN19 GXE	MER	Stobart	Samantha Emily	Sittingbourne
L 8148	GN19 GXF	MER	Stobart	Alexandra Jane	Sittingbourne
L 8149	GN19 GXG	MER	Stobart	Sally Jane	Sittingbourne
L 8150	GN19 GXH	MER	Stobart	Bethany Sarah	Sittingbourne
L 8151	GN19 GXJ	MER	Stobart	Philippa Anne	Sittingbourne
L 8152	GN19 GXK	MER	Stobart	Margaret Campbell	Sittingbourne
L 8153	GN19 GXL	MER	Stobart	Diane Rose	Sittingbourne
L 8154	GN19 GXM	MER	Stobart	Laura Chelsie	Sittingbourne
L 8155	GN19 GXO	MER	Stobart	Sandy Rose	Sittingbourne
L 8157	GN19 GXR	MER	Stobart	Lucy Elizabeth	Sittingbourne
L 8158	GN19 GXS	MER	Stobart	Jean Maureen	Sittingbourne
L 8159	GN19 GXT	MER	Stobart	Inya Elizabeth	Sittingbourne
L 8160	GN19 GXU	MER	Stobart	Lucy Gail	Sittingbourne
L 8161	GN19 GVC	MER	Stobart	Lizzie	Sittingbourne
L 8162	GN73 YZE	MER	Great Bear		Stoke
L 8163	GN73 YZD	MER	Stobart		Sittingbourne
L 8164	GN73 YZF	MER	Great Bear		Stoke
L 8165	GN73 YZG	MER	Great Bear		Stoke
L 8166	GN73 YZH	MER	Great Bear		Stoke
L 8167	GN73 ZBU	MER	Stobart		Sittingbourne
L 8168	GN73 ZBT	MER	Stobart		Sittingbourne
L 8169	GN73 ZBV	MER	Stobart		Sittingbourne
L 8170	GN73 ZCO	MER	Stobart		Sittingbourne
L 8171	GN73 ZBW	MER	Stobart		Sittingbourne
L 8172	GN73 ZBX	MER	Stobart		Sittingbourne
L 8173	GN73 ZCT	MER	Stobart		Sittingbourne
L 8174	GN73 ZBY	MER	Stobart		Sittingbourne
L 8175	GN73 ZBZ	MER	Stobart		Sittingbourne
L 8176	GN73 ZCA	MER	Stobart		Sittingbourne
L 8177	GN73 ZCE	MER	Stobart		Sittingbourne
L 8178		MER	Stobart		Sittingbourne
L 8179	GN73 ZCF	MER	Stobart		Sittingbourne
L 8180	GN73 ZCU	MER	Stobart		Sittingbourne
L 8181		MER	Stobart		Sittingbourne
L 8182		MER	Stobart		Sittingbourne
L 8183	GN73 ZDA	MER	Stobart		Sittingbourne
L 8184	GN73 ZCY	MER	Stobart		Sittingbourne
L 8185	GN73 ZDC	MER	Stobart		Sittingbourne
L 8186		MER	Stobart		Sittingbourne
L 8187	GN73 ZCJ	MER	Stobart		Sittingbourne
L 8188		MER	Stobart		Sittingbourne
L 8189	GN73 ZCK	MER	Stobart		Sittingbourne
L 8190		MER	Stobart		Sittingbourne
L 8191	GN73 ZCL	MER	Stobart		Sittingbourne
L 8300	PF73 RFE	SCA	Stobart		Walkers, Birchwood
L 8301	PF73 RFJ	SCA	Stobart		Walkers, Leicester
L 8302	PF73 RFK	SCA	Stobart		Walkers, Birchwood
L 8303	PF73 RGY	SCA	Stobart		Walkers, Birchwood
L 8304	PF73 RFL	SCA	Stobart		Walkers, Leicester
L 8305	PF73 RFN	SCA	Stobart		Walkers, Birchwood
L 8306	PF73 RFO	SCA	Stobart		Walkers, Leicester
L 8307	PF73 RFX	SCA	Stobart		Walkers, Birchwood
L 8308	PF73 RFY	SCA	Stobart		Walkers, Leicester

L 8309	PF73 RFZ	SCA	Stobart	Walkers, Leicester
L 8310	PF73 RGO	SCA	Stobart	Walkers, Leicester
L 8311	PF73 RGU	SCA	Stobart	Walkers, Birchwood
L 8312	PF73 RGV	SCA	Stobart	Walkers, Birchwood
L 8313	PF73 RGX	SCA	Stobart	Walkers, Birchwood
L 8314	PF73 RGZ	SCA	Stobart	Walkers, Leicester
L 8315	PF73 RHA	SCA	Stobart	Walkers, Birchwood
L 8316	PF73 RHE	SCA	Stobart	Walkers, Birchwood
L 8317	PF73 RHJ	SCA	Stobart	Walkers, Birchwood
L 8318	PF73 RHK	SCA	Stobart	Walkers, Birchwood
L 8319	PF73 RHO	SCA	Stobart	Walkers, Birchwood
L 8320	PL73 HDO	SCA	Stobart	Walkers, Birchwood
L 8321	PJ73 XUB	SCA	Stobart	Walkers, Birchwood
L 8322	PJ73 YLC	SCA	Stobart	Walkers, Leicester
L 8323	PJ73 YLD	SCA	Stobart	Walkers, Birchwood
L 8324	PL73 HDU	SCA	Stobart	Walkers, Birchwood
L 8325	PL73 HDY	SCA	Stobart	Walkers, Birchwood
L 8326	PL73 HDZ	SCA	Stobart	Walkers, Birchwood
L 8327	PL73 HDX	SCA	Stobart	Walkers, Birchwood
L 8328	PL73 HDV	SCA	Stobart	Walkers, Birchwood
L 8329	PL73 HEJ	SCA	Stobart	Walkers, Leicester
L 8330	PL73 HEU	SCA	Stobart	Walkers, Leicester
L 8331	PL73 HFO	SCA	Stobart	Walkers, Leicester
L 8332	PL73 HFG	SCA	Stobart	Walkers, Leicester
L 8333	PL73 HEV	SCA	Stobart	Walkers, Leicester
L 8334	PL73 HFA	SCA	Stobart	Walkers, Leicester
L 8335	PL73 HFC	SCA	Stobart	Walkers, Leicester
L 8337	PF73 CGO	SCA	Stobart	Walkers, Leicester
L 8338	PL73 HFB	SCA	Stobart	Walkers, Leicester
L 8339	PL73 HFF	SCA	Stobart	Walkers, Leicester
L 8340	PL73 HFH	SCA	Stobart	Walkers, Leicester
L 8341	PL73 HFP	SCA	Stobart	Walkers, Leicester
L 8342	PJ73 XUE	SCA	Stobart	Walkers, Leicester
L 8343	PL73 HFM	SCA	Stobart	Walkers, Leicester
L 8344	PL73 HFR	SCA	Stobart	Walkers, Leicester
L 8345	PF73 EKV	SCA	Stobart	Walkers, Leicester
L 8346	PL73 HFJ	SCA	Stobart	Walkers, Leicester
L 8347	PF73 EKP	SCA	Stobart	Walkers, Leicester
L 8348	PL73 HFK	SCA	Stobart	Walkers, Leicester
L 8349	PL73 HFE	SCA	Stobart	Walkers, Leicester
L 8350	PL73 HFN	SCA	Stobart	Walkers, Leicester
L 8351	PF73 EHE	SCA	Stobart	Walkers, Leicester
L 8352	PF73 KTC	SCA	Stobart	Walkers, Leicester
L 8353	PF73 EHL	SCA	Stobart	Walkers, Leicester
L 8354	PF73 RDV	SCA	Stobart	Tesco Goole
L 8355	PF73 EKK	SCA	Stobart	Walkers, Leicester
L 8356	PJ73 XVX	SCA	Stobart	Walkers, Leicester
L 8358	PL73 HJY	SCA	Stobart	Tesco Goole
L 8360	PF73 KTO	SCA	Stobart	Walkers, Leicester
L 8360	PF73 KWH	SCA	Stobart	Tesco Doncaster
L 8361	PF73 KVM	SCA	Stobart	Tesco Daventry 1
L 8362	PF73 KVK	SCA	Stobart	Daventry 1
L 8364	PL73 HHJ	SCA	Stobart	Tesco Doncaster
L 8365	PF73 KTK	SCA	Stobart	Walkers, Leicester
L 8367	PF73 KVZ	SCA	Stobart	Burton Latimer
L 8368	PL73 HHR	SCA	Stobart	Tesco Doncaster
L 8369	PL73 HGE	SCA	Stobart	Tesco Goole
L 8370	PF73 KVA	SCA	Stobart	Tesco Goole
L 8371	PL73 HHS	SCA	Stobart	Tesco Doncaster
L 8372	PL73 HGG	SCA	Stobart	Tesco Daventry 1

L 8373	PF73 KWJ	SCA	Stobart	Tesco Goole
L 8374	PL73 HJZ	SCA	Stobart	Tesco Goole
L 8375	PL73 HGJ	SCA	Stobart	Tesco Doncaster
L 8376	PF73 KTP	SCA	Stobart	Walkers, Leicester
L 8378	PL73 HHK	SCA	Stobart	Tesco Goole
L 8379	PL73 HHM	SCA	Stobart	Tesco Goole
L 8380	PL73 HJJ	SCA	Stobart	Tesco Doncaster
L 8381	PF73 KTL	SCA	Stobart	Walkers, Leicester
L 8382	PF73 KVO	SCA	Stobart	Tesco Goole
L 8383	PL73 HFX	SCA	Stobart	Tesco Goole
L 8384	PF73 KWD	SCA	Stobart	Burton Latimer
L 8385	PL73 HGF	SCA	Stobart	Tesco Goole
L 8386	PL73 HGM	SCA	Stobart	Tesco Doncaster
L 8387	PL73 HJV	SCA	Stobart	Tesco Goole
L 8388	PL73 HGK	SCA	Stobart	
L 8389	PL73 HHT	SCA	Stobart	Tesco Goole
L 8390	PL73 HHN	SCA	Stobart	Tesco Goole
L 8391	PL73 HGD	SCA	Stobart	Tesco Doncaster
L 8392	PL73 HJG	SCA	Stobart	Tesco Goole
L 8393	PL73 HGO	SCA	Stobart	Tesco Goole
L 8394	PL73 HHF	SCA	Stobart	Tesco Doncaster
L 8395	PF73 EKJ	SCA	Stobart	Tesco Goole
L 8396	PF73 KVP	SCA	Stobart	Tesco Goole
L 8397	PF73 KVR	SCA	Stobart	Carlisle
L 8398	PF73 KVS	SCA	Stobart	Tesco Goole
L 8399	PF73 KVY	SCA	Stobart	Carlisle
L 8400	PF73 EKY	SCA	Stobart	Tesco Doncaster
L 8401	PF73 KUT	SCA	Stobart	Walkers, Leicester
L 8403	PF73 EKD	SCA	Stobart	Walkers, Leicester
L 8404	PF73 KUV	SCA	Stobart	Walkers, Leicester
L 8405	PF73 KVT	SCA	Stobart	Tesco Doncaster
L 8406	PL73 HJK	SCA	Stobart	Tesco Doncaster
L 8407	PF73 KVL	SCA	Stobart	Tesco Doncaster
L 8408	PL73 HHG	SCA	Stobart	Daventry 1
L 8409	PL73 HGP	SCA	Stobart	Tesco Doncaster
L 8410	PL73 HFY	SCA	Stobart	Tesco Doncaster
L 8411	PF73 KWA	SCA	Stobart	Tesco Goole
L 8412	PL73 HHO	SCA	Stobart	Tesco Doncaster
L 8413	PL73 HFZ	SCA	Stobart	Tesco Doncaster
L 8414	PF73 KTN	SCA	Stobart	Walkers, Leicester
L 8415	PF73 KVU	SCA	Stobart	Tesco Goole
L 8416	PL73 HHP	SCA	Stobart	Tesco Doncaster
L 8417	PL73 HGA	SCA	Stobart	Tesco Doncaster
L 8418	PL73 HJO	SCA	Stobart	Tesco Doncaster
L 8419	PF73 KVW	SCA	Stobart	Tesco Goole
L 8420	PF73 ELC	SCA	Stobart	Tesco Doncaster
L 8421	PF73 KVC	SCA	Stobart	Walkers, Leicester
L 8422	PJ73 XSE	SCA	Stobart	Tesco Doncaster
L 8423	PL73 HJN	SCA	Stobart	Tesco Doncaster
L 8424	PF73 KVH	SCA	Stobart	Walkers, Leicester
L 8426	PL73 HGU	SCA	Stobart	Tesco Goole
L 8428	PF73 KWC	SCA	Stobart	Tesco Goole
L 8429	PF73 KVG	SCA	Stobart	Tesco Doncaster
L 8431	PL73 HKB	SCA	Stobart	Tesco Doncaster
L 8432	PL73 HHC	SCA	Stobart	Tesco Doncaster
L 8433	PL73 HHD	SCA	Stobart	Tesco Doncaster
L 8434	PL73 HKA	SCA	Stobart	Tesco Doncaster
L 8435	PL73 HHV	SCA	Stobart	Tesco Doncaster
L 8436	PL73 HHW	SCA	Stobart	Tesco Doncaster
L 8437	PL73 HHY	SCA	Stobart	Tesco Goole

L 8438	PL73 HKC	SCA	Stobart		Tesco Doncaster
L 8439	PL73 YBM	SCA	Stobart		Tesco Doncaster
L 8440	PL73 HJC	SCA	Stobart		Tesco Doncaster
L 8441	PL73 HJA	SCA	Stobart		Tesco Doncaster
L 8442	PL73 HGX	SCA	Stobart		Tesco Doncaster
L 8443	PL73 HJD	SCA	Stobart		Tesco Doncaster
L 8445	PL73 HJA	SCA	Stobart		Tesco Goole
L 8446	PL73 HGZ	SCA	Stobart		Tesco Doncaster
L 8447	PL73 HKD	SCA	Stobart		Tesco Doncaster
L 8448	PL73 HGY	SCA	Stobart		Tesco Goole
M 480	PN20 AYX	SCA	Stobart	Ciara Leigh	Carlisle
M 481	PE69 FSN	SCA	Stobart	Helena Charlotte	Carlisle
M 482	PN20 AYY	SCA	Stobart	Alicia Jayne	Carlisle
M 483	PE69 FSG	SCA	Stobart	Amber Rose	Carlisle
M 484	PK69 KWY	SCA	Stobart	Valerie May	Carlisle
M 485	PK69 KWD	SCA	Stobart	Beverley Jayne	Carlisle
M 486	PE69 FSJ	SCA	Stobart	Liana Rose	Carlisle
M 487	PN20 AYZ	SCA	Stobart	Sheila Mary	Carlisle
M 488	PN20 AZA	SCA	Stobart	Anna Zilpha	Carlisle
M 489	PK69 KWM	SCA	Stobart	Julie Annette	Carlisle
M 490	PK21 OZV	SCA	Stobart	Lyla Molly	Carlisle
M 491	PK21 RBF	SCA	Stobart	Azayila Diamond Cain	Carlisle
M 492	PK21 RBX	SCA	Stobart	Iris Ellise	Carlisle
M 493	PK21 RBV	SCA	Stobart	Josephine	Carlisle
M 494	PK21 RCO	SCA	Stobart	Janice Rosemary	Carlisle
M 495	PK21 RBO	SCA	Stobart	Julie Ann	Carlisle
M 496	PK21 OZW	SCA	Stobart	Afiya Cadence	Carlisle
M 497	PK21 RBZ	SCA	Stobart	Gabrielle Winifred	Carlisle
M 498	PK21 RCF	SCA	Stobart	Wendy Hannah	Carlisle
M 499	PK21 RBU	SCA	Stobart	Sheila Margaret	Carlisle
PTU	839 WX08 UYK	MER	Walkers		Leicester
TV 5	NA23 HXV	MER	Stairs Property		
TV 6	KU23 XYC	MER	Stairs Property		
TV 7	NA23 HYP	MER	Stairs Property		
TV 9	NA23 JFO	MER	Stairs Property		
TV 10	NA23 JFU	MER	Stairs Property		
TV 14	PK23 NTU	MER	Stairs Property		
TV 20	PF23 ADZ	MER	Stairs Property		
TV 21	PF23 AEA	MER	Tech Wash		
TV 22	PF23 AEB	MER	Tech Wash		
TV 23	PF23 AED	MER	Tech Wash		Goresbrook
V 1500	V9 ESL (18)	Volkswagon	Black		
V 1501	GK18 XUF	Volkswagon	White		
V 1667	NU17 OJA	Peugeot	White		
V 1669	NU17 OHT	Peugeot	White		
V 1676	FL17 VZA	Ford	White		
V 1685	WP17 BPE	Ford	White		
V 1696	WP17 BOF	Ford	White		
V 1712	MT17 WI ID	Peugeot	White		
V 1714	NV17 MSO	Peugeot	White		
V 1766	NV67 DZP	Peugeot	White		
V 1769	WR67 YCA	Ford	White		
V 1809	MK19 YRG	Peugeot	White		
V 1827	WV17 XJL	Fiat	White		
V 1871	CP18 BVN	Ford	White		
V 1881	MM17 MVU	Peugeot	Silver		
V 1884	WM68 EPY	Fiat	White		
V 1887	GD67 XZA	Volkswagon	Silver		
V 1889	BP68 UAX	Ford	White		
V 1890	WM68 EVJ	Fiat	White		

Culina Group (cont)

V 1895	WM68 ETE	Fiat	White
V 1896	WM68 ERV	Fiat	White
V 1897	WM68 ETR	Fiat	White
V 1898	WM68 EWF	Fiat	White
V 1904	GL67 ZZH	Volkswagon	White
V 1905	CT68 KLC	Ford	White
V 1906	CT68 KKP	Ford	White
V 1907	CT68 VSC	Ford	White
V 1908	CT68 VSD	Ford	White
V 1910	WM68 WAU	Fiat	White
V 1911	CV68 ANR	Ford	White
V 1913	T20 ESL (17)	Ford	Blue
V 1914	EU19 NBY	Ford	White
V 1915	EU19 MYW	Ford	White
V 1920	G8 ESL (68)	Volkswagon	Grey
V 1922	BJ19 LXX	Ford	White
V 1924	MF19 JDK	Peugeot	White
V 1925	CP19 UBK	Ford	White
V 1928	EF19 HCD	Ford	White
V 1929	EF19 HCE	Ford	White
V 1930	EF19 HCG	Ford	White
V 1931	X7 ESL (19)	Ford	White
V 1932	C2 ESL (19)	Ford	Grey
V 1933	BW19 XGA	Ford	White
V 1934	CT19 JLU	Ford	White
V 1940	EU19 NGE	Ford	White
V 1941	N13 ESL (19)	Ford	White
V 1942	CP19 PSX	Ford	White
V 1943	MC19 YCM	Peugeot	White
V 1948	CA19 TVF	Ford	White
V 1955	GH19 LLF	Volkswagon	White
V 1958	X4 ESL (18)	Volkswagon	Blue
V 1959	X5 ESL (68)	Volkswagon	White
V 1965	T22 ESL (18)	Volkswagon	Black
V 1971	NH19 NGF	MER	White
V 1973	NH19 NHJ	MER	White
V 1974	DL19 PJV	Vauxhall	Grey
V 1976	KX19 PWE	MER	White
V 1977	KM19 PCO	MER	White
V 1980	CV69 UUE	Ford	Silver
V 1984	CV69 UUP	Ford	Silver
V 1985	CV69 UUO	Ford	Silver
V 1986	CV69 VCN	Ford	Silver
V 1989	CV69 WEP	Ford	Silver
V 1991	MB19 OVJ	Peugeot	White
V 1992	DT19 OVD	Vauxhall	White
V 1998	GL69 NWY	Volkswagon	Silver
V 1999	GF69 UEY	Volkswagon	White
V 2000	CV69 WKP	Ford	Silver
V 2002	KJ19 RVM	MER	White
V 2003	S55 ESL (69)	Volkswagon	Black
V 2005	GL69 XGS	Volkswagon	Silver
V 2012	HW69 OEL	Ford	Silver
V 2018	MA69 ZWC	Peugeot	White
V 2023	DN69 LFH	Vauxhall	Black
V 2027	HW20 SUU	Ford	White
V 2046	GL12 CEO	MER	Steady Eddie
V 2048	YT70 VFZ	Ford	White
V 2049	DY69 ZBW	Vauxhall	White
V 2050	DS20 VLD	Vauxhall	Grey

Culina Group (cont)

BN21GCF   ~~MER~~ MMiD

V 2051	DS20 WDK	Vauxhall	White
V 2053	BK68 ZFR	Ford	White
V 2054	DP18 PXH	Nissan	White
V 2055	DS20 VRC	Vauxhall	White
V 2056	KJ68 HNC	MER	White
V 2057	MD18 PJJ	Peugeot	White
V 2058	DS20 VUC	Vauxhall	Grey
V 2059	MC19 YBU	Peugeot	Grey
V 2060	DY70 WYK	Vauxhall	White
V 2066	WN70 DME	Ford	Silver
V 2068	WM19 CWR	Fiat	White
V 2069	HW70 URO	Ford	White
V 2070	HW70 UOX	Ford	White
V 2071	HW70 UPV	Ford	White
V 2073	WR70 OVH	Mitsubishi	Orange
V 2079	MA69 ZVO	Peugeot	White
V 2080	HT70 LDU	Ford	Silver
V 2082	FH70 LHG	Toyota	Grey
V 2083	HW70 YMR	Ford	White
V 2085	DT70 HZB	Vauxhall	White
V 2093	BX18 TZF	Ford	Silver
V 2110	MF71 PDY	Peugeot	White
V 2111	MF71 PFD	Peugeot	White
V 2157	FL71 MLK	Toyota	White
V 2190	FL22 XUM	Toyota	White
V 2199	LC72 BVX	Ford	White
V 2221	DY72 KFL	Ford	White
V	YF13 FRP	Ford	Stobart
V	WR71 FMC	Fiat	White
V	DY70 FUU	Ford	Logistics People
V	EW19 LPE	Ford	Black
V	BJ20 NWZ	Ford	Black
V	KM20 EOB	Ford	Logistics People
V	KR20 BBJ	Ford	Logistics People
V	KR20 TWD	Ford	Logistics People
V	KR20 TWS	Ford	Logistics People
V	KR20 PFO	Ford	Logistics People
V	KS20 ANF	Ford	Logistics People
V	KS20 ETF	Ford	Logistics People
V	KS20 HTN	Ford	Logistics People
V	VN20 YHC	Volkswagon	Grey
V	VN20 YHP	Volkswagon	Black
V	BN21 FCD	MER	MMiD
V	BN21 FMZ	MER	MMiD
V	CX21 YYM	Ford	Logistics People
V	FL20 NVC	Ford	Stairs Property
V	FL20 NVE	Ford	Stairs Property
V	STA 12S (70)	Ford	Stairs Property
V	AK70 HND	Ford	Stairs Property
V	EJ70 KKB	Ford	Stairs Property
V	STA 15S (70)	Ford	Stairs Property
V	PJ70 EHB	Ford	Stairs Property
V	PJ70 FDV	Ford	Stairs Property
V	CY70 AAO	Ford	Stairs Property
V	FG71 UMJ	Ford	Stairs Property
V	FL71 VFS	Ford	Stairs Property
V	OY21 WDP	Ford	Fowler Welch
V	BJ22 LTK	Ford	Fowler Welch
V	FL22 WCN	Toyota	Silver
V	FL22 WDR	Toyota	Silver

V	FL22 WFG	Toyota	Grey	
V	NA22 RZJ	Ford	Stairs Property	
V	NA22 RZL	Ford	Stairs Property	
V	SD22 OJW	Ford	Stairs Property	
V	SD22 ONH	Ford	Stairs Property	
V	PO22 MVN	Ford	Logistics People	
V	PO22 MVU	Ford	Logistics People	
V	PO22 MVW	Ford	Logistics People	
V	PO22 MWG	Ford	Logistics People	
V	LD23 OPM	Ford	Culina	
V	LD23 OMR	Ford	Culina	
V	LD23 OPR	Ford	Culina	
V	NA23 HVH	MER	Stairs Property	
V	NA23 HWN	MER	Stairs Property	
V	PO73 MGJ	Ford	Logistics People	
V	PO73 MHE	Ford	Logistics People	
V	PO73 MHL	Ford	Logistics People	
S 064	YK08 DHF	Terberg	Unknown	Burton Latimer
S 088	YK60 AFA	Terberg	Unknown	Wakefield
S 096	YJ62 ODH	Terberg	Unknown	Burton Latimer
S 98	YJ09 VPW	Terberg	Yellow	Sittingbourne
S 100	YJ14 KFO	Terberg	Unknown	Bridgwater
S 104	YA15 FYJ	Terberg	Unknown	Stockton
S 105	YA15 GJU	Terberg	Unknown	Sittingbourne
S 110	YJ65 UXR	Terberg	Unknown	Burton Latimer
S 111	YJ66 MWL	Terberg	Unknown	Sittingbourne
S 112	YE66 WXM	Terberg	Unknown	Sittingbourne
S 113	YE66 WXO	Terberg	Unknown	Sittingbourne
S 114	YE66 WXP	Terberg	Unknown	Burton Latimer
S 115	YH66 FZG	Terberg	Unknown	Burton Latimer
S 121	YC68 EAX	Terberg	Unknown	Burton Latimer
S 122	YC68 DYX	Terberg	Unknown	Burton Latimer
S 128	YF68 FRK	Terberg	Unknown	Bridgwater
S 129	YK71 ZBC	Terberg	Unknown	Stockton
S 130	YK71 ZBD	Terberg	Unknown	Stockton
S 131	YK71 ZBN	Terberg	Unknown	Burton Latimer
S 133	YK71 ZBW	Terberg	Unknown	Bridgwater
S 134	YB71 OJT	Terberg	Unknown	Wakefield
S 136	YB71 OJS	Terberg	Unknown	Wakefield
S	YG65 UYP	Terberg	Unknown	Stockton
S	YJ09 VPZ	Terberg	Unknown	Stockton
DS	1701	YE67 URU	Terberg	Yellow (Walkers)	Leicester
DS	1702	YE67 URW	Terberg	Yellow (Walkers)	Leicester
DS	1703	YE67 URS	Terberg	Yellow (Walkers)	Leicester
DS	1704	YE67 YZZ	Terberg	Yellow (Walkers)	Leicester
DS	1705	YE67 YZV	Terberg	Yellow (Walkers)	Leicester
DS	1706	YE67 YZY	Terberg	Yellow	Skelmersdale
DS	1707	YF67 OSP	Terberg	Yellow (Walkers)	Leicester
DS	1708	No Reg	Terberg	Yellow	Coventry
DS	1709	No Reg	Terberg	Yellow	Coventry
DS	1710	No Reg	Terberg	Yellow	Lincoln
DS	1711	No Reg	Terberg	Yellow	Skelmersdale
DS	1712	No Reg	Terberg	Yellow	Coupar Fife
DS	9122	No Reg	Terberg	Yellow	Peterlee
DS	9124	YK59 BGE	Terberg	Yellow (Walkers)	Leicester
X 0021	W351 VNY	SCA	Stobart White	
X 0022	W373 VNY	SCA	Stobart White	Lillyhall
X 0023	W837 ANH	SCA	Stobart White	Appleton
X 0024	W839 ANH	SCA	Stobart White	Goresbrook
X 0069	YK11 CTE	Terberg	Yellow	Crick

Culina Group (cont)

X 0106	YJ61 NZA	Terberg	Battenberg		Widnes
X 0111	YJ61 NZD	Terberg	Tesco Battenberg		Bardon
X 0118	R712 MJU	Daf	James Irlam		Stoke
X 0119	No Reg	Terberg	Yellow		Appleton
X 0146	YJ14 KGA	Terberg	Yellow		Swansea
X 0149	YJ64 PXL	Terberg	Yellow		Hemel Hempstead
X 0150	YJ64 PXM	Terberg	Yellow		Ridgmount
X 0151	YJ64 PXA	Terberg	Yellow		Doncaster
X 0159	YJ64 NHO	Terberg	Tesco Battenberg		Teesport
X 0160	YJ64 NHX	Terberg	Tesco Battenberg		Teesport
X 0173	YB65 JFE	Terberg	Tesco Battenberg		Daventry
X 0174	YB65 DUJ	Terberg	Tesco Battenberg		Daventry
X 0176	YB65 KJO	Terberg	Tesco Battenberg		Widnes
X 0177	YJ64 NHP	Terberg	Tesco Battenberg		Daventry
X 0178	YB65 AZA	Terberg	Tesco Battenberg		Daventry
X 0187	YJ60 NPA	Terberg	Battenberg		Coventry
X 0188	YJ60 NOU	Terberg	Yellow		Coventry
X 0192	YJ61 NSE	Terberg	Yellow		Daventry
X 0200	YH63 MYU	Terberg	Yellow		Altrincham
X 0201	YH63 MYT	Terberg	Yellow		Altrincham
X 0203	YC68 EAJ	Terberg	Tesco Battenberg		Daventry
X 0214	YF66 UJG	Terberg	Tesco Battenberg		Daventry
X 0216	YF66 UJC	Terberg	Yellow		Goresbrook
X 0220	YL61 NXR	Terberg	Yellow		
X 0223	YE17 EKF	Terberg	Tesco (Battenberg)		Daventry
X 0224	YC17 UOY	Terberg	Tesco (Battenberg)		Daventry
X 0226	YC17 UOX	Terberg	Tesco (Battenberg)		Widnes
X 0228	YK61 BNJ	Terberg	Yellow		Corby
X 0229	YL61 NTD	Terberg	Yellow		Goresbrook
X 0234	YJ57 UEE	Terberg	Yellow		Tilbury
X 0243	YJ61 NPA	Terberg	Battenberg		Dunstable
X 0245	YK12 CNE	Terberg	White/Blue		Bardon
X 0250	YA67 LVB	Terberg	Tesco Battenberg		Daventry
X 0251	YA67 LVZ	Terberg	Tesco Battenberg		Daventry
X 0257	WA57 TZG	Terberg	Yellow		Bardon
X 0259	YJ62 ANX	Terberg	Battenberg		Workington
X 0260	YJ62 AFX	Terberg	Battenberg		Daventry
X 0262	YK11 CPY	Terberg	Yellow		Sherburn
X 0264	YJ61 NXZ	Terberg	Yellow		Rugby
X 0265	No Reg	Terberg	Yellow		Thirsk
X 0269	YN16 GRX	Terberg	Yellow		Bolton
X 0272	YF66 VOA	Terberg	Tesco Battenberg		Teesport
X 0275	YH65 DDJ	Terberg	Yellow		Bolton
X 0282	YF68 KDX	Terberg	Yellow		Tilbury
X 0287	YF68 FHJ	Terberg	Tesco Battenberg		Widnes
X 0288	YC68 EAE	Terberg	Yellow		Warrington
X 0290	YF66 JZV	Terberg	Unknown		Daventry
X 0292	No Reg	Terberg	Yellow		Stoke
X 0293	YK12 CNC	Terberg	White/Blue		Daventry
X 0294	MF63 BXJ	Terberg	Yellow Battenberg		Corby
X 0296	YC68 DYS	Terberg	Tesco Battenberg		Daventry
X 0297	YC13 MYX	Terberg	Yellow		Silvertown
X 0299	YF69 EEM	Terberg	Yellow		Northampton
X 0302	YJ14 SBX	Terberg	White		Rugeley
X 0307	YH63 JZC	Terberg	White		Crick
X 0308	YF69 EEX	Terberg	Tesco		Widnes
X 0309	YK69 OZU	Terberg	Tesco		Daventry
X 0310	YF69 EFE	Terberg	Tesco		Teesport
X 0311	YF69 KPP	Terberg	Tesco		Daventry
X 0313	YK69 PAO	Terberg	Yellow		Gourock

YJ 23 PEF   YK70 XCU   YC73 NHY   YE73 AVS   YC73 MSE
YB 68 DKe   YL72 NBU   YH71 XZH   YC73 NKY6   YC73 NJJ
                                     YC73 NJF9   YC73 NJ411

Culina Group (cont)

X 0314	YK69 PCX	Terberg	Yellow		Dunfermline
X 0315	YK61 CTF	Terberg	Yellow		Goresbrook
X 0317	MF63 BXN	Terberg	Yellow Battenberg		Crick
X 0319	YB69 MGE	Terberg	Yellow Battenberg		Widnes
X 0321	YH63 MYP	Terberg	Yellow		Bardon
X 0322	YC68 EBA	Terberg	Tesco Battenberg		Teesport
X 0323	YF69 EEY	Terberg	Tesco Battenberg		Teesport
X 0324	YB66 DJO	Terberg	Tesco Battenberg		Doncaster
X 0325	YB66 DJK	Terberg	Tesco Battenberg		Doncaster
X 0326	YK18 JJT	Terberg	Yellow		Peterborough
X 0327	YJ14 RPO	Terberg	Unknown		Trafford Park
X 0330	YJ64 NHD	Terberg	Unknown		Tilbury
X 0331	YJ13 SKR	Terberg	Unkown		Dunstable
X 0332	YJ61 NZP	Terberg	Unknown		Milton Keynes
X 0333	YJ64 NGG	Terberg	Unknown		Tilbury
X 0334	No Reg	Terberg	Unknown		Braunstone
X 0335	YK61 CVE	Terberg	White		Bardon
X 0336	YA15 FYL	Terberg	Unknown		Dunfermline
X 0338	YK07 HRH	Terberg	Unknown		Altrincham
X 0339	YJ64 AMK	Terberg	Unknown		Daventry
X 0340	YK11 BJJ	Terberg	Unknown		Rugeley
X 0341	No Reg	Terberg	Unknown		Ridgmount
X 0342	No Reg	Terberg	Unknown		Sittingbourne
X 0346	YF70 WXR	Terberg	Unknown		Widnes
X 0350	YF70 WXU	Terberg	Unknown		Daventry
X 0351	YF70 WXZ	Terberg	Unknown		Daventry
X 0354	No Reg	Terberg	Yellow		Bardon
X 0355	YJ14 KGV	Terberg	Yellow		Trafford Park
X 0356	No Reg	Terberg	Yellow		Newport
X	2 APT 449	Terberg	White	William	Genk
X	2 BTE 919	Terberg	White	Francis	Genk
X	2 CKD 184	Terberg	White	Edward	Genk
X	No Reg	Terberg	Yellow		Raunds
X	No Reg	Terberg	Black		Raunds
X	YF70 WAY	Terberg	Unknown		Daventry
X	YF70 WXL	Terberg	Unknown		Teesport
X	YF70 WXT	Terberg	Unknown		Daventry
X	YJ64 NHE	Terberg	Unknown		Doncaster
X	YK12 BXH	Terberg	Yellow		Birchwood
X	YK61 BNL	Terberg	Yellow		Rugby
X	YJ14 KGO	Terberg	Yellow		Droitwich
X	YA67 OSM	Terberg	Yellow		Rugby
X	YA69 ONK	Terberg	White		Goresbrook
X	YF69 EFA	Terberg	White		Magna Park
X	YC71 RMX	Terberg	White / Yellow		
X	YC71 RMZ	Terberg	White / Yellow		
X	YK71 XYO	Terberg	White / Yellow		Daventry
X	YK71 XYP	Terberg	White / Yellow		
X	YK71 XYS	Terberg	White / Yellow		Widnes
X	YK70 XCC	Terberg	Great Bear		Bourneville
X	YK70 XDA	Terberg	Culina		
X	YA22 MYJ	Terberg	White / Yellow		Warrens, Rugby
X	YE72 UBL	Terberg	Fowler Welch		Evesham
X	YE72 UBM	Terberg	Fowler Welch		Evesham
X	YE72 TZX	Terberg	White / Yellow		Warrens, Rugby
	NXZ 4991 (69)	Volvo	Morgan McLernon		
	NXZ 4994 (69)	Volvo	Morgan McLernon		
	NXZ 8777 (69)	Volvo	Morgan McLernon		
	NXZ 8778 (69)	Volvo	Morgan McLernon		
	NXZ 8779 (69)	Volvo	Morgan McLernon		

Culina Group (cont)

Reg	Make	Operator		Reg	Make	Livery
NXZ 8780 (69)	Volvo	Morgan McLernon		8 AU 9919	MER	Stardes White
NXZ 8783 (69)	Volvo	Morgan McLernon		8 AZ 8244	MER	Stardes White
NXZ 8784 (69)	Volvo	Morgan McLernon		9 AL 6985	MER	Stardes White
NXZ 8786 (69)	Volvo	Morgan McLernon		9 AM 4390	MER	Stardes White
OXZ 1205 (20)	Volvo	Morgan McLernon		9 AN 8552	MER	Stardes White
OXZ 2905 (20)	SCA	Scania V8 Red		9 AP 1312	MER	Stardes White
OXZ 2907 (20)	SCA	Scania V8 Red		WX06 OFO	Man	Culina
OXZ 2908 (20)	SCA	Scania V8 Red		YK57 TCA	Terberg	Yellow
OXZ 2909 (20)	SCA	Scania V8 Red		E12 BTL (12)	SCA	Ball Trucking
OXZ 4461 (20)	Volvo	Morgan McLernon		KY63 ZRP	SCA	Ball Trucking
OXZ 4462 (20)	Volvo	Morgan McLernon		BK65 OLX	SCA	Ball Trucking
OXZ 4463 (20)	Volvo	Morgan McLernon		BK65 OMA	SCA	Ball Trucking
OXZ 4464 (20)	Volvo	Morgan McLernon		BK65 OMF	SCA	Ball Trucking
OXZ 4465 (20)	Volvo	Morgan McLernon		EK65 GUD	Daf	Culina
OXZ 4467 (20)	Volvo	Morgan McLernon		Y111 BTL (16)	SCA	Ball Trucking
OXZ 4468 (20)	Volvo	Morgan McLernon		DX16 ATZ	Daf	Culina
OXZ 4469 (20)	Volvo	Morgan McLernon		PE16 HVC	Volvo	Great Bear (White)
OXZ 6115 (20)	Volvo	Morgan McLernon		PE16 HVD	Volvo	White
OXZ 6116 (20)	Volvo	Morgan McLernon		PE16 HVF	Volvo	White
OXZ 6394 (70)	Volvo	Morgan McLernon		PE16 HVH	Volvo	White
OXZ 6396 (70)	Volvo	Morgan McLernon		PE16 HVJ	Volvo	Great Bear (White)
OXZ 6397 (70)	Volvo	Morgan McLernon		PE16 HVM	Volvo	Great Bear (White)
OXZ 6398 (70)	Volvo	Morgan McLernon		PE16 HVN	Volvo	Great Bear (White)
OXZ 6915 (70)	Volvo	Morgan McLernon		PE16 HVO	Volvo	Great Bear (White)
OXZ 6917 (70)	Volvo	Morgan McLernon		PE16 HVP	Volvo	Great Bear (White)
OXZ 6918 (70)	Volvo	Morgan McLernon		PE16 HVR	Volvo	Great Bear (White)
OXZ 6920 (70)	Volvo	Morgan McLernon		PE16 HVS	Volvo	Great Bear (White)
OXZ 6921 (70)	Volvo	Morgan McLernon		PE16 HVT	Volvo	Great Bear (White)
OXZ 6923 (70)	Volvo	Morgan McLernon		PE16 HVU	Volvo	Great Bear (White)
OXZ 8012 (70)	Volvo	Morgan McLernon		PE16 HVV	Volvo	Great Bear (White)
OXZ 8013 (70)	Volvo	Morgan McLernon		PE16 HVW	Volvo	Great Bear (White)
OXZ 8014 (70)	Volvo	Morgan McLernon		PE16 HVX	Volvo	Great Bear (White)
OXZ 8016 (70)	Volvo	Morgan McLernon		PE16 HVY	Volvo	Great Bear (White)
OXZ 8017 (70)	Volvo	Morgan McLernon		KX66 YUJ	MER	White
OXZ 8018 (70)	Volvo	Morgan McLernon		KX66 YUU	MER	White
OXZ 8020 (70)	Volvo	Morgan McLernon		KX66 YVP	MER	White
OXZ 8021 (70)	Volvo	Morgan McLernon		KX66 YWR	MER	White
OXZ 8022 (70)	Volvo	Morgan McLernon		MX66 ENF	Daf	White
OXZ 8503 (70)	Volvo	Morgan McLernon		MX66 EOM	Daf	White
OXZ 8504 (70)	Volvo	Morgan McLernon		MX66 EVG	Daf	White
OXZ 8506 (70)	Volvo	Morgan McLernon		MX66 EWC	Daf	White
OXZ 8728 (70)	Volvo	Morgan McLernon		MX66 FEU	Daf	White
OXZ 8912 (21)	Volvo	Morgan McLernon		SF17 KAX	Volvo	Culina - Mmi
K50 STA (19)	Daf	Stardes		FP67 HCV	Volkswagon	Stairs Property
L5 STA (18)	Daf	Stardes		FX67 UHA	REN	Robsons of Spalding
L6 STA (68)	Daf	Stardes		FX67 UHC	REN	Robsons of Spalding
R10 STA (72)	Daf	Stardes		FX67 UHE	REN	Robsons of Spalding
R60 STA (23)	Daf	Williams		LX67 EWN	Terberg	Yellow
S80 STA (18)	Daf	Stardes		GD18 KMO	Volvo	White
W70 STA (19)	Daf	Stardes		KN18 ULU	Daf	White
Y5 STA (19)	Daf	Stardes		YA18 YZB	Terberg	White
Y7 STA (19)	Daf	Stardes		YB18 LVY	Volvo	Great Bear
YO15 ZRK	Daf	Blue		YB18 LVZ	Volvo	Great Bear
MX20 MWJ	Daf	Stardes		YB18 LWA	Volvo	Great Bear
YS20 FNF	Daf	Stardes		YB18 LWC	Volvo	Great Bear
YS20 FPG	Daf	Stardes		YB18 LWD	Volvo	Great Bear

4M 18 x FT

Reg	Make	Operator		Reg	Make	Operator
YB18 LWE	Volvo	Great Bear		PJ19 FME	SCA	Fowler Welch
YB18 LWF	Volvo	Great Bear		PJ19 FMG	SCA	White
YB18 LXA	Volvo	Great Bear		PJ19 FMO	SCA	White
YD18 CNA	Terberg	White		PJ19 LDN	SCA	White
YD18 TXC	SCA	Ball Trucking		PJ19 LDV	SCA	Fowler Welch
YH18 SNB	Terberg	White		PJ19 LDZ	SCA	White
YN18 XYE	SCA	Ball Trucking		PJ19 LFF	SCA	White
DG68 AVD	MER	Culina		PJ19 LFG	SCA	White
DG68 AWJ	MER	Culina		PJ19 LFH	SCA	White
DG68 BMO	MER	Great Bear		PJ19 LFK	SCA	White
DG68 BMU	MER	Great Bear		PJ19 LFL	SCA	White
DG68 BMV	MER	Great Bear		PJ19 LFM	SCA	White
DG68 BMY	MER	Great Bear		PJ19 LFT	SCA	White
DK68 WRN	Man	Fowler Welch		PJ19 LFU	SCA	White
DK68 WRP	Man	Fowler Welch		PN19 FHG	SCA	White
DK68 WRX	Man	Fowler Welch		PN19 FHH	SCA	White
DK68 WRZ	Man	Fowler Welch		PN19 FHJ	SCA	White
DK68 WSD	Man	Fowler Welch		PN19 FHU	SCA	White
DK68 WSE	Man	Fowler Welch		PN19 FJZ	SCA	White
DK68 WSF	Man	Fowler Welch		PN19 FKG	SCA	Fowler Welch
DK68 WSJ	Man	Fowler Welch		PN19 FKH	SCA	Fowler Welch
DK68 WSL	Man	Fowler Welch		SK19 BKX	SCA	Robert Burns
DK68 WSO	Man	Fowler Welch		BP69 CNC	Ford	White
DK68 WSU	Man	Fowler Welch		DA69 BVC	MER	Great Bear
DK68 WSZ	Man	Fowler Welch		DA69 BVG	MER	Great Bear
DK68 WTE	Man	Fowler Welch		DA69 BVH	MER	Great Bear
DK68 WTF	Man	Fowler Welch		DA69 BVJ	MER	Great Bear
GD68 WPZ	Volvo	White		DA69 BVL	MER	Great Bear
MM68 XPW	SCA	Culina - CML		DA69 CKC	MER	Culina - MMI
MX68 BNN	Daf	White		DA69 CZK	MER	Culina - MMI
PO68 YBS	SCA	Fowler Welch		DA69 CZN	MER	Culina - MMI
PO68 YCA	SCA	Fowler Welch		DA69 CZO	MER	Culina - MMI
PO68 YCW	SCA	White		DA69 CZP	MER	Culina - MMI
PO68 YRT	SCA	White		DA69 ECT	MER	Culina - MMI
DK19 WLA	MIT	Great Bear		DA69 ECV	MER	Culina - MMI
DK19 WLB	MIT	Great Bear		DA69 ECW	MER	Culina - MMI
DK19 WLC	MIT	Great Bear		DA69 ECX	MER	Culina - MMI
DX19 YCA	Volvo	Culina		DA69 HYJ	MER	Culina - MMI
GF19 WNH	Volvo	White		DA69 HYS	MER	Culina - MMI
GK19 BBV	Volvo	Silver		DA69 HYY	MER	Culina - MMI
MD19 OYS	SCA	Culina - CML		DA69 JWJ	MER	Culina - MMI
ML19 FLR	SCA	Morgan McLernon		DA69 JWK	MER	Culina - MMI
ML19 FMP	SCA	Morgan McLernon		DA69 JWL	MER	Culina - MMI
ML19 FMZ	SCA	Morgan McLernon		DA69 JWN	MER	Culina - MMI
PF19 TKC	Daf	Great Bear		DA69 JWU	MER	Culina - MMI
PF19 TKT	Daf	Great Bear		DA69 JWW	MER	Culina - MMI
PF19 TKY	Daf	Great Bear		DA69 JWX	MER	Culina - MMI
PJ19 FHP	SCA	Fowler Welch		DA69 JWY	MER	Culina - MMI
PJ19 FKT	SCA	White		DA69 JXC	MER	Culina - MMI
PJ19 FKU	SCA	Fowler Welch		DA69 KBO	MER	Culina - MMI
PJ19 FKV	SCA	Fowler Welch		DA69 KJK	MER	Culina - MMI
PJ19 FLF	SCA	White		DA69 KJU	MER	Culina - MMI
PJ19 FLH	SCA	Fowler Welch		DA69 KJV	MER	Culina - MMI
PJ19 FLK	SCA	White		DA69 KKB	MER	Culina - MMI
PJ19 FLP	SCA	White		DA69 KKD	MER	Culina - MMI
PJ19 FMA	SCA	Fowler Welch		DA69 KKE	MER	Culina - MMI

Reg	Make	Fleet	Reg	Make	Fleet
DA69 NHX	MER	Great Bear	FN69 AKZ	Daf	Fowler Welch
DA69 NHY	MER	Great Bear	FN69 ALU	Daf	Fowler Welch
DA69 NKE	MER	Great Bear	FX69 RZK	SCA	Fowler Welch
DA69 NKF	MER	Great Bear	FX69 RZL	SCA	Fowler Welch
DA69 NKG	MER	Great Bear	FX69 RZM	SCA	Fowler Welch
DA69 NKH	MER	Great Bear	FX69 RZN	SCA	Fowler Welch
DA69 NKJ	MER	Great Bear	FX69 RZO	SCA	Fowler Welch
DA69 NKK	MER	Great Bear	FX69 RZP	SCA	Fowler Welch
DA69 NKM	MER	Great Bear	GD69 PZP	Volvo	AIM
DA69 NKP	MER	Great Bear	GD69 PZR	Volvo	AIM
DA69 OZC	MER	Great Bear	GN69 WYY	MER	Fowler Welch
DA69 OZD	MER	Great Bear	GN69 WYZ	MER	Fowler Welch
DE69 TKA	MER	Culina - MMI	GN69 WZA	MER	Fowler Welch
DE69 TKC	MER	Culina - MMI	GN69 WZB	MER	Fowler Welch
DE69 TKD	MER	Culina - MMI	GN69 WZC	MER	Fowler Welch
DE69 TKK	MER	Culina - MMI	GN69 WZD	MER	Fowler Welch
DE69 TKN	MER	Culina - MMI	GN69 WZE	MER	Fowler Welch
DE69 TYU	MER	Culina - MMI	GN69 WZF	MER	Fowler Welch
DE69 UNF	MER	Culina - MMI	GN69 WZG	MER	Fowler Welch
DE69 XVG	MER	Culina - MMI	GN69 WZH	MER	Fowler Welch
DE69 XWS	MER	Culina - MMI	GN69 WZJ	MER	Fowler Welch
DE69 XXN	MER	Culina - MMI	GN69 WZK	MER	Fowler Welch
DE69 XZF	MER	Culina - MMI	GN69 WZL	MER	Fowler Welch
DE69 YAH	MER	Culina - MMI	GN69 XNE	Volvo	AIM
DE69 YAK	MER	Culina - MMI	GN69 XNF	Volvo	AIM
DE69 YBJ	MER	Culina - MMI	GN69 XOK	Volvo	AIM
DE69 YCB	MER	Culina - MMI	GN69 XOL	Volvo	AIM
DE69 YCP	MER	Culina - MMI	MV69 KNX	SCA	Morgan McLernon
DE69 YCV	MER	Culina - MMI	MV69 KOD	SCA	Morgan McLernon
DE69 YEK	MER	Culina - MMI	MV69 KOJ	SCA	Morgan McLernon
DE69 YGA	MER	Culina - MMI	MV69 KPE	SCA	Morgan McLernon
DE69 YRF	MER	Culina - MMI	MV69 KPG	SCA	Morgan McLernon
DX69 TTF	Volvo	Culina	MV69 KPJ	SCA	Culina - CML
FN69 ABF	Daf	Fowler Welch	MV69 KPL	SCA	Culina - CML
FN69 ABO	Daf	Fowler Welch	MV69 KPP	SCA	Culina - CML
FN69 ACZ	Daf	Fowler Welch	MV69 KPT	SCA	Culina - CML
FN69 ADO	Daf	Fowler Welch	DK20 YGO	MER	Great Bear
FN69 AEB	Daf	Fowler Welch	DK20 YJN	MER	Fowler Welch
FN69 AEC	Daf	Fowler Welch	DK20 YKJ	MER	Great Bear
FN69 AED	Daf	Fowler Welch	DX20 UTA	Volvo	Culina
FN69 AEE	Daf	Fowler Welch	DX20 UUN	Volvo	Culina
FN69 AEF	Daf	Fowler Welch	DX20 UUR	Volvo	Culina
FN69 AEK	Daf	Fowler Welch	DX20 VEH	Volvo	Culina
FN69 AET	Daf	Fowler Welch	DX20 VEK	Volvo	Culina
FN69 AFA	Daf	Fowler Welch	DX20 VEO	Volvo	Culina
FN69 AFK	Daf	Fowler Welch	DX20 VEP	Volvo	Culina
FN69 AFY	Daf	Fowler Welch	DX20 VEU	Volvo	Culina
FN69 AGV	Daf	Fowler Welch	DX20 VEV	Volvo	Culina
FN69 AHA	Daf	Fowler Welch	DX20 VEW	Volvo	Culina
FN69 AHD	Daf	Fowler Welch	DX20 VEY	Volvo	Culina
FN69 AHE	Daf	Fowler Welch	FJ20 ZWD	Daf	Fowler Welch
FN69 AHY	Daf	Fowler Welch	MT20 XAS	SCA	Morgan McLernon
FN69 AJY	Daf	Fowler Welch	MT20 XAU	SCA	Morgan McLernon
FN69 AKJ	Daf	Fowler Welch	MT20 XBC	SCA	Morgan McLernon
FN69 AKU	Daf	Fowler Welch	SJ20 HRE	Volvo	Robert Burns
FN69 AKV	Daf	Fowler Welch	YK20 PKE	Volvo	Great Bear

Culina Group (cont)

Reg	Make	Operator		Reg	Make	Operator
YK20 PUA	Volvo	Great Bear		MX70 MVW	Daf	White
YK20 PUJ	Volvo	Great Bear		MX70 MWE	Daf	White
YK20 PUO	Volvo	Great Bear		PJ70 DFU	Daf	Culina - MMI
YK20 PUV	Volvo	Great Bear		PJ70 DFV	Daf	Culina - MMI
YK20 PUX	Volvo	Great Bear		PJ70 DFX	Daf	Culina - MMI
BU70 XZG	Daf	Culina - MMI		PJ70 DFY	Daf	Culina - MMI
BU70 XZN	Daf	Culina - MMI		PJ70 DFZ	Daf	Culina - MMI
BU70 XZP	Daf	Culina - MMI		PJ70 DGF	Daf	Culina - MMI
BU70 XZR	Daf	Culina - MMI		PJ70 DGO	Daf	Culina - MMI
BU70 XZS	Daf	Culina - MMI		PJ70 DGU	Daf	Culina - MMI
BU70 XZT	Daf	Culina - MMI		PJ70 DGV	Daf	Culina - MMI
BU70 XZV	Daf	Culina - MMI		PJ70 DGX	Daf	Culina - MMI
BU70 XZW	Daf	Culina - MMI		PK70 XPR	Daf	Culina - MMI
BU70 XZX	Daf	Culina - MMI		PK70 XPT	Daf	Culina - MMI
BU70 XZY	Daf	Culina - MMI		PK70 XPU	Daf	Culina - MMI
BU70 XZZ	Daf	Culina - MMI		PK70 XPV	Daf	Culina - MMI
DA70 ARX	MER	Culina - MMI		PK70 XPW	Daf	Culina - MMI
DA70 CDO	MER	Culina - MMI		PK70 XPX	Daf	Culina - MMI
DA70 EXB	MER	Culina - MMI		PK70 XPY	Daf	Culina - MMI
DA70 EXG	MER	Culina - MMI		PK70 XPZ	Daf	Culina - MMI
DA70 EXM	MER	Culina - MMI		PN70 CSF	Daf	Culina - MMI
DA70 EXV	MER	Culina - MMI		PN70 CSO	Daf	Culina - MMI
DA70 EXW	MER	Culina - MMI		PN70 CSU	Daf	Culina - MMI
DE70 OCG	MER	Culina - MMI		PO70 ZKH	SCA	White
DE70 OCH	MER	Culina - MMI		YK70 UUB	Volvo	Great Bear
DE70 OCJ	MER	Culina - MMI		YK70 UUC	Volvo	Great Bear
DE70 OCK	MER	Culina - MMI		YK70 UUD	Volvo	Great Bear
DE70 OCL	MER	Culina - MMI		YK70 UUE	Volvo	Great Bear
DE70 OCM	MER	Culina - MMI		YK70 VDC	Volvo	Great Bear
DE70 OCN	MER	Culina - MMI		YK70 VDF	Volvo	Great Bear
DE70 OCO	MER	Culina - MMI		YK70 VDJ	Volvo	Great Bear
DE70 OCR	MER	Culina - MMI		YK70 VDL	Volvo	Great Bear
DE70 OCS	MER	Culina - MMI		YK70 XCH	Terberg	White
DE70 OCU	MER	Culina - MMI		YK70 XCO	Terberg	White
DE70 OCV	MER	Culina		MK21 BVU	SCA	Culina - MMI
DE70 OCW	MER	Culina - MMI		MK21 BVV	SCA	Culina - MMI
DE70 OCX	MER	Culina - MMI		MK21 BVW	SCA	Culina - MMI
DE70 OCY	MER	Culina - MMI		MK21 BVX	SCA	Culina - MMI
DE70 OCZ	MER	Culina - MMI		MK21 BVZ	SCA	Culina - MMI
DE70 ODJ	MER	Culina - CML		MK21 BWN	SCA	Culina - MMI
DE70 ODP	MER	Culina - CML		MK21 BWO	SCA	Culina - MMI
DE70 ODY	MER	Culina - CML		MK21 BWP	SCA	Culina - MMI
DK70 YSF	MER	Great Bear		MK21 BWU	SCA	Culina - MMI
DX70 UPB	Volvo	Culina		MK21 BWV	SCA	Culina - MMI
MV70 VPK	SCA	Culina - MMI		MK21 BWW	SCA	Culina - MMI
MV70 VPM	SCA	Culina - MMI		MK21 BWX	SCA	Culina - MMI
MV70 VPN	SCA	Culina - MMI		SJ21 KWA	Volvo	Robert Burns
MV70 VRP	SCA	Culina - MMI		SJ21 KWB	Volvo	Robert Burns
MV70 VYH	SCA	Culina - MMI		SJ21 KWC	Volvo	Robert Burns
MV70 VYW	SCA	Culina - MMI		PK71 TWV	Daf	Culina - MMI
MV70 WBJ	SCA	Culina - MMI		PK71 TXH	Daf	Culina - MMI
MV70 WBK	SCA	Culina - MMI		PK71 TXJ	Daf	Culina - MMI
MV70 WBL	SCA	Culina - MMI		PK71 TXL	Daf	Culina - MMI
MX70 KNU	Daf	White		PK71 TXM	Daf	Culina - MMI
MX70 KNV	Daf	White		PN71 FSY	Daf	Culina - MMI
MX70 LPF	REN	White		PN71 FSZ	Daf	Culina - MMI

YP07 BSM ?
YN70 XDB
YK71 X24
YK73 2EX

Reg	Make	Operation	Reg	Make	Operation
PN71 FTA	Daf	Culina - MMI	PN22 DPY	SCA	MMiD Culina
PN71 FTC	Daf	Culina - MMI	PN22 DRV	SCA	MMiD Culina
BV22 LHB	SCA	Ball Trucking	PN22 DRX	SCA	MMiD Culina
WU02 YBW	Daf	Stobart White	PN22 DSO	SCA	MMiD Culina
YK08 DWL	Dulevo	White	PN22 DTK	SCA	MMiD Culina
YC13 LGG	Terberg	Great Bear	PN22 DTU	SCA	MMiD Culina
YC13 LGK	Terberg	Great Bear	PN22 DTV	SCA	MMiD Culina
MT69 EJE	REN	White	PN22 DTX	SCA	MMiD Culina
MT69 EJX	REN	White	PN22 DTY	SCA	MMiD Culina
MT69 ENF	REN	White	PN22 DUH	SCA	MMiD Culina
MX69 BKG	Daf	White	PN22 DUJ	SCA	MMiD Culina
SJ68 ZLY	Citroen	Muller Milk	PN22 DUU	SCA	MMiD Culina
BN21 FGA	MER	Culina Group	PN22 DUY	SCA	MMiD Culina
YK08 CWW	Terberg	Culina Group	PN22 DVA	SCA	MMiD Culina
YB67 XJX	Terberg	White	PN22 DVB	SCA	MMiD Culina
YB68 NFJ	Terberg	White	PN72 DTK	SCA	MMiD Culina
YC71 RNE	Terberg	White/Yellow goole	PJ23 URV	Daf	White - MMiD
YE71 UJL	Terberg	White/Yellow goole	PJ23 URY	Daf	MMiD Culina
YH71 UGB	Terberg	White/Yellow	PF73 JYM	Daf	MMiD Culina
YK22 WZR	Terberg	White/Yellow goole	PF73 JYR	Daf	MMiD Culina
PO70 ZTN	SCA	MMiD Culina	PF73 JYT	Daf	MMiD Culina
PJ71 MZP	SCA	MMiD Culina	PF73 JYU	Daf	MMiD Culina
PJ71 MZT	SCA	MMiD Culina	PF73 JYV	Daf	MMiD Culina
PJ71 MZV	SCA	MMiD Culina	PF73 JYX	Daf	MMiD Culina
PJ71 MZW	SCA	MMiD Culina	PF73 JZG	Daf	MMiD Culina
PK71 VKA	SCA	MMiD Culina	PF73 JZH	Daf	MMiD Culina
PK71 VKE	SCA	MMiD Culina	PF73 JZJ	Daf	MMiD Culina
PK71 VKG	SCA	MMiD Culina	PF73 JZK	Daf	MMiD Culina
PK71 VKM	SCA	MMiD Culina	PF73 JZL	Daf	MMiD Culina
PK71 VKN	SCA	MMiD Culina	PF73 JZM	Daf	MMiD Culina
PK71 VKO	SCA	MMiD Culina	PF73 JZN	Daf	MMiD Culina
PK71 VKP	SCA	MMiD Culina	PF73 JZO	Daf	MMiD Culina
PK71 VKR	SCA	MMiD Culina	PF73 JZP	Daf	MMiD Culina
PK71 VKT	SCA	MMiD Culina	PF73 JZR	Daf	MMiD Culina
PK71 VKW	SCA	MMiD Culina	PF73 JZT	Daf	MMiD Culina
PK71 VKZ	SCA	MMiD Culina	PF73 RXX	Daf	MMiD Culina
PK71 VLB	SCA	MMiD Culina	PF73 RXY	Daf	MMiD Culina
PN71 DZT	SCA	MMiD Culina	PF73 RXZ	Daf	MMiD Culina
PN71 DZU	SCA	MMiD Culina	PF73 RYA	Daf	MMiD Culina
PN71 DZW	SCA	MMiD Culina	PF73 RYB	Daf	MMiD Culina
PN71 DZY	SCA	MMiD Culina	PF73 RYC	Daf	MMiD Culina
PN71 EAM	SCA	MMiD Culina	PF73 RYM	Daf	MMiD Culina
PN71 EBM	SCA	MMiD Culina	PF73 RYO	Daf	MMiD Culina
PN71 ECD	SCA	MMiD Culina	PF73 RYP	Daf	MMiD Culina
PN71 ECJ	SCA	MMiD Culina	PF73 RYR	Daf	MMiD Culina
PN22 DMZ	SCA	MMiD Culina	PJ73 JMV	SCA	MMiD Culina
PN22 DND	SCA	MMiD Culina	PJ73 JMX	SCA	MMiD Culina
PN22 DNE	SCA	MMiD Culina	PJ73 JNF	SCA	MMiD Culina
PN22 DNF	SCA	MMiD Culina	PJ73 JNK	SCA	MMiD Culina
PN22 DNJ	SCA	MMiD Culina	PJ73 JNL	SCA	MMiD Culina
PN22 DNO	SCA	MMiD Culina	PJ73 JWE	SCA	MMiD Culina
PN22 DNU	SCA	MMiD Culina	PJ73 JWF	SCA	MMiD Culina
PN22 DNX	SCA	MMiD Culina	PJ73 YXV	Daf	MMiD Culina
PN22 DNY	SCA	MMiD Culina	PJ73 YXW	Daf	MMiD Culina
PN22 DOA	SCA	MMiD Culina	PJ73 YXY	Daf	MMiD Culina
PN22 DPO	SCA	MMiD Culina	PJ73 YYA	Daf	MMiD Culina

Culina Group (cont)

PJ73 YYZ

Reg	Make	Body		Reg	Make	Body
PJ73 YYB	Daf	MMiD Culina		PJ73 YZN	Daf	MMiD Culina
PJ73 YYC	Daf	MMiD Culina		PK73 XWN	SCA	MMiD Culina
PJ73 YYD	Daf	MMiD Culina		PK73 XWS	SCA	MMiD Culina
PJ73 YYF	Daf	MMiD Culina		PK73 XWT	SCA	MMiD Culina
PJ73 YYG	Daf	MMiD Culina		PL73 EXF	Daf	MMiD Culina
PJ73 YYP	Daf	MMiD Culina		PL73 ZXW	Daf	MMiD Culina
PJ73 YYR	Daf	MMiD Culina		PL73 ZXY	Daf	MMiD Culina
PJ73 YYS	Daf	MMiD Culina		PL73 ZXZ	Daf	MMiD Culina
PJ73 YYT	Daf	MMiD Culina		PL73 ZYA	Daf	MMiD Culina
PJ73 YYV	Daf	MMiD Culina		PL73 ZYB	Daf	MMiD Culina
PJ73 YYW	Daf	MMiD Culina		PL73 ZYC	Daf	MMiD Culina
PJ73 YYX	Daf	MMiD Culina		PN73 ELC	SCA	MMiD Culina
PJ73 YZA	Daf	MMiD Culina		PN73 EYX	SCA	MMiD Culina
PJ73 YZB	Daf	MMiD Culina		PN73 EYY	SCA	MMiD Culina
PJ73 YZK	Daf	MMiD Culina		PN73 EYZ	SCA	MMiD Culina
PJ73 YZL	Daf	MMiD Culina		PN73 EZA	SCA	MMiD Culina
PJ73 YZM	Daf	MMiD Culina		PN73 EZB	SCA	MMiD Culina

Culina Group (European)

Fleet	Reg	Make	Operator	Name	Location
865	BT ZJ 37	MER	Automotive		
1601	1 NBC 769	SCA	Stobart	Nina	
1602	1 NBC 771	SCA	Stobart	Tatiana Maria	
1603	1 NBC 774	SCA	Stobart	Sabrina Patricia	
1604	1 NBC 779	SCA	Stobart	Sabrina Maria	
1605	1 NBC 766	SCA	Stobart	Karin	
1606	1 NBC 783	SCA	Stobart	Helga	
1613	1 RDV 385	Man	White		Genk
1701	1 RPJ 271	SCA	Stobart	Wousje	
1702	1 SCZ 083	SCA	Stobart	Lore	
1703	1 RPJ 035	SCA	Stobart	Kristen	
1704	1 RPJ 208	SCA	Stobart	Lien	
1705	89 BJG 5	Man	White		
1706	87 BJG 8	Man	White		
1707	2 AMF 206	Man	White		Vilvoorde
1801	15 BKL 5	Man	White		
1802	1 XUR 792	Volvo	White	Christel	
1901	1 WHN 243	MER	Stobart	Daisy	
1902	1 WHN 417	MER	Stobart	Lizzy	
1903	1 WHR 731	MER	Stobart	Annelies	
1904	8 AS 0846	MER	Stobart	Fatme	
1905	8 AS 0847	MER	Stobart	Patricia	
1906	8 AS 2975	MER	Stobart	Wendy	
1907	8 AS 0845	MER	Stobart	Nathalie	
1908	8 AS 9998	MER	Stobart	Catty	
1909	5L9 3846	MER	Stobart	Candida-Chrsitina	
1910	5L9 3842	MER	Stobart	Nici-Ela	
1911	5L9 3841	MER	Stobart	Ramona Sofia	
1912	5L9 3845	MER	Stobart	Claudia-Karoline	
1913	5L9 3847	MMER	Stobart	Stephanie	
1914	5L7 8971	MER	Stobart	Anne-Sophie	
1915	5L7 8970	MER	Stobart	Lenka	
1916	5L7 8972	MER	Stobart	Jasmina	
1917	5L7 8974	MER	Stobart	Ivana	
1918	5L7 8975	MER	Stobart	Maria	
1919	5L7 8973	MER	Stobart	Sabrina	
1920	5L7 8976	MER	Stobart	Lieve	
1921	5L7 8977	MER	Stobart	Dominique	
1922	5L7 8978	MER	Stobart	Imane	
1924	5SL 6745	MER	Stobart	Olinka	

Culina Group (European)

1925	5L7 8968	MER	Stobart	Marcela
1926	5L7 8966	MER	Stobart	Isabela
1927	5L7 8967	MER	Stobart	Amalka
1928	1 XAE 226	MER	White	
1929	1 XAT 408	MER	White	
2101	2 ACL 225	MER	Stobart	Valérienne
2102	2 ACL 211	MER	Stobart	Marie-Alix
2103	2 ACL 185	MER	Stobart	Renate
2104	2 ACL 146	MER	Stobart	Anja
2105	2 ACL 174	MER	Stobart	Yasmina
2106	2 ACL 107	MER	Stobart	Romina
2107	2 ACL 128	MER	Stobart	Feyza
2108	2 ACL 160	MER	Stobart	Manou
2109	2 ADA 864	MER	Stobart	Britt Lucia
2110	2 AGU 322	MER	Stobart	Emma
2111	2 ADA 881	MER	Stobart	Noor
2112	2 ADA 902	MER	Stobart	Lena
2113	2 ADA 915	MER	Stobart	Maud
2114	2 ADA 843	MER	Stobart	Fauve
2115	2 AFF 300	MER	Stobart	Thanee
2116	2 AFF 322	MER	Stobart	Josephine
2117	2 AFK 772	MER	Stobart	Melanie
2118	2 AFK 336	MER	Stobart	Nore
2119	2 AFK 367	MER	Stobart	Lorena
2120	2 AFK 784	MER	Stobart	Sienna Maria
2121	2 AFF 391	MER	Stobart	Jacqueline
2122	2 AGU 330	MER	Stobart	Sarah
2123	2 AHQ 887	MER	Stobart	Roin
2124	2 AHQ 902	MER	Stobart	Iman
2125	2 AGU 366	MER	Stobart	Elina
2201	9AD 6757	MER	Stobart	Albina
2202	9AD 6762	MER	Stobart	Ayse
2203	5ST 3233	MER	Stobart	Bohuslava
2204	5ST 3232	MER	Stobart	Stepanka
2205	9AD 6759	MER	Stobart	Renata
2206	9AF 4842	MER	Stobart	Eva
2207	9AD 6758	MER	Stobart	Alena
2208	9AD 6761	MER	Stobart	Tatana
2209	5ST 3231	MER	Stobart	Paulina
2210	9AD 6760	MER	Stobart	Cornelia
2211	5ST 3230	MER	Stobart	Hanka
2212	9AF 5725	MER	Stobart	Martina
2213	9AF 5724	MER	Stobart	Tamara
2214	9AF 4841	MER	Stobart	Ariane
2215	9AF 4843	MER	Stobart	Pascale
2216	9AI 0401	MER	Stobart	Fran
2217	9AI 0393	MER	Stobart	Nasia
2218	9AI 0400	MER	Stobart	Iza
2219	5SX 3778	MER	Stobart	Risa
2220	9AI 0390	MER	Stobart	Morgan
2221	5SX 2294	MER	Stobart	Anna-Maria
2222	5SX 3779	MER	Stobart	Caroline
2223	5SX 2295	MER	Stobart	Yuliya
2224	5SX 2293	MER	Stobart	Gloria
2225	5SX 3780	MER	Stobart	Ecrin
2226	5SX 2296	MER	Stobart	Saschia
2227	2 CBH 419	MER	Stobart	Giulia
2228	2 CBN 640	MER	Stobart	Isabel
2229	2 CCQ 999	MER	Stobart	Daphne
2230	2 CDL 552	MER	Stobart	Anouck
2231	2 CDL 544	MER	Stobart	Katrien
2232	2 CDL 562	MER	Stobart	Celine

Culina Group (European)

2301	2 DQR 778	MER	Stobart	Valerie
2302	2 DQS 173	MER	Stobart	Joelle
2303	2 DSJ 879	MER	Stobart	Faustine
2304	2 DWG 989	MER	Stobart	Leana
2305	2 DSR 649	MER	Stobart	Emmul
2306	2 DSJ 951	MER	Stobart	Marie-Julie
2307	2 DXT 260	MER	Stobart	Zoubida
2308	2 DSJ 900	MER	Stobart	Camile Victoria
2309	2 DXT 272	MER	Stobart	Vanessa
2310	2 DWH 020	MER	Stobart	Megan
		MER	Stobart	Laura
		MER	Stobart	Barbora
		MER	Stobart	Sandra of Sany
2314	6 SH 3498	MER	Stobart	Mikina
		MER	Stobart	Zanna
		MER	Stobart	Konnie
ESE 21179	AC ES 263	MER	Stobart	Iva
ESE 21180	AC ES 516	MER	Stobart	Nataliya
ESE 21181	AC ES 525	MER	Stobart	Patricia
ESE 21182	AC ES 264	MER	Stobart	Adriana
ESE 21183	AC ES 526	MER	Stobart	Vasilena
ESE 21184	AC ES 265	MER	Stobart	Lidia
ESE 21185	AC ES 540	MER	Stobart	Gloria
ESE 21186	AC ES 541	MER	Stobart	Greta
ESE 21187	AC ES 266	MER	Stobart	Siana
ESE 21188	AC ES 269	MER	Stobart	Krisiya
ESE 21189	AC ES 542	MER	Stobart	Tichka
ESE 21190	AC ES 276	MER	Stobart	Vanya
ESE 21191	AC ES 543	MER	Stobart	Silvina
ESE 21192	AC ES 277	MER	Stobart	Krasimira
ESE 21193	AC ES 279	MER	Stobart	Milena
ESE 21194	AC ES 280	MER	Stobart	Nina
ESE 21195	AC ES 213	MER	Stobart	Radostina
ESE 21196	AC ES 552	MER	Stobart	Ryukie
ESE 21197	AC ES 402	MER	Stobart	Firdes
ESE 21198	AC ES 556	MER	Stobart	Ana
ESE 21199	AC ES 565	MER	Stobart	Marinka
ESE 21200	AC ES 558	MER	Stobart	Elena
ESE 21201	AC ES 563	MER	Stobart	Neda
ESE 21202	AC ES 413	MER	Stobart	Rada
ESE 21203	AC ES 403	MER	Stobart	Elitsa
ESE 21204	AC ES 405	MER	Stobart	Gena
ESE 21205	AC ES 419	MER	Stobart	Silviya
ESE 21206	AC ES 420	MER	Stobart	Stanimira
ESE 21207	AC ES 409	MER	Stobart	Dariya
ESE 21208	AC ES 407	MER	Stobart	Aleksandra
ESE 22209	AC ES 177	MER	Stobart	Elza
ESE 22210	AC ES 169	MER	Stobart	Kylie
ESE 22211	AC ES 165	MER	Stobart	Evi
ESE 22212	AC ES 163	MER	Stobart	Noortje
ESE 22213	AC ES 122	MER	Stobart	Emilie
ESE 22214	AC ES 194	MER	Stobart	Myrthe
ESE 22215	AC ES 184	MER	Stobart	Andreia
ESE 22216	AC ES 158	MER	Stobart	Rebecca
ESE 22217	AC ES 138	MER	Stobart	Gerty
ESE 22218	AC ES 156	MER	Stobart	Janne
ESE 22219	AC ES 142	MER	Stobart	Dana
ESE 22220	AC ES 130	MER	Stobart	LIse
ESE 22221	AC ES 154	MER	Stcbart	Ann-Lien
ESE 22222	AC ES 152	MER	Stobart	Lotte
ESE 22223	AC ES 185	MER	Stobart	Erika
ESE 22224	AC ES 179	MER	Stobart	Paulien

ESE 22225	AC ES 143	MER	Stobart	Laura
ESE 22226	AC ES 172	MER	Stobart	Yuliya
ESE 22227	AC ES 145	MER	Stobart	Ann-Sophie
ESE 22228	AC ES 157	MER	Stobart	Carolien
ESE 22229	AC ES 1041	MER	Stobart	
ESE 22230	AC ES 1048	MER	Stobart	
ESE 22231	AC ES 1036	MER	Stobart	
ESE 22232	AC ES 1047	MER	Stobart	
ESE 22233	AC ES 1049	MER	Stobart	
ESE 22234	AC ES 1045	MER	Stobart	
ESE 22235	AC ES 1045	MER	Stobart	
ESE 22236	AC ES 1052	MER	Stobart	
ESE 22237	AC ES 1037	MER	Stobart	
ESE 22238	AC ES 1038	MER	Stobart	
ESE 22239	AC ES 1042	MER	Stobart	
ESE 22240	AC ES 1015	Ford	Stobart	
ESE 22241	AC ES 1017	Ford	Stobart	
ESE 22242	AC ES 1019	Ford	Stobart	
ESE 22243	AC ES 1021	Ford	Stobart	
ESE 22244	AC ES 1022	Ford	Stobart	
ESE 22245	AC ES 1034	Ford	Stobart	
ESE 22246	AC ES 1033	Ford	Stobart	
ESE 22247	AC ES 1002	Ford	Stobart	
ESE 22248	AC ES 1023	Ford	Stobart	
ESE 22249	AC ES 1035	Ford	Stobart	
ESE 22250	AC ES 1044	MER	Stobart	
ESE 23251	AC ES 1053	MER	Stobart	
ESE 23252	AC ES 1054	MER	Stobart	
ESE 23253	AC ES 1068	MER	Stobart	
ESE 23254	AC ES 1057	MER	Stobart	
ESE 23255	AC ES 1060	MER	Stobart	
ESE 23256	AC ES 1063	MER	Stobart	
ESE 23257	AC ES 1061	MER	Stobart	
ESE 23258	AC ES 1059	MER	Stobart	
ESE 23259	AC ES 1062	MER	Stobart	
ESE 23260	AC ES 1067	MER	Stobart	
ESE 23261	AC ES 1056	MER	Stobart	
ESE 23262	AC ES 3262	MER	Stobart	
ESE 23263	AC ES 3263	MER	Stobart	
ESE 23264	AC ES 3264	MER	Stobart	
ESE 23265	AC ES 1265	MER	Stobart	
ESE 23266	AC ES 3266	MER	Stobart	
ESE 23267	AC ES 3267	MER	Stobart	
ESE 23268	AC ES 3268	MER	Stobart	
ESE 23269	AC ES 3269	MER	Stobart	
ESE 23270	AC ES 3270	MER	Stobart	
ESE 23271	AC ES 3271	MER	Stobart	
ESE 23272	AC ES 3272	MER	Stobart	
ESE 23273	AC ES 3273	MER	Stobart	
ESE 23274	AC ES 3274	MER	Stobart	
ESE 23275	AC ES 3275	MER	Stobart	
ESE 23276	AC ES 3276	MER	Stobart	
ESE 23277	AC ES 3277	MER	Stobart	
ESE 23278	AC ES 3278	MER	Stobart	
ESE 23279	AC ES 3279	MER	Stobart	
ESE 23280	AC ES 3280	MER	Stobart	
ESE 23281	AC ES 3281	MER	Stobart	
ESE 23282	AC ES 3282	MER	Stobart	
ESE 23283	AC ES 3283	MER	Stobart	
ESE 23284	AC ES 3284	MER	Stobart	
ESE 23285	AC ES 3285	MER	Stobart	
ESE 23286	AC ES 3286	MER	Stobart	

ESE 23287	AC ES 3287	MER	Stobart	
ESE 23288	AC ES 3288	MER	Stobart	
ESE 23289	AC ES 3289	MER	Stobart	
ESE 23290	AC ES 3290	MER	Stobart	
ESE 23291	AC ES 3291	MER	Stobart	
ESE 23292	AC ES 3292	MER	Stobart	
ESE 23293	AC ES 3293	MER	Stobart	
ESE 23294	AC ES 3294	MER	Stobart	
ESE 23295	AC ES 3295	MER	Stobart	
ESE 23296	AC ES 3296	MER	Stobart	
ESE 23297	AC ES 3297	MER	Stobart	
ESE 23298	AC ES 3298	MER	Stobart	
ESE 23299	AC ES 3299	MER	Stobart	
ESE 23300	AC ES 3300	MER	Stobart	
ESE 23301	AC ES 3301	MER	Stobart	
ESE 23302	AC ES 3302	MER	Stobart	
ESE 23303	AC ES 2330	MER	Stobart	
ESE 23304	AC ES 3304	MER	Stobart	
ESE 24305	AC ES 4305	MER	Stobart	
ESE 24306	AC ES 4306	MER	Stobart	
ESE 24307	AC ES 4307	MER	Stobart	
ESE 24308		MER	Stobart	
ESE 24309	AC ES 4309	MER	Stobart	
ESE 24310	AC ES 4310	MER	Stobart	
ESE 24311		MER	Stobart	
ESE 24312		MER	Stobart	
ESE 24313	AC ES 4313	MER	Stobart	
ESE 24314	AC ES 4314	MER	Stobart	
ESE 24315		MER	Stobart	
ESE 24316	AC ES 4316	MER	Stobart	
ESE 24317	AC ES 4317	MER	Stobart	
ESE 24318	AC ES 4318	MER	Stobart	
ESE 24319	AC ES 4319	MER	Stobart	
ESE 24320	AC ES 4320	MER	Stobart	
ESE 24321	AC ES 2432	MER	Stobart	
ESE 24322	AC ES 4322	MER	Stobart	
ESE 24323	AC ES 4323	MER	Stobart	
ESE 24324	AC ES 4324	MER	Stobart	
MSE 18225	AC ES 7599	MER	Stobart	Roxana
MSE 18226	AC ES 7501	MER	Stobart	Ilinca
MSE 18227	AC ES 7502	MER	Stobart	Iulia
MSE 18228	AC ES 7503	MER	Stobart	Virginia
MSE 18229	AC ES 7504	MER	White	
MSE 18230	AC ES 7505	MER	White	
MSE 18231	AC ES 7506	MER	Stobart	Oana
MSE 18232	AC ES 7507	MER	Stobart	Sanziana
MSE 18233	AC ES 7508	MER	Stobart	Sorina
MSE 18234	AC ES 7509	MER	Stobart	Eva
MSE 18235	AC ES 7510	MER	Stobart	Corina
MSE 18236	AC ES 7511	MER	Stobart	Adelina
MSE 21001	AC ES 7512	MER	Stobart	Nikol
MSE 21002	AC ES 7513	MER	Stobart	Bogomila
MSE 21003	AC ES 301	MER	Stobart	Bisera
MSE 21004	AC ES 303	MER	Stobart	Blaga
MSE 21005	AC ES 7514	MER	Stobart	Anna-Maria
MSE 21006	AC ES 215	MER	Stobart	Vesela
MSE 21007	AC ES 214	MER	Stobart	Venera
MSE 21008	AC ES 306	MER	Stobart	Doroteya
MSE 21009	AC ES 313	MER	Stobart	Dilyana
MSE 21010	AC ES 1223	MER	Stobart	Lazarina
MSE 21011	AC ES 216	MER	Stobart	Zhivka
MSE 21012	AC ES 329	MER	Stobart	Mira

Culina Group (European)

MSE 21013	AC ES 421	MER	Stobart	Marta
MSE 21014	AC ES 229	MER	Stobart	Ivelina
MSE 21015	AC ES 228	MER	Stobart	Tanya
MSE 21016	AC ES 423	MER	Stobart	Tsveta
MSE 21017	AC ES 426	MER	Stobart	Madlen
MSE 21018	AC ES 225	MER	Stobart	Boryana
MSE 21019	AC ES 501	MER	Stobart	Lyubka
MSE 21020	AC ES 430	MER	Stobart	Donka
MSE 21021	AC ES 433	MER	Stobart	Petranka
MSE 21022	AC ES 502	MER	Stobart	Svetla
MSE 21023	AC ES 503	MER	Stobart	Velimira
MSE 21024	AC ES 217	MER	Stobart	Stefani
MSE 21025	AC ES 504	MER	Stobart	Plamena
MSE 21026	AC ES 506	MER	Stobart	Martina
MSE 21027	AC ES 220	MER	Stobart	Deyana
MSE 21028	AC ES 262	MER	Stobart	Marinela
MSE 21029	AC ES 510	MER	Stobart	Viktoriya
MSE 21030	AC ES 512	MER	Stobart	Nikolina
MSE 22031	AC ES 134	MER	White	
MSE 22032	AC ES 149	MER	White	
MSE 22033	AC ES 117	MER	White	
MSE 22034	AC ES 174	MER	White	
MSE 22035	AC ES 136	MER	White	
MSE 22036	AC ES 146	MER	White	
MSE 23037	AC ES 3037	MER	White	
MSE 23038	AC ES 3038	MER	White	
MSE 23039	AC ES 3039	MER	White	
MSE 23040	AC ES 3040	MER	White	
MSE 23041	AC ES 3041	MER	White	
MSE 23042	AC ES 3043	MER	White	
MSE 23043	AC ES 3043	MER	White	
MSE 23044	AC ES 3044	MER	Stobart	
MSE 23045	AC ES 3045	MER	Stobart	
MSE 23046	AC ES 3046	MER	Stobart	
MSE 23047	AC ES 3047	MER	Stobart	
MSE 23048	AC ES 3048	MER	White	

Notes

David Watson

Fleet No	Registration	Make	Specification	Name	Allocation
SH1	AY08 EER	Daf	FTGCF85 460 6x2 SC	Vulcan	Brandon
V001	AV18 WKP	Volvo	FM 410 6w G Flatbed	Hercules	Northampton
V002	AY23 VWH	Daf	FTG 530 6x2 XG	Poseidon	
V003	AY73 UHS	Daf	FAN 480 6w (XF) Flatbed	Pegasus	
V004	AY68 PXT	Volvo	FM 410 6w G Flatbed	Oceanus	Earls Colne
V005	KM64 BTU	Volvo	FM 330 4w G Flatbed	Theia	Medway
V006	AY13 EFL	Daf	FANCF85 410 6w SC Flatbed	Olympus	York
V007	AV21 VOO	Daf	FTGXF 530 6x2 SSC	Zeus	Brandon
V008	AV70 OWZ	Volvo	FH 460 8w G Flatbed	Apollo	Earls Colne
V009	AV16 UCZ	Daf	FTGXF 510 6x2 SSC	Iris	Brandon
V010	AY65 PVO	Volvo	FH 540 6x4 G	Chimera	York
V011	KU64 CZN	Scania	G410 6w HL Flatbed	Hera	York
V012	AY73 UHX	Daf	FTG 480 6x2 (XF)	Ceres	
V013					
V014	AY23 VWJ	Daf	FTG 530 6x2 XG	Juno	
V015	KP65 UTE	Scania	G410 6w HL Flatbed	Crius	Stafford
V016	KW14 NUO	Volvo	FM 370 6w G Flatbed	Baldr	Medway
V017	KY12 VGR	Volvo	FM 460 8w G Flatbed	Deimos	Wellingborough
V018	AY23 VWK	Daf	FTG 530 6x2 XG	Maia	
V019	AY17 VYF	Daf	FAXCF 460 8w SC Flatbed	Lucina	Medway
V020	AY71 XUD	Scania	500S 6x2 (NG) HL	Fulgora	Earls Colne
V021	AY71 XUC	Scania	500S 6x2 (NG) HL	Medusa	Brandon
V022	AY23 WVG	Volvo	FH 460 8w G Flatbed	Adonis	
V023	AV68 CKY	Daf	FTGXF 510 6x2 SSC	Mimir	York
V024	AV67 EZR	Daf	FTPCF 530 6x2 SC	Vesta	Medway
V025	KX64 TOJ	Volvo	FH 540 6x4 GXL	Gladiator	Brandon
V026	AV66 NFE	Volvo	FM 460 8w G Flatbed	Trojan	Northampton
V027	KM64 BSO	Volvo	FM 410 8w G Flatbed	Androcles	York
V028	AV70 RZB	Daf	FTGXF 530 6x2 SSC	Vulcan	Brandon
V029	AY71 XUA	Scania	500S 6x2 (NG) HL	Zephyrus	Earls Colne
V030	AY72 YWA	Scania	R500 8w HL Flatbed	Pantheon	Earls Colne
V031	AV70 OXA	Volvo	FM 460 8w G Flatbed	Tara	Earls Colne
V032	BD23 WMT	Volvo	FH16 750 8x4 GXL	Goliath	
V033	AY67 NNL	Volvo	FM 370 6w G Flatbed	Kari	Stafford
V034	AY21 UMU	Daf	FAXCF 460 8w SC Flatbed	Sostratos	Medway
V035	AV16 FGM	Daf	FTGXF 510 6x2 SSC	Juventas	York
V036	AY15 UFC	Daf	FTGXF 510 6x2 SSC	Rhea	Brandon
V037	KT15 VRW	Scania	G410 6w HL Flatbed	Frey	York
V038	KU15 UUY	Volvo	FH 540 6x4 G	Typhon	Medway
V039	AY71 XUB	Scania	500S 6x2 (NG) HL	Perseus	Wellingborough
V040	AY70 TZD	Volvo	FH 460 8w G Flatbed	Grace	Northampton
V041	AY71 XUE	Scania	500S 6x2 (NG) HL	Heimdall	York
V042	AX19 FZY	Volvo	FH 540 6x4 G	Velkyrie	Wellingborough
V043	AY68 PZO	Volvo	FH 540 6x4 G	Odysseus	Stafford
V044	AY22 UUM	Volvo	FH 540 6x2 GXL	Nemesis	
V045	AX19 GAU	Volvo	FH 540 6w GXL Curtainside	Minerva	Northampton
V046	KX14 LPZ	Volvo	FM 410 6w G Flatbed	Aurora	Medway
V047	AY66 TKK	Volvo	FM 460 8w G Flatbed	Palaemon	Stafford
V048	AY23 WVH	Volvo	FH 460 8w G Flatbed	Aphrodite	
V049	KX65 PYD	Scania	G410 6w HL Flatbed	Medea	Northampton
V050	AY66 NRO	Mercedes	Actros 2551 6x2 BSC	Atlas	Earls Colne
V051	AV67 FNL	Volvo	FM 460 8w G Flatbed	Ulysses	Medway
V052	AY73 UHT	Daf	FAN 480 6w (XF) Flatbed	Astarte	
V053	AV66 NFD	Volvo	FM 460 8w G Flatbed	Freya	Medway
V054	AV70 RZC	Daf	FTGXF 530 6x2 SSC	Faunus	York
V055	AV22 OWA	Volvo	FH 540 6x4 G	Genesis	
V056	KY19 GPO	Scania	S650 6x2 (NG) HL	Corra	Brandon
V057	KX64 TKF	Volvo	FM 370 6w G Flatbed	Kronos	Stafford

V058	AY71 XUF	Scania	500S 6x2 (NG) HL	Taranis	Brandon
V059	AY18 PVE	Daf	FTPCF 530 6x2 SC	Jupiter	Wellingborough
V060	AY18 PVF	Daf	FTPCF 530 6x2 SC	Selene	Medway
V061					
V062	AY22 UGU	Daf	FTG 530 6x2 XF	Spartacus	
V063	AY68 PXS	Volvo	FM 410 6w G Flatbed	Vidar	Earls Colne
V064	AY23 VWM	Daf	FTG 530 6x2 XG	Vali	
V065	AV17 UWW	Volvo	FM 460 8w G Flatbed	Centaur	Earls Colne
V066	KX18 WDW	Scania	R450 6w HL Flatbed	Magnus	Brandon
V067	KX64 TNN	Volvo	FM 370 6w G Flatbed	Orpheus	York
V068	KV64 LBO	Volvo	FM 420 8w G Flatbed	Maximus	Earls Colne
V069	KM64 BUU	Volvo	FM 370 6w G Flatbed	Pygmalion	Earls Colne
V070	KX16 ZZR	Scania	G410 6w HL Flatbed	Prometheus	Brandon
V071	KU15 FGO	Scania	G410 6w HL Flatbed	Honos	Brandon
V072	KN64 RWW	Volvo	FH 540 6x4 GXL	Triton	York
V073	KX64 TOA	Volvo	FM 330 4w G Flatbed	Heracles	Brandon
V074	AY72 YWT	Scania	R500 8w HL Flatbed	Persephone	Stafford
V075	KW14 NTM	Volvo	FM 370 6w G Flatbed	Dionysus	Stafford
V076	AY69 OZN	Daf	FAXXF 480 8w SC Flatbed	Eos	Brandon
V077	AY13 BMO	Scania	G400 6w HL Flatbed	Thor	York
V078	KX64 TLV	Volvo	FH 540 6w GXL Curtainside	Andromeda	Brandon
V079	KX16 ZZP	Scania	G410 6w HL Flatbed	Venus	Stafford
V080	AX19 GCO	Volvo	FH 540 6x2 G	Patroclus	Stafford
V081	AY67 NSN	Volvo	FM 370 6w G Flatbed	Woden	Northampton
V082	KP65 UTC	Scania	G450 8w HL Flatbed	Talos	York
V083	AV16 WYG	Volvo	FH 540 6x4 G	Eileithyia	Northampton
V084	KX65 PYF	Scania	G450 8w HL Flatbed	Gryphon	Northampton
V085	AV69 LUJ	Volvo	FM 460 8w G Flatbed	Camalus	Earls Colne
V086	AV22 OWB	Volvo	FH 540 6x4 G	Arete	Earls Colne
V087	AY16 ZNS	Daf	FTGXF 510 6x2 SSC	Morgan	York
V088	AY66 SZW	Volvo	FH 540 6x4 G	Midas	Earls Colne
V089	DX71 OVP	Volvo	FH 460 8w G Flatbed	Forseti	York
V090	AV71 RUC	Volvo	FH 500 6x2 GXL	Mars	Brandon
V091	AV66 NFC	Volvo	FM 460 8w G Flatbed	Colossus	Earls Colne
V092					
V093	AY73 UHZ	Daf	FTG 480 6x2 (XF)	Menelaus	
V094					
V095	AY16 LUH	Mercedes	Atego 1523 4w Curtainside	Loki	Earls Colne
V096					
V097	AV71 RUH	Volvo	FH 500 6x2 GXL	Bellona	Wellingborough
V098	KW16 KTV	Scania	G410 6w HL Flatbed	Artemis	Northampton
V099	AY17 VYG	Daf	FANCF 410 6w SC Flatbed	Ares	Medway
V100	AY20 TTE	Volvo	FH 460 8w G Flatbed	Centurion	Earls Colne
V101	AY68 PXU	Volvo	FM 410 6w G Flatbed	Theseus	York
V102	AY23 VWN	Daf	FTG 530 6x2 XG	Astrlid	
V103	KM15 FBK	Scania	G410 6w HL Flatbed	Athena	Wellingborough
V104	KU64 EAO	Scania	G410 6w HL Flatbed	Orion	Northampton
V105	KU64 CZO	Scania	G410 6w HL Flatbed	Tyr	Brandon
V106	AV67 FNM	Volvo	FM 460 8w G Flatbed	Melia	York
V107	AV18 WLG	Volvo	FM 410 6w G Flatbed	Vanir	Stafford
V108	MF64 EPC	Scania	G410 8w Flatbed	Agamemnon	York
V109	KU69 WZO	Scania	R500 8w HL Flatbed	Alexis	Brandon
V110	AY19 TZH	Volvo	FH 460 8w G Flatbed	Skymir	Earls Colne
V111	AY19 TCJ	Daf	FAXXF 480 8w SC Flatbed	Morpheus	Medway
V112	AV71 RUO	Volvo	FH 500 6x2 GXL	Staurn	Stafford
V113	MF64 EPJ	Scania	G410 8w Flatbed	Freyja	Wellingborough
V114	KU15 GKC	Scania	G410 6w HL Flatbed	Bacchus	Wellingborough
V115	KP15 OVF	Volvo	FM 420 8w G Flatbed	Atalanta	Medway
V116	AY20 TPX	Volvo	FH16 650 6x2 GXL	Magni	Brandon
V117	AY71 TYX	Daf	FTGXF 530 6x2 SSC	Demetrius	York
	AY23 VWL	Daf	FTG 530 6x2 XG		

Dent Logistics (Penrith)

Note: All vehicles are Scania - R450 6x2 (NG) HL

PV19 EJL	PY69 KHG	PK21 OYL	PK71 VJU	PJ72 UBP	PK23 ECT	
PV19 EKA	PY69 KHM	PK21 OYM	PK71 VJV	PJ72 UBR	PK23 LRU	
PV19 EKC	PY69 KHR	PK21 OYN	PK71 VJX	PJ72 UBS	PK23 LRV	
PV19 ELW	PX20 LTA	PK21 OYO	PK71 VJY	PJ72 UBT	PK23 LRX	
PV19 KTL	PX20 LTE	PK21 OYP	PK71 VJZ	PJ72 UBU	PK23 LUW	
PV19 KTO	PX20 LTF	PK21 OYR	PN22 ECD	PJ72 UBV	PK23 LUZ	
PX19 KXA	PX20 LTJ	PK21 OYT	PJ72 FGO	PJ72 UBW	PK23 LVL	
PX19 KXE	PX20 LTK	PK21 OYU	PJ72 FGP	PJ72 UBX	PK23 LVN	
PX19 KXG	PX20 LTN	PN21 FFT	PJ72 UBC	PJ72 UBY	PF73 CFM	
PX19 LBP	PX20 LUH	PN21 FFU	PJ72 UBD	PJ72 UBZ	PF73 LBU	
PX19 LBV	PX20 LUJ	PN21 FFV	PJ72 UBE	PJ72 UCE	PF73 LBZ	
PX69 KYB	PX20 LUL	PN21 FFW	PJ72 UBF	PJ72 UCF	PF73 LCO	
PX69 KYC	PX20 LUP	PN21 FFX	PJ72 UBG	PF23 ELO	PL73 HFV	
PX69 KYF	PX20 LUR	PE71 WJU	PJ72 UBH	PF23 EOM	PL73 YBO	
PY69 AKF	PX20 LUT	PE71 WJV	PJ72 UBK	PF23 EPX	PN73 EWY	
PY69 AKG	PX20 LUW	PK71 VJM	PJ72 UBL	PK23 EPX	PN73 EWZ	
PY69 AKK	PX20 LUY	PK71 VJN	PJ72 UBM	PK23 ECC	PN73 EXH	
PY69 KHC	PK21 OYH	PK71 VJO	PJ72 UBN	PK23 ECD	PN73 EXJ	
PY69 KHF	PK21 OYJ	PK71 VJP	PJ72 UBO	PK23 ECN		

D.G. Noble (Wootton Bedfordshire)

Reg	Make	Description	Reg	Make	Description
L2 HAB (18)	Scania	G360 6w HL Curtainside	KM18 GVT	Volvo	FM 460 8W (G) Curtainside
Y994 PRP	Volvo	FM7 6w Flatbed	KT18 TCJ	Volvo	FM 500 6W (G) Flatbed
DG11 OWV	Man	TGX 26.480 6x2 XLX	KX18 XDG	Scania	G450 8W (HL) Flatbed
KR62 DXL	Volvo	FH 500 6x2 (GXL)	KY68 HDG	Scania	R500 6x2 (HL)
KP14 FNR	Volvo	FH 460 6x2 G	KY68 HDN	Scania	R500 8W (HL) Flatbed
KX14 EKE	Scania	G360 6W (HL) Curtainside	KM19 YVH	Volvo	FH 460 8W (G) Flatbed
KY14 CXG	Scania	R450 8W (HL) Tanker	KM19 YVJ	Volvo	FH 460 8W (G) Curtainside
KP64 XYL	Volvo	FM 370 6W (G) Flatbed	KY19 GDO	Scania	R500 8W (HL) Flatbed
KU64 DOJ	Scania	R490 6x2 (HL)	KY19 JPO	Volvo	FH 460 6x2 GXL
KU15 FLH	Scania	G370 6W (HL) Flatbed	KU69 XDG	Scania	G450 8W (HL) Curtainside
GN65 OCD	Volvo	FH 500 6x2 (GXL)	KU69 XDN	Scania	G450 8W (HL) Hooklift
KM65 KPE	Volvo	FH 500 6x2 (G)	KU70 YOP	Volvo	FH 540 8W (GXL) Flatbed
KP65 KXJ	Volvo	FH 500 8w GXL Curtainside	KU70 YOW	Volvo	FH 500 8W (G) Tanker
KX65 RBU	Scania	R490 8W (HL) Flatbed	KY21 FDG	Scania	R500 8W (HL) Curtainside
KT16 KJE	Scania	G450 8W (HL) Flatbed	KY21 FDN	Scania	R450 8W (HL) Curtainside
KX16 ZRJ	Scania	G450 8W (HL) Flatbed	KY21 HTT	Volvo	FH 500 6x2 (G)
KX16 ZRP	Scania	G450 8W (HL) Curtainside	KY71 BND	Scania	R450 8W (HL) Flatbed
KX16 ZTM	Scania	R580 6x2 (Top)	KY71 CDN	Scania	R500 8W (HL) Flatbed
KU66 AJX	Scania	G450 8W (HL) Curtainside	KY22 ELW	Scania	540S 6x4 (HL)
KN17 ZKR	Scania	R450 6x2 (HL)	KM72 DGX	Volvo	FMX 460 8w G Curtainside
KX17 BXD	Scania	R450 8W (Top) Flatbed	KM72 DGY	Volvo	FMX 460 8w G Flatbed
KX17 BXF	Scania	R450 8W (Top) Flatbed	KY72 FLV	Scania	R500 6x2 (HL)
KX17 BXL	Scania	R450 8W (Top) Tanker	KY72 JGZ	Volvo	FH 500 6x2 (GXL)
KX17 SKF	Mercedes	Atego 1221 4W Flatbed	KY23 FZK	Scania	R450 8w (NG) HL Flatbed
KM67 LLT	Volvo	FH 500 6x2 (G)	KY23 HDG	Scania	R450 8w (NG) HL Flatbed
KM67 LLU	Volvo	FH 500 6x2 (G)	KY23 HDN	Scania	R450 8w (NG) HL Flatbed

D Steven & Sons (Scrabster)

No.	Reg	Make	Name	No.	Reg	Make	Name
3	SK23 ESK	Scania	Highland Lady X	18	SK23 GTS	Scania	Highland Fox VI
4	SK70 FGY	Scania	Highland Lassie XV	19	SK20 SSS	Scania	Highland Fox VI
5	SK23 FSK	Scania		20	SK73 USK	Scania	
6	SK73 MSK	Scania		21	SK23 BSK	Scania	Highland Warrior VII
7	SK21 BXF	Scania	Highland Ranger X	22	SK21 BXC	Scania	Highland Contender X
8	SK21 BXE	Scania	Highland Duchess XII	23	SK20 WSK	Scania	Caithness Emperor V
9	SK70 GUL	Scania	Highland Duchess XII	26	SK70 DSK	Scania	Highland Reiver XI
10	SK21 BXG	Scania	Caithness Emperor XI	28	SK21 BXH	Scania	Highland Cheiftan IX
11	SK73 JSK	Scania		29	SK21 BXA	Scania	Highland Express XI
12	SK21 BXD	Scania	Caithness Prince VII	31	SK73 NSK	Scania	
14	SK23 GSK	Scania	Highland Challender IV	32	SK23 DSK	Scania	
15	SK73 OSK	Scania		34	SK70 ROE	Scania	Highland Challender IX
16	SK21 BXB	Scania	Highland Prince VIII	40	SK70 BOW	Scania	Silver Fox XII
17	SK21 BXJ	Scania	Caithness Contender VIII	55	SK71 CSK	Scania	Caithness Empress

Esken Renewables

Fleet	Reg	Make	Livery	Fleet	Reg	Make	Livery
R 3	PK 20 HWJ	Scania	Megaskips	H 8553	PV 19 KPK	Scania	Esken (White)
R 4	PN 70 ACU	Scania	Megaskips	H 8554	PV 19 KPL	Scania	Esken
H 8511	PX 68 UNJ	Scania	Esken (White)	H 8555	PV 19 KPN	Scania	Esken (White)
H 8512	PX 68 UNK	Scania	Esken (White)	H 8556	PV 19 KPO	Scania	Esken
H 8513	PX 68 UNL	Scania	Esken (White)	H 8557	PV 19 KPP	Scania	Esken (White)
H 8514	PX 68 UNM	Scania	Esken (White)	H 8558	PV 19 KPR	Scania	Esken (White)
H 8515	PX 68 UNN	Scania	Esken (White)	H 8559	PV 19 KPT	Scania	Esken (White)
H 8516	PX 68 ZJU	Scania	Esken (White)	H 8560	PV 19 KPU	Scania	Esken (White)
H 8517	PX 68 ZJV	Scania	Esken	H 8561	PV 19 KPX	Scania	Esken (White)
H 8518	PX 68 ZJY	Scania	Esken (White)	H 8562	PV 19 KPY	Scania	Esken (White)
H 8520	PX 68 ZKA	Scania	Esken (White)	H 8563	PV 19 KPZ	Scania	Esken (White)
H 8521	PX 68 ZKB	Scania	Esken (White)	H 8564	PV 19 UUA	Scania	Esken (White)
H 8522	PX 68 ZKC	Scania	Esken (White)	H 8565	PV 19 UUB	Scania	Esken
H 8523	PX 68 ZKD	Scania	White	H 8566	PV 19 UUC	Scania	Esken (White)
H 8524	PX 68 ZKH	Scania	Esken (White)	H 8567	PV 19 UUD	Scania	Esken (White)
H 8525	PX 68 ZKJ	Scania	Esken (White)	H 8568	PV 19 UUE	Scania	Esken (White)
H 8526	PX 68 ZKK	Scania	Esken (White)	H 8569	PV 19 UUG	Scania	Esken
H 8527	PX 68 ZKM	Scania	Esken (White)	H 8570	PV 19 UUH	Scania	Esken (White)
H 8529	PX 68 ZKE	Scania	Esken	H 8571	PV 19 UUF	Scania	White
H 8530	PX 68 ZKF	Scania	Esken (White)	H 8572	PX 69 LFA	Scania	Esken
H 8531	PX 68 ZKG	Scania	Esken (White)	H 8573	PX 69 LFB	Scania	Esken (White)
H 8532	PY 68 SWK	Scania	Esken	H 8574	PX 69 LFD	Scania	Esken (White)
H 8533	PY 68 SWF	Scania	Esken (White)	H 8575	PX 69 LFE	Scania	Esken (White)
H 8534	PY 68 SWN	Scania	White	H 8576	PX 69 LFF	Scania	Esken
H 8535	PY 68 SWO	Scania	Esken (White)	H 8577	PX 69 LFG	Scania	Esken (White)
H 8536	PY 68 SWJ	Scania	Esken	H 8578	PX 69 LEF	Scania	Esken (White)
H 8537	PY 68 SWU	Scania	Esken (White)	H 8579	PX 69 LEJ	Scania	Esken (White)
H 8538	PY 68 SWW	Scania	White	H 8580	PX 69 LDD	Scania	Esken (White)
H 8539	PY 68 SWV	Scania	Esken (White)	H 8581	PX 69 LDJ	Scania	Esken (White)
H 8540	PX 19 KZC	Scania	Esken (White)	H 8582	PX 69 LDA	Scania	Esken (White)
H 8541	PX 19 KZD	Scania	Esken	H 8583	PX 69 LDL	Scania	White
H 8542	PX 19 KZE	Scania	Esken (White)	H 8584	PX 69 LDN	Scania	Esken
H 8543	PX 19 KZF	Scania	Esken	H 8585	PX 69 LDV	Scania	Esken
H 8544	PX 19 KZG	Scania	Esken (White)	H 8586	PX 69 LEU	Scania	Esken (White)
H 8545	PX 19 KZH	Scania	White	H 8587	PX 69 LDC	Scania	Esken (White)
H 8546	PX 19 KZJ	Scania	Esken (White)	H 8588	PX 69 LDE	Scania	Esken (White)
H 8547	PX 19 KZK	Scania	Esken (White)	H 8589	PX 69 LDF	Scania	Esken (White)
H 8548	PV 19 KPA	Scania	Esken (White)	H 8590	PX 69 LDK	Scania	Esken (White)
H 8549	PV 19 KPE	Scania	Esken (White)	H 8591	PX 69 LDO	Scania	White
H 8550	PV 19 KPF	Scania	Esken (White)	H 8592	PX 69 LDU	Scania	Esken
H 8551	PV 19 KPG	Scania	Esken	H 8593	PY 69 AMK	Scania	Esken (White)
H 8552	PV 19 KPJ	Scania	Esken	H 8594	PY 69 AMO	Scania	Esken (White)

Esken Renewables (cont)

H 8595	PY 69 AMU	Scania	Esken (White)	H 8707	KY 19 HLW	Volvo	Esken (White)
H 8596	PY 69 AMV	Scania	Esken (White)	H 8708	KY 19 HLV	Volvo	Esken
H 8597	PY 69 AMX	Scania	Esken (White)	H 8709	KY 19 HMF	Volvo	Esken (White)
H 8598	PY 69 ANF	Scania	Esken (White)	H 8710	KY 19 HLR	Volvo	Esken (White)
H 8599	PY 69 ANP	Scania	White	H 8711	KY 19 HLP	Volvo	Esken (White)
H 8600	DK 67 WHD	Man	White/Red	H 8712	KY 19 HLO	Volvo	Esken (White)
H 8601	PY 69 ANR	Scania	Esken (White)	H 8713	KY 19 HLN	Volvo	Esken (White)
H 8602	PY 69 ANU	Scania	Esken (White)	H 8714	KY 19 HLM	Volvo	Esken
H 8603	PY 69 ANV	Scania	Esken (White)	H 8715	KY 19 HLK	Volvo	Esken (White)
H 8604	PY 69 ANX	Scania	Esken (White)	H 8716	KY 19 HLJ	Volvo	Esken (White)
H 8605	PY 69 AOA	Scania	Esken (White)	H 8717	KY 19 HLH	Volvo	Esken (White)
H 8700	KY 19 HLU	Volvo	Esken (White)	H 8718	KY 19 HLG	Volvo	Esken (White)
H 8701	KY 19 HME	Volvo	Esken (White)	H 8719	KY 19 HLF	Volvo	Esken (White)
H 8702	KY 19 HMD	Volvo	Esken (White)	H 8721	KY 19 HLD	Volvo	Esken (White)
H 8703	KY 19 HMC	Volvo	Esken (White)	H 8722	KY 19 HLC	Volvo	Esken (White)
H 8704	KY 19 HMA	Volvo	Esken (White)	H 8723	KY 19 HLA	Volvo	Esken (White)
H 8705	KY 19 HLZ	Volvo	Esken (White)	H 8724	KY 19 HKZ	Volvo	Esken (White)
H 8706	KY 19 HLX	Volvo	Esken (White)				

Fagan & Whalley

Registration	Make	Specification	Livery	Allocation
S90 FAW (17)	Scania	S450 6x2 (HL)	Fagan & Whalley	Burnley
RCZ 8996 (13)	Renault	Premium 420 dci 4x2	Alan R Jones	Newport
EU06 ECT	Scania	R420 4x2	Fagan & Whalley	Burnley
PN57 PHO	Scania	R420 6x2 (HL)	Fagan & Whalley	Burnley
PG08 CHH	Scania	R420 4x2 (HL)	Fagan & Whalley	Burnley
PG08 XCN	Scania	R420 4x2 (Top)	Fagan & Whalley	Burnley
PN08 HLO	Scania	R420 4x2 (HL)	Knauf	Burnley
PN08 HLP	Scania	R420 4x2 (HL)	Knauf	Exhall
FJ58 XYO	Renault	Midlum 240 Dxi 6w Curtainside	Alan R Jones	Newport
PE10 JKX	Scania	R420 6x2	Fagan & Whalley	Burnley
PE10 YGZ	Scania	R440 6x2 (HL)	Fagan & Whalley	Burnley
JC60 TTC (60)	Scania	P230 4W Curtainside	Palletforce	Burnley
PJ11 UBO	Scania	R440 6x2 (HL)	Fagan & Whalley	Exhall
PK11 NKT	Scania	R440 6x2 (HL)	Fagan & Whalley	Burnley
NJ61 CJO	Scania	R440 4x2 (Top)	Fagan & Whalley	Burnley
NJ61 CJV	Scania	R440 4x2 (Top)	Fagan & Whalley	Not Known
BX12 MHL	Renault	Premium 460 Dxi 6x2	Alan R Jones	Newport
PJ62 RDV	Scania	R440 6x2 (HL)	Fagan & Whalley	Coventry
PJ63 JFA	Scania	R440 6x2 (HL)	Fagan & Whalley	Burnley
PJ63 JFE	Scania	R440 6x2 (HL)	Fagan & Whalley	Exhall
PJ63 SXK	Scania	R440 6x2 (HL)	Fagan & Whalley	Burnley
PJ63 SXL	Scania	R440 6x2 (HL)	Fagan & Whalley	Burnley
PK63 YHR	Scania	R440 6x2 (HL)	Fagan & Whalley	Burnley
PK63 YHS	Scania	R440 6x2 (HL)	Fagan & Whalley	Burnley
PK63 ZCT	Scania	R440 6x2 (HL)	Fagan & Whalley	Burnley
PO63 PJX	Scania	R440 6x2 (HL)	Fagan & Whalley	Burnley
PO63 PJY	Scania	R440 6x2 (HL)	Knauf	Exhall
PO63 PVD	Scania	R440 6x2 (HL)	Fagan & Whalley	Burnley
AU14 CCA	Renault	D250 4w Curtainside	Alan R Jones	Newport
AU14 CEA	Renault	D250 4w Curtainside	Alan R Jones	Newport
PF14 LFS	Scania	R450 6x2 (HL)	Fagan & Whalley	Burnley
PF14 LFT	Scania	R450 6x2 (HL)	Fagan & Whalley	Burnley
PJ14 RLX	Scania	R450 6x2 (HL)	Fagan & Whalley	Burnley
PJ14 RLY	Scania	R450 6x2 (HL)	Fagan & Whalley	Burnley
PK14 KAU	Scania	R440 6x2 (HL)	Fagan & Whalley	Burnley
PK14 KAX	Scania	R440 6x2 (HL)	Fagan & Whalley	Burnley
PK14 VSJ	Scania	R440 6x2 (HL)	Fagan & Whalley	Coventry

PN14 TGV	Daf	FALF 180 4W Curtainside	Palletforce	Coventry
PN14 TGX	Daf	FALF 150 4W Curtainside	Fagan & Whalley	Burnley
PO14 FJU	Renault	T460 6x2	Alan R Jones	Newport
PO14 VKF	Scania	R440 6x2 (HL)	Fagan & Whalley	Burnley
PO14 VKG	Scania	R440 6x2 (HL)	Fagan & Whalley	Burnley
PO14 VKP	Scania	R440 6x2 (HL)	Fagan & Whalley	Burnley
DK64 EHC	Renault	T460 6x2	Alan R Jones	Newport
PE64 MVW	Scania	R450 6x2 (HL)	Fagan & Whalley	Burnley
PE64 MVX	Scania	R450 6x2 (HL)	Fagan & Whalley	Burnley
PE64 MWF	Scania	R410 4x2 (HL)	Fagan & Whalley	Coventry
PE64 MWG	Scania	R410 4x2 (HL)	Fagan & Whalley	Burnley
PE64 MXA	Scania	P280 4W Curtainside	Fagan & Whalley	Burnley
PE64 MXB	Scania	P280 4W Curtainside	Fagan & Whalley	Burnley
PE64 MXN	Scania	R450 6x2 (HL)	Fagan & Whalley	Burnley
PE64 MXO	Scania	R450 6x2 (HL)	Fagan & Whalley	Burnley
PK64 YDX	Scania	R410 6x2 (HL)	Fagan & Whalley	Burnley
PK64 YEY	Scania	R410 6x2 (HL)	Fagan & Whalley	Burnley
PK64 YFA	Scania	R450 6x2 (HL)	Fagan & Whalley	Burnley
PK64 YGL	Scania	R450 6x2 (HL)	Fagan & Whalley	Burnley
PO64 DVT	Renault	T460 6x2	Alan R Jones	Newport
PO64 VMT	Scania	R450 6x2 (HL)	Fagan & Whalley	Burnley
PO64 VMU	Scania	R450 6x2 (HL)	Fagan & Whalley	Burnley
LX15 DVZ	Renault	T460 6x2	Alan R Jones	Newport
LX15 DWJ	Renault	T460 6x2	Alan R Jones	Newport
LX15 DWW	Renault	T460 6x2	Alan R Jones	Newport
LX15 DXG	Renault	T460 6x2	Alan R Jones	Newport
LX15 DXJ	Renault	T460 6x2	Alan R Jones	Newport
PO15 UGE	Scania	R450 6x2 (HL)	Fagan & Whalley	Burnley
PO15 UGF	Scania	R450 6x2 (HL)	Fagan & Whalley	Burnley
PO15 UGG	Scania	G320 6W Curtainside	Fagan & Whalley	Burnley
PO15 UGH	Scania	G320 6W Curtainside	Fagan & Whalley	Burnley
PO15 ULH	Scania	R450 6x2 (HL)	Fagan & Whalley	Burnley
PO15 ULJ	Scania	R450 6x2 (HL)	Fagan & Whalley	Burnley
PO15 ULZ	Scania	R450 6x2 (HL)	Fagan & Whalley	Burnley
PO15 UMA	Scania	R450 6x2 (HL)	Fagan & Whalley	Burnley
PO15 UMB	Scania	R450 6x2 (HL)	Fagan & Whalley	Burnley
PO15 UUW	Scania	R450 6x2 (Top)	Fagan & Whalley	Cwmbran
YX15 DVV	Renault	D280 4w Curtainside	Alan R Jones	Newport
LX65 BVY	Renault	D280 4w Curtainside	Alan R Jones	Newport
NK65 SFN	Scania	G410 4x2	Fagan & Whalley	Burnley
PJ65 JBE	Daf	FTGXF 460 6x2 (SSC)	Fagan & Whalley	Burnley
PO65 VBX	Scania	R450 6x2 (Top)	Fagan & Whalley	Burnley
PO65 VBY	Scania	R450 6x2 (Top)	Fagan & Whalley	Burnley
PO65 VGF	Scania	R450 6x2 (Top)	Fagan & Whalley	Burnley
PO65 VGG	Scania	P410 4x2 (Day Cab)	Mike England	Burnley
PO65 VKD	Scania	R450 6x2 (Top)	Fagan & Whalley	Burnley
PO65 VKU	Scania	R450 6x2 (Top)	Fagan & Whalley	Burnley
EU16 GBY	Scania	R450 6x2	Fagan & Whalley	Burnley
PK16 LVE	Scania	R450 6x2 (Top)	Fagan & Whalley	Burnley
PN16 OAB	Scania	R450 0x2 (Top)	Fagan & Whalley	Burnley
PN16 OAC	Scania	R450 6x2 (Top)	Fagan & Whalley	Burnley
PN16 OTG	Scania	G320 4W (HL) Curtainside	Fagan & Whalley	Burnley
PN16 OTJ	Scania	R450 6x2 (Top)	Fagan & Whalley	Burnley
PN16 OTK	Scania	R450 6x2 (Top)	Fagan & Whalley	Burnley
PN16 OXC	Scania	R450 6x2 (Top)	Fagan & Whalley	Burnley
PN16 OXD	Scania	G320 4W (HL) Curtainside	Fagan & Whalley	Burnley
PN16 OZW	Scania	R450 6x2 (Top)	Fagan & Whalley	Burnley
PO16 FJC	Renault	D280 4w Curtainside	Alan R Jones	Newport
AU66 BYD	Renault	T460 6x2	Alan R Jones	Newport

EU66 XCX	Scania	R450 6x2 (HL)	Fagan & Whalley	Burnley
EU66 XDD	Scania	R450 6x2 (HL)	Fagan & Whalley	Burnley
PG66 VFK	Renault	D250 4w Curtainside	Alan R Jones	Newport
PG66 VFL	Renault	D250 4w Curtainside	Alan R Jones	Newport
PN66 HJU	Mercedes	Actros 2545 6x2 (SSC)	Fagan & Whalley	Burnley
PN66 HJV	Mercedes	Actros 2545 6x2 (BSC)	Fagan & Whalley	Burnley
PO66 UGH	Scania	R450 6x2 (Top)	Fagan & Whalley	Burnley
PO66 UKK	Scania	R450 6x2 (Top)	Fagan & Whalley	Burnley
PO66 UKL	Scania	R450 6x2 (Top)	Fagan & Whalley	Burnley
PO66 ULV	Scania	R450 6x2 (Top)	Fagan & Whalley	Burnley
PO66 UTU	Scania	G450 6x2 (Day)	Fagan & Whalley	Burnley
PO66 UTV	Scania	P250 4W Curtainside	Palletforce	Burnley
PO66 VAK	Scania	R450 6x2 (Top)	Fagan & Whalley	Burnley
AU17 CJV	Renault	T460 6x2	Alan R Jones	Newport
PO17 UFW	Scania	R450 6x2 (Top)	Fagan & Whalley	Burnley
PO17 UFX	Scania	R450 6x2 (Top)	Fagan & Whalley	Burnley
PO17 UFY	Scania	R450 6x2 (Top)	Fagan & Whalley	Burnley
PO67 UZN	Scania	R410 4x2	Fagan & Whalley	Burnley
PO67 VDA	Scania	R450 6x2 (HL)	Fagan & Whalley	Burnley
PO67 VDE	Scania	R450 6x2 (HL)	Fagan & Whalley	Burnley
PO67 VFV	Scania	P250 4W Curtainside	Palletforce	Burnley
PO67 VFW	Scania	P250 4W Curtainside	Palletforce	Burnley
PO18 MLX	Scania	R450 6x2 (NG) HL	Fagan & Whalley	Burnley
PO18 MLY	Scania	R450 6x2 (NG) HL	Fagan & Whalley	Burnley
PO18 MMA	Scania	R450 6x2 (NG) HL	Fagan & Whalley	Burnley
PO18 MMF	Scania	R450 6x2 (NG) HL	Fagan & Whalley	Burnley
PO18 MMJ	Scania	R450 6x2 (NG) HL	Fagan & Whalley	Burnley
PO18 MMK	Scania	R450 6x2 (NG) HL	Fagan & Whalley	Burnley
PO18 MMU	Scania	R450 6x2 (NG) HL	Fagan & Whalley	Burnley
PO18 MMV	Scania	R450 6x2 (NG) HL	Fagan & Whalley	Burnley
PO18 MMX	Scania	R450 6x2 (NG) HL	Fagan & Whalley	Burnley
PO18 MOV	Scania	R450 6x2 (NG) HL	Fagan & Whalley	Burnley
PF68 XAB	Scania	R450 6x2 (NG) HL	Fagan & Whalley	Burnley
PN68 RPV	Mercedes	Actros 1842 4x2 (BSC)	Fagan & Whalley	Burnley
PN68 XXH	Daf	FALF 180 4W Curtainside	Fagan & Whalley	Burnley
PO68 XLH	Scania	R450 6x2 (NG) HL	Fagan & Whalley	Burnley
PO68 XRH	Scania	R450 6x2 (NG) HL	Fagan & Whalley	Burnley
PO68 XRJ	Scania	R450 6x2 (NG) HL	Fagan & Whalley	Burnley
PO68 XRL	Scania	R450 6x2 (NG) HL	Fagan & Whalley	Burnley
PO68 XRM	Scania	R450 6x2 (NG) HL	Fagan & Whalley	Burnley
PO68 XRN	Scania	R450 6x2 (NG) HL	Fagan & Whalley	Burnley
PO68 XRR	Scania	R410 4x2 (NG) HL	Fagan & Whalley	Burnley
PN19 DZB	Mercedes	Actros 2545 6x2 (BSC)	Fagan & Whalley	Burnley
PN19 DZC	Mercedes	Actros 2545 6x2 (BSC)	Fagan & Whalley	Burnley
PN19 DZD	Mercedes	Actros 2545 6x2 (BSC)	Fagan & Whalley	Burnley
PN19 DZE	Mercedes	Actros 2545 6x2 (BSC)	Fagan & Whalley	Burnley
PN19 FNA	Scania	R450 6x2 (NG) HL	Fagan & Whalley	Burnley
PN19 FNC	Scania	G280 4W (HL) Curtainside	Fagan & Whalley	Burnley
PN19 FWW	Scania	G450 6x2 (NG) HL	Fagan & Whalley	Burnley
PK69 XSA	Scania	R450 6x2 (NG) HL	Fagan & Whalley	Burnley
PK69 XSB	Scania	R450 6x2 (NG) HL	Fagan & Whalley	Burnley
PK69 XSD	Scania	R450 6x2 (NG) HL	Fagan & Whalley	Burnley
PK69 XSE	Scania	R450 6x2 (NG) HL	Fagan & Whalley	Burnley
PK69 XWE	Scania	S450 6x2 (NG) HL	Fagan & Whalley	Burnley
PO69 YDV	Scania	R450 6x2 (NG) HL	Fagan & Whalley	Burnley
PO69 YJS	Scania	R450 6x2 (NG) HL	Fagan & Whalley	Burnley
PN20 AUR	Scania	R450 6x2 (NG) HL	Fagan & Whalley	Burnley
PN20 AUT	Scania	S450 6x2 (NG) HL	Fagan & Whalley	Burnley
PN20 AUU	Scania	R450 6x2 (NG) HL	Fagan & Whalley	Burnley

Reg	Make	Model	Operator	Location
PN20 AUV	Scania	R450 6x2 (NG) HL	Fagan & Whalley	Burnley
PN20 AUW	Scania	R450 6x2 (NG) HL	Fagan & Whalley	Burnley
PN20 AVC	Scania	G450 8W (NG) HL Curtainside	Fagan & Whalley	Burnley
PN20 AVD	Scania	G280 4W (NG) HL Curtainside	Fagan & Whalley	Burnley
PN20 AEA	Scania	S450 6x2 (NG) HL	Fagan & Whalley	Burnley
PN70 AED	Scania	R450 6x2 (NG) NL	Fagan & Whalley	Burnley
PN70 AEF	Scania	R450 6x2 (NG) NL	Fagan & Whalley	Burnley
PN21 FWA	Scania	R450 6x2 (NG) HL	Fagan & Whalley	Burnley
PN21 FWB	Scania	R450 6x2 (NG) HL	Fagan & Whalley	Burnley
PN21 FWF	Scania	R450 6x2 (NG) HL	Fagan & Whalley	Burnley
PN71 EFF	Scania	R450 6x2 (NG) HL	Fagan & Whalley	Burnley
PN71 EFG	Scania	R450 6x2 (NG) HL	Fagan & Whalley	Burnley
PN71 EFH	Scania	R450 6x2 (NG) HL	Fagan & Whalley	Burnley
PN71 EFK	Scania	R450 6x2 (NG) HL	Fagan & Whalley	Burnley
PN71 EFL	Scania	R450 6x2 (NG) HL	Fagan & Whalley	Burnley
PN71 EFM	Scania	R450 6x2 (NG) HL	Fagan & Whalley	Burnley
PN71 EFO	Scania	R450 6x2 (NG) HL	Fagan & Whalley	Burnley
PN71 EFP	Scania	R450 6x2 (NG) HL	Fagan & Whalley	Burnley
PN71 EFR	Scania	R450 6x2 (NG) HL	Fagan & Whalley	Burnley
PN71 EFS	Scania	R450 6x2 (NG) HL	Fagan & Whalley	Burnley
PN71 EFT	Scania	R450 6x2 (NG) HL	Fagan & Whalley	Burnley
PN71 EFU	Scania	R450 6x2 (NG) HL	Fagan & Whalley	Burnley
PN71 EFV	Scania	R450 6x2 (NG) HL	Fagan & Whalley	Burnley
PN71 EFW	Scania	R450 6x2 (NG) HL	Fagan & Whalley	Burnley
PN71 EFX	Scania	R450 6x2 (NG) HL	Fagan & Whalley	Burnley
PN71 EGJ	Scania	P280 4W HL Curtainside	Fagan & Whalley	Burnley
PN71 EGK	Scania	L280 4w HL Curtainside	Fagan & Whalley	Burnley
MF22 LNH	Daf	FTG 480 6x2 XF	Fagan & Whalley	Burnley
MF22 LNJ	Daf	FTG 480 6x2 XF	Fagan & Whalley	Burnley
MF22 LNK	Daf	FTG 480 6x2 XF	Fagan & Whalley	Burnley
MF22 LNN	Daf	FTG 480 6x2 XF	Fagan & Whalley	Burnley
MF22 LNO	Daf	FTG 480 6x2 XF	Fagan & Whalley	Coventry
MW22 WEO	Daf	FALF 260 4w Curtainside	Fagan & Whalley	Burnley
PN22 EFA	Scania	450S 6x2 (NG) HL	Fagan & Whalley	Burnley
PN22 EFC	Scania	P450 6x2 (NG) HL	Fagan & Whalley	Burnley
PN22 EFD	Scania	P450 6x2 (NG) HL	Fagan & Whalley	Burnley
CA72 JVR	Daf	FTG 480 6x2 XG	Alan R Jones	Newport
CA72 JVT	Daf	FTG 480 6x2 XG	Alan R Jones	Newport
MF72 OOD	Daf	FALF 260 4w Curtainside	Fagan & Whalley	Burnley
MF72 OOG	Daf	FTG 480 6x2 XF	Fagan & Whalley	Burnley
PJ72 DXB	Scania	460R 6x2 (NG) HL	Fagan & Whalley	Burnley
CA23 OXR	Daf	FALF 230 4w Curtainside	Alan R Jones	Newport
CE23 FNX	Daf	FTG 480 6x2 XG	Alan R Jones	Newport
CE23 FNW	Daf	FTG 480 6x2 XG	Alan R Jones	Newport
MX23 AYE	Scania	P450 6x2 (NG) HL	Fagan & Whalley	Burnley
MX23 AYF	Scania	P450 6x2 (NG) HL	Fagan & Whalley	Burnley
PN23 EKU	Scania	460R 6x2 (NG) HL	Fagan & Whalley	Burnley
PN23 EKV	Scania	460R 6x2 (NG) HL	Fagan & Whalley	Burnley
PN23 EKW	Scania	460R 6x2 (NG) HL	Fagan & Whalley	Burnley
PN23 EKX	Scania	460R 6x2 (NG) HL	Fagan & Whalley	Burnley
PN23 EKY	Scania	460R 6x2 (NG) HL	Fagan & Whalley	Burnley
PN23 ELJ	Scania	460R 6x2 (NG) HL	Fagan & Whalley	Burnley
PN23 ELO	Scania	450G 6x2 (NG) HL	Fagan & Whalley	Burnley
PN23 ELW	Scania	450G 6x2 (NG) HL	Fagan & Whalley	Burnley
PN73 DYX	Scania	460R 6x2 (NG) HL	Fagan & Whalley	Burnley
PN73 DYY	Scania	460R 6x2 (NG) HL	Fagan & Whalley	Burnley
PN73 DZA	Scania	460R 6x2 (NG) HL	Fagan & Whalley	Burnley

FlyByNite (Redditch & Europe)

Reg	Make	Reg	Make	Reg	Make	Reg	Make
10 BSP 9	Daf	181 D 52850	Daf	201 D 29636	Daf	JN15 FBN	Daf
11 BSP 9	Daf	181 D 53564	Daf	201 D 29645	Daf	AN65 FBN	Daf
14 BSP 9	Daf	181 D 53632	Daf	201 D 29651	Daf	BV65 HSG	Mercedes
16 BBV 6	Daf	181 D 53765	Daf	201 D 29652	Daf	CN65 RGY	Daf
17 BSP 9	Daf	181 D 53766	Daf	231 D 36828	Daf	AN16 FBN	Volvo
20 BSP 9	Daf	181 D 53936	Daf	231 D 37260	Daf	BN16 FBN	Volvo
23 BSP 9	Daf	181 D 54315	Daf	231 D 39399	Daf	CN16 FBN	Volvo
30 BST 4	Daf	181 D 54758	Daf	231 D 39654	Daf	DN16 FBN	Volvo
31 BST 4	Daf	181 D 55106	Daf	231 D 43511	Daf	EN16 FBN	Volvo
33 BST 4	Daf	181 D 55277	Volvo	231 D 43528	Daf	FN16 FBN	Volvo
86 BDB 5	Daf	181 D 55278	Volvo	55 24 EL	Volvo	HN16 FBN	Daf
88 BPJ 6	Daf	181 D 55307	Volvo	K155 FBN (19)	Daf	JN16 FBN	Daf
IF 13 RKF	Scania	181 D 55309	Volvo	P1 FBN (19)	Volvo	KN16 FBN	Daf
CJ 17 NED	Volvo	182 D 25712	Daf	S100 PBC	Daf	LN16 FBN	Daf
CJ 18 NED	Volvo	182 D 25947	Daf	S200 PBC	Daf	AN66 FBN	Daf
CJ 19 NED	Volvo	182 D 26030	Daf	S700 PBC	Daf	BN66 FBN	Daf
CJ 20 NED	Volvo	182 D 26253	Daf	S900 PBC	Daf	CN66 FBN	Daf
CJ 22 NED	Volvo	182 D 26259	Daf	T100 PBC	Daf	DN66 FBN	Daf
CJ 23 NED	Volvo	182 D 26260	Daf	T200 PBC	Daf	EN66 FBN	Daf
CJ 24 NED	Volvo	182 D 26261	Daf	T400 PBC	Daf	FN66 FBN	Daf
CJ 26 NED	Volvo	182 D 26766	Volvo	T500 PBC	Daf	GN66 FBN	Daf
CJ 28 NED	Volvo	182 D 26768	Volvo	T600 PBC	Daf	HN66 FBN	Daf
CJ 29 NED	Daf	191 D 49321	Volvo	T800 PBC	Daf	JN66 FBN	Daf
CJ 32 NED	Daf	191 D 49384	Daf	V100 PBC	Volvo	KN66 FBN	Volvo
CJ 36 NED	Daf	191 D 49461	Volvo	DC07 CYG	Volvo	PN66 FBN	Daf
CJ 37 NED	Daf	191 D 49521	Volvo	AN11 FBN	Daf	RN66 FBN	Daf
CJ 40 NED	Daf	191 D 49526	Volvo	DN11 FBN	Daf	AN17 FBN	Daf
CJ 46 NED	Daf	191 D 49527	Volvo	FN11 FBN	Daf	AX17 CHN	Daf
CJ 60 NED	Daf	191 D 49581	Volvo	BN12 FBN	Daf	BN17 EKR	Mercedes
CJ 93 NED	Daf	191 D 49587	Volvo	DN12 FBN	Daf	BN17 FBN	Daf
10 D 120305	Mercedes	191 D 49608	Volvo	EN12 FBN	Daf	CA17 FBN	Daf
12 D 64492	Daf	191 D 49697	Daf	FN12 FBN	Daf	CN17 FBN	Daf
131 D 28985	Mercedes	191 D 49894	Daf	NN12 FBN	Daf	DN17 FBN	Daf
151 D 55900	Daf	191 D 49895	Daf	SN12 FBN	Daf	EN17 FBN	Daf
151 D 55901	Daf	191 D 49896	Daf	TN12 FBN	Daf	FN17 FBN	Daf
151 D 55903	Daf	191 D 49897	Daf	VN12 FBN	Daf	AN67 FBN	Volvo
161 D 64242	Daf	191 D 49898	Daf	AN13 FBN	Daf	AN18 FBN	Volvo
161 D 64256	Daf	191 D 49899	Volvo	BN13 FBN	Daf	BN18 FBN	Volvo
162 D 33305	Daf	191 D 49900	Volvo	CN13 FBN	Daf	CN18 FBN	Volvo
162 D 33090	Daf	191 D 49980	Daf	DN13 FBN	Daf	DN18 FBN	Volvo
162 D 33102	Daf	191 D 49981	Daf	EN13 FBN	Daf	EN18 FBN	Volvo
162 D 33863	Daf	191 D 49982	Daf	GN13 FBN	Daf	FN18 FBN	Daf
162 D 33865	Daf	191 D 49984	Daf	HN13 FBN	Daf	HN18 FBN	Daf
162 D 33866	Daf	191 D 49985	Daf	JN13 FBN	Daf	JN18 FBN	Daf
162 D 33877	Daf	191 D 50031	Daf	KN13 FBN	Daf	KN18 FBN	Daf
162 D 33880	Daf	201 D 29193	Daf	LN13 FDN	Daf	LN18 FBN	Daf
162 D 33882	Daf	201 D 29224	Daf	RN13 FBN	Daf	NN18 FBN	Daf
162 D 33912	Daf	201 D 29225	Daf	AN63 FBN	Daf	PN18 FBN	Daf
162 D 33913	Daf	201 D 29285	Daf	BU14 ZWB	Daf	RN18 FBN	Daf
162 D 33922	Daf	201 D 29286	Daf	BG64 NWN	Mercedes	AN68 FBN	Volvo
162 D 35478	Daf	201 D 29356	Daf	DE64 HJY	Daf	BF68 FZL	Daf
162 D 35484	Volvo	201 D 29357	Volvo	AN15 FBN	Daf	BN68 FBN	Volvo
162 D 35488	Volvo	201 D 29482	Daf	BN15 FBN	Daf	CN68 FBN	Volvo
171 D 59184	Daf	201 D 29504	Volvo	CN15 FBN	Daf	DN68 FBN	Volvo
172 D 29672	Daf	201 D 29515	Volvo	DG15 AEJ	Daf	EN68 FBN	Volvo
172 D 29947	Daf	201 D 29516	Volvo	DN15 FBN	Daf	FN68 FBN	Volvo
172 D 29952	Daf	201 D 29581	Volvo	EN15 FBN	Daf	GN68 FBN	Daf
172 D 29967	Daf	201 D 29582	Volvo	FN15 FBN	Daf	HN68 FBN	Daf
172 D 29968	Daf	201 D 29632	Volvo	GN15 FBN	Daf	JN68 FBN	Daf
172 D 29969	Daf	201 D 29634	Daf	HN15 FBN	Daf	KN68 FBN	Daf

FlyByNite (Redditch & Europe)

Reg	Make	Reg	Make	Reg	Make	Reg	Make
LN68 FBN	Daf	XN19 FBN	Daf	BU22 ZTE	Daf	BV23 FKT	Daf
NN68 FBN	Daf	YN19 FBN	Daf	BU22 ZTN	Daf	BV23 FKU	Daf
PN68 FBN	Daf	BW69 LDD	Daf	BU22 ZVB	Daf	BV23 FKX	Daf
RN68 FBN	Daf	AH20 FBN	Daf	BU22 ZVC	Daf	BV23 FKY	Daf
SN68 FBN	Volvo	AL20 FBN	Daf	BU22 ZVE	Daf	BV23 FKZ	Daf
TN68 FBN	Volvo	BU20 OEH	Daf	BU22 ZVF	Daf	BV23 FLJ	Daf
UN68 FBN	Volvo	BY20 FBN	Daf	BU22 ZVG	Daf	BV23 FLL	Daf
VN68 FBN	Volvo	DJ20 FBN	Daf	BU22 ZVJ	Daf	BV23 FLZ	Daf
AN19 FBN	Volvo	ED20 FBN	Daf	BU22 ZVK	Daf	BP73 USB	Daf
BN19 FBN	Volvo	EH20 FBN	Daf	BT72 XWF	Daf	BP73 USC	Daf
CN19 FBN	Volvo	FN20 FBN	Volvo	BT72 XWG	Daf	BP73 USD	Daf
DN19 FBN	Volvo	GB20 FBN	Volvo	BW72 XTA	Daf	BP73 USE	Daf
EN19 FBN	Daf	GN20 FBN	Volvo	BW72 XTB	Daf	BP73 USF	Daf
FN19 FBN	Daf	HN20 FBN	Volvo	BW72 XTC	Daf	BP73 USG	Daf
GN19 FBN	Daf	JN20 FBN	Volvo	BW72 XTD	Daf	BP73 USJ	Daf
HN19 FBN	Daf	KN20 FBN	Volvo	BW72 XTE	Daf	BP73 USL	Daf
JN19 FBN	Daf	LN20 FBN	Daf	BW72 XTH	Daf	BP73 USM	Daf
KN19 FBN	Volvo	MG20 FBN	Daf	BD23 UTK	Daf	BP73 USO	Daf
LN19 FBN	Volvo	MY20 FBN	Volvo	BD23 UUE	Daf	BP73 USS	Daf
NN19 FBN	Volvo	NN20 FBN	Volvo	BD23 UUF	Daf	BP73 USU	Daf
PN19 FBN	Volvo	DA70 FVS	Man	BD23 UUG	Daf	BP73 USV	Daf
RN19 FBN	Volvo	DA70 FVW	Man	BV23 FGK	Daf	BP73 USW	Daf
SN19 FBN	Daf	DA70 FVY	Man	BV23 FGO	Daf	BP73 USX	Daf
TN19 FBN	Daf	DA70 FVZ	Man	BV23 FHU	Daf	BP73 USY	Daf
UN19 FBN	Daf	DA70 FWL	Man	BV23 FHW	Daf	BP73 USZ	Daf
VN19 FBN	Daf	BU22 ZTC	Daf	BV23 FKS	Daf	BP73 UTA	Daf
WN19 FBN	Daf						

Gregory Group

Reg	Make	Livery	Reg	Make	Livery
Y 366 KBA	Daf	Yellow	WX 63 FUV	Scania	Kay Transport (2)
RX 07 CWN	Daf	Green	WX 63 FVA	Scania	Gregory (White)
AE 10 HPX	Daf	Yellow	WX 63 FVB	Scania	Gregory (White)
MX 60 CVM	Daf	White	WX 63 FVC	Scania	Gregory (White)
NX 11 CXK	Daf	Greggs (Gregory)	WX 63 FVD	Scania	Gregory (White)
WR 62 GHH	Scania	Gregory	WX 63 FVE	Scania	Gregory (White)
WR 62 GHJ	Scania	Gregory	WX 63 FVF	Scania	Gregory (White)
WR 62 GHK	Scania	Gregory	WX 63 FVG	Scania	Gregory (White)
WA 13 BJY	Volvo	Red	WX 63 FVH	Scania	Gregory (White)
WP 13 TXK	Scania	Gregory	WX 63 FVJ	Scania	Gregory (White)
WP 13 TXL	Scania	Gregory	WX 63 FWR	Scania	Gregory Environmental
WP 13 TXM	Scania	Gregory	WX 63 FWW	Scania	Gregory
WP 13 TXS	Scania	Gregory	WX 63 FWY	Scania	Gregory
WP 13 TXU	Scania	Gregory	WX 63 FXB	Scania	Kay Transport (2)
WP 13 TXV	Scania	Gregory	WX 63 FXC	Scania	Kay Transport (2)
WP 13 TXW	Scania	Gregory	HK 14 DLN	Daf	White
WP 13 TXX	Scania	Gregory	WA 14 HLR	Volvo	Kay Transport (2)
WV 13 GFK	Scania	Gregory (White)	WX 14 VTZ	Scania	Gregory
WV 13 GFO	Scania	Gregory (White)	DG64 JYL	Man	White
WV 13 GFU	Scania	Gregory (White)	DG64 JYN	Man	White
WV 13 GYT	Scania	Gregory (White)	DG64 JYS	Man	White
WR 63 VBU	Scania	Gregory	DG64 JYT	Man	White
WR 63 VBX	Scania	Gregory	VA 64 ONJ	Daf	White
WR 63 VCL	Scania	Gregory (White)	WA 64 CGU	Volvo	Kay Transport (2)
WV 63 FWT	Scania	Gregory	WA 64 HZG	Volvo	Palletline (Gregory)
WV 63 FWU	Scania	Palletline (Gregory)	WJ 64 JWU	Daf	Gregory Environmental
WV 63 FWX	Scania	Palletline (Gregory)	WR 64 VRC	Scania	Palletline (Gregory)
WV 63 FWY	Scania	Gregory	WR 64 VRD	Scania	Palletline (Gregory)
WV 63 FWZ	Scania	Palletline (Gregory)	WR 64 VRE	Scania	Gregory
WX 63 FSJ	Scania	Gregory	WR 64 VRF	Scania	Gregory

Reg	Make	Operator	Reg	Make	Operator
WR 64 VRG	Scania	Gregory	SV 66 KBN	Daf	ARR Craib
WR 64 VRJ	Scania	Gregory	SV 66 KBY	Daf	Boxshop (ARR Craib)
WU 64 BJF	Scania	Gregory (White)	SV 66 KBZ	Daf	Boxshop (ARR Craib)
WU 64 BJJ	Scania	Gregory	SV 66 LLC	Man	White
DG 15 VVE	Man	White	WG 66 AAF	Volvo	Gregory
NK 15 ZNL	Scania	Greggs (Gregory)	WJ 66 DXA	Volvo	Gregory
WJ 15 EHW	Daf	Gregory (Red)	WJ 66 DXB	Volvo	Gregory
WJ 15 EJA	Daf	Gregory (Red)	WJ 66 DXC	Volvo	Gregory
WJ 15 EJC	Daf	Gregory (Red)	WJ 66 DXD	Volvo	Gregory
WJ 15 EJD	Daf	Gregory (Red)	WJ 66 DXE	Volvo	Gregory
WJ 15 EJE	Daf	Gregory (Red)	WJ 66 DXF	Volvo	Gregory
WJ 15 EJF	Daf	Gregory (Red)	WJ 66 NGX	Daf	Palletline (Gregory)
WJ 15 EJK	Daf	Gregory (Red)	WJ 66 NGY	Daf	Palletline (Gregory)
WJ 15 EJL	Daf	Gregory (Red)	WM 66 BJK	Scania	Gregory
WJ 15 EJN	Daf	Gregory (Red)	WM 66 BJO	Scania	Gregory
WJ 15 EJX	Daf	Gregory (Red)	WM 66 BJV	Scania	Gregory
WJ 15 EJY	Daf	Gregory (Red)	WM 66 BJX	Scania	Gregory
WJ 15 EJZ	Daf	Gregory (Red)	WP 66 OTA	Scania	Gregory
WP 15 ERY	Scania	Gregory	WP 66 OTD	Scania	Gregory
WP 15 ERZ	Scania	Gregory	WP 66 OTF	Scania	Gregory
WR 15 WXG	Scania	Gregory	WP 66 OTK	Scania	Gregory
WU 15 UBY	Scania	Gregory	WU 66 ATN	Scania	Gregory (White)
WU 15 UBZ	Scania	Gregory	WU 66 AZG	Scania	Gregory
WU 15 UDH	Scania	Kay Transport (2)	WU 66 AZJ	Scania	Gregory
WU 15 UDJ	Scania	Kay Transport (2)	WU 66 AZL	Scania	Gregory
SV 65 HKC	Daf	Palletline (ARR Craib)	WU 66 AZN	Scania	Gregory
WF 65 EZN	Daf	Gregory (White)	WU 66 AZO	Scania	Palletline (Gregory)
WF 65 EZO	Daf	Gregory (White)	WU 66 AZR	Scania	Palletline (Gregory)
WF 65 EZR	Daf	Gregory	FM 17 HFS	Daf	Antalis (Gregory)
WF 65 EZS	Daf	Gregory (White)	FM 17 HFT	Daf	Antalis (Gregory)
WR 65 WVB	Scania	Gregory	FM 17 HFU	Daf	Antalis (Gregory)
WR 65 WVC	Scania	Gregory	FM 17 HFX	Daf	Antalis (Gregory)
WR 65 WVD	Scania	Gregory	FM 17 HFY	Daf	Antalis (Gregory)
WR 65 WVE	Scania	Gregory	FM 17 HGF	Daf	Antalis (Gregory)
WR 65 WVG	Scania	Gregory	FM 17 HGG	Daf	Antalis (Gregory)
WR 65 WVK	Scania	Gregory	FM 17 HHA	Daf	Antalis (Gregory)
WR 65 WVM	Scania	Gregory	FP 17 OAL	Daf	White
WU 65 NND	Scania	Gregory (White)	FP 17 OAY	Daf	Antalis (Gregory)
WU 65 NNF	Scania	Gregory	FP 17 OBA	Daf	Antalis (Gregory)
WA 16 FWG	Daf	Coulthard (2)	FP 17 OBC	Daf	Antalis (Gregory)
WA 16 FWY	Daf	Gregory	FP 17 YJJ	Daf	Antalis (Gregory)
WP 16 TPU	Scania	Gregory	FP 17 YJL	Daf	Antalis (Gregory)
WP 16 TPX	Scania	Gregory	FP 17 YJN	Daf	Antalis (Gregory)
WP 16 TVT	Scania	Gregory (White)	FP 17 YJU	Daf	Antalis (Gregory)
WP 16 TVV	Scania	Gregory (White)	SV 17 HGF	Daf	Boxshop (ARR Craib)
WV 16 VDG	Scania	Gregory	SV 17 HGJ	Daf	Walkers Shortbread
WV 16 VDR	Scania	Gregory	WJ 17 WNH	Volvo	Gregory
WX 16 YRE	Scania	Gregory	WJ 17 WNL	Volvo	Gregory
WX 16 YRF	Scania	Gregory	WX 17 WUD	Scania	Gregory
WX 16 YRG	Scania	Gregory	WX 17 WVL	Scania	Gregory
WX 16 YRV	Scania	Gregory	WX 17 WVM	Scania	Gregory
WX 16 YRW	Scania	Gregory	WX 17 WVO	Scania	Gregory
WX 16 YRZ	Scania	Gregory	WX 17 WXZ	Scania	Gregory
WX 16 YSD	Scania	Gregory	WX 17 WZY	Scania	Gregory (White)
WX 16 YSE	Scania	Gregory	WX 17 XAA	Scania	Gregory (White)
WX 16 YSG	Scania	Greggs	WX 17 XAB	Scania	Gregory (White)
WX 16 YSH	Scania	Gregory	WX 17 XAC	Scania	Gregory (White)
WX 16 YSJ	Scania	Gregory	WX 17 XAD	Scania	Gregory (White)
WX 16 YSK	Scania	Gregory	WX 17 XAE	Scania	Gregory (White)
WX 16 YTM	Scania	Gregory	FN 67 UTA	Daf	White
WX 16 YUB	Scania	Kay Transport (2)	FN 67 UTE	Daf	White

Reg	Make	Livery	Reg	Make	Livery
FN 67 UTZ	Daf	White	WU 18 BXE	Scania	Gregory
FN 67 UUJ	Daf	White	WU 18 BXF	Scania	Gregory
FN 67 UUK	Daf	White	WU 18 BXH	Scania	Gregory
FN 67 UVB	Daf	White	WU 18 BXJ	Scania	Gregory
SV 67 HHE	Daf	Augean	WU 18 BXK	Scania	Gregory
SV 67 HHF	Daf	Augean	WU 18 BXX	Scania	Gregory
SV 67 HJK	Daf	Kuehne + Nagel	WU 18 BYL	Scania	Arla (Gregory)
SV 67 JLX	Mercedes	John Lawrie (2)	WU 18 BYM	Scania	Arla (Gregory)
WA 67 UKJ	Volvo	Gregory	WU 18 BYN	Scania	Gregory (White)
WP 67 LXU	Scania	Gregory (White)	WU 18 BYO	Scania	Gregory (White)
WP 67 LYS	Scania	Gregory	WU 18 BYV	Scania	Arla (Gregory)
WP 67 LYT	Scania	Gregory	WU 18 BZA	Scania	Gregory (White)
WP 67 LYU	Scania	Gregory	WU 18 CFE	Scania	Gregory
WP 67 LYV	Scania	Gregory	WU 18 CFF	Scania	Gregory
WP 67 LYX	Scania	Gregory	WU 18 CHJ	Scania	The Range
WP 67 LYY	Scania	Gregory	WU 18 CHK	Scania	The Range
WP 67 LYZ	Scania	Gregory	WU 18 CKA	Scania	Gregory
WR 67 WHW	Scania	Gregory	WU 18 CKC	Scania	Gregory
WR 67 WJC	Scania	Gregory	WU 18 CKD	Scania	Gregory
WU 67 KFP	Scania	Gregory	WU 18 CKE	Scania	Gregory
WU 67 KJJ	Scania	Arla (Gregory)	WU 18 CKF	Scania	Gregory
WU 67 KJK	Scania	Arla (Gregory)	WU 18 CKG	Scania	Gregory
WU 67 KJO	Scania	Arla (Gregory)	WU 18 CKJ	Scania	Gregory
WU 67 KUG	Scania	Arla (Gregory)	WU 18 CKK	Scania	Gregory
WU 67 KUH	Scania	Arla (Gregory)	WU 18 CKL	Scania	Gregory
WU 67 KUJ	Scania	Gregory	DG 68 YYM	Man	White
WU 67 KUK	Scania	Gregory	FN 68 HUY	Daf	Gregory (White)
WU 67 KUN	Scania	Gregory	GF 68 VRV	Volvo	Gregory
WU 67 KUO	Scania	Gregory	GF 68 VRW	Volvo	Gregory
WU 67 KUP	Scania	Gregory	GJ 68 FDP	Volvo	Gregory
WU 67 KUT	Scania	Gregory	GJ 68 FDU	Volvo	Gregory
WV 67 VXW	Scania	Gregory	GJ 68 FDV	Volvo	Gregory
WV 67 VXX	Scania	Gregory	GN 68 YRV	Volvo	Coulthard (2)
WV 67 VXZ	Scania	Gregory	KU 68 GNV	Scania	Gregory (White)
YD 67 VLP	Daf	White	KU 68 GRX	Scania	Gregory (White)
YD 67 VLS	Daf	White	KU 68 GUD	Scania	Gregory (White)
FL 18 CKK	Daf	Gregory (White)	KU 68 GUE	Scania	Gregory (Pollock)
GC 18 DYO	Volvo	Coulthard (2)	KU 68 GUH	Scania	Gregory (White)
GC 18 DYS	Volvo	Coulthard (2)	KU 68 GUK	Scania	Gregory (White)
KR 18 XNM	Daf	Gregory (White)	KU 68 GWP	Scania	Gregory (Pollock)
KX 18 WCN	Scania	Gregory (White)	KU 68 GWW	Scania	Gregory (White)
KX 18 WCZ	Scania	Gregory (White)	KU 68 GXS	Scania	Gregory (White)
KX 18 WDK	Scania	Gregory (White)	KU 68 GXT	Scania	Gregory (White)
SJ 18 JHO	Mercedes	ARR Craib (White/2)	KU 68 GYE	Scania	Gregory (White)
SJ 18 JHU	Mercedes	ARR Craib (White/2)	KU 68 GYG	Scania	Gregory (Pollock)
SJ 18 JHV	Mercedes	ARR Craib (White/2)	KU 68 GYK	Scania	Gregory (White)
SJ 18 JHX	Mercedes	ARR Craib (White/2)	PF 68 UFS	Daf	Gregory (White)
SJ 18 JHY	Mercedes	ARR Craib (White/2)	PJ 68 UGL	Daf	Gregory (White)
SJ 18 JHZ	Mercedes	ARR Craib (White/2)	PJ 68 UGP	Daf	Gregory (White)
SJ 68 JJE	Mercedes	Palletline (ARR Craib)	PJ 68 UGT	Daf	Gregory (White)
WA 18 SVZ	Volvo	Gregory	PO 68 YBT	Scania	Gregory (Pollock)
WJ 18 KBK	Volvo	Gregory	PO 68 YDE	Scania	Gregory (ARR Craib)
WJ 18 KBN	Volvo	Gregory	PO 68 YGC	Scania	Gregory (ARR Craib)
WJ 18 KBO	Volvo	Gregory	PO 68 YGK	Scania	Gregory (ARR Craib)
WJ 18 KBP	Volvo	Gregory	PO 68 YGM	Scania	Gregory (ARR Craib)
WJ 18 KBU	Volvo	Gregory	PO 68 YGN	Scania	Gregory (Pollock)
WJ 18 KBV	Volvo	Gregory	PO 68 YGT	Scania	Gregory (White)
WP 18 KHO	Scania	Gregory	PO 68 YHB	Scania	Gregory (ARR Craib)
WP 18 KHV	Scania	Gregory	PO 68 YHG	Scania	Gregory (ARR Craib)
WU 18 BXA	Scania	Gregory	PO 68 YHP	Scania	Gregory (ARR Craib)
WU 18 BXD	Scania	Gregory	PO 68 YHV	Scania	Gregory (Pollock)

Reg	Make	Operator	Reg	Make	Operator
PO 68 YHY	Scania	Gregory (ARR Craib)	WU 68 XRS	Scania	Gregory
PO 68 YJP	Scania	Gregory (ARR Craib)	WU 68 XRT	Scania	The Range
PO 68 YJR	Scania	Gregory (ARR Craib)	WU 68 XSC	Scania	Gregory (White)
PO 68 YKN	Scania	Gregory (ARR Craib)	WU 68 XSD	Scania	Gregory (White)
PO 68 YKR	Scania	Gregory (ARR Craib)	WU 68 XSE	Scania	Gregory (White)
PO 68 YNS	Scania	Gregory (ARR Craib)	WU 68 XSF	Scania	Gregory (White)
PO 68 YNU	Scania	Gregory (ARR Craib)	WU 68 XSH	Scania	Gregory (White)
PO 68 YOE	Scania	Gregory (ARR Craib)	WU 68 XSJ	Scania	Gregory
PO 68 YOH	Scania	Gregory (ARR Craib)	WU 68 XTB	Scania	Arla (Gregory)
PO 68 YPC	Scania	Gregory (ARR Craib)	WU 68 XXA	Scania	Gregory (White)
PO 68 YPN	Scania	Gregory (Pollock)	WU 68 XXB	Scania	Gregory (White)
PO 68 YPP	Scania	Gregory (Pollock)	WU 68 XXC	Scania	Gregory (White)
PO 68 YPV	Scania	Gregory (Pollock)	WU 68 XXD	Scania	Gregory (White)
PO 68 YPX	Scania	Gregory (ARR Craib)	WU 68 XXE	Scania	Gregory (White)
PO 68 YPZ	Scania	Gregory (Pollock)	WU 68 XXF	Scania	Gregory (White)
PO 68 YRE	Scania	Gregory (ARR Craib)	WU 68 XXG	Scania	Gregory (White)
PO 68 YRP	Scania	Gregory (Pollock)	KY 19 FSL	Scania	Gregory (White)
RX 68 YHM	Mitsubishi	Gregory (White)	KY 19 FTU	Scania	Gregory (White)
SJ 68 OUM	Man	Coulthard (2)	KY 19 FVH	Scania	Gregory (ARR Craib)
WA 68 XUO	Volvo	Coulthard (2)	KY 19 FWL	Scania	Gregory (White)
WJ 68 GVW	Daf	Gregory	KY 19 FXB	Scania	Gregory (ARR Craib)
WJ 68 GVX	Daf	Gregory	KY 19 FXG	Scania	Gregory (ARR Craib)
WJ 68 GVY	Daf	Gregory	KY 19 FXH	Scania	Gregory (ARR Craib)
WJ 68 GVZ	Daf	Gregory	KY 19 FXM	Scania	Gregory (ARR Craib)
WJ 68 GWA	Daf	Gregory	KY 19 FXV	Scania	Gregory (ARR Craib)
WJ 68 GWC	Daf	Gregory	KY 19 FXW	Scania	Gregory (ARR Craib)
WJ 68 GWD	Daf	Gregory	KY 19 FXZ	Scania	Gregory (White)
WJ 68 GWE	Daf	Gregory	KY 19 FYR	Scania	Gregory (White)
WJ 68 GWF	Daf	Gregory	KY 19 FYU	Scania	Gregory (White)
WJ 68 GWG	Daf	Gregory	KY 19 FZM	Scania	Gregory (ARR Craib)
WJ 68 GWK	Daf	Gregory	KY 19 FZO	Scania	Gregory (White)
WJ 68 GWP	Daf	Gregory	KY 19 FZT	Scania	Gregory (White)
WJ 68 GWU	Daf	Gregory	KY 19 FZW	Scania	Gregory (White)
WJ 68 GWV	Daf	Gregory	KY 19 GEJ	Scania	Gregory (White)
WJ 68 GWX	Daf	Gregory	KY 19 GVV	Scania	Gregory (White)
WJ 68 GWZ	Daf	Gregory	MT19 ZJX	Man	Gregory (White)
WJ 68 GXA	Daf	Gregory	SM 19 BXU	Scania	Gregory (Red)
WJ 68 GXB	Daf	Gregory	SM 19 BXV	Scania	Gregory (Red)
WJ 68 GXC	Daf	Gregory	SM 19 BXW	Scania	HH Distribution
WJ 68 GXD	Daf	Gregory	SM 19 BXX	Scania	HH Distribution
WJ 68 GXE	Daf	Gregory	SM 19 BXY	Scania	HH Distribution
WJ 68 GXF	Daf	Gregory	SM 19 BXZ	Scania	HH Distribution
WJ 68 GXG	Daf	Gregory	SM 19 BYA	Scania	Gregory (Red)
WJ 68 GXH	Daf	Gregory	SM 19 BYB	Scania	Gregory (Red)
WJ 68 GXK	Daf	Gregory	SV 19 LZD	Daf	Augean
WJ 68 GXL	Daf	Gregory	WL 19 EKK	Man	Gregory
WJ 68 GXM	Daf	Gregory	WL 19 EKM	Man	Gregory
WJ 68 GXN	Daf	Gregory	WN 19 HWT	Scania	Gregory (White)
WJ 68 GXO	Daf	Gregory	WN 19 VFT	Scania	Gregory
WJ 68 GXP	Daf	Gregory	WN 19 VFU	Scania	Gregory
WJ 68 GXR	Daf	Gregory	WN 19 VFV	Scania	Gregory
WJ 68 GXS	Daf	Gregory	WN 19 VFW	Scania	Gregory
WJ 68 GXT	Daf	Gregory	WN 19 VFX	Scania	Gregory
WJ 68 GXU	Daf	Gregory	WN 19 VGK	Scania	Gregory (White)
WJ 68 GXV	Daf	Gregory	WN 19 VGL	Scania	Gregory (White)
WJ 68 GXW	Daf	Gregory	WN 19 VGM	Scania	Gregory (White)
WJ 68 GXX	Daf	Gregory	WN 19 VGO	Scania	Gregory (White)
WJ 68 GXY	Daf	Gregory	WN 19 VGP	Scania	Gregory (White)
WJ 68 GXZ	Daf	Gregory	WN 19 VGR	Scania	Gregory (White)
WM 68 HMV	Scania	Gregory	WN 19 VGT	Scania	Gregory (White)
WM 68 HNG	Scania	Gregory	WN 19 VGU	Scania	Gregory (White)

Reg	Make	Operator	Reg	Make	Operator
WN 19 VGV	Scania	Gregory (White)	WU 69 AUK	Scania	Gregory
WN 19 VGY	Scania	Gregory (White)	WU 69 AUL	Scania	Gregory
WN 19 VGZ	Scania	Gregory (White)	WU 69 AUM	Scania	Gregory
WN 19 VHA	Scania	Gregory	WU 69 AWA	Scania	Gregory
WN 19 VHB	Scania	Gregory	WU 69 AWC	Scania	Gregory
WN 19 VHC	Scania	Gregory	WU 69 AWF	Scania	Gregory
WN 19 VHD	Scania	Gregory	WU 69 AWG	Scania	Gregory
WU 19 KSE	Scania	Gregory	WU 69 AWH	Scania	Gregory
WU 19 KSF	Scania	Gregory	WU 69 AWJ	Scania	Gregory
WU 19 KSJ	Scania	Gregory	WU 69 AWM	Scania	Gregory
WU 19 KSK	Scania	Gregory	WU 69 AWO	Scania	Gregory
WU 19 KUB	Scania	Gregory	WU 69 AWP	Scania	Gregory
WU 19 KUC	Scania	Gregory	WU 69 AWR	Scania	Gregory
MV 69 LYZ	Man	Gregory (White)	HY 20 BLF	Daf	The Range
MV 69 LZP	Man	Gregory (White)	MV20 UHE	Man	Gregory (White)
MV 69 LZS	Man	Gregory (White)	MV20 UHG	Man	Gregory (White)
MV 69 LZW	Man	Gregory (White)	MV20 UHM	Man	Gregory (White)
MV 69 MDE	Man	Gregory (White)	MV20 UHR	Man	Gregory (White)
MV 69 MDX	Man	Gregory (White)	MV20 UHS	Man	Gregory (White)
MV 69 MDY	Man	Gregory (White)	MV20 UHW	Man	Gregory (White)
SN 69 XNH	Scania	HH Distribution	MV20 UJB	Man	Gregory (White)
SV 69 AAU	Scania	Coulthard (2)	MV20 UJN	Man	Gregory (White)
SV 69 AAY	Scania	Coulthard (2)	MV20 UJO	Man	Gregory (White)
SV 69 AAZ	Scania	Coulthard (2)	MV20 UJU	Man	Gregory (White)
SV 69 ABO	Scania	ARR Craib	MV20 UJY	Man	Gregory (White)
SV 69 ABU	Scania	ARR Craib	SF 20 CZA	Scania	Coulthard (2)
SV 69 ABX	Scania	ARR Craib	SF 20 CZB	Scania	Coulthard (2)
SV 69 ABZ	Scania	ARR Craib	SF 20 CZC	Scania	Coulthard (2)
SV 69 ACJ	Scania	Coulthard (2)	SF 20 CZD	Scania	Coulthard (2)
SV 69 ACO	Scania	Coulthard (2)	SF 20 CZE	Scania	Coulthard (2)
WJ 69 AVT	Daf	The Range	SV 20 AYD	Scania	ARR Craib
WJ 69 AVV	Daf	The Range	SV 20 AYE	Scania	ARR Craib
WJ 69 AVW	Daf	The Range	SV 20 AYF	Scania	ARR Craib
WJ 69 AVX	Daf	The Range	SV 20 AYG	Scania	ARR Craib
WM 69 DWA	Scania	Gregory (White)	SV 20 MFJ	Daf	Augean
WM 69 DWC	Scania	Gregory (White)	SV 20 MFK	Daf	Augean
WM 69 DWD	Scania	Gregory (White)	WU 20 BTV	Scania	Gregory
WM 69 DWF	Scania	Gregory (White)	WU 20 BTX	Scania	Gregory
WM 69 DWG	Scania	Gregory (White)	WU 20 BTY	Scania	Gregory
WM 69 DWJ	Scania	Gregory (White)	WU 20 BTZ	Scania	Gregory
WM 69 DWK	Scania	Gregory (White)	WU 20 BVC	Scania	Gregory (White)
WM 69 DWL	Scania	Gregory (White)	WU 20 BVP	Scania	Gregory (White)
WN 69 CTE	Scania	Gregory (White)	WU 20 BVS	Scania	Gregory (White)
WN 69 CTF	Scania	Gregory (White)	WU 20 BWA	Scania	Gregory
WN 69 CTK	Scania	Gregory (White)	WU 20 BWB	Scania	Gregory
WN 69 CTO	Scania	Gregory (White)	WU 20 BWC	Scania	Gregory
WN 69 CTU	Scania	Gregory (White)	WU 20 BWD	Scania	Gregory
WN 69 CTV	Scania	Gregory (White)	WU 20 BWE	Scania	Gregory
WN 69 ZSE	Scania	Gregory (White)	WU 20 BWF	Scania	Crediton Dairy
WN 69 ZSF	Scania	Gregory (White)	WU 20 BWG	Scania	Crediton Dairy
WN 69 ZTD	Scania	Gregory	WU 20 BWH	Scania	Gregory (White)
WN 69 ZTE	Scania	Gregory	WU 20 BWJ	Scania	Gregory (White)
WN 69 ZTF	Scania	Gregory	WU 20 BWK	Scania	Gregory (White)
WN 69 ZTJ	Scania	Gregory (White)	WU 20 BWL	Scania	Gregory (White)
WU 69 ASO	Scania	Gregory	WU 20 BWM	Scania	Gregory (White)
WU 69 ASV	Scania	Gregory	WU 20 BWX	Scania	Gregory (White)
WU 69 ASX	Scania	Gregory	WU 20 BWY	Scania	Gregory (White)
WU 69 ASZ	Scania	Gregory	WU 20 BXA	Scania	Gregory (White)
WU 69 AUF	Scania	Gregory (White)	WU 20 BXB	Scania	Gregory (White)
WU 69 AUH	Scania	Greggs (Gregory)	HY 70 BHK	Daf	Gregory
WU 69 AUJ	Scania	Gregory	HY 70 BHL	Daf	Gregory

Gregory Group (cont)

HY 70 BHN	Daf	Gregory		SN 70 XXY	Daf	Pollock (White)
HY 70 BHO	Daf	Gregory		SV 70 NGE	Man	ARR Craib
HY 70 BHP	Daf	Gregory		SV 70 NGF	Man	ARR Craib
HY 70 BHU	Daf	Gregory		SV 70 NGG	Man	ARR Craib
HY 70 BHV	Daf	Gregory		SV 70 NGJ	Man	ARR Craib
HY 70 BWH	Daf	Gregory		SV 70 NGO	Man	ARR Craib
HY 70 BWJ	Daf	Gregory		SV 70 NGU	Man	ARR Craib
HY 70 BWK	Daf	Gregory		SV 70 NGX	Man	ARR Craib
HY 70 BWL	Daf	Gregory		SV 70 NGY	Man	ARR Craib
HY 70 BWM	Daf	Gregory		SV 70 NGZ	Man	ARR Craib
HY 70 BWN	Daf	Gregory		SV 70 NHK	Man	ARR Craib
HY 70 BWO	Daf	Gregory		SV 70 NZA	Scania	ARR Craib
HY 70 BWP	Daf	Gregory		SV 70 NZB	Scania	ARR Craib
HY 70 BWU	Daf	Gregory		SV 70 NZC	Scania	ARR Craib
HY 70 BWV	Daf	Gregory		SV 70 NZD	Scania	ARR Craib
HY 70 BWW	Daf	Gregory		SV 70 NZE	Scania	ARR Craib
HY 70 BWX	Daf	Gregory		SV 70 NZF	Scania	ARR Craib
HY 70 BWZ	Daf	Gregory		SV 70 NZG	Scania	ARR Craib
HY 70 BXA	Daf	Gregory		SV 70 NZH	Scania	ARR Craib
HY 70 BXB	Daf	Gregory		WK 70 KXB	Man	Gregory
HY 70 BXC	Daf	Gregory		WK 70 KXC	Man	Gregory
HY 70 BXD	Daf	Gregory		WK 70 KXD	Man	Gregory
HY 70 BXE	Daf	Gregory		WK 70 KXE	Man	Thatchers (Gregory)
HY 70 BXZ	Daf	The Range		WK 70 KXF	Man	Thatchers (Gregory)
HY 70 BYA	Daf	The Range		WK 70 KXG	Man	Gregory
HY 70 BYB	Daf	The Range		WK 70 KXH	Man	Gregory
HY 70 BYC	Daf	The Range		WK 70 KXJ	Man	Gregory
HY 70 BYD	Daf	The Range		WK 70 KXL	Man	Gregory
HY 70 BYF	Daf	The Range		WK 70 KXM	Man	Gregory
HY 70 BYG	Daf	The Range		WK 70 KXN	Man	Gregory
HY 70 BYH	Daf	The Range		WK 70 KXO	Man	Gregory
HY 70 BYJ	Daf	The Range		WU 70 DJK	Scania	Arla (Gregory)
HY 70 BYK	Daf	The Range		WU 70 DJO	Scania	Arla (Gregory)
HY 70 BYL	Daf	The Range		WU 70 DJV	Scania	Arla (Gregory)
HY 70 BYM	Daf	The Range		WU 70 DJX	Scania	Arla (Gregory)
HY 70 BYN	Daf	The Range		WU 70 DJY	Scania	Arla (Gregory)
HY 70 BYO	Daf	The Range		WU 70 DJZ	Scania	Gregory
HY 70 BYP	Daf	The Range		WU 70 DKA	Scania	Gregory
KM70 YBH	Mitsubishi	Gregory (White)		WU 70 DKD	Scania	Gregory
KU 70 XWN	Volvo	Gregory		WU 70 DKE	Scania	Gregory
KU 70 XWO	Volvo	Gregory		WU 70 DKF	Scania	Gregory
KU 70 XWP	Volvo	Gregory		WU 70 DKJ	Scania	Gregory
KU 70 XWR	Volvo	Gregory		WU 70 DKK	Scania	Gregory
KU 70 XWS	Volvo	Gregory		WU 70 DKL	Scania	Gregory
KU 70 XWT	Volvo	Gregory		WU 70 DLE	Scania	Gregory
KU 70 XWV	Volvo	Gregory		WU 70 DPE	Scania	Gregory
KU 70 XXA	Volvo	Gregory		WU 70 DPF	Scania	Gregory
KU 70 XXB	Volvo	Gregory		WU 70 DPK	Scania	Gregory
KU 70 XXC	Volvo	Gregory		WU 70 DPN	Scania	Gregory
KU 70 XXD	Volvo	Gregory		WU 70 DPO	Scania	Gregory
KU 70 XXE	Volvo	Gregory		WU 70 DTF	Scania	Gregory
KU 70 XXF	Volvo	Gregory		WU 70 DTK	Scania	Gregory
KU 70 XYT	Volvo	The Range		WU 70 DTN	Scania	Gregory
KU 70 XYV	Volvo	The Range		WU 70 DTO	Scania	Gregory
KU 70 XYW	Volvo	The Range		WU 70 DTV	Scania	Gregory
KU 70 XYX	Volvo	The Range		WU 70 DTX	Scania	Gregory
KU 70 XYZ	Volvo	Gregory		WU 70 DTY	Scania	Gregory
KU 70 XZA	Volvo	Gregory		WU 70 DTZ	Scania	Gregory
KU 70 XZB	Volvo	Gregory		WU 70 DUH	Scania	Gregory
MV 70 XEW	Man	Gregory (White)		WU 70 DUJ	Scania	Gregory
NV70 EEA	Iveco	White		WU 70 DUV	Scania	Gregory

Reg	Make	Operator		Reg	Make	Operator
WU 70 DUY	Scania	Gregory		SN 71 ZJO	Scania	Coulthard (2)
FE 21 HJX	IVECO	Gregory (White)		SN 71 ZJU	Scania	Coulthard (2)
HY 21 FZH	Daf	The Range		SN 71 ZJV	Scania	Coulthard (2)
HY 21 FZJ	Daf	The Range		SN 71 ZJX	Scania	Coulthard (2)
HY 21 FZK	Daf	The Range		SN 71 ZJY	Scania	Coulthard (2)
HY 21 FZL	Daf	Gregory (White)		WA 71 XTU	Volvo	Gregory
HY 21 FZM	Daf	Gregory (White)		WA 71 XTV	Volvo	Gregory
HY 21 FZN	Daf	Gregory (White)		WA 71 XTW	Volvo	Gregory
HY 21 FZO	Daf	Gregory		WA 71 XTX	Volvo	Gregory
HY 21 FZP	Daf	Gregory		WA 71 XTZ	Volvo	Gregory
NU21 WFV	Iveco	White		WA 71 XUB	Volvo	Gregory
NU21 WFV	Iveco	White		WA 71 XUC	Volvo	Gregory
WU 21 HPV	Scania	Gregory		WA 71 XUD	Volvo	Gregory
WU 21 HPX	Scania	Gregory		WA 71 XUE	Volvo	Gregory
WU 21 HRJ	Scania	Gregory		WA 71 XUF	Volvo	Gregory
WU 21 HRK	Scania	Gregory		WA 71 XUG	Volvo	Gregory
WU 21 HRL	Scania	Gregory		WA 71 XUH	Volvo	Gregory
WU 21 HRN	Scania	Gregory		WM 71 AAE	Scania	Gregory
WU 21 HRO	Scania	Gregory		WM 71 AAF	Scania	Gregory
WU 21 HRP	Scania	Gregory		WM 71 AAJ	Scania	Gregory
WU 21 HRR	Scania	Gregory		WM 71 AAK	Scania	Gregory
WU 21 HRW	Scania	Gregory		WM 71 AAN	Scania	Gregory
WU 21 HTA	Scania	Gregory		WM 71 AAO	Scania	Gregory
WU 21 HTC	Scania	Gregory		WM 71 AAU	Scania	Gregory
WU 21 HTD	Scania	Gregory		WM 71 AAV	Scania	Gregory
WU 21 HTE	Scania	Gregory		WM 71 AVB	Scania	Gregory
WU 21 HTF	Scania	Gregory		WM 71 AVC	Scania	Gregory
WU 21 HTG	Scania	Gregory		WM 71 AVD	Scania	Gregory
WU 21 HTJ	Scania	Gregory		WM 71 AVE	Scania	Gregory
WU 21 HTK	Scania	Gregory		WM 71 AVF	Scania	Gregory
WU 21 HTL	Scania	Gregory		WM 71 AVG	Scania	Gregory
WU 21 HTN	Scania	Gregory		WM 71 AVJ	Scania	Gregory
WU 21 HWA	Scania	Gregory (White)		WM 71 AVK	Scania	Gregory
WU 21 HWB	Scania	Gregory (White)		WM 71 AVL	Scania	Gregory
WU 21 HWC	Scania	Gregory (White)		WM 71 AVN	Scania	Gregory
WU 21 HWD	Scania	Gregory (White)		WM 71 AVO	Scania	Gregory
WU 21 HWE	Scania	Gregory (White)		WP 71 LUA	Scania	Gregory
HY 71 DSU	Daf	The Range		WP 71 LUH	Scania	Gregory
HY 71 DSX	Daf	The Range		WP 71 LVA	Scania	Gregory
KY 71 DWD	Volvo	The Range		WP 71 LVB	Scania	Gregory
KY 71 DWE	Volvo	The Range		WP 71 LVC	Scania	Gregory
KY 71 DWF	Volvo	The Range		WP 71 LVD	Scania	Gregory
PK71 TWX	Daf	White		WP 71 LVE	Scania	Gregory
SJ 71 GVM	Man	Coulthard (2)		WP 71 LVF	Scania	Gregory
SJ 71 GVN	Man	Coulthard (2)		WP 71 LVG	Scania	Gregory
SJ 71 GVO	Man	Coulthard (2)		WP 71 LVH	Scania	Gregory
SJ 71 GVP	Man	Coulthard (2)		WP 71 LVJ	Scania	Gregory
SJ 71 GVR	Man	Coulthard (2)		WP 71 LVK	Scania	Gregory
SN 71 ZHA	Scania	Pollock (2)		WP 71 LVL	Scania	Gregory
SN 71 ZHB	Scania	Pollock (2)		WP 71 LVM	Scania	Gregory
SN 71 ZHC	Scania	Pollock (2)		WP 71 LVN	Scania	Gregory
SN 71 ZHD	Scania	Pollock (2)		WP 71 LVO	Scania	Gregory
SN 71 ZHE	Scania	Pollock (2)		WP 71 LVR	Scania	Gregory
SN 71 ZHF	Scania	Pollock (2)		WP 71 LVS	Scania	Gregory
SN 71 ZHG	Scania	Pollock (2)		WP 71 LVT	Scania	Gregory
SN 71 ZHH	Scania	Pollock (2)		WP 71 LVU	Scania	Gregory
SN 71 ZHJ	Scania	Pollock (2)		WP 71 LVV	Scania	Gregory
SN 71 ZHK	Scania	Pollock (2)		WU 71 RVM	IVECO	Gregory (White)
SN 71 ZJE	Scania	Coulthard (2)		WU 71 RVN	IVECO	Gregory (White)
SN 71 ZJJ	Scania	Coulthard (2)		WU 71 RVO	IVECO	Gregory (White)
SN 71 ZJK	Scania	Coulthard (2)		WU 71 RXX	IVECO	Gregory (White)

WX 71 XRA	Scania	Gregory	SN 22 YXC	Scania	Coulthard (2)
WX 71 XRB	Scania	Gregory	SN 22 YXD	Scania	Coulthard (2)
WX 71 XRC	Scania	Gregory	SV 22 AVN	Daf	ARR Craib
WX 71 XRD	Scania	Gregory	SV 22 AVO	Daf	ARR Craib
WX 71 XRE	Scania	Gregory	SV 22 AVP	Daf	ARR Craib
WX 71 XRF	Scania	Gregory	SV 22 AVR	Daf	ARR Craib
WX 71 XRG	Scania	Gregory	SV 22 AVT	Daf	ARR Craib
WX 71 XRH	Scania	Gregory	SV 22 AVU	Daf	ARR Craib
WX 71 XRJ	Scania	Gregory	SV 22 AVW	Daf	ARR Craib
WX 71 XSA	Scania	Gregory	SV 22 AVX	Daf	ARR Craib
WX 71 XSB	Scania	Gregory	SV 22 AVY	Daf	ARR Craib
WX 71 XSC	Scania	Gregory	SV 22 AVZ	Daf	ARR Craib
WX 71 XSD	Scania	Gregory	WU 22 EFA	Scania	Gregory
WX 71 XSE	Scania	Gregory	WU 22 EFB	Scania	Gregory
WX 71 XSF	Scania	Gregory	WU 22 EFC	Scania	Gregory
WX 71 XSG	Scania	Gregory	WU 22 EFD	Scania	Gregory
WX 71 XSH	Scania	Gregory	WU 22 EFO	Scania	Gregory (White)
WX 71 XSJ	Scania	Gregory	WU 22 EHB	Scania	Gregory
WX 71 XSK	Scania	Gregory	WU 22 EHC	Scania	Gregory
WX 71 XSL	Scania	Gregory	WU 22 EHD	Scania	Gregory
WX 71 XSM	Scania	Gregory (White)	WU 22 EHE	Scania	Gregory
WX 71 XSN	Scania	Gregory (White)	WU 22 EHF	Scania	Gregory
WX 71 XSO	Scania	Gregory (White)	WU 22 EHG	Scania	Gregory
WX 71 XSP	Scania	Gregory (White)	WU 22 EHH	Scania	Gregory
WX 71 XSZ	Scania	Gregory	WU 22 EHJ	Scania	Gregory
YX 71 NCZ	Daf	White	WU 22 EHK	Scania	Gregory
FJ 22 CPY	Renault	White	WU 22 EHL	Scania	Gregory
FJ 22 DKL	Scania	The Range	HY 72 DZB	Daf	Gregory
HY 22 CMF	Daf	The Range	HY72 EAM	Daf	The Range
HY 22 CMK	Daf	The Range	HY72 EAO	Daf	The Range
HY 22 CMO	Daf	The Range	HY72 EAW	Daf	The Range
HY 22 CMU	Daf	The Range	HY72 EAX	Daf	The Range
HY 22 CMV	Daf	The Range	HY72 EBA	Daf	The Range
HY 22 CMX	Daf	The Range	HY72 EBC	Daf	The Range
HY 22 CMZ	Daf	The Range	HY72 EBD	Daf	The Range
HY 22 CNA	Daf	The Range	HY72 EBF	Daf	The Range
HY 22 CNC	Daf	Gregory	HY72 EBG	Daf	The Range
HY 22 CNE	Daf	Gregory	HY72 EBJ	Daf	The Range
HY 22 CNF	Daf	Gregory	JY72 EBK	Daf	The Range
HY 22 CNK	Daf	Gregory	HY72 EBL	Daf	The Range
HY 22 CNN	Daf	Gregory	HY72 EBM	Daf	The Range
HY 22 CNO	Daf	Gregory	HY72 EBN	Daf	The Range
HY 22 CNU	Daf	Gregory	HY 72 EEX	Daf	Gregory
HY 22 CNV	Daf	Gregory	HY 72 EEZ	Daf	Gregory
HY 22 CNX	Daf	Gregory	HY 72 EFA	Daf	Gregory
HY 22 CNZ	Daf	Gregory	HY 72 EFB	Daf	Gregory
HY 22 COA	Daf	Gregory	HY 72 EFC	Daf	Gregory
HY 22 COH	Daf	Gregory	HY 72 EFD	Daf	Gregory
HY 22 COJ	Daf	The Range	HY 72 EFE	Daf	Gregory
HY 22 COU	Daf	The Range	HY 72 EFF	Daf	Gregory
HY 22 CPE	Daf	The Range	HY 72 EFG	Daf	Gregory
HY 22 CPF	Daf	The Range	HY 72 EFH	Daf	Gregory
HY 22 CPK	Daf	The Range	HY 72 EFJ	Daf	Gregory
HY 22 CPN	Daf	The Range	HY 72 EFK	Daf	Gregory
KM 22 UUG	Volvo	Gregory (Pollock)	HY 72 EFL	Daf	Gregory
KM 22 UUK	Volvo	Gregory (Pollock)	HY 72 EFM	Daf	Gregory
SN 22 YWX	Scania	Coulthard (2)	HY 72 EFN	Daf	Gregory
SN 22 YWY	Scania	Coulthard (2)	HY 72 EFO	Daf	Gregory
SN 22 YWZ	Scania	Coulthard (2)	SF 72 CZB	Daf	Coulthard (2)
SN 22 YXA	Scania	Coulthard (2)	SF 72 CZC	Daf	Coulthard (2)
SN 22 YXB	Scania	Coulthard (2)	SF 72 CZD	Daf	Coulthard (2)

Reg	Make	Operator	Reg	Make	Operator
SF 72 CZE	Daf	Coulthard (2)	SV 72 NZH	Scania	ARR Craib
SF 72 CZG	Daf	Coulthard (2)	SV 72 NZJ	Scania	ARR Craib
SF 72 CZH	Daf	Coulthard (2)	SV 72 NZK	Scania	ARR Craib
SF 72 CZJ	Daf	Coulthard (2)	WU 72 FMM	Scania	Gregory
SF 72 CZK	Daf	Coulthard (2)	WU 72 FMO	Scania	Gregory
SF 72 CZL	Daf	Coulthard (2)	WU 72 FNP	Scania	Gregory
SF 72 CZM	Daf	Coulthard (2)	WU 72 FNR	Scania	Gregory
SF 72 CZN	Daf	Coulthard (2)	WU 72 FPA	Scania	Gregory
SF 72 CZO	Daf	Coulthard (2)	WU 72 FPC	Scania	Gregory
SF 72 CZP	Daf	Coulthard (2)	WU 72 FPD	Scania	Gregory
SM 72 EGK	Scania	Coulthard (2)	WU 72 FPE	Scania	Gregory
SM 72 EGU	Scania	Coulthard (2)	WU 72 FPF	Scania	Gregory
SM 72 EGV	Scania	Coulthard (2)	WU 72 FPG	Scania	Gregory
SM 72 EGX	Scania	Coulthard (2)	WU 72 FPJ	Scania	Gregory
SN 72 BYR	Daf	Pollock (2)	WU 72 FPK	Scania	Gregory
SN 72 BYS	Daf	Pollock (2)	WU 72 FPL	Scania	Gregory
SN 72 BYT	Daf	Pollock (2)	WU 72 FPN	Scania	Gregory
SN 72 BYU	Daf	Pollock (2)	WU 72 FPO	Scania	Gregory
SN 72 BYV	Daf	Pollock (2)	WU 72 FPP	Scania	Gregory
SN 72 BYW	Daf	Pollock (2)	WU 72 FPT	Scania	Gregory
SN 72 BYX	Daf	Pollock (2)	WU 72 FPV	Scania	Gregory
SN 72 BYY	Daf	Pollock (2)	WU 72 FPX	Scania	Gregory
SN 72 BYZ	Daf	Pollock (2)	HY23 DYX	Daf	The Range
SN 72 BZA	Daf	Pollock (2)	NJ23 BHU	Mercedes	White
SN 72 ZNA	Scania	Brewdog (ARR Craib)	NJ23 BHW	Mercedes	White
SN 72 ZNB	Scania	Brewdog (ARR Craib)	SJ23 FXA	Volvo	Coulthard (2)
SN 72 ZNK	Scania	Coulthard (2)	SJ23 FXB	Volvo	Coulthard (2)
SN 72 ZNL	Scania	Coulthard (2)	SJ23 FXC	Volvo	Coulthard (2)
SN 72 ZNM	Scania	Coulthard (2)	SJ23 FXD	Volvo	Coulthard (2)
SN 72 ZNO	Scania	Coulthard (2)	SJ23 FXE	Volvo	Coulthard (2)
SN 72 ZNP	Scania	Coulthard (2)	SJ23 FXF	Volvo	Coulthard (2)
SN 72 ZNR	Scania	Coulthard (2)	SJ23 FXG	Volvo	Coulthard (2)
SN 72 ZPF	Scania	Pollock (2)	SJ23 FXH	Volvo	Coulthard (2)
SN 72 ZPG	Scania	Pollock (2)	SJ23 FXK	Volvo	Coulthard (2)
SN 72 ZPH	Scania	Pollock (2)	SJ23 GUD	Renault	Coulthard (2)
SN 72 ZPJ	Scania	Pollock (2)	SJ23 HGM	Man	Coulthard (2)
SN 72 ZPK	Scania	Pollock (2)	SJ23 HGN	Man	Coulthard (2)
SN 72 ZPL	Scania	Pollock (2)	SJ23 HGO	Man	Coulthard (2)
SN 72 ZPM	Scania	Pollock (2)	SO23 AHA	Scania	Coulthard (2)
SN 72 ZPO	Scania	Pollock (2)	SO23 AHC	Scania	Coulthard (2)
SN 72 ZPP	Scania	Pollock (2)	SO23 AHD	Scania	Coulthard (2)
SN 72 ZPR	Scania	Pollock (2)	SO23 AHK	Scania	Coulthard (2)
SN 72 ZPS	Scania	Pollock (2)	SO23 AHL	Scania	Coulthard (2)
SV 72 BNE	Daf	ARR Craib	WJ23 GDU	Volvo	Gregory
SV 72 BNF	Daf	ARR Craib	WJ23 GDV	Volvo	Gregory
SV 72 NJF	Man	ARR Craib	WJ23 GDX	Volvo	Gregory
SV 72 NJJ	Man	ARR Craib	WJ23 GDY	Volvo	Gregory
SV 72 NJK	Man	ARR Craib	WJ23 GDZ	Volvo	Gregory
SV 72 NJN	Man	ARR Craib	WJ23 GEU	Volvo	Gregory
SV 72 NJO	Man	ARR Craib	WJ23 GUD	Scania	Gregory
SV 72 NJU	Man	ARR Craib	WU23 GUE	Scania	Gregory
SV 72 NJX	Man	ARR Craib	WU23 GUF	Scania	Gregory
SV 72 NJY	Man	ARR Craib	WU23 GUG	Scania	Gregory
SV 72 NJZ	Man	ARR Craib	WU23 GWL	Scania	Gregory
SV 72 NZA	Scania	ARR Craib	WU23 GWM	Scania	Gregory
SV 72 NZB	Scania	ARR Craib	WU23 GXE	Scania	Gregory (White)
SV 72 NZC	Scania	ARR Craib	WU23 GXF	Scania	Gregory
SV 72 NZD	Scania	ARR Craib	WU23 GYC	Scania	Gregory
SV 72 NZE	Scania	ARR Craib	WU23 GYH	Scania	Gregory
SV 72 NZF	Scania	ARR Craib	WU23 GYJ	Scania	Gregory
SV 72 NZG	Scania	ARR Craib	WU23 GYK	Scania	Gregory

Reg	Make	Operator	Reg	Make	Operator
WU23 GYN	Scania	Gregory	F 10 GDR (65)	Scania	Garador (Gregory)
WU23 GYO	Scania	Gregory	F 11 GDR (65)	Scania	Garador (Gregory)
WU23 GYR	Scania	Gregory	F 11 PSL (70)	Volvo	William Pollock
WU23 GYT	Scania	Gregory	F 12 GDR (65)	Scania	Garador (Gregory)
WU23 GYV	Scania	Gregory	F 13 GDR (65)	Scania	Garador (Gregory)
DE73 VPJ	Man	Gregory (White)	F 14 GDR (65)	Scania	Garador (Gregory)
SN73 ZPY	Scania	Coulthard (2)	F 15 GDR (65)	Scania	Garador (Gregory)
SN73 ZPZ	Scania	Coulthard (2)	J60 HCT (23)	Man	Coulthard (2)
SV73 NMM	Man	ARR Craib	J 80 PSL (70)	Volvo	Pollock (1)
WD73 NVB	Volvo	Gregory (White)	K 30 PSL (69)	Man	Pollock (1)
WD73 NVC	Volvo	Gregory (White)	K 33 PSL (69)	Man	Pollock (1)
WJ73 EUA	Volvo	Gregory (White)	K 80 PSL (70)	Volvo	Pollock (1)
WJ73 EUB	Volvo	Gregory (White)	K 100 PSL (69)	Man	Pollock (1)
WJ73 EUC	Volvo	Gregory (White)	K 200 PSL (69)	Man	Pollock (1)
WK73 KXO	Man	Gregory	K 300 PSL (69)	Man	Pollock (1)
WK73 KXS	Man	Gregory	K 400 PSL (69)	Man	Pollock (1)
WK73 KXY	Man	Gregory	L 80 PSL (70)	Volvo	Pollock (1)
WK73 KYA	Man	Gregory	M 80 PSL (70)	Volvo	Pollock (1)
WK73 KYC	Man	Gregory	M 800 PSL (18)	Daf	Pollock (White)
WK73 KYF	Man	Gregory	M 900 PSL (18)	Daf	Pollock (L&S)
WK73 KYH	Man	Gregory	N 33 PSL (70)	Daf	Pollock (White)
WU73 GDA	Scania	Gregory	N 44 PSL (70)	Daf	Pollock (White)
WU73 GDE	Scania	Gregory	N 55 PSL (70)	Daf	Pollock (White)
WU73 GDF	Scania	Gregory	N 80 PSL (70)	Volvo	Pollock (1)
WU73 GDJ	Scania	Gregory	R 1 PSL (69)	Daf	Pollock (White)
WU73 GDK	Scania	Gregory	R 2 PSL (69)	Daf	Pollock (White)
WU73 GDO	Scania	Gregory	R 3 PSL (69)	Daf	Pollock (White)
WU73 GDV	Scania	Gregory	R 4 PSL (69)	Daf	Pollock (White)
WU73 GDZ	Scania	Gregory	R 6 PSL (69)	Daf	Pollock (White)
WU73 GFA	Scania	Gregory	R 7 PSL (69)	Daf	Pollock (White)
WU73 GFJ	Scania	Gregory	R 8 PSL (70)	Renault	Pollock (1)
WU73 GFK	Scania	Gregory	R 9 PSL (70)	Renault	Pollock (1)
WU73 GGK	Scania	Gregory	R 10 PSL (70)	Renault	Pollock (1)
WU73 GGO	Scania	Gregory	R 11 PSL (70)	Renault	Pollock (1)
WU73 GGP	Scania	Gregory	S 90 PSL (18)	Mercedes	Pollock (1)
WU73 GGV	Scania	Gregory	T 1 PSL (68)	Daf	(Red - Pollock)
WU73 GGX	Scania	Gregory	T 3 KTL (15)	Scania	Gregory (White)
WU73 GGZ	Scania	Gregory	T 4 KTL (02)	MITS	Gregory (White)
WU73 GHA	Scania	Gregory (White)	T 6 KTL (63)	Scania	Gregory
WU73 GHD	Scania	Gregory (White)	T 40 PSL (18)	Man	Pollock (1)
WU73 GHF	Scania	Gregory (White)	T 55 PSL (70)	Daf	Pollock (1)
WU73 GHG	Scania	Gregory (White)	T 66 PSL (70)	Daf	Pollock (1)
WU73 GHH	Scania	Gregory	T 88 PSL (70)	Daf	Pollock (1)
WU73 GKK	Scania	Garador (Gregory)	T 99 PSL (70)	Daf	Pollock (1)
WU73 GLK	Scania	Gregory (White)	T 200 PSL (20)	Daf	Pollock (1)
WU73 GLV	Scania	Gregory (White)	T 300 PSL (20)	Daf	Pollock (1)
WU73 GNK	Scania	Gregory (White)	T 400 PSL (20)	Daf	Pollock (1)
WU73 GNO	Scania	Gregory (White)	T 500 PSL (20)	Daf	Pollock (1)
WU73 GNP	Scania	Gregory (White)	T 600 PSL (20)	Daf	Pollock (1)
WX73 CXU	Scania	Gregory	T 700 PSL (20)	Daf	Pollock (1)
WX73 CXV	Scania	Gregory	T 800 PSL (20)	Daf	Pollock (1)
WX73 CXW	Scania	Gregory	T 900 PSL (20)	Daf	Pollock (1)
WX73 CXY	Scania	Gregory	V 4 PSL (68)	Renault	Pollock (1)
F 2 GDR (15)	Scania	Garador (Gregory)	V 5 KTL (15)	Scania	Kay Transport (2)
F 3 GDR (15)	Scania	Garador (Gregory)	W 66 PSL (18)	Daf	Pollock (L&S)
F 4 GDR (15)	Scania	Garador (Gregory)	W 77 PSL (18)	Daf	Pollock (L&S)
F 5 GDR (15)	Scania	Garador (Gregory)	X 1 PSL (69)	Renault	Pollock (1)
F 6 GDR (15)	Scania	Garador (Gregory)	X 2 PSL (19)	Renault	Pollock (1)
F 7 GDR (15)	Scania	Garador (Gregory)	X 3 PSL (16)	Volvo	MSP (2)
F 8 GDR (15)	Scania	Garador (Gregory)	Y 5 PSL (18)	Man	Pollock (1)
F 9 GDR (65)	Scania	Garador (Gregory)	Y 11 PSL (69)	Man	Pollock (1)

Gregory Group (cont)

Y 100 GDL (68)	Scania	Gregory	Y 111 PSL (69)	Man	Pollock (1)
Y 100 HCT (16)	Volvo	Coulthard (2)			

Hawkins Logistics (Rugeley)

G 497 SGB	Leyland	FG 20 MYZ	Daf	MT 21 TZV	Scania
V 5 WCK (71)	Volvo	FG 20 MZO	Daf	MT 21 TZW	Scania
KU 10 EYS	Scania	MA 20 TFV	Scania	DX 71 ORY	Volvo
BU 64 HVX	Daf	MA 20 TFX	Scania	DX 71 ORZ	Volvo
YD 17 YUV	Scania	MA 20 TFY	Scania	DX 22 VHA	Volvo
DX 18 HWK	Volvo	MA 20 TFZ	Scania	DX 22 VHB	Volvo
DX 18 HWL	Volvo	MV 20 RSY	Scania	DX 22 VHC	Volvo
DX 18 HWM	Volvo	MV 20 RSZ	Scania	FL 22 UHK	Daf
DX 18 HWN	Volvo	BV 70 HKL	Scania	HL 22 DAF (22)	Daf
FJ 18 HVV	Daf	FN 70 BKD	Daf	BG72 MWV	Scania
FP 18 WTF	Daf	FN 70 BKE	Daf	BV72 NTO	Scania
KF 18 EJN	Daf	FN 70 BKF	Daf	BV72 NVZ	Scania
BG 68 HHW	Man	FN 70 BKG	Daf	BV72 NZZ	Scania
FN 68 EVV	Daf	FN70 BKJ	Daf	EX72 NJK	Scania
DX 19 YHJ	Volvo	MX 70 LHB	Scania	EX72 NJO	Scania
DX 19 YHK	Volvo	BV 21 TWP	Scania	MV72 WUL	Scania
DX 19 YHL	Volvo	BV 21 TYK	Scania	MV72 WUM	Scania
FN 19 KTE	Daf	BV 21 TYX	Scania	BV23 MYT	Renault
FN 19 KTF	Daf	DX 21 WWA	Volvo	DS23 ULX	Volvo
FN 19 KTG	Daf	DX 21 WWB	Volvo	DS23 ULY	Volvo
MV 19 UGF	Scania	DX 21 WWC	Volvo	DS23 ULZ	Volvo
MV 19 UGG	Scania	DX 21 WWD	Volvo	HL23 HLL	Scania
DX 69 UHH	Volvo	DX 21 WWE	Volvo	BK73 XAJ	Man
FN 69 ARZ	Daf	DX 21 WWF	Volvo	BV73 LKZ	Renault
HL 69 HLL (69)	Volvo	DX 21 WWG	Volvo	DX73 VHK	Volvo
NK 69 XMW	Mercedes	KC 21 FXU	Scania	DX73 VHL	Volvo
NK 69 XNW	Mercedes	KC 21 GHJ	Scania	FJ73 SXA	Mercedes
NK 69 XOA	Mercedes	KC 21 GHO	Scania	FJ73 SXB	Mercedes
PO 69 XDR	Mercedes	MK 21 BVR	Scania	FJ73 SXC	Mercedes
PO 69 XDS	Mercedes	MK 21 BVT	Scania	FJ73 SXD	Mercedes
BU 20 XTB	Scania	MT 21 TZU	Scania		

Lantern Recovery (South Mimms)

No	Reg	Make	No	Reg	Make	No	Reg	Make
42	SS18 LRS (18)	Isuzu	79	VD67 LRS (67)	Isuzu	191	SS68 LRS (68)	Volvo
43	NS13 LRS (13)	Isuzu	80	BU17 LRS (17)	Man	192	GS19 LRS (19)	Volvo
44	GB72 LRS (72)	Daf	81	JS19 LRS (19)	Man	193	KY14 CYA	Scania
45	LN64 NVP	Isuzu	82	JC21 LRS (21)	Daf	195	JS69 LRS (69)	Volvo
46	AH70 LRS (70)	Daf	86	MY71 LRS (71)	Volvo	196	TS21 LRS (21)	Man
47	LE65 LRS (65)	Daf	87	SS66 LRS (66)	Man	197	VD19 LRS (19)	Daf
48	MY22 LRS (22)	Daf	91	AT20 LRS (20)	Man		AB11 LRS (11)	Daf
49	YS68 LRS (68)	Man	93	MY72 LRS (72)	Volvo		DA22 LRS (22)	Daf
50	TG21 LRS (21)	Man	94	US56 LRS (56)	Man		GB21 LRS (21)	Isuzu
51	BS68 LRS (68)	Man	95	SK19 LRS (19)	Daf		GB22 LRS (22)	Man
52	AE71 LRS (71)	Man	96	HW13 BGX	Volvo		LE22 LRS (22)	Daf
55	JB21 LRS (21)	Isuzu	97	FH07 LRS (07)	Volvo		LF23 LRS (23)	Daf
57	BU66 LRS (66)	Daf	98	SB70 LRS (70)	Man		LH10 AFE	Isuzu
58	LS14 LRS (14)	Daf	131	BS18 LRS (18)	Daf		LK08 AFN	Isuzu
60	MG71 LRS (71)	Daf	132	FV66 EJO	Scania		LR71 LRS (71)	Daf
61	LS61 LRS (61)	Isuzu	133	MY70 LRS (70)	Daf		LS68 LRS (68)	Daf
62	ON22 LRS (22)	Daf	141	PH21 LRS (21)	Volvo		MC21 LRS (21)	Daf
63	HE17 LRS (17)	Daf	142	NU71 LRS (71)	Volvo		NS65 LRS (65)	Isuzu
64	MH21 LRS (21)	Daf	143	CF63 LRS (63)	Daf		NS67 LRS (67)	Man
65	AO71 LRS (71)	Man	144	LR72 LRS (72)	Daf		PN21 JTU	Daf
66	AE 72 LRS (72)	Man	146	LM08 KWB	Daf		PN22 CAO	Mercedes
67	AS66 LRS (66)	Man	152	PX16 BMO	Volvo		SF21 LRS (21)	Isuzu
68	WN62 YPD	Man	153	PX17 BYA	Volvo		TS08 LRS (08)	Renault
69	UP71 LRS (71)	Isuzu	156	OW15 AWM	Man		UM72 LRS (72)	Isuzu
70	CA17 LRS (17)	Daf	160	L333 KAW (14)	Scania		UP72 LRS (72)	Daf
71	GE21 LRS (21)	Man	179	HS19 LRS (19)	Daf		UR22 LRS (22)	Isuzu
72	OG12 LRS (12)	Isuzu	186	KN12 WVT	Volvo		UR72 URS (72)	Volvo
74	TG66 LRS (66)	Daf	187	JB67 LRS (67)	Volvo		YS59 LRS (59)	Renault
76	CF21 LRS (21)	Daf	188	AU67 LRS (67)	Volvo		GE73 LRS (73)	Daf
77	GN09 HBF	Iveco	190	VD18 LRS (18)	Volvo			

Leicester Heavy Haulage

Reg	Make	Model	Reg	Make	Model
L4 LHH (69)	Daf	FTTXF106 510 6x4 SSC	X3 LHH (69)	Daf	FTTXF106 530 6x4 SSC
M1 LHH (61)	Daf	FTGXF105 460 6x2 SSC	X4 LHH (71)	Man	TGX 41.580 8x4 GX
M2 LHH (72)	Daf	FTTXF 530 6x4 SSC	X6 LHH (69)	Daf	FTTXF106 510 6x4 SSC
R1 LHH (22)	Daf	FTGXF 530 6x2 SSC	X7 LHH (22)	Daf	FTTXF 530 6x4 SSC
R2 LHH (22)	Daf	FTGXF 480 6x2 SSC	Y1 LHH (68)	Daf	FTGXF106 530 6x2 SSC
S1 LHH (65)	Daf	FAXCF 460 8w Flatbed	Y2 LHH (68)	Daf	FTGXF106 530 6x2 SSC
S2 LHH (65)	Daf	FAXCF 460 8w Flatbed	Y3 LHH (68)	Daf	FTGXF106 530 6x2 SSC
V1 LHH (69)	Daf	FTGXF106 480 6x2 SSC	Y4 LHH (68)	Daf	FTGXF106 530 6x2 SSC
X1 LHH (69)	Man	TGX 41.640 8x4 XXL	FP64 LHH (64)	Daf	FTGXF105 460 6x2 SSC
X2 LHH (69)	Man	TGX 41.640 8x4 XXL			

Lomas (Buxton)

Reg	Make	Reg	Make	Reg	Make	Reg	Make
J521 TOP	Volvo	LD 69 YEH	Scania	KS 71 MDV	Volvo	LD 22 LOR	Scania
WAZ 66 (64)	Scania	LD 69 YEM	Scania	LD 71 FAV	Scania	LD 22 LOS	Scania
A 10 HVO	Scania	LD 69 YOS	Scania	LD 71 FAX	Scania	LD 22 LOV	Scania
D 10 LDL	Scania	LD 20 JAM	Scania	LD 71 FAZ	Scania	LD 22 LSD	Scania
E 10 LDL	Scania	LD 20 JAR	Scania	LD 71 FOD	Scania	LD 22 LTD	Scania
K 21 LDL	Mercedes	LD 20 JAT	Scania	LD 71 FUS	Scania	LD 22 LUD	Scania
M 21 LDL	Mercedes	LD 20 JAV	Scania	LD 71 FYD	Scania	LD 22 LYD	Scania
N 10 LDL	Mercedes	LD 20 JAW	Scania	LD 71 GUM	Scania	LD 22 LYL	Scania
N 21 LDL	Mercedes	LD 20 JAX	Scania	LD 71 HAN	Scania	LD 22 MAB	Scania
P 21 LDL	Mercedes	LD 20 PAD	Scania	LD 71 HAZ	Scania	LD 22 MAR	Scania
T 10 LDL	Scania	LD 20 PAK	Scania	LD 71 HED	Scania	LD 22 MEN	Scania
T 21 LDL	Mercedes	LD 20 PAR	Scania	LD 71 HET	Scania	LD 22 MOD	Scania
V 10 LDL	Mercedes	LD 20 PAV	Scania	LD 71 HEY	Scania	LD 22 MOL	Scania
V 21 LDL	Mercedes	LD 20 PAW	Scania	LD 71 HOD	Scania	LD 22 MON	Scania
V 80 JLO	Scania	LD 20 PED	Scania	LD 71 HOL	Scania	LD 22 MOO	Scania
W 10 LDL	Mercedes	LD 20 PEG	Scania	LD 71 HON	Scania	LD 22 MOP	Scania
Y 21 LDL	Mercedes	LD 20 PEK	Scania	LD 71 HUG	Scania	LD 22 MOW	Scania
Y 30 LDL	Scania	LD 20 PEN	Scania	LD 71 HUM	Scania	LD 22 MUD	Scania
GH 09 TOW	Mercedes	LD 20 PUD	Scania	LD 71 KAL	Scania	LD 22 MUK	Scania
WC 10 MAS	Scania	LD 20 PUN	Scania	LD 71 KAR	Scania	LD 22 MUL	Scania
LD 16 XXX	Volvo	LD 20 PUP	Scania	LD 71 KAS	Scania	LD 22 MUX	Scania
VB 16 LAD	Volvo	LD 20 PUR	Scania	LD 71 KAT	Scania	LD 22 NAN	Volvo
LD 66 UNA	Volvo	LD 20 PUT	Scania	LD 71 KEE	Scania	LD 22 NAS	Volvo
LD 17 XAD	Volvo	LD 20 PYD	Scania	LD 71 KEZ	Scania	LD 22 NET	Volvo
LD 18 ADE	Volvo	LD 20 PYE	Scania	LD 71 KOP	Scania	LD 22 NEV	Volvo
LD 18 AKE	Volvo	LD 20 PYM	Scania	LD 71 KOY	Scania	LD 22 NEW	Volvo
LD 18 ANJ	Volvo	LD 20 SOX	Volvo	LD 71 KYD	Scania	LD 22 NOD	Volvo
LD 18 ART	Volvo	LD 20 SUS	Volvo	LD 71 KYL	Scania	LD 22 NOM	Volvo
LD 18 AVA	Volvo	LD 20 SUZ	Volvo	LD 71 RAF	Scania	LD 22 NOT	Volvo
LD 18 AXE	Volvo	LD 20 SYL	Volvo	LD 71 RAK	Scania	LD 22 NOV	Volvo
LD 18 CAM	Volvo	LD 20 SYM	Volvo	LD 71 RAS	Scania	LD 22 NOW	Volvo
LD 18 CEC	Volvo	LD 70 ALL	Mercedes	LD 71 REV	Scania	LD 22 PAN	Volvo
LD 18 COP	Volvo	LD 70 AUB	Mercedes	LD 71 RUB	Scania	LD 22 PAP	Volvo
LD 18 CRY	Volvo	LD 70 AVE	Mercedes	LD 71 RUM	Scania	LD 22 PAY	Volvo
LD 18 CUE	Volvo	LD 70 CAB	Scania	LD 71 RUS	Scania	LD 22 PEP	Volvo
LD 18 CYB	Volvo	LD 70 CAD	Scania	LD 71 RXE	Scania	LD 22 PEU	Volvo
LD 18 NAX	Volvo	LD 70 CAG	Scania	LD 71 RYE	Scania	LD 22 TAG	Scania
LD 68 BAB	Scania	LD 70 COB	Scania	HG 22 AAA	Scania	LD 22 TAM	Scania
LD 68 BOS	Scania	LD 70 COO	Scania	HG 22 CCC	Scania	LD 22 TAN	Scania
LD 68 DUX	Scania	LD 70 COS	Scania	HG 22 DDD	Scania	LD 22 TAP	Scania
LD 68 DYL	Scania	LD 70 GAL	Scania	HG 22 EEE	Scania	LD 22 TAR	Scania
LD 68 EAK	Scania	LD 70 GEF	Scania	LD 22 DAR	Mercedes	LD 22 TAT	Scania
LD 68 ESE	Scania	LD 70 GEL	Scania	LD 22 DAW	Mercedes	LD 22 TEE	Scania
LD 68 LAV	Volvo	LD 70 GET	Scania	LD 22 DEX	Mercedes	LD 22 TES	Scania
LD 68 LOZ	Volvo	LD 70 GGG	Scania	LD 22 DEZ	Mercedes	LD 22 TOD	Scania
LD 68 LUV	Volvo	LD 70 GOG	Scania	LD 22 DOB	Mercedes	LD 22 TOR	Scania
LD 68 TOO	Volvo	LD 70 GUM	Scania	LD 22 DOD	Mercedes	LD 22 TOT	Scania
LD 68 WHY	Volvo	LD 21 BAK	Scania	LD 22 DOE	Mercedes	LD 22 TUC	Scania
LD 19 MAP	Scania	LD 21 BAP	Scania	LD 22 DOL	Mercedes	LD 22 TUG	Scania
LD 19 MAW	Scania	LD 21 BAS	Scania	LD 22 DOT	Mercedes	LD 22 TUN	Scania
LD 19 OAK	Scania	LD 21 BEE	Scania	LD 22 DUK	Mercedes	LD 22 WOT	Scania
LD 19 OAR	Scania	LD 21 BET	Scania	LD 22 LAR	Scania	LD 22 ZAC	Scania
LD 19 OAT	Scania	LD 21 BEX	Scania	LD 22 LAS	Scania	LD 22 ZEB	Scania
LD 19 OLY	Scania	LD 21 WOW	Mercedes	LD 22 LAY	Scania	LD 22 ZEN	Scania
LD 69 AGG	Volvo	LD 21 ZEE	Scania	LD 22 LED	Scania	LD 72 JEB	Volvo
LD 69 SAO	Volvo	LD 21 ZEF	Scania	LD 22 LEV	Scania	LD 72 JED	Volvo
LD 69 SAZ	Volvo	LD 21 ZEG	Scania	LD 22 LEZ	Scania	LD 72 JEM	Volvo
LD 69 SOL	Volvo	LD 21 ZEO	Scania	LD 22 LON	Scania	LD 72 JER	Volvo
LD 69 VED	Scania	LD 21 ZER	Scania	LD 22 LOO	Scania	LD 72 JEZ	Volvo

Lomas (cont)

LD 72 JOB	Volvo	LD 23 ATE	Volvo	LD 23 OCK	Volvo	LD 23 ZOO	Volvo
LD 72 JOC	Volvo	LD 23 ATT	Volvo	LD 23 ORE	Volvo	LD 23 ZUD	Volvo
LD 72 JOD	Volvo	LD 23 AYR	Volvo	LD 23 ORS	Volvo	LD73 HUD	Volvo
LD 72 JOG	Volvo	LD 23 BEA	Scania	LD 23 OTT	Volvo	LD73 LAB	Scania
LD 72 JOX	Volvo	LD 23 BEB	Scania	LD 23 SAN	Volvo	LD73 LAC	Scania
LD 72 JOZ	Volvo	LD 23 BEC	Scania	LD 23 SAS	Volvo	LD73 LAH	Scania
LD 72 VAG	Volvo	LD 23 CER	Volvo	LD 23 SEB	Volvo	LD73 LAX	Scania
LD 72 VAZ	Volvo	LD 23 CHE	Volvo	LD 23 SED	Volvo	LD73 LEA	Scania
LD 72 VOE	Volvo	LD 23 CHR	Volvo	LD 23 SEN	Volvo	LD73 LEC	Scania
LD 72 VOW	Volvo	LD 23 COE	Volvo	LD 23 SEV	Volvo	LD73 LEJ	Scania
LD 72 VOX	Volvo	LD 23 COG	Volvo	LD 23 SHY	Volvo	LD73 LEL	Scania
LD 72 YAM	Scania	LD 23 CUB	Volvo	LD 23 SKY	Volvo	LD73 LEP	Scania
LD 72 YAR	Scania	LD 23 CUS	Volvo	LD 23 SOY	Volvo	LD73 LOG	Scania
LD 72 YEO	Scania	LD 23 ELT	Scania	LD 23 STE	Volvo	LD73 LOJ	Scania
LD 72 YEP	Scania	LD 23 ERN	Scania	LD 23 STY	Volvo	LD73 LOL	Scania
LD 72 YES	Scania	LD 23 EYE	Scania	LD 23 UDD	Scania	LD73 REN	Volvo
FL 23 VLD	Scania	LD 23 GAP	Scania	LD 23 UMP	Scania	LD73 RES	Volvo
FL 23 VLE	Scania	LD 23 GEN	Scania	LD 23 UNN	Scania	LD73 REY	Volvo
LD 23 ANO	Volvo	LD 23 GUD	Scania	LD 23 USH	Scania	LD73 ROL	Volvo
LD 23 ARA	Volvo	LD 23 GUZ	Scania	LD 23 UUU	Scania	LD73 ROO	Volvo
LD 23 ARL	Volvo						

Longs of Leeds

Fleet No	Registration	Make	Specification	Livery	Allocation
303	YJ13 USX	Daf	FALF45 160 4w Curtain	Pallex	Leeds
309	YH13 PMV	Daf	FARCF75 310 6w SC Curtain	Longs	Leeds
318	YA67 AGY	Daf	FTGXF 480 6x2 SSC	Longs	Unknown
319	YA67 AGZ	Daf	FTGXF 480 6x2 SSC	Longs	Hull
320	YA67 XPK	Daf	FTGXF 480 6x2 SSC	Longs	Leeds
321	YA67 XPL	Daf	FTGXF 480 6x2 SSC	Longs	Leeds
322	YK18 BKA	Daf	FTGXF 480 6x2 SSC	Longs	Hull
323	YK18 BKD	Daf	FTGXF 480 6x2 SSC	Longs	Hull
324	YK18 BKE	Daf	FTGXF 480 6x2 SSC	Longs	Hull
326	YK18 BKG	Daf	FTGXF 480 6x2 SSC	Longs	Hull
327	YK18 BKJ	Daf	FTGXF 480 6x2 SSC	Longs	Hull
328	YK18 BKL	Daf	FTGXF 480 6x2 SSC	Longs	Hull
329	YK18 BKN	Daf	FTGXF 480 6x2 SSC	Longs	Hull
330	YK18 BKO	Daf	FTGXF 480 6x2 SSC	Longs	Hull
331	YG68 LWA	Daf	FTGXF 480 6x2 SSC	Longs	Hull
332	YG68 LWC	Daf	FTGXF 480 6x2 SSC	Longs	Hull
333	YG68 LWD	Daf	FTGXF 480 6x2 SSC	Longs	Hull
334	YG68 LWE	Daf	FTGXF 480 6x2 SSC	Longs	Hull
335	YG68 LWF	Daf	FTGXF 480 6x2 SSC	Longs	Hull
336	YG68 LWH	Daf	FTGXF 480 6x2 SSC	Longs	Hull
337	YK19 WEJ	Daf	FTGXF 480 6x2 SSC	Longs	Hull
338	YK19 WEH	Daf	FTGXF 480 6x2 SSC	Longs	Hull
339	YK19 WEP	Daf	FTGXF 480 6x2 SSC	Longs	Leeds
340	YK19 WEO	Daf	FTGXF 480 6x2 SSC	Longs	Hull
341	YK19 WFS	Daf	FTGXF 480 6x2 SSC	Longs	Leeds
342	YK19 WFT	Daf	FTGXF 480 6x2 SSC	Longs	Leeds
343	YK19 WFU	Daf	FTGXF 480 6x2 SSC	Longs	Leeds
344	YK19 WFV	Daf	FTGXF 480 6x2 SSC	Longs	Leeds
351	YK17 VKB	Daf	FTGXF 460 6x2 SSC	Longs	Leeds
353	YK17 VKD	Daf	FTGXF 460 6x2 SSC	Longs	Leeds
354	YK17 VKE	Daf	FTGXF 460 6x2 SSC	Longs	Leeds
355	YK17 VKF	Daf	FTGXF 460 6x2 SSC	Longs	Leeds
356	YK17 VKH	Daf	FTGXF 460 6x2 SSC	Longs	Leeds
357	YK17 VKJ	Daf	FTGXF 460 6x2 SSC	Longs	Leeds

358	YK17 VKL	Daf	FTGXF 460 6x2 SSC	Longs	Leeds
359	YK17 VKM	Daf	FTGXF 460 6x2 SSC	Longs	Leeds
360	YK17 VKN	Daf	FTGXF 460 6x2 SSC	Longs	Leeds
361	YK17 VKO	Daf	FTGXF 460 6x2 SSC	Longs	Leeds
362	YK17 VKP	Daf	FTGXF 460 6x2 SSC	Longs	Leeds
363	YK17 VKR	Daf	FTGXF 460 6x2 SSC	Longs	Leeds
364	YK17 VKS	Daf	FTGXF 460 6x2 SSC	Longs	Leeds
365	YK17 VKT	Daf	FTGXF 460 6x2 SSC	Longs	Leeds
366	YK17 VKU	Daf	FTGXF 460 6x2 SSC	Longs	Leeds
367	YK17 VKV	Daf	FTGXF 460 6x2 SSC	Longs	Leeds
368	YK17 VKW	Daf	FTGXF 460 6x2 SSC	Longs	Leeds
369	YK17 VKX	Daf	FTGXF 460 6x2 SSC	Longs	Leeds
370	YK17 VKZ	Daf	FTGXF 460 6x2 SSC	Longs	Leeds
371	YK17 VLA	Daf	FTGXF 460 6x2 SSC	Longs	Leeds
372	YK17 VLB	Daf	FTGXF 460 6x2 SSC	Longs	Leeds
373	YK17 VLC	Daf	FTGXF 460 6x2 SSC	Longs	Leeds
374	YK17 VLD	Daf	FTGXF 460 6x2 SSC	Longs	Leeds
375	YK17 VLE	Daf	FTGXF 460 6x2 SSC	Longs	Leeds
376	YK17 VLF	Daf	FTGXF 460 6x2 SSC	Longs	Leeds
377	YK17 VLG	Daf	FTGXF 460 6x2 SSC	Longs	Leeds
378	YK17 VLH	Daf	FTGXF 460 6x2 SSC	Longs	Leeds
379	YK17 VLJ	Daf	FTGXF 460 6x2 SSC	Longs	Leeds
380	YK17 VLL	Daf	FTGXF 460 6x2 SSC	Longs	Leeds
381	YK17 VLM	Daf	FTGXF 460 6x2 SSC	Longs	Leeds
383	YK17 VLO	Daf	FTGXF 460 6x2 SSC	Longs	Leeds
384	YK17 VLP	Daf	FTGXF 460 6x2 SSC	Longs	Leeds
385	YK17 VLR	Daf	FTGXF 460 6x2 SSC	Longs	Leeds
386	YK17 VLS	Daf	FTGXF 460 6x2 SSC	Longs	Leeds
401	YW23 HBD	Daf	FTG 480 6x2 (XF)	Longs	Hull
402	YX23 NUW	Daf	FTG 480 6x2 (XF)	Longs	Hull
403	YY23 NYZ	Daf	FTG 480 6x2 (XF)	Longs	Hull
404	YY23 NYC	Daf	FTG 480 6x2 (XF)	Longs	Hull
405	YY23 NYP	Daf	FTG 480 6x2 (XF)	Longs	Hull
406	YX73 NYH	Daf	FTG 480 6x2 (XF)	Longs	Leeds
407	YY23 NZJ	Daf	FTG 480 6x2 (XF)	Longs	Hull
408	YY23 UZW	Daf	FTG 480 6x2 (XF)	Longs	Hull
409	YY23 NYT	Daf	FTG 480 6x2 (XF)	Longs	Hull
410	YY23 NYU	Daf	FTG 480 6x2 (XF)	Longs	Hull
411	YY23 VWJ	Daf	FTG 480 6x2 (XF)	Longs	Hull
412	YY23 NZH	Daf	FTG 480 6x2 (XF)	Longs	Hull
413	YY23 UZV	Daf	FTG 480 6x2 (XF)	Longs	Hull
414	YW23 HBE	Daf	FTG 480 6x2 (XF)	Longs	Hull
415	YW23 FMG	Daf	FTG 480 6x2 (XF)	Longs	Leeds
416	YW23 FMJ	Daf	FTG 480 6x2 (XF)	Longs	Hull
417	YW23 AJU	Daf	FTG 480 6x2 (XF)	Longs	Leeds
418	YW23 HAX	Daf	FTG 480 6x2 (XF)	Longs	Hull
419	YW23 FMK	Daf	FTG 480 6x2 (XF)	Longs	Hull
420	YW23 HBA	Daf	FTG 480 6x2 (XF)	Longs	Hull
421		Daf	FTG 480 6x2 (XF)	Longs	
422		Daf	FTG 480 6x2 (XF)	Longs	
423	YY23 VWK	Daf	FTG 480 6x2 (XF)	Longs	Hull
424		Daf	FTG 480 6x2 (XF)	Longs	
425	YX73 NTE	Daf	FTG 480 6x2 (XF)	Longs	Leeds
426	YY73 NSZ	Daf	FTG 480 6x2 (XF)	Longs	Leeds
427	YY73 NTA	Daf	FTG 480 6x2 (XF)	Longs	Leeds
428		Daf	FTG 480 6x2 (XF)	Longs	
429		Daf	FTG 480 6x2 (XF)	Longs	
430	YY73 NUP	Daf	FTG 480 6x2 (XF)	Longs	Leeds
431		Daf	FTG 480 6x2 (XF)	Longs	
432	YY73 EKJ	Daf	FTG 480 6x2 (XF)	Longs	Leeds
433		Daf	FTG 480 6x2 (XF)	Longs	

434	YX73 NTD	Daf	FTG 480 6x2 (XF)	Longs	Leeds
435		Daf	FTG 480 6x2 (XF)	Longs	
436		Daf	FTG 480 6x2 (XF)	Longs	
437		Daf	FTG 480 6x2 (XF)	Longs	
438	YX73 NUU	Daf	FTG 480 6x2 (XF)	Longs	Leeds
439	YX73 NYG	Daf	FTG 480 6x2 (XF)	Longs	Leeds
440	YY73 NUO	Daf	FTG 480 6x2 (XF)	Longs	Leeds
441		Daf	FTG 480 6x2 (XF)	Longs	
442	YX73 NVA	Daf	FTG 480 6x2 (XF)	Longs	Leeds
861	YK17 VLT	Daf	FTGXF 460 6x2 SSC	Longs	Hull
862	YK17 VLU	Daf	FTGXF 460 6x2 SSC	Longs	Hull
863	YK17 VLV	Daf	FTGXF 460 6x2 SSC	Longs	Hull
864	YK17 VLW	Daf	FTGXF 460 6x2 SSC	Longs	Hull
865	YK17 VLX	Daf	FTGXF 460 6x2 SSC	Longs	Hull
866	YK17 VLY	Daf	FTGXF 460 6x2 SSC	Longs	Hull
867	YK17 VLZ	Daf	FTGXF 460 6x2 SSC	Longs	Hull
868	YK17 VMA	Daf	FTGXF 460 6x2 SSC	Longs	Hull
869	YK17 VMC	Daf	FTGXF 460 6x2 SSC	Longs	Hull
870	YK17 VMD	Daf	FTGXF 460 6x2 SSC	Longs	Hull
871	YK17 VME	Daf	FTGXF 460 6x2 SSC	Longs	Hull
872	YK17 VMF	Daf	FTGXF 460 6x2 SSC	Longs	Hull
873	YK17 VMG	Daf	FTGXF 460 6x2 SSC	Longs	Hull
874		Daf	FTG 480 6x2 (XF)	Longs	
875		Daf	FTG 480 6x2 (XF)	Longs	
876	YW23 HAO	Daf	FTG 480 6x2 (XF)	Longs	Hull
877	YW23 HAE	Daf	FTG 480 6x2 (XF)	Longs	Hull
878	YW23 HBC	Daf	FTG 480 6x2 (XF)	Longs	Hull
879	YW23 HBB	Daf	FTG 480 6x2 (XF)	Longs	Hull
880	YY23 NYV	Daf	FTG 480 6x2 (XF)	Longs	Hull
881	YY23 NZG	Daf	FTG 480 6x2 (XF)	Longs	Hull
882	YX73 NSZ	Daf	FTG 480 6x2 (XF)	Longs	Leeds
883	YX73 NTV	Daf	FTG 480 6x2 (XF)	Longs	Leeds
884		Daf	FTG 480 6x2 (XF)	Longs	
885	YY23 NYO	Daf	FTG 480 6x2 (XF)	Longs	Hull
886	YY23 NZF	Daf	FTG 480 6x2 (XF)	Longs	Hull
887		Daf	FTG 480 6x2 (XF)	Longs	
888	YY23 XMX	Daf	FTG 480 6x2 (XF)	Longs	Hull
889		Daf	FTG 480 6x2 (XF)	Longs	
890	YY73 NTK	Daf	FTG 480 6x2 (XF)	Longs	Leeds
891	YY23 UZG	Daf	FTG 480 6x2 (XF)	Longs	Hull
892	YX73 NTU	Daf	FTG 480 6x2 (XF)	Longs	Leeds
900	YK19 WGJ	Daf	FARCF 340 6w SC Curtain	Longs	Leeds
901	YK19 WFL	Daf	FARCF 340 6w SC Curtain	Longs	Leeds
902	YK19 WFN	Daf	FARCF 340 6w SC Curtain	Longs	Leeds
903	YK19 WFO	Daf	FARCF 340 6w SC Curtain	Longs	Leeds
904	YK19 WFP	Daf	FARCF 340 6w SC Curtain	Longs	Leeds
905	YK19 WFR	Daf	FARCF 340 6w SC Curtain	Longs	Leeds
906	YK69 HAA	Daf	FARCF 340 6w SC Curtain	Longs	Leeds
907	YK69 HAE	Daf	FARCF 340 6w SC Curtain	Longs	Leeds
908	YK69 HAO	Daf	FARCF 340 6w SC Curtain	Longs	Leeds
909	YK20 LFT	Daf	FALF 180 4w Curtain	Pallex	Leeds
910	YK20 LFU	Daf	FALF 260 4w Curtain	Pallex	Leeds
911	YK21 VVT	Daf	FALF 180 4w Curtain	Pallex	Leeds
912	YK21 VVU	Daf	FALF 180 4w Curtain	Pallex	Leeds
913	YK21 VVW	Daf	FALF 260 4w Curtain	Pallex	Leeds
914	YK21 VVX	Daf	FALF 260 4w Curtain	Pallex	Leeds
915	YK21 VVZ	Daf	FALF 260 4w Curtain	Pallex	Leeds
916	YK23 POF	Daf	FALF 260 4w Curtain	Pallex	Leeds
	YX73 NSY	Daf	FTG 480 6x2 (XF)	Longs	Leeds
	YX73 NTO	Daf	FTG 480 6x2 (XF)	Longs	Leeds

Maritime

Depot Codes

AL	Alconbury	**IP**	Ipswich	**PE**	Peterborough
BI	Birmingham	**IS**	Islip	**RE**	Reading
BR	Bristol	**LE**	Leeds	**SO**	Southampton
DS	Desborough	**LV**	Liverpool	**ST**	Stanford le Hope
DO	Doncaster	**LG**	London Gateway	**TM**	Tamworth
EM	East Mids Gateway	**MA**	Manchester	**TH**	Thrapston
EL	Ellistown	**ME**	Medway	**TI**	Tilbury
FX	Felixstowe	**MI**	Middlesbrough	**WI**	Widnes
HH	Hams Hall	**MK**	Milton Keynes	**WK**	Wakefield
IM	Immingham	**NO**	Northampton		

2936	KX17 RHV	Scania	DO	3480	KY19 GEK	Scania	NO
3332	KY19 FSK	Scania	LE	3481	KU69 XAO	Scania	MI
3334	KY19 FSU	Scania	EM	3482	KU69 XAP	Scania	LV
3339	KY19 FTV	Scania	MA	3483	KU69 XAV	Scania	BR
3344	KY19 FUD	Scania	MA	3484	KU69 XAW	Scania	EM
3345	KU69 XBW	Scania	BR	3485	KU69 XAX	Scania	AL
3346	KU69 XAB	Scania	LE	3486	KU69 XAY	Scania	TM
3347	KY19 FUG	Scania	EM	3487	KU69 XAZ	Scania	WI
3349	KY19 FUJ	Scania	DS	3488	KU69 XBA	Scania	FX
3352	KU69 XAD	Scania	IP	3489	KU69 XBB	Scania	IM
3353	KY19 FUT	Scania	MK	3490	KU69 XBC	Scania	MA
3354	KY19 FUU	Scania	EL	3491	KU69 XBD	Scania	AL
3355	KU69 XAE	Scania	TH	3492	KU69 XBF	Scania	LE
3356	KY19 FUW	Scania	EL	3493	KU69 XBG	Scania	IP
3357	KY19 FVA	Scania	MK	3494	KU69 XBH	Scania	NO
3358	KY19 FVB	Scania	IM	3495	KU69 XBJ	Scania	LV
3359	KY19 FVC	Scania	WI	3498	KU69 XBM	Scania	BR
3360	KY19 FVD	Scania	WI	3499	KU69 XBN	Scania	TM
3361	KY19 FVE	Scania	NO	3500	KU69 XBO	Scania	MA
3363	KY19 FVG	Scania	LE	3501	KY19 GHU	Scania	EL
3365	KY19 FVJ	Scania	IM	3503	KY19 GHX	Scania	LE
3367	KY19 FVL	Scania	IM	3504	KY19 GHZ	Scania	MK
3368	KU69 XAF	Scania	SO	3505	KY19 GJE	Scania	NO
3370	KU69 XAH	Scania	TM	3506	KY19 GJF	Scania	DS
3371	KY19 FVP	Scania	EL	3508	KY19 GJJ	Scania	EL
3372	KU69 XAJ	Scania	IM	3509	KY19 GJU	Scania	WI
3377	KY19 FVW	Scania	WI	3510	KY19 GJV	Scania	NO
3380	KY19 FWA	Scania	LV	3512	KU69 XBP	Scania	NO
3383	KY19 FWD	Scania	LV	3513	KU69 XBS	Scania	LE
3398	KY19 FWX	Scania	LV	3514	KU69 XBT	Scania	MI
3405	KY19 FXF	Scania	WI	3515	KU69 XBV	Scania	AL
3415	KY19 FXS	Scania	MA	3516	KU69 XBX	Scania	AL
3423	KY19 FYB	Scania	LE	3517	KU69 XBY	Scania	AL
3425	KY19 FYD	Scania	LV	3518	KU69 XBZ	Scania	MA
3434	KY19 FYN	Scania	LV	3519	KU69 XCB	Scania	LE
3435	KY19 FYP	Scania	BR	3521	KU69 XCD	Scania	IP
3469	KY19 GBO	Scania	EM	3522	KU69 XCF	Scania	MI
3470	KY19 GBU	Scania	NO	3523	KU69 XCF	Scania	MI
3471	KU69 XAL	Scania	LV	3524	KU69 XCG	Scania	BR
3472	KY19 GBX	Scania	PE	3525	KU69 XCH	Scania	LV
3473	KU69 XAM	Scania	IM	3539	KU69 YJS	Volvo	PE
3474	KU69 XAN	Scania	IP	3551	KU69 XER	Scania	FX
3475	KY19 GCK	Scania	ME	3552	KU69 XES	Scania	MI
3476	KY19 GCO	Scania	EL	3553	KU69 XHZ	Scania	AL
3477	KY19 GCU	Scania	LV	3555	KU69 XEY	Scania	LE
3478	KY19 GDZ	Scania	MA	3556	KU69 XFB	Scania	ME

Maritime (cont)

3557	KU69 XFD	Scania	MI	3620	KU69 XLJ	Scania	SO
3558	KU69 XFE	Scania	MA	3621	KU69 XLK	Scania	FX
3559	KU69 XFG	Scania	MI	3622	KU69 XLL	Scania	MA
3560	KU69 XFH	Scania	LE	3623	KU69 XLM	Scania	EM
3561	KU69 XFJ	Scania	TM	3624	KU69 XLN	Scania	FX
3562	KU69 XFK	Scania	EM	3625	KU69 XLO	Scania	IP
3564	KU69 XFN	Scania	MA	3626	KU69 XLP	Scania	LV
3565	KU69 XFO	Scania	WI	3627	KU69 XLS	Scania	TI
3566	KU69 XFP	Scania	TI	3628	KU69 XLT	Scania	LV
3567	KU69 XFW	Scania	FX	3629	KU69 XLV	Scania	AL
3569	KU69 XGO	Scania	IP	3630	KU69 XLW	Scania	NO
3570	KU69 XGP	Scania	MA	3631	KU69 XLX	Scania	ME
3571	KU69 XGS	Scania	AL	3632	KU69 XLY	Scania	LV
3572	KU69 XGV	Scania	EM	3633	KU69 XLZ	Scania	SO
3573	KU69 XGW	Scania	LE	3634	KU69 XOA	Scania	BR
3574	KU69 XGX	Scania	LE	3635	KU69 XOB	Scania	TM
3575	KU69 XGY	Scania	SO	3636	KU69 XOD	Scania	IM
3576	KU69 XGZ	Scania	BR	3637	KU69 XOE	Scania	DO
3577	KU69 XHJ	Scania	WI	3638	KU69 XOF	Scania	ME
3578	KU69 XHK	Scania	FX	3639	KU69 XOG	Scania	FX
3579	KU69 XHL	Scania	PE	3670	KU69 XRA	Scania	IL
3580	KU69 XHM	Scania	FX	3671	KU69 XRD	Scania	DO
3581	KU69 XHN	Scania	DO	3672	KU69 XRE	Scania	AL
3582	KU69 XHO	Scania	MA	3673	KU69 XRH	Scania	IP
3583	KU69 XHP	Scania	EM	3674	KU69 XRJ	Scania	NO
3584	KU69 XHW	Scania	AL	3675	KU69 XRK	Scania	AL
3585	KU69 XHX	Scania	IL	3676	KU69 XRM	Scania	LE
3587	KU69 XJB	Scania	MI	3677	KU69 XRN	Scania	AL
3588	KU69 XJC	Scania	NO	3678	KU69 XRP	Scania	NO
3589	KU69 XJE	Scania	MA	3679	KU69 XRR	Scania	SO
3590	KU69 XJF	Scania	MI	3680	KU70 WXA	Scania	MA
3591	KU69 XJG	Scania	IM	3681	KU70 WXB	Scania	ST
3593	KU69 XJK	Scania	NO	3682	KU70 WXC	Scania	MA
3594	KU69 XJM	Scania	AL	3683	KU70 WXD	Scania	ST
3595	KU69 XJN	Scania	TI	3684	KU70 WXE	Scania	ST
3596	KU69 XJO	Scania	BR	3685	KU70 WXF	Scania	ST
3597	KU69 XJP	Scania	FX	3686	KU70 WXG	Scania	SO
3598	KU69 XJT	Scania	SO	3687	KU70 WXH	Scania	SO
3599	KU69 XJV	Scania	MI	3688	KU70 WXJ	Scania	TM
3600	KU69 XJX	Scania	BR	3689	KU70 WXK	Scania	ME
3601	KU69 XJY	Scania	TM	3690	KU70 WXL	Scania	ST
3602	KU69 XJZ	Scania	MA	3691	KU70 WXM	Scania	ST
3603	KU69 XKK	Scania	EM	3692	KU70 WXN	Scania	ME
3604	KU69 XKM	Scania	EM	3693	KU70 WXO	Scania	MI
3605	KU69 XKN	Scania	AL	3694	KU70 WXP	Scania	ST
3606	KU69 XKO	Scania	EM	3695	KU70 WXR	Scania	FX
3607	KU69 XKP	Scania	TI	3696	KU70 WXS	Scania	FX
3608	KU69 XKS	Scania	NO	3697	KU70 WXT	Scania	MI
3609	KU69 XKV	Scania	LE	3698	KU70 WXV	Scania	MI
3610	KU69 XKW	Scania	BR	3699	KU70 WXW	Scania	BR
3611	KU69 XKX	Scania	IL	3700	KU70 WXX	Scania	SO
3612	KU69 XKY	Scania	FX	3701	KU70 WXY	Scania	SO
3613	KU69 XKZ	Scania	MA	3702	KU70 WXZ	Scania	TH
3614	KU69 XLB	Scania	SO	3703	KU70 WYA	Scania	TM
3615	KU69 XLC	Scania	AL	3704	KU70 WYB	Scania	TM
3616	KU69 XLD	Scania	TH	3705	KM70 ZGU	Volvo	FX
3617	KU69 XLE	Scania	NO	3706	KM70 ZGV	Volvo	FX
3618	KU69 XLF	Scania	MA	3708	KM70 ZGX	Volvo	FX
3619	KU69 XLH	Scania	LV	3709	KM70 ZGY	Volvo	FX

3712	KM70 ZHB	Volvo	FX	3772	KU70 WTY	Scania	FX
3713	KM70 ZHC	Volvo	FX	3773	KU70 WTZ	Scania	IM
3714	KM70 ZHD	Volvo	FX	3774	KY21 EUV	Scania	TM
3716	KM70 ZHF	Volvo	FX	3775	KU70 WUB	Scania	FX
3717	KM70 ZHP	Volvo	ST	3777	KU70 WUE	Scania	FX
3718	KM70 ZHR	Volvo	DO	3778	KU70 WUK	Scania	FX
3719	KM70 ZHG	Volvo	FX	3779	KY21 EUW	Scania	TM
3720	KM70 ZHO	Volvo	ST	3780	KY21 EUX	Scania	BR
3721	KM70 ZHK	Volvo	ST	3781	KU70 WUP	Scania	LE
3722	KM70 ZHN	Volvo	ST	3782	KU70 WUR	Scania	SO
3723	KM70 ZHH	Volvo	LE	3783	KY21 EUZ	Scania	FX
3724	KM70 ZHT	Volvo	DO	3784	KY21 EVB	Scania	SO
3725	KM70 ZHL	Volvo	ST	3785	KU70 WUW	Scania	LV
3726	KM70 ZHJ	Volvo	ST	3786	KY21 EVC	Scania	ST
3727	KM70 ZHZ	Volvo	SO	3787	KY21 EVD	Scania	ST
3728	KM70 ZHU	Volvo	DO	3788	KY21 EVF	Scania	IM
3729	KM70 ZHV	Volvo	DO	3789	KU70 WVO	Scania	TM
3730	KM70 ZHX	Volvo	MA	3790	KY21 EVG	Scania	FX
3731	KM70 ZHY	Volvo	MA	3791	KU70 WVR	Scania	TM
3732	KM70 ZJE	Volvo	SO	3792	KY21 EVH	Scania	ST
3733	KM70 ZJJ	Volvo	LE	3793	KU70 WVV	Scania	FX
3734	KM70 ZHW	Volvo	LV	3794	KY21 EVJ	Scania	FX
3735	KU70 XUA	Volvo	SO	3795	KY21 EVK	Scania	IM
3736	KU70 XUC	Volvo	SO	3796	KY21 EVL	Scania	IM
3737	KM70 ZGP	Volvo	ST	3797	KY21 EVM	Scania	IM
3738	KM70 ZGR	Volvo	ST	3798	KU70 WZA	Scania	SO
3739	KP70 THX	Volvo	SO	3799	KY21 EVN	Scania	FX
3740	KY21 GZD	Volvo	ST	3800	KY21 EVP	Scania	ST
3741	KM70 ZJN	Volvo	ST	3801	KU70 WZD	Scania	FX
3742	KP70 THZ	Volvo	SO	3802	KY21 EVR	Scania	FX
3743	KU70 XTZ	Volvo	SO	3803	KU70 WZF	Scania	FX
3744	KU70 XUB	Volvo	SO	3804	KY21 EVT	Scania	FX
3745	KU70 XTX	Volvo	SO	3805	KY21 EVU	Scania	SO
3746	KY21 GZE	Volvo	ST	3806	KU70 WZK	Scania	TM
3747	KY21 GZF	Volvo	ST	3807	KU70 WZL	Scania	FX
3748	KY21 GZG	Volvo	ST	3808	KY21 EVV	Scania	NO
3749	KY21 GZH	Volvo	ST	3809	KU70 WZO	Scania	ST
3750	KY21 GZJ	Volvo	ST	3810	KY21 EVW	Scania	FX
3751	KY21 GZK	Volvo	SO	3811	KY21 EVX	Scania	MI
3752	KY21 GZL	Volvo	SO	3812	KY21 EWE	Scania	ST
3753	KY21 GZM	Volvo	SO	3813	KU70 WZT	Scania	SO
3754	KY21 GZN	Volvo	SO	3814	KY21 EWF	Scania	SO
3755	KU70 WPW	Scania	FX	3815	KY21 EWG	Scania	FX
3756	KU70 WPX	Scania	FX	3816	KU70 WZX	Scania	ST
3757	KY21 EUN	Scania	FX	3817	KY21 EWH	Scania	FX
3758	KU70 WPZ	Scania	FX	3818	KU70 WZZ	Scania	SO
3759	KU70 WRA	Scania	FX	3819	KY21 EWJ	Scania	MA
3760	KU70 WRP	Scania	FX	3820	KR70 KRX	Scania	FX
3761	KU70 WRR	Scania	FX	3821	KR70 KRZ	Scania	TI I
3762	KU70 WRW	Scania	FX	3822	KR70 KSE	Scania	TH
3763	KY21 EUO	Scania	FX	3823	KR70 KSF	Scania	FX
3764	KU70 WRZ	Scania	FX	3824	KR70 KSJ	Scania	FX
3765	KU70 WSZ	Scania	FX	3825	KY21 EWK	Scania	MA
3766	KU70 WTF	Scania	FX	3826	KR70 KSO	Scania	AL
3767	KU70 WTR	Scania	FX	3827	KR70 KSU	Scania	SO
3768	KY21 EUP	Scania	SO	3828	KR70 KSV	Scania	SO
3769	KY21 EUR	Scania	ST	3829	KY21 EWL	Scania	SO
3770	KY21 EUT	Scania	FX	3830	KY21 EWM	Scania	MI
3771	KY21 EUU	Scania	FX	3831	KR70 KSZ	Scania	FX

Maritime (cont)

3832	KR70 KVL	Scania	SO		3891	AY21 TSV	Mercedes	ST
3833	KY21 EWN	Scania	ST		3892	AY21 TSX	Mercedes	ST
3834	KR70 KVO	Scania	SO		3893	AY21 TSZ	Mercedes	TM
3835	KY21 EWO	Scania	SO		3894	AY21 TTE	Mercedes	ST
3836	KY21 EWP	Scania	FX		3895	AY21 TTF	Mercedes	SO
3837	KR70 KVT	Scania	FX		3896	AY21 TTJ	Mercedes	SO
3838	KY21 EWR	Scania	SO		3897	AY21 TTK	Mercedes	SO
3839	KR70 KVV	Scania	AL		3898	AY21 TTO	Mercedes	SO
3840	KR70 KVW	Scania	FX		3899	AY21 TTU	Mercedes	TM
3841	KR70 KVX	Scania	SO		3900	AY21 TTV	Mercedes	SO
3842	KY21 EWT	Scania	MA		3901	AY21 TTX	Mercedes	SO
3843	KR70 KWA	Scania	FX		3902	AY21 TTZ	Mercedes	LE
3844	KR70 KWB	Scania	FX		3903	AY21 TUA	Mercedes	TM
3845	KY21 EWU	Scania	NO		3904	AY21 TUH	Mercedes	SO
3846	KY21 EWV	Scania	FX		3905	AY21 TUJ	Mercedes	SO
3847	KR70 KWE	Scania	FX		3906	AY21 TUO	Mercedes	LE
3848	KR70 KWF	Scania	SO		3907	AY21 TUP	Mercedes	FX
3849	KY21 EWW	Scania	FX		3908	AY21 TUU	Mercedes	SO
3850	KY21 EWX	Scania	NO		3909	AY21 TUV	Mercedes	LE
3851	KY21 EWZ	Scania	SO		3910	AY21 TUW	Mercedes	TM
3852	KY21 EXB	Scania	SO		3911	AY21 TVA	Mercedes	TM
3853	KY21 EXC	Scania	LE		3912	AY21 TVC	Mercedes	TM
3854	KR70 KSK	Scania	FX		3913	AY21 TVD	Mercedes	TM
3855	AY21 TLO	Mercedes	SO		3914	AY21 TVE	Mercedes	IM
3856	AY21 TLU	Mercedes	PE		3915	AY21 TVF	Mercedes	FX
3857	AY21 TLV	Mercedes	FX		3916	AY21 TVJ	Mercedes	FX
3858	AY21 TLZ	Mercedes	ST		3917	AY21 TVK	Mercedes	FX
3859	AY21 TMO	Mercedes	SO		3918	AY21 TVL	Mercedes	SO
3860	AY21 TMU	Mercedes	SO		3919	AY21 TVM	Mercedes	SO
3861	AY21 TMV	Mercedes	IM		3920	AY21 TVN	Mercedes	LE
3862	AY21 TMX	Mercedes	SO		3921	AY21 TVO	Mercedes	SO
3863	AY21 TMZ	Mercedes	MA		3922	AY21 TVP	Mercedes	SO
3864	AY21 TNE	Mercedes	DO		3923	AY21 TVT	Mercedes	SO
3865	AY21 TNF	Mercedes	LE		3924	AY21 TVU	Mercedes	IM
3866	AY21 TNJ	Mercedes	IM		3925	AV21 HFH	Mercedes	LE
3867	AY21 TNK	Mercedes	LE		3926	AV21 HFJ	Mercedes	ST
3868	AY21 TNL	Mercedes	FX		3927	AV21 HYB	Mercedes	TM
3869	AY21 TNN	Mercedes	ST		3928	AV21 HYC	Mercedes	FX
3870	AY21 TNO	Mercedes	DO		3929	AV21 HYJ	Mercedes	ST
3871	AY21 TNU	Mercedes	DO		3930	AV21 HYK	Mercedes	ST
3872	AY21 TNV	Mercedes	ST		3931	AV21 KLC	Mercedes	ST
3873	AY21 TNX	Mercedes	DO		3932	AV21 KLK	Mercedes	ST
3874	AY21 TNZ	Mercedes	LE		3933	AV21 KLL	Mercedes	LE
3875	AY21 TOA	Mercedes	FX		3934	AV21 KLM	Mercedes	LE
3876	AY21 TOH	Mercedes	FX		3935	AV21 KRU	Mercedes	ST
3877	AY21 TOJ	Mercedes	ST		3936	AV21 LDJ	Mercedes	ST
3878	AY21 TOU	Mercedes	FX		3937	AV21 LDU	Mercedes	FX
3879	AY21 TOV	Mercedes	SO		3938	AV21 LDX	Mercedes	FX
3880	AY21 TPF	Mercedes	FX		3939	AV21 LVZ	Mercedes	ST
3881	AY21 TPO	Mercedes	FX		3940	AV21 LWA	Mercedes	ST
3882	AY21 TPU	Mercedes	TM		3941	AV21 MDN	Mercedes	ST
3883	AY21 TPV	Mercedes	TM		3942	AV21 NCE	Mercedes	ST
3884	AY21 TPX	Mercedes	TM		3943	AV21 OLU	Mercedes	SO
3885	AY21 TPZ	Mercedes	ST		3944	AV21 OLW	Mercedes	SO
3886	AY21 TRV	Mercedes	ST		3945	AV21 OMF	Mercedes	ST
3887	AY21 TRX	Mercedes	IM		3946	AY21 TLK	Mercedes	ST
3888	AY21 TRZ	Mercedes	ST		3947	AV21 OWX	Mercedes	SO
3889	AY21 TSO	Mercedes	SO		3948	AV21 OXA	Mercedes	DO
3890	AY21 TSU	Mercedes	TM		3949	AV21 OZD	Mercedes	FX

3950	AY21 TLX	Mercedes	ST		4009	KY71 DDV	Volvo	ME
3951	AV21 PVK	Mercedes	FX		4010	KY71 DDX	Volvo	LE
3952	AV21 YHW	Mercedes	FX		4011	KY17 DDZ	Volvo	IP
3953	AV21 YHX	Mercedes	FX		4012	KY71 DFA	Volvo	LE
3954	KY21 HJA	Volvo	MI		4013	KY71 DFC	Volvo	MA
3955	KY21 HJC	Volvo	DO		4014	KY71 DFD	Volvo	LE
3956	KY21 HJD	Volvo	DO		4015	KY71 DFE	Volvo	LE
3957	KY21 HJE	Volvo	IP		4016	KY71 DFF	Volvo	LG
3958	KY21 HJF	Volvo	ST		4017	KY71 DFG	Volvo	DO
3959	KY21 HJG	Volvo	DO		4018	KY71 DFJ	Volvo	MA
3960	KY21 HJJ	Volvo	MI		4019	KY71 DFK	Volvo	AL
3961	KY21 HJK	Volvo	IL		4020	KY71 DFL	Volvo	LE
3962	KY21 HJN	Volvo	SO		4021	KY71 DFN	Volvo	ME
3963	KY21 HJO	Volvo	SO		4022	KY71 DZZ	Volvo	IP
3964	KY21 HJU	Volvo	AL		4023	KY71 EAA	Volvo	IP
3965	KY21 GVA	Volvo	SO		4024	KY71 EAC	Volvo	PE
3966	KY21 GVC	Volvo	SO		4025	KY71 EAE	Volvo	IP
3967	KY21 GVD	Volvo	TM		4026	KY71 EAF	Volvo	IP
3968	AY21 TLN	Mercedes	ST		4027	KY71 EAG	Volvo	MA
3969	KY21 GVF	Volvo	TM		4028	KY71 EAJ	Volvo	MA
3970	KY21 GVG	Volvo	BR		4029	KY71 EAK	Volvo	BI
3971	KY21 GVJ	Volvo	LV		4030	KY71 EAM	Volvo	FX
3972	KY21 GVK	Volvo	FX		4031	KY71 EAO	Volvo	MA
3973	KY21 GVL	Volvo	LV		4032	KY71 EAP	Volvo	LE
3974	KY21 GVM	Volvo	LE		4033	KY71 EAW	Volvo	LE
3975	KY21 GVN	Volvo	SO		4034	KY71 EAX	Volvo	MI
3976	KY21 GVO	Volvo	TM		4035	KY71 EBA	Volvo	FX
3977	KY21 GVP	Volvo	ST		4036	KY71 EBC	Volvo	FX
3978	KY21 GVR	Volvo	DO		4037	KY71 EBD	Volvo	FX
3979	KY21 GVT	Volvo	LE		4038	KY71 EBF	Volvo	MA
3980	KY21 GVX	Volvo	SO		4039	KY71 EBG	Volvo	DO
3981	KY21 GVZ	Volvo	AL		4040	KY71 EBJ	Volvo	ME
3982	KY71 CZW	Volvo			4041	KY71 EBK	Volvo	RE
3983	KY71 CZX	Volvo			4042	KY71 DHA	Volvo	DO
3984	KY71 CZZ	Volvo			4043	KY71 DHC	Volvo	DO
3985	KY71 DAA	Volvo			4044	KY71 DHD	Volvo	LV
3986	KY71 DAO	Volvo			4045	KY71 DHE	Volvo	PE
3987	KY71 DAU	Volvo			4046	KY71 DHF	Volvo	LV
3988	KY71 DBO	Volvo			4047	KY71 DHG	Volvo	LV
3989	KY71 DBU	Volvo			4048	KY71 DHJ	Volvo	LV
3990	KY71 DBV	Volvo			4049	KY71 DHK	Volvo	LE
3991	KY71 DBX	Volvo			4050	KY71 DHL	Volvo	SO
3992	KY71 DBZ	Volvo			4051	KY71 DHM	Volvo	SO
3993	KY71 DCE	Volvo			4052	KY71 DHN	Volvo	SO
3994	KY71 DCF	Volvo	IP		4053	KY71 DHO	Volvo	PE
3995	KY71 DCO	Volvo	IP		4054	KY71 DHP	Volvo	ME
3996	KY71 DCU	Volvo	IP		4055	KY71 DHU	Volvo	WI
3997	KY71 DCV	Volvo	IP		4056	KY71 DHV	Volvo	MI
3008	KY71 DCX	Volvo	DO		4057	KY71 DHX	Volvo	DO
3999	KY71 DCZ	Volvo	MA		4058	KY71 DHZ	Volvo	SO
4000	KY71 DDA	Volvo	PE		4059	KY71 DJD	Volvo	SO
4001	KY71 DDE	Volvo	PE		4060	KY71 DJE	Volvo	AL
4002	KY71 DDF	Volvo	LE		4061	KY71 DJF	Volvo	AL
4003	KY71 DDJ	Volvo	IP		4062	KY71 DJJ	Volvo	FX
4004	KY71 DDK	Volvo	ME		4063	KY71 DJK	Volvo	FX
4005	KY71 DDL	Volvo	LE		4064	KY71 DJO	Volvo	FX
4006	KY71 DDN	Volvo	DO		4065	KY71 DJU	Volvo	SO
4007	KY71 DDO	Volvo	LE		4066	KY71 DJV	Volvo	MA
4008	KY71 DDU	Volvo	DO		4067	KY71 DJX	Volvo	LG

4068	KY71 DJZ	Volvo	LV	4128	KM71 OOF	Volvo	LE
4069	KY71 DKA	Volvo	LV	4129	KM71 OOG	Volvo	AL
4070	KY71 DKD	Volvo	WI	4130	KM71 OOH	Volvo	FX
4071	KY71 DTZ	Volvo	MI	4131	KM71 OOJ	Volvo	FX
4072	KY71 DTX	Volvo	MI	4132	KR71 DKJ	Volvo	FX
4073	KY71 DTV	Volvo	MI	4133	KR71 DKK	Volvo	NO
4074	KY71 DTU	Volvo	MI	4134	KR71 DKL	Volvo	FX
4075	KY71 DTO	Volvo	TM	4135	KR71 DKN	Volvo	LG
4076	KY71 DTN	Volvo	TM	4136	KR71 DKO	Volvo	TM
4077	KY71 DTK	Volvo	TM	4137	KR71 DKU	Volvo	MA
4078	KY71 DTF	Volvo	TM	4138	KR71 DKV	Volvo	AL
4079	KY71 DSZ	Volvo	SO	4139	KR71 DKX	Volvo	LE
4080	KY71 DSX	Volvo	SO	4140	KR71 DKY	Volvo	SO
4081	KY71 DRV	Volvo	SO	4141	KR71 DLD	Volvo	AL
4082	KY71 DRO	Volvo	SO	4142	KR71 DLE	Volvo	TM
4083	KY71 DPV	Volvo	SO	4143	KR71 DLF	Volvo	SO
4084	KY71 DPU	Volvo	SO	4144	KR71 DLJ	Volvo	LE
4085	KY71 DPO	Volvo	MA	4145	KR71 DLK	Volvo	PE
4086	KY71 DPN	Volvo	SO	4146	KR71 DLN	Volvo	TM
4087	KY71 DPK	Volvo	MI	4147	KR71 DLO	Volvo	EM
4088	KY71 DOU	Volvo	MA	4148	KR71 DLU	Volvo	LV
4089	KY71 DOJ	Volvo	MA	4149	KR71 DLV	Volvo	MI
4090	KY71 DOH	Volvo	SO	4150	KR71 DLX	Volvo	NO
4091	KY71 DOA	Volvo	SO	4151	KR71 DLY	Volvo	AL
4092	KY71 DNX	Volvo	LG	4152	KR71 DME	Volvo	AL
4093	KY71 DNV	Volvo	SO	4153	KR71 DMF	Volvo	LE
4094	KY71 DNU	Volvo	DO	4154	KR71 DMO	Volvo	LE
4095	KY71 DNO	Volvo	MA	4155	KR71 DMU	Volvo	AL
4096	KY71 BXA	Scania	IM	4156	KR71 DMV	Volvo	PE
4097	KY71 BXB	Scania	NO	4157	KR71 DMX	Volvo	MA
4098	KY71 BXC	Scania	FX	4158	KR71 DMY	Volvo	ME
4099	KY71 BXD	Scania	BR	4159	KR71 DMZ	Volvo	SO
4100	KY71 BXE	Scania	NO	4160	KR71 DUA	Volvo	EM
4101	KY71 BXF	Scania	SO	4161	KR71 DUH	Volvo	MA
4102	KY71 BXG	Scania	MA	4162	KR71 DUJ	Volvo	LE
4104	KY71 BXJ	Scania	BR	4163	KR71 DUU	Volvo	FX
4105	KY71 BXK	Scania	TM	4164	KR71 DUV	Volvo	AL·
4106	KY71 BXL	Scania	MI	4165	KR71 DUY	Volvo	EM
4107	KY71 BXM	Scania	BR	4166	KR71 DVA	Volvo	BR
4108	KY71 BXN	Scania	ME	4167	KR71 DVB	Volvo	FX
4109	KY71 BXO	Scania	FX	4168	KR71 DVC	Volvo	LG
4110	KY71 BXP	Scania	FX	4169	KY22 FLP	Volvo	LG
4111	KY71 BXR	Scania	LG	4170	KY71 DFU	Volvo	WI
4112	KY71 BXU	Scania	FX	4171	KY71 DFV	Volvo	FX
4113	KY71 BXV	Scania	LE	4172	KY71 DFX	Volvo	TM
4114	KY71 BXW	Scania	PE	4173	KY71 DGU	Volvo	SO
4115	KY71 BXX	Scania	LV	4174	KY71 DGV	Volvo	IL
4116	KY71 BXZ	Scania	IM	4175	KY71 DGX	Volvo	AL
4117	KY71 BYA	Scania	NO	4176	KY71 DGZ	Volvo	LG
4118	KY71 BYB	Scania	NO	4177	KY71 DKE	Volvo	LE
4119	KY71 BYC	Scania	EM	4178	KY71 DKF	Volvo	MA
4120	KY71 BYD	Scania	LE	4179	KY71 DNN	Volvo	WI
4121	KM71 ONX	Volvo	DO	4180	KY71 EDK	Volvo	LE
4122	KM71 ONZ	Volvo	FX	4181	KY71 EDJ	Volvo	LG
4123	KM71 OOA	Volvo		4182	KY71 EDF	Volvo	PE
4124	KM71 OOB	Volvo	LV	4183	KY71 EDC	Volvo	ME
4125	KM71 OOC	Volvo	AL	4184	KY71 ECZ	Volvo	IP
4126	KM71 OOD	Volvo		4185	KY71 ECX	Volvo	TM
4127	KM71 OOE	Volvo		4186	KY71 ECW	Volvo	DO

4187	KY71 ECV	Volvo	LE	4286	KY22 FLE	Volvo	SO
4188	KY71 ECT	Volvo	DO	4287	KY22 FLF	Volvo	SO
4189	KY71 ECN	Volvo	DO	4288	KY22 FLG	Volvo	SO
4190	KY71 ECJ	Volvo	DO	4289	KY22 FLH	Volvo	WK
4191	KY71 ECF	Volvo	TM	4290	KY22 FLJ	Volvo	TM
4192	KY71 ECE	Volvo	AL	4291	KY22 FLK	Volvo	TM
4193	KY71 DWX	Volvo	TH	4292	KY22 FLL	Volvo	IP
4194	KY71 DWW	Volvo	TH	4293	KY22 FLM	Volvo	IP
4195	KY71 DWV	Volvo	LG	4294	KY22 FLN	Volvo	EM
4196	KY71 DWU	Volvo	LG	4295	KY22 FLV	Volvo	AL
4197	KY71 DWP	Volvo	LG	4296	KY22 FVH	Volvo	TM
4198	KY71 DWO	Volvo	MI	4297	KY22 FVM	Volvo	SO
4199	KY71 DWN	Volvo	IP	4298	KY22 FVN	Volvo	DO
4200	KY71 DWM	Volvo	IP	4299	KY22 FVO	Volvo	WK
4201	KY71 DWL	Volvo	TM	4300	KY22 FVR	Volvo	MA
4202	KY71 DWK	Volvo	MI	4301	KY22 FEW	Volvo	LG
4203	KY71 DWJ	Volvo	SO	4302	KY22 FWJ	Volvo	FX
4204	KY71 DWG	Volvo	SO	4303	KY22 FWK	Volvo	FX
4245	KS71 LVJ	Volvo	SO	4304	KY22 FWL	Volvo	PE
4246	KS71 LVK	Volvo	SO	4305	KY22 FWU	Volvo	SO
4247	KS71 LVL	Volvo	MA	4306	KY22 FXA	Volvo	FX
4248	KS71 LVM	Volvo	NO	4307	KY22 FXB	Volvo	WK
4249	KS71 LVN	Volvo	MA	4308	KY22 FRR	Volvo	WK
4250	KS71 LVO	Volvo	FX	4309	KY22 FRU	Volvo	WK
4251	KS71 LVP	Volvo	FX	4310	KY22 FRX	Volvo	DO
4252	KS71 LVR	Volvo	FX	4311	KY22 FRZ	Volvo	LG
4253	KS71 LVT	Volvo	FX	4312	KY22 FSA	Volvo	LG
4254	KS71 LVU	Volvo	FX	4313	KY22 FSC	Volvo	LG
4255	KS71 LVV	Volvo	FX	4314	KY22 FSD	Volvo	LG
4256	KS71 LVW	Volvo	FX	4315	KY22 FSE	Volvo	SO
4257	KS22 GFJ	Volvo	SO	4316	KY22 FSF	Volvo	SO
4258	KS71 LVY	Volvo	FX	4317	KY22 FSG	Volvo	DO
4259	KS71 LWC	Volvo	FX	4318	KY22 FSJ	Volvo	MA
4260	KS71 LWD	Volvo	FX	4319	KY22 FSL	Volvo	BR
4261	KS71 LWE	Volvo	AL	4320	KY22 FSN	Volvo	BR
4262	KS71 LWF	Volvo	AL	4321	KY22 FSO	Volvo	BR
4263	KS71 LWG	Volvo	AL	4322	KY22 FSP	Volvo	BR
4264	KS71 LWH	Volvo	WK	4323	KY22 FSS	Volvo	TM
4265	KS71 LWJ	Volvo	EM	4324	KY22 FSV	Volvo	AL
4266	KS71 LWK	Volvo	EM	4325	KY22 FSX	Volvo	LV
4267	KS71 LWL	Volvo	TM	4326	KY22 FSZ	Volvo	DO
4268	KS71 LWM	Volvo	TM	4327	KY22 FTA	Volvo	MI
4269	KS71 LWN	Volvo	TM	4328	KY22 FTC	Volvo	IM
4270	KS71 LWO	Volvo	TM	4329	KY22 FTD	Volvo	DO
4271	KS71 LWP	Volvo	SO	4330	KY22 FTE	Volvo	DO
4272	KS71 LWR	Volvo	WK	4331	KY22 FTF	Volvo	TI
4273	KS71 LWT	Volvo	LV	4332	KY22 FTK	Volvo	NO
4274	KS71 LWU	Volvo	MA	4333	KY22 FTN	Volvo	ST
4275	KS71 MDZ	Volvo	LV	4334	KY22 FTO	Volvo	WK
4276	KY22 FKT	Volvo	SO	4335	KY22 FTP	Volvo	NO
4277	KY22 FKU	Volvo	EM	4336	KY22 FTU	Volvo	DO
4278	KY22 FKV	Volvo	AL	4337	KY22 FUE	Volvo	ST
4279	KY22 FKW	Volvo	AL	4338	KY22 FUF	Volvo	FX
4280	KY22 FKX	Volvo	MA	4339	KY22 FUP	Volvo	DO
4281	KY22 FKZ	Volvo	WI	4340	KY22 FUV	Volvo	DO
4282	KY22 FLA	Volvo	MI	4341	KY22 FXZ	Volvo	IM
4283	KY22 FLB	Volvo	SO	4342	KY22 FYA	Volvo	EM
4284	KY22 FLC	Volvo	SO	4343	KY22 FYF	Volvo	FX
4285	KY22 FLD	Volvo	SO	4344	KY22 FLW	Volvo	EM

4345	KY22 FLX	Volvo	BR	4404	KY72 HKG	Volvo	FX
4346	KY22 FLZ	Volvo	MA	4405	KY72 HKH	Volvo	FX
4347	KY22 FYR	Volvo	LV	4406	KY72 HKJ	Volvo	FX
4348	KY22 FYU	Volvo	TM	4407	KY72 HKK	Volvo	SO
4349	KY22 FZB	Volvo	MA	4408	KY72 HKL	Volvo	TM
4350	KY22 FZJ	Volvo	TH	4409	KY72 HKM	Volvo	SO
4351	KY22 FZM	Volvo	IM	4410	KY72 HKN	Volvo	ST
4352	KY22 FZO	Volvo	MI	4411	KY72 HKO	Volvo	FX
4353	KY22 FZT	Volvo	WK	4412	KY72 HKP	Volvo	DO
4354	KY22 FZV	Volvo	TM	4413	KY72 HKT	Volvo	DO
4355	KY22 FZW	Volvo	WK	4414	KY72 HDF	Volvo	SO
4356	KY22 GAA	Volvo	WK	4415	KY72 HDG	Volvo	TM
4357	KY22 GAU	Volvo	BR	4416	KY72 HDH	Volvo	DO
4358	KY22 GAX	Volvo	NO	4417	KY72 HDJ	Volvo	MI
4359	KY22 GBE	Volvo	WI	4418	KY72 HDK	Volvo	DO
4360	KY22 GBF	Volvo	MA	4419	KY72 HDL	Volvo	NO
4361	KY22 GBV	Volvo	WI	4420	KY72 HDN	Volvo	NO
4362	KY22 GBZ	Volvo	WK	4421	KY72 HDO	Volvo	FX
4363	KY22 GCF	Volvo	WK	4422	KY72 HDU	Volvo	TM
4364	KY22 GCV	Volvo	MA	4423	KY72 HDV	Volvo	ST
4365	KY22 FMA	Volvo	EM	4424	KY72 HDX	Volvo	SO
4366	KY22 FMC	Volvo	EM	4425	KY72 HDZ	Volvo	LV
4367	KY22 FMD	Volvo	MI	4426	KY72 HEJ	Volvo	LV
4368	KY22 FME	Volvo	MI	4427	KY72 HEU	Volvo	MA
4369	KY72 HGP	Volvo	FX	4428	KY72 HEV	Volvo	WK
4370	KY72 HGU	Volvo	FX	4429	KY72 HFA	Volvo	RE
4371	KY72 HGX	Volvo	FX	4430	KY72 HFB	Volvo	MI
4372	KY72 HGZ	Volvo	FX	4431	KY72 HFC	Volvo	TM
4373	KY72 HHA	Volvo	FX	4432	KY72 HFD	Volvo	MA
4374	KY72 HHB	Volvo	FX	4433	KY72 HFE	Volvo	LV
4375	KY72 HHC	Volvo	FX	4434	KY72 HFF	Volvo	LV
4376	KY72 HHD	Volvo	SO	4435	KY72 HFG	Volvo	LV
4377	KY72 HHE	Volvo	SO	4436	KY72 HFK	Volvo	MA
4378	KY72 HHF	Volvo	SO	4437	KY72 HFL	Volvo	DO
4379	KY72 HHG	Volvo	SO	4438	KY72 HFM	Volvo	DO
4380	KY72 HHJ	Volvo	DO	4439	KY72 HFN	Volvo	FX
4381	KY72 HHK	Volvo	WK	4440	KY72 HFO	Volvo	FX
4382	KY72 HHL	Volvo	DO	4441	KY72 HFP	Volvo	FX
4383	KY72 HHM	Volvo	DO	4442	KY72 HFR	Volvo	LV
4384	KY72 HHN	Volvo	WK	4443	KY72 HFS	Volvo	FX
4385	KY72 HHO	Volvo	WK	4445	KY72 HFU	Volvo	DO
4386	KY72 HHP	Volvo	TM	4446	KY72 HFV	Volvo	ST
4387	KY72 HHR	Volvo	TM	4447	KY72 HFW	Volvo	ST
4388	KY72 HHS	Volvo	TM	4448	KY72 HFX	Volvo	IP
4389	KY72 HHT	Volvo	HH	4449	KY72 HFZ	Volvo	DO
4390	KY72 HHU	Volvo	FX	4450	KY72 HGA	Volvo	MI
4391	KY72 HHV	Volvo	WK	4451	KY72 HGC	Volvo	EM
4392	KY72 HHW	Volvo	DO	4452	KY72 HGD	Volvo	DO
4393	KY72 HHX	Volvo	DO	4453	KY72 HGE	Volvo	MI
4394	KY72 HHZ	Volvo	DO	4454	KY72 HGF	Volvo	EM
4395	KY72 HJV	Volvo	WI	4455	KY72 HGG	Volvo	TM
4396	KY72 HJX	Volvo	FX	4456	KY72 HGJ	Volvo	BR
4397	KY72 HJZ	Volvo	HH	4457	KY72 HGK	Volvo	NO
4398	KY72 HKA	Volvo	WK	4458	KY72 HGL	Volvo	IP
4399	KY72 HKB	Volvo	DO	4459	KY72 HGM	Volvo	IP
4400	KY72 HKC	Volvo	DO	4460	KY72 HGN	Volvo	FX
4401	KY72 HKD	Volvo	MI	4461	KY72 HGO	Volvo	RE
4402	KY72 HKE	Volvo	MA	4462	KY72 HAA	Volvo	DO
4403	KY72 HKF	Volvo	WK	4463	KY72 HAE	Volvo	DO

4464	KY72 HAO	Volvo	TM	4523	KY72 FFJ	Scania	LV
4465	KY72 HAU	Volvo	TM	4524	KY72 FFK	Scania	WK
4466	KY72 HAX	Volvo	WK	4525	KY23 GXO	Scania	NO
4467	KY72 HBA	Volvo	WK	4526	KY23 GXR	Scania	NO
4468	KY72 HBB	Volvo	MA	4527	KY23 GXS	Scania	NO
4469	KY72 HBC	Volvo	MA	4528	KY72 FFO	Scania	NO
4470	KY72 HBD	Volvo	IP	4529	KY23 GXT	Scania	NO
4471	KY72 HBE	Volvo	IP	4530	KY23 GXU	Scania	NO
4472	KY72 HBF	Volvo	BR	4531	KY72 FFS	Scania	NO
4473	KY72 HBG	Volvo	BR	4532	KY72 FFT	Scania	NO
4474	KY72 HBH	Volvo	IP	4533	KY23 GYD	Scania	NO
4475	KY72 HBJ	Volvo	IP	4534	KY23 GYE	Scania	NO
4476	KY72 HBK	Volvo	BR	4535	AY23 VAA	Mercedes	DO
4477	KY72 HBL	Volvo	DO	4536	AY23 VAD	Mercedes	BR
4478	KY72 HBN	Volvo	PE	4537	AY23 VAE	Mercedes	BR
4479	KY23 JXD	Volvo	BR	4538	AY23 VAF	Mercedes	DO
4480	KY23 JXE	Volvo	PE	4539	AY23 VAH	Mercedes	FX
4481	KY23 JXF	Volvo	PE	4540	AY23 VAJ	Mercedes	FX
4482	KY23 JXG	Volvo	AL	4541	AY23 VAK	Mercedes	DO
4483	KY23 JXH	Volvo	FX	4542	AY23 VAM	Mercedes	IP
4484	KY23 JXJ	Volvo	AL	4543	AY23 VAO	Mercedes	SO
4485	KY23 JXK	Volvo	FX	4544	AY23 VAU	Mercedes	DO
4486	KY23 JXL	Volvo	MA	4545	AY23 VAV	Mercedes	FX
4487	KY23 JXM	Volvo	SO	4546	AY73 TFA	Mercedes	MI
4488	KY23 JXN	Volvo	PE	4547	AY23 VBA	Mercedes	DO
4489	KY23 JXO	Volvo	WK	4548	AY73 TFE	Mercedes	ST
4490	KY23 JXP	Volvo	MA	4549	AY23 VBC	Mercedes	FX
4491	KY23 JXR	Volvo	MA	4550	AY23 VBD	Mercedes	DO
4492	KY23 JXS	Volvo	MA	4551	AY73 TFF	Mercedes	FX
4493	KY23 JXT	Volvo	DO	4552	AY73 TFK	Mercedes	TI
4494	KY23 JXU	Volvo	IM	4553	AY73 TFN	Mercedes	DO
4495	KY72 FDJ	Scania	NO	4554	AY23 VBJ	Mercedes	IP
4496	KY72 FDK	Scania	NO	4555	AY73 TFO	Mercedes	DO
4497	KY72 FDL	Scania	NO	4556	AY73 TFU	Mercedes	TI
4498	KY72 FDM	Scania	NO	4557	AY73 TFV	Mercedes	FX
4499	KY72 FDN	Scania	NO	4558	AY73 TFX	Mercedes	MI
4500	KY72 FDO	Scania	NO	4559	AY73 TFZ	Mercedes	TI
4501	KY23 GXH	Scania	NO	4560	AY73 TGE	Mercedes	IP
4502	KY23 GXK	Scania	NO	4561	AY73 TGF	Mercedes	DO
4503	KY72 FDX	Scania	NO	4562	AY73 TGJ	Mercedes	DO
4504	KY23 GXL	Scania	NO	4563	AY73 TGK	Mercedes	TI
4505	KY72 FEF	Scania	ST	4564	AY73 TGN	Mercedes	FX
4506	KY72 FEG	Scania	FX	4565	AY73 TGO	Mercedes	DO
4507	KY72 FEH	Scania	DO	4566	AY73 TGU	Mercedes	TI
4508	KY72 FEJ	Scania	DO	4567	AY73 TGV	Mercedes	
4509	KY72 FEK	Scania	ST	4568	AY73 TGX	Mercedes	FX
4510	KY72 FEM	Scania	FX	4569	AY73 TGZ	Mercedes	DO
4511	KY72 FEO	Scania	SO	4570	AY73 THF	Mercedes	FX
4512	KY72 FEP	Scania	ST	4571	AY73 TKA	Mercedes	IP
4513	KY72 FET	Scania	ST	4572	AY73 TKC	Mercedes	BR
4514	KY72 FEU	Scania	DO	4573	AY73 TKD	Mercedes	IP
4515	KY72 FEV	Scania	FX	4574	AY73 TKE	Mercedes	MA
4516	KY72 FEX	Scania	WK	4575	AY73 TKF	Mercedes	FX
4517	KY72 FFB	Scania	FX	4576	AY73 TKJ	Mercedes	MA
4518	KY72 FFC	Scania	SO	4577	AY73 TKK	Mercedes	MA
4519	KY72 FFD	Scania	SO	4578	AY73 TKN	Mercedes	FX
4520	KY72 FFE	Scania	MA	4579	AY73 TKT	Mercedes	BR
4521	KY72 FFG	Scania	TM	4580	AY73 TKU	Mercedes	TI
4522	KY72 FFH	Scania	SO	4581	AY73 TKV	Mercedes	DO

4582	AY73 TKX	Mercedes	MI	4625	AY23 VVX	Daf	SO
4583	AY73 TFJ	Mercedes	MI	4626	AY73 YXC	Scania	DO
4584	AY73 TKO	Mercedes	MA	4627	AY73 YXD	Scania	WK
4585	KY23 GYG	Scania	WK	4628	AY73 YXE	Scania	FX
4586	KY23 GYK	Scania	BR	4629	AY73 YXF	Scania	FX
4587	KY23 GYP	Scania	TM	4630	AY73 YXG	Scania	FX
4588	KY23 GYR	Scania	MA	4631		Scania	
4589	KY23 GYT	Scania	PE	4632	AY73 YXJ	Scania	TM
4590	KY23 GYU	Scania	SO	4633	AY73 YXK	Scania	TM
4591	KY23 GYW	Scania	NO	4634	AY73 YXL	Scania	IP
4592	KY23 GZO	Scania	TM	4635		Scania	
4593	KY23 GZP	Scania	ST	4636	AY73 YXN	Scania	BR
4594	KY23 GZR	Scania	EM	4637	AY73 YXO	Scania	WK
4595	KY23 GZS	Scania	ST	4638	AY73 YXP	Scania	
4596	KY23 GZT	Scania	SO	4639	AY73 YXR	Scania	FX
4597	KY23 GZU	Scania	TM	4640	AY73 YXS	Scania	MA
4598	KY23 GZV	Scania	TM	4641	AY73 YXT	Scania	TM
4599	KY23 GZW	Scania	WK	4642	AY73 YXU	Scania	TM
4600	AY73 YWA	Scania	LV	4643	AY73 YXV	Scania	TM
4601	AY73 YWB	Scania	ST	4644	AY73 YXW	Scania	TM
4602	AY73 YWC	Scania	MA	4645	AY73 YXZ	Scania	TM
4603	AY73 YWD	Scania	AL	4646	AY73 YYA	Scania	
4604	AY73 YWE	Scania	AL	4647	AY73 YYB	Scania	
4605	AY73 YWF	Scania	MI	4648	AY73 YYC	Scania	IP
4606	AY23 YWG	Scania	DO	4649	AY73 YYD	Scania	IP
4607	AY73 YWH	Scania	PE	4650	AY73 YYE	Scania	TM
4608	AY73 YWJ	Scania	PE	4651	AY73 YYF	Scania	DO
4609	AY73 YWK	Scania		4652	AY73 YYG	Scania	NO
4610	AY73 YWL	Scania	PE	4653	AY73 YYH	Scania	DO
4611	AY73 YWM	Scania	ME	4654	AY73 YYJ	Scania	SO
4612	AY73 YWN	Scania	MA	4655	AY73 YYK	Scania	SO
4613	AY73 YWO	Scania	DO	4656	AY73 YYL	Scania	SO
4614	AY73 YWP	Scania	WK	4657	AY73 YYM	Scania	MA
4615	AY73 YWR	Scania	DO	4658	AY73 YYN	Scania	MA
4616	AY73 YWS	Scania	NO	4659	AY73 YYO	Scania	DO
4617	AY73 YWT	Scania	FX	4660	AY73 YYP	Scania	DO
4618	AY73 YWU	Scania	DO	4661	AY73 YYR	Scania	IP
4619	AY73 YWV	Scania	DO	4662	AY73 YYS	Scania	TM
4620	AY73 YWW	Scania	ST	4663	AY73 YYT	Scania	WK
4621	AY73 YWX	Scania	ST	4664	AY73 YYU	Scania	TM
4622	AY73 YWZ	Scania	MA	4665	AY73 YYV	Scania	EM
4623	AY73 YXA	Scania	IP	4666	AY73 YYW	Scania	IP
4624	AY73 YXB	Scania	MA	4667	AY73 YYX	Scania	IP

Metcalfe Farms

M21 MET (68)	Scania	Metcalfe Farms	W25 MET (15)	Scania	Metcalfe Farms
M24 MET (15)	Volvo	Metcalfe Farms	W26 MET (72)	Daf	Metcalfe Farms
M25 MET (68)	Scania	Metcalfe Farms	W30 MET (71)	Daf	Metcalfe Farms
M26 MET (68)	Scania	Metcalfe Farms	W33 MET (72)	Daf	Metcalfe Farms
M27 MET (68)	Scania	Metcalfe Farms	W40 MET (18)	Volvo	Metcalfe Farms
M28 MET (67)	Daf	Metcalfe Farms	W50 MET (18)	Volvo	Metcalfe Farms
M80 MET (19)	Scania	Metcalfe Farms	W55 MET (15)	Scania	Metcalfe Farms
M90 MET (19)	Scania	Metcalfe Farms	W60 MET (15)	Volvo	Metcalfe Farms
N30 MET (65)	Scania	Metcalfe Farms	W66 MET (66)	Volvo	Metcalfe Farms
N40 MET (15)	Scania	Metcalfe Farms	W70 MET (71)	Daf	Metcalfe Farms
N50 MET (15)	Volvo	Metcalfe Farms	W88 MET (65)	Scania	Metcalfe Farms
N70 MET (66)	Volvo	Metcalfe Farms	W99 MET (71)	Daf	Metcalfe Farms
N90 MET (15)	Scania	Metcalfe Farms	X16 MET (70)	Daf	Metcalfe Farms
P40 MET (23)	Daf	Metcalfe Farms	X17 MET (70)	Daf	Metcalfe Farms
P60 MET (23)	Daf	Metcalfe Farms	X19 MET (70)	Daf	Metcalfe Farms
P70 MET (15)	Scania	Metcalfe Farms	X20 MET (72)	Daf	Metcalfe Farms
P90 MET (23)	Daf	Metcalfe Farms	X22 MET (70)	Daf	Metcalfe Farms
R40 MET (70)	Volvo	Metcalfe Farms	X25 MET (70)	Daf	Metcalfe Farms
R70 MET (15)	Volvo	Metcalfe Farms	X29 MET (19)	Scania	Metcalfe Farms
R80 MET (65)	Scania	Metcalfe Farms	X33 MET (65)	Scania	Metcalfe Farms
R90 MET (15)	Scania	Metcalfe Farms	X40 MET (72)	Daf	Metcalfe Farms
S60 MET (15)	Scania	Metcalfe Farms	X66 MET (65)	Scania	Metcalfe Farms
S70 MET (15)	Volvo	Metcalfe Farms	X70 MET (71)	Daf	Metcalfe Farms
S80 MET (70)	Volvo	Green	X77 MET (71)	Daf	Metcalfe Farms
T22 MET (66)	Volvo	Metcalfe Farms	X80 MET (16)	Daf	Metcalfe Farms
V13 MET (21)	Daf	Metcalfe Farms	X90 MET (65)	Scania	Metcalfe Farms
V17 MET (19)	Scania	Metcalfe Farms	Y10 MET (64)	Scania	Metcalfe Farms
V19 MET (15)	Volvo	Metcalfe Farms	Y16 MET (63)	Scania	Metcalfe Farms
V22 MET (65)	Scania	Metcalfe Farms	Y17 MET (16)	Volvo	M S Ellis
V25 MET (19)	Scania	Metcalfe Farms	Y18 MET (66)	Volvo	Metcalfe Farms
V26 MET (14)	Volvo	Metcalfe Farms	Y22 MET (15)	Scania	Metcalfe Farms
V28 MET (14)	Volvo	Metcalfe Farms	Y24 MET (66)	Volvo	Metcalfe Farms
V29 MET (14)	Volvo	Metcalfe Farms	Y30 MET (15)	Volvo	M S Ellis
V31 MET (14)	Volvo	Metcalfe Farms	Y31 MET (16)	Volvo	M S Ellis
V33 MET (15)	Scania	Metcalfe Farms	Y33 MET (66)	Volvo	Metcalfe Farms
V40 MET (21)	Daf	Metcalfe Farms	Y40 MET (19)	Volvo	Metcalfe Farms
V44 MET (65)	Scania	Metcalfe Farms	Y44 MET (66)	Volvo	Metcalfe Farms
V50 MET (18)	Volvo	Metcalfe Farms	Y50 MET (19)	Volvo	Metcalfe Farms
V60 MET (67)	Volvo	Metcalfe Farms	Y55 MET (15)	Scania	Metcalfe Farms
V70 MET (67)	Volvo	Metcalfe Farms	Y77 MET (65)	Scania	Metcalfe Farms
V77 MET (21)	Daf	Metcalfe Farms	Y80 MET (18)	Daf	M S Ellis
V80 MET (15)	Volvo	Metcalfe Farms	Y88 MET (15)	Man	Metcalfe Farms
V88 MET (65)	Scania	Metcalfe Farms	Y99 MET (15)	Scania	Metcalfe Farms
V90 MET (21)	Daf	Metcalfe Farms	GL04 MET (19)	Scania	Glovis
V99 MET (21)	Daf	Metcalfe Farms	KU06 MET (69)	Volvo	Kubota
W10 MET (65)	Scania	Metcalfe Farms	KU08 MET (69)	Volvo	Kubota
W17 MET (72)	Daf	Metcalfe Farms	FH16 MET (18)	Volvo	Metcalfe Farms
W20 MET (65)	Scania	Metcalfe Farms	NV66 ZNH	Volvo	Metcalfe Farms
W23 MET (15)	Scania	Metcalfe Farms	PO66 VMM	Volvo	M S Ellis

Muller

Livery Codes

FL	Fresh 'n' Lo	MM	Milk & More	MU	Muller (White)	MW	Muller Wiseman

Reg	Make	Code	Reg	Make	Code	Reg	Make	Code
MX58 DNV	Daf	MU	SD16 HYA	Volvo	MU	SH16 SUX	Volvo	MU
SN13 PCO	Scania	MW	SD16 HYB	Volvo	MU	SH16 SUY	Volvo	MU
SF63 RXY	Daf	MW	SD16 HYC	Volvo	MU	SH16 SVA	Volvo	MU
SF63 RYW	Daf	MW	SD16 HYF	Volvo	MU	SH16 SVC	Volvo	MU
KX14 LKC	Volvo	MW	SD16 HYG	Volvo	MU	SH16 SVE	Volvo	MU
KW64 AYK	Volvo	FL	SD16 HYH	Volvo	MU	SH16 SVF	Volvo	MU
KW64 AYL	Volvo	MW	SD16 HYJ	Volvo	MU	SH16 SVJ	Volvo	MU
KW64 AYM	Volvo	MW	SD16 HYK	Volvo	MU	SH16 SVL	Volvo	MU
KW64 AYN	Volvo	MW	SD16 HYL	Volvo	MU	SH16 SVN	Volvo	MU
KW64 AYO	Volvo	MW	SE16 UXX	Daf	MU	SH16 SVP	Volvo	MU
KW64 AYP	Volvo	MW	SE16 UXY	Daf	MU	SH16 SVR	Volvo	MU
KX15 MWE	Volvo	MW	SE16 UYA	Daf	MW	SH16 SVS	Volvo	MU
KX15 MWG	Volvo	MW	SE16 UYB	Daf	MW	SH16 SVT	Volvo	MU
KX15 MWL	Volvo	MW	SF16 CAC	Daf	MU	SJ16 TJD	Daf	MU
KX15 MWM	Volvo	MW	SF16 CAH	Daf	MU	SJ16 TJL	Daf	MU
KX15 MWN	Volvo	MW	SF16 CBA	Daf	MU	SN16 NZH	Scania	MU
SC15 VDG	Volvo	MW	SF16 CBB	Daf	MU	SN16 NZJ	Scania	MU
SC15 VDN	Volvo	MW	SF16 CBC	Daf	MU	SN16 NZM	Scania	MU
SC15 VDO	Volvo	MW	SF16 VGE	Volvo	MU	SN16 NZO	Scania	MU
SC15 VDP	Volvo	MW	SF16 VGG	Volvo	MU	SN16 NZP	Scania	MU
SC15 VDR	Volvo	MW	SF16 VGJ	Volvo	MU	DG66 JWU	Mercedes	MU
SK15 WYA	Scania	MW	SF16 VGK	Volvo	MU	SA66 FXE	Daf	MU
SK15 WYG	Scania	MW	SF16 VGL	Volvo	MU	SA66 FXF	Daf	MU
SK15 WYH	Scania	MW	SF16 VGM	Volvo	MU	SA66 FXG	Daf	MU
SK15 WYL	Scania	MW	SF16 VGN	Volvo	MU	SA66 FXH	Daf	MU
SK15 WYM	Scania	MW	SF16 VGO	Volvo	MU	SA66 FXU	Daf	MU
MX65 GYD	Daf	MU	SF16 VGP	Volvo	MU	SF66 YGO	Volvo	MU
SF65 TNZ	Volvo	MW	SF16 VGR	Volvo	MU	SF66 YGP	Volvo	MU
SF65 TOA	Volvo	MW	SF16 VGT	Volvo	MU	SF66 YGU	Volvo	MU
SF65 TPO	Volvo	MW	SH16 NBK	Daf	MU	SF66 YGV	Volvo	MU
SF65 TPU	Volvo	MW	SH16 NBX	Daf	MU	SF66 YGW	Volvo	MU
SF65 TPV	Volvo	MW	SH16 NBY	Daf	MU	SH66 FCY	Volvo	MU
SF65 TPZ	Volvo	MW	SH16 NBZ	Daf	MU	SH66 FCZ	Volvo	MU
SF65 TRV	Volvo	MW	SH16 PZM	Daf	MU	SH66 FDA	Volvo	MU
SF65 TRZ	Volvo	MW	SH16 PZN	Daf	MU	SH66 FDC	Volvo	MU
SF65 TSV	Volvo	MW	SH16 SOU	Volvo	MU	SH66 FDD	Volvo	MU
SF65 TTO	Volvo	MW	SH16 SPU	Volvo	MU	SH66 FDE	Volvo	MU
SN65 NDJ	Scania	MW	SH16 SPV	Volvo	MU	SH66 FDG	Volvo	MU
SN65 NDK	Scania	MW	SH16 SPX	Volvo	MU	SH66 FDJ	Volvo	MU
SN65 NDL	Scania	MW	SH16 SPZ	Volvo	MU	SH66 FDK	Volvo	MU
MX16 BNZ	Daf	MU	SH16 SRO	Volvo	MU	SH66 FDV	Volvo	MU
SA16 FBN	Daf	MU	SH16 SRU	Volvo	MU	SH66 FDX	Volvo	MU
SA16 FBO	Daf	MU	SH16 SRV	Volvo	MU	SH66 FDY	Volvo	MU
SA16 FBU	Daf	MU	SH16 SRX	Volvo	MU	SH66 FDZ	Volvo	MU
SA16 FBV	Daf	MU	SH16 SRY	Volvo	MU	SH66 FEG	Volvo	MU
SA16 FBX	Daf	MU	SH16 SRZ	Volvo	MU	SH66 FEJ	Volvo	MU
SA16 FBZ	Daf	MU	SH16 SSJ	Volvo	MU	SH66 FEK	Volvo	MU
SA16 FCC	Daf	MU	SH16 SSK	Volvo	MU	SH66 FEM	Volvo	MU
SA16 GHY	Daf	MU	SH16 SSO	Volvo	MU	SJ66 HFX	Daf	MU
SC16 TWZ	Daf	MU	SH16 SUO	Volvo	MU	SJ66 HFY	Daf	MU
SD16 HXY	Volvo	MU	SH16 SUU	Volvo	MU	SJ66 HFZ	Daf	MU
SD16 HXZ	Volvo	MU	SH16 SUV	Volvo	MU	SJ66 HHW	Daf	MU

Reg	Make	Fleet	Reg	Make	Fleet	Reg	Make	Fleet
SJ66 HHX	Daf	MU	SF17 KAO	Volvo	MU	SG67 UKV	Volvo	MU
SJ66 HHY	Daf	MU	SF17 KAU	Volvo	MU	SG67 UKW	Volvo	MU
SJ66 HHZ	Daf	MU	SF17 KBE	Volvo	MU	SG67 UKX	Volvo	MU
SJ66 HJG	Daf	MU	SF17 KBJ	Volvo	MU	SG67 UKY	Volvo	MU
SJ66 HJO	Daf	MU	SF17 KBK	Volvo	MU	SG67 UKZ	Volvo	MU
SN66 NMJ	Scania	MU	SF17 KBN	Volvo	MU	SG67 ULA	Volvo	MU
SN66 NMK	Scania	MU	SF17 KBO	Volvo	MU	SG67 ULB	Volvo	MU
SN66 NMM	Scania	MU	SF17 KBP	Volvo	MU	SG67 ULD	Volvo	MU
SN66 NMO	Scania	MU	SF17 KBU	Volvo	MU	SG67 ULE	Volvo	MU
SN66 NMU	Scania	MU	SF17 KBV	Volvo	MU	SG67 ULF	Volvo	MU
SN66 NMV	Scania	MU	SF17 KBX	Volvo	MU	SG67 ULH	Volvo	MU
DG17 BFO	Mercedes	MU	SF17 KBY	Volvo	MU	SG67 ULJ	Volvo	MU
DG17 BFU	Mercedes	MU	SF17 KBZ	Volvo	MU	SG67 ULK	Volvo	MU
DG17 BFV	Mercedes	MU	SF17 KCA	Volvo	MU	SG67 ULL	Volvo	MU
DG17 BFX	Mercedes	MU	SF17 KCC	Volvo	MU	SG67 ULM	Volvo	MU
DG17 BFZ	Mercedes	MU	SF17 KCE	Volvo	MU	SG67 ULN	Volvo	MU
DG17 BGF	Mercedes	MU	SF17 KCG	Volvo	MU	SG67 ULO	Volvo	MU
DG17 BGK	Mercedes	MU	SF17 KCJ	Volvo	MU	SG67 ULR	Volvo	MU
DG17 BGO	Mercedes	MU	SM17 CUG	Scania	MU	SG67 ULS	Volvo	MU
DG17 BGU	Mercedes	MU	SM17 CUH	Scania	MU	SG67 ULT	Volvo	MU
DG17 BGV	Mercedes	MU	SM17 CUK	Scania	MU	SG67 ULU	Volvo	MU
DG17 BGX	Mercedes	MU	DG67 CZL	Mercedes	MU	SG67 ULV	Volvo	MU
DG17 BGY	Mercedes	MU	DG67 EDK	Mercedes	MU	SG67 ULW	Volvo	MU
DG17 BHD	Mercedes	MU	DG67 EDL	Mercedes	MU	SG67 ULX	Volvo	MU
DG17 BHE	Mercedes	MU	DG67 EDO	Mercedes	MU	SG67 ULY	Volvo	MU
DG17 BHJ	Mercedes	MU	DG67 EDR	Mercedes	MU	SG67 ULZ	Volvo	MU
DG17 BHK	Mercedes	MU	DG67 EDU	Mercedes	MU	SG67 UMA	Volvo	MU
DG17 BHL	Mercedes	MU	DG67 EDV	Mercedes	MU	SG67 UMB	Volvo	MU
DG17 BHP	Mercedes	MU	DG67 EDX	Mercedes	MU	SG67 UMC	Volvo	MU
DG17 BHV	Mercedes	MU	DG67 EEA	Mercedes	MU	SN67 SPV	Scania	MU
DG17 BHW	Mercedes	MU	DG67 EEB	Mercedes	MU	SN67 SPX	Scania	MU
DG17 BHX	Mercedes	MU	DG67 EEF	Mercedes	MU	SN67 SPZ	Scania	MU
DG17 BJE	Mercedes	MU	DG67 EEH	Mercedes	MU	SN67 SUA	Scania	MU
DG17 BNA	Mercedes	MU	DG67 EEJ	Mercedes	MU	SN67 SUF	Scania	MU
DG17 BNB	Mercedes	MU	DG67 EEN	Mercedes	MU	SN67 SUH	Scania	MU
DG17 BNE	Mercedes	MU	DG67 EEO	Mercedes	MU	DG18 JPO	Mercedes	MU
DG17 BNF	Mercedes	MU	DG67 EEP	Mercedes	MU	DG18 JPV	Mercedes	MU
DG17 BNJ	Mercedes	MU	DG67 EES	Mercedes	MU	DG18 JPX	Mercedes	MU
DG17 BNN	Mercedes	MU	DG67 EFA	Mercedes	MU	DG18 JPY	Mercedes	MU
DG17 BNO	Mercedes	MU	SF67 MPX	Volvo	MU	DG18 JRO	Mercedes	MU
DG17 BNX	Mercedes	MU	SF67 MPY	Volvo	MU	DG18 KHL	Mercedes	MU
DG17 BNZ	Mercedes	MU	SF67 MPZ	Volvo	MU	DG18 KHM	Mercedes	MU
DG17 BOF	Mercedes	MU	SF67 MRO	Volvo	MU	DG18 KHO	Mercedes	MU
DG17 BOH	Mercedes	MU	SF67 MRU	Volvo	MU	DG18 KHP	Mercedes	MU
DG17 BOJ	Mercedes	MU	SF67 MRV	Volvo	MU	DG18 KHR	Mercedes	MU
DG17 BOV	Mercedes	MU	SF67 MRX	Volvo	MU	DG18 KHT	Mercedes	MU
DG17 BPE	Mercedes	MU	SF67 MUA	Volvo	MU	DG18 KHU	Mercedes	MU
DG17 BPK	Mercedes	MU	SF67 MUC	Volvo	MU	DG18 KHV	Mercedes	MU
DG17 BPO	Mercedes	MU	SG67 UKK	Volvo	MU	DG18 KHW	Mercedes	MU
DG17 BPU	Mercedes	MU	SG67 UKM	Volvo	MU	DG18 KHY	Mercedes	MU
DG17 BPV	Mercedes	MU	SG67 UKN	Volvo	MU	DG18 KHZ	Mercedes	MU
DG17 BPX	Mercedes	MU	SG67 UKO	Volvo	MU	DG18 KJA	Mercedes	MU
SF17 KAA	Volvo	MU	SG67 UKP	Volvo	MU	DG18 KJE	Mercedes	MU
SF17 KAE	Volvo	MU	SG67 UKR	Volvo	MU	DG18 KJF	Mercedes	MU
SF17 KAJ	Volvo	MU	SG67 UKT	Volvo	MU	DG18 KJJ	Mercedes	MU
SF17 KAK	Volvo	MU	SG67 UKU	Volvo	MU	DG18 KJK	Mercedes	MU

Muller (cont)

Reg	Make	Fleet	Reg	Make	Fleet	Reg	Make	Fleet
DG18 KJN	Mercedes	MU	DG68 BGX	Mercedes	MU	SJ68 HZC	Volvo	MM
DG18 KJO	Mercedes	MU	DG68 BGY	Mercedes	MU	SJ68 HZD	Volvo	MM
DG18 KJU	Mercedes	MU	DG68 BHD	Mercedes	MU	SJ68 HZE	Volvo	MM
DG18 KJV	Mercedes	MU	DG68 BHE	Mercedes	MU	SJ68 HZF	Volvo	MM
DG18 KJX	Mercedes	MU	DG68 BHJ	Mercedes	MU	SJ68 HZG	Volvo	MM
DG18 KJY	Mercedes	MU	DG68 BHK	Mercedes	MU	SJ68 HZH	Volvo	MM
SB18 DPZ	Volvo	MU	DG68 BHL	Mercedes	MU	SJ68 HZK	Volvo	MM
SB18 DRO	Volvo	MU	DG68 BHN	Mercedes	MU	SJ68 HZL	Volvo	MM
SB18 DRV	Volvo	MU	DG68 BHO	Mercedes	MU	SJ68 HZM	Volvo	MM
SB18 DRX	Volvo	MU	DG68 BHP	Mercedes	MU	SJ68 HZN	Volvo	MM
SB18 DRZ	Volvo	MU	DG68 BHU	Mercedes	MU	SJ68 HZP	Volvo	MM
SB18 DSE	Volvo	MU	DG68 BHV	Mercedes	MU	SJ68 HZR	Volvo	MM
SB18 DSO	Volvo	MU	DG68 BHW	Mercedes	MU	SJ68 HZS	Volvo	MM
SB18 DSU	Volvo	MU	DG68 BHX	Mercedes	MU	SJ68 HZT	Volvo	MM
SB18 DSV	Volvo	MU	DG68 BHY	Mercedes	MU	SJ68 HZU	Volvo	MM
SF18 WVT	Volvo	MU	DG68 BJE	Mercedes	MU	SJ68 HZV	Volvo	MM
SF18 WVU	Volvo	MU	DG68 BJF	Mercedes	MU	SJ68 HZW	Volvo	MM
SF18 WWJ	Volvo	MU	DG68 BJJ	Mercedes	MU	SJ68 HZX	Volvo	MM
SF18 WWK	Volvo	MU	DG68 BJK	Mercedes	MU	SJ68 HZY	Volvo	MM
SF18 WWL	Volvo	MU	DG68 BJO	Mercedes	MU	SJ68 HZZ	Volvo	MM
SF18 WWM	Volvo	MU	DG68 BJU	Mercedes	MU	SJ68 JAU	Volvo	MM
SF18 WWN	Volvo	MU	DG68 BJV	Mercedes	MU	SN68 XMA	Scania	MU
SF18 WWO	Volvo	MU	SJ68 HVF	Volvo	MU	SN68 XMB	Scania	MU
SF18 WWP	Volvo	MU	SJ68 HVG	Volvo	MU	SN68 XMC	Scania	MU
SF18 WWR	Volvo	MU	SJ68 HVH	Volvo	MU	SN68 XMD	Scania	MU
SF18 WWS	Volvo	MU	SJ68 HVK	Volvo	MU	SN68 XME	Scania	MU
SF18 WWT	Volvo	MU	SJ68 HVL	Volvo	MU	SN68 XMF	Scania	MU
SF18 WWU	Volvo	MU	SJ68 HVM	Volvo	MU	SN68 XMG	Scania	MU
SF18 WWV	Volvo	MU	SJ68 HVW	Volvo	MU	SN68 XMH	Scania	MU
DG68 BGF	Mercedes	MU	SJ68 HVX	Volvo	MU	SN68 XMJ	Scania	MU
DG68 BGK	Mercedes	MU	SJ68 HVY	Volvo	MU	SN68 XMK	Scania	MU
DG68 BGO	Mercedes	MU	SJ68 HYZ	Volvo	MM	SN68 XML	Scania	MU
DG68 BGU	Mercedes	MU	SJ68 HZA	Volvo	MM	MV70 VSG	Scania	MU
DG68 BGV	Mercedes	MU	SJ68 HZB	Volvo	MM			

Owens

Reg	Make	Fleet	Reg	Make	Fleet
999 TVO (22)	Volvo	Owens	FG 63 UDH	Daf	Owens White
L 700 DRS (17)	Dennis	Dyfed Recycling	FG 63 UDJ	Daf	Owens
R400 ERF	ERF	Owens	CN 14 JXD	Man	Owens White
W 7 ORS (22)	Volvo	Owens	DF 14 EWM	Man	Owens White
W 8 ORS (23)	Daf	Owens	HX 14 XUK	Mercedes	Owens (Black)
X 582 EER	Volvo	Owens	WP 14 ZHL	Man	Owens White
X 700 DRS (65)	Scania	Dyfed Recycling	WP 14 ZHM	Man	Owens White
Y 700 EVS (11)	Dennis	Dyfed Recycling	WP 14 ZHN	Man	Owens White
NJ 58 KZA	Volvo	Owens White	WP 14 ZHU	Man	Owens White
MX 09 KXO	Mercedes	Owens White	WP 14 ZHX	Man	Owens White
MX 09 KXP	Mercedes	Owens White	WP 14 ZHZ	Man	Owens White
DK 61 UHT	Man	Owens White	WX 14 ZKY	Man	Owens White
GK61 XTL	Mercedes	White	WX 14 ZNU	Man	Owens White
CA 12 WPO	Mercedes	Owens White	WX 14 ZPL	Man	Owens White
NX 62 RUJ	Man	Owens White	WX 14 ZPM	Man	Owens White
DG 13 AHU	Man	Owens White	WX 14 ZPO	Man	Owens White
YN 13 RZZ	Mercedes	Owens White	WX 14 ZPS	Man	Owens White
YN 13 SBU	Mercedes	Owens White	WX 14 ZPW	Man	Owens White
FD 63 URY	Daf	Owens White	FG 64 FKB	Daf	Owens White
FD 63 URZ	Daf	Owens White	FG 64 FKD	Daf	Owens White

Reg	Make	Livery	Reg	Make	Livery
FG 64 FKJ	Daf	Owens White	CK 68 ZZP	Daf	Owens White
FG 64 FKM	Daf	Owens White	CK 68 ZZR	Daf	Owens White
FL 15 YOW	Daf	Dyfed Recycling	CK 68 ZZS	Daf	Owens White
GN65 MZL	Daf	Dyfed Recycling	CK 68 ZZU	Daf	Owens White
GN65 MZU	Daf	Dyfed Recycling	CK 68 ZZV	Daf	Owens White
SK 65 BSV	Daf	Owens White	CK 68 ZZW	Daf	Owens White
BG 66 HKU	Man	Owens White	CK 68 ZZX	Daf	Owens White
BP 66 MFU	Man	Owens White	CK 68 ZZY	Daf	Owens White
CN 66 YMF	Man	Dyfed Recycling	DK 68 UAC	Daf	Owens White
CN 66 YMG	Man	Dyfed Recycling	FL 68 EPU	Renault	Celtic Couriers
CN 66 YMH	Man	Dyfed Recycling	FL 68 EPV	Renault	Celtic Couriers
GD66 VJG	Volvo	Owens White	FN 68 EYV	Daf	Celtic Couriers
GN 66 XUY	Man	Owens White	GN 68 YSJ	Volvo	Dyfed Recycling
NV 66 KCE	Man	Owens White	KP 68 AUM	Daf	Owens White
NV 66 KCJ	Man	Owens White	LN68 ZPY	Daf	Dyfed Recycling
CN 17 OLA	Scania	Owens	CE 19 FBZ	Man	Owens White
CN 17 OLB	Scania	Owens	CE 19 FCY	Man	Owens White
MV 17 AHK	Scania	Owens White	CE 19 FDA	Man	Owens White
MX 17 ZVA	Scania	Owens White	CE 19 FDD	Man	Owens White
MX 17 ZWA	Scania	Owens White	CE 19 FDK	Man	Owens White
MX 17 ZWD	Scania	Owens White	CE 19 FDN	Man	Owens White
SN 17 OWK	Man	Owens White	CE 19 FEG	Man	Owens White
SN 17 OYB	Man	Owens White	CE 19 FEP	Man	Owens White
YD 17 ZBT	Scania	Dyfed Recycling	CE 19 FEX	Man	Owens White
FP 67 SMO	Daf	Owens White	CE 19 FFO	Man	Owens White
WV67 FMD	Volvo	Owens	CE 19 FGA	Man	Owens White
CN 18 ZKO	Man	Owens White	CE 19 FGJ	Man	Owens White
FD 18 AHV	Daf	Owens White	CE 19 FGK	Man	Owens White
FD 18 AHX	Daf	Owens White	CE 19 FGX	Man	Owens White
CA 68 FAJ	Daf	Owens White	CE 19 FGZ	Man	Owens White
CA 68 FAK	Daf	Owens White	CE 19 FHA	Man	Owens White
CA 68 FAM	Daf	Owens	CE 19 FHC	Man	Owens White
CA 68 FAO	Daf	Owens White	CE 19 FHD	Man	Owens White
CA 68 FAU	Daf	Owens White	CE 19 FHF	Man	Owens White
CA 68 FBB	Daf	Owens White	CF 19 TVP	Man	Dyfed Recycling
CE 68 DHD	Daf	Owens White	CV 19 FLL	Man	Owens White
CE 68 DHF	Daf	Owens White	CV 19 FLM	Man	Owens White
CE 68 DHG	Daf	Owens White	FM 19 YRZ	Daf	Owens White
CE 68 DHK	Daf	Owens White	CE 69 AKN	Man	Owens White
CE 68 DHL	Daf	Owens White	CE 69 AKP	Man	Owens White
CE 68 DHM	Daf	Owens White	CE 69 AKU	Man	Owens White
CK 68 ZYV	Daf	Owens White	CE 69 AKV	Man	Owens White
CK 68 ZYW	Daf	Owens White	CE 69 AKY	Man	Owens White
CK 68 ZYX	Daf	Owens White	FG 69 VOV	Daf	Owens White
CK 68 ZYY	Daf	Owens White	FG 69 VPC	Daf	Owens White
CK 68 ZYZ	Daf	Owens White	FG 69 VPF	Daf	Owens White
CK 68 ZZA	Daf	Owens White	FG 69 VPM	Daf	Owens White
CK 68 ZZB	Daf	Owens White	FG 69 VPP	Daf	Owens White
CK 68 ZZC	Daf	Owens White	FG 69 VPV	Daf	Owens White
CK 68 ZZD	Daf	Owens White	FG 69 VPY	Daf	Owens White
CK 68 ZZF	Daf	Owens White	FN 69 AYO	Daf	Owens White
CK 68 ZZH	Daf	Owens White	FN 69 BFJ	Daf	Owens White
CK 68 ZZJ	Daf	Owens White	FN 69 BFL	Daf	Owens White
CK 68 ZZL	Daf	Owens White	FN 69 BFM	Daf	Owens White
CK 68 ZZM	Daf	Owens White	FN 69 BFO	Daf	Owens White
CK 68 ZZN	Daf	Owens White	FN 69 BFP	Daf	Owens White
CK 68 ZZO	Daf	Owens White	FN 69 BFV	Daf	Owens White

FN 69 BFY	Daf	Owens White		CE 21 FKO	Man	Owens
FN 69 BFZ	Daf	Owens White		CE 21 FKP	Man	Owens White
CE 70 AEZ	Man	Owens White		CE 21 FKT	Man	Owens White
CN 70 ZYB	Man	Dyfed Recycling		CE 21 FKU	Man	Owens White
MV 70 VUA	Scania	Owens		CE 21 FKV	Man	Owens White
MV 70 VUB	Scania	Owens		CE 21 FKW	Man	Owens White
MV 70 VUC	Scania	Owens		CE 21 FKX	Man	Owens White
MV 70 VUD	Scania	Owens		CE 21 FKZ	Man	Owens White
MV 70 VUE	Scania	Owens		CE 21 FLA	Man	Owens White
CA 21 NXB	Man	Owens White		CE 21 FLD	Man	Owens
CA 21 NXC	Man	Owens White		CE 21 FLF	Man	Owens White
CA 21 NXD	Man	Owens White		CE 21 FLG	Man	Owens White
CA 21 NXE	Man	Owens White		CE 21 FLH	Man	Owens White
CA 21 NXF	Man	Owens White		CE 21 FLJ	Man	Owens White
CA 21 NXG	Man	Owens White		CE 21 FLM	Man	Owens White
CA 21 NXH	Man	Owens White		CE 21 FLN	Man	Owens White
CA 21 NXJ	Man	Owens White		CE 21 FLP	Man	Owens White
CA 21 NXK	Man	Owens White		CE 21 FLR	Man	Owens
CA 21 NXL	Man	Owens White		CE 21 FLV	Man	Owens
CE 21 FGU	Man	Owens White		CF 21 FTK	Daf	Owens
CE 21 FGZ	Man	Owens White		CF 21 FTN	Daf	Owens
CE 21 FHA	Man	Owens White		CF 21 FTO	Daf	Owens
CE 21 FHB	Man	Owens White		CF 21 FTT	Daf	Owens White
CE 21 FHC	Man	Owens White		CF 21 FTU	Daf	Owens White
CE 21 FHD	Man	Owens		CF 21 FTV	Daf	Owens
CE 21 FHF	Man	Owens White		CK 21 WGA	Daf	Owens
CE 21 FHG	Man	Owens White		CK 21 WGC	Daf	Owens
CE 21 FHH	Man	Owens		CK 21 WGD	Daf	Owens
CE 21 FHJ	Man	Owens White		CK 21 WGE	Daf	Owens White
CE 21 FHK	Man	Owens		CK 21 WGF	Daf	Owens White
CE 21 FHL	Man	Owens		CK 21 WGG	Daf	Owens
CE 21 FHM	Man	Owens White		CK 21 WGJ	Daf	Owens White
CE 21 FHN	Man	Owens White		CK 21 WGM	Daf	Owens White
CE 21 FHO	Man	Owens		CK 21 WGN	Daf	Owens
CE 21 FHP	Man	Owens White		CK 21 WGO	Daf	Owens White
CE 21 FHR	Man	Owens White		CK 21 WGP	Daf	Owens White
CE 21 FHT	Man	Owens		CK 21 WGU	Daf	Owens White
CE 21 FHU	Man	Owens White		CK 21 WGV	Daf	Owens White
CE 21 FHV	Man	Owens		CK 21 WGW	Daf	Owens White
CE 21 FHX	Man	Owens White		CK 21 WGX	Daf	Owens White
CE 21 FHZ	Man	Owens White		CK 21 WGZ	Daf	Owens White
CE 21 FJA	Man	Owens White		CK 21 WHA	Daf	Owens White
CE 21 FJC	Man	Owens White		CK 21 WHB	Daf	Owens White
CE 21 FJP	Man	Owens		CK 21 WHC	Daf	Owens White
CE 21 FJU	Man	Owens		CK 21 WHD	Daf	Owens White
CE 21 FJV	Man	Owens White		CK 21 WHE	Daf	Owens White
CE 21 FJX	Man	Owens White		CK 21 WHF	Daf	Owens White
CE 21 FJZ	Man	Owens White		CN 21 WXU	Mercedes	Dyfed Recycling
CE 21 FKA	Man	Owens White		GK 21 BXN	Volvo	Dyfed Recycling
CE 21 FKB	Man	Owens White		CN 71 OZS	Man	Dyfed Recycling
CE 21 FKF	Man	Owens White		CN 71 SMX	Daf	Owens
CE 21 FKG	Man	Owens White		CN 71 SNF	Daf	Owens
CE 21 FKH	Man	Owens White		CN 71 SNJ	Daf	Owens
CE 21 FKJ	Man	Owens White		CN 71 SNK	Daf	Owens
CE 21 FKL	Man	Owens White		CN 71 SNU	Daf	Owens
CE 21 FKM	Man	Owens White		CN 71 SNV	Daf	Owens
CE 21 FKN	Man	Owens White		CN 71 SNX	Daf	Owens

Reg	Make	Body	Reg	Make	Body
CN 71 SNY	Daf	Owens	PN 22 GYA	Volvo	Owens
CN 71 SNZ	Daf	Owens	PN 22 GYB	Volvo	Owens
CN 71 SOA	Daf	Owens	PN 22 GYC	Volvo	Owens
CN 71 SOC	Daf	Owens	PN 22 GYE	Volvo	Owens
CN 71 SOE	Daf	Owens	PN 22 GYG	Volvo	Owens
PN 71 HHA	Volvo	Owens	PN 22 GYH	Volvo	Owens
PN 71 HHB	Volvo	Owens	CA 72 JVC	Daf	Rockwool
PN 71 HHC	Volvo	Owens	CA 72 JVF	Daf	Owens
PN 71 HHD	Volvo	Owens	CA 72 JVG	Daf	Owens
PN 71 HHE	Volvo	Owens	CA 72 JVH	Daf	Owens
PN 71 HHF	Volvo	Owens	CA 72 JVJ	Daf	Owens
PN 71 HHG	Volvo	Owens	CA 72 JVK	Daf	Owens
PN 71 HHJ	Volvo	Owens	CA 72 JVO	Daf	Rockwool
PN 71 HHK	Volvo	Owens	CA 72 JVP	Daf	Rockwool
PN 71 HHL	Volvo	Owens	CA 72 JVU	Daf	Rockwool
PN 71 HHM	Volvo	Owens	CA 72 JVV	Daf	Owens
PN 71 HHO	Volvo	Owens	CA 72 JVW	Daf	Rockwool
PN 71 HHP	Volvo	Owens	CA 72 ZCV	Daf	Owens
PN 71 HHR	Volvo	Owens	CA 72 ZCX	Daf	Owens
PN 71 HHS	Volvo	Owens	CA 72 ZCZ	Daf	Owens
PN 71 HHT	Volvo	Owens	CA 72 ZDD	Daf	Rockwool
PN 71 HHU	Volvo	Owens	CA 72 ZDE	Daf	Rockwool
PN 71 HHV	Volvo	Owens	CF 72 SSJ	Daf	Rockwool
PN 71 HHX	Volvo	Owens	CF 72 SSK	Daf	Rockwool
PN 71 HHY	Volvo	Owens	CF 72 SSO	Daf	Rockwool
PN 22 GWM	Volvo	Owens	CF 72 SSU	Daf	Rockwool
PN 22 GWO	Volvo	Owens	CF 72 SSV	Daf	Rockwool
PN 22 GWP	Volvo	Owens	CF 72 SSX	Daf	Rockwool
PN 22 GWU	Volvo	Owens	CF 72 SSZ	Daf	Rockwool
PN 22 GWV	Volvo	Owens	CF 72 STZ	Daf	Rockwool
PN 22 GWW	Volvo	Owens	CF 72 SUA	Daf	Rockwool
PN 22 GWX	Volvo	Owens	CF 72 SUH	Daf	Rockwool
PN 22 GWY	Volvo	Owens	CF 72 SUV	Daf	Rockwool
PN 22 GWZ	Volvo	Owens	CJ 72 BWN	Daf	Rockwool
PN 22 GXA	Volvo	Owens	DX 72 TZD	Daf	Dyfed Recycling
PN 22 GXB	Volvo	Owens	CE 23 FLM	Daf	Rockwool
PN 22 GXC	Volvo	Owens	CE 23 FLN	Daf	Rockwool
PN 22 GXD	Volvo	Owens	CE 23 FLP	Daf	Rockwool
PN 22 GXE	Volvo	Owens	CE 23 FLR	Daf	Rockwool
PN 22 GXF	Volvo	Owens	CE 23 FLX	Daf	Rockwool
PN 22 GXG	Volvo	Owens	CE 23 FLZ	Daf	Rockwool
PN 22 GXH	Volvo	Owens	CE 23 FMA	Daf	Rockwool
PN 22 GXJ	Volvo	Owens	CE 23 FMC	Daf	Rockwool
PN 22 GXK	Volvo	Owens	CE 23 FMD	Daf	Rockwool
PN 22 GXL	Volvo	Owens	CE 23 FMF	Daf	Rockwool
PN 22 GXM	Volvo	Owens	CE 23 FMG	Daf	Rockwool
PN 22 GXO	Volvo	Owens	CE73 DVA	Man	Owens
PN 22 GXP	Volvo	Owens	CE73 DVB	Man	Owens
PN 22 GXR	Volvo	Owens	CE73 DVC	Man	Owens
PN 22 GXS	Volvo	Owens	CE73 DVK	Man	Owens White
PN 22 GXT	Volvo	Owens	CE73 DXP	Man	Owens
PN 22 GXU	Volvo	Owens	CE73 FNH	Daf	Owens White
PN 22 GXV	Volvo	Owens	CE73 FNL	Daf	Owens White
PN 22 GXW	Volvo	Owens	CE73 FPF	Daf	Owens
PN 22 GXX	Volvo	Owens	CF73 EZR	Daf	Owens
PN 22 GXY	Volvo	Owens	WU73 JZA	Volvo	Owens
PN 22 GXZ	Volvo	Owens	WU73 JZC	Volvo	Owens

Owens (cont)

WU73 JZD	Volvo	Owens	WU73 JZJ	Volvo	Owens
WU73 JZE	Volvo	Owens	WU73 JZK	Volvo	Owens
WU73 JZF	Volvo	Owens	WU73 JZL	Volvo	Owens
WU73 JZG	Volvo	Owens	WU73 JZM	Volvo	Owens
WU73 JZH	Volvo	Owens	WU73 JZN	Volvo	Owens White

SG Haulage (Saxilby)

N489 HFV	Scania	143M 450 6x2	PO65 UUB	Scania	R450 6x2 HL
V10 SGH (67)	Scania	R450 6x2 HL	PO65 UUC	Scania	R450 6x2 HL
V13 SGH (73)	Volvo	FH 500 8w G Flatbed	FX16 KHK	Scania	R450 6x2 Top
V25 SGH (18)	Scania	S650 6x2 (NG) HL	FX66 KAA	Scania	R450 6x2 Top
XL08 BEN (17)	Scania	R580 6x2 Top LHD	WN66 KGG	Scania	R450 6x2 Top
SG71 SGH (71)	Scania	530S 4x2 (NG) HL LHD	WN66 KGU	Scania	R450 6x2 Top
PM65 FLY (22)	Scania	R500 8w HL Flatbed	FX17 KUK	Scania	S500 6x2 (NG) HL
FX04 ADU	Scania	R124L 420 6x2 Top	FX67 NUF	Scania	S500 6x2 (NG) HL
FJ08 AFU	Scania	R420 6x2 Top	SG19 FLY	Scania	R450 8w (NG) NL Flatbed
NV60 KHL	Man	TGS 18.400 4w LX Flatbed	SM19 XTV	Scania	R450 6x2 (NG) HL
SK60 GXN	Scania	R560 6x2 Top	YK69 NKH	Volvo	FH 500 6x2 G
FX12 CTY	Scania	R480 8w HL Flatbed	FX20 TUY	Scania	R500 6x2 (NG) HL
PX12 RVY	Daf	FASCF85 510 Flatbed	FX70 UGE	Scania	R500 6x2 (NG) HL
FN14 LVA	Scania	R410 4w HL Flatbed	FX22 UNK	Scania	500S 6x2 (NG) HL
FN14 LVH	Scania	R410 4w HL Flatbed	FX23 VDA	Scania	R500 6x2 (NG) HL
BL64 BKV	Scania	R450 6x2 Top	PF23 WNC	Daf	FTS 530 6x2 (XG)
YK64 ZTO	Scania	R450 6x2 Top			

Spiers & Hartwell (Blackminster)

Note: All Vehicles are Scania's

J111 EDC (73)	P555 EDC (19)	R999 EDC (20)	V444 EDC (21)	X555 EDC (23)
J222 EDC (73)	P666 EDC (19)	S222 EDC (21)	V555 EDC (71)	Y111 EDC (23)
M666 EDC (71)	P999 EDC (19)	S333 EDC (21)	V666 EDC (71)	Y222 EDC (23)
M777 EDC (22)	R111 EDC (19)	T111 EDC (21)	W222 EDC (22)	Y333 EDC (23)
M888 EDC (22)	R222 EDC (69)	T222 EDC (21)	W333 EDC (22)	Y444 EDC (23)
N333 EDC (19)	R333 EDC (69)	T333 EDC (21)	W444 EDC (22)	Y555 EDC (23)
N555 EDC (19)	R444 EDC (20)	T444 EDC (21)	X111 EDC (22)	Y666 EDC (23)
P111 EDC (19)	R555 EDC (20)	V111 EDC (21)	X222 EDC (22)	Y777 EDC (73)
P222 EDC (19)	R666 EDC (20)	V222 EDC (21)	X333 EDC (22)	Y888 EDC (73)
P333 EDC (19)	R777 EDC (20)	V333 EDC (21)	X444 EDC (72)	Y999 EDC (73)
P444 EDC (19)	R888 EDC (70)			

Stuart Nicol (Shotts)

3 SNT (18)	Volvo	N 40 SNT (23)	Volvo	N 333 SNT (71)	Scania	S 27 SNT (17)	Merc
G20 SNT (68)	Scania	N 44 SNT (66)	Daf	N 444 SNT (19)	Scania	S 28 SNT (68)	Volvo
N 3 SNT (70)	Volvo	N 50 SNT (71)	Scania	N 500 SNT (21)	Volvo	S 33 SNT (69)	Merc
N 6 SNT (66)	Scania	N 55 SNT (16)	Scania	N 555 SNT (23)	Volvo	S 80 SNT (17)	Scania
N 8 SNT (66)	Scania	N 60 SNT (65)	Volvo	N 600 SNT (18)	Scania	T 18 SNT (19)	Daf
N 9 SNT (19)	Scania	N 66 SNT (64)	Volvo	N 700 SNT (22)	Scania	T 500 SNT (18)	Renault
N 11 SNT (16)	Scania	N 77 SNT (73)	Scania	N 777 SNT (71)	Renault	V 25 SNT (19)	Volvo
N 12 SNT (22)	Volvo	N 80 SNT (17)	Scania	N 888 SNT (17)	Volvo	V 26 SNT (19)	Volvo
N 14 SNT (72)	Volvo	N 88 SNT (15)	Scania	N 900 SNT (23)	Volvo	W 33 DAF (20)	Daf
N 16 SNT (66)	Volvo	N 90 SNT (73)	Scania	N 999 SNT (22)	Scania	NO 02 SNT (65)	Volvo
N 17 SNT (23)	Volvo	N 99 SNT (17)	Scania	R 5 SNT (18)	Scania	NO 04 SNT (65)	Volvo
N 18 SNT (72)	Renault	N 100 SNT (68)	Scania	S 12 SNT (71)	Scania	NY 09 REE (63)	Volvo
N 19 SNT (17)	Renault	N 111 SNT (23)	Renault	S 20 SNT (23)	Renault	NN10 COL (21)	Scania
N 20 SNT (16)	Scania	N 200 SNT (68)	Volvo	S 24 SNT (16)	Daf	SN 10 COL (16)	Scania
N 30 SNT (17)	Volvo	N 222 SNT (23)	Volvo	S 25 SNT (66)	Scania	BA 11 SNT (17)	Scania
N 33 SNT (73)	Scania	N 300 SNT (19)	Scania	S 26 SNT (16)	Scania	PH 11 SNT (21)	Scania

Major UK HGV Fleets 2024

Turners Group

Reg	Make	Operator	Reg	Make	Operator
B 13 MKT (16)	Volvo	Kibble	AV 16 XZC	Daf	Turners
D 13 MKT (68)	Daf	Kibble	AV 16 XZD	Daf	Hanson (White)
E 13 MJK (67)	Volvo	Kibble	AV 16 XZE	Daf	Hanson (White)
E 18 FFS (18)	Volvo	Kibble	AV 16 XZF	Daf	Turners
G 13 MJK (68)	Volvo	Kibble	AV 16 XZG	Daf	Francis Flower
K 13 MKT (68)	Volvo	Kibble	AV 16 XZH	Daf	Turners
N 13 MKT (68)	Volvo	Kibble	AV 16 XZK	Daf	LKAB (Turners)
P 13 MKT (22)	Daf	Kibble	AV 16 XZL	Daf	Francis Flower
R 13 MJK (15)	Volvo	Kibble	AV 16 XZM	Daf	LKAB (Turners)
S 13 MKT (17)	Volvo	Kibble	AX 16 HYH	Daf	Francis Flower
T 100 FTP (66)	Daf	Turners	AX 16 HYJ	Daf	Turners
T 200 FTP (66)	Daf	Turners	AX 16 HYK	Daf	Turners
T 300 FTP (18)	Daf	Turners	AX 16 HYL	Daf	Turners
T 400 FTP (69)	Daf	Turners	AX 16 HYM	Daf	Turners
T 500 FTP (23)	Daf	Turners	AX 16 HYN	Daf	Turners
T 600 FTP (73)	Daf	MFG Turners	AY 16 LSC	Mercedes	Macintyre
T 700 FTP (67)	Daf	Turners	AY 16 LSD	Mercedes	Macintyre
T 800 FTP (19)	Daf	Turners	AY 16 LSE	Mercedes	Macintyre
T 900 FTP (70)	Daf	Turners	AY 16 LSF	Mercedes	Macintyre
T 999 FTP (22)	Daf	Turners	AY 16 LWD	Mercedes	Turners
W 888 LJH (19)	Scania	Dowse	AY 16 LWE	Mercedes	Turners
Y 9 THC (21)	Mercedes	Clements (2)	AY 16 LWF	Mercedes	Turners
Y 10 THC (21)	Mercedes	Clements (2)	AY 16 LWG	Mercedes	Turners
Y 13 MJK (67)	Volvo	Kibble	AY 16 LWH	Mercedes	Turners
AV 52 HFN	Scania	Turners	AY 16 LWK	Mercedes	Turners
AY 11 AHO	Scania	Turners	AY 16 LWL	Mercedes	Turners
DE 62 EUP	Daf	Weedon	AY 16 LWM	Mercedes	Turners
CK 13 BLE (70)	Volvo	Kibble	AY 16 LWN	Mercedes	Turners
DE 13 WKJ	Daf	Blue	AY 16 LWO	Mercedes	Turners
DG 13 SXC	Daf	Blue	AY 16 LWP	Mercedes	Turners
AY 65 UYW	Daf	BWOC	AY 16 LWR	Mercedes	Turners
AY 65 UYX	Daf	BWOC	AY 16 LWS	Mercedes	Turners
AY 65 UYZ	Daf	BWOC	AY 16 LWT	Mercedes	Turners
AY 65 VBC	Daf	Lynx Fuels	AY 16 LWU	Mercedes	Turners
AY 65 VBD	Daf	Lynx Fuels	AY 16 MDE	Daf	Turners
DK 65 UBY	Daf	Taylor Wimpey	AY 16 MDF	Daf	Turners
DK 65 UBZ	Daf	Taylor Wimpey	AY 16 MDJ	Daf	Turners
DK 65 UCA	Daf	Taylor Wimpey	AY 16 MDK	Daf	Turners
DK 65 UCB	Daf	Taylor Wimpey	AY 16 MDN	Daf	Turners
FL 65 YBT	Daf	Lynn Star	AY 16 MDO	Daf	Turners
FP 65 MVD	Daf	Lynn Star	AY 16 MDU	Daf	Turners
KX 65 RGY	Scania	R & R Haulage	AY 16 MDV	Daf	Turners
KX 65 RGZ	Scania	R & R Haulage	AY 16 MDX	Daf	Turners
AV 16 CFX	Daf	Turners	AY 16 MDZ	Daf	Turners
AV 16 UCL	Daf	Turners	AY 16 MEU	Daf	Turners
AV 16 VDE	Mercedes	Macintyre	AY 16 MGZ	Daf	Lynx Fuels
AV 16 VDF	Mercedes	Macintyre	AY 16 MHJ	Daf	Turners
AV 16 VDG	Mercedes	Macintyre	AY 16 MHK	Daf	Turners
AV 16 XYT	Daf	Turners	AY 16 MHL	Daf	Turners
AV 16 XYU	Daf	Hanson (White)	AY 16 YCN	Daf	Turners
AV 16 XYW	Daf	LKAB (Turners)	AY 16 YCO	Daf	Turners
AV 16 XYX	Daf	LKAB (Turners)	AY 16 YCP	Daf	Turners
AV 16 XYY	Daf	LKAB (Turners)	AY 16 YCR	Daf	Turners
AV 16 XYZ	Daf	LKAB (Turners)	AY 16 YCS	Daf	Turners
AV 16 XZA	Daf	Francis Flower	AY 16 YCT	Daf	Turners
AV 16 XZB	Daf	Turners	AY 16 YCU	Daf	Turners

Reg	Make	Operator	Reg	Make	Operator
AY 16 YCV	Daf	Turners	PE 16 HMO	Volvo	Fullforce
AY 16 YCW	Daf	Turners	PN16 FMK	Volvo	Kibble
AY 16 YCX	Daf	Turners	SJ 16 NVF	Mitsubishi Fuso	Turners
AY 16 YCZ	Daf	Turners	AY 66 LPV	Daf	LKAB (Turners)
AY 16 YDA	Daf	Turners	AY 66 LWR	Daf	BWOC
AY 16 YDB	Daf	Turners	AY 66 LWS	Daf	BWOC
AY 16 YDC	Daf	Turners	AY 66 LWT	Daf	BWOC
AY 16 YDD	Daf	Turners	AY 66 LWU	Daf	BWOC
AY 16 YDF	Daf	Turners	AY 66 LWW	Daf	Turners
AY 16 YDG	Daf	Turners	AY 66 LWX	Daf	Turners
AY 16 YDH	Daf	Turners	AY 66 LWZ	Daf	Turners
AY 16 YDJ	Daf	Turners	AY 66 NTJ	Mercedes	Turners
AY 16 YDK	Daf	Turners	AY 66 NTK	Mercedes	Turners
AY 16 YDL	Daf	Hanson (White)	AY 66 NTL	Mercedes	Turners
AY 16 YDM	Daf	Turners	AY 66 NTM	Mercedes	Turners
AY 16 YDN	Daf	Turners	AY 66 NXD	Mercedes	Macintyre
AY 16 YDO	Daf	Turners	AY 66 NXE	Mercedes	Macintyre
AY 16 YDP	Daf	Hanson (White)	AY 66 NXF	Mercedes	Macintyre
AY 16 YDR	Daf	Turners	AY 66 NXG	Mercedes	Macintyre
AY 16 YDS	Daf	Turners	AY 66 NXH	Mercedes	Macintyre
AY 16 YDT	Daf	Hanson (White)	AY 66 NXJ	Mercedes	Macintyre
AY 16 YDU	Daf	Hanson (White)	AY 66 NXK	Mercedes	Macintyre
AY 16 YED	Daf	Turners	AY 66 NXL	Mercedes	Macintyre
AY 16 YEE	Daf	Lynx Fuels	AY 66 NXM	Mercedes	Macintyre
DK 16 YTB	Daf	Jack Richards	AY 66 NXO	Mercedes	Macintyre
DK 16 YTC	Daf	Jack Richards	AY 66 NXR	Mercedes	Macintyre
DK 16 YTD	Daf	Jack Richards	AY 66 NXS	Mercedes	Macintyre
DK 16 YTF	Daf	Jack Richards	AY 66 NXT	Mercedes	Macintyre
DK 16 YTG	Daf	Jack Richards	AY 66 NXU	Mercedes	Macintyre
DK 16 YTH	Daf	Jack Richards	AY 66 NXV	Mercedes	Macintyre
DK 16 YTJ	Daf	Jack Richards	AY 66 NXW	Mercedes	Macintyre
DK 16 YTL	Daf	Jack Richards	AY 66 URK	Daf	LKAB (Turners)
FX 16 KGO	Scania	Turners	AY 66 URS	Daf	LKAB (Turners)
FX 16 KGP	Scania	Turners	AY 66 ZWD	Daf	Francis Flower
FX 16 KGU	Scania	Turners	AY 66 ZWE	Daf	Francis Flower
FX 16 KGV	Scania	Turners	FX 66 KAO	Scania	Clements (2)
FX 16 KGY	Scania	Turners	FX 66 KGY	Scania	Dowse
FX 16 KGZ	Scania	Turners	FX 66 KGZ	Scania	Dowse
KU 16 AAK	Scania	Turners	KU 66 AEW	Scania	Turners
KU 16 AAN	Scania	Turners	KU 66 AEX	Scania	Turners
KU 16 AAO	Scania	Turners	KU 66 AEY	Scania	Turners
KU 16 AAV	Scania	Turners	KU 66 AEZ	Scania	Turners
KU 16 AAZ	Scania	Turners	KU 66 MHZ	Scania	Turners
KU 16 ABF	Scania	Turners	KU 66 MLY	Scania	Turners
KU 16 ABN	Scania	Turners	KU 66 MLZ	Scania	Turners
KU 16 ABO	Scania	Turners	KU 66 MMO	Scania	R & R Haulage
KU 16 ABV	Scania	Turners	KU 66 MMV	Scania	R & R Haulage
KX 16 ZXF	Scania	Turners	KU 66 MMX	Scania	R & R Haulage
KX 16 ZXG	Scania	Turners	KU 66 XLE	Mercedes	Turners
KX 16 ZXH	Scania	Turners	KU 66 XLF	Mercedes	Turners
KX 16 ZXJ	Scania	Turners	KU 66 XLG	Mercedes	Turners
KX 16 ZXK	Scania	Turners	KU 66 XLH	Mercedes	Turners
KX 16 ZXL	Scania	Turners	PN 66 PPY	Daf	Kibble
KX 16 ZXM	Scania	OOCL (Turners)	PO66 VHA	Volvo	Kibble
KX 16 ZXR	Scania	Turners	PO66 VHB	Volvo	Kibble
MV 16 SEY	Man	Goldstar	PO66 VHC	Volvo	Kibble
OE 16 UJH	Daf	Turners	AV 17 DXK	Daf	Turners

Reg	Make	Operator	Reg	Make	Operator
AV 17 DXO	Daf	Turners	AV 17 EUZ	Mercedes	MSC (Goldstar)
AV 17 DXP	Daf	Turners	AV 17 EVB	Mercedes	MSC (Goldstar)
AV 17 EHH	Mercedes	Turners	AV 17 EVD	Mercedes	MSC (Goldstar)
AV 17 EHJ	Mercedes	Turners	AV 17 EVF	Mercedes	MSC (Goldstar)
AV 17 EHK	Mercedes	Turners	AV 17 EVG	Mercedes	MSC (Goldstar)
AV 17 EHL	Mercedes	Turners	AV 17 EVJ	Mercedes	MSC (Goldstar)
AV 17 EHM	Mercedes	Turners	AV 17 EVK	Mercedes	MSC (Goldstar)
AV 17 EHN	Mercedes	Turners	AV 17 EVL	Mercedes	MSC (Goldstar)
AV 17 EHO	Mercedes	Turners	AV 17 EVM	Mercedes	MSC (Goldstar)
AV 17 EHP	Mercedes	Turners	AV 17 EVN	Mercedes	MSC (Goldstar)
AV 17 EHR	Mercedes	Turners	AV 17 EVP	Mercedes	MSC (Goldstar)
AV 17 EHS	Mercedes	Turners	AV 17 EVT	Mercedes	MSC (Goldstar)
AV 17 EHT	Mitsubishi Fuso	Turners	AV 17 EVU	Mercedes	MSC (Goldstar)
AV 17 EKA	Mercedes	MSC (Turners)	AV 17 EVW	Mercedes	MSC (Goldstar)
AV 17 EKB	Mercedes	MSC (Turners)	AV 17 EVX	Mercedes	MSC (Goldstar)
AV 17 EKC	Mercedes	Macintyre	AV 17 EVY	Mercedes	MSC (Goldstar)
AV 17 EKD	Mercedes	MSC (Turners)	AV 17 EWB	Mercedes	MSC (Goldstar)
AV 17 EKE	Mercedes	Macintyre	AV 17 EWC	Mercedes	MSC (Goldstar)
AV 17 EKF	Mercedes	MSC (Turners)	AV 17 EWD	Mercedes	MSC (Goldstar)
AV 17 EKG	Mercedes	Macintyre	AV 17 EWE	Mercedes	MSC (Goldstar)
AV 17 EKH	Mercedes	MSC (Turners)	AV 17 EWF	Mercedes	MSC (Goldstar)
AV 17 EKJ	Mercedes	Macintyre	AV 17 EWG	Mercedes	MSC (Goldstar)
AV 17 EKK	Mercedes	MSC (Turners)	AV 17 EWH	Mercedes	MSC (Goldstar)
AV 17 EKL	Mercedes	MSC (Turners)	AV 17 EWJ	Mercedes	MSC (Goldstar)
AV 17 EKM	Mercedes	MSC (Turners)	AV 17 EWK	Mercedes	MSC (Goldstar)
AV 17 EKO	Mercedes	Macintyre	AV 17 EWL	Mercedes	MSC (Goldstar)
AV 17 EKP	Mercedes	MSC (Turners)	AV 17 EWM	Mercedes	MSC (Goldstar)
AV 17 EKW	Mercedes	Macintyre	AV 17 EWN	Mercedes	MSC (Goldstar)
AV 17 ETA	Mercedes	MSC (Goldstar)	AV 17 EWO	Mercedes	MSC (Goldstar)
AV 17 ETD	Mercedes	Goldstar	AV 17 EWP	Mercedes	MSC (Goldstar)
AV 17 ETE	Mercedes	Goldstar	AV 17 EWR	Mercedes	MSC (Goldstar)
AV 17 ETF	Mercedes	MSC (Goldstar)	AV 17 EWS	Mercedes	MSC (Goldstar)
AV 17 ETJ	Mercedes	MSC (Goldstar)	AV 17 EWT	Mercedes	MSC (Goldstar)
AV 17 ETK	Mercedes	MSC (Goldstar)	AV 17 EWU	Mercedes	MSC (Goldstar)
AV 17 ETL	Mercedes	MSC (Goldstar)	AV 17 EWW	Mercedes	MSC (Goldstar)
AV 17 ETO	Mercedes	MSC (Goldstar)	AV 17 EWX	Mercedes	MSC (Goldstar)
AV 17 ETR	Mercedes	MSC (Goldstar)	AV 17 EWY	Mercedes	MSC (Goldstar)
AV 17 ETT	Mercedes	MSC (Goldstar)	AV 17 EWZ	Mercedes	MSC (Goldstar)
AV 17 ETX	Mercedes	MSC (Goldstar)	AV 17 EXA	Mercedes	MSC (Goldstar)
AV 17 ETY	Mercedes	MSC (Goldstar)	AV 17 EXB	Mercedes	MSC (Goldstar)
AV 17 EUA	Mercedes	MSC (Goldstar)	AV 17 EXC	Mercedes	MSC (Goldstar)
AV 17 EUB	Mercedes	MSC (Goldstar)	AV 17 EXD	Mercedes	MSC (Goldstar)
AV 17 EUC	Mercedes	MSC (Goldstar)	AV 17 EXE	Mercedes	MSC (Goldstar)
AV 17 EUD	Mercedes	MSC (Goldstar)	AV 17 EXF	Mercedes	MSC (Goldstar)
AV 17 EUE	Mercedes	MSC (Goldstar)	AV 17 EXG	Mercedes	MSC (Goldstar)
AV 17 EUF	Mercedes	MSC (Goldstar)	AV 17 EXH	Mercedes	MSC (Goldstar)
AV 17 EUH	Mercedes	MSC (Goldstar)	AV 17 EXJ	Mercedes	MSC (Goldstar)
AV 17 EUJ	Mercedes	MSC (Goldstar)	AV 17 EXK	Mercedes	MSC (Goldstar)
AV 17 EUK	Mercedes	MSC (Goldstar)	AV 17 EXL	Mercedes	MSC (Goldstar)
AV 17 EUL	Mercedes	MSC (Goldstar)	AV 17 EXM	Mercedes	MSC (Goldstar)
AV 17 EUO	Mercedes	MSC (Goldstar)	AV 17 EXN	Mercedes	MSC (Goldstar)
AV 17 EUP	Mercedes	MSC (Goldstar)	AV 17 EXO	Mercedes	MSC (Goldstar)
AV 17 EUR	Mercedes	MSC (Goldstar)	AV 17 EXP	Mercedes	MSC (Goldstar)
AV 17 EUT	Mercedes	MSC (Goldstar)	AV 17 EXR	Mercedes	MSC (Goldstar)
AV 17 EUU	Mercedes	MSC (Goldstar)	AV 17 EXS	Mercedes	MSC (Goldstar)
AV 17 EUW	Mercedes	MSC (Goldstar)	AV 17 EXT	Mercedes	MSC (Goldstar)
AV 17 EUY	Mercedes	MSC (Goldstar)	AV 17 EXU	Mercedes	MSC (Goldstar)

AV 17 EXW	Mercedes	MSC (Goldstar)	DF 17 PYX	Daf	Jack Richards
AV 17 EXX	Mercedes	MSC (Goldstar)	DF 17 PYY	Daf	Jack Richards
AV 17 EXZ	Mercedes	MSC (Goldstar)	DF 17 PYZ	Daf	Jack Richards
AV 17 EYA	Mercedes	MSC (Goldstar)	DF 17 VKD	Daf	Jack Richards
AV 17 EYB	Mercedes	MSC (Goldstar)	DF 17 VKE	Daf	Jack Richards
AV 17 EYC	Mercedes	MSC (Goldstar)	DF 17 VKG	Daf	Jack Richards
AV 17 EYD	Mercedes	MSC (Goldstar)	DF 17 VKK	Daf	Jack Richards
AV 17 EYF	Mercedes	MSC (Goldstar)	DG 17 KFP	Daf	Smurfit Kappa
AV 17 EYG	Mercedes	MSC (Goldstar)	DG 17 KFR	Daf	Smurfit Kappa
AV 17 EYH	Mercedes	MSC (Goldstar)	DG 17 KLJ	Daf	Jack Richards
AV 17 EYJ	Mercedes	MSC (Goldstar)	DG 17 KLK	Daf	Jack Richards
AV 17 EYK	Mercedes	MSC (Goldstar)	DG 17 KLL	Daf	Jack Richards
AV 17 WUX	Daf	Turners	DG 17 KLM	Daf	Jack Richards
AV 17 WUY	Daf	Turners	DG 17 KOU	Daf	Jack Richards
AV 17 WVA	Daf	Turners	DG 17 KOV	Daf	Jack Richards
AV 17 WVB	Daf	Turners	DG 17 KOX	Daf	Jack Richards
AV 17 WVC	Daf	Turners	DG 17 KPA	Daf	Jack Richards
AV 17 WVD	Daf	Turners	DG 17 KSE	Daf	Jack Richards
AV 17 WVE	Daf	Turners	DG 17 KSF	Daf	Jack Richards
AV 17 WVF	Daf	Turners	DG 17 KSJ	Daf	Jack Richards
AV 17 WVG	Daf	Turners	DG 17 KSK	Daf	Jack Richards
AV 17 ZWT	Mercedes	Turners	FD 17 XPW	Daf	Turners
AX 17 DVK	Daf	Turners	FX 17 KHA	Scania	Dowse
AX 17 DVL	Daf	Turners	FX 17 KJA	Scania	Dowse
AX 17 DVM	Daf	Turners	FX 17 KTO	Scania	Dowse
AX 17 DVN	Daf	Turners	FX 17 KUP	Scania	Red
AX 17 DVO	Daf	Turners	FX 17 KVA	Scania	Clements
AX 17 DVP	Daf	Turners	FX 17 KVB	Scania	Clements
AX 17 DVR	Daf	Turners	NK 17 UEZ	Scania	Macintyre
AX 17 FEP	Daf	Turners	NK 17 UKD	Scania	Macintyre
AX 17 FET	Daf	Turners	PJ 17 USE	Scania	Macintyre
AX 17 FEU	Daf	Turners	SP 17 MXN	Iveco	White
AX 17 FEV	Daf	Turners	SP 17 MXO	Iveco	White
AX 17 FFA	Daf	Turners	AV 67 EYJ	Daf	Turners
AX 17 FFB	Daf	Turners	AV 67 EYK	Daf	Hanson (White)
AX 17 FFC	Daf	Turners	AV 67 EYL	Daf	Turners
AX 17 FFD	Daf	Turners	AV 67 EYM	Daf	Hanson (White)
AX 17 FFE	Daf	Turners	AV 67 EYO	Daf	Turners
AX 17 FFG	Daf	Turners	AV 67 EYP	Daf	Turners
AX 17 FFH	Daf	Turners	AV 67 EYR	Daf	Turners
AX 17 FFJ	Daf	Turners	AV 67 EYS	Daf	Turners
AX 17 FFK	Daf	Turners	AV 67 EYT	Daf	Turners
AX 17 FFL	Daf	Turners	AV 67 EYU	Daf	Turners
AX 17 FFM	Daf	Turners	AV 67 EYW	Daf	Hanson (White)
AX 17 LSF	Daf	Turners	AV 67 EYX	Daf	Hanson (White)
AX 17 LSJ	Daf	Turners	AV 67 EZT	Daf	Turners
AX 17 LSK	Daf	Turners	AV 67 EZW	Daf	Turners
AX 17 LSL	Daf	Turners	AV 67 EZX	Daf	Turners
AX 17 LSN	Daf	Turners	AV 67 EZZ	Daf	Turners
AY 17 WDA	Daf	Macintyre	AY 67 RZA	Mercedes	Turners
AY 17 WDC	Daf	Macintyre	AY 67 RZB	Mercedes	Turners
AY 17 WDK	Daf	Turners	AY 67 RZC	Mercedes	Turners
AY 17 WDL	Daf	UK Fuels	AY 67 RZD	Mercedes	Turners
AY 17 WDM	Daf	Turners	AY 67 RZE	Mercedes	Turners
DF 17 PJV	Daf	Jack Richards	AY 67 RZF	Mercedes	Turners
DF 17 PJX	Daf	Jack Richards	AY 67 RZG	Mercedes	Turners

Reg	Make	Operator	Reg	Make	Operator
AY 67 RZH	Mercedes	Turners	BG 67 XRX	Daf	Goldstar
AY 67 RZJ	Mercedes	Turners	BG 67 XRY	Daf	Goldstar
AY 67 RZK	Mercedes	Turners	DE 67 UHJ	Daf	Jack Richards
AY 67 RZL	Mercedes	Turners	DE 67 UHK	Daf	Jack Richards
AY 67 RZN	Mercedes	Turners	DE 67 UHL	Daf	Jack Richards
AY 67 RZO	Mercedes	Turners	DE 67 UHM	Daf	Jack Richards
AY 67 RZP	Mercedes	Turners	DE 67 UHN	Daf	Jack Richards
AY 67 RZR	Mercedes	Turners	DE 67 UHO	Daf	Jack Richards
AY 67 RZS	Mercedes	Turners	DE 67 UHP	Daf	Jack Richards
AY 67 RZT	Mercedes	Turners	DE 67 UKC	Daf	Smurfit Kappa
AY 67 RZU	Mercedes	Turners	DE 67 UKD	Daf	Smurfit Kappa
AY 67 RZV	Mercedes	Turners	DE 67 ULT	Daf	Jack Richards
AY 67 SXA	Mercedes	MSC (Turners)	DE 67 ULU	Daf	Jack Richards
AY 67 SXB	Mercedes	MSC (Turners)	DE 67 UML	Daf	Jack Richards
AY 67 SXC	Mercedes	Macintyre	DE 67 UMM	Daf	Jack Richards
AY 67 SYA	Mercedes	Macintyre	DE 67 UMO	Daf	Jack Richards
AY 67 SYC	Mercedes	Macintyre	DE 67 UMR	Daf	Jack Richards
AY 67 SYE	Mercedes	Macintyre	DF 67 JXA	Daf	Jack Richards
AY 67 SYF	Mercedes	Macintyre	DF 67 JXB	Daf	Jack Richards
AY 67 SYG	Mercedes	Macintyre	DF 67 JXC	Daf	Jack Richards
AY 67 SYH	Mercedes	Macintyre	DF 67 JXD	Daf	Jack Richards
AY 67 TVC	Mercedes	Goldstar	DF 67 JXE	Daf	Smurfit Kappa
AY 67 TVE	Mercedes	Goldstar	DF 67 JXG	Daf	Smurfit Kappa
AY 67 TVF	Mercedes	Goldstar	DF 67 JXH	Daf	Smurfit Kappa
AY 67 TVJ	Mercedes	Goldstar	DF 67 JXJ	Daf	Jack Richards
AY 67 TVK	Mercedes	Goldstar	DF 67 JXK	Daf	Jack Richards
AY 67 TVL	Mercedes	Goldstar	DF 67 JXL	Daf	Jack Richards
AY 67 TVM	Mercedes	Goldstar	DF 67 JXM	Daf	Jack Richards
AY 67 TVN	Mercedes	Goldstar	DF 67 JXN	Daf	Smurfit Kappa
AY 67 TVO	Mercedes	Goldstar	DF 67 JXO	Daf	Smurfit Kappa
AY 67 TVP	Mercedes	Goldstar	DF 67 JXP	Daf	Smurfit Kappa
AY 67 TVT	Mercedes	Goldstar	DK 67 UVA	Daf	Jack Richards
AY 67 TVU	Mercedes	Goldstar	DK 67 UVB	Daf	Jack Richards
AY 67 TVV	Mercedes	Goldstar	DK 67 UVC	Daf	Jack Richards
AY 67 TVW	Mercedes	Goldstar	DK 67 UVD	Daf	Jack Richards
AY 67 TVX	Mercedes	Goldstar	DK 67 UVE	Daf	Jack Richards
AY 67 TVZ	Mercedes	Goldstar	DK 67 UVG	Daf	Jack Richards
AY 67 TWA	Mercedes	Goldstar	DK 67 UVH	Daf	Jack Richards
AY 67 TWC	Mercedes	Goldstar	DK 67 UVJ	Daf	Jack Richards
AY 67 TWD	Mercedes	Goldstar	DK 67 UVL	Daf	Jack Richards
AY 67 TWK	Mercedes	Macintyre	DK 67 UVM	Daf	Jack Richards
AY 67 VAH	Daf	Turners	DK 67 UWU	Daf	Jack Richards
AY 67 VAJ	Daf	Turners	DK 67 UXB	Daf	Jack Richards
AY 67 VAK	Daf	Turners	DK 67 UXC	Daf	Jack Richards
AY 67 VAM	Daf	Turners	DK 67 UXD	Daf	Jack Richards
AY 67 VAO	Daf	Turners	DK 67 UXE	Daf	Jack Richards
AY 67 VAU	Daf	Greenchem	DK 67 UZN	Daf	Jack Richards
AY 67 VAV	Daf	Turners	DK 67 VBM	Daf	Jack Richards
AY 67 VAX	Daf	Turners	DK 67 VBP	Daf	Jack Richards
AY 67 VBA	Daf	AdBlue	DK 67 VBT	Daf	Jack Richards
AY 67 VBB	Daf	Turners	DK 67 VBV	Daf	Jack Richards
AY 67 VBC	Daf	Turners	DK 67 VBY	Daf	Jack Richards
AY 67 VBD	Daf	Turners	FX 67 NUM	Scania	Dowse
AY 67 VBE	Daf	Turners	FX 67 NZT	Scania	Dowse
AY 67 VBF	Daf	BWOC	FX 67 OCA	Scania	Dowse
AY 67 VBG	Daf	BWOC	KX 67 TXA	Scania	R & R Haulage

Reg	Make	Operator	Reg	Make	Operator
KX 67 TXH	Scania	R & R Haulage	AY 18 PUK	Daf	Turners
KX 67 TXR	Scania	R & R Haulage	AY 18 PUO	Daf	Turners
OY 67 KVJ	Daf	Turners (Blue)	AY 18 PUU	Daf	Turners
OY 67 KVK	Daf	Turners (Blue)	AY 18 PUV	Daf	Turners
PF 67 EDK	Volvo	Kibble	AY 18 PUX	Daf	Turners
PO 67 UDP	Volvo	Kibble	AY 18 PVA	Daf	Turners
TY 67 DAF (67)	Daf	Ocean Trailers	AY 18 PVD	Daf	Turners
YH 67 JNF	Iveco	White	AY 18 RAX	Daf	Turners
AE 18 RZJ	Isuzu	Jack Richards	AY 18 RBU	Daf	Lynx Fuels
AV 18 BFF	Daf	Turners	AY 18 RBV	Daf	Lynx Fuels
AV 18 BFJ	Daf	Turners	AY 18 RBX	Daf	Turners
AV 18 BFK	Daf	Macintyre	AY 18 RCX	Daf	Turners
AV 18 BFL	Daf	Macintyre	CN 18 UDX	Daf	Goldstar
AV 18 BFM	Daf	Macintyre	CN 18 UDY	Daf	Goldstar
AV 18 BFN	Daf	Macintyre	DC 18 LVX	Daf	Jack Richards
AV 18 BFO	Daf	Macintyre	DC 18 LVY	Daf	Jack Richards
AV 18 BFP	Daf	Macintyre	DC 18 LVZ	Daf	Jack Richards
AV 18 BFU	Daf	Macintyre	DC 18 LWA	Daf	Jack Richards
AV 18 BFX	Daf	Turners	DC 18 LWD	Daf	Jack Richards
AV 18 BFY	Daf	Turners	DC 18 LWH	Daf	Jack Richards
AV 18 BFZ	Daf	Turners	DC 18 LWL	Daf	Jack Richards
AV 18 BGE	Daf	Turners	DF 18 GFZ	Daf	Smurfit Kappa
AV 18 BGF	Daf	Turners	DF 18 GGA	Daf	Smurfit Kappa
AV 18 BGK	Daf	Turners	DF 18 GGE	Daf	Smurfit Kappa
AV 18 BGO	Daf	Turners	DF 18 GGJ	Daf	Smurfit Kappa
AV 18 BGU	Daf	Turners	DF 18 GGK	Daf	Smurfit Kappa
AV 18 BGX	Daf	Turners	DF 18 GGO	Daf	Smurfit Kappa
AV 18 BGY	Daf	Turners	DF 18 GGP	Daf	Smurfit Kappa
AV 18 BGZ	Daf	Turners	DF 18 GGU	Daf	Smurfit Kappa
AV 18 BHA	Daf	Turners	DF 18 GGV	Daf	Smurfit Kappa
AV 18 BHD	Daf	Turners	DF 18 GGX	Daf	Smurfit Kappa
AV 18 BHE	Daf	Turners	DF 18 GGY	Daf	Smurfit Kappa
AV 18 BHF	Daf	Turners	DF 18 GGZ	Daf	Smurfit Kappa
AV 18 BHJ	Daf	Turners	DF 18 GHD	Daf	Smurfit Kappa
AV 18 GZL	Daf	Turners	DG 18 YEJ	Daf	Jack Richards
AV 18 GZM	Daf	Turners	DG 18 YEK	Daf	Jack Richards
AV 18 GZN	Daf	Turners	DG 18 YEL	Daf	Jack Richards
AV 18 GZO	Daf	Turners	DG 18 YEU	Daf	Jack Richards
AV 18 RZC	Daf	Turners	DG 18 YEV	Daf	Jack Richards
AV 18 RZD	Daf	Turners	DG 18 YEX	Daf	Jack Richards
AV 18 RZE	Daf	Turners	DG 18 YEY	Daf	Jack Richards
AV 18 RZF	Daf	Turners	DG 18 YFA	Daf	Jack Richards
AV 18 RZG	Daf	Turners	DG 18 YFB	Daf	Jack Richards
AV 18 RZH	Daf	Turners	DG 18 YFC	Daf	Jack Richards
AV 18 RZJ	Daf	Turners	DK 18 HFZ	Daf	Smurfit Kappa
AV 18 RZK	Daf	Turners	DK 18 HGA	Daf	Smurfit Kappa
AV 18 RZL	Daf	Turners	DK 18 HGC	Daf	Jack Richards
AV 18 RZM	Daf	Turners	DK 18 HGD	Daf	Jack Richards
AV 18 RZN	Daf	Turners	DK 18 HGE	Daf	Jack Richards
AV 18 RZO	Daf	Turners	DK 18 HKE	Daf	Jack Richards
AY 18 KDJ	Mitsubishi	Turners	DK 18 HKF	Daf	Jack Richards
AY 18 PUA	Daf	Turners	DK 18 HKG	Daf	Jack Richards
AY 18 PUE	Daf	Turners	DK 18 HKH	Daf	Jack Richards
AY 18 PUF	Daf	Turners	DK 18 HKJ	Daf	Jack Richards
AY 18 PUH	Daf	Turners	DK 18 HKL	Daf	Jack Richards
AY 18 PUJ	Daf	Turners	DK 18 HKM	Daf	Jack Richards

DK 18 HKN	Daf	Jack Richards	DK 18 HWU	Daf	Jack Richards
DK 18 HKO	Daf	Jack Richards	DK 18 HWV	Daf	Jack Richards
DK 18 HKP	Daf	Jack Richards	DK 18 HWW	Daf	Jack Richards
DK 18 HKT	Daf	Jack Richards	DK 18 HWX	Daf	Jack Richards
DK 18 HKU	Daf	Jack Richards	DK 18 HWY	Daf	Jack Richards
DK 18 HKV	Daf	Jack Richards	DK 18 HWZ	Daf	Jack Richards
DK 18 HKW	Daf	Jack Richards	DK 18 HXA	Daf	Jack Richards
DK 18 HKX	Daf	Jack Richards	DK 18 HXB	Daf	Jack Richards
DK 18 HKY	Daf	Jack Richards	DK 18 HYV	Daf	Jack Richards
DK 18 HKZ	Daf	Jack Richards	DK 18 HYW	Daf	Jack Richards
DK 18 HMJ	Daf	Jack Richards	DK 18 HYX	Daf	Jack Richards
DK 18 HMO	Daf	Jack Richards	DK 18 HYY	Daf	Jack Richards
DK 18 HMU	Daf	Jack Richards	DK 18 HYZ	Daf	Smurfit Kappa
DK 18 HMV	Daf	Jack Richards	DK 18 HZA	Daf	Smurfit Kappa
DK 18 HMX	Daf	Jack Richards	DK 18 HZB	Daf	Smurfit Kappa
DK 18 HMY	Daf	Jack Richards	DK 18 HZC	Daf	Smurfit Kappa
DK 18 HMZ	Daf	Jack Richards	DK 18 HZD	Daf	Smurfit Kappa
DK 18 HNA	Daf	Jack Richards	DK 18 HZE	Daf	Smurfit Kappa
DK 18 HNB	Daf	Jack Richards	DK 18 HZF	Daf	Smurfit Kappa
DK 18 HNC	Daf	Jack Richards	DK 18 HZG	Daf	Smurfit Kappa
DK 18 HND	Daf	Jack Richards	FX 18 TFF	Scania	Dowse
DK 18 HNE	Daf	Jack Richards	KX 18 WLR	Scania	R & R Haulage
DK 18 HNF	Daf	Jack Richards	KX 18 WOR	Scania	R & R Haulage
DK 18 HNG	Daf	Jack Richards	KX 18 WVH	Scania	R & R Haulage
DK 18 HNM	Daf	Jack Richards	KX 18 WVL	Scania	R & R Haulage
DK 18 HNN	Daf	Jack Richards	PO 18 TVD	Volvo	Kibble
DK 18 HSY	Daf	Jack Richards	YJ18 SDU	Mercedes	Turners
DK 18 HSZ	Daf	Jack Richards	AV 68 CHJ	Daf	MFG (Turners)
DK 18 HTA	Daf	Jack Richards	AV 68 CHK	Daf	MFG (Turners)
DK 18 HTC	Daf	Jack Richards	AV 68 CHL	Daf	MFG (Turners)
DK 18 HTD	Daf	Jack Richards	AV 68 CKA	Daf	Goldstar
DK 18 HVP	Daf	Smurfit Kappa	AV 68 CKG	Daf	Goldstar
DK 18 HVR	Daf	Smurfit Kappa	AV 68 EPJ	Daf	Turners
DK 18 HVS	Daf	Smurfit Kappa	AV 68 EPK	Daf	Turners
DK 18 HVT	Daf	Smurfit Kappa	AV 68 EPO	Daf	Goldstar
DK 18 HVU	Daf	Smurfit Kappa	AV 68 EPP	Daf	Goldstar
DK 18 HVV	Daf	Smurfit Kappa	AV 68 EPU	Daf	Goldstar
DK 18 HVW	Daf	Jack Richards	AV 68 EPX	Daf	Goldstar
DK 18 HVX	Daf	Jack Richards	AV 68 EPY	Daf	Goldstar
DK 18 HVY	Daf	Jack Richards	AV 68 KPF	Daf	Turners
DK 18 HVZ	Daf	Jack Richards	AV 68 KPG	Daf	BWOC
DK 18 HWC	Daf	Jack Richards	AV 68 KPJ	Daf	Turners
DK 18 HWD	Daf	Jack Richards	AV 68 KPK	Daf	BWOC
DK 18 HWE	Daf	Jack Richards	AV 68 KPL	Daf	Turners
DK 18 HWF	Daf	Jack Richards	AV 68 KPN	Daf	Turners
DK 18 HWG	Daf	Smurfit Kappa	AV 68 KPP	Daf	Goldstar
DK 18 HWH	Daf	Smurfit Kappa	AV 68 KPR	Daf	Goldstar
DK 18 HWJ	Daf	Smurfit Kappa	AV 68 KPT	Daf	Goldstar
DK 18 HWL	Daf	Jack Richards	AV 68 KPU	Daf	Goldstar
DK 18 HWM	Daf	Jack Richards	AV 68 RNX	Daf	Macintyre
DK 18 HWN	Daf	Jack Richards	AV 68 RNY	Daf	Macintyre
DK 18 HWO	Daf	Jack Richards	AV 68 RNZ	Daf	Turners
DK 18 HWP	Daf	Jack Richards	AV 68 ROH	Daf	Turners
DK 18 HWR	Daf	Jack Richards	AV 68 RPO	Daf	Turners
DK 18 HWS	Daf	Jack Richards	AV 68 RPU	Daf	Turners
DK 18 HWT	Daf	Jack Richards	AV 68 RPX	Daf	Turners

AV 68 RPY	Daf	Turners	AY 68 TCV	Daf	Macintyre
AV 68 RPZ	Daf	Turners	AY 68 TCX	Daf	Macintyre
AV 68 RRO	Daf	Turners	AY 68 TCZ	Daf	Macintyre
AV 68 RRU	Daf	Turners	AY 68 TDO	Daf	Macintyre
AV 68 RRX	Daf	Turners	AY 68 TDU	Daf	Macintyre
AV 68 RRZ	Daf	Turners	AY 68 TDV	Daf	Macintyre
AV 68 RSU	Daf	Turners	AY 68 TDX	Daf	Macintyre
AV 68 RSX	Daf	Macintyre	AY 68 TDZ	Daf	Macintyre
AV 68 RSY	Daf	Macintyre	AY 68 TEJ	Daf	BWOC
AV 68 RSZ	Daf	Macintyre	AY 68 TEO	Daf	Ford Fuel Oils
AV 68 RTO	Daf	Macintyre	AY 68 TEU	Daf	BWOC
AV 68 VVA	Daf	Turners	AY 68 TEV	Daf	Turners
AV 68 VVB	Daf	Turners	AY 68 TFA	Daf	BWOC
AV 68 VVC	Daf	Turners	AY 68 TFE	Daf	BWOC
AV 68 VVD	Daf	Turners	AY 68 TFF	Daf	MFG (Turners)
AV 68 VVE	Daf	Turners	AY 68 TFJ	Daf	Turners
AX 68 MXZ	Mercedes	Goldstar	AY 68 TFK	Daf	Harvest Energy
AX 68 MYA	Mercedes	Goldstar	AY 68 TFN	Daf	Turners
AX 68 MYB	Mercedes	Goldstar	AY 68 TGJ	Daf	Goldstar
AX 68 MYC	Mercedes	Goldstar	AY 68 TGK	Daf	Goldstar
AX 68 MYD	Mercedes	Goldstar	AY 68 TGN	Daf	Goldstar
AX 68 MYF	Mercedes	Goldstar	AY 68 TGO	Daf	Goldstar
AX 68 MYG	Mercedes	Goldstar	AY 68 TGU	Daf	Goldstar
AX 68 MYH	Mercedes	Goldstar	AY 68 TGV	Daf	Goldstar
AX 68 MYJ	Mercedes	Goldstar	AY 68 TGX	Daf	MFG (Turners)
AX 68 MYK	Mercedes	Goldstar	AY 68 TGZ	Daf	MFG (Turners)
AX 68 MYL	Mercedes	Goldstar	AY 68 THF	Daf	MFG (Turners)
AX 68 NKH	Mercedes	Turners	AY 68 THG	Daf	MFG (Turners)
AX 68 NKJ	Mercedes	Turners	AY 68 THK	Daf	Turners
AX 68 NKK	Mercedes	Turners	AY 68 THN	Daf	Turners
AX 68 NKL	Mercedes	Turners	AY 68 THU	Daf	Turners
AX 68 NKM	Mercedes	Turners	AY 68 THV	Daf	Turners
AX 68 NKN	Mercedes	Turners	AY 68 THX	Daf	MFG (Turners)
AX 68 NKO	Mercedes	Turners	AY 68 THZ	Daf	Turners
AX 68 NKP	Mercedes	Turners	AY 68 TJO	Daf	MFG (Turners)
AX 68 NKR	Mercedes	Turners	AY 68 TJU	Daf	Turners
AX 68 NKT	Mercedes	Turners	AY 68 TJV	Daf	Turners
AX 68 NKU	Mercedes	Turners	AY 68 TJX	Daf	Turners
AX 68 NKW	Mercedes	Turners	AY 68 YNV	Daf	Turners
AX 68 NKZ	Mercedes	Turners	AY 68 YNW	Daf	Turners
AX 68 NLA	Mercedes	Turners	AY 68 YNX	Daf	Turners
AX 68 NLC	Mercedes	Turners	BF 68 UVG	Iveco	Lynn Star
AX 68 NLD	Mercedes	Turners	DK 68 TUO	Daf	Jack Richards
AX 68 NLE	Mercedes	Turners	DK 68 TUP	Daf	Jack Richards
AX 68 NLF	Mercedes	Turners	DK 68 TUU	Daf	Jack Richards
AX 68 RDO	Daf	Turners	DK 68 TUV	Daf	Jack Richards
AX 68 RHU	Daf	Turners	DK 68 TUW	Daf	Jack Richards
AX 68 RNN	Daf	Turners	DK 68 TUY	Daf	Jack Richards
AX 68 RNY	Daf	Turners	DK 68 TVA	Daf	Jack Richards
AY 68 TBV	Daf	Macintyre	DK 68 TVZ	Daf	Jack Richards
AY 68 TBX	Daf	Macintyre	DK 68 TWA	Daf	Jack Richards
AY 68 TBZ	Daf	Macintyre	DK 68 TWC	Daf	Jack Richards
AY 68 TCJ	Daf	Macintyre	DK 68 TWD	Daf	Jack Richards
AY 68 TCK	Daf	Macintyre	DK 68 TWE	Daf	Jack Richards
AY 68 TCO	Daf	Macintyre	FD 68 ODF	Daf	Lynn Star
AY 68 TCU	Daf	Macintyre	FD 68 ODK	Daf	Lynn Star

Reg	Make	Operator	Reg	Make	Operator
FD 68 OEA	Daf	Lynn Star	KY 68 GHZ	Scania	Turners
FD 68 OEB	Daf	Lynn Star	KY 68 GJE	Scania	Turners
FN 68 HRJ	Daf	Turners	KY 68 GJF	Scania	Turners
FP 68 LGU	Daf	Lynn Star	KY 68 GJG	Scania	Turners
FP 68 LGW	Daf	Lynn Star	KY 68 GJJ	Scania	Turners
FP 68 LGX	Daf	Lynn Star	KY 68 GJK	Scania	Turners
FP 68 LGY	Daf	Lynn Star	KY 68 GJO	Scania	Turners
FP 68 LGZ	Daf	Lynn Star	KY 68 GJU	Scania	Turners
FP 68 LHA	Daf	Lynn Star	KY 68 GJV	Scania	Turners
FP 68 LHB	Daf	Lynn Star	KY 68 GJX	Scania	Turners
FP 68 LHE	Daf	Lynn Star	KY 68 GJZ	Scania	Turners
FX 68 OMG	Scania	Dowse	KY 68 GKA	Scania	Turners
FX 68 ONK	Scania	Dowse	KY 68 GKC	Scania	Turners
FX 68 OPC	Scania	Dowse	KY 68 GKD	Scania	Turners
KT 68 OKB	Scania	Turners	KY 68 GKE	Scania	Turners
KT 68 OKC	Scania	Turners	KY 68 GKF	Scania	Turners
KT 68 OKD	Scania	Turners	KY 68 GKG	Scania	Turners
KT 68 OKE	Scania	Turners	KY 68 GKJ	Scania	Turners
KT 68 OKF	Scania	Turners	KY 68 GKK	Scania	Turners
KT 68 OKG	Scania	Turners	KY 68 GKL	Scania	Turners
KT 68 OKH	Scania	Turners	KY 68 GKN	Scania	Turners
KT 68 OKJ	Scania	Turners	KY 68 GKO	Scania	Turners
KT 68 OKK	Scania	Macintyre	KY 68 GKP	Scania	Turners
KT 68 OKL	Scania	Macintyre	KY 68 GKU	Scania	Turners
KT 68 OKM	Scania	Macintyre	KY 68 GKV	Scania	Turners
KT 68 OKN	Scania	Macintyre	KY 68 GKX	Scania	Turners
KT 68 OKO	Scania	Macintyre	KY 68 GKZ	Scania	Turners
KT 68 OKP	Scania	Macintyre	KY 68 GLF	Scania	Turners
KT 68 PHV	Scania	Turners	KY 68 GZU	Scania	Turners
KT 68 PHZ	Scania	Turners	KY 68 GZV	Scania	Turners
KT 68 PKA	Scania	Turners	KY 68 GZW	Scania	Turners
KT 68 PKK	Scania	Turners	KY 68 GZX	Scania	Turners
KT 68 PKU	Scania	Turners	KY 68 GZZ	Scania	Turners
KT 68 PLJ	Scania	Turners	YL 68 ANF	Mercedes	White
KY 68 GGF	Scania	Turners	YL 68 ANV	Mercedes	White
KY 68 GGJ	Scania	Turners	AW 19 KWR	Daf	Turners
KY 68 GGK	Scania	Turners	AW 19 KWS	Daf	Turners
KY 68 GGO	Scania	Turners	AW 19 KWT	Daf	Turners
KY 68 GGP	Scania	Turners	AW 19 KWU	Daf	Turners
KY 68 GGU	Scania	Turners	AW 19 KWV	Daf	Turners
KY 68 GGV	Scania	Turners	AW 19 KWX	Daf	Turners
KY 68 GGX	Scania	Turners	AW 19 KWY	Daf	Turners
KY 68 GGZ	Scania	Turners	AW 19 KWZ	Daf	Turners
KY 68 GHA	Scania	Turners	AW 19 KXA	Daf	Turners
KY 68 GHB	Scania	Turners	AW 19 KXB	Daf	Turners
KY 68 GHD	Scania	Turners	AW 19 KXC	Daf	Turners
KY 68 GHF	Scania	Turners	AW 19 KXD	Daf	Turners
KY 68 GHG	Scania	Turners	AW 19 KXE	Daf	Turners
KY 68 GHH	Scania	Turners	AW 19 KXF	Daf	Turners
KY 68 GHJ	Scania	Turners	AW 19 KXG	Daf	Turners
KY 68 GHK	Scania	Turners	AW 19 KXH	Daf	Turners
KY 68 GHN	Scania	Turners	AW 19 KXJ	Daf	Turners
KY 68 GHO	Scania	Turners	AW 19 KXK	Daf	Turners
KY 68 GHU	Scania	Turners	AW 19 KXL	Daf	Turners
KY 68 GHV	Scania	Turners	AW 19 KXM	Daf	Turners
KY 68 GHX	Scania	Turners	AW 19 KXN	Daf	Turners

Reg	Make	Operator	Reg	Make	Operator
AW 19 KXO	Daf	Turners	AY 19 THU	Daf	Hanson (White)
AW 19 KXP	Daf	Turners	AY 19 THV	Daf	Hanson (White)
AW 19 MHY	Daf	Turners	AY 19 THX	Daf	Turners
AW 19 MHZ	Daf	Turners	AY 19 THZ	Daf	Turners
AX 19 JNJ	Daf	Goldstar	AY 19 TJO	Daf	Turners
AX 19 JNK	Daf	Goldstar	AY 19 TJU	Daf	Turners
AX 19 JNL	Daf	Macintyre	AY 19 TJV	Daf	Hanson (White)
AX 19 JNN	Daf	Macintyre	AY 19 TJX	Daf	Turners
AX 19 JRO	Daf	Macintyre	AY 19 TJZ	Daf	Turners
AX 19 JRV	Daf	Macintyre	AY 19 TKA	Daf	Turners
AX 19 XEW	Daf	Turners	AY 19 TKC	Daf	Turners
AX 19 XEY	Daf	Turners	AY 19 TKD	Daf	Turners
AX 19 XEZ	Daf	Turners	AY 19 TKE	Daf	Turners
AX 19 XFA	Daf	Turners	AY 19 TKF	Daf	Hanson (White)
AX 19 XFB	Daf	Turners	AY 19 TKJ	Daf	Turners
AX 19 XFC	Daf	Turners	AY 19 TKK	Daf	Turners
AX 19 XFD	Daf	Turners	AY 19 TKN	Daf	Turners
AX 19 XFE	Daf	Turners	AY 19 TKO	Daf	Turners
AX 19 XFF	Daf	Turners	AY 19 TKT	Daf	Hanson (White)
AX 19 XFG	Daf	Turners	AY 19 TKU	Daf	Hanson (White)
AX 19 XFH	Daf	Turners	AY 19 TKV	Daf	Turners
AX 19 XFJ	Daf	Turners	AY 19 TKX	Daf	Turners
AX 19 XFK	Daf	Turners	AY 19 TKZ	Daf	Turners
AX 19 XFL	Daf	Turners	AY 19 TLF	Daf	Turners
AX 19 XFM	Daf	Turners	AY 19 TLJ	Daf	Turners
AX 19 XFN	Daf	Turners	AY 19 TLK	Daf	Turners
AX 19 XFO	Daf	Turners	AY 19 TLN	Daf	Hanson (White)
AX 19 XFP	Daf	Turners	AY 19 TLO	Daf	Turners
AX 19 XFR	Daf	Turners	AY 19 TLU	Daf	Hanson (White)
AX 19 XFS	Daf	Turners	AY 19 TLV	Daf	Hanson (White)
AX 19 XFT	Daf	Goldstar	AY 19 TLX	Daf	Hanson (White)
AX 19 XFU	Daf	Goldstar	AY 19 TLZ	Daf	Turners
AX 19 XFV	Daf	Goldstar	AY 19 TMO	Daf	Hanson (White)
AX 19 XFW	Daf	Goldstar	AY 19 TMU	Daf	Hanson (White)
AX 19 XFY	Daf	Goldstar	AY 19 TMV	Daf	Hanson (White)
AX 19 XFZ	Daf	Goldstar	AY 19 TMX	Daf	Turners
AX 19 XGA	Daf	Goldstar	AY 19 TMZ	Daf	Turners
AX 19 XGB	Daf	Goldstar	AY 19 TNE	Daf	Hanson (White)
AX 19 XGC	Daf	Goldstar	AY 19 TNF	Daf	Turners
AX 19 XGD	Daf	Goldstar	AY 19 TNJ	Daf	Hanson (White)
AX 19 XGE	Daf	Goldstar	AY 19 TNK	Daf	Turners
AY 19 RWV	Mercedes	Turners	AY 19 TNL	Daf	Turners
AY 19 RWX	Mercedes	Turners	AY 19 TNN	Daf	Goldstar
AY 19 RXJ	Mercedes	Turners	AY 19 TNO	Daf	Goldstar
AY 19 RXK	Mercedes	Turners	AY 19 TNU	Daf	Goldstar
AY 19 RXL	Mercedes	Turners	AY 19 TNV	Daf	Goldstar
AY 19 RXR	Mercedes	Turners	AY 19 TNX	Daf	Goldstar
AY 19 RXS	Mercedes	Turners	AY 19 TNZ	Daf	Goldstar
AY 19 RXV	Mercedes	Turners	AY 19 TOA	Daf	Goldstar
AY 19 RXZ	Mercedes	Turners	AY 19 TOH	Daf	Goldstar
AY 19 RYD	Mercedes	Turners	AY 19 TOJ	Daf	Goldstar
AY 19 RYF	Mercedes	Turners	AY 19 TOV	Daf	Goldstar
AY 19 RYG	Mercedes	Turners	AY 19 TPF	Daf	Goldstar
AY 19 SDU	Mercedes	Turners	BV 19 JKN	Mitsubishi Fuso	Turners
AY 19 SNF	Mercedes	Turners	BV 19 JKO	Mitsubishi Fuso	Turners
AY 19 SNV	Mercedes	Vesty Foods	DA 19 YBX	Daf	Jack Richards

Reg	Make	Operator	Reg	Make	Operator
DA 19 YBY	Daf	Jack Richards	DK 19 XSU	Daf	Jack Richards
DA 19 YBZ	Daf	Jack Richards	DK 19 XSV	Daf	Jack Richards
DA 19 YCB	Daf	Jack Richards	DK 19 XSW	Daf	Smurfit Kappa
DA 19 YCC	Daf	Jack Richards	DK 19 XSX	Daf	Smurfit Kappa
DA 19 YCD	Daf	Jack Richards	DK 19 XSY	Daf	Smurfit Kappa
DA 19 YCE	Daf	Jack Richards	DK 19 XSZ	Daf	Smurfit Kappa
DF 19 ZJX	Daf	Jack Richards	DK 19 XTA	Daf	Smurfit Kappa
DF 19 ZJY	Daf	Jack Richards	DK 19 XTB	Daf	Smurfit Kappa
DF 19 ZJZ	Daf	Jack Richards	DK 19 XTC	Daf	Smurfit Kappa
DF 19 ZKA	Daf	Jack Richards	DK 19 XTD	Daf	Smurfit Kappa
DF 19 ZKB	Daf	Jack Richards	DK 19 XTE	Daf	Smurfit Kappa
DF 19 ZKC	Daf	Jack Richards	DK 19 XTF	Daf	Smurfit Kappa
DF 19 ZKD	Daf	Jack Richards	DK 19 XTG	Daf	Smurfit Kappa
DF 19 ZKE	Daf	Jack Richards	DK 19 XTH	Daf	Smurfit Kappa
DF 19 ZKG	Daf	Jack Richards	DK 19 XTJ	Daf	Smurfit Kappa
DF 19 ZKH	Daf	Jack Richards	DK 19 XTL	Daf	Smurfit Kappa
DF 19 ZKJ	Daf	Jack Richards	DK 19 XTS	Daf	Smurfit Kappa
DF 19 ZKK	Daf	Jack Richards	DK 19 XTT	Daf	Smurfit Kappa
DF 19 ZLN	Daf	Smurfit Kappa	DK 19 XTU	Daf	Smurfit Kappa
DF 19 ZLO	Daf	Jack Richards	DK 19 XTV	Daf	Jack Richards
DF 19 ZLU	Daf	Jack Richards	DK 19 XTW	Daf	Smurfit Kappa
DF 19 ZLV	Daf	Smurfit Kappa	DK 19 XTX	Daf	Jack Richards
DF 19 ZNL	Daf	Jack Richards	DK 19 XTY	Daf	Smurfit Kappa
DF 19 ZNM	Daf	Jack Richards	DK 19 XTZ	Daf	Jack Richards
DF 19 ZNN	Daf	Jack Richards	DK 19 XUA	Daf	Jack Richards
DF 19 ZNO	Daf	Jack Richards	DK 19 XUB	Daf	Smurfit Kappa
DF 19 ZNP	Daf	Jack Richards	DK 19 XUC	Daf	Jack Richards
DF 19 ZNR	Daf	Jack Richards	DK 19 XUD	Daf	Smurfit Kappa
DF 19 ZNS	Daf	Jack Richards	DK 19 XUE	Daf	Jack Richards
DF 19 ZNT	Daf	Jack Richards	DK 19 XUF	Daf	Jack Richards
DH 19 UNX	Daf	Jack Richards	DK 19 XUG	Daf	Smurfit Kappa
DH 19 UNY	Daf	Jack Richards	DK 19 XUH	Daf	Jack Richards
DH 19 UNZ	Daf	Jack Richards	FL 19 VDZ	Daf	Lynn Star
DH 19 UOA	Daf	Jack Richards	FX 19 UHT	Scania	Dowse
DH 19 UOF	Daf	Jack Richards	FX 19 UKG	Scania	Dowse
DH 19 UOG	Daf	Jack Richards	FX 19 UKL	Scania	Dowse
DH 19 UOJ	Daf	Jack Richards	FX 19 UKS	Scania	Dowse
DH 19 UOK	Daf	Jack Richards	KJ 19 TMY	Scania	Macintyre
DH 19 UOL	Daf	Jack Richards	KJ 19 TMZ	Scania	Macintyre
DH 19 UOM	Daf	Jack Richards	KJ 19 TNK	Scania	Macintyre
DH 19 UON	Daf	Jack Richards	KJ 19 TNL	Scania	Macintyre
DK 19 XNW	Daf	Jack Richards	KJ 19 TNN	Scania	Macintyre
DK 19 XNX	Daf	Jack Richards	KJ 19 TNU	Scania	Macintyre
DK 19 XNY	Daf	Jack Richards	KJ 19 TNV	Scania	Macintyre
DK 19 XNZ	Daf	Jack Richards	KJ 19 TPV	Scania	Turners
DK 19 XOD	Daf	Jack Richards	KJ 19 TPX	Scania	Turners
DK 19 XOE	Daf	Jack Richards	KJ 19 TSU	Scania	Turners
DK 19 XOF	Daf	Jack Richards	KJ 19 TSV	Scania	Macintyre
DK 19 XPZ	Daf	Jack Richards	KJ 19 TSX	Scania	Macintyre
DK 19 XRA	Daf	Jack Richards	KJ 19 TSY	Scania	Macintyre
DK 19 XRB	Daf	Jack Richards	KJ 19 TSZ	Scania	Macintyre
DK 19 XRC	Daf	Jack Richards	KJ 19 TTE	Scania	Macintyre
DK 19 XRD	Daf	Jack Richards	KJ 19 TTF	Scania	Macintyre
DK 19 XRE	Daf	Jack Richards	KJ 19 TTK	Scania	Turners
DK 19 XSR	Daf	Jack Richards	KJ 19 TXV	Scania	Turners
DK 19 XST	Daf	Jack Richards	KJ 19 TXX	Scania	Turners

Reg	Make	Operator	Reg	Make	Operator
KJ 19 TXY	Scania	Turners	KW 19 OLN	Scania	Goldstar
KJ 19 TXZ	Scania	Turners	KW 19 OLO	Scania	Goldstar
KJ 19 TYB	Scania	Turners	KW 19 OLP	Scania	Goldstar
KJ 19 TYD	Scania	Turners	KW 19 OLR	Scania	Goldstar
KJ 19 TYG	Scania	Turners	KW 19 OLT	Scania	Goldstar
KM 19 UHA	Scania	Goldstar	KW 19 OLU	Scania	Goldstar
KM 19 UHB	Scania	Goldstar	KW 19 OLV	Scania	Goldstar
KM 19 UHC	Scania	Goldstar	KW 19 OLX	Scania	Goldstar
KM 19 UHD	Scania	Goldstar	KW 19 OMA	Scania	Goldstar
KM 19 UHE	Scania	Goldstar	KW 19 OMD	Scania	Goldstar
KM 19 UHF	Scania	Goldstar	KW 19 OMF	Scania	Goldstar
KM 19 UHG	Scania	Goldstar	KW 19 OMG	Scania	Goldstar
KM 19 UHH	Scania	Goldstar	KW 19 OMH	Scania	Goldstar
KM 19 UHJ	Scania	Goldstar	KW 19 OMJ	Scania	Goldstar
KM 19 UHK	Scania	Goldstar	KW 19 OMK	Scania	Goldstar
KM 19 UHL	Scania	Goldstar	KW 19 OML	Scania	Goldstar
KM 19 UHN	Scania	Goldstar	KW 19 OMM	Scania	Goldstar
KM 19 UHO	Scania	Goldstar	KW 19 OMO	Scania	Goldstar
KM 19 UHP	Scania	Goldstar	KW 19 OMP	Scania	Goldstar
KM 19 UHR	Scania	Goldstar	KW 19 OMR	Scania	Goldstar
KM 19 UHS	Scania	Goldstar	KW 19 OMS	Scania	Goldstar
KM 19 UHT	Scania	Goldstar	KW 19 OMT	Scania	Goldstar
KM 19 UHU	Scania	Goldstar	KW 19 OMU	Scania	Goldstar
KM 19 UHV	Scania	Goldstar	KW 19 OMV	Scania	Goldstar
KM 19 UHW	Scania	Goldstar	KW 19 OMX	Scania	Goldstar
KM 19 UHX	Scania	Goldstar	KW 19 OMY	Scania	Goldstar
KM 19 UHY	Scania	Goldstar	KW 19 OMZ	Scania	Goldstar
KM 19 UHZ	Scania	Goldstar	KW 19 ONA	Scania	Goldstar
KM 19 UJA	Scania	Goldstar	KW 19 ONB	Scania	Goldstar
KM 19 UJB	Scania	Goldstar	KW 19 ONC	Scania	Goldstar
KM 19 UJC	Scania	Goldstar	KW 19 OND	Scania	Goldstar
KM 19 UJD	Scania	Goldstar	KW 19 ONF	Scania	Goldstar
KM 19 UJE	Scania	Goldstar	KW 19 ONH	Scania	Goldstar
KM 19 UJF	Scania	Goldstar	KW 19 ONJ	Scania	Goldstar
KM 19 UJG	Scania	Goldstar	KW 19 ONK	Scania	Goldstar
KM 19 UJH	Scania	Goldstar	KY 19 GDK	Scania	Turners
KM 19 UJJ	Scania	Goldstar	AE 69 DDA	Daf	Turners
KM 19 UJK	Scania	Goldstar	AE 69 DDF	Daf	Turners
KM 19 UJL	Scania	Goldstar	AE 69 DDJ	Daf	Turners
KM 19 UJN	Scania	Goldstar	AV 69 XRF	Daf	Turners
KM 19 UJO	Scania	Goldstar	AV 69 XRG	Daf	Turners
KM 19 UJP	Scania	Goldstar	AV 69 XRH	Daf	Turners
KM 19 UJR	Scania	Goldstar	AV 69 XRJ	Daf	Turners
KM 19 UJS	Scania	Goldstar	AV 69 XRK	Daf	Turners
KM 19 UJT	Scania	Goldstar	AV 69 XRL	Daf	Turners
KM 19 UJU	Scania	Goldstar	AY 69 OJG	Mitsubishi	Turners
KM 19 UJV	Scania	Goldstar	AY 69 OJH	Mitsubishi	Turners
KW 19 OJS	Scania	Goldstar	AY 69 OZD	Daf	Lynx Fuels
KW 19 OJT	Scania	Goldstar	AY 69 OZE	Daf	Lynx Fuels
KW 19 OJU	Scania	Goldstar	AY 69 PGX	Daf	Turners
KW 19 OJV	Scania	Goldstar	AY 69 PGZ	Daf	Turners
KW 19 OJX	Scania	Goldstar	AY 69 PHA	Daf	Turners
KW 19 OJY	Scania	Goldstar	AY 69 PHF	Daf	Turners
KW 19 OJZ	Scania	Goldstar	AY 69 PHJ	Daf	Turners
KW 19 OLK	Scania	Goldstar	AY 69 PHK	Daf	Turners
KW 19 OLM	Scania	Goldstar	AY 69 PHN	Daf	Turners

Reg	Make	Operator	Reg	Make	Operator
AY 69 PHO	Daf	Turners	DK 69 ZGG	Daf	Jack Richards
AY 69 PHU	Daf	Turners	DK 69 ZGH	Daf	Jack Richards
AY 69 PHV	Daf	Turners	DK 69 ZGJ	Daf	Jack Richards
AY 69 PHX	Daf	Turners	DK 69 ZGL	Daf	Jack Richards
AY 69 PKJ	Daf	Turners	FG 69 UBM	Daf	Lynn Star
AY 69 PKK	Daf	Turners	FG 69 UBT	Daf	Lynn Star
AY 69 PKN	Daf	Turners	FG 69 UBU	Daf	Lynn Star
AY 69 PKO	Daf	Turners	FG 69 UBV	Daf	Lynn Star
AY 69 PKU	Daf	Turners	FJ 69 WKH	Daf	Lynn Star
AY 69 PKV	Daf	Turners	FJ 69 WSU	Daf	Lynn Star
AY 69 PKX	Daf	Turners	FJ 69 WSV	Daf	Lynn Star
AY 69 PKZ	Daf	Turners	FJ 69 WSW	Daf	Lynn Star
AY 69 PLF	Daf	Turners	FJ 69 WSX	Daf	Lynn Star
AY 69 PLJ	Daf	Turners	FJ 69 WSY	Daf	Lynn Star
AY 69 PLN	Daf	Turners	FJ 69 WSZ	Daf	Lynn Star
AY 69 PUA	Daf	Jack Richards	FJ 69 WTA	Daf	Lynn Star
AY 69 PUE	Daf	Jack Richards	FJ 69 WTC	Daf	Lynn Star
AY 69 PUH	Daf	Jack Richards	FJ 69 WTD	Daf	Lynn Star
AY 69 PUJ	Daf	Jack Richards	FJ 69 WTE	Daf	Lynn Star
AY 69 PUK	Daf	Jack Richards	FX 69 RRO	Scania	Dowse
AY 69 PUO	Daf	Jack Richards	FX 69 RRU	Scania	Dowse
AY 69 PUU	Daf	Turners	FX 69 RSU	Scania	Dowse
AY 69 PUV	Daf	Turners	FX 69 RSV	Scania	Dowse
AY 69 PVA	Daf	Turners	FX 69 RYT	Scania	Dowse
AY 69 PVD	Daf	Turners	FX 69 RZD	Scania	Dowse
AY 69 PVE	Daf	Hanson (White)	FX 69 RZF	Scania	Dowse
AY 69 PVF	Daf	Turners	FX 69 SKF	Scania	Dowse
AY 69 PWJ	Daf	Goldstar	FX 69 SNN	Scania	Dowse
AY 69 PWK	Daf	Goldstar	KR 69 RNA	Scania	Turners
AY 69 PWL	Daf	Goldstar	KR 69 RNE	Scania	Turners
AY 69 PWN	Daf	Goldstar	KR 69 RNF	Scania	Turners
AY 69 PWO	Daf	Goldstar	KR 69 RNJ	Scania	Turners
AY 69 PWU	Daf	Goldstar	KR 69 RNN	Scania	Turners
AY 69 PWV	Daf	Goldstar	KR 69 RNO	Scania	Turners
AY 69 PWX	Daf	Goldstar	KR 69 RNU	Scania	Turners
AY 69 PWZ	Daf	Goldstar	KR 69 RNV	Scania	Turners
AY 69 PXA	Daf	Goldstar	KR 69 RNX	Scania	Turners
BU 69 ZZF	Scania	Macintyre	KR 69 RNY	Scania	Turners
DE 69 GVR	Daf	Jack Richards	KR 69 RPV	Scania	Turners
DE 69 GVU	Daf	Jack Richards	KR 69 RPX	Scania	Turners
DE 69 GVV	Daf	Jack Richards	KR 69 RPY	Scania	Turners
DE 69 GVW	Daf	Jack Richards	KR 69 RPZ	Scania	Turners
DE 69 GWA	Daf	Jack Richards	KR 69 RTV	Scania	Turners
DE 69 GWC	Daf	Jack Richards	KR 69 RTX	Scania	Turners
DE 69 GWN	Daf	Jack Richards	KR 69 RTZ	Scania	Turners
DK 69 YZS	Daf	Jack Richards	KU 69 XCN	Scania	Macintyre
DK 69 YZT	Daf	Jack Richards	KU 69 XCS	Scania	Macintyre
DK 69 YZU	Daf	Jack Richards	KU 69 XCT	Scania	Macintyre
DK 69 YZV	Daf	Jack Richards	KU 69 XCV	Scania	Macintyre
DK 69 YZW	Daf	Jack Richards	KU 69 XCW	Scania	Macintyre
DK 69 YZX	Daf	Jack Richards	KU 69 XCX	Scania	Macintyre
DK 69 YZY	Daf	Jack Richards	KU 69 XCY	Scania	Macintyre
DK 69 YZZ	Daf	Jack Richards	KU 69 XCZ	Scania	Macintyre
DK 69 ZBC	Daf	Jack Richards	KU 69 XDA	Scania	Macintyre
DK 69 ZBD	Daf	Jack Richards	KU 69 XDB	Scania	Macintyre
DK 69 ZGF	Daf	Jack Richards	KU 69 XDD	Scania	Macintyre

Reg	Make	Fleet	Reg	Make	Fleet
KU 69 XDE	Scania	Turners (R & R)	AY 20 PZV	Mercedes	Goldstar
KU 69 XDF	Scania	Turners (R & R)	AY 20 PZW	Mercedes	Goldstar
KU 69 XDS	Scania	Turners	AY 20 PZX	Mercedes	Goldstar
KU 69 XDT	Scania	Turners	AY 20 PZZ	Mercedes	Goldstar
KU 69 XDV	Scania	Turners	AY 20 RAU	Mercedes	Goldstar
KU 69 XDW	Scania	Turners	AY 20 RAX	Mercedes	Goldstar
KU 69 XDX	Scania	Turners	AY 20 RBF	Mercedes	Goldstar
KU 69 XDY	Scania	Turners	AY 20 RBO	Mercedes	Goldstar
KU 69 XDZ	Scania	Turners	AY 20 RBU	Mercedes	Goldstar
KU 69 XEA	Scania	Turners	AY 20 RBV	Mercedes	Goldstar
KU 69 XEB	Scania	Turners	AY 20 RBX	Mercedes	Goldstar
KU 69 XEC	Scania	Turners	AY 20 RBZ	Mercedes	Goldstar
KU 69 XED	Scania	Turners	AY 20 RCF	Mercedes	Goldstar
KU 69 XEE	Scania	Turners	AY 20 RCO	Mercedes	Goldstar
KU 69 XEF	Scania	Turners	AY 20 RCU	Mercedes	Goldstar
KU 69 XEG	Scania	Turners	AY 20 RCV	Mercedes	Goldstar
KU 69 XEH	Scania	Turners	AY 20 RCX	Mercedes	Goldstar
KU 69 XEJ	Scania	Turners	AY 20 RCZ	Mercedes	Goldstar
KU 69 XEK	Scania	Turners	AY 20 RDO	Mercedes	Goldstar
KU 69 XEL	Scania	Turners	AY 20 RDU	Mercedes	Goldstar
PE 69 OPF	Volvo	Kibble	AY 20 RDV	Mercedes	Goldstar
PE 69 OPG	Volvo	Kibble	AY 20 RDX	Mercedes	Goldstar
PE 69 OPH	Volvo	Kibble	AY 20 RDZ	Mercedes	Goldstar
PJ 69 TCU	Volvo	Kibble	AY 20 REU	Mercedes	Goldstar
AV 20 GHA	Scania	Turners	AY 20 RFE	Mercedes	Goldstar
AV 20 GHB	Scania	Turners	AY 20 RFF	Mercedes	Goldstar
AV 20 GHD	Scania	Turners	AY 20 RFJ	Mercedes	Goldstar
AV 20 GHF	Scania	Turners	AY 20 RFK	Mercedes	Goldstar
AV 20 GHG	Scania	Turners	AY 20 RFL	Mercedes	Goldstar
AV 20 GHH	Scania	Turners	AY 20 RFN	Mercedes	Goldstar
AV 20 GHJ	Scania	Macintyre	AY 20 RFO	Mercedes	Goldstar
AV 20 GHK	Scania	Macintyre	AY 20 RFX	Mercedes	Goldstar
AV 20 GXA	Scania	Jack Richards	AY 20 RFZ	Mercedes	Goldstar
AV 20 GXB	Scania	Jack Richards	AY 20 RLU	Mercedes	Macintyre
AV 20 GXC	Scania	Jack Richards	AY 20 SMV	Daf	Turners
AV 20 GXD	Scania	Turners (R & R)	AY 20 SMX	Daf	Turners
AV 20 GXE	Scania	Turners (R & R)	AY 20 SPZ	Daf	Turners
AV 20 GXF	Scania	Turners (R & R)	AY 20 SRU	Daf	Turners
AV 20 GXG	Scania	Jack Richards	AY 20 SRV	Daf	Turners
AV 20 GXH	Scania	Jack Richards	AY 20 SRX	Daf	Turners
AV 20 GXJ	Scania	Jack Richards	AY 20 SWJ	Daf	Turners
AV 20 GXK	Scania	Jack Richards	AY 20 SWK	Daf	Turners
AY 20 PZF	Mercedes	Macintyre	AY 20 TCZ	Daf	Turners
AY 20 PZG	Mercedes	Macintyre	AY 20 TDO	Daf	Turners
AY 20 PZH	Mercedes	Macintyre	AY 20 TDV	Daf	Turners
AY 20 PZJ	Mercedes	Macintyre	AY 20 TDX	Daf	Turners
AY 20 PZK	Mercedes	Macintyre	AY 20 TDZ	Daf	Turners
AY 20 PZL	Mercedes	Macintyre	AY 20 TEO	Daf	Turners
AY 20 PZM	Mercedes	Macintyre	AY 20 TEV	Daf	Turners
AY 20 PZN	Mercedes	Macintyre	AY 20 TFA	Daf	Turners
AY 20 PZO	Mercedes	Macintyre	FX 20 TVL	Scania	Dowse
AY 20 PZP	Mercedes	Goldstar	FX 20 TWA	Scania	Dowse
AY 20 PZR	Mercedes	Goldstar	FX 20 TWP	Scania	Dowse
AY 20 PZS	Mercedes	Goldstar	FX 20 TXH	Scania	Dowse
AY 20 PZT	Mercedes	Goldstar	FX 20 TYO	Scania	Dowse
AY 20 PZU	Mercedes	Goldstar	FX 20 TYT	Scania	Dowse

Reg	Make	Operator	Reg	Make	Operator
FX 20 TZE	Scania	Dowse	AV 70 RSX	Daf	Turners
AV 70 PNY	Daf	Jack Richards	AV 70 RSY	Daf	Turners
AV 70 RFX	Daf	Jack Richards	AV 70 RYG	Daf	Turners
AV 70 RFY	Daf	Jack Richards	AV 70 RYH	Daf	Turners
AV 70 RFZ	Daf	Jack Richards	AV 70 RYK	Daf	Turners
AV 70 RGO	Daf	Jack Richards	AV 70 RYM	Daf	Turners
AV 70 RGU	Daf	Jack Richards	AV 70 RYN	Daf	Turners
AV 70 RGX	Daf	Jack Richards	AV 70 RYO	Daf	Turners
AV 70 RHF	Daf	Jack Richards	AV 70 RYP	Daf	Turners
AV 70 RHJ	Daf	Turners	AV 70 RYR	Daf	Turners
AV 70 RHK	Daf	Turners	AV 70 RYT	Daf	Goldstar
AV 70 RHO	Daf	Turners	AV 70 RYU	Daf	Turners
AV 70 RHU	Daf	Turners	AV 70 RYW	Daf	Turners
AV 70 RHX	Daf	Turners	AV 70 RYX	Daf	Turners
AV 70 RHY	Daf	Turners	AV 70 RYY	Daf	Turners
AV 70 RHZ	Daf	Turners	AV 70 RYZ	Daf	Turners
AV 70 RJJ	Daf	Turners	AV 70 RZM	Daf	Goldstar
AV 70 RJO	Daf	Turners	AV 70 RZN	Daf	Goldstar
AV 70 RJU	Daf	Turners	AV 70 RZO	Daf	Goldstar
AV 70 RJX	Daf	Turners	AV 70 SEY	Daf	Goldstar
AV 70 RJY	Daf	Turners	AV 70 SFE	Daf	Goldstar
AV 70 RJZ	Daf	Turners	AV 70 XVH	Daf	Goldstar
AV 70 RKA	Daf	Turners	AV 70 XVJ	Daf	Goldstar
AV 70 RKE	Daf	Turners	AV 70 XVK	Daf	Goldstar
AV 70 RKF	Daf	Turners	AV 70 XVL	Daf	Goldstar
AV 70 RKJ	Daf	Turners	AV 70 XVM	Daf	Goldstar
AV 70 RKK	Daf	Turners	AV 70 XVN	Daf	Goldstar
AV 70 RKN	Daf	Turners	AV 70 XVO	Daf	Goldstar
AV 70 RKO	Daf	Turners	AV 70 XVP	Daf	Goldstar
AV 70 RKU	Daf	Turners	AV 70 XVR	Daf	Goldstar
AV 70 RKX	Daf	Turners	AV 70 XVS	Daf	Goldstar
AV 70 RKY	Daf	Turners	AV 70 XVT	Daf	Turners
AV 70 RKZ	Daf	Hanson (White)	AV 70 XVU	Daf	Turners
AV 70 RLO	Daf	Hanson (White)	AV 70 XVW	Daf	Turners
AV 70 RLU	Daf	Turners	AV 70 ZVW	Daf	Turners
AV 70 RLX	Daf	Turners	AV 70 ZVX	Daf	Turners
AV 70 RLY	Daf	Turners	AV 70 ZVY	Daf	Turners
AV 70 RLZ	Daf	Turners	AV 70 ZVZ	Daf	Turners
AV 70 RMO	Daf	Turners	AV 70 ZWA	Daf	Turners
AV 70 RMU	Daf	Turners	AV 70 ZWB	Daf	Turners
AV 70 RMX	Daf	Turners	AV 70 ZWC	Daf	Turners
AV 70 RMY	Daf	Turners	AV 70 ZWH	Daf	Clements
AV 70 RMZ	Daf	Turners	AV 70 ZWJ	Daf	Clements
AV 70 RNA	Daf	Turners	AV 70 ZWK	Daf	Clements
AV 70 RNE	Daf	Turners	AV 70 ZWL	Daf	Clements
AV 70 RNF	Daf	Turners	AV 70 ZWM	Daf	Turners
AV 70 RNJ	Daf	Turners	AV 70 ZWN	Daf	Turners
AV 70 RNN	Daf	Turners	AV 70 ZWP	Daf	Turners
AV 70 RPU	Daf	Turners	AV 70 ZWR	Daf	Turners
AV 70 RPX	Daf	Turners	AV 70 ZWS	Daf	Turners
AV 70 RPY	Daf	Turners	AV 70 ZWT	Daf	Turners
AV 70 RPZ	Daf	Turners	AV 70 ZWU	Daf	Goldstar
AV 70 RRU	Daf	Turners	AV 70 ZWW	Daf	Goldstar
AV 70 RRX	Daf	Turners	AV 70 ZWX	Daf	Goldstar
AV 70 RRZ	Daf	Turners	AV 70 ZWY	Daf	Goldstar
AV 70 RSU	Daf	Turners	AV 70 ZWZ	Daf	Goldstar

AV 70 ZXA	Daf	Goldstar	AY 70 TTE	Daf	Jack Richards
AV 70 ZXB	Daf	Goldstar	AY 70 TVN	Daf	Turners
AV 70 ZXC	Daf	Goldstar	AY 70 TVO	Daf	Turners
AV 70 ZXD	Daf	Goldstar	AY 70 TVP	Daf	Turners
AV 70 ZXE	Daf	Goldstar	AY 70 TVT	Daf	Turners
AV 70 ZYA	Daf	Goldstar	AY 70 TVU	Daf	Turners
AV 70 ZYB	Daf	Goldstar	AY 70 TVV	Daf	Turners
AV 70 ZYC	Daf	Goldstar	AY 70 TVW	Daf	Turners
AV 70 ZYD	Daf	Goldstar	AY 70 TVX	Daf	Turners
AV 70 ZYE	Daf	Goldstar	AY 70 TVZ	Daf	Turners
AY 70 SYW	Daf	Turners	AY 70 TWA	Daf	Turners
AY 70 SYT	Daf	Jack Richards	AY 70 TWC	Daf	Turners
AY 70 SYU	Daf	Jack Richards	AY 70 TWD	Daf	Turners
AY 70 SYV	Daf	Jack Richards	AY 70 TWE	Daf	Turners
AY 70 SYZ	Daf	Turners	AY 70 TWF	Daf	Turners
AY 70 SZF	Daf	Turners	AY 70 TWG	Daf	Turners
AY 70 SZG	Daf	Turners	AY 70 TWJ	Daf	Turners
AY 70 SZJ	Daf	Turners	FN 70 AEJ	Daf	Macintyre
AY 70 SZK	Daf	Turners	FN 70 AEK	Daf	Macintyre
AY 70 SZL	Daf	Turners	FN 70 AEL	Daf	Macintyre
AY 70 SZV	Daf	Turners	FN 70 AEM	Daf	Macintyre
AY 70 SZW	Daf	Turners	FN 70 AEP	Daf	Macintyre
AY 70 TGE	Daf	Turners	FN 70 AET	Daf	Macintyre
AY 70 TGF	Daf	Turners	FN 70 AWW	Daf	Turners
AY 70 TGJ	Daf	Turners	FN 70 AWY	Daf	Turners
AY 70 TGK	Daf	Turners	FN 70 AXF	Daf	Turners
AY 70 TGN	Daf	Turners	FN 70 AXH	Daf	Turners
AY 70 TGO	Daf	Turners	FN 70 AXJ	Daf	Turners
AY 70 TGU	Daf	Hanson (White)	FN 70 AXK	Daf	Turners
AY 70 TGV	Daf	Hanson (White)	FN 70 AXM	Daf	Macintyre
AY 70 TGX	Daf	Hanson (White)	FN 70 AXO	Daf	Macintyre
AY 70 TGZ	Daf	Hanson (White)	FN 70 AXP	Daf	Macintyre
AY 70 THF	Daf	Hanson (White)	FN 70 AXR	Daf	Macintyre
AY 70 THG	Daf	Hanson (White)	FN 70 BEJ	Daf	Macintyre
AY 70 THK	Daf	Turners	FN 70 BEO	Daf	Macintyre
AY 70 THN	Daf	Turners	FX 70 UBY	Scania	Dowse
AY 70 THU	Daf	Turners	FX 70 UDZ	Scania	Dowse
AY 70 THV	Daf	Turners	FX 70 UEK	Scania	Dowse
AY 70 TNZ	Daf	Turners	FX 70 UEW	Scania	Dowse
AY 70 TOA	Daf	Turners	FX 70 UFY	Scania	Dowse
AY 70 TOH	Daf	Jack Richards	FX 70 UGR	Scania	Dowse
AY 70 TOJ	Daf	Jack Richards	GK 70 EAG	Daf	Macintyre
AY 70 TOV	Daf	Jack Richards	GK 70 EAJ	Daf	Turners
AY 70 TPF	Daf	Jack Richards	GK 70 EAM	Daf	Macintyre
AY 70 TPO	Daf	Jack Richards	PJ 70 NTK	Volvo	Kibble
AY 70 TPU	Daf	Jack Richards	PJ 70 NTL	Volvo	Kibble
AY 70 TPV	Daf	Jack Richards	PN 70 DXY	Volvo	Kibble
AY 70 TPX	Daf	Jack Richards	PN 70 DYV	Volvo	Kibble
AY 70 TPZ	Daf	Jack Richards	AV 21 KSF	Mercedes	Jack Richards
AY 70 TRV	Daf	Jack Richards	AY 21 UPB	Daf	Jack Richards
AY 70 TRX	Daf	Jack Richards	AY 21 UPC	Daf	Jack Richards
AY 70 TSO	Daf	Jack Richards	AY 21 UPD	Daf	Jack Richards
AY 70 TSU	Daf	Jack Richards	AY 21 UPE	Daf	Jack Richards
AY 70 TSV	Daf	Jack Richards	AY 21 UPF	Daf	Jack Richards
AY 70 TSX	Daf	Jack Richards	AY 21 UPG	Daf	Jack Richards
AY 70 TSZ	Daf	Jack Richards	AY 21 UPH	Daf	Jack Richards

Reg	Make	Operator	Reg	Make	Operator
AV 21 UYN	Mercedes	Macintyre	AY 21 URJ	Daf	Hapag-Lloyd
AV 21 UYO	Mercedes	Macintyre	AY 21 URK	Daf	Hapag-Lloyd
AV 21 UYP	Mercedes	Macintyre	AY 21 UST	Daf	Turners
AV 21 UYU	Mercedes	Macintyre	AY 21 USU	Daf	Turners
AV 21 UZU	Mercedes	Macintyre	AY 21 USV	Daf	Turners
AV 21 UZW	Mercedes	Macintyre	AY 21 USW	Daf	Turners
AV 21 UZX	Mercedes	Macintyre	AY 21 USX	Daf	Turners
AV 21 VBA	Mercedes	Macintyre	AY 21 USZ	Daf	Turners
AV 21 VBB	Mercedes	Macintyre	AY 21 UTA	Daf	Turners
AV 21 VBC	Mercedes	Macintyre	AY 21 UTB	Daf	Turners
AV 21 VBD	Mercedes	Macintyre	AY 21 UTC	Daf	Turners
AV 21 VBE	Mercedes	Macintyre	AY 21 UTE	Daf	Turners
AV 21 VBF	Mercedes	Macintyre	AY 21 UTF	Daf	Turners
AV 21 VBG	Mercedes	Macintyre	AY 21 UTG	Daf	Turners
AV 21 VBJ	Mercedes	Macintyre	AY 21 UTH	Daf	Turners
AV 21 VBK	Mercedes	Macintyre	AY 21 UTJ	Daf	Turners
AV 21 VBL	Mercedes	Macintyre	DG 21 CLV	Man	Turners
AV 21 VBO	Mercedes	Turners	DG 21 CLX	Man	Turners
AV 21 VBP	Mercedes	Turners	FX 21 WPZ	Scania	Dowse
AV 21 VBT	Mercedes	Turners	FX 21 WRG	Scania	Dowse
AV 21 VBX	Mercedes	Turners	FX 21 WRU	Scania	Dowse
AV 21 VBZ	Mercedes	Turners	FX 21 WSJ	Scania	Turners
AV 21 VCA	Mercedes	Turners	FX 21 WSK	Scania	Dowse
AV 21 VCC	Mercedes	Turners	FX 21 WTL	Scania	Dowse
AV 21 VCD	Mercedes	Turners	FX 21 WTO	Scania	Dowse
AV 21 VCE	Mercedes	Turners	FX 21 WTT	Scania	Dowse
AV 21 VCF	Mercedes	Turners	FX 21 WUP	Scania	Dowse
AV 21 VCG	Mercedes	Macintyre	FX 21 WUW	Scania	Dowse
AV 21 VCJ	Mercedes	Macintyre	FX 21 WVA	Scania	Turners
AV 21 VCK	Mercedes	Macintyre	FX 21 WWB	Scania	Dowse
AV 21 VCL	Mercedes	Macintyre	FX 21 WWJ	Scania	Dowse
AV 21 VCM	Mercedes	Macintyre	MK 21 EWM	Man	Kibble
AV 21 VPF	Daf	Lynx Fuels	OY 21 CXB	Daf	Turners
AV 21 VRG	Daf	Lynx Fuels	PN 21 KLJ	Volvo	Kibble
AY 21 UNZ	Daf	Goldstar	PN 21 KLK	Volvo	Kibble
AY 21 UOB	Daf	Goldstar	PN 21 KLL	Volvo	Kibble
AY 21 UOC	Daf	Goldstar	PN 21 KLX	Volvo	Kibble
AY 21 UOD	Daf	Goldstar	AV 71 VNL	Daf	Jack Richards
AY 21 UOE	Daf	Goldstar	AV 71 VNM	Daf	Jack Richards
AY 21 UOF	Daf	Goldstar	AV 71 VNN	Daf	Jack Richards
AY 21 UOG	Daf	Goldstar	AV 71 VNO	Daf	Jack Richards
AY 21 UOH	Daf	Goldstar	AV 71 VNP	Daf	Jack Richards
AY 21 UOJ	Daf	Goldstar	AV 71 VNR	Daf	Jack Richards
AY 21 UOK	Daf	Goldstar	AV 71 VNS	Daf	Jack Richards
AY 21 UOL	Daf	Goldstar	AV 71 VNU	Daf	Jack Richards
AY 21 UOM	Daf	Goldstar	AV 71 VNW	Daf	Jack Richards
AY 21 UON	Daf	Goldstar	AV 71 VNX	Daf	Jack Richards
AY 21 UPW	Daf	Turners	AV 71 VOA	Daf	Jack Richards
AY 21 URA	Daf	Turners	AV 71 VOB	Daf	Jack Richards
AY 21 URB	Daf	Turners	AV 71 VOC	Daf	Jack Richards
AY 21 URC	Daf	Hapag-Lloyd	AV 71 VOD	Daf	Jack Richards
AY 21 URD	Daf	Hapag-Lloyd	AV 71 VOH	Daf	Jack Richards
AY 21 URE	Daf	Hapag-Lloyd	AV 71 VOJ	Daf	Jack Richards
AY 21 URF	Daf	Hapag-Lloyd	AV 71 VOK	Daf	Jack Richards
AY 21 URG	Daf	Hapag-Lloyd	AV 71 VOM	Daf	Jack Richards
AY 21 URH	Daf	Hapag-Lloyd	AV 71 VOO	Daf	Jack Richards

Turners Group (cont)

AV 71 VOP	Daf	Jack Richards	AY 71 TPV	Daf	Turners
AV 71 VOT	Daf	Jack Richards	AY 71 TPX	Daf	Turners
AV 71 VOU	Daf	Jack Richards	AY 71 TVZ	Daf	Turners
AV 71 VOY	Daf	Jack Richards	AY 71 TXB	Daf	Turners
AV 71 VPA	Daf	Jack Richards	AY 71 TXC	Daf	Turners
AV 71 VPC	Daf	Jack Richards	AY 71 TXD	Daf	Turners
AV 71 VPX	Daf	Macintyre	AY 71 TXE	Daf	Turners
AV 71 VRW	Daf	Macintyre	AY 71 TXF	Daf	Turners
AV 71 VRX	Daf	Macintyre	AY 71 TXG	Daf	Turners
AV 71 VRY	Daf	Macintyre	AY 71 TXH	Daf	Turners
AV 71 VRZ	Daf	Macintyre	AY 71 TXJ	Daf	Turners
AX 71 CWK	Daf	Macintyre	AY 71 TXK	Daf	Turners
AX 71 CWL	Daf	Goldstar	AY 71 TXL	Daf	Hanson (White)
AX 71 CWM	Daf	Goldstar	AY 71 TXM	Daf	Turners
AX 71 CWN	Daf	Goldstar	AY 71 TXN	Daf	Turners
AX 71 CWO	Daf	Goldstar	AY 71 TXO	Daf	Turners
AX 71 CWP	Daf	Goldstar	AY 71 TXP	Daf	Turners
AX 71 CWR	Daf	Goldstar	AY 71 TXR	Daf	Turners
AY 71 RYB	Mercedes	Turners	AY 71 TYC	Daf	Turners
AY 71 RYM	Mercedes	Turners	AY 71 TYD	Daf	Turners
AY 71 RYN	Mercedes	Turners	AY 71 TYF	Daf	Turners
AY 71 RYO	Mercedes	Turners	AY 71 TYG	Daf	Turners
AY 71 RYP	Mercedes	Turners	AY 71 TYH	Daf	Turners
AY 71 RYR	Mercedes	Turners	AY 71 TYK	Daf	Turners
AY 71 RYT	Mercedes	Turners	AY 71 UAJ	Daf	Turners
AY 71 RYU	Mercedes	Turners	AY 71 UAK	Daf	Turners
AY 71 RYV	Mercedes	Turners	AY 71 UAL	Daf	Turners
AY 71 RYW	Mercedes	Turners	AY 71 UAM	Daf	Turners
AY 71 RYX	Mercedes	Turners	AY 71 UAN	Daf	Turners
AY 71 RYZ	Mercedes	Macintyre	AY 71 UAO	Daf	Turners
AY 71 RZA	Mercedes	Macintyre	AY 71 UAP	Daf	Turners
AY 71 RZB	Mercedes	Macintyre	AY 71 UAR	Daf	Hanson (White)
AY 71 RZC	Mercedes	Macintyre	AY 71 UAS	Daf	Turners
AY 71 RZD	Mercedes	Macintyre	AY 71 UAT	Daf	Hanson (White)
AY 71 RZE	Mercedes	Macintyre	AY 71 UAU	Daf	Hanson (White)
AY 71 RZF	Mercedes	Turners	AY 71 UAV	Daf	Turners
AY 71 RZG	Mercedes	Jack Richards	AY 71 UBN	Daf	Turners
AY 71 TMU	Daf	Turners	AY 71 UBT	Daf	Turners
AY 71 TMV	Daf	Turners	AY 71 UBU	Daf	Turners
AY 71 TMX	Daf	Turners	AY 71 UBV	Daf	Turners
AY 71 TMZ	Daf	Turners	AY 71 UBW	Daf	Turners
AY 71 TNE	Daf	Turners	AY 71 UBX	Daf	Turners
AY 71 TNF	Daf	Turners	AY 71 UBZ	Daf	Turners
AY 71 TNJ	Daf	Turners	AY 71 UCA	Daf	Turners
AY 71 TNK	Daf	Turners	AY 71 UCB	Daf	Turners
AY 71 TNL	Daf	Turners	AY 71 UCC	Daf	Turners
AY 71 TNN	Daf	Turners	AY 71 UCD	Daf	Turners
AY 71 TNO	Daf	Turners	AY 71 UCE	Daf	Turners
AY 71 TNU	Daf	Turners	AY 71 UCF	Daf	Turners
AY 71 TNV	Daf	Turners	AY 71 UCG	Daf	Turners
AY 71 TNX	Daf	Turners	AY 71 UCH	Daf	Turners
AY 71 TOH	Daf	Lynx Fuels	AY 71 UCJ	Daf	Turners
AY 71 TOJ	Daf	Lynx Fuels	AY 71 UCL	Daf	Turners
AY 71 TPF	Daf	Turners	AY 71 UCM	Daf	Turners
AY 71 TPO	Daf	Turners	AY 71 UCN	Daf	Turners
AY 71 TPU	Daf	Turners	AY 71 UCO	Daf	Turners

AY 71 UCP	Daf	Turners	AV 22 TBU	Daf	Turners
AY 71 UCR	Daf	Turners	AV 22 TBY	Daf	Goldstar
AY 71 UCS	Daf	Turners	AV 22 TBZ	Daf	Goldstar
AY 71 UCT	Daf	Turners	AV 22 TCJ	Daf	Turners
AY 71 UCU	Daf	Turners	AV 22 TCO	Daf	Turners
AY 71 UCV	Daf	Turners	AV 22 TCY	Daf	Goldstar
AY 71 UCW	Daf	Turners	AV 22 TCZ	Daf	Turners
AY 71 UCX	Daf	Turners	AV 22 TDO	Daf	Turners
AY 71 UCZ	Daf	Turners	AV 22 TDU	Daf	Turners
AY 71 UDB	Daf	Turners	AV 22 TDX	Daf	Macintyre
AY 71 UDD	Daf	Turners	AV 22 VSU	Daf	Macintyre
AY 71 UDE	Daf	Turners	AV 22 VSX	Daf	Turners
AY 71 UDG	Daf	Turners	AV 22 VSY	Daf	Turners
AY 71 UDH	Daf	Turners	AV 22 VSZ	Daf	Macintyre
AY 71 UDJ	Daf	Turners	AV 22 VTA	Daf	Turners
AY 71 UDK	Daf	Turners	AV 22 VTC	Daf	Turners
AY 71 UDL	Daf	Turners	AV 22 VTD	Daf	Turners
AY 71 UDM	Daf	Turners	AV 22 VTE	Daf	Turners
AY 71 UDO	Daf	Turners	AV 22 VTF	Daf	Turners
AY 71 UDP	Daf	Turners	AV 22 VTG	Daf	Turners
AY 71 XVA	Scania	Turners	AV 22 VTJ	Daf	Turners
AY 71 XVB	Scania	Turners	AV 22 VTK	Daf	Turners
AY 71 XVC	Scania	Turners	AV 22 VTN	Daf	Hanson (White)
AY 71 XVD	Scania	Turners	AV 22 VTO	Daf	Turners
AY 71 XVE	Scania	Turners	AV 22 VTP	Daf	Turners
AY 71 XVF	Scania	Turners	AV 22 VTT	Daf	Goldstar
AY 71 XVG	Scania	Turners	AV 22 VTU	Daf	Turners
AY 71 XVH	Scania	Turners	AV 22 VTW	Daf	Macintyre
AY 71 XVJ	Scania	Turners (R & R)	AV 22 VTX	Daf	Goldstar
AY 71 XVM	Scania	Goldstar	AV 22 VTY	Daf	Goldstar
AY 71 XVN	Scania	Goldstar	AV 22 VUA	Daf	Clements
AY 71 XVP	Scania	Turners (R & R)	AV 22 VUC	Daf	Goldstar
AY 71 XVT	Scania	Goldstar	AV 22 YCJ	Daf	Goldstar
AY 71 XVU	Scania	Goldstar	AV 22 YCK	Daf	Goldstar
AY 71 XVV	Scania	Turners	AV 22 YCL	Daf	Goldstar
AY 71 XVW	Scania	Goldstar	AV 22 YCN	Daf	Goldstar
AY 71 XVZ	Scania	Turners	AV 22 YCO	Daf	Goldstar
AY 71 XWA	Scania	Turners	AV 22 ZDZ	Daf	Goldstar
AY 71 XWD	Scania	Turners	AV 22 ZFK	Daf	Goldstar
AY 71 XWF	Scania	Macintyre	AV 22 ZYX	Mercedes	Goldstar
AY 71 XXV	Scania	Turners (R & R)	AV 22 ZYZ	Mercedes	Goldstar
AY 71 XXW	Scania	Turners (R & R)	AX 22 AHU	Mercedes	Goldstar
BU 71 XBK	Scania	Kibble	AX 22 AHV	Mercedes	Goldstar
BU 71 XBL	Scania	Kibble	AX 22 GZZ	Daf	Turners
BU 71 XBM	Scania	Kibble	AY 22 TSV	Mercedes	Turners
FX 71 VDD	Scania	Dowse	AY 22 TSX	Mercedes	Goldstar
FX 71 VDT	Scania	Dowse	AY 22 YSZ	Mercedes	Goldstar
PN71 FWJ	Daf	Kibble	AY 22 TTE	Mercedes	Goldstar
PN71 FWK	Daf	Kibble	AY 22 TTF	Mercedes	Goldstar
PN71 FWL	Daf	Kibble	AY 22 TTJ	Mercedes	Goldstar
PN71 FWM	Daf	Kibble	AY 22 TTK	Mercedes	Goldstar
PN 71 GJJ	Daf	Kibble	AY 22 TTO	Mercedes	Goldstar
PN 71 GJK	Daf	Kibble	AY 22 TTU	Mercedes	Goldstar
PN 71 GJO	Daf	Kibble	AY 22 TTV	Mercedes	Goldstar
AV 22 TAU	Daf	Goldstar	AY 22 TUW	Mercedes	Goldstar
AV 22 TBO	Daf	Turners	AY 22 TVE	Mercedes	Goldstar

Reg	Make	Operator	Reg	Make	Operator
AY 22 TVF	Mercedes	Goldstar	AY 22 UOO	Daf	Turners
AY 22 TVL	Mercedes	Goldstar	AY 22 UOT	Daf	Dowse
AY 22 TVM	Mercedes	Goldstar	AY 22 UOU	Daf	Dowse
AY 22 TVN	Mercedes	Goldstar	AY 22 UOV	Daf	Hanson (White)
AY 22 TVP	Mercedes	Goldstar	AY 22 UOW	Daf	Hanson (White)
AY 22 UGZ	Daf	Turners	AY 22 UOX	Daf	Hanson (White)
AY 22 UHA	Daf	Turners	AY 22 UPA	Daf	Hanson (White)
AY 22 UHB	Daf	Macintyre	AY 22 UPB	Daf	Hanson (White)
AY 22 UHC	Daf	Macintyre	AY 22 UPC	Daf	Turners
AY 22 UHD	Daf	Turners	AY 22 UPD	Daf	Turners
AY 22 UHE	Daf	Macintyre	AY 22 UPE	Daf	Turners
AY 22 UHF	Daf	Hanson (White)	AY 22 UPG	Daf	Turners
AY 22 UHG	Daf	Turners	AY 22 URU	Daf	Turners
AY 22 UHH	Daf	Hanson (White)	AY 22 URV	Daf	Macintyre
AY 22 UHJ	Daf	Hanson (White)	AY 22 URW	Daf	Turners
AY 22 UHK	Daf	Turners	AY 22 URX	Daf	Turners
AY 22 UHL	Daf	Turners	AY 22 URZ	Daf	Turners
AY 22 UHM	Daf	Turners	AY 22 USB	Daf	Turners
AY 22 UHN	Daf	Turners	AY 22 USC	Daf	Macintyre
AY 22 UHO	Daf	Goldstar	AY 22 USD	Daf	Turners
AY 22 UHP	Daf	Macintyre	AY 22 USE	Daf	Macintyre
AY 22 UHR	Daf	Macintyre	AY 22 USF	Daf	Macintyre
AY 22 UHS	Daf	Macintyre	AY 22 YJA	Scania	Turners
AY 22 UHT	Daf	Macintyre	AY 22 YJB	Scania	Turners (R & R)
AY 22 UHU	Daf	Goldstar	AY 22 YJC	Scania	Turners
AY 22 UHV	Daf	Turners	AY 22 YJD	Scania	Turners
AY 22 UHW	Daf	Turners	AY 22 YJE	Scania	Turners
AY 22 UHZ	Daf	Turners	AY 22 YJF	Scania	Turners
AY 22 UJK	Daf	Turners	AY 22 YJG	Scania	Turners
AY 22 UJL	Daf	Turners	AY 22 YJH	Scania	Turners
AY 22 UJM	Daf	Turners	AY 22 YJJ	Scania	Turners
AY 22 UJO	Daf	Turners	AY 22 YLA	Scania	Goldstar
AY 22 UJP	Daf	Turners	AY 22 YLB	Scania	Goldstar
AY 22 UJR	Daf	Turners	AY 22 YLC	Scania	Goldstar
AY 22 UJS	Daf	Turners	AY 22 YLD	Scania	Goldstar
AY 22 UJT	Daf	Turners	AY 22 YLE	Scania	Goldstar
AY 22 UJV	Daf	Goldstar	AY 22 YLF	Scania	Turners (R & R)
AY 22 UJW	Daf	Goldstar	FX 22 UGV	Scania	Dowse
AY 22 ULA	Daf	Macintyre	FX 22 UGY	Scania	Dowse
AY 22 ULB	Daf	Macintyre	FX 22 UHK	Scania	Dowse
AY 22 ULC	Daf	Macintyre	FX 22 UHR	Scania	Dowse
AY 22 ULD	Daf	Macintyre	FX 22 UHS	Scania	Turners
AY 22 ULE	Daf	Goldstar	FX 22 UHT	Scania	Turners
AY 22 ULF	Daf	Goldstar	FX 22 UJB	Scania	Dowse
AY 22 ULG	Daf	Goldstar	FX 22 UJO	Scania	Dowse
AY 22 ULH	Daf	Goldstar	FX 22 UKC	Scania	Dowse
AY 22 ULJ	Daf	Turners	FX 22 UKK	Scania	Dowse
AY 22 ULW	Daf	Turners	FX 22 UKM	Scania	Dowse
AY 22 ULX	Daf	Turners	FX 22 UKW	Scania	Dowse
AY 22 ULZ	Daf	Turners	FX 22 ULA	Scania	Dowse
AY 22 UMA	Daf	Jack Richards	FX 22 ULB	Scania	Dowse
AY 22 UMB	Daf	Jack Richards	PN 22 FPU	Daf	Kibble
AY 22 UMC	Daf	Jack Richards	PN 22 FPV	Daf	Kibble
AY 22 UMD	Daf	Jack Richards	PN 22 FPX	Daf	Kibble
AY 22 UME	Daf	Jack Richards	PN 22 FSO	Daf	Kibble
AY 22 UON	Daf	Macintyre	PN 22 FYG	Daf	Kibble

Reg	Make	Body	Reg	Make	Body
PN 22 GJV	Daf	Kibble	AV 72 SXT	Daf	Goldstar
PN 22 GJX	Daf	Kibble	AV 72 SXU	Daf	Turners
PN 22 GJY	Daf	Kibble	AV 72 SXW	Daf	Turners
PN 22 GJZ	Daf	Kibble	AV 72 SXX	Daf	Macintyre
AV 72 GVA	Daf	Turners	AV 72 SXY	Daf	Macintyre
AV 72 GVC	Daf	Turners	AV 72 SXZ	Daf	Turners
AV 72 GVD	Daf	Turners	AV 72 TFO	Daf	Turners
AV 72 GVE	Daf	Ocean Trailers	AV 72 TFU	Daf	Turners
AV 72 GVF	Daf	Turners	AV 72 TFX	Daf	Turners
AV 72 GVG	Daf	Ocean Trailers	AV 72 TGE	Daf	Turners
AV 72 GVJ	Daf	Turners	AV 72 TGF	Daf	Turners
AV 72 GVK	Daf	Turners	AV 72 TGJ	Daf	Goldstar
AV 72 GVL	Daf	Ocean Trailers	AV 72 TGK	Daf	Goldstar
AV 72 GVM	Daf	Turners	AV 72 TGN	Daf	Goldstar
AV 72 GVU	Daf	Turners	AV 72 TGO	Daf	Turners
AV 72 SBO	Daf	Turners	AV 72 TGU	Daf	Turners
AV 72 SBX	Daf	Goldstar	AV 72 TGX	Daf	Turners
AV 72 SBY	Daf	Turners	AV 72 TGY	Daf	Clements
AV 72 SCX	Daf	Turners	AV 72 TGZ	Daf	Turners
AV 72 SCZ	Daf	Turners	AV 72 THF	Daf	Turners
AV 72 SDO	Daf	Goldstar	AV 72 THG	Daf	Turners
AV 72 SDU	Daf	Goldstar	AV 72 THK	Daf	Macintyre
AV 72 SDX	Daf	Turners	AV 72 THN	Daf	Turners
AV 72 SFN	Daf	Turners	AV 72 THU	Daf	Turners
AV 72 SFO	Daf	Turners	AV 72 THZ	Daf	Turners
AV 72 SFU	Daf	Turners	AV 72 TJO	Daf	Turners
AV 72 SFY	Daf	Turners	AV 72 TJU	Daf	Goldstar
AV 72 SFZ	Daf	Turners	AV 72 TJX	Daf	Turners
AV 72 SGO	Daf	Turners	AV 72 TJY	Daf	Turners
AV 72 SGU	Daf	Turners	AX 72 EXG	Daf	Goldstar
AV 72 SGX	Daf	Turners	AX 72 EXJ	Daf	Goldstar
AV 72 SOH	Daf	Macintyre	AX 72 EXL	Daf	Goldstar
AV 72 SOJ	Daf	Macintyre	AX 72 EXN	Daf	Goldstar
AV 72 SOU	Daf	Turners	AX 72 EXS	Daf	Goldstar
AV 72 SPU	Daf	Turners	AX 72 EXT	Daf	Goldstar
AV 72 SPX	Daf	Turners	AX 72 EXU	Daf	Turners
AV 72 SPZ	Daf	Turners	AX 72 EXV	Daf	Goldstar
AV 72 SRO	Daf	Goldstar	AX 72 EXW	Daf	Turners
AV 72 SRU	Daf	Goldstar	AX 72 EXZ	Daf	Turners
AV 72 SSJ	Daf	Turners	AX 72 EYA	Daf	Turners
AV 72 SSK	Daf	Goldstar	AX 72 EYB	Daf	Goldstar
AV 72 SVT	Daf	Turners	AX 72 EYC	Daf	Ocean Trailers
AV 72 SVU	Daf	Macintyre	AX 72 EYF	Daf	Turners
AV 72 SVW	Daf	Turners	AX 72 EYG	Daf	Turners
AV 72 SVX	Daf	Turners	AX 72 EYH	Daf	Turners
AV 72 SVY	Daf	Kibble	AY 72 SXK	Mercedes	Goldstar
AV 72 SVZ	Daf	Turners	AY 72 SXL	Mercedes	Goldstar
AV 72 SWK	Daf	Turners	AY 72 SXM	Mercedes	Goldstar
AV 72 SWN	Daf	Turners	AY 72 SXN	Mercedes	Goldstar
AV 72 SWO	Daf	Kibble	AY 72 SZN	Mercedes	Goldstar
AV 72 SWU	Daf	Turners	AY 72 SZO	Mercedes	Goldstar
AV 72 SWW	Daf	Goldstar	AY 72 SZP	Mercedes	Goldstar
AV 72 SWX	Daf	Turners	AY 72 SZR	Mercedes	Goldstar
AV 72 SWZ	Daf	Turners	AY 72 SZT	Mercedes	Goldstar
AV 72 SXP	Daf	Macintyre	AY 72 SZU	Mercedes	Goldstar
AV 72 SXR	Daf	Goldstar	AY 72 SZV	Mercedes	Goldstar

Turners Group (cont)

Reg	Make	Operator	Reg	Make	Operator
AY 72 TCK	Mercedes	Goldstar	AY 72 UNZ	Daf	Turners
AY 72 TCO	Mercedes	Goldstar	AY 72 UOA	Daf	Turners
AY 72 TCU	Mercedes	Goldstar	AY 72 UOB	Daf	Turners
AY 72 TCV	Mercedes	Goldstar	AY 72 UOC	Daf	Turners
AY 72 UGA	Daf	Turners	AY 72 UPT	Daf	Goldstar
AY 72 UGB	Daf	Turners	AY 72 UPV	Daf	Goldstar
AY 72 UGC	Daf	Goldstar EWL	AY 72 YGT	Scania	Turners (R & R)
AY 72 UGD	Daf	Goldstar EWL	AY 72 YGU	Scania	Turners
AY 72 UGE	Daf	Goldstar	AY 72 YGV	Scania	Turners
AY 72 UGF	Daf	Goldstar EWL	AY 72 YGW	Scania	Turners
AY 72 UGG	Daf	Goldstar EWL	AY 72 YGX	Scania	Turners
AY 72 UGH	Daf	Goldstar EWL	AY 72 YGZ	Scania	Turners
AY 72 UGJ	Daf	Goldstar EWL	AY 72 YHA	Scania	Turners
AY 72 UGK	Daf	Goldstar EWL	AY 72 YHB	Scania	Turners
AY 72 UGL	Daf	Turners	AY 72 YHC	Scania	Turners
AY 72 UGM	Daf	Turners	AY 72 YHD	Scania	Turners
AY 72 UGN	Daf	Turners	AY 72 YHE	Scania	Turners (R & R)
AY 72 UGO	Daf	Turners	AY 72 YHF	Scania	Turners (R & R)
AY 72 UGZ	Daf	Goldstar	AY 72 YHG	Scania	Turners (R & R)
AY 72 UKA	Daf	Goldstar	AY 72 YHH	Scania	Turners (R & R)
AY 72 UKB	Daf	Goldstar	AY 72 YHJ	Scania	Turners
AY 72 UKC	Daf	LKAB (Turners)	AY 72 YHK	Scania	Turners
AY 72 UKD	Daf	LKAB (Turners)	AY 72 YHL	Scania	Turners
AY 72 UKE	Daf	LKAB (Turners)	AY 72 YHM	Scania	Turners
AY 72 UKF	Daf	LKAB (Turners)	AY 72 YHN	Scania	Goldstar
AY 72 UKG	Daf	LKAB (Turners)	AY 72 YHO	Scania	Turners
AY 72 UKH	Daf	Turners	AY 72 YHP	Scania	Goldstar
AY 72 UKJ	Daf	BWOC	AY 72 YHR	Scania	Goldstar
AY 72 UKK	Daf	BWOC	AY 72 YHS	Scania	Goldstar
AY 72 UKL	Daf	Turners	AY 72 YHU	Scania	Goldstar
AY 72 UKM	Daf	Turners	AY 72 YHW	Scania	Turners
AY 72 UKN	Daf	Turners	AY 72 YHX	Scania	Turners
AY 72 UKO	Daf	Turners	AY 72 YHZ	Scania	Goldstar
AY 72 UKP	Daf	BWOC	AY 72 YJA	Scania	Goldstar
AY 72 UKR	Daf	Turners	AY 72 YJC	Scania	Goldstar
AY 72 UKS	Daf	BWOC	AY 72 YJD	Scania	Goldstar
AY 72 UKT	Daf	BWOC	AX 23 HLM	DAF	Lynn Star
AY 72 UKU	Daf	BWOC	AX 23 HLN	DAF	Turners
AY 72 UKV	Daf	Turners	AX 23 HLO	DAF	Lynn Star
AY 72 UKX	Daf	Turners	AX 23 HLR	DAF	Turners
AY 72 UKZ	Daf	Turners	AX 23 HLU	DAF	Turners
AY 72 UNB	Daf	Turners	AX 23 HLW	DAF	Turners
AY 72 UNE	Daf	Turners	AX 23 HLZ	DAF	Turners
AY 72 UNF	Daf	LKAB (Turners)	AX 23 HME	DAF	Turners
AY 72 UNG	Daf	Turners	AX 23 HMF	DAF	Turners
AY 72 UNH	Daf	Turners	AX 23 HMG	DAF	Turners
AY 72 UNJ	Daf	Turners	AX 23 HMH	DAF	Turners
AY 72 UNL	Daf	Turners	AX 23 HMO	DAF	Turners
AY 72 UNM	Daf	Turners	AX 23 HMU	DAF	Turners
AY 72 UNP	Daf	Turners	AX 23 HMV	DAF	Turners
AY 72 UNR	Daf	Turners	AX 23 HNC	DAF	Turners
AY 72 UNS	Daf	Turners	AX 23 HND	DAF	Turners
AY 72 UNU	Daf	Turners	AX 23 HND	DAF	Turners
AY 72 UNV	Daf	Turners	AX 23 HNE	DAF	Turners
AY 72 UNW	Daf	Turners	AX 23 HNH	DAF	Macintyre
AY 72 UNX	Daf	Turners	AX 23 HNJ	DAF	Macintyre

AX 23	HNK	DAF	Turners	AY 23	WBW	DAF	Turners
AX 23	HNL	DAF	Turners	AY 23	WBX	DAF	Turners
AX 23	HNM	DAF	Turners	AY 23	WBZ	DAF	Turners
AX 23	HNN	DAF	Macintyre	AY 23	WCA	DAF	Turners
AX 23	HNO	DAF	Turners	AY 23	WCC	DAF	Goldstar
AX 23	HNP	DAF	Turners	AY 23	WCD	DAF	Turners
AX 23	HNR	DAF	Turners	AY 23	WCE	DAF	Goldstar
AX 23	OVG	DAF	Clements	AY 23	WCF	DAF	Turners
AY 23	VRF	DAF	Goldstar	AY 23	WCG	DAF	Kibble
AY 23	VRG	DAF	Goldstar	AY 23	WCJ	DAF	Kibble
AY 23	VRJ	DAF	Goldstar	AY 23	WCK	DAF	Turners
AY 23	VRK	DAF	Goldstar	AY 23	WFA	DAF	Turners
AY 23	VWA	DAF	Turners	AY 23	WFB	DAF	Turners
AY 23	VWB	DAF	Ocean Trailers	AY 23	WFC	DAF	Turners
AY 23	VWC	DAF	Turners	AY 23	WFD	DAF	Turners
AY 23	VWD	DAF	Turners	AY 23	WFE	DAF	Turners
AY 23	VWE	DAF	Turners	AY 23	WFG	DAF	Turners
AY 23	VWF	DAF	Turners	AY 23	WFK	DAF	Harvest
AY 23	VWG	DAF	Turners	AY 23	WFL	DAF	Turners
AY 23	VYF	DAF	Turners	AY 23	WFN	DAF	Turners
AY 23	VYG	DAF	Turners	AY 23	WFR	DAF	Turners
AY 23	VYH	DAF	Turners	AY 23	WFS	DAF	Turners
AY 23	VYJ	DAF	Turners	AY 23	WFT	DAF	Turners
AY 23	VYK	DAF	Turners	AY 23	WFX	DAF	Turners
AY 23	VYL	DAF	Turners	AY 23	WFZ	DAF	Turners
AY 23	VYM	DAF	Turners	AY 23	WGE	DAF	Turners
AY 23	VYN	DAF	Turners	AY 23	WGF	DAF	Turners
AY 23	VYO	DAF	Turners	AY 23	WGG	DAF	Turners
AY 23	VYP	DAF	Turners	AY 23	WGJ	DAF	Turners
AY 23	VYR	DAF	Turners	AY 23	WGK	DAF	Goldstar
AY 23	VYS	DAF	Turners	AY 23	WGM	DAF	Turners
AY 23	VYT	DAF	Turners	AY 23	WGN	DAF	Turners
AY 23	VYU	DAF	Turners	AY 23	WGP	DAF	Goldstar
AY 23	VYV	DAF	Turners	AY 23	WGU	DAF	Goldstar
AY 23	VYW	DAF	Turners	AY 23	WGV	DAF	Turners
AY 23	VYX	DAF	Turners	AY 23	WGW	DAF	Goldstar
AY 23	VYZ	DAF	Turners	AY 23	WGX	DAF	Goldstar
AY 23	VZA	DAF	Turners	AY 23	WGZ	DAF	Turners
AY 23	VZB	DAF	Turners	AY 23	WHA	DAF	Turners
AY 23	WAA	DAF	Turners	AY 23	WHB	DAF	Turners
AY 23	WAE	DAF	Goldstar	AY 23	WHC	DAF	Turners
AY 23	WAJ	DAF	Goldstar	AY 23	WHD	DAF	Goldstar
AY 23	WAO	DAF	Turners	AY 23	WHF	DAF	Turners
AY 23	WAU	DAF	Goldstar	AY 23	WHG	DAF	Turners
AY 23	WBE	DAF	Turners	AY 23	WHH	DAF	Turners
AY 23	WBG	DAF	Turners	AY 23	WHJ	DAF	Turners
AY 23	WBJ	DAF	Goldstar	AY 23	WHK	DAF	Turners
AY 23	WBK	DAF	Turners	AY 23	WHL	DAF	Turners
AY 23	WBL	DAF	Goldstar	AY 23	WHM	DAF	Turners
AY 23	WBM	DAF	Turners	AY 23	WHN	DAF	Turners
AY 23	WBN	DAF	Turners	AY 23	WHP	DAF	Goldstar
AY 23	WBO	DAF	Goldstar	AY 23	WHR	DAF	Goldstar
AY 23	WBP	DAF	Goldstar	AY 23	WHS	DAF	Goldstar
AY 23	WBT	DAF	Kibble	AY 23	WHT	DAF	Goldstar
AY 23	WBU	DAF	Turners	AY 23	WHV	DAF	Turners
AY 23	WBV	DAF	Goldstar	AY 23	WHW	DAF	Goldstar

Turners Group (cont)

Reg	Make	Livery		Reg	Make	Livery
AY 23 WHX	DAF	Goldstar		FX 23 VKR	SCANIA	Dowse
AY 23 WHZ	DAF	Goldstar		FX 23 VKT	SCANIA	Dowse
AY 23 WJA	DAF	Goldstar		FX 23 VLC	SCANIA	Dowse
AY 23 WJC	DAF	Goldstar		FX 23 VLF	SCANIA	Dowse
AY 23 WJD	DAF	Goldstar		PN 23 FVY	DAF	Kibble
AY 23 WJE	DAF	Turners		AY 73 UXA	DAF	Goldstar
AY 23 WJF	DAF	Kibble		AY 73 UXB	DAF	Goldstar
AY 23 WJG	DAF	Turners		AY 73 UXC	DAF	Goldstar
AY 23 WJJ	DAF	Macintyre		AY 73 UXD	DAF	Goldstar
AY 23 WJK	DAF	Goldstar		AY 73 UXJ	DAF	Turners
AY 23 WJM	DAF	Turners		AY 73 UXM	DAF	Turners
AY 23 WJN	DAF	Turners		AY 73 UXR	DAF	Turners
AY 23 WJO	DAF	Goldstar		AY 73 UXT	DAF	Turners
AY 23 WJU	DAF	Goldstar		AY 73 UXU	DAF	Turners
AY 23 WJV	DAF	Turners		AY 73 UXV	DAF	Turners
AY 23 WJX	DAF	Turners		AY 73 UXW	DAF	Turners
AY 23 WJZ	DAF	Turners		AY 73 UXX	DAF	Turners
AY 23 WKZ	DAF	Goldstar		AY 73 UXZ	DAF	Turners
AY 23 WLW	DAF	Goldstar		AY 73 UYA	DAF	BWOC
AY 23 WLX	DAF	Goldstar		AY 73 UYB	DAF	BWOC
AY 23 WLZ	DAF	Turners		AY 73 UYC	DAF	BWOC
AY 23 WMA	DAF	Goldstar		AY 73 UYD	DAF	BWOC
AY 23 WMC	DAF	Goldstar		AY 73 UYE	DAF	BWOC
AY 23 WMD	DAF	Goldstar		AY 73 UYF	DAF	BWOC
AY 23 WME	DAF	Goldstar		AY 73 UYH	DAF	BWOC
AY 23 WMF	DAF	Goldstar		AY 73 UYJ	DAF	BWOC
AY 23 WMG	DAF	Goldstar		AY 73 UYL	DAF	Turners
AY 23 WMJ	DAF	Goldstar		AY 73 UYN	DAF	Turners
AY 23 WMK	DAF	Turners		AY 73 UYP	DAF	Turners
AY 23 WML	DAF	Lynn Star		AY 73 UYR	DAF	Turners
AY 23 WMM	DAF	Turners		AY 73 UYS	DAF	Turners
AY 23 WMO	DAF	Turners		AY 73 UYT	DAF	Heidelberg
AY 23 WMP	DAF	Turners		AY 73 UYU	DAF	Heidelberg
DF 23 TWA	MAN	Goldstar		AY 73 UYX	DAF	Turners
DF 23 TWC	MAN	Macintyre		AY 73 UYZ	DAF	Goldstar
DF 23 TWD	DAF	Goldstar		AY 73 UZA	DAF	Turners
DF 23 TWE	DAF	Goldstar		AY 73 UZB	DAF	Turners
DF 23 TWG	DAF	Goldstar		AY 73 UZC	DAF	Turners
DF 23 TWJ	DAF	Goldstar		AY 73 UZD	DAF	Turners
DF 23 TWK	MAN	Turners		AY 73 UZE	DAF	Goldstar
DF 23 TWL	MAN	Turners		AY 73 UZF	DAF	Goldstar
DF 23 TWM	MAN	Goldstar		AY 73 UZG	DAF	Goldstar
DF 23 TWN	MAN	Macintyre		AY 73 UZL	DAF	Goldstar
FX 23 VEW	SCANIA	Dowse		AY 73 UZO	DAF	Turners
FX 23 VFM	SCANIA	Dowse		AY 73 UZP	DAF	Turners
FX 23 VFN	SCANIA	Turners		AY 73 UZR	DAF	Turners
FX 23 VFO	SCANIA	Turners		AY 73 UZV	DAF	Turners
FX 23 VFS	SCANIA	Dowse		AY 73 UZW	DAF	Turners
FX 23 VFT	SCANIA	Dowse		AY 73 UZX	DAF	Turners
FX 23 VFZ	SCANIA	Dowse		AY 73 VAA	DAF	Turners
FX 23 VGV	SCANIA	Dowse		AY 73 VAD	DAF	Turners
FX 23 VJC	SCANIA	Dowse		AY 73 VAE	DAF	Turners
FX 23 VJJ	SCANIA	Dowse		AY 73 VAF	DAF	Turners
FX 23 VJP	SCANIA	Dowse		AY 73 VAH	DAF	Turners
FX 23 VKA	SCANIA	Dowse		AY 73 VAJ	DAF	Turners
FX 23 VKD	SCANIA	Dowse		AY 73 VAO	DAF	Logwin

Turners Group (cont)

Reg	Make	Operator	Reg	Make	Operator
AY 73 VAX	DAF	Turners	AY 73 ZDF	SCANIA	Turners
AY 73 VBA	DAF	Turners	AY 73 ZDG	SCANIA	Turners
AY 73 VBD	DAF	Turners	AY 73 ZDJ	SCANIA	Turners
AY 73 VBE	DAF	Turners	AY 73 ZDK	SCANIA	Turners
AY 73 VBF	DAF	Turners	AY 73 ZDL	SCANIA	Turners
AY 73 YZW	SCANIA	Turners	AY 73 ZDM	SCANIA	Turners
AY 73 YZX	SCANIA	Macintyre	AY 73 ZDN	SCANIA	Turners
AY 73 ZBD	SCANIA	Macintyre	AY 73 ZDO	SCANIA	Turners
AY 73 ZBF	SCANIA	Turners (R&R)	AY 73 ZDP	SCANIA	Turners
AY 73 ZBG	SCANIA	Turners	AY 73 ZDR	SCANIA	Turners
AY 73 ZBJ	SCANIA	Turners	AY 73 ZDS	SCANIA	Turners
AY 73 ZBL	SCANIA	Macintyre	DE 73 YGG	MAN	Macintyre
AY 73 ZBN	SCANIA	Turners	DF 73 KFO	MAN	Macintyre
AY 73 ZBP	SCANIA	Turners	FX 73 UYY	SCANIA	Dowse
AY 73 ZBT	SCANIA	Macintyre	FX 73 UZA	SCANIA	Dowse
AY 73 ZBU	SCANIA	Macintyre	FX 73 UZB	SCANIA	Dowse
AY 73 ZBV	SCANIA	Turners	FX 73 UZD	SCANIA	Dowse
AY 73 ZCA	SCANIA	Macintyre	FX 73 UZE	SCANIA	Dowse
AY 73 ZCE	SCANIA	Turners	FX 73 UZO	SCANIA	Dowse
AY 73 ZCF	SCANIA	Turners	FX 73 UZT	SCANIA	Dowse
AY 73 ZCU	SCANIA	Turners	FX 73 UZU	SCANIA	Dowse
AY 73 ZCV	SCANIA	Turners	FX 73 UZW	SCANIA	Dowse
AY 73 ZCX	SCANIA	Turners	FX 73 UZY	SCANIA	Dowse
AY 73 ZCZ	SCANIA	Turners	FX 73 VAD	SCANIA	Dowse
AY 73 ZDA	SCANIA	Turners	FX 73 VAH	SCANIA	Turners
AY 73 ZDC	SCANIA	Turners	FX 73 VAY	SCANIA	Dowse
AY 73 ZDD	SCANIA	Turners	FX 73 VBD	SCANIA	Dowse
AY 73 ZDE	SCANIA	Turners	FX 73 VBK	SCANIA	Dowse

William Nicol (Portleven)

No	Reg	Make	Name	No	Reg	Make	Name
1	ABZ 2706 (69)	Scania	Natasha	27	V 27 WNT (17)	Daf	Heather
2	V 9 WNT (20)	Scania	Flora	28	V 28 WNT (17)	Daf	Alma
3	V 6 WNT (69)	Scania		29	V 29 WNT (67)	Scania	Nicola
4	V 1 WNT (68)	Scania		30	V 30 WNT (67)	Scania	Sandra
4	V 10 WNT (20)	Scania	Margaret	40	V 40 WNT (18)	Scania	Kerry
5	V 5 WNT (20)	Daf	Babs	50	V 50 WNT (18)	Scania	Beverley
8	V 8 WNT (20)	Daf		60	V 60 WNT (66)	Scania	
11	N 11 COL (72)	Scania		70	V 70 WNT (66)	Scania	Glynis
15	V 15 WNT (21)	Scania		80	V 80 WNT (66)	Scania	
17	V 17 WNT (22)	Renault			N 15 JTT (R)	Scania	
18	V 18 WNT (72)	Renault			R 4 WNT (72)	Scania	
19	V 19 WNT (72)	Daf			R 11 WNT (73)	Renault	
20	V 20 WNT (19)	Renault			V 2 WNT (73)	Renault	
21	V 21 WNT (72)	Daf			V 11 GFL (07)	Scania	
23	V 23 WNT (63)	Scania	Pamela		V 14 WNT (21)	Scania	
24	V 24 WNT (63)	Scania	Sara		SV 56 HGF	Man	
25	V 25 WNT (63)	Scania	Patti		DX 07 FFW	Scania	
26	V 26 WNT (63)	Scania	Margaret		SW 17 YZC	Mercedes	

W.H. Malcolm

F/No	Reg	Make	Specification	Livery	Allocation
C 012	S12 WHM (10)	Volvo	FL 240 4w Sweeper LHD	Construction	Linwood
C 013	S13 WHM (14)	Scania	P230 4w Sweeper LHD	Construction	Clydeside
C 018	S18 WHM (62)	Scania	P230 4w Sweeper LHD	Construction	Shewalton
C 019	N3 WHM (52)	Renault	Midlum 150 4w Flatbed	Construction	Newhouse
C 021	S21 WHM (68)	Scania	P250 4w Sweeper LHD	Construction	
C 025	SJ21 KZU	Volvo	FMX 420 6w Hooklift	Construction	
C 026	SM19 BYP	Scania	P410 XT 8w Hooklift	Construction	
C 027	SM19 BYR	Scania	P410 XT 8w Hooklift	Construction	
C 028	SF68 OPM	Scania	P410 XT 8w Hooklift	Construction	
C 030	SL63 YSV	Scania	P400 6w Hooklift	Construction	Clydeside
C 131	SJ20 HVC	Volvo	FL 250 4w Skip	Construction	
C 301	SK21 BVL	Scania	R450 6x2 (NG) NL E6	Construction	
C 302	SK21 BVM	Scania	R450 6x2 (NG) NL E6	Construction	
C 303	SK21 BVN	Scania	R450 6x2 (NG) NL E6	Construction	
C 304	SK21 KZT	Volvo	FH 460 6x2	Construction	
C 311	SC61 FFA	Man	TGM 15.250 4w (L) Dropside	Construction	Clydeside
C 312	R19 WHM (11)	Scania	R560 6x2 (Top)	Construction	Clydeside
C 313	SF13 DHL	Volvo	FL 240 4w Dropside	Construction	
C 314	SJ13 KXO	Mercedes	Atego 1218 4w Tipper	Construction	
C 315	PX18 UUG	Scania	R450 6x2 HL SL Opti E6	Construction	
C 316	PX18 UUB	Scania	R450 6x2 HL SL Opti E6	Construction	
C 317	PX18 UUC	Scania	R450 6x2 HL SL Opti E6	Construction	
C 318	SN16 NYY	Scania	R450 6x2 HL SL Opti E6	Construction	Clydeside
C 319	SN16 NYX	Scania	R450 6x2 HL SL Opti E6	Construction	Loanhead
C 321	PX15 UMV	Scania	R450 6x2 HL SL Opti E6	Construction	Clydeside
C 322	PX15 UNJ	Scania	R450 6x2 HL SL Opti E6	Construction	Clydeside
C 323	PX15 UNB	Scania	R450 6x2 HL SL Opti E6	Construction	Clydeside
C 431	EY64 CKX	Scania	P410 8w Tipper	Construction	Loanhead
C 500	SN72 ZMO	Scania	P410 XT 8w Tipper	Construction	
C 501	SJ21 MGU	Man	TGS 35.430 8w (NN) Tipper	Construction	
C 503	SJ22 FHK	Volvo	FMX 420 8w Tipper	Construction	
C 504	SJ22 FHH	Volvo	FMX 420 8w Tipper	Construction	
C 505	SJ72 FUO	Volvo	FMX 420 8w Tipper	Construction	
C 506	SJ72 GMU	Renault	C460 8w Tipper	Construction	
C 509	SJ73 HKE	Man	TGS 35.430 8w (NN) Tipper	Construction	
C 529	SN67 SYG	Scania	P410 8w Tipper	Construction	Clydeside
C 530	SN67 SOU	Scania	P410 8w Tipper	Construction	
C 537	SN67 SXX	Scania	P410 8w Tipper	Construction	
C 538	SN68 XLU	Scania	P410 XT 8w Tipper	Construction	
C 539	SN68 XLV	Scania	P410 XT 8w Tipper	Construction	
C 540	SJ19 NZR	Volvo	FMX 420 8w Tipper	Construction	
C 541	SJ19 NZK	Volvo	FMX 420 8w Tipper	Construction	
C 542	SN68 XLX	Scania	P410 XT 8w Tipper	Construction	
C 544	SJ69 CVE	Volvo	FMX 420 8w Tipper	Construction	
C 545	SJ20 HMV	Volvo	FMX 420 8w Tipper	Construction	
C 547	SN68 XPX	Scania	P410 XT 8w Tipper	Construction	
C 548	SK19 BOF	Scania	P410 XT 8w Tipper	Construction	
C 549	SJ20 HMK	Volvo	FMX 420 8w Tipper	Construction	
C 550	SK19 BRV	Scania	P410 XT 8w Tipper	Construction	
C 551	SJ69 CVF	Volvo	FMX 420 8w Tipper	Construction	
C 552	SJ69 CVH	Volvo	FMX 420 8w Tipper	Construction	
C 553	SJ20 HNG	Volvo	FMX 420 8w Tipper	Construction	
C 554	SJ20 HUH	Volvo	FMX 420 8w Hooklift	Construction	
C 600	SN72 ZMU	Scania	P410 (NG) XT 8w Tipper	Construction	
C 601	SF72 BDO	Scania	P410 (NG) XT 8w Tipper	Construction	
C 602	SF72 BDU	Scania	P410 (NG) XT 8w Tipper	Construction	
C 603	SN72 ZMV	Scania	P410 (NG) XT 8w Tipper	Construction	
C 604	SN72 ZMX	Scania	P410 (NG) XT 8w Tipper	Construction	

C 606	SF71 CFV	Scania	P410 (NG) XT 8w Tipper	Construction	
C 607	SF71 CFX	Scania	P410 (NG) XT 8w Tipper	Construction	
C 624	SN67 SXO	Scania	P410 8w Tipper	Construction	
C 625	SN67 SYF	Scania	P410 8w Tipper	Construction	
C 626	SN67 SXP	Scania	P410 8w Tipper	Construction	
C 627	SN68 XLT	Scania	P410 XT 8w Tipper	Construction	
C 628	SN68 XLW	Scania	P410 XT 8w Tipper	Construction	
C 629	SK19 BNO	Scania	P410 XT 8w Tipper	Construction	Loanhead
C 630	SK19 BNU	Scania	P410 XT 8w Tipper	Construction	Loanhead
C 631	SK19 BOH	Scania	P410 XT 8w Tipper	Construction	
C 632	SK19 BWZ	Scania	P410 XT 8w Tipper	Construction	Loanhead
C 633	SK19 BXA	Scania	P410 XT 8w Tipper	Construction	Loanhead
C 634	SM19 BWH	Scania	P410 XT 8w Tipper	Construction	Loanhead
C 664	SA66 ENP	Volvo	FMX 370 8w Tipper	Construction	
C 666	SF18 WTM	Volvo	FMX 420 8w Tipper	Construction	
C 667	SF18 WTO	Volvo	FMX 420 8w Tipper	Construction	
C 668	SF18 WTL	Volvo	FMX 420 8w Tipper	Construction	
C 669	SF18 WTJ	Volvo	FMX 420 8w Tipper	Construction	
C 670	SF18 WTN	Volvo	FMX 420 8w Tipper	Construction	
C 671	SF18 WTK	Volvo	FMX 420 8w Tipper	Construction	
C 672	SJ19 NZU	Volvo	FMX 420 8w Tipper	Construction	
C 673	SJ19 NZX	Volvo	FMX 420 8w Tipper	Construction	
C 674	SJ19 NZZ	Volvo	FMX 420 8w Tipper	Construction	
C 675	SJ19 NZN	Volvo	FMX 420 8w Tipper	Construction	
C 676	SJ19 NZW	Volvo	FMX 420 8w Tipper	Construction	
C 679	SJ21 KXK	Volvo	FMX 420 8w Tipper	Construction	
C 680	SJ21 KXL	Volvo	FMX 420 8w Tipper	Construction	
C 681	SJ21 KXM	Volvo	FMX 420 8w Tipper	Construction	
C 682	SJ21 KXN	Volvo	FMX 420 8w Tipper	Construction	
C 725	Y100 RLH (10)	Man	TGM 15.250 4w (L) Dropside	Construction	Shewalton
C 730	T20 WHM (02)	Volvo	FM9 260 4w Flatbed	Construction	Linwood
C	SF60 CCZ	Volvo	FL 280 4w Gritter	Yellow	Linwood
C	SJ20 HMO	Volvo	FMX 420 8w Tipper	Construction	
C	SJ20 HVB	Volvo	FL 250 4w Skip	Construction	
C	SJ70 FWV	Volvo	FMX 420 8w Tipper	Construction	
C	R7 WHM	Scania	P410 (NG) XT 8w Tanker	Construction	
C	N900 TAR (22)	Man	TGL 8.190 4w CC Tipper	Construction	
C	SJ73 HKD	Man	TGS 25.400 82 NN	Construction	
F 195	F195 FHS	Scania	P93M 240 4x2	Malcolm Group	Gatenby
L 001	R200 WHM (17)	Scania	R450 6x2 (NG) HL E6	Malbart	Bristol
L 002	N16 WHM (13)	Volvo	FH 460 6x2 GXL	Malcolm Group	Linwood
L 003	SH19 VWS	Daf	FTGCF 480 6x2 SC	Malcolm Group	
L 005	SK21 BVJ	Scania	R450 6x2 (NG) NL E6	Malcolm Group	
L 007	LO07 WHM (21)	Man	TGX 26.470 6x2 GM	Malcolm Group	
L 008	KX14 LKN	Volvo	FM 450 6x2 G	Malcolm Group	Alloa
L 013	T11 WHM (05)	Scania	P380 4x2	Malcolm Group	Linwood
L 040	T9 WHM (63)	Volvo	FM 450 6x2 G	Malcolm Group	Linwood
L 047	KX15 MVT	Volvo	FH 460 6x2 G	Malcolm Group	Linwood
L 097	N191 JGG	Volvo	FL10 4x2	Malcolm Group	Linwood
L 098	J183 JYS	Volvo	FL10 4x2	Malcolm Group	Linwood
L 099	J879 JNS	Volvo	FL10 4x2	Malcolm Group	Linwood
L 100	L100 WHM (71)	Scania	R500 6x2 (NG) HL E6	100 Years	
L 101	GJ18 HVW	Volvo	FH 460 6x2 GXL	Malcolm Group	
L 117	H892 HSJ	Volvo	FL10 4x2	Malcolm Group	Linwood
L 150	SF65 TUW	Volvo	FM 410 4x2 G	Malcolm Group	Newhouse
L 151	M856 YSM	Scania	P113M 320 6x2	Malcolm Group	Grangemouth
L 152	M859 YSM	Scania	P113M 320 6x2	Malcolm Group	Grangemouth
L 172	SJ69 DXA	Man	TGX 26.460 6x2 XLX	Malcolm Group	
L 173	SJ69 DXB	Man	TGX 26.460 6x2 XLX	Malcolm Group	

L 174	SJ69 DXC	Man	TGX 26.460 6x2 XLX	Malcolm Group	
L 175	SJ69 DXD	Man	TGX 26.460 6x2 XLX	Malcolm Group	
L 176	SJ69 DXE	Man	TGX 26.460 6x2 XLX	Malcolm Group	
L 177	SJ69 DXF	Man	TGX 26.460 6x2 XLX	Malcolm Group	
L 178	SJ69 DXG	Man	TGX 26.460 6x2 XLX	Malcolm Group	
L 179	SJ69 DXH	Man	TGX 26.460 6x2 XLX	Malcolm Group	
L 180	SJ69 DXK	Man	TGX 26.460 6x2 XLX	Malcolm Group	
L 181	SJ69 DXL	Man	TGX 26.460 6x2 XLX	Malcolm Group	
L 182	SJ72 HGG	Man	TGX 26.470 6x2 GM	Malcolm Group	
L 183	SJ72 HGC	Man	TGX 26.470 6x2 GM	Malcolm Group	
L 185	SJ72 HGF	Man	TGX 26.470 6x2 GM	Malcolm Group	
L 186	SJ72 HGE	Man	TGX 26.470 6x2 GM	Malcolm Group	
L 187	SJ72 HFS	Man	TGX 26.470 6x2 GM	Malcolm Group	
L 188	SJ72 HFT	Man	TGX 26.470 6x2 GM	Malcolm Group	
L 189	SJ72 HFU	Man	TGX 26.470 6x2 GM	Malcolm Group	
L 191	SJ72 HFW	Man	TGX 26.470 6x2 GM	Malcolm Group	
L 194	SJ72 HFZ	Man	TGX 26.470 6x2 GM	Malcolm Group	
L 197	D19 WHM	Daf	FTG 530 6x2 (XG)	Malcolm Group	
L 200	V19 WHM (64)	Volvo	FH16 750 6x2 GXL	Malcolm Group	Grangemouth
L 201	T18 WHM (11)	Man	TGX 26.440 6x2 XL	Malcolm Group	Harlow
L 202	SJ21 LNR	Renault	T520 6x2 HSC	Malcolm Group	
L 203	KX19 BZE	Scania	R410 4x2 (NG) NL E6	Malcolm Group	
L 204	SJ71 GBX	Renault	T480 6x2 HSC	Malcolm Group	
L 208	K705 LHS	Scania	P113M 320 6x2 Day	Malcolm Group	Grangemouth
L 209	K706 LHS	Scania	P113M 320 6x2 Day	Malcolm Group	Grangemouth
L 213	SF17 WCJ	Volvo	FE 320 6w Curtainside	Malcolm Group	
L 214	SF17 WCK	Volvo	FE 320 6w Curtainside	Malcolm Group	
L 215	SF17 WCL	Volvo	FE 320 6w Curtainside	Malcolm Group	
L 216	SN68 XLA	Scania	G450 6X2 HL	Malcolm Group	
L 217	SN68 XLB	Scania	G450 6X2 HL	Malcolm Group	
L 218	SN68 XLC	Scania	G450 6X2 HL	Malcolm Group	
L 219	SN68 XLD	Scania	G450 6X2 HL	Malcolm Group	
L 220	SN68 XLE	Scania	G450 6X2 HL	Malcolm Group	
L 221	SN68 XLF	Scania	G450 6X2 HL	Malcolm Group	
L 222	SN68 XLG	Scania	G450 6X2 HL	Malcolm Group	
L 223	SN68 XLH	Scania	G450 6X2 HL	Malcolm Group	
L 224	SN68 XLJ	Scania	G450 6X2 HL	Malcolm Group	
L 225	SN68 XLK	Scania	G450 6X2 HL	Malcolm Group	
L 226	SN18 GXA	Scania	R450 6x2 Top	Malcolm Group	
L 227	SN18 GXB	Scania	R450 6x2 Top	Malcolm Group	
L 228	SN18 GXC	Scania	R450 6x2 Top	Malcolm Group	
L 229	SN18 GXD	Scania	R450 6x2 Top	Malcolm Group	
L 230	SN18 GXE	Scania	R450 6x2 Top	Malcolm Group	
L 231	SN18 GXF	Scania	R450 6x2 Top	Malcolm Group	
L 232	SN18 GXG	Scania	R450 6x2 Top	Malcolm Group	
L 233	SN18 GXH	Scania	R450 6x2 Top	Malcolm Group	
L 234	SN18 GXJ	Scania	R450 6x2 Top	Malcolm Group	
L 235	SN18 GXK	Scania	R450 6x2 Top	Malcolm Group	
L 236	SN68 XLL	Scania	R450 6x2 Top	Malcolm Group	
L 237	SN68 XLM	Scania	R450 6x2 Top	Malcolm Group	
L 238	SN68 XLO	Scania	R450 6x2 Top	Malcolm Group	
L 239	SN68 XLP	Scania	R450 6x2 Top	Malcolm Group	
L 240	SN68 XLR	Scania	R450 6x2 Top	Malcolm Group	
L 241	PN21 FGK	Scania	R450 6x2 (NG) HL E6	Malcolm Group	
L 242	PN21 FGM	Scania	R450 6x2 (NG) HL E6	Malcolm Group	
L 243	PN21 FGU	Scania	R450 6x2 (NG) HL E6	Malcolm Group	
L 244	PN21 FHB	Scania	R450 6x2 (NG) HL E6	Malcolm Group	
L 245	PN21 FHD	Scania	R450 6x2 (NG) HL E6	Malcolm Group	
L 249	T30 WHM (60)	Volvo	FM 410 6x2 Day	Malcolm Group	Glenrothes

L 251	T27 WHM (60)	Volvo	FM 410 6x2 Day	Malcolm Group	Grangemouth
L 252	T28 WHM (60)	Volvo	FM 410 6x2 Day	Malcolm Group	Glenrothes
L 253	T31 WHM (60)	Volvo	FM 410 6x2 Day	Malcolm Group	Glenrothes
L 254	T29 WHM (60)	Volvo	FM 410 6x2 Day	Malcolm Group	Glenrothes
L 257	T14 WHM (58)	Scania	R420 6x2 Day	Malcolm Group	Crick
L 260	SJ71 FMP	Volvo	FH 500 6x2 G	Malcolm Group	
L 261	SJ71 FMO	Volvo	FH 500 6x2 G	Malcolm Group	
L 262	SJ71 FMV	Volvo	FH 500 6x2 G	Malcolm Group	
L 263	SJ71 FMZ	Volvo	FH 500 6x2 G	Malcolm Group	
L 264	SJ71 FNA	Volvo	FH 500 6x2 G	Malcolm Group	
L 265	SJ71 FMU	Volvo	FH 500 6x2 G	Malcolm Group	
L 266	SJ71 FMM	Volvo	FH 500 6x2 G	Malcolm Group	
L 269	T16 WHM (58)	Scania	R420 6x2 Day	Malcolm Group	Grangemouth
L 270	SJ70 HFN	Man	TGX 26.470 6x2 XLX	Malcolm Group	Glenrothes
L 271	SJ70 HFO	Man	TGX 26.470 6x2 XLX	Malcolm Group	Grangemouth
L 272	SJ70 HFS	Man	TGX 26.470 6x2 XLX	Malcolm Group	
L 273	SJ70 HFH	Man	TGX 26.470 6x2 XLX	Malcolm Group	Glenrothes
L 274	SJ70 HFK	Man	TGX 26.470 6x2 XLX	Malcolm Group	Glenrothes
L 275	SJ70 HFM	Man	TGX 26.470 6x2 XLX	Malcolm Group	
L 276	SJ70 HFR	Man	TGX 26.470 6x2 XLX	Malcolm Group	Glenrothes
L 277	SJ70 HBU	Man	TGX 26.470 6x2 XLX	Malcolm Group	
L 278	SJ70 HFT	Man	TGX 26.470 6x2 XLX	Malcolm Group	
L 279	SJ70 HFP	Man	TGX 26.470 6x2 XLX	Malcolm Group	
L 280	SJ71 GVT	Man	TGX 26.470 6x2 XLX	Malcolm Group	
L 281	SJ71 GVU	Man	TGX 26.470 6x2 XLX	Malcolm Group	
L 282	SJ71 GVV	Man	TGX 26.470 6x2 XLX	Malcolm Group	
L 283	SJ71 GVW	Man	TGX 26.470 6x2 XLX	Malcolm Group	
L 285	SJ21 LZT	Man	TGX 26.470 6x2 GM	Malcolm Group	
L 286	SJ21 LZR	Man	TGX 26.470 6x2 GM	Malcolm Group	
L 287	SJ22 GPE	Man	TGX 26.470 6x2 GM	Malcolm Group	
L 288	SJ22 GPF	Man	TGX 26.470 6x2 GM	Malcolm Group	
L 289	SJ22 GPK	Man	TGX 26.470 6x2 GM	Malcolm Group	
L 290	SJ22 GPO	Man	TGX 26.470 6x2 GM	Malcolm Group	
L 291	SJ22 GPU	Man	TGX 26.470 6x2 GM	Malcolm Group	
L 292	SJ22 GPV	Man	TGX 26.470 6x2 GM	Malcolm Group	
L 293	SJ22 GRF	Man	TGX 26.470 6x2 GM	Malcolm Group	
L 294	SJ22 GRK	Man	TGX 26.470 6x2 GM	Malcolm Group	
L 295	SJ22 GRU	Man	TGX 26.470 6x2 GM	Malcolm Group	
L 296	SJ22 GRX	Man	TGX 26.470 6x2 GM	Malcolm Group	
L 300	SN09 DFG	Man	TGL 8.180 4w C Dropside	Malcolm Group	Glenrothes
L 450	T456 TSC	Scania	P94D 310 4x2 Day	Malcolm Group	Irvine
L 451	T457 TSC	Scania	P94D 310 4x2 Day	Malcolm Group	Glenrothes
L 459	T432 KJV	Scania	P94D 310 4x2 Day	Malcolm Group	Crick
L 469	T427 KJV	Scania	P94D 310 4x2 Day	Malcolm Group	Grangemouth
L 470	T428 KJV	Scania	P94D 310 4x2 Day	Malcolm Group	Irvine
L 471	SV04 LSH	Volvo	FM9 260 4x2 Day	Red	Newhouse
L 472	SV04 LSM	Volvo	FM9 260 4x2 Day	Red	Sheildhall
L 473	SV04 LSP	Volvo	FM9 260 4x2 Day	Red	Linwood
L 474	SV04 LSR	Volvo	FM9 260 4x2 Day	Red	Newhouse
L 475	DX57 DOA	Daf	FTGXF105 460 6x2 SC	Malcolm Group	Linwood
L 476	T450 TTW	Scania	P94D 310 4x2 Day	Malcolm Group	Haydock
L 477	T451 TTW	Scania	P94D 310 4x2 Day	Malcolm Group	Haydock
L 478	T452 TTW	Scania	P94D 310 4x2 Day	Malcolm Group	Linwood
L 479	T453 TTW	Scania	P94D 310 4x2 Day	Malcolm Group	Castleford
L 480	SF05 KMZ	Volvo	FM12 380 4x2 Day	Malcolm Group	Castleford
L 481	SF05 KNC	Volvo	FM12 380 4x2 Day	Malcolm Group	Alloa
L 482	SF05 KMY	Volvo	FM12 380 4x2 Day	Malcolm Group	Alloa
L 483	SF05 NUU	Volvo	FM12 380 4x2 Day	Malcolm Group	Leven
L 484	SF05 NUK	Volvo	FM12 380 4x2 Day	Malcolm Group	Castleford

L 485	SF05 NUM	Volvo	FM12 380 4x2 Day	Malcolm Group	Leven
L 508	SN15 LWA	Scania	R450 6x2 HL	Malcolm Group	Penrith
L 509	SN15 LWC	Scania	R450 6x2 HL	Malcolm Group	Penrith
L 510	SN15 LWE	Scania	R450 6x2 HL	Malcolm Group	Penrith
L 511	SN15 LWF	Scania	R450 6x2 HL	Malcolm Group	Penrith
L 515	SN65 MYW	Scania	R450 6x2 HL	Malcolm Group	Penrith
L 516	SN65 MYX	Scania	R450 6x2 HL	Malcolm Group	Penrith
L 517	SN65 MYY	Scania	R450 6x2 HL	Malcolm Group	Penrith
L 528	SF16 VDA	Volvo	FM 450 6x2 G	Malcolm Group	Castleford
L 529	SF17 WCY	Volvo	FH 460 6x2 G	Malcolm Group	
L 530	SF67 WBP	Volvo	FH 460 6x2 G	Malcolm Group	
L 534	SF67 WBT	Volvo	FH 460 6x2 G	Malcolm Group	
L 537	SF67 WBU	Volvo	FH 460 6x2 G	Malcolm Group	
L 543	PX18 UTR	Scania	R450 6x2 (NG) HL E6	Malcolm Group	
L 544	PX18 UTT	Scania	R450 6x2 (NG) HL E6	Malcolm Group	
L 546	PX18 UUA	Scania	R450 6x2 (NG) HL E6	Malcolm Group	
L 547	PX18 UUF	Scania	R450 6x2 (NG) HL E6	Malcolm Group	
L 548	PX18 UTP	Scania	R450 6x2 (NG) HL E6	Malcolm Group	
L 549	PX18 UTV	Scania	R450 6x2 (NG) HL E6	Malcolm Group	
L 550	SJ23 HHA	Man	TGX 26.470 6x2 GM	Malcolm Group	
L 551	SJ23 HHB	Man	TGX 26.470 6x2 GM	Malcolm Group	
L 552	SJ23 HHC	Man	TGX 26.470 6x2 GM	Malcolm Group	
L 553	SJ23 HHD	Man	TGX 26.470 6x2 GM	Malcolm Group	
L 554	SJ23 HHE	Man	TGX 26.470 6x2 GM	Malcolm Group	
L 555	SJ23 HHF	Man	TGX 26.470 6x2 GM	Malcolm Group	
L 556	SJ23 HHG	Man	TGX 26.470 6x2 GM	Malcolm Group	
L 558	SJ73 HLP	Man	TGX 26.470 6x2 GM	Malcolm Group	
L 564	SJ73 HLX	Man	TGX 26.470 6x2 GM	Malcolm Group	
L 565	SJ23 HJE	Man	TGX 26.470 6x2 GM	Malcolm Group	
L 568	KX15 MVU	Volvo	FH 460 6x2 G	Malcolm Group	Gatenby
L 569	KX15 MVV	Volvo	FH 460 6x2 G	Malcolm Group	Gatenby
L 570	SJ73 HLF	Man	TGX 26.470 6x2 GM	Malcolm Group	
L 571	SJ73 HMO	Man	TGX 26.470 6x2 GX	Malcolm Group	
L 572	SJ73 HMG	Man	TGX 26.470 6x2 GX	Malcolm Group	
L 573	SJ73 HMK	Man	TGX 26.470 6x2 GX	Malcolm Group	
L 574	SJ73 HJN	Man	TGX 26.470 6x2 GX	Malcolm Group	
L 575	SJ73 HJX	Man	TGX 26.470 6x2 GX	Malcolm Group	
L 576	SJ73 HLR	Man	TGX 26.470 6x2 GX	Malcolm Group	
L 577	SJ73 HMF	Man	TGX 26.470 6x2 GX	Malcolm Group	
L 578	SJ73 HMH	Man	TGX 26.470 6x2 GX	Malcolm Group	
L 579	SJ73 HJV	Man	TGX 26.470 6x2 GX	Malcolm Group	
L 580	SJ73 HLO	Man	TGX 26.470 6x2 GX	Malcolm Group	
L 581		Man	TGX 26.470 6x2 GX	Malcolm Group	
L 582	SJ73 HLH	Man	TGX 26.470 6x2 GX	Malcolm Group	
L 583	SJ73 HME	Man	TGX 26.470 6x2 GX	Malcolm Group	
L 584	SJ73 HLM	Man	TGX 26.470 6x2 GX	Malcolm Group	
L 585	SJ73 HJY	Man	TGX 26.470 6x2 GX	Malcolm Group	
L 586	SJ73 HJO	Man	TGX 26.470 6x2 GX	Malcolm Group	
L 587	SJ73 HJU	Man	TGX 26.470 6x2 GX	Malcolm Group	
L 588		Man	TGX 26.470 6x2 GX	Malcolm Group	
L 589		Man	TGX 26.470 6x2 GX	Malcolm Group	
L 590	SJ73 HJG	Man	TGX 26.470 6x2 GX	Malcolm Group	
L 591	SJ73 HJK	Man	TGX 26.470 6x2 GX	Malcolm Group	
L 600	SN15 LWO	Scania	R450 6x2 HL	Malcolm Group	Avonmouth
L 613	SN65 MYZ	Scania	G450 6X2 HL	Malcolm Group	Haydock
L 614	SN65 NAA	Scania	G450 6X2 HL	Malcolm Group	Haydock
L 615	SN65 NAE	Scania	G450 6X2 HL	Malcolm Group	Haydock
L 616	SN65 NAO	Scania	G450 6X2 HL	Malcolm Group	Haydock
L 617	SN65 NAU	Scania	G450 6X2 HL	Malcolm Group	Haydock

L 638	SN15 LWP	Scania	R450 6x2 HL	Malcolm Group	Haydock
L 639	SN67 SXR	Scania	G450 6X2 HL	Malcolm Group	
L 640	SL17 DMU	Scania	G450 6X2 HL	Malcolm Group	Grangemouth
L 641	SN67 SXS	Scania	G450 6X2 HL	Malcolm Group	
L 642	SN67 SXT	Scania	G450 6X2 HL	Malcolm Group	
L 643	SN67 SXU	Scania	G450 6X2 HL	Malcolm Group	
L 645	SN67 SXV	Scania	G450 6X2 HL	Malcolm Group	
L 646	SN67 SXW	Scania	G450 6X2 HL	Malcolm Group	
L 647	SN67 SXX	Scania	G450 6X2 HL	Malcolm Group	
L 648	SL17 DMF	Scania	G450 6X2 HL	Malcolm Group	Glenrothes
L 649	SN67 RYA	Scania	G450 6X2 HL	Malcolm Group	
L 655	SN67 SXY	Scania	G450 6X2 HL	Malcolm Group	
L 656	SL17 UHT	Scania	G450 6X2 HL	Malcolm Group	Glenrothes
L 657	SL17 UKU	Scania	G450 6X2 HL	Malcolm Group	Glenrothes
L 658	SL17 UKS	Scania	G450 6X2 HL	Malcolm Group	Glenrothes
L 659	SN67 SXZ	Scania	G450 6X2 HL	Malcolm Group	
L 660	SL17 UKV	Scania	G450 6X2 HL	Malcolm Group	Glenrothes
L 661	SL17 UKW	Scania	G450 6X2 HL	Malcolm Group	Leven
L 662	SL17 UKX	Scania	G450 6X2 HL	Malcolm Group	Leven
L 663	SL17 UKY	Scania	G450 6X2 HL	Malcolm Group	Grangemouth
L 664	SL17 ULS	Scania	G450 6X2 HL	Malcolm Group	Haydock
L 665	SN67 SYA	Scania	G450 6X2 HL	Malcolm Group	
L 666	SN67 RYB	Scania	G450 6X2 HL	Malcolm Group	
L 667	SN67 RYC	Scania	G450 6X2 HL	Malcolm Group	
L 668	SN67 RYD	Scania	G450 6X2 HL	Malcolm Group	
L 670	SN67 RYG	Scania	G450 6X2 HL	Malcolm Group	
L 671	SN67 RYH	Scania	G450 6X2 HL	Malcolm Group	
L 672	SN67 RYJ	Scania	G450 6X2 HL	Malcolm Group	
L 673	SN67 RYK	Scania	G450 6X2 HL	Malcolm Group	
L 674	SN67 RYM	Scania	G450 6X2 HL	Malcolm Group	
L 675	SN67 SYH	Scania	R450 6x2 (NG) HL E6	Malcolm Group	
L 676	SN67 SOA	Scania	R450 6x2 (NG) HL E6	Malcolm Group	
L 677	SN67 SOC	Scania	R450 6x2 (NG) HL E6	Malcolm Group	
L 682	SN15 LWR	Scania	R450 6x2 HL	Malcolm Group	Avonmouth
L 683	SN15 LWS	Scania	R450 6x2 HL	Malcolm Group	Avonmouth
L 684	SN15 LWT	Scania	R450 6x2 HL	Malcolm Group	Avonmouth
L 700	K12 TRS	Erf	E14 320 6x2	Malcolm Group	Haydock
L 701	SN15 LWV	Scania	R450 6x2 HL	Malcolm Group	Haydock
L 702	SN15 LWW	Scania	R450 6x2 HL	Malcolm Group	Haydock
L 703	SN15 LWX	Scania	R450 6x2 HL	Malcolm Group	Avonmouth
L 704	SF51 NFK	Erf	ECS 6x2 Day	Malcolm Group	Leven
L 705	SN15 LWY	Scania	R450 6x2 HL	Malcolm Group	Avonmouth
L 706	SN20 YJF	Scania	R450 6x2 (NG) NL E6	Malcolm Group	
L 707	SN20 YJG	Scania	R450 6x2 (NG) NL E6	Malcolm Group	
L 708	SN20 YJH	Scania	R450 6x2 (NG) NL E6	Malcolm Group	
L 709	SN20 YJJ	Scania	R450 6x2 (NG) NL E6	Malcolm Group	
L 710	SN20 YJD	Scania	R450 6x2 (NG) NL E6	Malcolm Group	
L 711	SN20 YJE	Scania	R450 6x2 (NG) NL E6	Malcolm Group	
L 712	SN20 YJL	Scania	R450 6x2 (NG) NL E6	Malcolm Group	
L 713	SN20 YJM	Scania	R450 6x2 (NG) NL E6	Malcolm Group	
L 714	SN20 YJO	Scania	R450 6x2 (NG) NL E6	Malcolm Group	
L 715	SN20 YJP	Scania	R450 6x2 (NG) NL E6	Malcolm Group	
L 716	SN20 YJC	Scania	R450 6x2 (NG) NL E6	Malcolm Group	
L 717	SN20 YJR	Scania	R450 6x2 (NG) NL E6	Malcolm Group	
L 718	SN20 YKC	Scania	R450 6x2 (NG) NL E6	Malcolm Group	
L 719	SN70 YRY	Scania	R450 6x2 (NG) NL E6	Malcolm Group	Gatenby
L 720	SN20 YJK	Scania	R450 6x2 (NG) NL E6	Malcolm Group	
L 721	SN70 YRU	Scania	R450 6x2 (NG) NL E6	Malcolm Group	Gatenby
L 722	SN70 YRV	Scania	R450 6x2 (NG) NL E6	Malcolm Group	Gatenby

W.H. Malcolm (cont)

L 723	SN70 YRW	Scania	R450 6x2 (NG) NL E6	Malcolm Group	Gatenby
L 724	SN20 YKG	Scania	R450 6x2 (NG) NL E6	Malcolm Group	
L 725	SN20 YKH	Scania	R450 6x2 (NG) NL E6	Malcolm Group	
L 726	SN70 YRX	Scania	R450 6x2 (NG) NL E6	Malcolm Group	Gatenby
L 727	SN20 YKA	Scania	R450 6x2 (NG) NL E6	Malcolm Group	
L 728	SN20 YKK	Scania	R450 6x2 (NG) NL E6	Malcolm Group	
L 729	SN20 YKL	Scania	R450 6x2 (NG) NL E6	Malcolm Group	
L 730	SN20 YKM	Scania	R450 6x2 (NG) NL E6	Malcolm Group	
L 731	SK21 BZA	Scania	R450 6x2 (NG) NL E6	Malcolm Group	
L 732	SK21 BZB	Scania	R450 6x2 (NG) NL E6	Malcolm Group	
L 733	SK21 BZC	Scania	R450 6x2 (NG) NL E6	Malcolm Group	
L 734	SK21 BZD	Scania	R450 6x2 (NG) NL E6	Malcolm Group	
L 735	SK21 BZE	Scania	R450 6x2 (NG) NL E6	Malcolm Group	
L 736	SK21 BZF	Scania	R450 6x2 (NG) NL E6	Malcolm Group	
L 737	SK21 BZG	Scania	R450 6x2 (NG) NL E6	Malcolm Group	
L 738	SK21 BZH	Scania	R450 6x2 (NG) NL E6	Malcolm Group	
L 739	SN22 YSG	Scania	R450 6x2 (NG) NL E6	Malcolm Group	Unknown
L 740	SN22 YSM	Scania	R450 6x2 (NG) NL E6	Malcolm Group	Unknown
L 741	SN22 YSJ	Scania	R450 6x2 (NG) NL E6	Malcolm Group	Unknown
L 742	SN22 YSL	Scania	R450 6x2 (NG) NL E6	Malcolm Group	Unknown
L 743	SN22 YSH	Scania	R450 6x2 (NG) NL E6	Malcolm Group	Unknown
L 744	SN22 YSF	Scania	R450 6x2 (NG) NL E6	Malcolm Group	Unknown
L 745	SN22 YSK	Scania	R450 6x2 (NG) NL E6	Malcolm Group	Unknown
L 746	SK21 BVF	Scania	R450 6x2 (NG) NL E6	Malcolm Group	
L 747	SK21 BVG	Scania	R450 6x2 (NG) NL E6	Malcolm Group	
L 748	SK21 BVH	Scania	R450 6x2 (NG) NL E6	Malcolm Group	
L 750	H19 WHM (64)	Man	TGX 26.440 6x2 XLX	Malcolm Group	
L 755	L10 WHM (16)	Scania	R450 6x2 Top	Malcolm Group	Haydock
L 756	L14 WHM (16)	Scania	R450 6x2 Top	Malcolm Group	Haydock
L 757	L16 WHM (16)	Scania	R450 6x2 Top	Malcolm Group	Haydock
L 758	L17 WHM (66)	Scania	R450 6x2 Top	Malcolm Group	Haydock
L 759	L18 WHM (16)	Scania	R450 6x2 Top	Malcolm Group	Haydock
L 760	L20 WHM (66)	Scania	R450 6x2 Top	Malcolm Group	Penrith
L 761	L25 WHM (16)	Scania	R450 6x2 Top	Malcolm Group	Haydock
L 762	L26 WHM (66)	Scania	R450 6x2 Top	Malcolm Group	
L 763	L27 WHM (16)	Scania	R450 6x2 Top	Malcolm Group	Haydock
L 764	L28 WHM (66)	Scania	R450 6x2 Top	Malcolm Group	
L 765	L29 WHM (16)	Scania	R450 6x2 Top	Malcolm Group	Penrith
L 766	L20 WHM (16)	Scania	R450 6x2 Top	Malcolm Group	Penrith
L 767	L31 WHM (66)	Scania	R450 6x2 Top	Malcolm Group	Penrith
L 768	L40 WHM (16)	Scania	R450 6x2 Top	Malcolm Group	Penrith
L 769	SF66 BMV	Scania	R450 6x2 Top	Malcolm Group	Penrith
L 770	L900 WHM (66)	Scania	R450 6x2 Top	Malcolm Group	
L 771	L70 WHM (66)	Scania	R450 6x2 Top	Malcolm Group	
L 772	L77 WHM (66)	Scania	R450 6x2 Top	Malcolm Group	
L 773	L80 WHM (66)	Scania	R450 6x2 Top	Malcolm Group	
L 774	L90 WHM (66)	Scania	R450 6x2 Top	Malcolm Group	
L 775	L60 WHM (66)	Scania	R450 6x2 Top	Malcolm Group	
L 776	L222 WHM (66)	Scania	R450 6x2 Top	Malcolm Group	
L 777	L300 WHM (66)	Scania	R450 6x2 Top	Malcolm Group	
L 778	L333 WHM (66)	Scania	R450 6x2 Top	Malcolm Group	
L 779	L444 WHM (66)	Scania	R450 6x2 Top	Malcolm Group	
L 780	L500 WHM (66)	Scania	R450 6x2 Top	Malcolm Group	
L 781	L600 WHM (66)	Scania	R450 6x2 Top	Malcolm Group	
L 782	L666 WHM (66)	Scania	R450 6x2 Top	Malcolm Group	Penrith
L 783	L700 WHM (66)	Scania	R450 6x2 Top	Malcolm Group	Haydock
L 784	SF17 AEB	Scania	R450 6x2 Top	Malcolm Group	Penrith
L 785	L777 WHM (16)	Scania	R450 6x2 Top	Malcolm Group	Penrith
L 786	L800 WHM (66)	Scania	R450 6x2 Top	Malcolm Group	Penrith

L 787	SF17 AEJ	Scania	R450 6x2 Top	Malcolm Group	
L 788	SF17 AEK	Scania	R450 6x2 Top	Malcolm Group	
L 789	SF17 AEL	Scania	R450 6x2 Top	Malcolm Group	
L 790	SF17 AEM	Scania	R450 6x2 Top	Malcolm Group	
L 791	SF17 AEN	Scania	R450 6x2 Top	Malcolm Group	
L 792	L888 WHM (16)	Scania	R450 6x2 Top	Malcolm Group	Penrith
L 793	SF17 AEC	Scania	R450 6x2 Top	Malcolm Group	Penrith
L 794	SF17 AED	Scania	R450 6x2 Top	Malcolm Group	
L 795	SF17 AEE	Scania	R450 6x2 Top	Malcolm Group	
L 796	SF17 AEG	Scania	R450 6x2 Top	Malcolm Group	Penrith
L 797	S19 WHM (17)	Scania	S730 6x2 (NG) HL E6	Malcolm Group	
L 798	M19 WHM (21)	Man	TGX 26.640 6x2 GX	Malcolm Group	
L 820	SJ18 GWF	Man	TGX 26.460 6x2 XXL	Malcolm Group	
L 821	SJ18 GWK	Man	TGX 26.460 6x2 XXL	Malcolm Group	
L 822	SJ18 GWL	Man	TGX 26.460 6x2 XXL	Malcolm Group	
L 823	SJ18 GWN	Man	TGX 26.460 6x2 XXL	Malcolm Group	
L 824	SJ18 GWO	Man	TGX 26.460 6x2 XXL	Malcolm Group	
L 831	SJ68 OPC	Man	TGX 26.460 6x2 XXL	Malcolm Group	Grangemouth
L 832	SJ68 OPD	Man	TGX 26.460 6x2 XXL	Malcolm Group	
L 846	SJ19 OCW	Volvo	FH 500 6x2 G	Malcolm Group	
L 847	SJ19 OCG	Volvo	FH 500 6x2 G	Malcolm Group	
L 848	SJ19 OCK	Volvo	FH 500 6x2 G	Malcolm Group	
L 849	SJ19 OBV	Volvo	FH 500 6x2 G	Malcolm Group	
L 850	SJ19 OCR	Volvo	FH 500 6x2 G	Malcolm Group	
L 851	SJ19 OBY	Volvo	FH 500 6x2 G	Malcolm Group	
L 852	SJ19 OCP	Volvo	FH 500 6x2 G	Malcolm Group	
L 853	SJ19 OBU	Volvo	FH 500 6x2 G	Malcolm Group	
L 854	SJ19 OCS	Volvo	FH 500 6x2 G	Malcolm Group	
L 855	SJ19 OCM	Volvo	FH 500 6x2 G	Malcolm Group	
L 856	SJ19 OCN	Volvo	FH 500 6x2 G	Malcolm Group	
L 857	SJ19 OBZ	Volvo	FH 500 6x2 G	Malcolm Group	
L 858	SJ19 OCV	Volvo	FH 500 6x2 G	Malcolm Group	
L 859	SJ19 OBC	Volvo	FH 500 6x2 G	Malcolm Group	
L 860	SJ19 OBM	Volvo	FH 500 6x2 G	Malcolm Group	
L 861	SJ19 OAM	Volvo	FH 500 6x2 G	Malcolm Group	
L 862	SJ19 OBL	Volvo	FH 500 6x2 G	Malcolm Group	
L 863	SJ19 OBK	Volvo	FH 500 6x2 G	Malcolm Group	
L 864	SJ19 OAX	Volvo	FH 500 6x2 G	Malcolm Group	
L 865	SJ19 OCH	Volvo	FH 500 6x2 G	Malcolm Group	
L 867	SJ19 OBB	Volvo	FH 500 6x2 G	Malcolm Group	
L 868	SJ19 OAW	Volvo	FH 500 6x2 G	Malcolm Group	
L 869	SJ19 OAP	Volvo	FH 500 6x2 G	Malcolm Group	Gatenby
L 870	SJ19 OAV	Volvo	FH 500 6x2 G	Malcolm Group	Gatenby
L 871	SJ19 OAU	Volvo	FH 500 6x2 G	Malcolm Group	
L 872	SJ19 OCE	Volvo	FH 500 6x2 G	Malcolm Group	
L 873	SJ19 OAY	Volvo	FH 500 6x2 G	Malcolm Group	
L 874	SJ19 OAO	Volvo	FH 500 6x2 G	Malcolm Group	
L 875	SJ19 OBT	Volvo	FH 500 6x2 G	Malcolm Group	
L 876	SJ19 OAS	Volvo	FH 500 6x2 G	Malcolm Group	
L 877	SJ19 OBN	Volvo	FH 500 6x2 G	Malcolm Group	
L 879	SJ19 OCB	Volvo	FH 500 6x2 G	Malcolm Group	
L 880	SJ19 OCO	Volvo	FH 500 6x2 G	Malcolm Group	
L 881	SJ19 OBH	Volvo	FH 500 6x2 G	Malcolm Group	
L 883	SJ19 OCL	Volvo	FH 500 6x2 G	Malcolm Group	
L 884	SJ19 OBW	Volvo	FH 500 6x2 G	Malcolm Group	
L 885	SJ19 OBF	Volvo	FH 500 6x2 G	Malcolm Group	
L 886	SJ19 OBR	Volvo	FH 500 6x2 G	Malcolm Group	
L 887	SJ19 OBO	Volvo	FH 500 6x2 G	Malcolm Group	
L 888	SJ69 CUO	Volvo	FH 500 6x2 G	Malcolm Group	

W.H. Malcolm (cont)

L 889	SJ19 OAZ	Volvo	FH 500 6x2 G	Malcolm Group	
L 890	SJ69 CUY	Volvo	FH 500 6x2 G	Malcolm Group	
L 891	SJ69 CUU	Volvo	FH 500 6x2 G	Malcolm Group	
L 892	SJ69 CVB	Volvo	FH 500 6x2 G	Malcolm Group	
L 893	SJ69 CUX	Volvo	FH 500 6x2 G	Malcolm Group	
L 894	SJ69 CUW	Volvo	FH 500 6x2 G	Malcolm Group	
L 895	SJ69 CUV	Volvo	FH 500 6x2 G	Malcolm Group	
L 896	SJ69 CUK	Volvo	FH 500 6x2 G	Malcolm Group	
L 897	SJ69 CUH	Volvo	FH 500 6x2 G	Malcolm Group	
L 898	SJ69 CVA	Volvo	FH 500 6x2 G	Malcolm Group	
L 899	SJ69 CVC	Volvo	FH 500 6x2 G	Malcolm Group	
L 900	X859 BFJ	Man	M2000 18.224 4w Gritter	Construction	Gatenby
L 901	X862 BFJ	Man	M2000 18.224 4w Gritter	Yellow	Grangemouth
L 902	X866 BFJ	Man	M2000 18.224 4w Gritter	Construction	Newhouse
L 903	X867 BFJ	Man	M2000 18.224 4w Gritter	Yellow	Avonmouth
L 904	HX05 DWM	Mercedes	Econic 1823 4w Gritter	Malcolm Group	Clydeside
L 910	YN53 MJK	Mercedes	Atego 1823 4w Gritter	Orange	Crick
L 911	YN53 MJX	Mercedes	Atego 1823 4w Gritter	Orange	Linwood
L 957	SN65 NBA	Scania	G450 6X2 HL	Malcolm Group	Crick
L 960	SN65 NBK	Scania	G450 6X2 HL	Malcolm Group	Crick
L 961	SN65 NBM	Scania	G450 6X2 HL	Malcolm Group	Crick
L 962	SN65 NBO	Scania	G450 6X2 HL	Malcolm Group	Crick
L 964	SN65 NBY	Scania	G450 6X2 HL	Malcolm Group	Crick
L 965	SN65 NBZ	Scania	G450 6X2 HL	Malcolm Group	Crick
L 966	SN65 NCA	Scania	G450 6X2 HL	Malcolm Group	Crick
L 967	SN65 NCC	Scania	G450 6X2 HL	Malcolm Group	Crick
L 969	SN65 NCE	Scania	G450 6X2 HL	Malcolm Group	Crick
L 970	SN65 NCF	Scania	G450 6X2 HL	Malcolm Group	Crick
L 972	SN65 NCO	Scania	G450 6X2 HL	Malcolm Group	Crick
L 973	SN65 NCU	Scania	G450 6X2 HL	Malcolm Group	Crick
L 975	SN65 NCY	Scania	G450 6X2 HL	Malcolm Group	Crick
L 976	SN65 NCZ	Scania	G450 6X2 HL	Malcolm Group	Crick
L 978	SN65 NDF	Scania	G450 6X2 HL	Malcolm Group	Crick
L 979	SN65 NDG	Scania	G450 6X2 HL	Malcolm Group	Crick
L 981	SN65 NDD	Scania	G450 6X2 HL	Malcolm Group	Crick
L	SJ72 HFX	Man	TGX 26.470 6x2 GM	Malcolm Group	
L	SJ72 HGD	Man	TGX 26.470 6x2 GM	Malcolm Group	
PL300	R16 WHM (11)	Volvo	FH16 600 8x4 GXL	Construction	
PL305	R11 WHM (63)	Volvo	FH 540 6x2	Construction	Clydeside
PL309	R9 WHM (22)	Volvo	FE 280 4w Flatbed	Construction	
PL312	R12 WHM (16)	Scania	R450 6x2 HL	Construction	Clydeside
PL313	R13 WHM (17)	Scania	R580 6x2 HL	Construction	
PL314	R14 WHM (21)	Scania	R580 XT 6x4	Construction	
PL315	R15 WHM (21)	Scania	R580 XT 6x4	Construction	
PL317	R17 WHM (66)	Scania	G410 8w HL Flatbed	Construction	Clydeside
PL318	R18 WHM (67)	Scania	G410 8w Flatbed	Construction	
PL320	R20 WHM (70)	Scania	G450 XT 8w Beavertail	Construction	
WHM40	R40 WHM (56)	Volvo	FH 520 8w GXL Recovery	Construction	Clydeside
WHM200	V200 WHM (V)	Volvo	FH12 6x2 G	Malcolm Group	Linwood
	L19 WHM	Scania	R580 4x2 (Longline)	Braveheart	
	N19 WHM (55)	Volvo	NH12 6x2	Black	
	R30 WHM (11)	Volvo	FH 460 6w GXL Recovery	Construction	Linwood
	S20 WHM (15)	Scania	P250 4w Sweeper LHD	Construction	
	T19 WHM	Scania	T 4x2 Top LHD	Construction	
	V100 WHM	Volvo	FH16 VTS 6x2 GXL	WHM Maroon	Linwood
	WHM 601 (64)	Volvo	FH 460 6w GXL Horsebox	Special	Linwood
	Q82 RDS	Scania	111 6w	Construction	Linwood
	FG58 YJS	Mercedes	Actros 2636 6w Skip	Green	
	SL64 ZVN	Daf	FTGCF 440 6x2 SC	White	

W.H. Malcolm (cont)

WR15 WVG	Scania	R450 6x2 HL	White
BV65 JUK	Mercedes	Actros 2545 6x2 SSC	White
MX65 FMV	Renault	T460 6x2	White
KX66 YUG	Mercedes	Actros 2545 6x2 BSC	White
KX66 YVZ	Mercedes	Actros 2545 6x2 SSC	White
MX67 ENM	Daf	FTGXF 460 6x2 SC	White
NK69 XMV	Mercedes	Actros 2548 6x2 BSC	White
RE69 FAA	Daf	FTGXF 530 6x2 SSC	Malcolm Group
RK69 DNV	Daf	FTGXF 530 6x2 SSC	Malcolm Group
BG21 RWF	Renault	T480 6x2 HSC	WHM White
FN71 CKF	Daf	FTGCF 480 6x2 SC	WHM White
RK72 FEX	Man	TGX 26.510 6x2 GX	WHM White
SJ73 HBH	Daf	FTG 530 6x2 (XG+)	Malcolm Group
SJ73 HLE	Man	TGX 26.470 6x2 GM	Malcolm Group
SJ73 HLG	Man	TGX 26.470 6x2 GM	Malcolm Group

W S Transportation & Explore

4x 113	WIW 113 (N)	Scania P113M 320 4x2	WS Transportation	Runcorn
6x 650	22 WS (20)	Scania S650 6x2 (NG) HL V8	WST V8 S/Edition	Penrith
6x 746	PN22 DPE	Scania S540 6x2 (NG) HL E6	WS Transportation	Bolton
6x 747	PN22 DOJ	Scania S540 6x2 (NG) HL E6	WS Transportation	Runcorn
6x 757	PN22 DSY	Scania R540 6x2 (NG) HL E6 (Tag)	WS Transportation	Coventry
6x 758	PN22 DTF	Scania S540 6x2 (NG) HL E6 (Tag)	WS Transportation	Thirsk
6x 766	PN22 DVK	Scania 660S 6x2 (NG) HL E6 V8 Tag	WS Transportation	Thirsk
6x 774	PN22 DVO	Scania 660S 6x2 (NG) HL E6 V8 Tag	White/Black	
6x 776	PN22 DVR	Scania 660S 6x2 (NG) HL E6 V8 Tag	WS Transportation	Runcorn
6x 781	PN22 DVX	Scania 660S 6x2 (NG) HL E6 V8 Tag	WS Transportation	Runcorn
6x 784	KY22 DZC	Scania R500 6x2 (NG) HL E6	WS Transportation	Bedford
6x 785	KY22 DZD	Scania S450 6x2 (NG) HL E6	WS Transportation	Runcorn
6x 786	KY22 DZE	Scania S450 6x2 (NG) HL E6	Autotrail	Thirsk
6x 787	KY22 DZF	Scania S450 6x2 (NG) HL E6	WS Transportation	Ireland
6x 790	PJ22 HDY	Scania R540 6x2 (NG) HL E6 (Tag)	WS Transportation	Thirsk
6x 791	PJ22 HFC	Scania R540 6x2 (NG) HL E6 (Tag)	WS Transportation	Immingham
6x 794	PJ22 HFX	Scania R540 6x2 (NG) HL E6 (Tag)	WS Transportation	Coventry
6x 795	S500 WST	Scania R540 6x2 (NG) HL E6 (Tag)	WS Transportation	Ireland
6x 796	PJ22 HFL	Scania R500 6x2 (NG) HL E6	WS Transportation	Ireland
6x 797	PJ22 HFM	Scania R540 6x2 (NG) HL E6 (Tag)	WS Transportation	Ireland
6x 800	PN72 DVY	Scania R500 6x2 (NG) HL E6	WS Transportation	Loughborough
6x 801	PN72 DVM	Scania R500 6x2 (NG) HL E6	WS Transportation	Runcorn
6x 803	PN72 DVO	Scania R500 6x2 (NG) HL E6	WS Transportation	Thirsk
6x 807	PN72 DWG	Scania R450 6x2 (NG) HL E6	WS Transportation	Ireland
6x 808				
6x 809	Y9 WST (72)	Scania 660S 6x2 (NG) HL E6 V8 Tag	WS Transportation	Wisbech
6x 815	PN72 DVW	Scania R500 6x2 (NG) HL E6	WS Transportation	Coventry
6x 817	PN72 DVR	Scania R500 6x2 (NG) HL E6	WS Transportation	Runcorn
6x 822	PN72 DPZ	Scania R540 6x2 (NG) HL E6 (Tag)	WS Transportation	Immingham
6x 824	PN72 DRO	Scania R540 6x2 (NG) HL E6 (Tag)	WS Transportation	Immingham
6x 825	PN72 DTZ	Scania R500 6x2 (NG) HL E6	WS Transportation	Thirsk
8x 828	PN72 DYA	Scania R500 6x2 (NG) HL E6	WS Transportation	Thirsk
6x 830	PN72 DYD	Scania R500 6x2 (NG) HL E6	WS Transportation	Ireland
6x 831	PN72 DXE	Scania R500 6x2 (NG) HL E6	WS Transportation	Thirsk
6x 836	PN72 DXC	Scania R500 6x2 (NG) HL E6	WS Transportation	Thirsk
6x 838	PN72 DZU	Scania R500 6x2 (NG) HL E6	WS Transportation	Thirsk
6x 839	PN72 DXD	Scania R500 6x2 (NG) HL E6	WS Transportation	Thirsk
6x 840	PN72 DZV	Scania R500 6x2 (NG) HL E6	WS Transportation	Thirsk
6x 842	PN72 EAW	Scania R500 6x2 (NG) HL E6	WS Transportation	Loughborough
6x 845	PK72 XJZ	Scania R500 6x2 (NG) HL E6	WS Transportation	Bootle
6x 850	PK72 XJW	Scania R500 6x2 (NG) HL E6	WS Transportation	Thirsk

6x 852	PK72 XKL	Scania R500 6x2 (NG) HL E6	WS Transportation	Runcorn
6x 853	PK72 XLH	Scania R500 6x2 (NG) HL E6	WS Transportation	Thirsk
6x 856	PK72 XKC	Scania R500 6x2 (NG) HL E6	WS Transportation	Loughborough
6x 857	PK72 XKG	Scania R500 6x2 (NG) HL E6	WS Transportation	Runcorn
6x 860	PK72 XJO	Scania R500 6x2 (NG) HL E6	WS Transportation	Immingham
6x 861	PK72 XKF	Scania R500 6x2 (NG) HL E6	WS Transportation	Immingham
6x 862	PK72 XLB	Scania R500 6x2 (NG) HL E6	WS Transportation	Immingham
6x 863	PK72 XKO	Scania R500 6x2 (NG) HL E6	WS Transportation	Runcorn
6x 864	PK72 XKM	Scania R500 6x2 (NG) HL E6	WS Transportation	Immingham
6x 865	PK72 XKP	Scania R500 6x2 (NG) HL E6	WS Transportation	Immingham
6x 866	PK72 XKU	Scania R500 6x2 (NG) HL E6	WS Transportation	Aveley
6x 867	PK72 XKZ	Scania R500 6x2 (NG) HL E6	WS Transportation	Immingham
6x 868	PK72 XKW	Scania R500 6x2 (NG) HL E6	WS Transportation	Immingham
6x 869	PK72 XKY	Scania R500 6x2 (NG) HL E6	WS Transportation	Runcorn
6x 872	PK72 XKT	Scania R500 6x2 (NG) HL E6	WS Transportation	Coventry
6x 874	PJ72 OOC	Scania R500 6x2 (NG) HL E6	WS Transportation	Coventry
6x 875	PN23 EAJ	Scania 500R 6x2 (NG) HL E6	WS Transportation	Runcorn
6x 876	PN23 EAG	Scania 500R 6x2 (NG) HL E6	WS Transportation	Runcorn
6x 877	PJ72 OOF	Scania R500 6x2 (NG) HL E6	WS Transportation	Runcorn
6x 878	PN23 DZU	Scania 500R 6x2 (NG) HL E6	WS Transportation	Coventry
6x 879	PN23 DZT	Scania 500R 6x2 (NG) HL E6	WS Transportation	Thirsk
6x 880	PN23 DZW	Scania 500R 6x2 (NG) HL E6	WS Transportation	Wyboston
6x 881	PJ72 OOV	Scania R500 6x2 (NG) HL E6	WS Transportation	Runcorn
6x 882	PN23 DZV	Scania 500R 6x2 (NG) HL E6	WS Transportation	Coventry
6x 884	PJ72 OOY	Scania R500 6x2 (NG) HL E6	WS Transportation	Runcorn
6x 885	PN23 EAM	Scania 500R 6x2 (NG) HL E6	WS Transportation	Wyboston
6x 886	PN23 EAK	Scania 500R 6x2 (NG) HL E6	WS Transportation	Wyboston
6x 888	PK72 XLC	Scania 540S 6x2 (NG) HL E6	WS Transportation	Loughborough
6x 889	PK72 XLE	Scania 540S 6x2 (NG) HL E6	Middlebrook	South Normanton
6x 890	PK72 XLG	Scania 540S 6x2 (NG) HL E6	Middlebrook	South Normanton
6x 892	PN72 DVA	Scania R500 6x2 (NG) HL E6	WS Transportation	Thirsk
6x 894	PN72 DSZ	Scania R500 6x2 (NG) HL E6	WS Transportation	Ireland
6x 897	PK72 XKN	Scania R500 6x2 (NG) HL E6	WS Transportation	Bolton
6x 899	PK72 XLA	Scania R500 6x2 (NG) HL E6	WS Transportation	Immingham
6x 900	PJ72 ONP	Scania S500 6x2 (NG) HL E6	Middlebrook	South Normanton
6x 901	PJ72 ONT	Scania S500 6x2 (NG) HL E6	WS Transportation	Ireland
6x 902	PJ72 OMY	Scania S500 6x2 (NG) HL E6	Middlebrook	South Normanton
6x 903	PJ72 ONA	Scania S500 6x2 (NG) HL E6	Middlebrook	South Normanton
6x 904	PJ72 ONL	Scania S500 6x2 (NG) HL E6	WS Transportation	Ireland
6x 905	PK72 XLF	Scania 540S 6x2 (NG) HL E6	Middlebrook	South Normanton
6x 906				
6x 907	PN23 DZL	Scania 660S 6x2 (NG) HL E6 V8 Tag	WS Transportation	Runcorn
6x 908	PN23 DZO	Scania 500R 6x2 (NG) HL E6	WS Transportation	Runcorn
6x 909	PN23 DZP	Scania 500R 6x2 (NG) HL E6	WS Transportation	Thirsk
6x 910	MY66 OVB (23)	Scania 660S 6x2 (NG) HL E6 V8 Tag	WS Transportation	Bolton
6x 911	PJ22 HGA	Scania R500 6x2 (NG) HL E6	WS Transportation	Middlesborough
6x 912	PJ22 HFF	Scania R500 6x2 (NG) HL E6	WS Transportation	Middlesborough
6x 913	PJ72 FEX	Scania R500 6x2 (NG) HL E6	WS Transportation	
6x 914	PJ22 HGC	Scania R500 6x2 (NG) HL E6	WS Transportation	
6x 915	PN72 DSE	Scania R500 6x2 (NG) HL E6	WS Transportation	Grangemouth
6x 916	PK72 XLJ	Scania R500 6x2 (NG) HL E6	WS Transportation	
6x 918	PJ72 FEU	Scania R500 6x2 (NG) HL E6	WS Transportation	
6x 919	PJ72 FEV	Scania R500 6x2 (NG) HL E6	WS Transportation	
6x 920	PJ72 FFA	Scania R500 6x2 (NG) HL E6	WS Transportation	
6x 921	PJ72 FFO	Scania R500 6x2 (NG) HL E6	WS Transportation	
6x 922	PJ72 FFL	Scania R500 6x2 (NG) HL E6	WS Transportation	
6x 923	PJ72 FFN	Scania R500 6x2 (NG) HL E6	WS Transportation	
6x 924	PJ72 FFC	Scania R500 6x2 (NG) HL E6	WS Transportation	
6x 926	PJ72 FFE	Scania R500 6x2 (NG) HL E6	WS Transportation	
6x 927	PJ72 FFK	Scania R500 6x2 (NG) HL E6	WS Transportation	
6x 928	PJ72 FFP	Scania R500 6x2 (NG) HL E6	WS Transportation	

Fleet	Reg	Vehicle	Operator	Location
6x 929	PJ72 FFB	Scania R500 6x2 (NG) HL E6	WS Transportation	
6x 930	PJ72 FFD	Scania R500 6x2 (NG) HL E6	WS Transportation	
6x 931	PJ72 OMU	Scania R500 6x2 (NG) HL E6	WS Transportation	
6x 932	PJ72 FFS	Scania R500 6x2 (NG) HL E6	WS Transportation	
6x 933	PJ72 FFT	Scania R500 6x2 (NG) HL E6	WS Transportation	
6x 934	PJ72 FFV	Scania R500 6x2 (NG) HL E6	WS Transportation	
6x 935	PJ72 FFW	Scania R500 6x2 (NG) HL E6	WS Transportation	
6x 936	PJ72 FFU	Scania R500 6x2 (NG) HL E6	WS Transportation	
6x 937	PJ72 OMR	Scania R500 6x2 (NG) HL E6	WS Transportation	
6x 938	PJ72 OMO	Scania R500 6x2 (NG) HL E6	WS Transportation	
6x 939	PJ72 OMP	Scania R500 6x2 (NG) HL E6	WS Transportation	
6x 940	PN72 DZP	Scania R500 6x2 (NG) HL E6	WS Transportation	
6x 941	PJ72 FFR	Scania R500 6x2 (NG) HL E6	WS Transportation	
6x 942	PN72 DSO	Scania R500 6x2 (NG) HL E6	WS Transportation	
6x 943	PJ72 FET	Scania R500 6x2 (NG) HL E6	WS Transportation	
6x 946	PN72 DWW	Scania R500 6x2 (NG) HL E6	WS Transportation	Wisbech
6x 950	PJ72 ONB	Scania R500 6x2 (NG) HL E6	Smith Bros Demo	
6x 951	PN23 EAW	Scania 460R 6x2 (NG) HL E6	WS Transportation	Loughborough
6x 952	PN23 EAX	Scania 460R 6x2 (NG) HL E6	WS Transportation	Runcorn
6x 953	PN23 EAY	Scania 460R 6x2 (NG) HL E6	WS Transportation	Wombourne
6x 954	PN23 EBA	Scania 460R 6x2 (NG) HL E6	WS Transportation	Runcorn
6x 955	PN23 EBC	Scania 460R 6x2 (NG) HL E6	WS Transportation	Wombourne
6x 956	PN23 EBD	Scania 460R 6x2 (NG) HL E6	WS Transportation	Runcorn
6x 957	PN23 EBF	Scania 460R 6x2 (NG) HL E6	WS Transportation	Wyboston
6x 958	PN23 EBG	Scania 460R 6x2 (NG) HL E6	Middlebrook	
6x 959	PN23 EBJ	Scania 460R 6x2 (NG) HL E6	Middlebrook	
6x 960	PN23 EBK	Scania 460R 6x2 (NG) HL E6	Middlebrook	
6x 961	PN23 EBL	Scania 460R 6x2 (NG) HL E6	Middlebrook	
6x 962	PN23 EBM	Scania 460R 6x2 (NG) HL E6	WS Transportation	Runcorn
6x 963	PN23 EBO	Scania 460R 6x2 (NG) HL E6	WS Transportation	Runcorn
6x 964	PN23 EBP	Scania 460R 6x2 (NG) HL E6	WS Transportation	Wyboston
6x 965	PN23 EBU	Scania 460R 6x2 (NG) HL E6	WS Transportation	Thirsk
6x 966	PN23 EBV	Scania 460R 6x2 (NG) HL E6	WS Transportation	Thirsk
6x 967	PN23 EBX	Scania 460R 6x2 (NG) HL E6	WS Transportation	Runcorn
6x 968	PN23 EBZ	Scania 460R 6x2 (NG) HL E6	WS Transportation	Runcorn
6x 969	PN23 ECA	Scania 460R 6x2 (NG) HL E6	WS Transportation	Thirsk
6x 970	PN23 ECC	Scania 460R 6x2 (NG) HL E6	WS Transportation	Runcorn
6x 971	PN23 ECD	Scania 460R 6x2 (NG) HL E6	WS Transportation	Winsford
6x 972	PN23 ECF	Scania 460R 6x2 (NG) HL E6	WS Transportation	Sherburn
6x 973	PN23 EVM	Scania 460R 6x2 (NG) HL E6	WS Transportation	Runcorn
6x 974	PN23 EVP	Scania 460R 6x2 (NG) HL E6	WS Transportation	Runcorn
6x 975	PN23 EVR	Scania 460R 6x2 (NG) HL E6	WS Transportation	Runcorn
6x 976	PN23 EVT	Scania 460R 6x2 (NG) HL E6	WS Transportation	Coventry
6x 977	PN23 EVU	Scania 460R 6x2 (NG) HL E6	WS Transportation	Wombourne
6x 978	PN23 EVV	Scania 460R 6x2 (NG) HL E6	WS Transportation	Runcorn
6x 979	PN23 EVW	Scania 460R 6x2 (NG) HL E6	WS Transportation	Runcorn
6x 980	PN23 EVX	Scania 460R 6x2 (NG) HL E6	WS Transportation	Thirsk
6x 981	PN23 EVY	Scania 460R 6x2 (NG) HL E6	WS Transportation	Loughborough
6x 982	PN23 EWA	Scania 460R 6x2 (NG) HL E6	WS Transportation	Wyboston
6x 983	PN23 EWB	Scania 460R 6x2 (NG) HL E6	WS Transportation	Runcorn
6x 984	PN23 EWC	Scania 460R 6x2 (NG) HL E6	WS Transportation	Wisbech
6x 985	PN23 EWD	Scania 460R 6x2 (NG) HL E6	WS Transportation	Runcorn
6x 986	PN23 EWE	Scania 460R 6x2 (NG) HL E6	WS Transportation	
6x 987	PN23 EWF	Scania 460R 6x2 (NG) HL E6	WS Transportation	Loughborough
6x 988	PN23 EWG	Scania 460R 6x2 (NG) HL E6	WS Transportation	Winsford
6x 989	PN23 EWH	Scania 460R 6x2 (NG) HL E6	WS Transportation	Wombourne
6x 990	PN23 EWJ	Scania 460R 6x2 (NG) HL E6	WS Transportation	Runcorn
6x 991	PN23 EWK	Scania 460R 6x2 (NG) HL E6	WS Transportation	Thirsk
6x 992	PN23 EWM	Scania 460R 6x2 (NG) HL E6	WS Transportation	Thirsk
6x 993	PN23 EWO	Scania 460R 6x2 (NG) HL E6	WS Transportation	Thirsk
6x 994				

6x 995				
6x 996				
6x 997	PN23 DZR	Scania 500R 6x2 (NG) HL E6	WS Transportation	Wombourne
6x 998	PN23 DZX	Scania 500R 6x2 (NG) HL E6	WS Transportation	Loughborough
6x 999	PN23 DZZ	Scania 500R 6x2 (NG) HL E6	WS Transportation	Coventry
6x 1000	PN23 EAF	Scania 500R 6x2 (NG) HL E6	WS Transportation	Runcorn
6x 1001	PN23 EAO	Scania 500R 6x2 (NG) HL E6	WS Transportation	Coventry
6x 1002	PN23 EAA	Scania 500R 6x2 (NG) HL E6	WS Transportation	Loughborough
6x 1003	PN23 EAC	Scania 500R 6x2 (NG) HL E6	WS Transportation	Runcorn
6x 1004	PN23 DZS	Scania 500R 6x2 (NG) HL E6	WS Transportation	Coventry
6x 1005	PN23 EAE	Scania 500R 6x2 (NG) HL E6	WS Transportation	Loughborough
6x 1006	PN23 EAP	Scania 500R 6x2 (NG) HL E6	WS Transportation	Coventry
6x 1007	PK23 LNG	Scania 500R 6x2 (NG) HL E6	Middlebrook	
6x 1008	PK23 LNJ	Scania 500R 6x2 (NG) HL E6	Middlebrook	
6x 1009	PK23 LNN	Scania 500R 6x2 (NG) HL E6	Middlebrook	
6x 1010	PK23 LNO	Scania 500R 6x2 (NG) HL E6	WS Transportation	
6x 1011				
6x 1012	PN73 EVJ	Scania 500R 6x2 (NG) HL E6	Middlebrook	
6x 1013	PK23 LRE	Scania 460R 6x2 (NG) HL E6	WS Transportation	Wyboston
6x 1014	PK23 LRF	Scania 460R 6x2 (NG) HL E6	WS Transportation	Wyboston
6x 1015	PK23 LRJ	Scania 460R 6x2 (NG) HL E6	WS Transportation	Wyboston
6x 1016	PK23 LRL	Scania 460R 6x2 (NG) HL E6	WS Transportation	Wyboston
6x 1017	PK23 LRN	Scania 460R 6x2 (NG) HL E6	WS Transportation	Wyboston
6x 1018	PK23 LRO	Scania 460R 6x2 (NG) HL E6	WS Transportation	Wyboston
6x 1019	PK23 LPJ	Scania 500R 6x2 (NG) HL E6	WS Transportation	Ireland
6x 1020	PJ23 MXK	Scania 460R 6x2 (NG) HL E6	WS Transportation	Runcorn
6x 1021	PK23 LPL	Scania 500R 6x2 (NG) HL E6	WS Transportation	Ireland
6x 1022	PJ23 MXL	Scania 500R 6x2 (NG) HL E6	WS Transportation	Runcorn
6x 1023	PJ23 MXT	Scania 460R 6x2 (NG) HL E6	WS Transportation	Immingham
6x 1024	PJ23 MXM	Scania 460R 6x2 (NG) HL E6	CLD Fencing	Bolton
6x 1025	PJ23 MXV	Scania 460R 6x2 (NG) HL E6	WS Transportation	
6x 1026	PJ23 MXR	Scania 460R 6x2 (NG) HL E6	Middlebrook	
6x 1027	PN21 FHU	Scania R500 6x2 (NG) HL E6	WS Transportation	
6x 1027	PF23 ESY	Scania 460R 6x2 (NG) HL E6	WS Transportation	
6x 1028	PF23 VNB	Scania 460R 6x2 (NG) HL E6	WS Transportation	
6x 1029	PF23 ESG	Scania 460R 6x2 (NG) HL E6	WS Transportation	
6x 1030	PF23 VMX	Scania 460R 6x2 (NG) HL E6	WS Transportation	
6x 1031	PF23 VMW	Scania 460R 6x2 (NG) HL E6	WS Transportation	
6x 1032	PF23 ESU	Scania 460R 6x2 (NG) HL E6	WS Transportation	Wisbech
6x 1033	PF23 ERO	Scania 460R 6x2 (NG) HL E6	WS Transportation	Runcorn
6x 1034	PF23 ESV	Scania 460R 6x2 (NG) HL E6	WS Transportation	Wisbech
6x 1035	PF23 VNA	Scania 460R 6x2 (NG) HL E6	WS Transportation	Wisbech
6x 1036	87 BVN 4	Scania R590 6x2 (NG) HL E6 V8	WS Transportation	Holland
6x 1037	PF23 VNE	Scania 500R 6x2 (NG) HL E6	WS Transportation	
6x 1038	PF23 VNC	Scania 500R 6x2 (NG) HL E6	WS Transportation	
6x 1039	PF23 VNG	Scania 500R 6x2 (NG) HL E6	WS Transportation	
6x 1040	PF23 VNH	Scania 500R 6x2 (NG) HL E6	WS Transportation	
6x 1041	PF23 VND	Scania 500R 6x2 (NG) HL E6	WS Transportation	
6x 1042	PF23 VNJ	Scania 500R 6x2 (NG) HL E6	WS Transportation	
6x 1043	PF23 VOD	Scania 500R 6x2 (NG) HL E6	WS Transportation	
6x 1044	PL23 JWD	Scania 500R 6x2 (NG) HL E6	Middlebrook	
6x 1045	PL23 LWG	Scania 500R 6x2 (NG) HL E6	Middlebrook	
6x 1046	PL23 JWY	Scania 500R 6x2 (NG) HL E6	WS Transportation	Coventry
6x 1047	PL23 JWE	Scania 500R 6x2 (NG) HL E6	WS Transportation	Ireland
6x 1048	PL23 JXC	Scania 500R 6x2 (NG) HL E6	WS Transportation	Toome
6x 1049				
6x 1050	WS10 RRY	Scania 660S 6x2 (NG) HL E6 V8 Tag	WS Transportation	Thirsk
6x 1051	PN73 EOJ	Scania 660S 6x2 (NG) HL E6 V8 Tag	WS Transportation	Gloucester
6x 1052	PN73 EOF	Scania 660S 6x2 (NG) HL E6 V8 Tag	WS Transportation	Bolton
6x 1053	PN73 EOE	Scania 660S 6x2 (NG) HL E6 V8 Tag	WS Transportation	Thirsk
6x 1054	PN73 EOS	Scania 660S 6x2 (NG) HL E6 V8 Tag	WS Transportation	Thirsk

6x 1055	PN73 EUK	Scania 660S 6x2 (NG) HL E6 V8 Tag	WS Transportation	Bolton
6x 1056	PN73 EOO	Scania 660S 6x2 (NG) HL E6 V8 Tag	WS Transportation	Bolton
6x 1057	PN73 EOP	Scania 660S 6x2 (NG) HL E6 V8 Tag	WS Transportation	Runcorn
6x 1058	13 BVR 7	Scania 660S 4x2 (NG) HL E6 V8	WS Transportation	Holand
6x 1059	PN73 EVR	Scania 500R 6x2 (NG) HL E6	Middlebrook	
6x 1060	PN73 EVK	Scania 500R 6x2 (NG) HL E6	WS Transportation	Immingham
6x 1061	PN73 EWK	Scania 500R 6x2 (NG) HL E6	WS Transportation	
6x 1062	PK73 XWO	Scania 500R 6x2 (NG) HL E6	WS Transportation	
6x 1063	PN73 EWL	Scania 500R 6x2 (NG) HL E6	WS Transportation	
6x 1064	PF73 EHV	Scania 500R 6x2 (NG) HL E6	WS Transportation	Immingham
6x 1065	PJ73 TEU	Scania 500R 6x2 (NG) HL E6	WS Transportation	Loughborough
6x 1066	PJ73 TFF	Scania 500R 6x2 (NG) HL E6	WS Transportation	Omagh
6x 1067	PJ73 TEY	Scania 500R 6x2 (NG) HL E6	WS Transportation	Ireland
6x 1068	PJ73 TFK	Scania 500R 6x2 (NG) HL E6	WS Transportation	Runcorn
6x 1069	PJ73 THU	Scania 500R 6x2 (NG) HL E6	WS Transportation	Chesterfield
6x 1070	PN73 EYV	Scania 500R 6x2 (NG) HL E6	WS Transportation	Coventry
6x 1071	PJ73 TFV	Scania 500R 6x2 (NG) HL E6	WS Transportation	Omagh
6x 1072	PN73 EYW	Scania 500R 6x2 (NG) HL E6	WS Transportation	Thirsk
6x 1073	PJ73 TFA	Scania 500R 6x2 (NG) HL E6	WS Transportation	Ireland
6x 1074	PJ73 TEV	Scania 500R 6x2 (NG) HL E6	WS Transportation	Thirsk
6x 1075				
6x 1076	PJ73 TFN	Scania 500R 6x2 (NG) HL E6	WS Transportation	Coventry
6x 1077	PF73 EHZ	Scania 500R 6x2 (NG) HL E6	WS Transportation	Runcorn
6x 1078	PJ73 THV	Scania 500R 6x2 (NG) HL E6	WS Transportation	Wyboston
6x 1079	PF73 CFX	Scania 500R 6x2 (NG) HL E6	WS Transportation	Wyboston
6x 1080	PJ73 TFZ	Scania 500R 6x2 (NG) HL E6	WS Transportation	Wyboston
6x 1081	PA55 WST (73)	Scania 500R 6x2 (NG) HL E6	WS Sherburns LGV	
6x 1082	PA22 WSS (73)	Scania 500R 6x2 (NG) HL E6	WS Sherburns LGV	
6x 1083	PF73 EGV	Scania 500R 6x2 (NG) HL E6	WS Transportation	Wisbech
6x 1084	PJ73 TGK	Scania 500R 6x2 (NG) HL E6	WS Transportation	Thirsk
6x 1084	PF73 EHX	Scania 500R 6x2 (NG) HL E6	WS Transportation	
6x 1085	PJ73 XRX	Scania 500R 6x2 (NG) HL E6	WS Transportation	Thirsk
6x 1086				
6x 1087	PF73 EHC	Scania 500R 6x2 (NG) HL E6	WS Transportation	Runcorn
6x 1088	PJ73 TMV	Scania 500R 6x2 (NG) HL E6	WS Transportation	Ireland
6x 1089	PN24 DWD			
6x 1090				
6x 1091	PF73 EHO	Scania 500R 6x2 (NG) HL E6	WS Transportation	Bootle
6x 1092	PJ73 XUC	Scania 500R 6x2 (NG) HL E6	WS Transportation	Thirsk
6x 1093	PF73 EKR	Scania 500R 6x2 (NG) HL E6	WS Transportation	Runcorn
6x 1094	PJ73 THG	Scania 500R 6x2 (NG) HL E6	WS Transportation	
6x 1095				
6x 1096	PF73 EHY	Scania 500R 6x2 (NG) HL E6	WS Transportation	Runcorn
6x 1097	PF73 RHK	Scania 500R 6x2 (NG) HL E6	WS Transportation	Immingham
6x 1098	PF73 CGV	Scania 500R 6x2 (NG) HL E6	WS Transportation	Immingham
6x 1099				
6x 1100				
6x 1101	PJ73 XSC	Scania 500R 6x2 (NG) HL E6	WS Transportation	Thirsk
6x 1102	PF73 EHB	Scania 500R 6x2 (NG) HL E6	WS Transportation	Thirsk
6x 1103	PJ73 XRV	Scania 500R 6x2 (NG) HL E6	WS Transportation	Runcorn
6x 1104	PJ73 XRY	Scania 500R 6x2 (NG) HL E6	WS Transportation	Wombourne
6x 1105	PN73 EUS	Scania 500R 6x2 (NG) HL E6	WS Transportation	
6x 1106	PJ73 XUL	Scania 500R 6x2 (NG) HL E6	WS Transportation	Wombourne
6x 1107	PN73 EWJ	Scania 500R 6x2 (NG) HL E6	WS Transportation	
6x 1108	PF73 EHG	Scania 500R 6x2 (NG) HL E6	WS Transportation	Thirsk
6x 1109	PJ73 TJO	Scania 500R 6x2 (NG) HL E6	WS Transportation	Runcorn
6x 1110	PJ73 XVV	Scania 500R 6x2 (NG) HL E6	WS Transportation	Runcorn
6x 1111	PK23 LNH	Scania 500R 6x2 (NG) HL E6	WS Transportation	Immingham
6x 1112	PK23 LNM	Scania 500R 6x2 (NG) HL E6	WS Transportation	Immingham
6x 1113	PF73 EKT	Scania 500R 6x2 (NG) HL E6	WS Transportation	Coventry
6x 1114	PF73 KTA	Scania 500R 6x2 (NG) HL E6	WS Transportation	Aveley

6x 1115	PF73 HER	Scania 500R 6x2 (NG) HL E6		WS Transportation	Thirsk
6x 1116	PF73 EJU	Scania 500R 6x2 (NG) HL E6		WS Transportation	Loughborough
6x 1117	PF73 EKL	Scania 500R 6x2 (NG) HL E6		WS Transportation	Wombourne
6x 1118	PF73 KSU	Scania 500R 6x2 (NG) HL E6		WS Transportation	Aveley
6x 1119					
6x 1120	PF73 EKZ	Scania 500R 6x2 (NG) HL E6		WS Transportation	Ireland
6x 1121	PJ73 XVY	Scania 500R 6x2 (NG) HL E6		WS Transportation	Runcorn
6x 1122	PF73 KTT	Scania 500R 6x2 (NG) HL E6		WS Transportation	Coventry
6x 1123	PF73 CFY	Scania 500R 6x2 (NG) HL E6		WS Transportation	Coventry
6x 1124	PF73 KTD	Scania 500R 6x2 (NG) HL E6		WS Transportation	
6x 1125	PF73 CGG	Scania 500R 6x2 (NG) HL E6		WS Transportation	Chesterfield
6x 1126	PF73 EKO	Scania 560R 6x2 (NG) HL E6		WS Transportation	
6x 1127	PF73 KUJ	Scania 500R 6x2 (NG) HL E6		WS Transportation	Runcorn
6x 1128	PF73 KTU	Scania 500R 6x2 (NG) HL E6		WS Transportation	Ireland
6x 1129					
6x 1130					
6x 1131					
6x 1132					
6x 1133	PF73 EJE	Scania 500R 6x2 (NG) HL E6		WS Transportation	Immingham
6x 1134					
6x 1135					
6x 1136	PF73 KUK	Scania 500R 6x2 (NG) HL E6		WS Transportation	Runcorn
6x 1137					
6x 1138	PF73 KTX	Scania 500R 6x2 (NG) HL E6		WS Transportation	
6x 1139	PF73 KSY	Scania 500R 6x2 (NG) HL E6		WS Transportation	Wombourne
6x 1140	PF73 CGK	Scania 500R 6x2 (NG) HL E6		WS Transportation	Sherburn
6x 1141	PF73 KSX	Scania 500R 6x2 (NG) HL E6		WS Transportation	
6x 1142	PF73 KUX	Scania 500R 6x2 (NG) HL E6		WS Transportation	
6x 1143	PF73 KTG	Scania 500R 6x2 (NG) HL E6		WS Transportation	Wyboston
6x 1144	PF73 KSK	Scania 500R 6x2 (NG) HL E6		WS Transportation	
6x 1145	PF73 KTV	Scania 500R 6x2 (NG) HL E6		WS Transportation	
6x 1146					
6x 1147	PF73 CFZ	Scania 500R 6x2 (NG) HL E6		WS Transportation	Runcorn
6x 1148					
6x 1149	PJ73 XSA	Scania 500R 6x2 (NG) HL E6		WS Transportation	Runcorn
6x 1150	PJ73 TNF	Scania 500R 6x2 (NG) HL E6		WS Transportation	Immingham
6x 1151					
6x 1152	PF73 ELO	Scania 500R 6x2 (NG) HL E6		WS Transportation	
6x 1153	PF73 KUC	Scania 500R 6x2 (NG) HL E6		WS Transportation	Runcorn
6x 1154	PF73 KVB	Scania 500R 6x2 (NG) HL E6		WS Transportation	Runcorn
6x 1155	PF73 KSN	Scania 500R 6x2 (NG) HL E6		WS Transportation	Wisbech
6x 1156	PF73 ELJ	Scania 500R 6x2 (NG) HL E6		WS Transportation	Wyboston
6x 1157	PF73 KTE	Scania 500R 6x2 (NG) HL E6		WS Transportation	Wyboston
6x 1158	PJ73 XSH	Scania 550S 6x2 (NG) HL E6		WS Transportation	Ipswich
6x 1159					
6x 1160					
6x 1161					
6x 1162					
6x 1163					
6x 1164					
6x 1165					
6x 1166	PJ73 XRZ	Scania 500R 6x2 (NG) HL E6		WS Transportation	Bolton
6x 1167	PJ73 XSD	Scania 500R 6x2 (NG) HL E6		WS Transportation	Wyboston
6x 1168	PJ73 XUM	Scania 500R 6x2 (NG) HL E6		WS Transportation	Coventry
6x 1169	PF73 EGK	Scania 500R 6x2 (NG) HL E6		WS Transportation	Wisbech
6x 1170	PJ73 XSF	Scania 500R 6x2 (NG) HL E6		WS Transportation	Runcorn
6x 1171					
6x 1172	PF73 EKU	Scania 500R 6x2 (NG) HL E6		WS Transportation	Wombourne
6x 1173	PF73 EGZ	Scania 500R 6x2 (NG) HL E6		WS Transportation	Wyboston
6x 1174	PF73 EKX	Scania 500R 6x2 (NG) HL E6		WS Transportation	
6x 1175					

6x 1176				
6x 1177				
6x 1178				
6x 1179				
6x 1180				
6x 1181				
6x 1182				
6x 1183				
6x 1184				
6x 1185				
6x 1186	*PK 24 APZ*			
6x 1187				
6x 1188	PK24 APY	Scania 500R 6x2 (NG) HL E6	WS Transportation	
6x 1189	PJ73 XUO	Scania 500R 6x2 (NG) HL E6	WS Transportation	Thirsk
6x 1190	PF73 KVD	Scania 500R 6x2 (NG) HL E6	WS Transportation	Thirsk
6x 1191	PL73 HFT	Scania 500R 6x2 (NG) HL E6	Middlebrook	
6x 1192	PL73 HFS	Scania 500R 6x2 (NG) HL E6	Middlebrook	
6x 1193	PJ73 TMX	Scania 500R 6x2 (NG) HL E6	WS Transportation	
6x 1194				
6x 1195				
6x 1196				
6x 1197	*PN 24 DSU*			
6x 1198				
6x 1199	PJ73 TEO	Scania 500R 6x2 (NG) HL E6	WS Transportation	
6x 1200				
6x 1201				
6x 1202				
6x 1203				
6x 1204				
6x 1205				
6x 1206				
6x 1207				
6x 1208				
6x 1209				
6x 1210				
6x 1211				
6x 1212				
6x 1213				
6x 1214	PN24 DYB	Scania 500R 6x2 (NG) HL E6	WS Transportation	
6x 1215				
6x 1216	PN24 DXW	Scania 500R 6x2 (NG) HL E6	WS Transportation	
6x 1217	PN24 DXO	Scania 500R 6x2 (NG) HL E6	WS Transportation	
6x 1218	PN24 DXU	Scania 500R 6x2 (NG) HL E6	WS Transportation	
6x 1219	*PN24 DVC*			
6x 1220	PN24 DWY	Scania 500R 6x2 (NG) HL E6	WS Transportation	
6x 1221	PL73 HFU	Scania 500R 6x2 (NG) HL E6	Middlebrook	
6x 1222	Pf73 EHH	Scania 500R 6x2 (NG) HL E6	WS Transportation	Wisbech
6x 1223	PF73 EHJ	Scania 500R 6x2 (NG) HL E6	WS Transportation	Wisbech
6x 1224	PF73 EHD	Scania 500R 6x2 (NG) HL E6	WS Transportation	Runcorn
6x 1225	PF73 EJA	Scania 500R 6x2 (NG) HL E6	WS Transportation	Thirsk
6x 1226	PF73 EJY	Scania 500R 6x2 (NG) HL F6	WS Transportation	Runcorn
6x 1227	PJ73 XVZ	Scania 500R 6x2 (NG) HL E6	WS Transportation	Loughborough
6x 1228	PF73 EJG	Scania 500R 6x2 (NG) HL E6	WS Transportation	Loughborough
6x 1229	PJ73 XSK	Scania 500R 6x2 (NG) HL E6	WS Transportation	Coventry
6x 1230	PF73 EHW	Scania 500R 6x2 (NG) HL E6	Middlebrook	
6x 1231	PF73 EHN	Scania 500R 6x2 (NG) HL E6	Middlebrook	
6x 1232	PF73 CGU	Scania 500R 6x2 (NG) HL E6	Middlebrook	
6x 1279	PN24 DVF	Scania 500R 6x2 (NG) HL E6	WS Transportation	
6x 1315	PN24 DXA	Scania 500R 6x2 (NG) HL E6	WS Transportation	
AH12	PN19 EYR	Scania R450 6x2 (NG) HL E6 Hiab Tag	WS Transportation	Heathrow
AH13	PN19 EYP	Scania R450 6x2 (NG) HL E6 Hiab Tag	WS Transportation	Runcorn

AH14	PO69 XZU	Scania R450 6x2 (NG) Hiab E6	WS Transportation	Sherburn
AH16	PO69 XZC	Scania R450 6x2 (NG) Hiab E6	WS Transportation	Dagenham
AH18	PJ19 FRL	Scania R450 6x2 (NG) HL E6 Hiab Tag	WS Transportation	Dagenham
AH21	PO70 ZPX	Scania R450 6x2 (NG) NL Hiab E6	WS Transportation	Dagenham
AH22	PO70 ZPW	Scania R450 6x2 (NG) NL Hiab E6	WS Transportation	Dagenham
AH23	PO70 ZPZ	Scania R450 6x2 (NG) NL Hiab E6	WS Transportation	Runcorn
RC01	PJ17 UST	Scania G410 4w Curtainside Rigid	WS Transportation	Winsford
RC02	PO18 NZY	Scania G410 4w Curtainside Rigid	WS Transportation	Loughborough
RC03	PO18 NZR	Scania G410 4w Curtainside Rigid	WS Transportation	Loughborough
RC04	PO18 NZN	Scania G410 4w Curtainside Rigid	WS Transportation	Loughborough
RC05	PO18 OAX	Scania G410 4w Curtainside Rigid	WS Transportation	Loughborough
RC06	PO18 OAY	Scania G410 4w Curtainside Rigid	WS Transportation	Wisbech
RC07	PO18 OHD	Scania G410 4w Curtainside Rigid	WS Transportation	Loughborough
RC08	PO18 OGV	Scania G410 4w Curtainside Rigid	WS Transportation	Appleton
RC09	PO18 OGU	Scania G410 4w Curtainside Rigid	WS Transportation	Wyboston
RC10	PO18 OBH	Scania G410 4w Curtainside Rigid	WS Transportation	Appleton
RC11	PO18 OBF	Scania G410 4w Curtainside Rigid	WS Transportation	Coventry
RC12	PO18 OAJ	Scania G410 4w Curtainside Rigid	WS Transportation	Coventry
RC13	PO18 OAD	Scania G410 4w Curtainside Rigid	WS Transportation	Coventry
RC14	PO18 OBK	Scania G410 4w Curtainside Rigid	WS Transportation	Loughborough
RC15	PO18 OGY	Scania G410 4w Curtainside Rigid	WS Transportation	Wyboston
RC16	PO18 OGK	Scania G410 4w Curtainside Rigid	WS Transportation	Coventry
RC17	PO18 OHB	Scania G410 4w Curtainside Rigid	WS Transportation	Loughborough
RC18	PO18 OHJ	Scania G410 4w Curtainside Rigid	WS Transportation	Coventry
RC19	PF73 CEN	Scania G360 4w (NG) Curtainside Rigid	WS Transportation	
RC20	PF73 CEO	Scania G360 4w (NG) Curtainside Rigid	WS Transportation	
RF01	PJ17 USW	Scania G410 4w Flatbed SL	WS Transportation	Thirsk
RF02	PJ17 USY	Scania G410 4w Flatbed SL	WS Transportation	Thirsk
RF03	PO18 OBZ	Scania G410 4w Flatbed SL	WS Transportation	Runcorn
RF100	PO18 OHW	Scania P450 6w SL Vehicle Transporter	WS Transportation	Runcorn
RF101	PO18 OHX	Scania P450 6w SL Vehicle Transporter	WS Transportation	Runcorn
RH45	PO68 YSD	Scania R450 8w (NG) NL E6 Rigid Hiab	WS Transportation	Heathrow
RH47	PJ19 FRX	Scania R450 8w (NG) NL E6 Rigid Hiab	WS Transportation	Dagenham
RH50	PN19 EYG	Scania R450 8w (NG) NL E6 Rigid Hiab	WS Transportation	Wakefield
RH51	PN19 EYH	Scania R450 8w (NG) NL E6 Rigid Hiab	WS Transportation	Heathrow
RH52	PJ19 FSA	Scania R450 8w (NG) NL E6 Rigid Hiab	WS Transportation	Runcorn
RH60	PO70 ZPY	Scania R450 6w (NG) NL E6 Rigid Hiab	WS Transportation	Runcorn
RH61	PE69 FWZ	Scania R450 6w NL Rgd Hiab E6	WS Transportation	Rugby
RH64	PN71 DYX	Scania R450 8w (NG) NL E6 Rigid Hiab	WS Transportation	Dagenham
RH65	PN71 DYY	Scania R450 8w (NG) NL E6 Rigid Hiab	WS Transportation	Dagenham
RH66	PN71 DZB	Scania R450 8w (NG) NL E6 Rigid Hiab	WS Transportation	Heathrow
RH68	PF23 ELH	Scania	WS Transportation	
RH73	PN24 DSV	Scania 500R 6w (NG) NL E6 Rigid Hiab	WS Transportation	
RH74	PN24 DSX	Scania 500R 6w (NG) NL E6 Rigid Hiab	WS Transportation	
RH75	PF73 KSO	Scania 500R 6w (NG) NL E6 Rigid Hiab	WS Transportation	Coventry
No F/No	PMN-109-K	Scania R450 6x2 (NG) NL E6	WS Mezeron	Ramsey
No F/No	PMN-705-T	Scania G410 4w Curtainside Rigid	WS Mezeron	Ramsey
No F/No	RMN-187-B	Scania R450 6x2 HL SL	WS Mezeron	
No F/No	770 WS (23)	Scania 770S 6w (NG) HL E6 V8 Rigid	Grey	
No F/No	S55 HGV (61)	Daf FACF 75.360 4w Rigid Curtainside	White	Markham Vale
No F/No	W200 WST (70)	Ford Transit Courier Sport TDC	Grey	
No F/No	W400 WST (19)	Audi Q5 Tdi S Line	Black	
No F/No	W500 WST (69)	Ford Transit Custom 320 Limited Ed	Black	
No F/No	W600 WST (70)	Ford Transit Courier Sport TDC	Grey	
No F/No	W700 WST (14)	Mercedes Sprinter 313 Cdi	White	
No F/No	W800 WST (70)	Ford Transit Courier Sport TDC	Grey	
No F/No	W900 WST (70)	Ford Transit Courier Sport TDC	Grey	
No F/No	W55 VAC (71)	Scania R500 6x2 (NG) HL E6	WS Transportation	
No F/No	W555 VAC (71)	Scania R500 6x2 (NG) HL E6	WS Transportation	
No F/No	PA55 WSS (16)	Mercedes Actros 1824 Rigid Box	Sherburns HGV	Markham Vale

No F/No	V500 WST (63)	Scania	R500 6x2 HL E5	WS Transportation	
No F/No	M471 MOJ	Scania	113M 360 4x2	White/Blue/WST	Runcorn
No F/No	CT18 CFE	Ford	Transit 350 Panel	White (WS Logo Blue)	
No F/No	DP18 PXU	Nissan	NV200 Acenta Dci	White (WS Logo Blue)	
No F/No	PO64 VRJ	Scania	R450 6X2 HL SL	WST Blue	Markham Vale
No F/No	PO64 VRN	Scania	R450 6X2 HL SL	WST Blue	Markham Vale
No F/No	MX16 HGP	Mercedes	Actros 1824 Rigid Box	Sherburns HGV	Markham Vale
No F/No	PK67 URS	Scania	R450 6X2 HL SL Tag	WST Blue	
No F/No	PX18 JUA	Scania	R450 6x2 HL SL	White	
No F/No	MC19 XLJ	Peugeot	Partner Professional	Grey (WS Logos)	
No F/No	PO70 ZTK	Scania	R450 6x2 (NG) HL E6	Sherburns HGV	Markham Vale
No F/No	MA21 OJO	Ford	Transit Custom 320 Limited Ed	Black (747 Logistics)	
No F/No	OV21 VRC	Man	TGE 3.140 Panel LWB	WS Fleet Services	
No F/No	PL21 FKG	Scania	R450 6x2 (NG) HL E6	WS Transportation	
No F/No	PL21 FKM	Scania	R450 6x2 (NG) HL E6	WS Transportation	
No F/No	PL21 FKX	Scania	R450 6x2 (NG) HL E6	WS Transportation	
No F/No	PN21 FHV	Scania	R500 6x2 (NG) HL E6	WS Transportation	
No F/No	PN21 FHW	Scania	R500 6x2 (NG) HL E6	WS Transportation	Middlesborough
No F/No	PN21 FLK	Scania	R500 6x2 (NG) HL E6	WS Transportation	
No F/No	PJ71 MYC	Scania	R500 6x2 (NG) HL E6	WS Transportation	Markham Vale
No F/No	PJ71 MYF	Scania	R500 6x2 (NG) HL E6	WS Transportation	
No F/No	PJ71 MYG	Scania	R500 6x2 (NG) HL E6	WS Transportation	
No F/No	PJ71 MYK	Scania	R500 6x2 (NG) HL E6	WS Transportation	
No F/No	PJ71 MYL	Scania	R500 6x2 (NG) HL E6	WS Transportation	
No F/No	PJ71 MYM	Scania	R500 6x2 (NG) HL E6	WS Transportation	
No F/No	PN71 EAW	Scania	R450 6x2 (NG) HL E6	WS Transportation	
No F/No	PN71 EAY	Scania	R500 6x2 (NG) HL E6	WS Transportation	Grangemouth
No F/No	PN71 EBA	Scania	R500 6x2 (NG) HL E6	WS Transportation	
No F/No	PN71 EBC	Scania	R500 6x2 (NG) HL E6	WS Transportation	Grangemouth
No F/No	PN71 EBD	Scania	R500 6x2 (NG) HL E6	WS Transportation	
No F/No	PN71 EBF	Scania	R500 6x2 (NG) HL E6	WS Transportation	
No F/No	PN71 EBL	Scania	R500 6x2 (NG) HL E6	WS Transportation	Markham Vale
No F/No	PN71 EBO	Scania	R500 6x2 (NG) HL E6	WS Transportation	
No F/No	PN71 EBU	Scania	R500 6x2 (NG) HL E6	WS Transportation	
No F/No	PN71 EBV	Scania	R500 6x2 (NG) HL E6	WS Transportation	
No F/No	PN71 EBX	Scania	R500 6x2 (NG) HL E6	WS Transportation	
No F/No	PN71 EBZ	Scania	R500 6x2 (NG) HL E6	WS Transportation	
No F/No	SM71 YKL	Citroen	Berlingo 1000 Eprise PRO Bhdi	WS Tankers (White)	
No F/No	FY22 PFK	Ford	Transit 350 Leader EcoBlu	WS Fleet Services	
No F/No	FY22 PGK	Ford	Transit 350 Leader EcoBlu	WS Fleet Services	
No F/No	FY23 TBV	Ford	Transit 350 Leader EcoBlu	WS Fleet Services	
No F/No	BJ71 BTS	Volvo	FH 500 6x2 GL E6	BTS	Congleton
No F/No	BK71 BTS	Volvo	FH 500 6x2 GL E6	BTS	Congleton

Explore

AT 095	FN64 XCS	Scania	R450 6x2 HL SL Tag	Explore White	
EP001	PO68 YDU	Scania	R410 8w Rigid SL Flatbed Tag	Explore	
EP002	PO68 YDV	Scania	R410 8w Rigid SL Flatbed Tag	Explore	
EP003	PN19 FCL	Scania	P410 8w Rigid SL Flatbed Tag	Explore	
EP004	PN19 FCG	Scania	P410 8w Rigid SL Flatbed Tag	Explore	
EP005	PN10 FCJ	Scania	P410 8w Rigid SL Flatbed Tag	Explore	
ET 271	PN71 DZE	Scania	R500 6x2 (NG) HL E6 (Tag)	Explore (Tarmac)	Merdien
ET 272	PN71 DZJ	Scania	R500 6x2 (NG) HL E6 (Tag)	Explore (Tarmac)	
ET 273	PK21 RKZ	Scania	R500 6x2 (NG) HL E6 (Tag)	Tarmac	Meriden
ET 276	PN71 DZG	Scania	R500 6x2 (NG) HL E6 (Tag)	Explore (Tarmac)	
ET 277	PN71 DZD	Scania	R500 6x2 (NG) HL E6 (Tag)	Explore	Merdien
ET 278	PN71 EAC	Scania	R500 6x2 (NG) HL E6 (Tag)	White	Newark
ET 279	PN71 EAE	Scania	R500 6x2 (NG) HL E6 (Tag)	Explore	
ET 342	PN72 DTV	Scania	R540 6x2 (NG) HL E6 (Tag)	Explore	
ET 346	PN72 EAK	Scania	R500 6x2 (NG) HL E6 (Tag)	Explore	

ET 348	PN72 EAE	Scania	R500 6x2 (NG) HL E6 (Tag)	Explore	
ET 349	PN72 DXY	Scania	R500 6x2 (NG) HL E6 (Tag)	Explore	Newark
ET 355	PN72 DZX	Scania	R500 6x2 (NG) HL E6 (Tag)	Explore	
ET 357	PN72 DZO	Scania	R500 6x2 (NG) HL E6 (Tag)	Explore	
ET 362	PN72 DYG	Scania	R500 6x2 (NG) HL E6 (Tag)	Explore	St Neots
ET 363	PN72 DZS	Scania	R500 6x2 (NG) HL E6 (Tag)	Explore	Newark
ET 364	PN72 DXS	Scania	R500 6x2 (NG) HL E6 (Tag)	Explore	St Neots
ET 365	PN72 DYH	Scania	R500 6x2 (NG) HL E6 (Tag)	Explore	Aveley
ET 366	PN72 DYJ	Scania	R500 6x2 (NG) HL E6 (Tag)	Explore	
ET 368	PN72 DXW	Scania	R500 6x2 (NG) HL E6 (Tag)	Explore	Aveley
ET 369	PN72 DXK	Scania	R500 6x2 (NG) HL E6 (Tag)	Explore	Newark
ET 373	PN72 DZY	Scania	R500 6x2 (NG) HL E6 (Tag)	Explore	Swadlincote
ET 374	PN72 DXH	Scania	R500 6x2 (NG) HL E6 (Tag)	Explore	
ET 384	PN72 EBF	Scania	R500 6x2 (NG) HL E6 (Tag)	Explore	Aveley
ET 390	PK72 XJC	Scania	R500 6x2 (NG) HL E6 (Tag)	Explore	
ET 391	PK72 XHV	Scania	R500 6x2 (NG) HL E6 (Tag)	Explore	
ET 395	PK72 XJB	Scania	R500 6x2 (NG) HL E6 (Tag)	Explore	
ET 397	PK72 XHW	Scania	R500 6x2 (NG) HL E6 (Tag)	Explore	St Neots
ET 401	PK72 XJF	Scania	R500 6x2 (NG) HL E6 (Tag)	Explore	
ET 402	PK72 XJJ	Scania	R500 6x2 (NG) HL E6 (Tag)	Explore	
ET 404	PK72 XJE	Scania	R500 6x2 (NG) HL E6 (Tag)	Explore	
ET 405	PK72 XJH	Scania	R500 6x2 (NG) HL E6 (Tag)	Explore	
ET 406	PK72 XJD	Scania	R500 6x2 (NG) HL E6 (Tag)	Explore	Aveley
ET 407	PK72 XJL	Scania	R500 6x2 (NG) HL E6 (Tag)	Explore	
ET 408	PK23 LNP	Scania	460R 6x2 (NG) HL E6	Explore	
ET 409	PK23 LNR	Scania	460R 6x2 (NG) HL E6	Explore	
ET 410	PK23 LNT	Scania	460R 6x2 (NG) HL E6	Explore	St Neots
ET 411	PK23 LNU	Scania	460R 6x2 (NG) HL E6	Explore	
ET 412	PK23 LNV	Scania	460R 6x2 (NG) HL E6	Explore	Aveley
ET 413	PK23 LNW	Scania	460R 6x2 (NG) HL E6	Explore	Aveley
ET 414	PK23 LNX	Scania	460R 6x2 (NG) HL E6	Explore	
ET 415	PK23 LNY	Scania	460R 6x2 (NG) HL E6	Explore	
ET 416	PK23 LNZ	Scania	460R 6x2 (NG) HL E6	Explore	
ET 417	PK23 LOA	Scania	460R 6x2 (NG) HL E6	Explore	
ET 418	PK23 LOD	Scania	460R 6x2 (NG) HL E6	Explore	St Neots
ET 419	PK23 LOF	Scania	460R 6x2 (NG) HL E6	Explore	
ET 420	PK23 LOH	Scania	460R 6x2 (NG) HL E6	Explore	Aveley
ET 421	PK23 LOJ	Scania	460R 6x2 (NG) HL E6	Explore	Aveley
ET 422	PK23 LPA	Scania	460R 6x2 (NG) HL E6	Explore	St Neots
ET 423	PK23 LPC	Scania	460R 6x2 (NG) HL E6	Explore	
ET 424	PK23 LPF	Scania	460R 6x2 (NG) HL E6	Explore	
ET 425					
ET 426					
ET 427	PK23 LVR	Scania	460R 6x2 (NG) HL E6	Explore	
ET 428	PJ23 MWY	Scania	460R 6x2 (NG) HL E6	Explore	Worksop
ET 429	PK23 LVU	Scania	460R 6x2 (NG) HL E6	Explore	
ET 430	PK23 LVT	Scania	460R 6x2 (NG) HL E6	Explore	
ET 431	PK23 LVP	Scania	460R 6x2 (NG) HL E6	Explore	
ET 432	PJ23 MXE	Scania	460R 6x2 (NG) HL E6	Explore	
ET 433	PJ23 MXA	Scania	460R 6x2 (NG) HL E6	Explore	
ET 434	PJ23 MXF	Scania	460R 6x2 (NG) HL E6	Explore	
ET 435	PJ23 MXG	Scania	460R 6x2 (NG) HL E6	Explore	St Neots
ET 436	PJ23 MXH	Scania	460R 6x2 (NG) HL E6	Explore	Aveley
ET 437	PK23 LVS	Scania	460R 6x2 (NG) HL E6	Explore	
ET 438	PJ23 MXC	Scania	460R 6x2 (NG) HL E6	Explore	
ET 439	PJ23 MXD	Scania	460R 6x2 (NG) HL E6	Explore	
ET 440	PJ23 MXN	Scania	460R 6x2 (NG) HL E6	Explore	
ET 441	PJ23 MWZ	Scania	460R 6x2 (NG) HL E6	Explore	
ET 442	PJ23 MXO	Scania	460R 6x2 (NG) HL E6	Explore	
ET 443	PJ23 MXP	Scania	460R 6x2 (NG) HL E6	Explore	
ET 444	PJ23 MXS	Scania	460R 6x2 (NG) HL E6	Explore	Aveley

ET445	PL23 JWN	Scania	460R 6x2 (NG) HL E6	Explore	
ET446	PL23 JWP	Scania	460R 6x2 (NG) HL E6	Explore	
ET447	PL23 JWV	Scania	460R 6x2 (NG) HL E6	Explore	
ET448	PL23 JWW	Scania	460R 6x2 (NG) HL E6	Explore	
ET449	PL23 JWO	Scania	460R 6x2 (NG) HL E6	Explore	
ET450	PN73 EVG	Scania	500R 6x2 (NG) HL E6	Explore	
ET451	PF73 EJN	Scania	500R 6x2 (NG) HL E6	Explore	
ET452	PJ73 THK	Scania	500R 6x2 (NG) HL E6	Explore	
ET453	PJ73 XVW	Scania	500R 6x2 (NG) HL E6	Explore	Newark
ET454	PF73 EKE	Scania	500R 6x2 (NG) HL E6	Explore	
ET455	PJ73 XWC	Scania	500R 6x2 (NG) HL E6	Explore	Aveley
ET456					
ET457	PJ73 XWA	Scania	500R 6x2 (NG) HL E6	Explore	
ET458	PF73 EJO	Scania	500R 6x2 (NG) HL E6	Explore	
ET459	PJ73 XRW	Scania	500R 6x2 (NG) HL E6	Explore	
ET460	PF73 EHT	Scania	500R 6x2 (NG) HL E6	Explore	
ET461					
ET462					
ET463					
ET464					
ET465	PN73 EVB	Scania	500R 6x2 (NG) HL E6	Explore	
ET466	PN73 EVC	Scania	500R 6x2 (NG) HL E6	Explore	
ET467	PN73 EVH	Scania	500R 6x2 (NG) HL E6	Explore	
ET468	PN73 EUX	Scania	500R 6x2 (NG) HL E6	Explore	
ET469	PJ73 XSL	Scania	500R 6x2 (NG) HL E6	Explore	
ET470	PF73 EJK	Scania	500R 6x2 (NG) HL E6	Explore	
ET471	PF73 EJK	Scania	500R 6x2 (NG) HL E6	Explore	
ET472	PJ73 XSB	Scania	500R 6x2 (NG) HL E6	Explore	
ET473	PN73 EUY	Scania	500R 6x2 (NG) HL E6	Explore	
ET474	PN73 EYP	Scania	500R 6x2 (NG) HL E6	Explore	
ET475	PN73 EWB	Scania	500R 6x2 (NG) HL E6	Explore	
ET476	PN73 EWF	Scania	500R 6x2 (NG) HL E6	Explore	
ET477	PN73 EWM	Scania	500R 6x2 (NG) HL E6	Explore	
ET478					
ET479					
ET480					
ET481					
ET482					
ET483					
ET484					
ET485					
ET486					
ET487					
ET488	PN73 EWD	Scania	500R 6x2 (NG) HL E6	Explore	St Neots
ET490	PN73 YET	Scania	500R 6x2 (NG) HL E6	Explore	
ET491	PN73 EWG	Scania	500R 6x2 (NG) HL E6	Explore	
ET492	PN73 EWO	Scania	500R 6x2 (NG) HL E6	Explore	
ET493	PN73 EVY	Scania	500R 6x2 (NG) HL E6	Explore	
ET494	PN73 EWH	Scania	500R 6x2 (NG) HL E6	Explore	
ET495	PN73 EVV	Scania	500R 6x2 (NG) HL E6	Explore	
ET496	PN73 EVW	Scania	500R 6x2 (NG) HL E6	Explore	
ET497	PN73 EVX	Scania	500R 6x2 (NG) HL E6	Explore	
ET498	PN73 EWP	Scania	500R 6x2 (NG) HL E6	Explore	
ET499	PN73 EYR	Scania	500R 6x2 (NG) HL E6	Explore	
ET500	PN73 EYO	Scania	500R 6x2 (NG) HL E6	Explore	Aveley
ET501	PN73 EVT	Scania	500R 6x2 (NG) HL E6	Explore	
ET502	PJ73 TDZ	Scania	500R 6x2 (NG) HL E6	Explore	
ET503	PN73 EWC	Scania	500R 6x2 (NG) HL E6	Explore	
ET504	PN73 EWE	Scania	500R 6x2 (NG) HL E6	Explore	
ET505	PN73 EWA	Scania	500R 6x2 (NG) HL E6	Explore	

ET 506	PJ73 TGO	Scania	500R 6x2 (NG) HL E6	Explore	
ET 507	PJ73 TGF	Scania	500R 6x2 (NG) HL E6	Explore	
ET 508	PN73 EYU	Scania	500R 6x2 (NG) HL E6	Explore	Aveley
ET 509					
ET 510	PJ73 TFX	Scania	500R 6x2 (NG) HL E6	Explore	
ET 511					
ET 512	PJ73 XUD	Scania	500R 6x2 (NG) HL E6	Explore	
ET 513	PF73 EKH	Scania	500R 6x2 (NG) HL E6	Explore	Aveley
ET 514	PF73 EHU	Scania	500R 6x2 (NG) HL E6	Explore	
ET 515	PJ73 TMO	Scania	500R 6x2 (NG) HL E6	Explore	
ET 516	PF73 EJC	Scania	500R 6x2 (NG) HL E6	Explore	
ET 517					
ET 518	PF73 KVE	Scania	500R 6x2 (NG) HL E6	Explore	St Neots
ET 519	PF73 EJL	Scania	500R 6x2 (NG) HL E6	Explore	
ET 520	PF73 EJD	Scania	500R 6x2 (NG) HL E6	Explore	St Neots
ET 521	PF73 EJJ	Scania	500R 6x2 (NG) HL E6	Explore	
ET 522	PF73 EKW	Scania	500R 6x2 (NG) HL E6	Explore	
ET 523					
ET 524	PF73 CGE	Scania	500R 6x2 (NG) HL E6	Explore	Worksop
ET 525	PF73 KUN	Scania	500R 6x2 (NG) HL E6	Explore	
ET 526	PF73 KUP	Scania	500R 6x2 (NG) HL E6	Explore	
ET 527					
ET 528	PF73 KTJ	Scania	500R 6x2 (NG) HL E6	Explore	
ET 529	PF73 KSZ	Scania	500R 6x2 (NG) HL E6	Explore	
ET 530	PF73 KUU	Scania	500R 6x2 (NG) HL E6	Explore	
ET 531	PF73 KUY	Scania	500R 6x2 (NG) HL E6	Explore	
ET 532	PF73 KUR	Scania	500R 6x2 (NG) HL E6	Explore	
ET 533	PF73 KUS	Scania	500R 6x2 (NG) HL E6	Explore	
ET 534	PF73 EHM	Scania	500R 6x2 (NG) HL E6	Explore	St Neots
ET 535	PF73 EHS	Scania	500R 6x2 (NG) HL E6	Explore	
ET 536					
ET 537	PJ73 XUN	Scania	500R 6x2 (NG) HL E6	Explore	
ET 538	PJ73 TNK	Scania	500R 6x2 (NG) HL E6	Explore	
ET 539	PF73 KUE	Scania	500R 6x2 (NG) HL E6	Explore	
ET 541	PN24 DVZ	Scania	500R 6x2 (NG) HL E6	Explore	
ET 562	PF73 KSV	Scania	500R 6x2 (NG) HL E6	Explore	
ET 563	PF73 EKN	Scania	500R 6x2 (NG) HL E6	Explore	
ET 564	PF73 ELH	Scania	500R 6x2 (NG) HL E6	Explore	
ET nnn	PF73 EKM	Scania	500R 6x2 (NG) HL E6	Explore	
ET nnn	PJ73 TFE	Scania	500R 6x2 (NG) HL E6	Explore	
ET nnn	PN73 EUZ	Scania	500R 6x2 (NG) HL E6	Explore	
ETAH 10	PN19 EYL	Scania	R450 6x2 (NG) HL E6 Hiab Tag	Explore	
ETAH 11	PN19 FAJ	Scania	R450 6x2 (NG) HL E6 Hiab Tag	Explore	
ETAH 13	PN19 EYM	Scania	R450 6x2 (NG) HL E6 Hiab Tag	Explore	Winsford
ETAH 15	PO69 XZA	Scania	R450 6x2 (NG) Hiab E6	Explore	Winsford
ETAH 16	PJ19 FRV	Scania	R450 6x2 (NG) HL E6 Hiab Tag	Explore	
ETAH 18	PO69 XZB	Scania	R450 6x2 (NG) Hiab E6	Explore	Newark
ETAH 19	PJ19 FRN	Scania	R450 6x2 (NG) HL E6 Hiab Tag	Explore	Worksop
ETM 01	PO67 VJJ	Scania	P410 8w SL Cement Mixer Tag	Cemex	Gorton
ETM 02	PO67 VJK	Scania	P410 8w SL Cement Mixer Tag	Cemex	Leicester
ETM 21	PO67 VOD	Scania	P410 8w SL Cement Mixer Tag	Explore Hire	Worksop
ETM 22	PK67 USD	Scania	P410 8w SL Cement Mixer Tag	Explore Hire	Worksop
ETM 25	PK67 USL	Scania	P410 8w SL Cement Mixer Tag	Explore Hire	Worksop
ETM 28	PY21 FHR	Renault	C Range 430.32 8w Cement Mixer	Tarmac	Meridan
ETM 29	PY21 FHP	Renault	C Range 430.32 8w Cement Mixer	Tarmac	Worksop
ETM 30	PY21 KPR	Renault	C Range 430.32 8w Cement Mixer	Tarmac	Meridan
ETM 31	PY21 KPL	Renault	C Range 430.32 8w Cement Mixer	Tarmac	Meridan
ETM 32	PY21 KPK	Renault	C Range 430.32 8w Cement Mixer	Tarmac	Meridan
ETM 33	PX71 LOD	Renault	C Range 430.32 8w Cement Mixer	Tarmac	Meridan
ETM 34	PX71 LNZ	Renault	C Range 430.32 8w Cement Mixer	Tarmac	Meridan

ETM 35	PX71 LPC	Renault	C Range 430.32 8w Cement Mixer	Explore	Meridan
ETM 36		Renault	C Range 430.32 8w Cement Mixer	Explore	
ETM 37	PX22 ZTO	Renault	C Range 430.32 8w Cement Mixer	Explore	Meridan
ETM 38	PX22 ZTP	Renault	C Range 430.32 8w Cement Mixer	Explore	Meridan
ETM 39	PX72 YJF	Renault	C Range 430.32 8w Cement Mixer	Tarmac	
ETM 40	PX72 YJG	Renault	C Range 430.32 8w Cement Mixer	Tarmac	
ETM 41	FJ22 PXG	Mercedes	Arocs 3243 B 8w Cement Mixer	Explore	Meridan
ETM 42	FJ22 PXH	Mercedes	Arocs 3243 B 8w Cement Mixer	Explore	Meridan
ETM 44	FJ22 PXL	Mercedes	Arocs 3243 B 8w Cement Mixer	Explore	Meridan
ETM 45	FJ22 PXM	Mercedes	Arocs 3243 B 8w Cement Mixer	Tarmac	Meridan
ETM 47	FJ22 PXR	Mercedes	Arocs 3243 B 8w Cement Mixer	Tarmac	
ETM 48	FJ22 PXS	Mercedes	Arocs 3243 B 8w Cement Mixer	Tarmac	
ETM 49	FJ22 PXT	Mercedes	Arocs 3243 B 8w Cement Mixer	Tarmac	
ETM 50	FJ22 PXZ	Mercedes	Arocs 3243 B 8w Cement Mixer	Tarmac	
ETM 51	FJ22 PXU	Mercedes	Arocs 3243 B 8w Cement Mixer	Explore	Meridan
ETM 52	FJ22 PXV	Mercedes	Arocs 3243 B 8w Cement Mixer	Explore	
ETM 53	FJ22 PXW	Mercedes	Arocs 3243 B 8w Cement Mixer	Cemex	
ETM 54	FJ22 PXX	Mercedes	Arocs 3243 B 8w Cement Mixer	Cemex	
ETM 55	FJ22 PXY	Mercedes	Arocs 3243 B 8w Cement Mixer	Explore	
ETM 56	FJ22 PXO	Mercedes	Arocs 3243 B 8w Cement Mixer	Explore	
ETM 57		Mercedes	Arocs 3243 B 8w Cement Mixer	Explore	
ETM 58	PY23 EBP	Renault	C Range 430.32 8w Cement Mixer	Explore	
ETM 59	PY23 EBU	Renault	C Range 430.32 8w Cement Mixer	Explore	
ETM 60	PY23 EBV	Renault	C Range 430.32 8w Cement Mixer	Explore	
ETRH 12	PN19 EZZ	Scania	R450 8w (NG) NL E6 Rigid Hiab Tag	Explore	Newark
ETRH 13	PJ19 FSD	Scania	R450 8w (NG) NL E6 Rigid Hiab Tag	Explore	Worksop
ETRH 14	PJ19 FSC	Scania	R450 8w (NG) NL E6 Rigid Hiab Tag	Explore	
ETRH 16	PJ19 FRZ	Scania	R450 8w (NG) NL E6 Rigid Hiab Tag	Explore	
ETRH 17	PN21 FFK	Scania	R450 8w (NG) NL E6 Rigid Hiab	Explore	
ETRH 18	PN71 DZA	Scania	R450 8w (NG) NL E6 Rigid Hiab Tag	Explore	
ETRH 19	PF23 EKZ	Scania	R500 6w (NG) HL Rigid Hiab Flatbed	Explore	
ETRH 20	PK73 XWM	Scania	R500 6w (NG) HL Rigid Hiab Flatbed	Explore	
ETRT 01	PO18 OJE	Scania	R410 8W Flatbed Tag	Select	
ETSH 01	SF17 AOE	Mercedes	Arocs 4163 8X4	Explore	
ETSH 02	EXP 102E	Mercedes	Arocs 4163 8X4 (LHD)	Explore	
ES 100	PN73 EVP	Scania	500R 6x2 (NG) HL E6	East Suffolk Logistics	
ES 101	PJ73 TGZ	Scania	500R 6x2 (NG) HL E6	East Suffolk Logistics	
ES 102	PJ73 TGE	Scania	500R 6x2 (NG) HL E6	East Suffolk Logistics	
ES 103	PJ73 TGX	Scania	500R 6x2 (NG) HL E6	East Suffolk Logistics	
ES 104	PJ73 TFY	Scania	500R 6x2 (NG) HL E6	East Suffolk Logistics	
ES 105		Scania	500R 6x2 (NG) HL E6	East Suffolk Logistics	
ES 106	PJ73 XTZ	Scania	500R 6x2 (NG) HL E6	East Suffolk Logistics	
ES 107		Scania	500R 6x2 (NG) HL E6	East Suffolk Logistics	
ES 108	PJ73 XWD	Scania	500R 6x2 (NG) HL E6	East Suffolk Logistics	
ESnnn	PN24 DYD	Scania	500R 6x2 (NG) HL E6	East Suffolk Logistics	
HH 816	WU23 FHX	Man	TGX 41.580 8x4 GX	Explore Heavy Haulage	
HH 817	MX73 DFJ	Scania	770S 6x4 (NG) HL V8 E6	Explore Heavy Haulage	
HH 818	MX73 DFK	Scania	770S 6x4 (NG) HL V8 E6	Explore Heavy Haulage	
HH 819	MX73 DFL	Scania	770S 6x4 (NG) HL V8 E6	Explore Heavy Haulage	
HH 820	MX73 DFN	Scania	770S 6x4 (NG) HL V8 E6	Explore Heavy Haulage	
HH 821	PF23 VNL	Scania	500S 8x4 (NG) HL E6	Explore Heavy Haulage	
HH 822	PF23 VNN	Scania	560S 6x4 (NG) HL E6	Explore Heavy Haulage	
HH 823	PF23 VNM	Scania	560S 6x4 (NG) HL E6	Explore Heavy Haulage	
HH 824	PF23 VNK	Scania	560S 6x4 (NG) HL E6	Explore Heavy Haulage	
ST 807	GN67 OZS	Mercedes	Arocs 3351S 6x2 (BSC)	Explore	
ST 808	GN67 OZT	Mercedes	Arocs 3351S 6x2 (BSC)	Explore	
ST 810	PN72 EBO	Scania	R540 6x4 (NG) HL E6	Explore Heavy Haulage	
ST 811	PN72 EBL	Scania	R540 6x4 (NG) HL E6	Explore Heavy Haulage	
ST 812	PN72 EBU	Scania	R540 6x4 (NG) HL E6	Explore Heavy Haulage	
ST 813	PN72 EBP	Scania	R540 6x4 (NG) HL E6	Explore Heavy Haulage	

ST 814	PN72 EBV	Scania	R540 6x4 (NG) HL E6	Explore Heavy Haulage
No F/No	VF06 CXZ	Terberg	YT-180 Tug	Yellow
No F/No	MM66 UDB	Ford	Transit Van	Select
No F/No	WN68 WPP	Ford	Transit 350 Leader EcoBlu	Select
No F/No	MJ19 LDA	Ford	Transit Custom 300 Base	Select
No F/No	MX19 WJZ	Ford	Transit Courier Base TDCI	Explore
No F/No	MF69 CCE	Ford	Transit 350 Leader EcoBlu	Select
No F/No	MT69 VKO	Ford	Transit 350 Leader EcoBlu	Select
No F/No	MT69 VMM	Ford	Transit Custom 340 Leader	Select
No F/No	MT69 WZH	Peugeot	Partner Professional	Select
No F/No	MX69 WZB	Mercedes	Vito	Select
No F/No	MK20 NVG	Peugeot	Partner Professional L1	Select
No F/No	MK20 NWN	Peugeot	Partner Professional L1	Select
No F/No	YF20 KKO	Toyota	Hilux Active 4WD Pick-Up	Select
No F/No	MF70 ZDJ	Ford	Transit 350 Leader P/V EcoBlue	Select
No F/No	MJ70 KUR	Ford	Transit 350 Leader P/V EcoBlue	Select
No F/No	YM70 WWU	Ford	Fiesta TDCi Car Derived Van	Explore
No F/No	YR70 JOJ	Ford	Transit 350 Leader P/V EcoBlue	Explore
No F/No	YR70 HJF	Ford	Transit 350 Leader P/V EcoBlue	Explore
No F/No	YR70 LFK	Ford	Transit 350 Leader P/V EcoBlue	Explore
No F/No	YR70 LRK	Ford	Transit 350 Leader P/V EcoBlue	Explore
No F/No	YR70 LUH	Ford	Transit 350 Leader P/V EcoBlue	Explore
No F/No	YR70 LUL	Ford	Transit 350 Leader P/V EcoBlue	Explore
No F/No	YR70 LUO	Ford	Transit 350 Leader P/V EcoBlue	Explore
No F/No	YR70 LUY	Ford	Transit 350 Leader P/V EcoBlue	Explore
No F/No	YR70 LVL	Ford	Transit 350 Leader P/V EcoBlue	Explore
No F/No	YR70 LVX	Ford	Transit 350 Leader P/V EcoBlue	Explore
No F/No	YS70 UFA	Ford	Transit 350 Leader P/V EcoBlue Dropside	Explore
No F/No	YS70 UPJ	Ford	Transit 350 Leader P/V EcoBlue Dropside	Explore
No F/No	YS70 USG	Ford	Transit 350 Leader P/V EcoBlue Dropside	Explore
No F/No	YS70 UTV	Ford	Transit 350 Leader P/V EcoBlue Dropside	Explore

WS Home Delivery

	182 D 12981	Renault	Traffic LL29 Dci 120 Business	HomeDel	Ireland
	182 D 19484	Renault	Traffic LL29 Dci 120 Business	HomeDel	Ireland
	182 D 19527	Renault	Traffic LL29 Dci 120 Business	HomeDel	Ireland
	182 D 22609	Mercedes	Sprinter 314 Cdi Box Van	HomeDel	Ireland
	182 D 22617	Mercedes	Sprinter 314 Cdi Box Van	HomeDel	Ireland
	182 D 22618	Mercedes	Sprinter 314 Cdi Box Van	HomeDel	Ireland
	182 D 22620	Mercedes	Sprinter 314 Cdi Box Van	HomeDel	Ireland
	182 D 22621	Mercedes	Sprinter 314 Cdi Box Van	HomeDel	Ireland
	192 D 16572	Mercedes	Sprinter 314 Cdi Panel Van	HomeDel	Ireland
	192 D 16574	Mercedes	Sprinter 314 Cdi Panel Van	HomeDel	Ireland
	HG21 VGC	Volkswagon	Crafter CR35 Startline TD Box Van	WS HomeDel	Unknown
HV1	DG16 XUP	Man	TGL 7.180 4w Curtainside	WS HomeDel	
LV 1	YY22 HMU	Volkswagon	Crafter CR35 Startline TD Box Van	WS HomeDel	Coventry
LV 2	YY22 NFC	Volkswagon	Crafter CR35 Startline TD Box Van	WS HomeDel	Coventry
LV 3	YY22 JXN	Volkswagon	Crafter CR35 Startline TD Box Van	WS HomeDel	Coventry
LV 4	YY22 OAZ	Volkswagon	Crafter CR35 Startline TD Box Van	WS HomeDel	Coventry
LV 5	YY22 NDU	Volkswagon	Crafter CR35 Startline TD Box Van	WS HomeDel	Coventry
LV 6	YY22 GWZ	Volkswagon	Crafter CR35 Startline TD Box Van	WS HomeDel	Coventry
LV 7	YY22 UGL	Volkswagon	Crafter CR35 Startline TD Box Van	WS HomeDel	Coventry
LV 8	YY22 RBF	Volkswagon	Crafter CR35 Startline TD Box Van	WS HomeDel	Coventry
LV 9	YY22 UGJ	Volkswagon	Crafter CR35 Startline TD Box Van	WS HomeDel	Coventry
LV 10	YY22 XZD	Volkswagon	Crafter CR35 Startline TD Box Van	WS HomeDel	Coventry
LV 11	YY22 XJG	Volkswagon	Crafter CR35 Startline TD Box Van	WS HomeDel	Coventry
LV 12	YY22 XOH	Volkswagon	Crafter CR35 Startline TD Box Van	WS HomeDel	Coventry
LV 13	YY22 XZS	Volkswagon	Crafter CR35 Startline TD Box Van	WS HomeDel	Coventry
LV 14	YY22 YDP	Volkswagon	Crafter CR35 Startline TD Box Van	WS HomeDel	Coventry
LV 16	YY22 NDV	Volkswagon	Crafter CR35 Startline TD Box Van	WS HomeDel	Coventry

LV 17	YY72 BZJ	Volkswagon	Crafter CR35 Startline TD Box Van	WS HomeDel
LV 18	YX72 TDU	Volkswagon	Crafter CR35 Startline TD Box Van	WS HomeDel
LV 19	YY72 AWO	Volkswagon	Crafter CR35 Startline TD Box Van	WS HomeDel
LV 20	YX72 TCY	Volkswagon	Crafter CR35 Startline TD Box Van	WS HomeDel
LV 21	YX72 TCZ	Volkswagon	Crafter CR35 Startline TD Box Van	WS HomeDel
LV 22	YX72 TCV	Volkswagon	Crafter CR35 Startline TD Box Van	WS HomeDel
LV 23	YY72 EKT	Volkswagon	Crafter CR35 Startline TD Box Van	WS HomeDel
LV 24	YY72 ERJ	Volkswagon	Crafter CR35 Startline TD Box Van	WS HomeDel
LV 25	YX72 TBY	Volkswagon	Crafter CR35 Startline TD Box Van	WS HomeDel
LV 26	YY72 CVA	Volkswagon	Crafter CR35 Startline TD Box Van	WS HomeDel
LV 27	YX72 TDO	Volkswagon	Crafter CR35 Startline TD Box Van	WS HomeDel
LV 28	YX72 TCK	Volkswagon	Crafter CR35 Startline TD Box Van	WS HomeDel
LV 29	YY72 EJK	Volkswagon	Crafter CR35 Startline TD Box Van	WS HomeDel
LV 30	YY72 ETU	Volkswagon	Crafter CR35 Startline TD Box Van	WS HomeDel
LV 31	YX72 TBZ	Volkswagon	Crafter CR35 Startline TD Box Van	WS HomeDel
LV 32	YY72 EPP	Volkswagon	Crafter CR35 Startline TD Box Van	WS HomeDel

Graylaw

NMN-293-X	Man	TGL 7.180 4w Curtainside	Graylaw Freight	Isle of Man
PMN-136-E	Scania	G410 4w SL Rgd Fridge	Graylaw Freight	Isle of Man
PMN-202-C	Ford	Transit 100 T350 FWD	Graylaw Freight	Isle of Man
PMN-353-F	Man	TGL 7.180 4w Rgd	Graylaw Freight	Isle of Man
PMN-722-K	Scania	G410 4w Fridge SL	Graylaw Freight	Skelmersdale
PMN-729-B	Scania	G410 4w SL Curtainside	Graylaw Freight	Isle of Man
PMN-730-B	Scania	G410 4w SL Curtainside	Graylaw Freight	Isle of Man
PMN-731-B	Scania	P320 6w SL Curtainside	Graylaw Freight	Isle of Man
PMN-732-B	Scania	R450 6x2 HL SL	Graylaw Freight	Isle of Man
PMN-733-B	Scania	R450 6x2 HL SL	Graylaw Freight	Isle of Man
PMN-734-B	Scania	R450 6x2 HL SL	Graylaw Freight	Isle of Man
PMN-735-B	Scania	R450 6x2 HL SL	Graylaw Freight	Isle of Man
PMN-736-B	Scania	R450 6x2 HL SL	Graylaw Freight	Isle of Man
PMN-793-G	Ford	Transit Leader 290 EcoBlue	Graylaw Freight	Isle of Man
PMN-794-G	Ford	Transit Leader 290 EcoBlue	Graylaw Freight	Isle of Man
PMN-928-C	Scania	G410 4w SL Rgd Curtainside	Graylaw Freight	Isle of Man
PMN-929-C	Scania	G410 4w SL Rgd Curtainside	Graylaw Freight	Isle of Man
PMN-930-C	Man	TG-L 7.180 4w Curtainside	Graylaw Freight	Isle of Man
PMN-932-G	Ford	Transit Leader 290 EcoBlue	Graylaw Freight	Isle of Man
PMN-933-G	Ford	Transit Leader 290 EcoBlue	Graylaw Freight	Isle of Man
CMN-318	Fiat	Ducato SWB	Graylaw Silver	Isle of Man
PN16 OBZ	Scania	G410 4w SL Rgd Curtainside	Graylaw Freight	Skelmersdale
PN16 OCD	Scania	G410 4w SL Rgd Fridge	Graylaw Freight	Skelmersdale
PN16 OCJ	Scania	G410 4w SL Rgd Curtainside	Graylaw Freight	Skelmersdale
PN16 OCL	Scania	G410 4w SL Rgd Curtainside	Graylaw Freight	Skelmersdale
PN16 OCP	Scania	G410 4w SL Rgd Curtainside	Graylaw Freight	Skelmersdale
PN16 OCZ	Scania	G410 4w SL Rgd Curtainside	Graylaw Freight	Skelmersdale
PN16 OJL	Scania	G410 4w SL Rgd Curtainside	Graylaw Freight	Skelmersdale
PN16 OKK	Scania	G410 4w SL Rgd Curtainside	Graylaw Freight	Skelmersdale
PN16 OKL	Scania	G410 4w SL Rgd Curtainside	Graylaw Freight	Skelmersdale
PN16 OKO	Scania	G410 4w SL Rgd Curtainside	Graylaw Freight	Skelmersdale
PN16 OKU	Scania	G410 4w SL Rgd Fridge	Graylaw Freight	Skelmersdale
PN16 OKW	Scania	G410 4w SL Rgd Curtainside	Graylaw Freight	Skelmersdale
PN16 OLG	Scania	G410 4w SL Rgd Fridge	Graylaw Freight	Skelmersdale
MM66 LBA	Scania	P320 6w Curtainside	Graylaw Freight	Skelmersdale
MM66 LBG	Scania	P320 6w Curtainside	Graylaw Freight	Skelmersdale
PJ17 USV	Scania	G410 4w Fridge SL	Graylaw Freight	Skelmersdale
MK67 NLN	Scania	P320 6w SL Curtainside	Graylaw Freight	Skelmersdale
MK67 NLO	Scania	P320 6w SL Curtainside	Graylaw Freight	Skelmersdale
PO18 NZU	Scania	G410 4w SL Curtainside	Graylaw Freight	Skelmersdale
PO18 NZV	Scania	G410 4w SL Curtainside	Graylaw Freight	Skelmersdale
PO18 OAV	Scania	G410 4w SL Curtainside	Graylaw Freight	Skelmersdale

PMN-935 M
PMN 936 M

PO18 OHG	Scania	G410 4w SL Curtainside	Graylaw Freight	Skelmersdale
PN71 EAO	Scania	R500 6x2 (NG) HL E6	Graylaw Freight	Skelmersdale
PN71 EBJ	Scania	R500 6x2 (NG) HL E6	Graylaw Freight	Skelmersdale
YY22 TXV	Volkswagon	Crafter CR35 Startline Box Van	Graylaw Freight	
PN72 DUH	Scania	R500 6x2 (NG) HL E6	Graylaw Freight	Skelmersdale
PN72 DUJ	Scania	R500 6x2 (NG) HL E6	Graylaw Freight	Skelmersdale
PN72 DUU	Scania	R500 6x2 (NG) HL E6	Graylaw Freight	Skelmersdale
PN72 EAP	Scania	R500 6x2 (NG) HL E6	Graylaw Freight	Skelmersdale
PN72 ECF	Scania	R500 6x2 (NG) HL E6	Graylaw Freight	Skelmersdale
PF23 ERV	Scania	460R 6x2 (NG) HL E6	Graylaw Freight	Skelmersdale
PK23 LPN	Scania	460R 6x2 (NG) HL E6	Graylaw Freight	Skelmersdale
PK23 LPX	Scania	460R 6x2 (NG) HL E6	Graylaw Freight	Skelmersdale
PK23 LPY	Scania	460R 6x2 (NG) HL E6	Graylaw Freight	Skelmersdale
PK23 LPZ	Scania	460R 6x2 (NG) HL E6	Graylaw Freight	Skelmersdale
PK23 LRA	Scania	460R 6x2 (NG) HL E6	Graylaw Freight	Skelmersdale
PF73 EGU	Scania	500R 6x2 (NG) HL E6	Graylaw Freight	Skelmersdale
PJ73 TGU	Scania	500R 6x2 (NG) HL E6	Graylaw Freight	Skelmersdale
PJ73 XSM	Scania	500R 6x2 (NG) HL E6	Graylaw Freight	Skelmersdale
PJ73 XWB	Scania	500R 6x2 (NG) HL E6	Graylaw Freight	Skelmersdale
PN73 EVM	Scania	500R 6x2 (NG) HL E6	Graylaw Freight	Skelmersdale
PN24 DVA	Scania	500R 6x2 (NG) HL E6	Graylaw Freight	Skelmersdale
PN24 DVB	Scania	500R 6x2 (NG) HL E6	Graylaw Freight	Skelmersdale

Related Fleets

AD16 LMJ	Daf	FTGXF 460 6x2 SSC	SCS Logistics
AD16 LMM	Daf	FTGXF 460 6x2 SSC	SCS Logistics
AV17 CZE	Volvo	FH 460 4x2 GXL	H E Payne
BF18 SNK	Iveco	Strailis XP 460 6x2 (HW)	Simmonds (White)
BF18 SNN	Iveco	Strailis XP 460 6x2 (HW)	Simmonds (White)
BF18 SNU	Iveco	Strailis XP 460 6x2 (HW)	Simmonds (White)
BF22 UJW	Iveco	EuroCargo 180E255 4w Curtainside	Simmonds (White)
BF23 YMS	Iveco	S-Way 340 6w AT Curtainside	Palletline
BF23 YST	Iveco	EuroCargo 180-250 4w Curtainside	Palletline
BG19 NZS	Renault	T380 6w Curtainside	Simmonds (White)
BT65 XLB	Iveco	Strailis 310 6w (HR) Curtainside	Simmonds (White)
BT65 XSC	Iveco	Strailis 310 6w (HR) Curtainside	Simmonds (White)
BT65 XSD	Iveco	Strailis 260 6w (HR) Curtainside	Simmonds (White)
BT72 XYX	Daf	FANCF 340 6w SC Curtainside	Simmonds (White)
BT72 XYY	Daf	FANCF 340 6w SC Curtainside	Simmonds (White)
BT72 XYZ	Daf	FANCF 340 6w SC Curtainside	Simmonds (White)
BU14 JVY	Daf	FALF45 180 4w Curtainside	SCS Logistics
BU69 XFM	Renault	T480 6x2	Simmonds (White)
BU69 XFN	Renault	T480 6x2	Simmonds (White)
BU69 XFO	Renault	T480 6x2	Simmonds (White)
BU69 XFP	Renault	T480 6x2	Simmonds (White)
BU69 XFR	Renault	T480 6x2	Simmonds (White)
BU69 XFS	Renault	T480 6x2	Simmonds (White)
BU69 XFT	Renault	T480 6x2	Simmonds (White)
BU69 XFV	Renault	T480 6x2	Simmonds (White)
BV23 FSD	Daf	FANCF 340 6w SC Curtainside	Simmonds (White)
BV23 FSE	Daf	FANCF 340 6w SC Curtainside	Simmonds (White)
BV23 FSF	Daf	FANCF 340 6w SC Curtainside	Simmonds (White)
BV23 FSG	Daf	FANCF 340 6w SC Curtainside	Simmonds (White)
BV65 YOH	Iveco	Strailis 460 6x2 (HW)	Simmonds (White)
BV66 ATK	Iveco	Strailis 460 6x2 (HW)	Simmonds (White)
BV66 ATN	Iveco	Strailis 460 6x2 (HW)	Simmonds (White)
BV66 ATY	Iveco	Strailis 460 6x2 (HW)	Simmonds (White)
BW17 TFY	Iveco	Strailis XP 460 6x2 (HW)	Simmonds (White)
BW17 TGE	Iveco	Strailis 460 6x2 (HW)	Simmonds (White)
BW65 DHY	Iveco	Strailis 460 6x2 (HW)	Simmonds (White)

W S Transportation & Explore (cont)

BW65 DHZ	Iveco	Strailis 460 6x2 (HW)	Simmonds (White)
BX14 EVP	Renault	Midlum 270 Dci 4w Curtainside	SCS Logistics
BX17 XCB	Iveco	EuroCargo 75.160 4w Rigid Curtainside	PE Logisitcs
BX17 XCC	Iveco	EuroCargo 75.160 4w Rigid Curtainside	PE Logisitcs
BX60 LNF	Renault	Midlum 270 Dci 4w Curtainside	SCS Logistics
DA16 VMM	Man	TGX 26.440 6x2 XLX	SCS Logistics
DK17 KUU	Man	TGX 26.460 6x2 XLX	SCS Logistics
DK17 KWE	Man	TGX 26.460 6x2 XLX	SCS Logistics
DK67 LZS	Mercedes	Vito 311 Cdi	White
DK67 MBV	Mercedes	Sprinter 313 Cdi	White
DK67 UXA	Daf	FTGXF 480 6x2 SSC	Simmonds (White)
DK69 YXU	Daf	FTGXF 530 6x2 SSC	Simmonds (White)
DK69 YXV	Daf	FTGXF 530 6x2 SSC	Simmonds (White)
DK69 YXW	Daf	FTGXF 530 6x2 SSC	Simmonds (White)
DK69 YXX	Daf	FTGXF 530 6x2 SSC	Simmonds (White)
DK70 TXA	Daf	FTGXF 530 6x2 SSC	Simmonds (White)
DX21 VDD	Daf	FANCF 340 6w SC Curtainside	Simmonds (White)
DX21 VDE	Daf	FANCF 340 6w SC Curtainside	Simmonds (White)
DX21 VDF	Daf	FANCF 340 6w SC Curtainside	Simmonds (White)
DX21 VDL	Daf	FTGXF 530 6x2 SSC	Simmonds (White)
DX21 VDM	Daf	FTGXF 530 6x2 SSC	Simmonds (White)
DX21 VDN	Daf	FTGXF 530 6x2 SSC	Simmonds (White)
DX70 TXB	Daf	FTGXF 530 6x2 SSC	Simmonds (White)
DX70 TXC	Daf	FTGXF 530 6x2 SSC	Simmonds (White)
DX70 TXD	Daf	FTGXF 530 6x2 SSC	Simmonds (White)
DX70 TXE	Daf	FTGXF 530 6x2 SSC	Simmonds (White)
DX70 TXF	Daf	FTGXF 530 6x2 SSC	Simmonds (White)
DX70 TXG	Daf	FTGXF 530 6x2 SSC	Simmonds (White)
DX70 TXH	Daf	FTGXF 530 6x2 SSC	Simmonds (White)
DX70 TXJ	Daf	FTGXF 530 6x2 SSC	Simmonds (White)
EU17 TNK	Daf	FTGXF 510 6x2 SSC	Simmonds (White)
FA19 SYS	Scania	S450 6x2 (NG) HL E6	Middlebrook Transport
FA19 SYT	Scania	S450 6x2 (NG) HL E6	Middlebrook Transport
FD14 CXW	Daf	FTGXF 105 460 6x2 SSC	Middlebrook Transport
FG18 VSX	Mercedes	Actros 2548 6x2 GSC	Middlebrook Transport
FG18 VSY	Mercedes	Actros 2548 6x2 GSC	Middlebrook Transport
FG18 VSZ	Mercedes	Actros 2548 6x2 GSC	Middlebrook Transport
FJ08 NWF	Iveco	Strailis 450 6x2 (AS)	Simmonds (White)
FJ21 URM	Mercedes	Actros 2548 6x2 GSC	Middlebrook Transport
FJ21 URN	Mercedes	Actros 2548 6x2 GSC	Middlebrook Transport
FJ21 URO	Mercedes	Actros 2548 6x2 GSC	Middlebrook Transport
FJ22 ZGB	Scania	500S 6x2 (NG) HL E6	Middlebrook Transport
FJ22 ZGO	Scania	500S 6x2 (NG) HL E6	Middlebrook Transport
FJ22 ZGS	Scania	500S 6x2 (NG) HL E6	Middlebrook Transport
FJ22 ZJE	Scania	540S 6x2 (NG) HL E6	Middlebrook Transport
FJ22 ZJO	Scania	500S 6x2 (NG) HL E6	Middlebrook Transport
FJ22 ZKE	Scania	500S 6x2 (NG) HL E6	Middlebrook Transport
FJ22 ZKR	Scania	500S 6x2 (NG) HL E6	Middlebrook Transport
FJ22 ZLO	Scania	540S 6x2 (NG) HL E6	Middlebrook Transport
FJ68 XAD	Mercedes	Actros 2548 6x2 GSC	Middlobrook Transport
FJ68 XAE	Mercedes	Actros 2548 6x2 GSC	Middlebrook Transport
FJ69 ZGH	Scania	S450 6x2 (NG) HL E6	Middlebrook Transport
FJ69 ZGM	Scania	S450 6x2 (NG) HL E6	Middlebrook Transport
FJ69 ZJZ	Scania	S450 6x2 (NG) HL E6	Middlebrook Transport
FJ70 PMO	Mercedes	Actros 2548 6x2 GSC	Middlebrook Transport
FJ70 PMU	Mercedes	Actros 2548 6x2 GSC	Middlebrook Transport
FJ70 PMV	Mercedes	Actros 2548 6x2 GSC	Middlebrook Transport
FJ70 PMX	Mercedes	Actros 2548 6x2 GSC	Middlebrook Transport
FJ70 PMY	Mercedes	Actros 2548 6x2 GSC	Middlebrook Transport
FJ71 SJV	Mercedes	Actros 2548 6x2 GSC	Middlebrook Transport

FJ71 SJX	Mercedes	Actros 2548 6x2 GSC	Middlebrook Transport
FJ71 SJY	Mercedes	Actros 2548 6x2 GSC	Middlebrook Transport
FN68 FGE	Daf	FTGCF 440 6x2 SC	SCS Logistics
FN69 AUU	Daf	FTGXF 106 480 6x2 SSC	Middlebrook Transport
FN70 AXS	Daf	FTGXF 106 480 6x2 SSC	Middlebrook Transport
FN70 AXT	Daf	FTGXF 106 480 6x2 SSC	Middlebrook Transport
FN70 AXU	Daf	FTGXF 106 480 6x2 SSC	Middlebrook Transport
FN70 AXV	Daf	FTGXF 106 480 6x2 SSC	Middlebrook Transport
FP64 CVW	Mercedes	Actros 2527 6w SSC Curtainside	Ken Mallinson
FP69 WWM	Scania	S450 6x2 (NG) HL E6	Middlebrook Transport
FX17 KOW	Scania	R450 6x2 HL SL	J Cutt & Son
FX18 RYR	Scania	R450 6x2 (NG) HL E6	Prigmore Haulage
FX18 RYT	Scania	R450 6x2 (NG) HL E6	Prigmore Haulage
FX19 UJJ	Scania	R450 6x2 (NG) HL E6	J Cutt & Son
FX66 KOA	Scania	R450 6x2 HL SL	J Cutt & Son
FX66 KOU	Scania	R450 6x2 HL SL	J Cutt & Son
GN63 FBB	Volvo	FL 260 4w Curtainside	Ken Mallinson
GO19 DVA	Iveco	Daily 35S16V	WMB Logistics
HV63 XSF	Mercedes	Sprinter 313 Cdi	Middlebrook Transport
J9 RWH (J)	Scania	R143M 470 4x2 Top	H E Payne
KMS 453 (22)	Scania	660S 6x2 (NG) HL E6 V8	Ken Mallinson
KP19 WNW	Mercedes	Actros 2448 6x2	H E Payne
KT68 OLH	Scania	S450 6x2 (NG) HL E6	Prigmore Haulage
KT68 OLP	Scania	S450 6x2 (NG) HL E6	Prigmore Haulage
KU20 XHP	Scania	S450 6x2 (NG) HL E6	Prigmore Haulage
KU64 EET	Scania	R450 6x2 HL SL	Prigmore Haulage
KU68 GVD	Scania	R500 6x2 (NG) HL E6	H E Payne
KU68 GVE	Scania	R500 6x2 (NG) HL E6	H E Payne
KU68 GVF	Scania	R500 6x2 (NG) HL E6	H E Payne
KU68 GVG	Scania	R500 6x2 (NG) HL E6	H E Payne
KU68 GVJ	Scania	R500 6x2 (NG) HL E6	H E Payne
KU68 GVK	Scania	R500 6x2 (NG) HL E6	H E Payne
KU68 GVL	Scania	R500 6x2 (NG) HL E6	H E Payne
KU68 GVN	Scania	R500 6x2 (NG) HL E6	H E Payne
KU68 GVO	Scania	R500 6x2 (NG) HL E6	H E Payne
KU68 GVP	Scania	R500 6x2 (NG) HL E6	H E Payne
KU70 WPM	Scania	S450 6x2 (NG) HL E6	Prigmore Haulage
KX08 AUP	Moffett	Lift Truck	Red
KX11 BGE	Scania	G320 6w Curtainside	Prigmore Haulage
KX18 WHO	Scania	R450 6x2 (NG) HL E6	Prigmore Haulage
KX18 WPR	Scania	S450 6x2 (NG) HL E6	Prigmore Haulage
KY22 EVP	Scania	R500 6x2 (NG) HL E6	Prigmore Haulage
MK67 NLP	Scania	P320 6w SL Curtainside	PE (WS) Blue
MV67 NKA	Daf	FANCF 330 6w Curtainside	MXL Logistics
MV67 NLA	Daf	FANCF 330 6w Curtainside	PE Logistics
MV67 NNO	Daf	FANCF 330 6w Curtainside	PE Logistics
MV67 NNR	Daf	FANCF 330 6w Curtainside	PE Logistics
MV67 NNT	Daf	FANCF 330 6w Curtainside	MXL Logistics
MX65 FGA	Daf	FTGXF 460 6x2 SC	SCS Logistics
MX66 FGM	Daf	FTGXF 460 6x2 SC	SCS Logistics
NJ21 EZW	Mercedes	Antos 1824 4w Rigid Curtainside	Ken Mallinson
NJ21 EZX	Mercedes	Antos 1824 4w Rigid Curtainside	Ken Mallinson
NJ22 AGU	Mercedes	Actros 2533LS 6w Rigid Curtainside Tag	Ken Mallinson
NL21 VHO	Mercedes	Antos 1824 4w Rigid Curtainside	Ken Mallinson
OO03 WMB (64)	Mercedes	Sprinter 316 Cdi	WMB Logistics
P11 YNE	Scania	R164L 580 6x2 Top	H E Payne
PJ23 MXB	Scania	500S 6x2 (NG) HL E6	Ken Mallinson
PJ23 MXU	Scania	560S 6x2 (NG) HL E6	Ken Mallinson
PJ23 MXW	Scania	500S 6x2 (NG) HL E6	Ken Mallinson
PJ23 MXX	Scania	500S 6x2 (NG) HL E6	Ken Mallinson
PJ23 MXY	Scania	560S 6x2 (NG) HL E6	Ken Mallinson

PJ23 MXZ	Scania	500S 6x2 (NG) HL E6	Ken Mallinson
PJ71 MZE	Scania	R500 6x2 (NG) HL E6	Ken Mallinson
PJ71 VCO	Scania	450S 6x2 (NG) HL E6 Tag	Ken Mallinson
PJ71 VCP	Scania	450S 6x2 (NG) HL E6 Tag	Ken Mallinson
PJ71 VCT	Scania	450S 6x2 (NG) HL E6 Tag	Ken Mallinson
PJ71 VCU	Scania	450S 6x2 (NG) HL E6 Tag	Ken Mallinson
PJ71 VCV	Scania	450S 6x2 (NG) HL E6 Tag	Ken Mallinson
PJ73 THN	Scania	500R 6x2 (NG) HL E6	Prigmore Haulage
PK18 YMD	Scania	R450 6x2 (NG) HL E6	Oliver Transport
PK21 RNV	Scania	R450 6x2 (NG) HL E6	MXL Logistics
PK23 LPE	Scania	500S 6x2 (NG) HL E6	Ken Mallinson
PL73 YBU	Scania	500R 6x2 (NG) HL E6	Ken Mallinson
PL73 YBV	Scania	500R 6x2 (NG) HL E6	Ken Mallinson
PL73 YBW	Scania	500R 6x2 (NG) HL E6	Ken Mallinson
PL73 YBX	Scania	500R 6x2 (NG) HL E6	Ken Mallinson
PN21 FHP	Scania	R500 6x2 (NG) HL E6	PE Logistics
PN21 FHR	Scania	R500 6x2 (NG) HL E6	PE Logistics
PN21 FHZ	Scania	R500 6x2 (NG) HL E6	PE Logistics
PN21 FJC	Scania	R500 6x2 (NG) HL E6	PE Logistics
PN21 FJD	Scania	R500 6x2 (NG) HL E6	PE Logistics
PN21 FJJ	Scania	R500 6x2 (NG) HL E6	PE Logistics
PN23 EWT	Scania	500S 6x2 (NG) HL E6	Ken Mallinson
PN23 EWU	Scania	540S 6x2 (NG) HL E6	Ken Mallinson
PN23 EWV	Scania	540S 6x2 (NG) HL E6	Ken Mallinson
PN23 EWW	Scania	540S 6x2 (NG) HL E6	Ken Mallinson
PN23 EWX	Scania	540S 6x2 (NG) HL E6	Ken Mallinson
PN23 EWY	Scania	500S 6x2 (NG) HL E6	Ken Mallinson
PN24 DTK	Scania	500R 6x2 (NG) HL E6	Simmonds Transport
PN24 DTO	Scania	500R 6x2 (NG) HL E6	Simmonds Transport
PN24 DTV	Scania	500R 6x2 (NG) HL E6	Simmonds Transport
PN24 DTX	Scania	500R 6x2 (NG) HL E6	Simmonds Transport
PN24 DTY	Scania	500R 6x2 (NG) HL E6	Simmonds Transport
PN24 DTZ	Scania	500R 6x2 (NG) HL E6	Simmonds Transport
PN24 DUA	Scania	500R 6x2 (NG) HL E6	Simmonds Transport
PN24 DUH	Scania	500R 6x2 (NG) HL E6	Simmonds Transport
PN24 DUJ	Scania	500R 6x2 (NG) HL E6	Simmonds Transport
PN24 DUU	Scania	500R 6x2 (NG) HL E6	Simmonds Transport
PN24 DUY	Scania	500R 6x2 (NG) HL E6	Simmonds Transport
PN24 DVJ	Scania	500R 6x2 (NG) HL E6	Simmonds Transport
PN24 DVK	Scania	500R 6x2 (NG) HL E6	Simmonds Transport
PN24 DVP	Scania	500R 6x2 (NG) HL E6	Simmonds Transport
PN71 DZP	Scania	500S 6x2 (NG) HL E6	Ken Mallinson
PN71 DZR	Scania	R500 6x2 (NG) HL E6	Ken Mallinson
PN71 DZS	Scania	500S 6x2 (NG) HL E6	Ken Mallinson
PN71 DZV	Scania	R500 6x2 (NG) HL E6	Ken Mallinson
PN71 DZX	Scania	500S 6x2 (NG) HL E6	Ken Mallinson
PN71 EAF	Scania	R500 6x2 (NG) HL E6	Ken Mallinson
PN71 EAG	Scania	R500 6x2 (NG) HL E6	Ken Mallinson
PN71 EAJ	Scania	500S 6x2 (NG) HL E6	Ken Mallinson
PN71 EAK	Scania	500S 6x2 (NG) HL E6	Ken Mallinson
PN71 EAX	Scania	R500 6x2 (NG) HL E6	Ken Mallinson
PN72 DTO	Scania	540S 6x2 (NG) HL E6	Middlebrook Transport
PN72 EAY	Scania	R540 6x2 (NG) HL E6 (Tag)	Ken Mallinson
PN72 EBA	Scania	R540 6x2 (NG) HL E6 (Tag)	Ken Mallinson
PN72 EBC	Scania	R540 6x2 (NG) HL E6 (Tag)	Ken Mallinson
PN72 EBD	Scania	R500 6x2 (NG) HL E6	Ken Mallinson
PN72 EBX	Scania	R500 6x2 (NG) HL E6	Ken Mallinson
PN72 EBZ	Scania	R450 6x2 (NG) HL E6	Ken Mallinson
PN72 ECA	Scania	R500 6x2 (NG) HL E6	Ken Mallinson
PN72 ECC	Scania	R450 6x2 (NG) HL E6	Ken Mallinson
PN72 ECD	Scania	R450 6x2 (NG) HL E6	Ken Mallinson

W S Transportation & Explore (cont)

Reg	Make	Model	Operator
PN73 EUL	Scania	500S 6x2 (NG) HL E6	Ken Mallinson
PN73 EUO	Scania	500S 6x2 (NG) HL E6	Ken Mallinson
PN73 EUP	Scania	560S 6x2 (NG) HL E6	Ken Mallinson
PN73 EUT	Scania	500S 6x2 (NG) HL E6	Ken Mallinson
PN73 EUU	Scania	500S 6x2 (NG) HL E6	Ken Mallinson
PN73 EUV	Scania	500S 6x2 (NG) HL E6	Ken Mallinson
PN73 EUW	Scania	500S 6x2 (NG) HL E6	Ken Mallinson
PN73 EVU	Scania	500R 6x2 (NG) HL E6	Ken Mallinson
PO18 NZT	Scania	G410 4w Curtainside Rigid	PE Logistics
PO18 NZW	Scania	G410 4w Curtainside Rigid	PE Logisitcs
PO18 OAA	Scania	G410 4w Curtainside Rigid	PE Logistics
PO18 OAH	Scania	G410 4w Curtainside Rigid	PE Logisitcs
PO18 OAM	Scania	G410 4w Curtainside Rigid	PE Logistics
PO18 OAP	Scania	G410 4w Curtainside Rigid	PE Logisitcs
PO18 OBD	Scania	G410 4w Curtainside Rigid	PE Logistics
PO18 OBE	Scania	G410 4w Curtainside Rigid	PE Logistics
PO18 OBG	Scania	G410 4w Curtainside Rigid	PE Logisitcs
PO18 OBM	Scania	G410 4w Curtainside Rigid	PE Logisitcs
PO18 OCA	Scania	G410 4w Curtainside Rigid	MXL Logistics
PO18 OCH	Scania	G410 4w Curtainside Rigid	PE Logisitcs
S22 KMS (19)	Mercedes	Sprinter 313 Cdi	White
SBM 132 (13)	Isuzu	D-Max D/C Intercooler TD	White
SC55 LOG (14)	Daf	FTGXF 460 6x2 SSC	SCS Logistics
T12 WMB (72)	Scania	S540 6x2 (NG) HL E6	WMB Logistics
T15 WMB (72)	Scania	S540 6x2 (NG) HL E6	WMB Logistics
T16 WMB (73)	Scania	560S 6x2 (NG) HL E6	WMB Logistics
T18 WMB (72)	Scania	660S 6x2 (NG) HL E6 V8	WMB Logistics
T19 WMB (72)	Scania	540S 6x2 (NG) HL E6	WMB Logistics
T20 WMB (72)	Scania	540S 6x2 (NG) HL E6	WMB Logistics
T21 WMB (70)	Scania	500S 6x2 (NG) HL E6	WMB Logistics
T23 WMB (73)	Scania	560S 6x2 (NG) HL E6	WMB Logistics
T24 WMB (73)	Scania	560S 6x2 (NG) HL E6	WMB Logistics
T29 WMB (73)	Scania	560S 6x2 (NG) HL E6	WMB Logistics
V25 WAY (71)	Iveco	S-Way 570 4x2	H E Payne
VU62 WYC	Volvo	FH500 6x2 GXL	WMB Logistics
W22 KMS (14)	Mercedes	Sprinter 313 Cdi	White
W29 KMS (16)	Mercedes	Citan 109 Cdi	White
W77 OTS (69)	Scania	R450 6x2 (NG) HL E6	Oliver Transport
WV68 CYC	Mercedes	Actros 2527 6w SSC Curtainside	Ken Mallinson
WV68 CYG	Mercedes	Actros 2527 6w SSC Curtainside	Ken Mallinson
X25 WAY (71)	Iveco	S-Way 570 4x2	H E Payne
Y444 SCS (15)	Daf	FTGXF 460 6x2 SC	SCS Logistics
Y800 HEP (16)	Scania	R450 6x2 Top	H E Payne
Y900 HEP (18)	Scania	G320 6w HL Curtainside Tag	H E Payne
YD67 KMJ	Mercedes	Actros 1824 4w CSC Curtainside	Ken Mallinson
YD67 KMM	Mercedes	Actros 1824 4w SSC Curtainside	Ken Mallinson
YE10 RYW	Mercedes	Axor 1824 4w Curtainside	Ken Mallinson
YE67 UYG	Daf	FTGCF 450 6x2	SCS Logistics
YF19 UYY	Mercedes	Actros 2533 6w SSC Flatbed	Ken Mallinson
YG68 DYA	Mercedes	Actros 2545 6x2 BSC	Ken Mallinson
YG68 DYB	Mercedes	Actros 2545 6x2 BSC	Ken Mallinson
YG68 DYC	Mercedes	Actros 2545 6x2 BSC	Ken Mallinson
YG68 DYD	Mercedes	Actros 2545 6x2 BSC	Ken Mallinson
YG68 DYF	Mercedes	Actros 2545 6x2 BSC	Ken Mallinson
YG68 DYH	Mercedes	Actros 2545 6x2 BSC	Ken Mallinson
YJ17 BHN	Renault	Master LL35 Business Dci Curtainside	PE Logisitcs
YK15 HJX	Mercedes	Actros 2545 6x2 BSC	Ken Mallinson
YK62 KSV	Mercedes	Axor 1824 4w Curtainside	Ken Mallinson
YT62 DJV	Volvo	FH 460 6x2 GXL	J Cutt & Son

Culina/WS Transport Groups Trailers

Culina Group Trailer Abbreviations

BDD – Box Trailer Double Decker
BIT – Box International Trailer
BTK – Bulk Powder Tanker
CL – Chipliner
CLD – Curtainside Low Double Deck
CT – Cage Trailer
ET – Euro Trailer
FLD – Fridge ? Trailer
FMT – Fridge Multi Temperature
FST – Fridge Single Temperature
HB – Homebase Trailer
HET – High Eco Trailer
HHT – High Volume High Trailer
HT – Hydraroll Trailer
HVT – High Volume Trailer
ICT – International Cage Trailer
IET – International Euro Trailer
MCIT – Mega Curtainside International Trailer
MIT – Mega International Trailer
MT – Mega Continental Trailer
MXT – Mixer Trailer

RBT – Retail Box Trailer
RT/WRT/PRTAF/R – Race Trailers
RTT – Retail Tail lift Trailer
RUT – Retail Urban Trailer
SCT – Steel Coil Trailer
SDT – Swivel Deck Trailer
SET – Secure European Trailer
SIT – Step Frame International Trailer
SK – Skeletal Trailer
SKG – Skeletal Trailer
SMT – Secure Mega Trailer
TCT – Tesco Cage Trailer
TET – Tesco Euro Trailer
TFT – Tesco Fridge Trailer
TK/ATK – Tanker Trailer
TP – Tipper Trailer
UDD – Urban Double Deck Trailer
WDD – Wedge Double Deck Trailer
WF – Walking Floor Trailer
XET – Cross Strap Euro Trailer

WS Transportation Trailer Abbreviations

WSBT – Bulk Tanker Trailer
WSC – Curtainside Trailer
WSCL – Chipliner Trailer
WSCT – Cage Trailer
WSDD – Double Deck Trailer
WSET – European Trailer

WSLT – Liquid Tanker Trailer
WSMT – Moffatt Trailer
WSRD – Raindrop Trailer
WSS – Steel Trailer
WSSE – ? Tanker Trailer
WSSDU – Silo Skeletal Trailer

WST – Flatbed Trombone Trailer
WSTSL – Low Loader Trailer
WSTT – Tanker Trailer
WSUSC – ? Trailer
WSUT – Urban Trailer
TT – Low Loader Trailer

Explore Trailer Abreviations

CMDT – ? Trailer
CORT – Curtainside Trailer
CST – ? Trailer
CSU – Urban Trailer

FB – Flatbed Trailer
FBTW – Flatbed Trombone Trailer
LL – Low Loader Trailer
SF – Step Frame Trailer

SFEX – Low Loader Trailer
SU – ? Trailer
TCMAX – Low Loader Trailer
TEX – Low Loader Trailer

Livery Codes

ASF	Angus Soft Fruits	CGV	Culina-Vimto	MSW	Muller Milk (Silver/White)
BAM	Black AMG	CWW	Culina-Warrens White	PIB	Pirelli Black
CAC	Cathedral City	CUW	Culina-White	RHA	RHA
CIN	Cinch	CUR	Culina Recruitment	ROB	Robert Burns
CIK	Circle K	DAN	Danepak	ROS	Robsons of Spalding
CML	CML	ESG	Eddie Stobart Green	SIL	Silver
GBW	Culina-Great Bear (White)	ESW	Eddie Stobart White	SML	Silver (Muller Logo)
CUA	Culina Ambient	FOW	Fowler Welch White	SAM	Silver AMG
CCA	Culina Chilled Ambient	GBB	Great Bear Blue	SDB	Stardes Dark Blue
CCW	Culina Chilled White	GBG	Culina-Great Bear Green	SPR	Stobart Ports Red
CUL	Culina Group	HEK	Heck	STP	Stobart Power
CFW	Culina-Fowler Welch White	IRB	IRF Blue	THS	Thistle Seafoods
CIG	Culina-I R F Green	JET	Jet2.com	WAL	Walkers
CGI	Culina-iForce	MMI	Muller MMiD	WIL	White (Williams)
CSB	Culina-Stobart Black	MML	Morgan McLernon	WHS	White / Silver
CSG	Culina-Stobart Green	MUM	Muller Milk	YOC	Yorkshire Creamery
CSW	Culina-Stobart White	MBW	Muller Milk (Black/White)		

Culina Group (New Livery)

AVD 11000	GBG	AVD 11060	GBG	BIT 0159	CSW	BIT 0219	CSW	BMT 0003	CSW
AVD 11001	GBG	AVD 11061	CSG	BIT 0160	CSW	BIT 0220	CSW	BMT 0004	CSW
AVD 11002	GBG	AVD 11062	CSG	BIT 0161	CSW	BIT 0221	CSW	BMT 0005	CSW
AVD 11003	GBG	AVD 11063	CSG	BIT 0162	CSW	BIT 0222	CSW	BMT 0006	CSW
AVD 11004	GBG	AVD 11064	CSG	BIT 0163	CSW	BIT 0223	CSW	BMT 0007	CSW
AVD 11005	GBG	AVD 11065	CSG	BIT 0164	CSW	BIT 0224	CSW	BMT 0008	CSW
AVD 11006	GBG	AVD 11066	CSG	BIT 0165	CSW	BIT 0225	CSW	BMT 0009	CSW
AVD 11007	GBG	AVD 11067	CSG	BIT 0166	CSW	BIT 0226	CSW	BMT 0010	CSW
AVD 11008	GBG	AVD 11068	CSG	BIT 0167	CSW	BIT 0227	CSW	BMT 0011	CSW
AVD 11009	GBG	AVD 11069	CSG	BIT 0168	CSW	BIT 0228	CSW	BMT 0012	CSW
AVD 11010	GBG	AVD 11070	CSG	BIT 0169	CSW	BIT 0229	CSW	BMT 0013	CSW
AVD 11011	GBG	AVD 11071	CSG	BIT 0170	CSW	BIT 0230	CSW	BMT 0014	CSW
AVD 11012	GBG	AVD 11072	CSG	BIT 0171	CSW	BIT 0231	CSW	BMT 0015	CSW
AVD 11013	GBG	AVD 11073	CSG	BIT 0172	CSW	BIT 0232	CSW	CT 3528	CSG
AVD 11014	GBG	AVD 11074	CSG	BIT 0173	CSW	BIT 0233	CSW	CT 3540	CSG
AVD 11015	GBG	AVD 11075	CSG	BIT 0174	CSW	BIT 0234	CSW	CT 3558	CSG
AVD 11016	GBG	AVD 11076	CSG	BIT 0175	CSW	BIT 0235	CSW	CT 3710	CSG
AVD 11017	GBG	AVD 11077	CSG	BIT 0176	CSW	BIT 0236	CSW	CT 3711	CSG
AVD 11018	GBG	AVD 11078	CSG	BIT 0177	CSW	BIT 0237	CSW	CT 3712	CSG
AVD 11019	GBG	AVD 11079	CSG	BIT 0178	CSW	BIT 0238	CSW	CT 3713	CSG
AVD 11020	GBG	AVD 11080	CSG	BIT 0179	CSW	BIT 0239	CSW	CT 3714	CSG
AVD 11021	GBG	AVD 11081	CSG	BIT 0180	CSW	BIT 0240	CSW	CT 3715	CSG
AVD 11022	GBG	AVD 11082	CSG	BIT 0181	CSW	BIT 0241	CSW	CT 3716	CSG
AVD 11023	GBG	AVD 11083	CSG	BIT 0182	CSW	BIT 0242	CSW	CT 3717	CSG
AVD 11024	GBG	AVD 11084	CSG	BIT 0183	CSW	BIT 0243	CSW	CT 3718	CSG
AVD 11025	GBG	AVD 11085	CSG	BIT 0184	CSW	BIT 0244	CSW	CT 3719	CSG
AVD 11026	GBG	AVD 11086	CSG	BIT 0185	CSW	BIT 0245	CSW	CT 3720	CSG
AVD 11027	GBG	AVD 11087	CSG	BIT 0186	CSW	BIT 0246	CSW	CT 3721	CSG
AVD 11028	GBG	AVD 11088	CSG	BIT 0187	CSW	BIT 0247	CSW	CT 3722	CSG
AVD 11029	GBG	AVD 11089	CSG	BIT 0188	CSW	BIT 0248	CSW	CT 3723	CSG
AVD 11030	GBG	AVD 11090	CSG	BIT 0189	CSW	BIT 0249	CSW	CT 3724	CSG
AVD 11031	GBG	AVD 11091	CSG	BIT 0190	CSW	BIT 0250	CSW	CT 3725	CSG
AVD 11032	GBG	AVD 11092	CSG	BIT 0191	CSW	BIT 0251	CSW	CT 3726	CSG
AVD 11033	GBG	AVD 11093	CSG	BIT 0192	CSW	BLD 2067	CWW	CT 3727	CSG
AVD 11034	GBG	AVD 11094	CSG	BIT 0193	CSW	BLD 2068	CWW	CT 3728	CSG
AVD 11035	GBG	AVD 11095	CSG	BIT 0194	CSW	BLD 2069	CWW	CT 3729	CSG
AVD 11036	GBG	AVD 11096	CSG	BIT 0195	CSW	BLD 2070	CWW	CT 3730	CSG
AVD 11037	GBG	AVD 11097	CSG	BIT 0196	CSW	BLD 2071	CWW	CT 3731	CSG
AVD 11038	GBG	AVD 11098	CSG	BIT 0197	CSW	BLD 2072	CWW	CT 3732	GBG
AVD 11039	GBG	AVD 11099	CSG	BIT 0198	CSW	BLD 2073	CWW	CT 3733	CSG
AVD 11040	GBG	AVD 11100	CSG	BIT 0199	CSW	BLD 2074	CWW	CT 3734	CSG
AVD 11041	GBG	AVD 11101	CSG	BIT 0200	CSW	BLD 2075	CWW	CT 3735	CSG
AVD 11042	GBG	AVD 11102	CSG	BIT 0201	CSW	BLD 2076	CWW	CT 3736	CSG
AVD 11043	GBG	AVD 11103	CSG	BIT 0202	CSW	BLD 2077	CWW	CT 3737	CSG
AVD 11044	GBG	AVD 11104	CSG	BIT 0203	CSW	BLD 2078	CWW	CT 3738	CSG
AVD 11045	GBG	AVD 11105	CSG	BIT 0204	CSW	BLD 2079	CWW	CT 3739	CSG
AVD 11046	GBG	AVD 11106	CSG	BIT 0205	CSW	BLD 2080	CWW	CT 3740	CSG
AVD 11047	GBG	AVD 11107	CSG	BIT 0206	CSW	BLD 2081	CWW	CT 3741	CSG
AVD 11048	GBG	AVD 11108	CSG	BIT 0207	CSW	BLD 2082	CWW	CT 3742	CSG
AVD 11049	GBG	AVD 11109	CSG	BIT 0208	CSW	BLD 2083	CWW	CT 3743	CSG
AVD 11050	GBG	AVD 11110	CSG	BIT 0209	CSW	BLD 2084	CWW	CT 3744	CSG
AVD 11051	GBG	AVD 11111	CSG	BIT 0210	CSW	BLD 2085	CWW	CT 3745	CSG
AVD 11052	GBG	AVD 11112	CSG	BIT 0211	CSW	BLD 2086	CWW	CT 3746	CSG
AVD 11053	GBG	BIT 0152	CSW	BIT 0212	CSW	BLD 2087	CWW	CT 3747	CSG
AVD 11054	GBG	BIT 0153	CSW	BIT 0213	CSW	BLD 2088	CWW	CT 3748	CSG
AVD 11055	GBG	BIT 0154	CSW	BIT 0214	CSW	BLD 2089	CWW	CT 3749	CSG
AVD 11056	GBG	BIT 0155	CSW	BIT 0215	CSW	BLD 2090	CWW	CT 3750	CSG
AVD 11057	GBG	BIT 0156	CSW	BIT 0216	CSW	BLD 2091	CWW	CT 3751	CSG
AVD 11058	GBG	BIT 0157	CSW	BIT 0217	CSW	BMT 0001	CSW	CT 3752	CSG
AVD 11059	GBG	BIT 0158	CSW	BIT 0218	CSW	BMT 0002	CSW	CT 3753	CSG

Culina Group (New Livery)

CT 3754	CSG	FSK 1001	CSB	FST 5564	CUW	FST 5624	CUW	FST 5684	CUW
CT 3755	CSG	FSK 1002	CSB	FST 5565		FST 5625	CUW	FST 5685	CUW
CT 3756	CSG	FSK 1003	CSB	FST 5566		FST 5626	CUW	FST 5686	CUW
CT 3757	CSG	FSK 1004	CSB	FST 5567		FST 5627	CUW	FST 5687	CUW
CT 3758	CSG	FSK 1005	CSB	FST 5568		FST 5628	CUW	FST 5688	CUW
CT 3759	CSG	FSK 1006	CSB	FST 5569		FST 5629	CUW	FST 5689	CUW
CT 3760	CSG	FSK 1007	CSB	FST 5570		FST 5630	CUW	FST 5690	CUW
CT 3761	CSG	FSK 1008	CSB	FST 5571		FST 5631	CUW	FST 5691	CUW
CT 3762	GBG	FSK 1009	CSB	FST 5572		FST 5632	CUW	FST 5692	CUW
CT 3763	CSG	FSK 1010	CSB	FST 5573	CUW	FST 5633	CUW	FST 5693	CUW
CT 3764	CSG	FSK 1011	CSB	FST 5574	CUW	FST 5634	CUW	FST 5694	CUW
CT 3765	CSG	FSK 1012	CSB	FST 5575	CUW	FST 5635	CUW	FST 5695	CUW
CT 3766	CSG	FSK 1013	CSB	FST 5576	CUW	FST 5636	CUW	FST 5696	CUW
CT 3767	CSG	FSK 1014	CSB	FST 5577	CUW	FST 5637	CUW	FST 5697	CUW
FLD 2037	CUW	FSK 1015	CSB	FST 5578	CUW	FST 5638	ROB	FST 5698	CUW
FLD 2040	CUW	FSK 1016	CSB	FST 5579	CUW	FST 5639	CUW	FST 5699	CUW
FLD 2044	CUW	FSK 1017	CSB	FST 5580	CUW	FST 5640	CUW	FST 5700	CUW
FMT 5880	CUW	FSK 1018	CSB	FST 5581	CUW	FST 5641	CUW	FST 5701	CUW
FMT 5881	CUW	FSK 1019	CSB	FST 5582	CUW	FST 5642	CUW	FST 5702	CUW
FMT 5882	CUW	FST 5523	CFW	FST 5583	CUW	FST 5643	CUW	FST 5703	CUW
FMT 5883	CUW	FST 5524		FST 5584	CUW	FST 5644	CUW	FST 5704	CUW
FMT 5884	CUW	FST 5525		FST 5585	CUW	FST 5645	CUW	FST 5705	CUW
FMT 5885	CUW	FST 5526		FST 5586	CUW	FST 5646	CUW	FST 5706	CUW
FMT 5886	CUW	FST 5527		FST 5587	CUW	FST 5647	CUW	FST 5707	CUW
FMT 5887	CUW	FST 5528	CCW	FST 5588	CUW	FST 5648	CUW	FST 5708	CUW
FMT 5888	CUW	FST 5529		FST 5589	CUW	FST 5649	CUW	FST 5709	CUW
FMT 5889	CUW	FST 5530		FST 5590	CUW	FST 5650	CUW	FST 5710	CUW
FMT 5890	CFW	FST 5531	CFW	FST 5591	CUW	FST 5651	CUW	FST 5711	CUW
FMT 5891	CFW	FST 5532		FST 5592	CUW	FST 5652	CUW	FST 5712	CUW
FMT 5892	CFW	FST 5533		FST 5593	CUW	FST 5653	CUW	FST 5713	CUW
FMT 5893	CFW	FST 5534		FST 5594	CUW	FST 5654	CUW	FST 5714	CUW
FMT 5894	CFW	FST 5535		FST 5595	CUW	FST 5655	CUW	FST 5715	CUW
FMT 5895	CFW	FST 5536		FST 5596	CUW	FST 5656	CUW	FST 5716	CUW
FMT 5896	CFW	FST 5537		FST 5597	CUW	FST 5657	CUW	FST 5717	CUW
FMT 5897	CFW	FST 5538		FST 5598	CUW	FST 5658	CUW	FST 5718	CUW
FMT 5898	CFW	FST 5539		FST 5599	CUW	FST 5659	CUW	FST 5719	CUW
FMT 5899	CFW	FST 5540		FST 5600	CUW	FST 5660	CUW	FST 5720	CUW
FMT 5900	CFW	FST 5541		FST 5601	CUW	FST 5661	CUW	FST 5721	CUW
FMT 5901	CFW	FST 5542		FST 5602	CUW	FST 5662	CUW	FST 5722	CUW
FMT 5902	CFW	FST 5543		FST 5603	CUW	FST 5663	CUW	FST 5723	CUW
FMT 5903	CFW	FST 5544		FST 5604	CUW	FST 5664	CUW	FST 5724	CUW
FMT 5904	CFW	FST 5545		FST 5605	CUW	FST 5665	CUW	FST 5725	CUW
FMT 5905	CFW	FST 5546		FST 5606	CUW	FST 5666	CUW	FST 5726	CUW
FMT 5906	CUW	FST 5547	CUW	FST 5607	CUW	FST 5667	CUW	FST 5727	CUW
FMT 5907	CUW	FST 5548		FST 5608	CUW	FST 5668	CUW	FST 5728	CUW
FMT 5908	CUW	FST 5549		FST 5609	CUW	FST 5669	CUW	FST 5729	CUW
FMT 5909	CUW	FST 5550		FST 5610	CUW	FST 5670	CUW	FST 5730	CUW
FMT 5910	CFW	FST 5551		FST 5611	CUW	FST 5671	CUW	FST 5731	CUW
FMT 5911	CUW	FST 5552		FST 5612	CUW	FST 5672	CUW	FST 5732	CUW
FMT 5912	CUW	FST 5553	CFW	FST 5613	CUW	FST 5673	CUW	FST 5733	CUW
FMT 5913	CUW	FST 5554		FST 5614	CUW	FST 5674	CUW	FST 5734	CUW
FMT 5914	CUW	FST 5555		FST 5615	CUW	FST 5675	CUW	FST 5735	CUW
FMT 5915	CUW	FST 5556		FST 5616	CUW	FST 5676	CUW	FST 5736	CUW
FMT 5916	CUW	FST 5557		FST 5617	CUW	FST 5677	CUW	FST 5737	CUW
FMT 5917	CFW	FST 5558		FST 5618	CUW	FST 5678	CUW	FST 5738	CUW
FMT 5918	CFW	FST 5559	CFW	FST 5619	CUW	FST 5679	CUW	FST 5739	CUW
FMT 5919	CFW	FST 5560		FST 5620	CUW	FST 5680	CUW	FST 5740	CUW
FMT 6106	CUW	FST 5561		FST 5621	CUW	FST 5681	CUW	FST 5741	CUW
FMT 6109	CUW	FST 5562		FST 5622	CUW	FST 5682	CUW	FST 5742	CUW
FMT 6116	CUW	FST 5563		FST 5623	CUW	FST 5683	CUW	FST 5743	CUW

Culina Group (New Livery)

5811

FST 5744	CUW	FST 5804	CUW	FST 20054	CUW	FST 20114	CUW	FST 20268	CUW
FST 5745	CUW	FST 5805	CUW	FST 20055	CUW	FST 20190	MUM	FST 20269	CUW
FST 5746	CUW	FST 5806	CUW	FST 20056	CUW	FST 20191	MUM	FST 20270	CUW
FST 5747	CUW	FST 5807	CUW	FST 20057	CUW	FST 20192	MUM	FST 20271	CUW
FST 5748	CUW	FST 5808	CUW	FST 20058	CUW	FST 20193	MUM	FST 20272	CUW
FST 5749	CUW	FST 5809	CUW	FST 20059	CUW	FST 20194	MUM	FST 20273	CUW
FST 5750	CUW	FST 20000	CUW	FST 20060	CUW	FST 20195	MUM	FST 20274	CUW
FST 5751	CUW	FST 20001	CUW	FST 20061	CUW	FST 20196	MUM	FST 20275	CUW
FST 5752	CUW	FST 20002	CUW	FST 20062	CUW	FST 20197	MUM	FST 20276	CUW
FST 5753	CUW	FST 20003	CUW	FST 20063	CUW	FST 20198	MUM	FST 20277	CUW
FST 5754	CUW	FST 20004	CUW	FST 20064	CUW	FST 20199	MUM	FST 20278	CUW
FST 5755	CUW	FST 20005	CUW	FST 20065	CUW	FST 20200	CUW	FST 20279	CUW
FST 5756	CUW	FST 20006	CUW	FST 20066	CUW	FST 20201	CUW	FST 20280	CUW
FST 5757	CUW	FST 20007	CUW	FST 20067	CUW	FST 20202	CUW	FST 20281	CUW
FST 5758	CUW	FST 20008	CUW	FST 20068	CUW	FST 20203	CUW	FST 20282	CUW
FST 5759	CUW	FST 20009	CUW	FST 20069	CUW	FST 20204	CUW	FST 20283	CUW
FST 5760	CUW	FST 20010	CUW	FST 20070	CUW	FST 20205	CUW	FST 20284	CUW
FST 5761	CUW	FST 20011	CUW	FST 20071	CUW	FST 20206	CUW	FST 20285	CUW
FST 5762	CUW	FST 20012	CUW	FST 20072	CUW	FST 20207	CUW	FST 20286	CUW
FST 5763	CUW	FST 20013	CUW	FST 20073	CUW	FST 20208	CUW	FST 20287	CUW
FST 5764	CUW	FST 20014	CUW	FST 20074	CUW	FST 20209	CUW	FST 20288	CUW
FST 5765	CUW	FST 20015	CUW	FST 20075	CUW	FST 20210	CUW	FST 20289	CUW
FST 5766	CUW	FST 20016	CUW	FST 20076	CUW	FST 20211	CUW	FST 20290	CUW
FST 5767	CUW	FST 20017	CUW	FST 20077	CUW	FST 20212	CUW	FST 20291	CUW
FST 5768	CUW	FST 20018	CUW	FST 20078	CUW	FST 20213	CUW	FST 20292	CUW
FST 5769	CUW	FST 20019	CUW	FST 20079	CUW	FST 20214	CUW	FST 20293	CUW
FST 5770	CUW	FST 20020	CUW	FST 20080	CUW	FST 20215	CUW	FST 20294	CUW
FST 5771	CUW	FST 20021	CUW	FST 20081	CUW	FST 20216	CUW	FST 20295	CUW
FST 5772	CUW	FST 20022	CUW	FST 20082	CUW	FST 20217	CUW	FST 20296	CUW
FST 5773	CUW	FST 20023	CUW	FST 20083	CUW	FST 20218	CUW	FST 20297	CUW
FST 5774	CUW	FST 20024	CUW	FST 20084	CUW	FST 20219	CUW	FST 20298	CUW
FST 5775	CUW	FST 20025	CUW	FST 20085	CUW	FST 20220	CUW	FST 20299	CUW
FST 5776	CUW	FST 20026	CUW	FST 20086	CUW	FST 20221	CUW	FST 23001	MUM
FST 5777	CUW	FST 20027	CUW	FST 20087	CUW	FST 20222	CUW	FST 23002	MUM
FST 5778	CUW	FST 20028	CUW	FST 20088	CUW	FST 20223	CUW	FST 23003	MUM
FST 5779	CUW	FST 20029	CUW	FST 20089	CUW	FST 20224	CUW	FST 23004	MUM
FST 5780	CUW	FST 20030	CUW	FST 20090	CUW	FST 20225	CUW	FST 23005	MUM
FST 5781	CUW	FST 20031	CUW	FST 20091	CUW	FST 20226	CUW	FST 23006	MUM
FST 5782	CUW	FST 20032	CUW	FST 20092	CUW	FST 20244	CUW	FST 23007	MUM
FST 5783	CUW	FST 20033	CUW	FST 20093	CUW	FST 20247	CUW	FST 23008	MUM
FST 5784	CUW	FST 20034	CUW	FST 20094	CUW	FST 20248	CUW	FST 23009	MUM
FST 5785	CUW	FST 20035	CUW	FST 20095	CUW	FST 20249	CUW	FST 23010	MUM
FST 5786	CUW	FST 20036	CUW	FST 20096	CUW	FST 20250	CUW	FST 23011	MUM
FST 5787	CUW	FST 20037	CUW	FST 20097	CUW	FST 20251	CUW	FST 23012	MUM
FST 5788	CUW	FST 20038	CUW	FST 20098	CUW	FST 20252	CUW	FST 23013	MUM
FST 5789	CUW	FST 20039	CUW	FST 20099	CUW	FST 20253	CUW	FST 23014	MUM
FST 5790	CUW	FST 20040	CUW	FST 20100	CUW	FST 20254	CUW	FST 23015	MUM
FST 5791	CUW	FST 20041	CUW	FST 20101	CUW	FST 20255	CUW	FST 23016	MUM
FST 5792	CUW	FST 20042	CUW	FST 20102	CUW	FST 20256	CUW	FST 23017	MUM
FST 5793	CUW	FST 20043	CUW	FST 20103	CUW	FST 20257	CUW	FST 23018	MUM
FST 5794	CUW	FST 20044	CUW	FST 20104	CUW	FST 20258	CUW	FST 23019	MUM
FST 5795	CUW	FST 20045	CUW	FST 20105	CUW	FST 20259	CUW	FST 23020	MUM
FST 5796	CUW	FST 20046	CUW	FST 20106	CUW	FST 20260	CUW	FST 23021	MUM
FST 5797	CUW	FST 20047	CUW	FST 20107	CUW	FST 20261	CUW	FST 23022	MUM
FST 5798	CUW	FST 20048	CUW	FST 20108	CUW	FST 20262	CUW	FST 23023	MUM
FST 5799	CUW	FST 20049	CUW	FST 20109	CUW	FST 20263	CUW	FST 23024	MUM
FST 5800	CUW	FST 20050	CUW	FST 20110	CUW	FST 20264	CUW	FST 23025	MUM
FST 5801	CUW	FST 20051	CUW	FST 20111	CUW	FST 20265	CUW	FST 23026	MUM
FST 5802	CUW	FST 20052	CUW	FST 20112	CUW	FST 20266	CUW	FST 23027	MUM
FST 5803	CUW	FST 20053	CUW	FST 20113	CUW	FST 20267	CUW	FST 23028	MUM

Culina Group (New Livery)

ieτ 2537
ieτ 2548

FST 23029	MUM	FST 25029	CUW	FST 25088	CUW	FTT 6102	MUM	FTT 6161	MUM
FST 23030	MUM	FST 25030	CUW	FST 25089	CUW	FTT 6103	MUM	G 063	CWW
FST 23031	MUM	FST 25031	CUW	FST 25090	CUW	FTT 6104	MUM	HT 3524	CSG
FST 23032	MUM	FST 25032	CUW	FST 25091	CUW	FTT 6105	MUM	HT 3531	CSG
FST 23033	MUM	FST 25033	CUW	FST 25092	CUW	FTT 6106	MUM	HT 3539	CSG
FST 23034	MUM	FST 25034	CUW	FST 25093	CUW	FTT 6107	MUM	HT 3546	CSG
FST 23035	MUM	FST 25035	CUW	FST 25094	CUW	FTT 6108	MUM	HT 3583	CSG
FST 23036	MUM	FST 25036	CUW	FST 25095	CUW	FTT 6109	MUM	HT 3596	CSG
FST 23037	MUM	FST 25037	CUW	FST 25096	CUW	FTT 6110	MUM	HT 3604	CSG
FST 23038	MUM	FST 25038	CUW	FST 25195	CUW	FTT 6111	MUM	HT 3615	CSG
FST 23039	MUM	FST 25039	CUW	FST 25196	CUW	FTT 6112	MUM	HT 3623	CSG
FST 23040	MUM	FST 25040	CUW	FST 25197	CUW	FTT 6113	MUM	HT 3625	CSG
FST 23041	MUM	FST 25041	CUW	FST 25198	CUW	FTT 6114	MUM	HT 3626	CSG
FST 23042	MUM	FST 25042	CUW	FST 25199	CUW	FTT 6115	MUM	HT 3677	CSG
FST 23043	MUM	FST 25043	CUW	FST 25200	CUW	FTT 6116	MUM	HT 3682	CSG
FST 23044	MUM	FST 25044	CUW	FST 25201	CUW	FTT 6117	MUM	HT 3687	CSG
FST 23045	MUM	FST 25045	CUW	FST 25202	CUW	FTT 6118	MUM	HT 3699	CSG
FST 23046	MUM	FST 25046	CUW	FST 25203	CUW	FTT 6119	MUM	HT 3701	CSG
FST 23047	MUM	FST 25047	CUW	FST 25204	CUW	FTT 6120	MUM	HT 3702	CSG
FST 23048	MUM	FST 25048	CUW	FST 25205	CUW	FTT 6121	MUM	HT 3703	CSG
FST 23049	MUM	FST 25049	CUW	FST 25206	CUW	FTT 6122	MUM	HT 3704	CSG
FST 23050	MUM	FST 25050	CUW	FTT 5922	CUW	FTT 6123	MUM	HT 3705	CSG
FST 23051	MUM	FST 25051	CUW	FTT 5930	CUW	FTT 6124	MUM	HT 3706	CSG
FST 23052	MUM	FST 25052	CUW	FTT 5931	CUW	FTT 6125	MUM	HT 3707	CSG
FST 23053	MUM	FST 25053	CUW	FTT 5932	CUW	FTT 6126	MUM	HT 3708	CSG
FST 23054	MUM	FST 25054	CUW	FTT 5933	CUW	FTT 6127	MUM	HT 3709	CSG
FST 23055	MUM	FST 25055	CUW	FTT 5934	CUW	FTT 6128	MUM	IET 2514	CSG
FST 23056	MUM	FST 25056	CUW	FTT 5935	CUW	FTT 6129	MUM	IET 2520	CGI
FST 23057	MUM	FST 25057	CUW	FTT 5936	CUW	FTT 6130	MUM	IET 2523	CSG
FST 23058	MUM	FST 25058	CUW	FTT 5937	CUW	FTT 6131	MUM	IET 2531	CSG
FST 25000	CUW	FST 25059	CUW	FTT 5938	CUW	FTT 6132	MUM	IET 2540	CSG
FST 25001	CUW	FST 25060	CUW	FTT 5939	CUW	FTT 6133	MUM	IET 2542	CSG
FST 25002	CUW	FST 25061	CUW	FTT 5940	CUW	FTT 6134	MUM	IET 2543	CSG
FST 25003	CUW	FST 25062	CUW	FTT 5941	CUW	FTT 6135	MUM	IET 2544	CSG
FST 25004	CUW	FST 25063	CUW	FTT 5942	CUW	FTT 6136	MUM	IET 2545	CSG
FST 25005	CUW	FST 25064	CUW	FTT 5943	CUW	FTT 6137	MUM	IET 2546	CSG
FST 25006	CUW	FST 25065	CUW	FTT 5944	CUW	FTT 6138	MUM	IET 2547	CGI
FST 25007	CUW	FST 25066	CUW	FTT 5945	CUW	FTT 6139	MUM	IET 2551	CSG
FST 25008	CUW	FST 25067	CUW	FTT 5946	CUW	FTT 6140	MUM	IET 2552	CSG
FST 25009	CUW	FST 25068	CUW	FTT 5947	CUW	FTT 6141	MUM	IET 2553	CGV
FST 25010	CUW	FST 25069	CUW	FTT 5948	CUW	FTT 6142	MUM	IET 2559	CSG
FST 25011	CUW	FST 25070	CUW	FTT 5949	CUW	FTT 6143	MUM	IET 2564	CSG
FST 25012	CUW	FST 25071	CUW	FTT 5950	CUW	FTT 6144	MUM	IET 2577	CSG
FST 25013	CUW	FST 25072	CUW	FTT 5951	CUW	FTT 6145	MUM	IET 2590	CSG
FST 25014	CUW	FST 25073	CUW	FTT 5952	CUW	FTT 6146	MUM	IET 2591	CSG
FST 25015	CUW	FST 25074	CUW	FTT 5953	CUW	FTT 6147	MUM	RTT 12022	CSG
FST 25016	CUW	FST 25075	CUW	FTT 5954	CUW	FTT 6148	MUM	SCT 0154	CSG
FST 25017	CUW	FST 25076	CUW	FTT 5955	MUM	FTT 6149	MUM	SCT 0155	CSG
FST 25018	CUW	FST 25077	CUW	FTT 5956	MUM	FTT 6150	MUM	SCT 0156	CSC
FST 26010	CUW	FST 26078	CUW	FTT 6067	MUM	FTT 6151	MUM	SK 885	CSB
FST 25020	CUW	FST 25079	CUW	FTT 5958	MUM	FTT 6152	MUM	SK 886	CSB
FST 25021	CUW	FST 25080	CUW	FTT 5959	MUM	FTT 6153	MUM	SK 887	CSB
FST 25022	CUW	FST 25081	CUW	FTT 5960	MUM	FTT 6154	MUM	SK 888	CSB
FST 25023	CUW	FST 25082	CUW	FTT 5961	MUM	FTT 6155	MUM	SK 889	CSB
FST 25024	CUW	FST 25083	CUW	FTT 5962	MUM	FTT 6156	MUM	SK 890	CSB
FST 25025	CUW	FST 25084	CUW	FTT 5963	MUM	FTT 6157	MUM	SK 891	CSB
FST 25026	CUW	FST 25085	CUW	FTT 5964	MUM	FTT 6158	MUM	SK 892	CSB
FST 25027	CUW	FST 25086	CUW	FTT 5965	MUM	FTT 6159	MUM	SK 893	CSB
FST 25028	CUW	FST 25087	CUW	FTT 6101	MUM	FTT 6160	MUM		

SCT 0157 CSG
SCT 2593 CSG

Culina Group (New Livery)

SK 894	CSB	TCT 7394	CSG	TCT 7869	CSG	TET 9989	CSG	TTMT 1188	MSW
SK 895	CSB	TCT 7401	CSG	TCT 7870	CSG	TET 9991	CSG	TTMT 1195	MSW
SK 896	CSB	TCT 7416	GBG	TCT 7871	CSG	TET 9993	CSG	TTMT 1196	MSW
SK 897	CSB	TCT 7417	CSG	TCT 7872	CSG	TET 10011	CSG	TTMT 1197	MSW
SK 898	CSB	TCT 7425	CSG	TCT 7873	CSG	TET 10039	CSG	TTMT 1198	MSW
SK 899	CSB	TCT 7440	CSG	TCT 7874	CSG	TET 10048	CSG	UFT 5932	MBW
SK 900	CSB	TCT 7449	CSG	TCT 7875	CSG	TET 10054	CSG	UFT 5933	MBW
SK 901	CSB	TCT 7469	CSG	TCT 7876	CSG	TET 10060	CSG	UFT 5934	MBW
SK 902	CSB	TCT 7471	GBG	TCT 7877	CSG	TET 10064	CSG	UFT 5935	MBW
SK 903	CSB	TCT 7478	CSG	TCT 7878	CSG	TET 10074	CSG	UFT 5936	MBW
SK 904	CSB	TCT 7528	CSG	TCT 7879	CSG	TET 10075	CSG	UFT 5937	MBW
SK 905	CSB	TCT 7537	CSG	TCT 7880	CSG	TET 10083	CSG	UFT 5938	MBW
SK 906	CSB	TCT 7541	CSG	TCT 7881	CSG	TET 10085	CSG	UFT 5939	MBW
SK 907	CSB	TCT 7548	CSG	TCT 7882	CSG	TET 10089	CSG	UFT 5940	MBW
SK 908	CSB	TCT 7562	CSG	TCT 7883	CSG	TET 10091	CSG	UFT 5941	MBW
SK 909	CSB	TCT 7563	CSG	TCT 7884	CSG	TET 10092	CSG	UFT 5942	MBW
SK 910	CSB	TCT 7567	CSG	TCT 7885	CSG	TET 10101	CSG	UFT 5943	MBW
SK 911	CSB	TCT 7571	CSG	TCT 7886	CSG	TET 10103	CSG	UFT 5944	MBW
SK 912	CSB	TCT 7582	CSG	TCT 7887	CSG	TET 10110	CSG	UFT 5945	MBW
SK 913	CSB	TCT 7584	CSG	TCT 7888	CSG	TET 10111	CSG	UFT 5946	MBW
SK 914	CSB	TTC 7592	CSG	TCT 7889	CSG	TET 10115	CSG	UFT 5947	MBW
SK 915	CSB	TCT 7595	CSG	TCT 7890	CSG	TET 10121	CSG	UFT 5948	MBW
SK 916	CSB	TCT 7611	CSG	TCT 7891	CSG	TET 10127	CSG	UFT 5949	MBW
SK 917	CSB	TCT 7630	CSG	TET 9902	CSG	TET 10145	CSG	UFT 5950	MBW
SK 918	CSB	TCT 7631	CSG	TET 9904	CSG	TET 10154	CSG	UFT 5951	MBW
SK 919	CSB	TCT 7640	CSG	TET 9906	CSG	TET 10159	CSG	UFT 5952	MBW
SK 920	CSB	TCT 7643	CSG	TET 9909	CSG	TET 10163	CSG	UFT 5953	MBW
SK 921	CSB	TCT 7681	CSG	TET 9916	CSG	TET 10166	CSG	UFT 5954	MBW
SK 922	CSB	TCT 7718	CSG	TET 9917	CSG	TET 10169	CSG	UFT 5955	MBW
SK 923	CSB	TCT 7748	CSG	TET 9920	CIG	TET 10170	CSG	UFT 5956	MBW
SK 924	CSB	TCT 7805	CSG	TET 9921	CSG	TET 10196	CSG	UFT 5957	MBW
SK 925	CSB	TCT 7820	CSG	TET 9924	CSG	TET 10205	CSG	UFT 5958	MBW
SK 926	CSB	TCT 7850	CSG	TET 9925	CSG	TET 10210	CSG	UFT 5959	MBW
SK 927	CSB	TCT 7853	CSG	TET 9926	CSG	TET 10211	CSG	UFT 5960	MBW
SK 928	CSB	TCT 7854	CSG	TET 9928	CSG	TET 10215	CSG	UFT 5961	MBW
SK 929	CSB	TCT 7855	CSG	TET 9931	CSG	TET 10239	CSG	UFT 5962	MBW
SK 930	CSB	TCT 7856	CSG	TET 9937	CSG	TET 10247	CSG	UFT 5963	MBW
SK 931	CSB	TCT 7857	CSG	TET 9942	CSG	TET 10248	CSG	UFT 5964	MBW
SK 932	CSB	TCT 7858	CSG	TET 9943	CSG	TET 10252	CSG	UFT 5965	MBW
SK 933	CSB	TCT 7859	CSG	TET 9944	CSG	TET 10258	CSG	UFT 5966	MBW
SK 934	CSB	TCT 7860	CSG	TET 9949	CSG	TET 10261	CSG	UFT 5967	MBW
SK 1010	CSB	TCT 7861	CSG	TET 9950	CSG	TET 10262	CSG	UFT 5968	MBW
STA/MV62	SDB	TCT 7862	CSG	TET 9962	CSG	TET 10279	CSG	UFT 5969	MBW
STA/MV81	SDB	TCT 7863	CSG	TET 9968	CSG	TET 10286	CSG	UFT 5970	MBW
TCT 7362	CSG	TCT 7864	CSG	TET 9970	CSG	TET 10299	CSG	UFT 5971	MBW
TCT 7382	CSG	TCT 7865	CSG	TET 9973	GBG	TET 10328	CSG	XET 15417	CSG
TCT 7385	CSG	TCT 7866	CSG	TET 9974	CSG	TET 10330	CSG	XET 15550	GBG
TCT 7389	CSG	TCT 7867	CSG	TET 9976	CSG	TET 10363	CSG	XET 15578	CSG
TCT 7390	CSG	TCT 7868	CSG	TET 9984	GBG	TET 10424	CSG		

9930
9913

Culina Group

TA9	SML	T274	MUM	T421	MUM	T480	MUM	T539	CUA		
TA25	SML	T277	CCW	T422	MUM	T481	MUM	T540	CUA		
TA35	SML	T280	MUM	T423	MUM	T482	MUM	T541	CUA		
TA40	SML	T325	MUM	T424	MUM	T483	MUM	T542	CUA		
T4	MUM	T334	MUM	T425	MUM	T484	MUM	T543	CUA		
T20	MUM	T354	MUM	T426	MUM	T485	MUM	T544	CUA		
T31	MUM	T359	MUM	T427	MUM	T486	MUM	T545	CUA		
T38	MUM	T369	MUM	T428	MUM	T487	MUM	T546	CUA		
T39	MUM	T370	MUM	T429	MUM	T488	MUM	T547	CUA		
T40	MUM	T371	MUM	T430	MUM	T489	MUM	T548	CUA		
T41	MUM	T372	MUM	T431	MUM	T490	MUM	T549	CUA		
T42	MUM	T373	MUM	T432	MUM	T491	MUM	T550	CUA		
T43	MUM	T374	MUM	T433	MUM	T492	MUM	T551	CUA		
T44	MUM	T375	MUM	T434	MUM	T493	MUM	T552	CUA		
T45	MUM	T376	MUM	T435	MUM	T494	MUM	T553	CUA		
T46	MUM	T377	MUM	T436	MUM	T495	MUM	T554	CUA		
T59	MUM	T378	MUM	T437	MUM	T496	MUM	T555	CUA		
T62	MUM	T379	MUM	T438	MUM	T497	MUM	T556	CUA		
T63	MUM	T380	MUM	T439	MUM	T498	MUM	T557	CUA		
T69	MUM	T381	MUM	T440	MUM	T499	MUM	T558	CUA		
T74	MUM	T382	MUM	T441	MUM	T500	MUM	T559	CUA		
T78	MUM	T383	MUM	T442	MUM	T501	MUM	T560	CUA		
T84	MUM	T384	MUM	T443	MUM	T502	MUM	T561	CUA		
T94	MUM	T385	MUM	T444	MUM	T503	MUM	T573	MUM		
T95	MUM	T386	MUM	T445	MUM	T504	MUM	T574	CUW		
T103	MUM	T387	MUM	T446	MUM	T505	MUM	T575	CUW		
T104	MUM	T388	MUM	T447	MUM	T506	MUM	T576	CUW		
T106	MUM	T389	MUM	T448	MUM	T507	MUM	T577	CUW		
T108	MUM	T390	MUM	T449	MUM	T508	MUM	T578	CUW		
T112	MUM	T391	MUM	T450	MUM	T509	CUA	T579	CUW		
T124	MUM	T392	MUM	T451	MUM	T510	CUA	T580	CUW		
T129	CCW	T393	MUM	T452	MUM	T511	CUA	T581	CUW		
T131	MUM	T394	MUM	T453	MUM	T512	CUA	232	CUA		
T140	MUM	T395	MUM	T454	MUM	T513	CUA	236	CUA		
T141	MUM	T396	MUM	T455	MUM	T514	CUA	237	CUA		
T146	MUM	T397	MUM	T456	MUM	T515	CUA	613	CCA		
T153	MUM	T398	MUM	T457	MUM	T516	CUA	618	CCA		
T155	MUM	T399	MUM	T458	MUM	T517	CUA	627	CCA		
T163	MUM	T400	MMI	T459	MUM	T518	CUA	1014	CCA		
T168	MUM	T401	CUR	T460	MUM	T519	CUA	1026	CCA		
T176	MUM	T402	MUM	T461	MUM	T520	CUA	1027	CCA		
T179	MUM	T403	MUM	T462	MUM	T521	CUA	1037	CCW		
T180	MUM	T404	MUM	T463	MUM	T522	CUA	1038	CCA		
T185	MUM	T405	MUM	T464	MUM	T523	CUA	1039	CCA		
T190	MUM	T406	MUM	T465	MUM	T524	CUA	1040	CCA		
T201	MUM	T407	MUM	T466	MUM	T525	CUA	1041	CCA		
T209	MUM	T408	MUM	T467	MUM	T526	CUA	1042	CCA		
T211	MUM	T409	MUM	T468	MUM	T527	CUA	1043	CCA		
T214	MUM	T410	MUM	T469	MUM	T528	CUA	1044	CCA		
T226	MUM	T411	MUM	T470	MUM	T529	CUA	1045	CCA		
T229	MUM	T412	MUM	T471	MUM	T530	CUA	1046	CCA		
T232	MUM	T413	MUM	T472	MUM	T531	CUA	1047	CCA		
T233	MUM	T414	MUM	T473	MUM	T532	CUA	1048	CCA		
T236	MUM	T415	MUM	T474	MUM	T533	CUA	1049	CCA		
T241	MUM	T416	MUM	T475	MUM	T534	CUA	1050	CCA		
T256	MUM	T417	MUM	T476	MUM	T535	CUA	1051	CCA		
T262	MUM	T418	MUM	T477	MUM	T536	CUA	1052	CCA		
T268	MUM	T419	MUM	T478	MUM	T537	CUA	1053	CCA		
T272	MUM	T420	MUM	T479	MUM	T538	CUA	1054	CCA		

Culina Group

Fleet	Code	Fleet	Code	Fleet	Code	Fleet	Code	Fleet	Code
1055	CCA	1226	CCW	1286	CCW	1395-19	CCW	13155-20	CCW
1056	CCA	1227	CCW	1287	CCW	1396-19	CCW	13156-20	CCW
1057	CCA	1228	CCW	1288	CCW	1397-19	CCW	13157-20	CCW
1058	CCA	1229	CCW	1289	CCW	1398-19	CCW	13158-20	CCW
1069	CCW	1230	CCW	1290	CCW	1399-19	CCW	13159-20	CCW
1075	CCW	1231	CCW	1291	CCW	13100-19	CCW	13160-20	CCW
1076	CCW	1232	CCW	1292	CCW	13101-19	CCW	13161-20	CCW
1077	CCW	1233	CCW	1293	CCW	13102-19	CCW	13162-20	CCW
1078	CCW	1234	CCW	1294	CCW	13103-19	CCW	13163-20	CCW
1079	CCW	1235	CCW	1295	CCW	13104-19	CCW	13164-20	CCW
1080	CCW	1236	CCW	1296	CCW	13105-19	CCW	13165-20	CCW
1081	CCW	1237	CCW	1297	CCW	13106-19	CCW	13166-20	CCW
1082	CCW	1238	CCW	1298	CCW	13107-19	CCW	13167-20	CCW
1083	CCW	1239	CCW	1299	CCW	13108-19	CCW	13168-20	CCW
1084	CCW	1240	CCW	1300	CCW	13110-19	CCW	13169-20	CCW
1085	CCW	1241	CCW	1301	CCW	13111-19	CCW	13170-20	CCW
1086	CCW	1242	CCW	1302	CCW	13112-19	CCW	13171-20	CCW
1087	CCW	1243	CCW	1303	CCW	13113-19	CCW	13172-20	CCW
1088	CCW	1244	CCW	1304	CCW	13114-19	CCW	13173-20	CCW
1089	CCW	1245	CCW	1305	CCW	13115-19	CCW	13174-20	CCW
1090	CCW	1246	CCW	1306	CCW	13116-19	CCW	13175-20	CCW
1091	CCW	1247	CCW	1307	CCW	13117-19	CCW	13176-20	CCW
1092	CCW	1248	CCW	1308	CCW	13118-19	CCW	13177-20	CCW
1093	CCW	1249	CCW	1309	CCW	13119-19	CCW	13178-20	CCW
1094	CCW	1250	CCW	1310	CCW	13120-19	CCW	13179-20	CCW
1095	CCW	1251	CCW	1311	CCW	13121-19	CCW	13180-20	CCW
1096	CCW	1252	CCW	1312	CCW	13122-19	CCW	13181-20	CCW
TK1103	CCW	1253	CCW	1313	CCW	13123-19	CCW	13182-20	CCW
TK1106	CCW	1254	CCW	1314	CCW	13124-19	CCW	13183-20	CCW
1108	CCW	1255	CCW	1315	CCW	13125-19	CCW	13184-20	CCW
TK1138	CCW	1256	CCW	1316	CCW	13126-19	CCW	13185-20	CCW
1156	CCW	1257	CCW	1317	CCW	13127-19	CCW	13186-20	CCW
1159	CCW	1258	CCW	1318-18	CCW	13128-19	CCW	13187-20	CCW
1160	CCW	1259	CCW	1319-18	CCW	13129-19	CCW	13188-20	CCW
1162	CCW	1260	CCW	1320-18	CCW	13130-19	CCW	13189-20	CCW
1201	CCW	1261	CCW	1321-18	CCW	13131-19	CCW	13190-20	CCW
1202	CCW	1262	CCW	1322-18	CCW	13132-19	CCW	13191-20	CCW
1203	CCW	1263	CCW	1323-18	CCW	13133-19	CCW	13192-20	CCW
1204	CCW	1264	CCW	1324-18	CCW	13134-19	CCW	13193-20	CCW
1205	CCW	1265	CCW	1325-18	CCW	13135-19	CCW	13194-20	CCW
1206	CCW	1266	CCW	1326-18	CCW	13136-19	CCW	13195-20	CCW
1207	CCW	1267	CCW	1327-18	CCW	13137-19	CCW	13196-20	CCW
1208	CCW	1268	CCW	1328-18	CCW	13138-19	CCW	13197-20	CCW
1209	CCW	1269	CCW	1330-18	CCW	13139-20	CCW	13198-20	CCW
1210	CCW	1270	CCW	1336-18	CCW	13140-20	CCW	13199-21	CCW
1211	CCW	1271	CCW	1353-19	CCW	13141-20	CCW	13200-21	CCW
1212	CCW	1272	CCW	1354-19	CCW	13142-20	CCW	13201-21	CCW
1213	CCW	1273	CCW	1355-19	CCW	13143-20	CCW	13202-21	CCW
1214	CCW	1274	CCW	1359-19	CCW	13144-20	CCW	13203-21	CCW
1215	CCW	1275	CCW	1360-19	CCW	13145-20	CCW	13204-21	CCW
1216	CCW	1276	CCW	1370-19	CCW	13146-20	CCW	13205-21	CCW
1217	CCW	1277	CCW	1371-19	CCW	13147-20	CCW	13206-21	CCW
1218	CCW	1278	CCW	1374-19	CCW	13148-20	CCW	13207-21	CCW
1219	CCW	1279	CCW	1375-19	CCW	13149-20	CCW	13208-21	CCW
1220	CCW	1280	CCW	1376-19	CCW	13150-20	CCW	13209-21	CCW
1221	CCW	1281	CCW	1378-19	CCW	13151-20	CCW	13210-21	CCW
1222	CCW	1282	CCW	1379-19	CCW	13151-20	CCW	13211-21	CCW
1223	CCW	1283	CCW	1381-19	CCW	13152-20	CCW	13212-21	CCW
1224	CCW	1284	CCW	1385-19	CCW	13153-20	CCW	13213-21	CCW
1225	CCW	1285	CCW	1394-19	CCW	13154-20	CCW	13214-21	CCW

Culina Group

13215-21	CCW	1440	CCW	1473-18	CCW	14106	CCW	17027TL	CCW
13216-21	CCW	1441	CCW	1474-18	CCW	14107-19	CCW	17028TL	CCW
13217-21	CCW	1442	CCW	1475-18	CCW	14108	CCW	17029TL	CCW
13218-21	CCW	1443	CCW	1476-18	CCW	14109	CCW	17030TL	CCW
13219-21	CCW	1444	CCW	1477-18	CCW	14110-19	CCW	17031TL	CCW
13220-21	CCW	1445	CCW	1478-18	CCW	14111-19	CCW	17032TL	CCW
13221-21	CCW	1446	CCW	1479-18	CCW	1506	FOW	17033TL	CCW
13222-21	CCW	1447	CCW	1480-18	CCW	1507	FOW	17034TL	CCW
13223-21	CCW	1448	CCW	1481-18	CCW	17002TL	CCW	17035TL	CCW
13224-21	CCW	1449	CCW	1482-18	CCW	17003TL	CCW	17036TL	CCW
13225-21	CCW	1450	CCW	1483-18	CCW	17004TL	CCW	17037TL	CCW
13226-21	CCW	1451	CCW	1484-18	CCW	17005TL	CCW	17038TL	CCW
13227-21	CCW	1452	CCW	1485-18	CCW	17006TL	CCW	17039TL	CCW
13228-21	CCW	1453	CCW	1486-18	CCW	17007TL	CCW	17040TL	CCW
13229-21	CCW	1454	CCW	1487-18	CCW	17008TL	CCW	17041	CCW
13230-21	CCW	1455-18	CCW	1488-18	CCW	17009TL	CCW	17042	CCW
13231-21	CCW	1456-18	CCW	1489-18	CCW	17010TL	CCW	17043	CCW
13232-21	CCW	1457-18	CCW	1490-18	CCW	17011TL	CCW	17044	CCW
1400	CCW	1458-18	CCW	1491-18	CCW	17012TL	CCW	17045	CCW
1401	CCW	1459-18	CCW	1492-18	CCW	17013TL	CCW	17046	CCW
1404	CCW	1460-18	CCW	1493-18	CCW	17014TL	CCW	17047	CCW
1405	CCW	1461-18	CCW	1494-18	CCW	17015TL	CCW	17048	CCW
1429	CCW	1462-18	CCW	1495-18	CCW	17016TL	CCW	17049	CCW
1430	CCW	1463-18	CCW	1496-18	CCW	17017TL	CCW	17050	CCW
1431	CCW	1464-18	CCW	1497-18	CCW	17018TL	CCW	17051	CCW
1432	CCW	1465-18	CCW	1498-18	CCW	17019TL	CCW	17052	CCW
1433	CCW	1466-18	CCW	1499-18	CCW	17020TL	CCW	17053	CCW
1434	CCW	1467-18	CCW	14100-18	CCW	17021TL	CCW	17054	CCW
1435	CCW	1468-18	CCW	14101-18	CCW	17022TL	CCW	17055	CCW
1436	CCW	1469-18	CCW	14102	CCW	17023TL	CCW	17061	CCW
1437	CCW	1470-18	CCW	14103	CCW	17024TL	CCW	2140	CCW
1438	CCW	1471-18	CCW	14104	CCW	17025TL	CCW	42018S	CUL
1439	CCW	1472-18	CCW	14105	CCW	17026TL	CCW	42053U	CUL

Fowler Welch

13123TU	FOW	16113NN	CAC	16205	FOW	16227	FOW	16249	FOW
13128	JET	16114NN	CAC	16206	FOW	16228	FOW	16250	FOW
13136WT	JET	16115NN	FOW	16207	FOW	16229	FOW	16251	FOW
13196-21	White	16118NN	CAC	16208	FOW	16230	FOW	16252	FOW
13209DE	FOW	16119NN	FOW	16209	FOW	16231	FOW	16253	FOW
13249SP	JET	16120NN	FOW	16210	FOW	16232	FOW	16254	FOW
13251SP	JET	16121NN	FOW	16211	FOW	16233	FOW	16255	FOW
13254SP	JET	16122NN	FOW	16212	FOW	16234	FOW	16256NN	FOW
13257KE	JET	16123NN	FOW	16213	FOW	16235	FOW	16257NN	FOW
13260SP	JET	16124NN	FOW	16214	FOW	16236	FOW	16258	FOW
13277DE	FOW	16125NN	FOW	16215	FOW	16237	FOW	16259	FOW
14206SC	FOW	16126NN	FOW	16216	FOW	16238	FOW	16260	FOW
14226SC	FOW	16127NN	FOW	16217	FOW	16239	FOW	16201	FOW
15211	White	16128NN	FOW	16218	FOW	16240	FOW	16262	FOW
15215	RHA	16134NN	FOW	16219	FOW	16241	FOW	16263	FOW
16100NN	CAC	16136NN	FOW	16220	FOW	16242	FOW	16264	FOW
16101NN	FOW	16139NN	FOW	16221	FOW	16243	FOW	16265NN	FOW
16102NN	FOW	16200	FOW	16222	FOW	16244	FOW	16266	FOW
16103NN	FOW	16201	FOW	16223	FOW	16245	FOW	16267NN	FOW
16104NN	FOW	16202	FOW	16224	FOW	16246	FOW	16268NN	FOW
16105NN	CAC	16203	FOW	16225	FOW	16247	FOW	16269	FOW
16108NN	CAC	16204	FOW	16226	FOW	16248	FOW	16270	FOW

Fowler Welch

16271	FOW	17244	FOW	19126	FOW	19257	FOW	20236	FOW
16272	FOW	17245	FOW	19127	FOW	19258	FOW	20237	FOW
16273	FOW	17246	FOW	19203	HEK	19259	FOW	20238	FOW
16274	FOW	17247	FOW	19204	HEK	19260	FOW	20239	FOW
16275	FOW	17248	FOW	19205	HEK	19261	FOW	20240	FOW
16276NN	FOW	17249	FOW	19206	HEK	19262	FOW	20241	FOW
16277	FOW	17250	FOW	19207	HEK	19263	FOW	20242	FOW
16278	FOW	17251	FOW	19208	HEK	19264	FOW	20243	FOW
16279	FOW	17252	FOW	19209	HEK	19265	FOW	20244	FOW
16280	FOW	17253	FOW	19210	HEK	19266	FOW	20245	FOW
16281	FOW	17254	FOW	19211	HEK	19267	FOW	20246	FOW
16282	FOW	17255	FOW	19212	HEK	19268	FOW	20247	FOW
16283NN	FOW	17256	FOW	19213	HEK	19269	FOW	20248	FOW
17201	FOW	17257	FOW	19214	HEK	19270	FOW	20249	FOW
17202	FOW	17258	FOW	19215	FOW	19271	FOW	20250	FOW
17203	FOW	17259	FOW	19216	FOW	19272	FOW	20251	FOW
17204	FOW	17260	FOW	19217	FOW	19273	FOW	20252	FOW
17205	FOW	17261	FOW	19218	FOW	19274	FOW	20253	FOW
17206	FOW	17262	FOW	19219	FOW	19275	FOW	20254	FOW
17207	FOW	17263	FOW	19220	FOW	19276	FOW	20255	FOW
17208	FOW	17264	FOW	19221	FOW	19277	FOW	20256	FOW
17209	FOW	17265	FOW	19222	FOW	20201	FOW	20257	FOW
17210	FOW	17266	FOW	19223	FOW	20202	FOW	20258	FOW
17211	FOW	17267	FOW	19224	FOW	20203	FOW	20259	FOW
17212	FOW	17268	FOW	19225	FOW	20204	FOW	20260	FOW
17213	FOW	17269	FOW	19226	FOW	20205	FOW	20261	FOW
17214	FOW	17270	FOW	19227	FOW	20206	FOW	20262	FOW
17215	FOW	17271	FOW	19228	FOW	20207	FOW	20263	FOW
17216	FOW	17272	FOW	19229	FOW	20208	FOW	20264	FOW
17217	FOW	17273	FOW	19230	FOW	20209	FOW	20265	FOW
17218	FOW	19100	FOW	19231	FOW	20210	FOW	20266	FOW
17219	FOW	19101	FOW	19232	FOW	20211	FOW	20267	FOW
17220	FOW	19102	FOW	19233	FOW	20212	FOW	20268	FOW
17221	FOW	19103	FOW	19234	FOW	20213	FOW	20269	FOW
17222	FOW	19104	FOW	19235	FOW	20214	FOW	20270	FOW
17223	FOW	19105	FOW	19236	FOW	20215	FOW	20271	FOW
17224	FOW	19106	FOW	19237	FOW	20216	FOW	20272	FOW
17225	FOW	19107	FOW	19238	FOW	20217	FOW	20273	FOW
17226	FOW	19108	FOW	19239	FOW	20218	FOW	20274	FOW
17227	FOW	19109	FOW	19240	FOW	20219	FOW	20275	FOW
17228	FOW	19110	FOW	19241	FOW	20220	FOW	20276	FOW
17229	FOW	19111	FOW	19242	FOW	20221	FOW	20277	FOW
17230	FOW	19112	FOW	19243	FOW	20222	FOW	20278	FOW
17231	FOW	19113	FOW	19244	FOW	20223	FOW	20279	FOW
17232	FOW	19114	FOW	19245	FOW	20224	FOW	20280	FOW
17233	FOW	19115	FOW	19246	FOW	20225	FOW	20281	FOW
17234	FOW	19116	FOW	19247	FOW	20226	FOW	20282	FOW
17235	FOW	19117	FOW	19248	FOW	20227	FOW	20283	FOW
17236	FOW	19118	FOW	19249	FOW	20228	FOW	20284	FOW
17237	FOW	19119	FOW	19250	FOW	20229	FOW	20285	FOW
17238	FOW	19120	FOW	19251	FOW	20230	FOW	20287	FOW
17239	FOW	19121	FOW	19252	FOW	20231	FOW	21200	FOW
17240	FOW	19122	FOW	19253	FOW	20232	FOW	21201	FOW
17241	FOW	19123	FOW	19254	FOW	20233	FOW	21202	FOW
17242	FOW	19124	FOW	19255	FOW	20234	FOW	21203	FOW
17243	FOW	19125	FOW	19256	FOW	20235	FOW	21204	FOW

Fowler Welch

21205	FOW	21232	FOW	21259	FOW	21285	FOW	22211	CFW
21206	FOW	21233	FOW	21260	FOW	21286	FOW	22212	CFW
21207	FOW	21234	FOW	21261	FOW	21287	FOW	22213	CFW
21208	FOW	21235	FOW	21262	FOW	21288	FOW	22214	CFW
21209	FOW	21236	FOW	21263	FOW	21289	FOW	22215	CFW
21210	FOW	21237	FOW	21264	FOW	21290	FOW	22216	CFW
21211	FOW	21238	FOW	21265	FOW	21291	FOW	22217	CFW
21212	FOW	21239	FOW	21266	FOW	21292	FOW	22218	CFW
21213	FOW	21240	FOW	21267	FOW	21293	FOW	22219	CFW
21214	FOW	21241	FOW	21268	FOW	21294	FOW	22220	CFW
21215	FOW	21242	FOW	21269	FOW	21295	FOW	22221	CFW
21216	FOW	21243	FOW	21270	FOW	21296	FOW	22222	CFW
21217	FOW	21244	FOW	21271	FOW	21297	YOC	22223	CFW
21218	FOW	21245	FOW	21272	FOW	21298	YOC	22224	CFW
21219	FOW	21246	FOW	21273	FOW	21299	YOC	22225	CFW
21220	FOW	21247	FOW	21274	FOW	22200	CFW	22226	CFW
21221	FOW	21248	FOW	21275	FOW	22201	CFW	22227	CFW
21222	FOW	21249	FOW	21276	FOW	22202	CFW	22228	CFW
21223	FOW	21250	FOW	21277	FOW	22203	CFW	22229	CFW
21224	FOW	21251	FOW	21278	FOW	22204	CFW	22230	CFW
21225	FOW	21252	FOW	21279	FOW	22205	CFW	22231	CFW
21226	FOW	21253	FOW	21280	FOW	22206	CFW	22232	CFW
21227	FOW	21254	FOW	21281	FOW	22207	CFW	22233	CFW
21228	FOW	21255	FOW	21282	FOW	22208	CFW	22234	CFW
21229	FOW	21256	FOW	21283	FOW	22209	CFW	22235	CFW
21230	FOW	21257	FOW	21284	FOW	22210	CFW	22236	CFW
21231	FOW	21258	FOW						

Great Bear

42-17000	GBB	42-17026	GBB	42-18019	GBB	42-21039	GBB	45-18012	GBB
42-17001	GBB	42-17027	GBB	42-18020	GBB	42-21040	GBB	45-18013	GBB
42-17002	GBB	42-17028	GBB	42-18021	GBB	42-21041	GBB	45-18014	GBB
42-17003	GBB	42-17029	GBB	42-18022	GBB	42-21042	GBB	45-18015	GBB
42-17004	GBB	42-17030	GBB	42-18023	GBB	42-21043	GBB	45-18016	GBB
42-17005	GBB	42-17031	GBB	42-18024	GBB	42-21044	GBB	45-18017	GBB
42-17006	GBB	42-17032	GBB	42-18025	GBB	42-21045	GBB	45-18018	GBB
42-17007	GBB	42-17108	GBB	42-18026	GBB	42-21046	GBB	45-18019	GBB
42-17008	GBB	42-18001	GBB	42-18027	GBB	42-21047	GBB	45-18020	GBB
42-17009	GBB	42-18002	GBB	42-18028	GBB	42-21048	GBB	45-18021	GBB
42-17010	GBB	42-18003	GBB	42-18029	GBB	42-21049	GBB	45-18022	GBB
42-17011	GBB	42-18004	GBB	42-18030	GBB	42-21050	GBB	45-18023	GBB
42-17012	GBB	42-18005	GBB	42-18031	GBB	42-21051	GBB	45-18024	GBB
42-17013	GBB	42-18006	GBB	42-18032	GBB	42-21052	GBB	45-18025	GBB
42-17014	GBB	42-18007	GBB	42-18033	GBB	45-17015	GBB	45-18026	GBB
42-17015	GBB	42-18008	GBB	42-18034	GBB	45-18001	GBB	45-18027	GBB
42-17016	GBB	42-18009	GBB	42-18035	GBB	45-18002	GBB	45-18028	GBB
42-17017	GBB	42-18010	GBB	42-18036	GBB	45-18003	GBB	45-18029	GBB
42-17018	GBB	42-18011	GBB	42-18037	GBB	45-18004	GBB	45-18030	GBB
42-17019	GBB	42-18012	GBB	42-21032	GBB	45-18005	GBB	45-18031	GBB
42-17020	GBB	42-18013	GBB	42-21033	GBB	45-18006	GBB	45-18032	GBB
42-17021	GBB	42-18014	GBB	42-21034	GBB	45-18007	GBB	45-18033	GBB
42-17022	GBB	42-18015	GBB	42-21035	GBB	45-18008	GBB	45-18034	GBB
42-17023	GBB	42-18016	GBB	42-21036	GBB	45-18009	GBB	45-18035	GBB
42-17024	GBB	42-18017	GBB	42-21037	GBB	45-18010	GBB	45-18036	GBB
42-17025	GBB	42-18018	GBB	42-21038	GBB	45-18011	GBB	45-18037	GBB

Great Bear

45-18038	GBB	45-18094	GBB	46-17022	GBB	46-17078	GBB	GB 107	GBB
45-18039	GBB	45-18095	GBB	46-17023	GBB	46-17079	GBB	GB 111	GBB
45-18040	GBB	45-18096	GBB	46-17024	GBB	46-17080	GBB	GB 112	GBB
45-18041	GBB	45-18097	GBB	46-17025	GBB	46-17081	GBB	GB 122	GBB
45-18042	GBB	45-18098	GBB	46-17026	GBB	46-17082	GBB	GB 179	GBB
45-18043	GBB	45-18099	GBB	46-17027	GBB	46-17083	GBB	GB 180	GBB
45-18044	GBB	45-18100	GBB	46-17028	GBB	46-18064	GBB	GB 181	GBB
45-18045	GBB	45-18101	GBB	46-17029	GBB	46-18068	GBB	GB 182	GBB
45-18046	GBB	45-18102	GBB	46-17030	GBB	46-18070	GBB	GB 183	GBB
45-18047	GBB	45-18103	GBB	46-17031	GBB	47-18006	GBB	GB 184	GBB
45-18048	GBB	45-19001	GBB	46-17032	GBB	47-18057	GBB	GB 185	GBB
45-18049	GBB	45-19002	GBB	46-17033	GBB	47-18060	GBB	GB 186	GBB
45-18050	GBB	45-19003	GBB	46-17034	GBB	47-18063	GBB	GB 187	GBB
45-18051	GBB	45-19004	GBB	46-17035	GBB	47-18066	GBB	GB 188	GBB
45-18052	GBB	45-19005	GBB	46-17036	GBB	47-18073	GBB	GB 189	GBB
45-18053	GBB	45-19006	GBB	46-17037	GBB	47-18074	GBB	GB 190	GBB
45-18054	GBB	45-19007	GBB	46-17038	GBB	47-18075	GBB	GB 191	GBB
45-18055	GBB	45-19008	GBB	46-17039	GBB	47-21001	GBB	GB 192	GBB
45-18056	GBB	45-19009	GBB	46-17040	GBB	47-21002	GBB	GB 193	GBB
45-18057	GBB	45-19010	GBB	46-17041	GBB	47-21003	GBB	GB 194	GBB
45-18058	GBB	45-19011	GBB	46-17042	GBB	47-21004	GBB	GB 195	GBB
45-18059	GBB	45-19012	GBB	46-17043	GBB	47-21005	GBB	GB 196	GBB
45-18060	GBB	45-19013	GBB	46-17044	GBB	47-21006	GBB	GB 197	GBB
45-18061	GBB	45-19014	GBB	46-17045	GBB	47-21007	GBB	GB 201	GBB
45-18062	GBB	45-19015	GBB	46-17046	GBB	47-21008	GBB	GB 202	GBB
45-18063	GBB	45-19016	GBB	46-17047	GBB	47-21009	GBB	GB 203	GBB
45-18064	GBB	45-19017	GBB	46-17048	GBB	47-21010	GBB	GB 204	GBB
45-18065	GBB	45-19018	GBB	46-17049	GBB	47-21011	GBB	GB 205	GBB
45-18066	GBB	45-19019	GBB	46-17050	GBB	47-21012	GBB	GB 206	GBB
45-18067	GBB	45-19020	GBB	46-17051	GBB	47-21013	GBB	GB 207	GBB
45-18068	GBB	45-19021	GBB	46-17052	GBB	47-21014	GBB	GB 208	GBB
45-18069	GBB	45-19022	GBB	46-17053	GBB	47-21015	GBB	GB 209	GBB
45-18070	GBB	45-19023	GBB	46-17054	GBB	47-21016	GBB	GB 210	GBB
45-18071	GBB	45-19024	GBB	46-17055	GBB	47-21017	GBB	GB 211	GBB
45-18072	GBB	45-19025	GBB	46-17056	GBB	47-21018	GBB	GB 212	GBB
45-18073	GBB	46-17001	GBB	46-17057	GBB	47-21019	GBB	GB 213	GBB
45-18074	GBB	46-17002	GBB	46-17058	GBB	47-21020	GBB	GB 214	GBB
45-18075	GBB	46-17003	GBB	46-17059	GBB	47-21021	GBB	GB 215	GBB
45-18076	GBB	46-17004	GBB	46-17060	GBB	47-21022	GBB	GB 216	GBB
45-18077	GBB	46-17005	GBB	46-17061	GBB	CML 562-17		GB 217	GBB
45-18078	GBB	46-17006	GBB	46-17062	GBB	MD	GBB	GB 218	GBB
45-18079	GBB	46-17007	GBB	46-17063	GBB	GB 20	GBB	GB 219	GBB
45-18080	GBB	46-17008	GBB	46-17064	GBB	GB 22	GBB	GB 220	GBB
45-18081	GBB	46-17009	GBB	46-17065	GBB	GB 29	GBB	GB 221	GBB
45-18082	GBB	46-17010	GBB	46-17066	GBB	GB 30	GBB	GB 222	GBB
45-18083	GBB	46-17011	GBB	46-17067	GBB	GB 31	GBB	GB 223	GBB
45-18084	GBB	46-17012	GBB	46-17068	GBB	GB 61	GBB	GB 224	GBB
45-18085	GBB	46-17013	GBB	46-17069	GBB	GB 64	GBB	GB 225	GBB
45-18086	GBB	46-17014	GBB	46-17070	GBB	GB 66	GBB	GB 226	GBB
45-18087	GBB	46-17015	GBB	46-17071	GBB	GB 67	GBB	GB 227	GBB
45-18088	GBB	46-17016	GBB	46-17072	GBB	GB 71	GBB	GB 228	GBB
45-18089	GBB	46-17017	GBB	46-17073	GBB	GB 72	GBB	GB 229	GBB
45-18090	GBB	46-17018	GBB	46-17074	GBB	GB 73	GBB	GB 230	GBB
45-18091	GBB	46-17019	GBB	46-17075	GBB	GB 74	GBB	GB 231	GBB
45-18092	GBB	46-17020	GBB	46-17076	GBB	GB 75	GBB	GB 232	GBB
45-18093	GBB	46-17021	GBB	46-17077	GBB	GB 78	GBB	GB 233	GBB

GB 24
GB 65 *(handwritten)*

GB 234	GBB	GB 290	GBB	GB 346	GBB	GB 414	GBB	GB 686	GBW
GB 235	GBB	GB 291	GBB	GB 347	GBB	GB 415	GBB	GB 695	GBW
GB 236	GBB	GB 292	GBB	GB 348	GBB	GB 416	GBB	GB 696	GBW
GB 237	GBB	GB 293	GBB	GB 349	GBB	GB 417	GBB	GB 697	GBW
GB 238	GBB	GB 294	GBB	GB 350	GBB	GB 418	GBB	GB 698	GBB
GB 239	GBB	GB 295	GBB	GB 351	GBB	GB 419	GBB	GB 699	GBB
GB 240	GBB	GB 296	GBB	GB 352	GBB	GB 420	GBB	GB 700	GBB
GB 241	GBB	GB 297	GBB	GB 353	GBB	GB 421	GBB	GB 701	GBB
GB 242	GBB	GB 298	GBB	GB 354	GBB	GB 422	GBB	GB 702	GBB
GB 243	GBB	GB 299	GBB	GB 355	GBB	GB 423	GBB	GB 703	GBB
GB 244	GBB	GB 300	GBB	GB 356	GBB	GB 424	GBB	GB 704	GBB
GB 245	GBB	GB 301	GBB	GB 357	GBB	GB 425	GBB	GB 705	GBB
GB 246	GBB	GB 302	GBB	GB 358	GBB	GB 505	GBB	GB 706	GBB
GB 247	GBB	GB 303	GBB	GB 359	GBB	GB 515	GBB	GB 707	GBB
GB 248	GBB	GB 304	GBB	GB 360	GBB	GB 561	GBB	GB 708	GBB
GB 249	GBB	GB 305	GBB	GB 361	GBB	GB 563	GBB	GB 709	GBB
GB 250	GBB	GB 306	GBB	GB 362	GBB	GB 564	GBB	GB 710	GBB
GB 251	GBB	GB 307	GBB	GB 363	GBB	GB 566	GBB	GB 711	GBB
GB 252	GBB	GB 308	GBB	GB 364	GBB	GB 585	GBB	GB 712	GBB
GB 253	GBB	GB 309	GBB	GB 365	GBB	GB 586	GBB	GB 713	GBB
GB 254	GBB	GB 310	GBB	GB 366	GBB	GB 587	GBB	GB 714	GBB
GB 255	GBB	GB 311	GBB	GB 367	GBB	GB 588	GBB	GB 715	GBB
GB 256	GBB	GB 312	GBB	GB 368	GBB	GB 589	GBB	GB 716	GBB
GB 257	GBB	GB 313	GBB	GB 369	GBB	GB 590	GBB	GB 717	GBB
GB 258	GBB	GB 314	GBB	GB 370	GBB	GB 591	GBB	GB 718	GBB
GB 259	GBB	GB 315	GBB	GB 371	GBB	GB 592	GBB	GB 719	GBB
GB 260	GBB	GB 316	GBB	GB 372	GBB	GB 593	GBB	GB 720	GBB
GB 261	GBB	GB 317	GBB	GB 373	GBB	GB 595	GBB	GB 721	GBB
GB 262	GBB	GB 318	GBB	GB 374	GBB	GB 605	White	GB 722	GBB
GB 263	GBB	GB 319	GBB	GB 375	GBB	GB 606	White	GB 723	GBB
GB 264	GBB	GB 320	GBB	GB 376	GBB	GB 612	White	GB 724	GBB
GB 265	GBB	GB 321	GBB	GB 377	GBB	GB 621	White	GB 725	GBB
GB 266	GBB	GB 322	GBB	GB 378	GBB	GB 623	White	GB 726	GBB
GB 267	GBB	GB 323	GBB	GB 379	GBB	GB 631	White	GB 727	GBB
GB 268	GBB	GB 324	GBB	GB 380	GBB	GB 633	White	GB 728	GBB
GB 269	GBB	GB 325	GBB	GB 381	GBB	GB 638	White	GB 729	GBB
GB 270	GBB	GB 326	GBB	GB 382	GBB	GB 639	White	GB 730	GBB
GB 271	GBB	GB 327	GBB	GB 383	GBB	GB 641	White	GB 731	GBB
GB 272	GBB	GB 328	GBB	GB 384	GBB	GB 645	White	GB 732	GBB
GB 273	GBB	GB 329	GBB	GB 385	GBB	GB 646	White	GB 733	GBB
GB 274	GBB	GB 330	GBB	GB 386	GBB	GB 650	White	GB 734	GBB
GB 275	GBB	GB 331	GBB	GB 387	GBB	GB 658	GBW	GB 735	GBB
GB 276	GBB	GB 332	GBB	GB 388	GBB	GB 663	GBW	GB 736	GBB
GB 277	GBB	GB 333	GBB	GB 389	GBB	GB 673	GBW	GB 737	GBB
GB 278	GBB	GB 334	GBB	GB 390	GBB	GB 674	GBW	GB 738	GBB
GB 279	GBB	GB 335	GBB	GB 391	GBB	GB 675	GBW	GB 739	GBB
GB 280	GBB	GB 336	GBB	GB 392	GBB	GB 676	GBW	GB 740	GBB
GB 281	GBB	GB 337	GBB	GB 393	GBB	GB 677	GBW	GB 741	GBB
GB 282	GBB	GB 338	GBB	GB 394	GBB	GB 678	GBW	GB 742	GBB
GB 283	GBB	GB 339	GBB	GB 395	GBB	GB 679	GBW	GB 743	GBB
GB 284	GBB	GB 340	GBB	GB 396	GBB	GB 680	GBW	GB 744	GBB
GB 285	GBB	GB 341	GBB	GB 397	GBB	GB 681	GBW	GB 745	GBB
GB 286	GBB	GB 342	GBB	GB 398	GBB	GB 682	GBW	GB 746	GBB
GB 287	GBB	GB 343	GBB	GB 411	GBB	GB 683	GBW	GB 747	GBB
GB 288	GBB	GB 344	GBB	GB 412	GBB	GB 684	GBW	GB 748	GBB
GB 289	GBB	GB 345	GBB	GB 413	GBB	GB 685	GBW	GB 749	GBB

GB 562 *(handwritten)*

Great Bear

(handwritten: GB782   GB803)

GB 750	GBB	GB 760	GBB	GB 770	GBB	GB 789	GBB	GB 804	GBB
GB 751	GBB	GB 761	GBB	GB 771	GBB	GB 790	GBB	GB 1043	GBW
GB 752	GBB	GB 762	GBB	GB 772	GBB	GB 791	GBB	GB 1047	GBW
GB 753	GBB	GB 763	GBB	GB 773	GBB	GB 792	GBB	GB 1049	GBW
GB 754	GBB	GB 764	GBB	GB 774	GBB	GB 793	GBB	GB 1066	GBW
GB 755	GBB	GB 765	GBB	GB 775	GBB	GB 794	GBB	GB 1069	GBW
GB 756	GBB	GB 766	GBB	GB 776	GBB	GB 795	GBB	GB 1078	GBW
GB 757	GBB	GB 767	GBB	GB 777	GBB	GB 796	GBB	GB 2123	GBW
GB 758	GBB	GB 768	GBB	GB 778	GBB	GB 797	GBB	GB 2134	GBW
GB 759	GBB	GB 769	GBB	GB 779	GBB	GB 798	GBB		

International Road Ferry

IRF 413	IRB	IRF 592	IRB	IRF 787	IRB	IRF 844	IRB	IRF 906	IRB
IRF 443	IRB	IRF 633	IRB	IRF 794	IRB	IRF 851	IRB	IRF 913	IRB
IRF 463	IRB	IRF 701	IRB	IRF 805	IRB	IRF 863	IRB	IRF 950	IRB
IRF 526	IRB	IRF 724	IRB	IRF 815	IRB	IRF 871	IRB	IRF 980	IRB
IRF 546	IRB	IRF 725	IRB	IRF 825	IRB	IRF 872	IRB	IRF 9038	Grey
IRF 568	IRB	IRF 726	IRB	IRF 829	IRB	IRF 876	IRB	IRF 9074	Grey
IRF 589	IRB	IRF 748	IRB						

Morgan McLernon

MT 106	MML	CML 423 MD	CML	CML 505 MD	CML	CML 582-19 TD	MML
MT 107	MML	CML 425 MD	MML	CML 507-20 MD	CML	CML 588-19 MD	MML
MT 108	MML	CML 427 MD	CML	CML 508 MD	CML	CML 591-19 MD	MML
MT 122	MML	CML 429 MD	MML	CML 510 MD	CML	CML 593-19 MD	MML
MT 131	MML	CML 430 MD	MML	CML 511 MD	MML	CML 594-19 MD	MML
MT 142	MML	MT 432-16S	MML	MT 512-17 T	MML	CML 598-19 MD	MML
MT 146	MML	MT 433	MML	MT 513-17 T	MML	CML 599-19 MD	MML
MT 151	MML	CML 441 MD	CML	MT 515-17T	MML	CML 602-20 MD	CML
MT 152	MML	CML 443	CML	MT 516-17 T	MML	CML 605-20 MD	CML
MT 153	MML	CML 444	CML	MT 517-17 T	MML	CML 606-20 MD	CML
MT 175	MML	CML 447	CML	MT 520-17 T	MML	CML 607-20 MD	CML
MT 184	MML	CML 450	CML	MT 523-17 T	MML	CML 608-20 MD	CML
MT 185	MML	CML 451	CML	MT 524-17 T	MML	CML 609-20 MD	CML
CML 186	MML	CML 453	CML	MT 526-17 T	MML	CML 610-20 MD	CML
CML 192	CML	CML 454	CML	MT 536-17 T	MML	CML 611-20 MD	CML
CML 352	MML	CML 455	CML	MTS 538-17 T	MML	CML 612-20 MD	CML
CML 354	MML	CML 458	MML	MT 541-17 S	MML	CML 613-20 MD	CML
CML 357	MML	CML 461	White	MT 542-17 S	MML	CML 615-21 MD	CML
CML 358	MML	CML 463	White	MT 543-17 S	MML	CML 616-21 MD	CML
CML 359	MML	CML 465	White	MT 544-17 S	MML	CML 618-21 MD	CML
CML 363 MD	MML	CML 469	MML	MT 549-17 S	MML	CML 619-21 MD	CML
CML 365	MML	CML 475	CML	MT 552-17 T	MML	CML 621-21 MD	CML
CML 366	MML	CML 477	CML	MTS 546-17 S	MML	CML 624-21MD	CUW
CML 369	MML	CML 480	CML	MTS 561-17 T	MML	CML 633-20MD	CUW
CML 374 MD	MML	CML 481	CML	CML 564-17 MD	MML	CML 634-22 MD	CUW
CML 376 MD	MML	CML 490	CML	CML 568-17 MD	MML	CML 635-22 MD	CUW
MT 388	MML	CML 491	CML	CML 569-17 MD	MML	CML 636-22 MD	CUW
MT 391	MML	CML 492	CML	CML 570-17 MD	MML	CML 639-22 MD	CUW
MT 392	MML	CML 499	CML	CML 575-17 MD	MML	MT 596-18 SC	MML
MT 404	MML	CML 500	CML	CML 576-17 MD	MML	MT 600-18 SC	CML
MT 406	MML	CML 501 MD	CML	CML 577-17 MD	MML	MT 602-18 SC	CML
MT 414	MML	CML 502 MD	CML	CML 578-19 MD	MML	MT 608-18 SC	CML
MT 419	MML	CML 503 MD	CML	CML 580-17 MD	MML	MT 614-18 T	CML

Morgan McLernon

MT 615-18 H	CML	MT 673-18 T	CML	MT 743-20T	MML	MT 814	White
MT 616-18 H	CML	MT 676-18 T	CML	MT 744-20T	MML	MT 820 CTS	White
MT 621-18 S	CML	MT 677-18 T	CML	MT 745-20T	MML	MT 836	White
MT 628-18 S	CML	MT 684-18 T	CML	MT 746-20T	MML	MT 842	White
MT 636-18 S	CML	MT 686-19 T	MML	MT 747-20T	MML	MT 853	White
MT 637-18 S	MML	MT 688-19 T	CML	MT 748-20T	MML	MT 855	White
MT 638-18 T	CML	MT 694-19 T	CML	MT 749-20 T	MML	MT 862-20S	MML
MT 639-18 T	CML	MT 700-19 T	CML	MT 753-20 T	MML	MT 872	MML
MT 646-18 T	MML	MM 706-19 T	CML	MT 754-20 T	MML	MT 876-205	MML
MT 647-18 T	MML	MM 711-19 T	CML	MT 760-20 T	MML	MT 881-20 S	MML
MT 648-18 T	CML	MM 713-19 T	CML	MT 766-20 T	MML	MT 884-20 S	MML
MT 651-18 T	CML	MM 718-20 T	CML	MT 769-20 T	MML	MT 889-20 S	MML
MT 656-18 T	CML	MT 719-20 T	White	MT 774-20 T	MML	MT 896-20S	MML
MT 659-18 T	CML	MT 721-20 T	ROS	MT 781-20 H	MML	MT 898-20 S	MML
MT 663-18 T	CML	MT 740-20T	MML	MT 784-21 H	MML	MT 900-20 S	MML
MT 666-18 T	CML	MT 741-20T	MML	MT 805 CTS	White	MT 918-20	MML
MT 671-18 T	CML	MT 742-20T	MML	MT 812 CTS	White	MT 920-20	MML

Robert Burns

RB122	ROB	RB158	ROB	RB189	DAN	RB212	ROB	RB230	ROB
RB123	ROB	RB160	ROB	RB195	ROB	RB213	ROB	RB233	ROB
RB129	ROB	RB161	ROB	RB196	ROB	RB216	ROB	RB235	ROB
RB132	ROB	RB163	ROB	RB197	ROB	RB218	ROB	RB236	ROB
RB133	ROB	RB168	ROB	RB199	THS	RB220	ROB	RB238	ROB
RB135	ROB	RB170	ROB	RB205	ASF	RB221	ROB	RB240	ROB
RB144	ROB	RB180	ROB	RB206	ASF	RB222	ROB	RB243	ROB
RB147	ROB	RB184	ROB	RB208	THS	RB224	ROB	RB246	ROB
RB151	ROB	RB185	DAN	RB209	THS	RB227	ROB	RB247	ROB
RB152	ROB	RB187	DAN	RB210	THS	RB229	ROB	RB248	ROB
RB155	ROB	RB188	DAN			RB223		RB234	

RB171

Eddie Stobart

BDD 1500	ESW	BDD 1522	ESW	BDD 1544	ESW	BDD 1566	ESW	BDD 1588	ESW
BDD 1501	ESW	BDD 1523	ESW	BDD 1545	ESW	BDD 1567	ESW	BDD 1589	ESW
BDD 1502	ESW	BDD 1524	ESW	BDD 1546	ESW	BDD 1568	ESW	BDD 1590	ESW
BDD 1503	ESW	BDD 1525	ESW	BDD 1547	ESW	BDD 1569	ESW	BDD 1591	ESW
BDD 1504	ESW	BDD 1526	ESW	BDD 1548	ESW	BDD 1570	ESW	BDD 1592	ESW
BDD 1505	ESW	BDD 1527	ESW	BDD 1549	ESW	BDD 1571	ESW	BDD 1593	ESW
BDD 1506	ESW	BDD 1528	ESW	BDD 1550	ESW	BDD 1572	ESW	BDD 1594	ESW
BDD 1507	ESW	BDD 1529	ESW	BDD 1551	ESW	BDD 1573	ESW	BDD 1595	ESW
BDD 1508	ESW	BDD 1530	ESW	BDD 1552	ESW	BDD 1574	ESW	BDD 1596	ESW
BDD 1509	ESW	BDD 1531	ESW	BDD 1553	ESW	BDD 1575	ESW	BDD 1597	ESW
BDD 1510	ESW	BDD 1532	ESW	BDD 1554	ESW	BDD 1576	ESW	BDD 1598	ESW
BDD 1511	ESW	BDD 1533	ESW	BDD 1555	ESW	BDD 1577	ESW	BDD 1599	ESW
BDD 1512	ESW	BDD 1534	ESW	BDD 1556	ESW	BDD 1578	ESW	BDD 1600	ESW
DDD 1513	ESW	BDD 1535	ESW	BDD 1557	ESW	BDD 1579	ESW	BDD 1601	ESW
BDD 1514	ESW	BDD 1536	ESW	BDD 1558	ESW	BDD 1580	ESW	BDD 1602	ESW
BDD 1515	ESW	BDD 1537	ESW	BDD 1559	ESW	BDD 1581	ESW	BDD 1603	ESW
BDD 1516	ESW	BDD 1538	ESW	BDD 1560	ESW	BDD 1582	ESW	BDD 1604	ESW
BDD 1517	ESW	BDD 1539	ESW	BDD 1561	ESW	BDD 1583	ESW	BDD 1605	ESW
BDD 1518	ESW	BDD 1540	ESW	BDD 1562	ESW	BDD 1584	ESW	BDD 1606	ESW
BDD 1519	ESW	BDD 1541	ESW	BDD 1563	ESW	BDD 1585	ESW	BDD 1607	ESW
BDD 1520	ESW	BDD 1542	ESW	BDD 1564	ESW	BDD 1586	ESW	BDD 1608	ESW
BDD 1521	ESW	BDD 1543	ESW	BDD 1565	ESW	BDD 1587	ESW	BDD 1609	ESW

Eddie Stobart

BIT 0001	ESW	BIT 0057	ESW	BIT 0113	ESW	CLD 2016	ESG	CT 3461	ESG
BIT 0002	ESW	BIT 0058	ESW	BIT 0114	ESW	CLD 2017	ESG	CT 3462	ESG
BIT 0003	ESW	BIT 0059	ESW	BIT 0115	ESW	CLD 2018	ESG	CT 3463	ESG
BIT 0004	ESW	BIT 0060	ESW	BIT 0116	ESW	CLD 2019	ESG	CT 3464	ESG
BIT 0005	ESW	BIT 0061	ESW	BIT 0117	ESW	CLD 2020	ESG	CT 3465	ESG
BIT 0006	ESW	BIT 0062	ESW	BIT 0118	ESW	CLD 2021	ESG	CT 3466	ESG
BIT 0007	ESW	BIT 0063	ESW	BIT 0119	ESW	CLD 2022	ESG	CT 3467	ESG
BIT 0008	ESW	BIT 0064	ESW	BIT 0120	ESW	CLD 2023	ESG	CT 3468	ESG
BIT 0009	ESW	BIT 0065	ESW	BIT 0121	ESW	CLD 2024	ESG	CT 3469	ESG
BIT 0010	ESW	BIT 0066	ESW	BIT 0122	ESW	CLD 2025	ESG	CT 3470	ESG
BIT 0011	ESW	BIT 0067	ESW	BIT 0123	ESW	CLD 2026	ESG	CT 3471	ESG
BIT 0012	ESW	BIT 0068	ESW	BIT 0124	ESW	CLD 2027	ESG	CT 3472	ESG
BIT 0013	ESW	BIT 0069	ESW	BIT 0125	ESW	CLD 2028	ESG	CT 3473	ESG
BIT 0014	ESW	BIT 0070	ESW	BIT 0126	ESW	CLD 2029	ESG	CT 3474	ESG
BIT 0015	ESW	BIT 0071	ESW	BIT 0127	ESW	CLD 2030	ESG	CT 3475	ESG
BIT 0016	ESW	BIT 0072	ESW	BIT 0128	ESW	CLD 2031	ESG	CT 3476	ESG
BIT 0017	ESW	BIT 0073	ESW	BIT 0129	ESW	CLD 2032	ESG	CT 3477	ESG
BIT 0018	ESW	BIT 0074	ESW	BIT 0130	ESW	CLD 2033	ESG	CT 3478	ESG
BIT 0019	ESW	BIT 0075	ESW	BIT 0131	ESW	CLD 2034	ESG	CT 3479	ESG
BIT 0020	ESW	BIT 0076	ESW	BIT 0132	ESW	CLD 2035	ESG	CT 3480	ESG
BIT 0021	ESW	BIT 0077	ESW	BIT 0133	ESW	CLD 2036	ESG	CT 3481	ESG
BIT 0022	ESW	BIT 0078	ESW	BIT 0134	ESW	CLD 2037	ESG	CT 3482	ESG
BIT 0023	ESW	BIT 0079	ESW	BIT 0135	ESW	CLD 2038	ESG	CT 3483	ESG
BIT 0024	ESW	BIT 0080	ESW	BIT 0136	ESW	CLD 2039	ESG	CT 3484	ESG
BIT 0025	ESW	BIT 0081	ESW	BIT 0137	ESW	CLD 2040	ESG	CT 3485	ESG
BIT 0026	ESW	BIT 0082	ESW	BIT 0138	ESW	CLD 2041	ESG	CT 3486	ESG
BIT 0027	ESW	BIT 0083	ESW	BIT 0139	ESW	CLD 2042	ESG	CT 3487	ESG
BIT 0028	ESW	BIT 0084	ESW	BIT 0140	ESW	CLD 2043	ESG	CT 3488	ESG
BIT 0029	ESW	BIT 0085	ESW	BIT 0141	ESW	CLD 2044	ESG	CT 3489	ESG
BIT 0030	ESW	BIT 0086	ESW	BIT 0142	ESW	CLD 2045	ESG	CT 3490	ESG
BIT 0031	ESW	BIT 0087	ESW	BIT 0143	ESW	CLD 2046	ESG	CT 3491	ESG
BIT 0032	ESW	BIT 0088	ESW	BIT 0144	ESW	CLD 2047	ESG	CT 3492	ESG
BIT 0033	ESW	BIT 0089	ESW	BIT 0145	ESW	CLD 2048	ESG	CT 3493	ESG
BIT 0034	ESW	BIT 0090	ESW	BIT 0146	ESW	CLD 2049	ESG	CT 3494	ESG
BIT 0035	ESW	BIT 0091	ESW	BIT 0147	ESW	CLD 2050	ESG	CT 3495	ESG
BIT 0036	ESW	BIT 0092	ESW	BIT 0148	ESW	CLD 2051	ESG	CT 3496	ESG
BIT 0037	ESW	BIT 0093	ESW	BIT 0149	ESW	CLD 2052	ESG	CT 3497	ESG
BIT 0038	ESW	BIT 0094	ESW	BIT 0150	ESW	CLD 2053	ESG	CT 3498	ESG
BIT 0039	ESW	BIT 0095	ESW	BIT 0151	ESW	CLD 2054	ESG	CT 3499	ESG
BIT 0040	ESW	BIT 0096	ESW	BLD 2000	ESW	CLD 2055	ESG	CT 3500	ESG
BIT 0041	ESW	BIT 0097	ESW	BLD 2001	ESW	CLD 2056	ESG	CT 3501	ESG
BIT 0042	ESW	BIT 0098	ESW	BLD 2002	ESW	CLD 2057	ESG	CT 3502	ESG
BIT 0043	ESW	BIT 0099	ESW	BLD 2003	ESW	CLD 2058	ESG	CT 3503	ESG
BIT 0044	ESW	BIT 0100	ESW	BLD 2004	ESW	CLD 2059	ESG	CT 3504	ESG
BIT 0045	ESW	BIT 0101	ESW	BLD 2005	ESW	CLD 2060	ESG	CT 3505	ESG
BIT 0046	ESW	BIT 0102	ESW	BLD 2006	ESW	CLD 2061	ESG	CT 3506	ESG
BIT 0047	ESW	BIT 0103	ESW	BLD 2007	ESW	CT 3451	ESG	CT 3507	ESG
BIT 0048	ESW	BIT 0104	ESW	BLD 2008	ESW	CT 3452	ESG	CT 3508	ESG
BIT 0049	ESW	BIT 0105	ESW	BLD 2009	ESW	CT 3453	ESG	CT 3509	ESG
BIT 0050	ESW	BIT 0106	ESW	BLD 2010	ESW	CT 3454	ESG	CT 3510	ESG
BIT 0051	ESW	BIT 0107	ESW	CDD 2010	ESG	CT 3455	ESG	CT 3511	ESG
BIT 0052	ESW	BIT 0108	ESW	CLD 2011	ESG	CT 3456	ESG	CT 3512	ESG
BIT 0053	ESW	BIT 0109	ESW	CLD 2012	ESG	CT 3457	ESG	CT 3513	ESG
BIT 0054	ESW	BIT 0110	ESW	CLD 2013	ESG	CT 3458	ESG	CT 3514	ESG
BIT 0055	ESW	BIT 0111	ESW	CLD 2014	ESG	CT 3459	ESG	CT 3515	ESG
BIT 0056	ESW	BIT 0112	ESW	CLD 2015	ESG	CT 3460	ESG	CT 3516	ESG

Eddie Stobart

CT 3517 ESG	CT 3576 ESG	HHT 1982 ESG	HT 3491 ESG	HT 3547 ESG
CT 3518 ESG	CT 3577 ESG	HHT 1983 ESG	HT 3492 ESG	HT 3548 ESG
CT 3519 ESG	CT 3578 ESG	HHT 1984 ESG	HT 3493 ESG	HT 3549 ESG
CT 3520 ESG	CT 3579 ESG	HHT 1985 ESG	HT 3494 ESG	HT 3550 ESG
CT 3521 ESG	CT 3580 ESG	HHT 1986 ESG	HT 3495 ESG	HT 3551 ESG
CT 3522 ESG	CT 3581 ESG	HHT 1987 ESG	HT 3496 ESG	HT 3552 ESG
CT 3523 ESG	CT 3582 ESG	HHT 1988 ESG	HT 3497 ESG	HT 3553 ESG
CT 3524 ESG	CT 3583 ESG	HHT 1989 ESG	HT 3498 ESG	HT 3554 ESG
CT 3525 ESG	CT 3584 ESG	HHT 1990 ESG	HT 3499 ESG	HT 3555 ESG
CT 3526 ESG	CT 3585 ESG	HHT 1991 ESG	HT 3500 ESG	HT 3556 ESG
CT 3527 ESG	CT 3586 ESG	HHT 1992 ESG	HT 3501 ESG	HT 3557 ESG
CT 3529 ESG	CT 3587 ESG	HHT 1993 ESG	HT 3502 ESG	HT 3558 ESG
CT 3530 ESG	CT 3588 ESG	HHT 1994 ESG	HT 3503 ESG	HT 3559 ESG
CT 3531 ESG	CT 3589 ESG	HHT 1995 ESG	HT 3504 ESG	HT 3560 ESG
CT 3532 ESG	CT 3590 ESG	HHT 1996 ESG	HT 3505 ESG	HT 3561 ESG
CT 3533 ESG	CT 3591 ESG	HT 3450 ESG	HT 3506 ESG	HT 3562 ESG
CT 3534 ESG	CT 3592 ESG	HT 3451 ESG	HT 3507 ESG	HT 3563 ESG
CT 3535 ESG	CT 3593 ESG	HT 3452 ESG	HT 3508 ESG	HT 3564 ESG
CT 3536 ESG	CT 3594 ESG	HT 3453 ESG	HT 3509 ESG	HT 3565 ESG
CT 3537 ESG	CT 3595 ESG	HT 3454 ESG	HT 3510 ESG	HT 3566 ESG
CT 3538 ESG	CT 3596 ESG	HT 3455 ESG	HT 3511 ESG	HT 3567 ESG
CT 3539 ESG	CT 3597 ESG	HT 3456 ESG	HT 3512 ESG	HT 3568 ESG
CT 3541 ESG	CT 3598 ESG	HT 3457 ESG	HT 3513 ESG	HT 3569 ESG
CT 3542 ESG	CT 3599 ESG	HT 3458 ESG	HT 3514 ESG	HT 3570 ESG
CT 3543 ESG	CT 3600 ESG	HT 3459 ESG	HT 3515 ESG	HT 3571 ESG
CT 3544 ESG	CT 3601 ESG	HT 3460 ESG	HT 3516 ESG	HT 3572 ESG
CT 3545 ESG	CT 3602 ESG	HT 3461 ESG	HT 3517 ESG	HT 3573 ESG
CT 3546 ESG	FLD 2001 ESG	HT 3462 ESG	HT 3518 ESG	HT 3574 ESG
CT 3547 ESG	FLD 2002 ESG	HT 3463 ESG	HT 3519 ESG	HT 3575 ESG
CT 3548 ESG	FLD 2003 ESG	HT 3464 ESG	HT 3520 ESG	HT 3576 ESG
CT 3549 ESG	FLD 2004 ESG	HT 3465 ESG	HT 3521 ESG	HT 3577 ESG
CT 3550 ESG	FLD 2005 ESG	HT 3466 ESG	HT 3522 ESG	HT 3578 ESG
CT 3551 ESG	FLD 2006 ESG	HT 3467 ESG	HT 3523 ESG	HT 3579 ESG
CT 3552 ESG	FLD 2007 ESG	HT 3468 ESG	HT 3524 ESG	HT 3580 ESG
CT 3553 ESG	FLD 2008 ESG	HT 3469 ESG	HT 3525 ESG	HT 3581 ESG
CT 3554 ESG	FLD 2009 ESG	HT 3470 ESG	HT 3526 ESG	HT 3582 ESG
CT 3555 ESG	FLD 2010 ESG	HT 3471 ESG	HT 3527 ESG	HT 3583 ESG
CT 3556 ESG	HHT 1963 ESG	HT 3472 ESG	HT 3528 ESG	HT 3584 ESG
CT 3557 ESG	HHT 1964 ESG	HT 3473 ESG	HT 3529 ESG	HT 3585 ESG
CT 3559 ESG	HHT 1965 ESG	HT 3474 ESG	HT 3530 ESG	HT 3586 ESG
CT 3560 ESG	HHT 1966 ESG	HT 3475 ESG	HT 3531 ESG	HT 3587 ESG
CT 3561 ESG	HHT 1967 ESG	HT 3476 ESG	HT 3532 ESG	HT 3588 ESG
CT 3562 ESG	HHT 1968 ESG	HT 3477 ESG	HT 3533 ESG	HT 3589 ESG
CT 3563 ESG	HHT 1969 ESG	HT 3478 ESG	HT 3534 ESG	HT 3590 ESG
CT 3564 ESG	HHT 1970 ESG	HT 3479 ESG	HT 3535 ESG	HT 3591 ESG
CT 3565 ESG	HHT 1971 ESG	HT 3480 ESG	HT 3536 ESG	HT 3592 ESG
CT 3566 ESG	HHT 1972 ESG	HT 3481 ESG	HT 3537 ESG	HT 3593 ESG
CT 3567 ESG	HHT 1073 ESG	HI 3482 ESG	HT 3538 ESG	HT 3594 ESG
CT 3568 ESG	HHT 1974 ESG	HT 3483 ESG	HT 3539 ESG	HT 3595 ESG
CT 3569 ESG	HHT 1975 ESG	HT 3484 ESG	HT 3540 ESG	HT 3597 ESG
CT 3570 ESG	HHT 1976 ESG	HT 3485 ESG	HT 3541 ESG	HT 3598 ESG
CT 3571 ESG	HHT 1977 ESG	HT 3486 ESG	HT 3542 ESG	HT 3599 ESG
CT 3572 ESG	HHT 1978 ESG	HT 3487 ESG	HT 3543 ESG	HT 3600 ESG
CT 3573 ESG	HHT 1979 ESG	HT 3488 ESG	HT 3544 ESG	HT 3601 ESG
CT 3574 ESG	HHT 1980 ESG	HT 3489 ESG	HT 3545 ESG	HT 3602 ESG
CT 3575 ESG	HHT 1981 ESG	HT 3490 ESG	HT 3546 ESG	HT 3603 ESG

Eddie Stobart

IET 2589

HT 3604	ESG	HT 3662	ESG	IET 2539	ESG	IFT 1581	ESW	IFT 1637	ESW
HT 3605	ESG	HT 3663	ESG	IET 2546	ESG	IFT 1582	ESW	IFT 1638	ESW
HT 3606	ESG	HT 3664	ESG	IET 2550	ESG	IFT 1583	ESW	IFT 1639	ESW
HT 3607	ESG	HT 3665	ESG	IET 2555	ESG	IFT 1584	ESW	IFT 1640	ESW
HT 3608	ESG	HT 3666	ESG	IET 2556	ESG	IFT 1585	ESW	IFT 1641	ESW
HT 3609	ESG	HT 3667	ESG	IET 2557	ESG	IFT 1586	ESW	IFT 1642	ESW
HT 3610	ESG	HT 3668	ESG	IET 2560	ESG	IFT 1587	ESW	IFT 1643	ESW
HT 3611	ESG	HT 3669	ESG	IET 2562	ESG	IFT 1588	ESW	IFT 1644	ESW
HT 3612	ESG	HT 3670	ESG	IET 2563	ESG	IFT 1589	ESW	IFT 1645	ESW
HT 3613	ESG	HT 3671	ESG	IET 2565	ESG	IFT 1590	ESW	IFT 1646	ESW
HT 3614	ESG	HT 3672	ESG	IET 2566	ESG	IFT 1591	ESW	IFT 1647	ESW
HT 3615	ESG	HT 3673	ESG	IET 2567	ESG	IFT 1592	ESW	IFT 1648	ESW
HT 3616	ESG	HT 3674	ESG	IET 2568	ESG	IFT 1593	ESW	IFT 1649	ESW
HT 3617	ESG	HT 3675	ESG	IET 2569	ESG	IFT 1594	ESW	IFT 1650	ESW
HT 3618	ESG	HT 3676	ESG	IET 2571	ESG	IFT 1595	ESW	IFT 1651	ESW
HT 3619	ESG	HT 3677	ESG	IET 2572	ESG	IFT 1596	ESW	IFT 1652	ESW
HT 3620	ESG	HT 3678	ESG	IET 2573	ESG	IFT 1597	ESW	IFT 1653	ESW
HT 3621	ESG	HT 3679	ESG	IET 2574	ESG	IFT 1598	ESW	IFT 1654	ESW
HT 3622	ESG	HT 3680	ESG	IET 2575	ESG	IFT 1599	ESW	IFT 1655	ESW
HT 3624	ESG	HT 3681	ESG	IET 2576	ESG	IFT 1600	ESW	IFT 1656	ESW
HT 3625	ESG	HT 3682	ESG	IET 2578	ESG	IFT 1601	ESW	IFT 1657	ESW
HT 3627	ESG	HT 3683	ESG	IET 2579	ESG	IFT 1602	ESW	IFT 1658	ESW
HT 3628	ESG	HT 3684	ESG	IET 2580	ESG	IFT 1603	ESW	IFT 1659	ESW
HT 3629	ESG	HT 3685	ESG	IET 2581	ESG	IFT 1604	ESW	IFT 1661	ESW
HT 3630	ESG	HT 3686	ESG	IET 2582	ESG	IFT 1605	ESW	IFT 1662	ESW
HT 3631	ESG	HT 3687	ESG	IET 2583	ESG	IFT 1606	ESW	IFT 1663	ESW
HT 3632	ESG	HT 3688	ESG	IET 2584	ESG	IFT 1607	ESW	IFT 1664	ESW
HT 3633	ESG	HT 3689	ESG	IET 2586	ESG	IFT 1608	ESW	IFT 1665	ESW
HT 3634	ESG	HT 3690	ESG	IET 2587	ESG	IFT 1609	ESW	IFT 1666	ESW
HT 3635	ESG	HT 3691	ESG	IET 2588	ESG	IFT 1610	ESW	IFT 1667	ESW
HT 3636	ESG	HT 3692	ESG	IFT 1550	ESW	IFT 1611	ESW	IFT 1668	ESW
HT 3637	ESG	HT 3693	ESG	IFT 1551	ESW	IFT 1612	ESW	IFT 1669	ESW
HT 3638	ESG	HT 3694	ESG	IFT 1552	ESW	IFT 1613	ESW	IFT 1670	ESW
HT 3639	ESG	HT 3695	ESG	IFT 1553	ESW	IFT 1614	ESW	IFT 1671	ESW
HT 3640	ESG	HT 3696	ESG	IFT 1554	ESW	IFT 1615	ESW	IFT 1672	ESW
HT 3641	ESG	HT 3697	ESG	IFT 1555	ESW	IFT 1616	ESW	IFT 1673	ESW
HT 3642	ESG	HT 3698	ESG	IFT 1556	ESW	IFT 1617	ESW	IFT 1674	ESW
HT 3643	ESG	IET 2512	ESG	IFT 1557	ESW	IFT 1618	ESW	IFT 1675	ESW
HT 3644	ESG	IET 2515	ESG	IFT 1558	ESW	IFT 1619	ESW	IFT 1676	ESW
HT 3645	ESG	IET 2516	ESG	IFT 1559	ESW	IFT 1620	ESW	IFT 1677	ESW
HT 3646	ESG	IET 2517	ESG	IFT 1560	ESW	IFT 1621	ESW	IFT 1678	ESW
HT 3647	ESG	IET 2518	ESG	IFT 1561	ESW	IFT 1622	ESW	IFT 1679	ESW
HT 3648	ESG	IET 2519	ESG	IFT 1562	ESW	IFT 1623	ESW	IFT 1680	ESW
HT 3649	ESG	IET 2521	ESG	IFT 1563	ESW	IFT 1624	ESW	IFT 1800	ESW
HT 3650	ESG	IET 2522	ESG	IFT 1564	ESW	IFT 1625	ESW	IFT 1801	ESW
HT 3651	ESG	IET 2524	ESG	IFT 1570	ESW	IFT 1626	ESW	IFT 1802	ESW
HT 3652	ESG	IET 2525	ESG	IFT 1571	ESW	IFT 1627	ESW	IFT 1803	ESW
HT 3653	ESG	IET 2526	ESG	IFT 1572	ESW	IFT 1628	ESW	IFT 1804	ESW
HT 3654	ESG	IET 2527	ESG	IFT 1573	ESW	IFT 1629	ESW	IFT 1805	ESW
HT 3655	ESG	IET 2529	ESG	IFT 1574	ESW	IFT 1630	ESW	IFT 1806	ESW
HT 3656	ESG	IET 2530	ESG	IFT 1575	ESW	IFT 1631	ESW	MCIT 0001	ESG
HT 3657	ESG	IET 2532	ESG	IFT 1576	ESW	IFT 1632	ESW	MCIT 0002	ESG
HT 3658	ESG	IET 2533	ESG	IFT 1577	ESW	IFT 1633	ESW	MCIT 0003	ESG
HT 3659	ESG	IET 2534	ESG	IFT 1578	ESW	IFT 1634	ESW	MCIT 0004	ESG
HT 3660	ESG	IET 2535	ESG	IFT 1579	ESW	IFT 1635	ESW	MCIT 0005	ESG
HT 3661	ESG	IET 2536	ESG	IFT 1580	ESW	IFT 1636	ESW	MCIT 0006	ESG

Eddie Stobart

MCIT 0007 ESG	MIT 0019 ESG	RBT 12524 CIN	RT 0036 ESG	RTT 12027 ESG
MCIT 0008 ESG	MIT 0020 ESG	RBT 12525 ESW	RT 0037 ESG	RTT 12028 ESG
MCIT 0009 ESG	MIT 0021 ESG	RBT 12526 ESW	RT 0038 ESG	RTT 12029 ESG
MCIT 0010 ESG	MIT 0022 ESG	RBT 12527 ESW	RT 0039 ESG	RTT 12030 ESG
MCIT 0011 ESG	MIT 0023 ESG	RBT 12528 CIN	RT 0040 ESG	RTT 12031 ESG
MCIT 0012 ESG	MIT 0024 ESG	RBT 12529 CIN	RT 0041 ESG	RTT 12032 ESG
MCIT 0013 ESG	MIT 0025 ESG	RBT 12530 ESW	RT 0042 ESG	RTT 12033 ESG
MCIT 0014 ESG	MIT 0026 ESG	RBT 12531 ESW	RT 0043 ESG	RTT 12034 ESG
MCIT 0015 ESG	MIT 0027 ESG	RBT 12532 ESW	RT 0044 WIL	RTT 12035 ESG
MCIT 0016 ESG	MIT 0028 ESG	RBT 12533 ESW	RT 0045 WIL	RTT 12036 ESG
MCIT 0017 ESG	MIT 0029 ESG	RBT 12534 ESW	RT 0046 WIL	RTT 12037 ESG
MCIT 0018 ESG	MIT 0030 ESG	RBT 12535 ESW	RT 0047 WIL	RTT 12038 ESG
MCIT 0019 ESG	MIT 0031 ESG	RBT 12536 ESW	RT 0048 WIL	RTT 12039 ESG
MCIT 0020 ESG	MIT 0032 ESG	RBT 12537 ESW	RT 0049 WIL	RTT 12040 ESG
MCIT 0021 ESG	MIT 0033 ESG	RBT 12538 ESW	RT 0050 WIL	RTT 12041 ESG
MCIT 0022 ESG	MIT 0034 ESG	RBT 12539 ESW	RT 0051 WIL	RTT 12042 ESG
MCIT 0023 ESG	MIT 0035 ESG	RBT 12540 ESW	RT 0052 WIL	RTT 12043 ESG
MCIT 0024 ESG	MIT 0036 ESG	RBT 12541 CIN	RT 0053 WIL	RTT 12044 ESG
MCIT 0025 ESG	MIT 0037 ESG	RBT 12542 ESW	RT 0054 WIL	RTT 12045 ESG
MCIT 0026 ESG	MIT 0038 ESG	RBT 12543 ESW	RT 0055 WIL	RTT 12046 ESG
MCIT 0027 ESG	MIT 0039 ESG	RBT 12544 ESW	AF 0059 White	RTT 12047 ESG
MCIT 0028 ESG	MIT 0040 ESG	RBT 12545 ESW	AF 0060 White	RTT 12048 ESG
MCIT 0029 ESG	MIT 0041 ESG	RBT 12546 CIN	FIA 0061 White	RTT 12049 ESG
MCIT 0030 ESG	MIT 0042 ESG	RBT 12547 CIN	FIA 0062 White	RTT 12050 ESG
MCIT 0031 ESG	MIT 0043 ESG	RBT 12548 ESW	LOWLOADER	RTT 12051 ESG
MCIT 0032 ESG	MIT 0044 ESG	RBT 12549 White	Red	RTT 12052 ESG
MCIT 0033 ESG	MIT 0045 ESG	RBT 12550 White	R 1 WIL	RTT 12053 ESG
MCIT 0034 ESG	MIT 0046 ESG	RT 0001 SAM	R 2 WIL	RTT 12054 ESG
MCIT 0035 ESG	MIT 0047 ESG	RT 0002 SAM	R 3 WIL	RTT 12055 ESG
MCIT 0036 ESG	MIT 0048 ESG	RT 0003 BAM	R 4 WIL	RTT 12056 ESG
MCIT 0037 ESG	MIT 0049 ESG	RT 0004 BAM	RTT 12000 ESG	RTT 12057 ESG
MCIT 0038 ESG	MIT 0050 ESG	RT 0005 BAM	RTT 12001 ESG	RTT 12058 ESG
MCIT 0039 ESG	RBT 12500 ESG	RT 0006 Green	RTT 12002 ESG	RTT 12059 ESG
MCIT 0040 ESG	RBT 12501 ESG	RT 0007 Green	RTT 12003 ESG	RTT 12060 ESG
MCIT 0041 ESG	RBT 12502 ESG	RT 0008 Green	RTT 12004 ESG	RTT 12061 ESG
MCIT 0042 ESG	RBT 12503 ESG	SP 0009 STP	RTT 12005 ESG	RTT 12062 ESG
MCIT 0043 ESG	RBT 12504 ESG	RT 0010 PIB	RTT 12006 ESG	RTT 12063 ESG
MCIT 0044 ESG	RBT 12505 ESG	RT 0011 PIB	RTT 12007 ESG	RTT 12064 ESG
MIT 0001 ESG	RBT 12506 ESG	PRT 0012 PIB	RTT 12008 ESG	RTT 12065 ESG
MIT 0002 ESG	RBT 12507 ESG	PRT 0013 PIB	RTT 12009 ESG	RTT 12066 ESG
MIT 0003 ESG	RBT 12508 ESG	PRT 0014 PIB	RTT 12010 ESG	RTT 12067 ESG
MIT 0004 ESG	RBT 12509 ESG	PRT 0015 PIB	RTT 12011 ESG	RTT 12068 ESG
MIT 0005 ESG	RBT 12510 ESG	PRT 0016 PIB	RTT 12012 ESG	RUT 11000 ESG
MIT 0006 ESG	RBT 12511 ESG	PRT 0017 PIB	RTT 12013 ESG	RUT 11001 ESG
MIT 0007 ESG	RBT 12512 ESG	PRT 0018 PIB	RTT 12014 ESG	RUT 11002 ESG
MIT 0008 ESG	RBT 12513 ESG	PRT 0019 PIB	RTT 12015 ESG	RUT 11003 ESG
MIT 0009 ESG	RBT 12514 CIN	PRT 0020 PIB	RTT 12016 ESC	RUT 11004 ESG
MIT 0010 ESG	RBT 12515 ESW	PRT 0021 PIB	RTT 12017 ESG	RUT 11005 ESG
MIT 0011 ESG	RBT 12516 ESW	PRT 0024 PIB	RTT 12018 ESG	RUT 11006 ESG
MIT 0012 ESG	RBT 12517 CIN	PRT 0025 PIB	RTT 12019 ESG	RUT 11007 ESG
MIT 0013 ESG	RBT 12518 ESW	RT 0030 ESG	RTT 12020 ESG	SCT 0150 ESG
MIT 0014 ESG	RBT 12519 ESW	RT 0031 ESG	RTT 12021 ESG	SCT 0151 ESG
MIT 0015 ESG	RBT 12520 CIN	RT 0032 ESG	RTT 12023 ESG	SCT 0152 ESG
MIT 0016 ESG	RBT 12521 ESW	RT 0033 ESG	RTT 12024 ESG	SCT 0153 ESG
MIT 0017 ESG	RBT 12522 ESW	RT 0034 ESG	RTT 12025 ESG	SCT 2594 ESG
MIT 0018 ESG	RBT 12523 ESW	RT 0035 ESG	RTT 12026 ESG	SCT 2595 ESG

Eddie Stobart

SCT 2596	ESG	SIT 0051	ESG	SIT 0107	ESG	SK 252	SPR	SK 308	SPR
SCT 2597	ESG	SIT 0052	ESG	SIT 0108	ESG	SK 253	SPR	SK 309	SPR
SCT 2598	ESG	SIT 0053	ESG	SIT 0109	ESG	SK 254	SPR	SK 310	SPR
SCT 2599	ESG	SIT 0054	ESG	SIT 0110	ESG	SK 255	SPR	SK 311	SPR
SCT 2600	ESG	SIT 0055	ESG	SIT 0111	ESG	SK 256	SPR	SK 312	SPR
SCT 2601	ESG	SIT 0056	ESG	SK 200	SPR	SK 257	SPR	SK 313	SPR
SIT 0001	ESG	SIT 0057	ESG	SK 201	SPR	SK 258	SPR	SK 314	SPR
SIT 0002	ESG	SIT 0058	ESG	SK 202	SPR	SK 259	SPR	SK 315	SPR
SIT 0003	ESG	SIT 0059	ESG	SK 204	SPR	SK 260	SPR	SK 316	SPR
SIT 0004	ESG	SIT 0060	ESG	SK 205	SPR	SK 261	SPR	SK 317	SPR
SIT 0005	ESG	SIT 0061	ESG	SK 206	SPR	SK 262	SPR	SK 318	SPR
SIT 0006	ESG	SIT 0062	ESG	SK 207	SPR	SK 263	SPR	SK 319	SPR
SIT 0007	ESG	SIT 0063	ESG	SK 208	SPR	SK 264	SPR	SK 320	SPR
SIT 0008	ESG	SIT 0064	ESG	SK 209	SPR	SK 265	SPR	SK 321	SPR
SIT 0009	ESG	SIT 0065	ESG	SK 210	SPR	SK 266	SPR	SK 322	SPR
SIT 0010	ESG	SIT 0066	ESG	SK 211	SPR	SK 267	SPR	SK 323	SPR
SIT 0011	ESG	SIT 0067	ESG	SK 212	SPR	SK 268	SPR	SK 324	SPR
SIT 0012	ESG	SIT 0068	ESG	SK 213	SPR	SK 269	SPR	SK 325	SPR
SIT 0013	ESG	SIT 0069	ESG	SK 214	SPR	SK 270	SPR	SK 326	SPR
SIT 0014	ESG	SIT 0070	ESG	SK 215	SPR	SK 271	SPR	SK 327	SPR
SIT 0015	ESG	SIT 0071	ESG	SK 216	SPR	SK 272	SPR	SK 328	SPR
SIT 0016	ESG	SIT 0072	ESG	SK 217	SPR	SK 273	SPR	SK 329	SPR
SIT 0017	ESG	SIT 0073	ESG	SK 218	SPR	SK 274	SPR	SK 330	SPR
SIT 0018	ESG	SIT 0074	ESG	SK 219	SPR	SK 275	SPR	SK 331	SPR
SIT 0019	ESG	SIT 0075	ESG	SK 220	SPR	SK 276	SPR	SK 332	SPR
SIT 0020	ESG	SIT 0076	ESG	SK 221	SPR	SK 277	SPR	SK 333	SPR
SIT 0021	ESG	SIT 0077	ESG	SK 222	SPR	SK 278	SPR	SK 334	SPR
SIT 0022	ESG	SIT 0078	ESG	SK 223	SPR	SK 279	SPR	SK 335	SPR
SIT 0023	ESG	SIT 0079	ESG	SK 224	SPR	SK 280	SPR	SK 336	SPR
SIT 0024	ESG	SIT 0080	ESG	SK 225	SPR	SK 281	SPR	SK 337	SPR
SIT 0025	ESG	SIT 0081	ESG	SK 226	SPR	SK 282	SPR	SK 338	SPR
SIT 0026	ESG	SIT 0082	ESG	SK 227	SPR	SK 283	SPR	SK 339	SPR
SIT 0027	ESG	SIT 0083	ESG	SK 228	SPR	SK 284	SPR	SK 340	SPR
SIT 0028	ESG	SIT 0084	ESG	SK 229	SPR	SK 285	SPR	SK 341	SPR
SIT 0029	ESG	SIT 0085	ESG	SK 230	SPR	SK 286	SPR	SK 342	SPR
SIT 0030	ESG	SIT 0086	ESG	SK 231	SPR	SK 287	SPR	SK 343	SPR
SIT 0031	ESG	SIT 0087	ESG	SK 232	SPR	SK 288	SPR	SK 344	SPR
SIT 0032	ESG	SIT 0088	ESG	SK 233	SPR	SK 289	SPR	SK 345	SPR
SIT 0033	ESG	SIT 0089	ESG	SK 234	SPR	SK 290	SPR	SK 346	SPR
SIT 0034	ESG	SIT 0090	ESG	SK 235	SPR	SK 291	SPR	SK 347	SPR
SIT 0035	ESG	SIT 0091	ESG	SK 236	SPR	SK 292	SPR	SK 348	SPR
SIT 0036	ESG	SIT 0092	ESG	SK 237	SPR	SK 293	SPR	SK 349	SPR
SIT 0037	ESG	SIT 0093	ESG	SK 238	SPR	SK 294	SPR	SK 350	SPR
SIT 0038	ESG	SIT 0094	ESG	SK 239	SPR	SK 295	SPR	SK 351	SPR
SIT 0039	ESG	SIT 0095	ESG	SK 240	SPR	SK 296	SPR	SK 352	SPR
SIT 0040	ESG	SIT 0096	ESG	SK 241	SPR	SK 297	SPR	SK 353	SPR
SIT 0041	ESG	SIT 0097	ESG	SK 242	SPR	SK 298	SPR	SK 354	SPR
SIT 0042	ESG	SIT 0098	ESG	SK 243	SPR	SK 299	SPR	SK 355	SPR
SIT 0043	ESG	SIT 0099	ESG	SK 244	SPR	SK 300	SPR	SK 356	SPR
SIT 0044	ESG	SIT 0100	ESG	SK 245	SPR	SK 301	SPR	SK 357	SPR
SIT 0045	ESG	SIT 0101	ESG	SK 246	SPR	SK 302	SPR	SK 358	SPR
SIT 0046	ESG	SIT 0102	ESG	SK 247	SPR	SK 303	SPR	SK 359	SPR
SIT 0047	ESG	SIT 0103	ESG	SK 248	SPR	SK 304	SPR	SK 360	SPR
SIT 0048	ESG	SIT 0104	ESG	SK 249	SPR	SK 305	SPR	SK 361	SPR
SIT 0049	ESG	SIT 0105	ESG	SK 250	SPR	SK 306	SPR	SK 362	SPR
SIT 0050	ESG	SIT 0106	ESG	SK 251	SPR	SK 307	SPR	SK 363	SPR

Eddie Stobart

SK 364	SPR	SK 420	SPR	SK 624	SPR	SK 683	SPR	SK 739	SPR
SK 365	SPR	SK 421	SPR	SK 625	SPR	SK 684	SPR	SK 740	SPR
SK 366	SPR	SK 422	SPR	SK 626	SPR	SK 685	SPR	SK 741	SPR
SK 367	SPR	SK 423	SPR	SK 627	SPR	SK 686	SPR	SK 742	SPR
SK 368	SPR	SK 424	SPR	SK 628	SPR	SK 687	SPR	SK 743	SPR
SK 369	SPR	SK 425	SPR	SK 629	SPR	SK 688	SPR	SK 744	SPR
SK 370	SPR	SK 426	SPR	SK 630	SPR	SK 689	SPR	SK 745	SPR
SK 371	SPR	SK 427	SPR	SK 631	SPR	SK 690	SPR	SK 746	SPR
SK 372	SPR	SK 428	SPR	SK 632	SPR	SK 691	SPR	SK 747	SPR
SK 373	SPR	SK 429	SPR	SK 633	SPR	SK 692	SPR	SK 748	SPR
SK 374	SPR	SK 430	SPR	SK 634	SPR	SK 693	SPR	SK 749	SPR
SK 375	SPR	SK 431	SPR	SK 635	SPR	SK 694	SPR	SK 750	SPR
SK 376	SPR	SK 432	SPR	SK 636	SPR	SK 695	SPR	SK 751	SPR
SK 377	SPR	SK 433	SPR	SK 637	SPR	SK 696	SPR	SK 752	SPR
SK 378	SPR	SK 434	SPR	SK 638	SPR	SK 697	SPR	SK 753	SPR
SK 379	SPR	SK 435	SPR	SK 639	SPR	SK 698	SPR	SK 754	SPR
SK 380	SPR	SK 436	SPR	SK 640	SPR	SK 699	SPR	SK 755	SPR
SK 381	SPR	SK 437	SPR	SK 641	SPR	SK 700	SPR	SK 756	SPR
SK 382	SPR	SK 438	SPR	SK 643	SPR	SK 701	SPR	SK 757	SPR
SK 383	SPR	SK 439	SPR	SK 644	SPR	SK 702	SPR	SK 758	SPR
SK 384	SPR	SK 440	SPR	SK 645	SPR	SK 703	SPR	SK 759	SPR
SK 385	SPR	SK 441	SPR	SK 646	SPR	SK 704	SPR	SK 760	SPR
SK 386	SPR	SK 442	SPR	SK 647	SPR	SK 705	SPR	SK 761	SPR
SK 387	SPR	SK 443	SPR	SK 648	SPR	SK 706	SPR	SK 762	SPR
SK 388	SPR	SK 444	SPR	SK 649	SPR	SK 707	SPR	SK 763	SPR
SK 389	SPR	SK 445	SPR	SK 651	SPR	SK 708	SPR	SK 764	SPR
SK 390	SPR	SK 446	SPR	SK 652	SPR	SK 709	SPR	SK 765	SPR
SK 391	SPR	SK 447	SPR	SK 653	SPR	SK 710	SPR	SK 766	SPR
SK 392	SPR	SK 448	SPR	SK 654	SPR	SK 711	SPR	SK 767	SPR
SK 393	SPR	SK 449	SPR	SK 655	SPR	SK 712	SPR	SK 768	SPR
SK 394	SPR	SK 450	SPR	SK 656	SPR	SK 713	SPR	SK 769	SPR
SK 395	SPR	SK 451	SPR	SK 657	SPR	SK 714	SPR	SK 770	SPR
SK 396	SPR	SK 600	SPR	SK 658	SPR	SK 715	SPR	SK 771	SPR
SK 397	SPR	SK 601	SPR	SK 659	SPR	SK 716	SPR	SK 772	SPR
SK 398	SPR	SK 602	SPR	SK 660	SPR	SK 717	SPR	SK 773	SPR
SK 399	SPR	SK 603	SPR	SK 661	SPR	SK 718	SPR	SK 774	SPR
SK 400	SPR	SK 604	SPR	SK 662	SPR	SK 719	SPR	SK 775	SPR
SK 401	SPR	SK 605	SPR	SK 663	SPR	SK 720	SPR	SK 776	SPR
SK 402	SPR	SK 606	SPR	SK 664	SPR	SK 721	SPR	SK 777	SPR
SK 403	SPR	SK 607	SPR	SK 665	SPR	SK 722	SPR	SK 778	SPR
SK 404	SPR	SK 608	SPR	SK 666	SPR	SK 723	SPR	SK 779	SPR
SK 405	SPR	SK 609	SPR	SK 667	SPR	SK 724	SPR	SK 780	SPR
SK 406	SPR	SK 610	SPR	SK 668	SPR	SK 725	SPR	SK 781	SPR
SK 407	SPR	SK 611	SPR	SK 669	SPR	SK 726	SPR	SK 782	SPR
SK 408	SPR	SK 612	SPR	SK 670	SPR	SK 727	SPR	SK 783	SPR
SK 409	SPR	SK 613	SPR	SK 672	SPR	SK 728	SPR	SK 784	SPR
SK 410	SPR	SK 614	SPR	SK 673	SPR	SK 729	SPR	SK 785	SPR
SK 411	3PR	SK 615	SPR	SK 674	SPR	SK 730	SPR	SK 786	SPR
SK 412	SPR	SK 616	SPR	SK 675	SPR	SK 731	SPR	SK 787	SPR
SK 413	SPR	SK 617	SPR	SK 676	SPR	SK 732	SPR	SK 788	SPR
SK 414	SPR	SK 618	SPR	SK 677	SPR	SK 733	SPR	SK 789	SPR
SK 415	SPR	SK 619	SPR	SK 678	SPR	SK 734	SPR	SK 790	SPR
SK 416	SPR	SK 620	SPR	SK 679	SPR	SK 735	SPR	SK 791	SPR
SK 417	SPR	SK 621	SPR	SK 680	SPR	SK 736	SPR	SK 792	SPR
SK 418	SPR	SK 622	SPR	SK 681	SPR	SK 737	SPR	SK 793	SPR
SK 419	SPR	SK 623	SPR	SK 682	SPR	SK 738	SPR	SK 794	SPR

Eddie Stobart

SK 795	SPR	SK 851	SPR	TCT 7379	ESG	TCT 7438	ESG	TCT 7498	ESG
SK 796	SPR	SK 852	SPR	TCT 7380	ESG	TCT 7439	ESG	TCT 7499	ESG
SK 797	SPR	SK 853	SPR	TCT 7381	ESG	TCT 7441	ESG	TCT 7500	ESG
SK 798	SPR	SK 854	SPR	TCT 7383	ESG	TCT 7442	ESG	TCT 7501	ESG
SK 799	SPR	SK 855	SPR	TCT 7384	ESG	TCT 7443	ESG	TCT 7502	ESG
SK 800	SPR	SK 856	SPR	TCT 7385	ESG	TCT 7444	ESG	TCT 7503	ESG
SK 801	SPR	SK 857	SPR	TCT 7386	ESG	TCT 7445	ESG	TCT 7504	ESG
SK 802	SPR	SK 858	SPR	TCT 7387	ESG	TCT 7446	ESG	TCT 7505	ESG
SK 803	SPR	SK 859	SPR	TCT 7388	ESG	TCT 7447	ESG	TCT 7506	ESG
SK 804	SPR	SK 860	SPR	TCT 7389	ESG	TCT 7448	ESG	TCT 7507	ESG
SK 805	SPR	SK 865	SPR	TCT 7390	ESG	TCT 7449	ESG	TCT 7508	ESG
SK 806	SPR	SK 866	SPR	TCT 7391	ESG	TCT 7450	ESG	TCT 7509	ESG
SK 807	SPR	SK 867	SPR	TCT 7392	ESG	TCT 7451	ESG	TCT 7510	ESG
SK 808	SPR	SK 868	SPR	TCT 7393	ESG	TCT 7452	ESG	TCT 7511	ESG
SK 809	SPR	SK 869	SPR	TCT 7394	ESG	TCT 7453	ESG	TCT 7512	ESG
SK 810	SPR	SK 870	SPR	TCT 7395	ESG	TCT 7454	ESG	TCT 7513	ESG
SK 811	SPR	SK 871	SPR	TCT 7396	ESG	TCT 7455	ESG	TCT 7514	ESG
SK 812	SPR	SK 872	SPR	TCT 7397	ESG	TCT 7456	ESG	TCT 7515	ESG
SK 813	SPR	SK 873	SPR	TCT 7398	ESG	TCT 7457	ESG	TCT 7516	ESG
SK 814	SPR	SK 874	SPR	TCT 7399	ESG	TCT 7458	ESG	TCT 7517	ESG
SK 815	SPR	SKG 875	SPR	TCT 7400	ESG	TCT 7459	ESG	TCT 7518	ESG
SK 816	SPR	SKG 876	SPR	TCT 7401	ESG	TCT 7460	ESG	TCT 7519	ESG
SK 817	SPR	SKG 877	SPR	TCT 7402	ESG	TCT 7461	ESG	TCT 7520	ESG
SK 818	SPR	SKG 878	SPR	TCT 7403	ESG	TCT 7462	ESG	TCT 7521	ESG
SK 819	SPR	SKG 879	SPR	TCT 7404	ESG	TCT 7463	ESG	TCT 7522	ESG
SK 820	SPR	SKG 880	SPR	TCT 7405	ESG	TCT 7464	ESG	TCT 7523	ESG
SK 821	SPR	SKG 881	SPR	TCT 7406	ESG	TCT 7465	ESG	TCT 7524	ESG
SK 822	SPR	SKG 882	SPR	TCT 7407	ESG	TCT 7466	ESG	TCT 7525	ESG
SK 823	SPR	SKG 883	SPR	TCT 7408	ESG	TCT 7467	ESG	TCT 7526	ESG
SK 824	SPR	SKG 884	SPR	TCT 7409	ESG	TCT 7468	ESG	TCT 7527	ESG
SK 825	SPR	SSK 100	SPR	TCT 7410	ESG	TCT 7470	ESG	TCT 7528	ESG
SK 826	SPR	SSK 101	SPR	TCT 7411	ESG	TCT 7472	ESG	TCT 7529	ESG
SK 827	SPR	SSK 102	SPR	TCT 7412	ESG	TCT 7473	ESG	TCT 7530	ESG
SK 828	SPR	SSK 103	SPR	TCT 7413	ESG	TCT 7474	ESG	TCT 7531	ESG
SK 829	SPR	SSK 104	SPR	TCT 7414	ESG	TCT 7475	ESG	TCT 7532	ESG
SK 830	SPR	SSK 105R	SPR	TCT 7415	ESG	TCT 7476	ESG	TCT 7533	ESG
SK 831	SPR	SSK 861	SPR	TCT 7418	ESG	TCT 7477	ESG	TCT 7534	ESG
SK 832	SPR	SSK 862	SPR	TCT 7419	ESG	TCT 7479	ESG	TCT 7535	ESG
SK 833	SPR	SSK 863	SPR	TCT 7420	ESG	TCT 7480	ESG	TCT 7536	ESG
SK 834	SPR	SSK 864	SPR	TCT 7421	ESG	TCT 7481	ESG	TCT 7537	ESG
SK 835	SPR	TCT 7363	ESG	TCT 7422	ESG	TCT 7482	ESG	TCT 7538	ESG
SK 836	SPR	TCT 7364	ESG	TCT 7423	ESG	TCT 7483	ESG	TCT 7539	ESG
SK 837	SPR	TCT 7365	ESG	TCT 7424	ESG	TCT 7484	ESG	TCT 7540	ESG
SK 838	SPR	TCT 7366	ESG	TCT 7425	ESG	TCT 7485	ESG	TCT 7541	ESG
SK 839	SPR	TCT 7367	ESG	TCT 7426	ESG	TCT 7486	ESG	TCT 7542	ESG
SK 840	SPR	TCT 7368	ESG	TCT 7427	ESG	TCT 7487	ESG	TCT 7543	ESG
SK 841	SPR	TCT 7369	ESG	TCT 7428	ESG	TCT 7488	ESG	TCT 7544	ESG
SK 842	SPR	TCT 7370	ESG	TCT 7429	ESG	TCT 7489	ESG	TCT 7545	ESG
SK 843	SPR	TCT 7371	ESG	TCT 7430	ESG	TCT 7490	ESG	TCT 7546	ESG
SK 844	SPR	TCT 7372	ESG	TCT 7431	ESG	TCT 7491	ESG	TCT 7547	ESG
SK 845	SPR	TCT 7373	ESG	TCT 7432	ESG	TCT 7492	ESG	TCT 7549	ESG
SK 846	SPR	TCT 7374	ESG	TCT 7433	ESG	TCT 7493	ESG	TCT 7550	ESG
SK 847	SPR	TCT 7375	ESG	TCT 7434	ESG	TCT 7494	ESG	TCT 7551	ESG
SK 848	SPR	TCT 7376	ESG	TCT 7435	ESG	TCT 7495	ESG	TCT 7552	ESG
SK 849	SPR	TCT 7377	ESG	TCT 7436	ESG	TCT 7496	ESG	TCT 7553	ESG
SK 850	SPR	TCT 7378	ESG	TCT 7437	ESG	TCT 7497	ESG	TCT 7554	ESG

Eddie Stobart

TCT 7555 ESG	TCT 7613 ESG	TCT 7673 ESG	TCT 7731 ESG	TCT 7788 ESG
TCT 7556 ESG	TCT 7614 ESG	TCT 7674 ESG	TCT 7732 ESG	TCT 7789 ESG
TCT 7557 ESG	TCT 7615 ESG	TCT 7675 ESG	TCT 7733 ESG	TCT 7790 ESG
TCT 7558 ESG	TCT 7616 ESG	TCT 7676 ESG	TCT 7734 ESG	TCT 7791 ESG
TCT 7559 ESG	TCT 7617 ESG	TCT 7677 ESG	TCT 7735 ESG	TCT 7792 ESG
TCT 7560 ESG	TCT 7618 ESG	TCT 7678 ESG	TCT 7736 ESG	TCT 7793 ESG
TCT 7561 ESG	TCT 7619 ESG	TCT 7679 ESG	TCT 7737 ESG	TCT 7794 ESG
TCT 7563 ESG	TCT 7620 ESG	TCT 7680 ESG	TCT 7738 ESG	TCT 7795 ESG
TCT 7564 ESG	TCT 7621 ESG	TCT 7682 ESG	TCT 7739 ESG	TCT 7796 ESG
TCT 7565 ESG	TCT 7622 ESG	TCT 7683 ESG	TCT 7740 ESG	TCT 7797 ESG
TCT 7566 ESG	TCT 7623 ESG	TCT 7684 ESG	TCT 7741 ESG	TCT 7798 ESG
TCT 7567 ESG	TCT 7624 ESG	TCT 7685 ESG	TCT 7742 ESG	TCT 7799 ESG
TCT 7568 ESG	TCT 7625 ESG	TCT 7686 ESG	TCT 7743 ESG	TCT 7800 ESG
TCT 7569 ESG	TCT 7626 ESG	TCT 7687 ESG	TCT 7744 ESG	TCT 7801 ESG
TCT 7570 ESG	TCT 7627 ESG	TCT 7688 ESG	TCT 7745 ESG	TCT 7802 ESG
TCT 7571 ESG	TCT 7628 ESG	TCT 7689 ESG	TCT 7746 ESG	TCT 7803 ESG
TCT 7572 ESG	TCT 7629 ESG	TCT 7690 ESG	TCT 7747 ESG	TCT 7804 ESG
TCT 7573 ESG	TCT 7632 ESG	TCT 7691 ESG	TCT 7749 ESG	TCT 7806 ESG
TCT 7574 ESG	TCT 7633 ESG	TCT 7692 ESG	TCT 7750 ESG	TCT 7807 ESG
TCT 7575 ESG	TCT 7634 ESG	TCT 7693 ESG	TCT 7751 ESG	TCT 7808 ESG
TCT 7576 ESG	TCT 7635 ESG	TCT 7694 ESG	TCT 7752 ESG	TCT 7809 ESG
TCT 7577 ESG	TCT 7636 ESG	TCT 7695 ESG	TCT 7753 ESG	TCT 7810 ESG
TCT 7578 ESG	TCT 7637 ESG	TCT 7696 ESG	TCT 7754 ESG	TCT 7811 ESG
TCT 7579 ESG	TCT 7638 ESG	TCT 7697 ESG	TCT 7755 ESG	TCT 7812 ESG
TCT 7580 ESG	TCT 7639 ESG	TCT 7698 ESG	TCT 7756 ESG	TCT 7813 ESG
TCT 7581 ESG	TCT 7641 ESG	TCT 7699 ESG	TCT 7757 ESG	TCT 7814 ESG
TCT 7583 ESG	TCT 7642 ESG	TCT 7700 ESG	TCT 7758 ESG	TCT 7815 ESG
TCT 7584 ESG	TCT 7644 ESG	TCT 7701 ESG	TCT 7759 ESG	TCT 7816 ESG
TCT 7585 ESG	TCT 7645 ESG	TCT 7702 ESG	TCT 7760 ESG	TCT 7817 ESG
TCT 7586 ESG	TCT 7646 ESG	TCT 7703 ESG	TCT 7761 ESG	TCT 7818 ESG
TCT 7587 ESG	TCT 7647 ESG	TCT 7704 ESG	TCT 7762 ESG	TCT 7819 ESG
TCT 7588 ESG	TCT 7648 ESG	TCT 7705 ESG	TCT 7763 ESG	TCT 7821 ESG
TCT 7589 ESG	TCT 7649 ESG	TCT 7706 ESG	TCT 7764 ESG	TCT 7822 ESG
TCT 7590 ESG	TCT 7650 ESG	TCT 7707 ESG	TCT 7765 ESG	TCT 7823 ESG
TCT 7591 ESG	TCT 7651 ESG	TCT 7708 ESG	TCT 7766 ESG	TCT 7824 ESG
TCT 7592 ESG	TCT 7652 ESG	TCT 7709 ESG	TCT 7767 ESG	TCT 7825 ESG
TCT 7593 ESG	TCT 7653 ESG	TCT 7710 ESG	TCT 7768 ESG	TCT 7826 ESG
TCT 7594 ESG	TCT 7654 ESG	TCT 7711 ESG	TCT 7769 ESG	TCT 7827 ESG
TCT 7595 ESG	TCT 7655 ESG	TCT 7712 ESG	TCT 7770 ESG	TCT 7828 ESG
TCT 7596 ESG	TCT 7656 ESG	TCT 7713 ESG	TCT 7771 ESG	TCT 7829 ESG
TCT 7597 ESG	TCT 7657 ESG	TCT 7714 ESG	TCT 7772 ESG	TCT 7830 ESG
TCT 7598 ESG	TCT 7658 ESG	TCT 7715 ESG	TCT 7773 ESG	TCT 7831 ESG
TCT 7599 ESG	TCT 7659 ESG	TCT 7716 ESG	TCT 7774 ESG	TCT 7832 ESG
TCT 7600 ESG	TCT 7660 ESG	TCT 7717 ESG	TCT 7775 ESG	TCT 7833 ESG
TCT 7601 ESG	TCT 7661 ESG	TCT 7719 ESG	TCT 7776 ESG	TCT 7834 ESG
TCT 7602 ESG	TCT 7662 ESG	TCT 7720 ESG	TCT 7777 ESG	TCT 7835 ESG
TCT 7603 ESG	TCT 7663 ESG	TCT 7721 FSG	TCT 7778 ESG	TCT 7836 ESG
TCT 7604 ESG	TCT 7664 ESG	TCT 7722 ESG	TCT 7779 ESG	TCT 7837 ESG
TCT 7605 ESG	TCT 7665 ESG	TCT 7723 ESG	TCT 7780 ESG	TCT 7838 ESG
TCT 7606 ESG	TCT 7666 ESG	TCT 7724 ESG	TCT 7781 ESG	TCT 7839 ESG
TCT 7607 ESG	TCT 7667 ESG	TCT 7725 ESG	TCT 7782 ESG	TCT 7840 ESG
TCT 7608 ESG	TCT 7668 ESG	TCT 7726 ESG	TCT 7783 ESG	TCT 7841 ESG
TCT 7609 ESG	TCT 7669 ESG	TCT 7727 ESG	TCT 7784 ESG	TCT 7842 ESG
TCT 7610 ESG	TCT 7670 ESG	TCT 7728 ESG	TCT 7785 ESG	TCT 7843 ESG
TCT 7611 ESG	TCT 7671 ESG	TCT 7729 ESG	TCT 7786 ESG	TCT 7844 ESG
TCT 7612 ESG	TCT 7672 ESG	TCT 7730 ESG	TCT 7787 ESG	TCT 7845 ESG

Eddie Stobart

TCT 7846 ESG	TET 9815 ESG	TET 9888 ESG	TET 9961 ESG	TET 10027 ESG
TCT 7847 ESG	TET 9816 ESG	TET 9891 ESG	TET 9963 ESG	TET 10028 ESG
TCT 7848 ESG	TET 9817 ESG	TET 9892 ESG	TET 9964 ESG	TET 10029 ESG
TCT 7849 ESG	TET 9819 ESG	TET 9893 ESG	TET 9965 ESG	TET 10030 ESG
TCT 7850 ESG	TET 9820 ESG	TET 9894 ESG	TET 9966 ESG	TET 10031 ESG
TCT 7851 ESG	TET 9821 ESG	TET 9895 ESG	TET 9967 ESG	TET 10032 ESG
TCT 7852 ESG	TET 9822 ESG	TET 9896 ESG	TET 9969 ESG	TET 10033 ESG
TET 9750 ESG	TET 9823 ESG	TET 9898 ESG	TET 9971 ESG	TET 10034 ESG
TET 9751 ESG	TET 9824 ESG	TET 9901 ESG	TET 9972 ESG	TET 10035 ESG
TET 9752 ESG	TET 9825 ESG	TET 9902 ESG	TET 9973 ESG	TET 10036 ESG
TET 9753 ESG	TET 9826 ESG	TET 9903 ESG	TET 9975 ESG	TET 10037 ESG
TET 9754 ESG	TET 9827 ESG	TET 9904 ESG	TET 9977 ESG	TET 10038 ESG
TET 9756 ESG	TET 9828 ESG	TET 9906 ESG	TET 9978 ESG	TET 10039 ESG
TET 9758 ESG	TET 9829 ESG	TET 9907 ESG	TET 9979 ESG	TET 10040 ESG
TET 9760 ESG	TET 9831 ESG	TET 9908 ESG	TET 9980 ESG	TET 10041 ESG
TET 9763 ESG	TET 9833 ESG	TET 9909 ESG	TET 9981 ESG	TET 10042 ESG
TET 9764 ESG	TET 9835 ESG	TET 9910 ESG	TET 9982 ESG	TET 10043 ESG
TET 9767 ESG	TET 9836 ESG	TET 9911 ESG	TET 9983 ESG	TET 10044 ESG
TET 9768 ESG	TET 9837 ESG	TET 9912 ESG	TET 9985 ESG	TET 10045 ESG
TET 9769 ESG	TET 9839 ESG	TET 9915 ESG	TET 9986 ESG	TET 10046 ESG
TET 9770 ESG	TET 9840 ESG	TET 9918 ESG	TET 9987 ESG	TET 10047 ESG
TET 9771 ESG	TET 9841 ESG	TET 9919 ESG	TET 9988 ESG	TET 10048 ESG
TET 9772 ESG	TET 9843 ESG	TET 9922 ESG	TET 9990 ESG	TET 10049 ESG
TET 9773 ESG	TET 9844 ESG	TET 9923 ESG	TET 9992 ESG	TET 10050 ESG
TET 9775 ESG	TET 9845 ESG	TET 9925 ESG	TET 9994 ESG	TET 10051 ESG
TET 9776 ESG	TET 9846 ESG	TET 9927 ESG	TET 9995 ESG	TET 10052 ESG
TET 9777 ESG	TET 9847 ESG	TET 9928 ESG	TET 9996 ESG	TET 10053 ESG
TET 9778 ESG	TET 9848 ESG	TET 9929 ESG	TET 9997 ESG	TET 10054 ESG
TET 9779 ESG	TET 9850 ESG	TET 9932 ESG	TET 9998 ESG	TET 10055 ESG
TET 9780 ESG	TET 9851 ESG	TET 9933 ESG	TET 9999 ESG	TET 10056 ESG
TET 9782 ESG	TET 9852 ESG	TET 9934 ESG	TET 10000 ESG	TET 10057 ESG
TET 9783 ESG	TET 9853 ESG	TET 9935 ESG	TET 10001 ESG	TET 10058 ESG
TET 9784 ESG	TET 9854 ESG	TET 9936 ESG	TET 10002 ESG	TET 10059 ESG
TET 9785 ESG	TET 9855 ESG	TET 9937 ESG	TET 10003 ESG	TET 10061 ESG
TET 9787 ESG	TET 9856 ESG	TET 9938 ESG	TET 10004 ESG	TET 10062 ESG
TET 9788 ESG	TET 9859 ESG	TET 9939 ESG	TET 10005 ESG	TET 10063 ESG
TET 9789 ESG	TET 9860 ESG	TET 9940 ESG	TET 10006 ESG	TET 10064 ESG
TET 9790 ESG	TET 9862 ESG	TET 9941 ESG	TET 10007 ESG	TET 10065 ESG
TET 9791 ESG	TET 9863 ESG	TET 9942 ESG	TET 10008 ESG	TET 10066 ESG
TET 9792 ESG	TET 9864 ESG	TET 9943 ESG	TET 10009 ESG	TET 10067 ESG
TET 9793 ESG	TET 9865 ESG	TET 9944 ESG	TET 10010 ESG	TET 10068 ESG
TET 9794 ESG	TET 9867 ESG	TET 9945 ESG	TET 10012 ESG	TET 10069 ESG
TET 9797 ESG	TET 9868 ESG	TET 9946 ESG	TET 10013 ESG	TET 10070 ESG
TET 9798 ESG	TET 9870 ESG	TET 9947 ESG	TET 10014 ESG	TET 10071 ESG
TET 9799 ESG	TET 9872 ESG	TET 9948 ESG	TET 10015 ESG	TET 10072 ESG
TET 9802 ESG	TET 9873 ESG	TET 9950 ESG	TET 10016 ESG	TET 10073 ESG
TET 9803 ESG	TET 9875 ESG	TET 9951 ESG	TET 10017 ESG	TET 10075 ESG
TET 9804 ESG	TET 9877 ESG	TET 9952 ESG	TET 10018 ESG	TET 10076 ESG
TET 9805 ESG	TET 9878 ESG	TET 9953 ESG	TET 10019 ESG	TET 10077 ESG
TET 9806 ESG	TET 9879 ESG	TET 9954 ESG	TET 10020 ESG	TET 10078 ESG
TET 9807 ESG	TET 9881 ESG	TET 9955 ESG	TET 10021 ESG	TET 10079 ESG
TET 9808 ESG	TET 9882 ESG	TET 9956 ESG	TET 10022 ESG	TET 10080 ESG
TET 9809 ESG	TET 9883 ESG	TET 9957 ESG	TET 10023 ESG	TET 10081 ESG
TET 9810 ESG	TET 9885 ESG	TET 9958 ESG	TET 10024 ESG	TET 10082 ESG
TET 9811 ESG	TET 9886 ESG	TET 9959 ESG	TET 10025 ESG	TET 10083 ESG
TET 9812 ESG	TET 9887 ESG	TET 9960 ESG	TET 10026 ESG	TET 10084 ESG

TET 10085 ESG	TET 10147 ESG	TET 10207 ESG	TET 10267 ESG	TET 10326 ESG
TET 10086 ESG	TET 10148 ESG	TET 10208 ESG	TET 10268 ESG	TET 10327 ESG
TET 10087 ESG	TET 10149 ESG	TET 10209 ESG	TET 10269 ESG	TET 10329 ESG
TET 10088 ESG	TET 10150 ESG	TET 10210 ESG	TET 10270 ESG	TET 10331 ESG
TET 10089 ESG	TET 10151 ESG	TET 10211 ESG	TET 10271 ESG	TET 10332 ESG
TET 10090 ESG	TET 10152 ESG	TET 10212 ESG	TET 10272 ESG	TET 10333 ESG
TET 10091 ESG	TET 10153 ESG	TET 10213 ESG	TET 10273 ESG	TET 10334 ESG
TET 10092 ESG	TET 10154 ESG	TET 10214 ESG	TET 10274 ESG	TET 10335 ESG
TET 10093 ESG	TET 10155 ESG	TET 10215 ESG	TET 10275 ESG	TET 10336 ESG
TET 10094 ESG	TET 10156 ESG	TET 10216 ESG	TET 10276 ESG	TET 10337 ESG
TET 10095 ESG	TET 10157 ESG	TET 10217 ESG	TET 10277 ESG	TET 10338 ESG
TET 10096 ESG	TET 10158 ESG	TET 10218 ESG	TET 10278 ESG	TET 10339 ESG
TET 10097 ESG	TET 10160 ESG	TET 10219 ESG	TET 10280 ESG	TET 10340 ESG
TET 10098 ESG	TET 10161 ESG	TET 10220 ESG	TET 10281 ESG	TET 10341 ESG
TET 10099 ESG	TET 10162 ESG	TET 10221 ESG	TET 10282 ESG	TET 10342 ESG
TET 10100 ESG	TET 10164 ESG	TET 10222 ESG	TET 10283 ESG	TET 10343 ESG
TET 10102 ESG	TET 10165 ESG	TET 10223 ESG	TET 10284 ESG	TET 10344 ESG
TET 10104 ESG	TET 10167 ESG	TET 10224 ESG	TET 10285 ESG	TET 10345 ESG
TET 10105 ESG	TET 10168 ESG	TET 10225 ESG	TET 10287 ESG	TET 10346 ESG
TET 10106 ESG	TET 10170 ESG	TET 10226 ESG	TET 10288 ESG	TET 10347 ESG
TET 10107 ESG	TET 10171 ESG	TET 10227 ESG	TET 10289 ESG	TET 10348 ESG
TET 10108 ESG	TET 10172 ESG	TET 10228 ESG	TET 10290 ESG	TET 10349 ESG
TET 10109 ESG	TET 10173 ESG	TET 10229 ESG	TET 10291 ESG	TET 10350 ESG
TET 10111 ESG	TET 10174 ESG	TET 10230 ESG	TET 10292 ESG	TET 10351 ESG
TET 10112 ESG	TET 10175 ESG	TET 10231 ESG	TET 10293 ESG	TET 10352 ESG
TET 10113 ESG	TET 10176 ESG	TET 10232 ESG	TET 10294 ESG	TET 10353 ESG
TET 10114 ESG	TET 10177 ESG	TET 10233 ESG	TET 10295 ESG	TET 10354 ESG
TET 10116 ESG	TET 10178 ESG	TET 10234 ESG	TET 10296 ESG	TET 10355 ESG
TET 10117 ESG	TET 10179 ESG	TET 10235 ESG	TET 10297 ESG	TET 10356 ESG
TET 10118 ESG	TET 10180 ESG	TET 10236 ESG	TET 10298 ESG	TET 10357 ESG
TET 10119 ESG	TET 10181 ESG	TET 10237 ESG	TET 10300 ESG	TET 10358 ESG
TET 10120 ESG	TET 10182 ESG	TET 10238 ESG	TET 10301 ESG	TET 10359 ESG
TET 10122 ESG	TET 10183 ESG	TET 10240 ESG	TET 10302 ESG	TET 10360 ESG
TET 10123 ESG	TET 10184 ESG	TET 10241 ESG	TET 10303 ESG	TET 10361 ESG
TET 10124 ESG	TET 10185 ESG	TET 10242 ESG	TET 10304 ESG	TET 10362 ESG
TET 10125 ESG	TET 10186 ESG	TET 10243 ESG	TET 10305 ESG	TET 10364 ESG
TET 10126 ESG	TET 10187 ESG	TET 10244 ESG	TET 10306 ESG	TET 10365 ESG
TET 10128 ESG	TET 10188 ESG	TET 10245 ESG	TET 10307 ESG	TET 10366 ESG
TET 10129 ESG	TET 10189 ESG	TET 10246 ESG	TET 10308 ESG	TET 10367 ESG
TET 10130 ESG	TET 10190 ESG	TET 10248 ESG	TET 10309 ESG	TET 10368 ESG
TET 10131 ESG	TET 10191 ESG	TET 10249 ESG	TET 10310 ESG	TET 10369 ESG
TET 10132 ESG	TET 10192 ESG	TET 10250 ESG	TET 10311 ESG	TET 10370 ESG
TET 10133 ESG	TET 10193 ESG	TET 10251 ESG	TET 10312 ESG	TET 10371 ESG
TET 10134 ESG	TET 10194 ESG	TET 10252 ESG	TET 10313 ESG	TET 10372 ESG
TET 10135 ESG	TET 10195 ESG	TET 10253 ESG	TET 10314 ESG	TET 10373 ESG
TET 10136 ESG	TET 10196 ESG	TET 10254 ESG	TET 10315 ESG	TET 10374 ESG
TET 10137 ESG	TET 10197 ESG	TET 10255 ESG	TET 10316 ESG	TET 10375 ESG
TET 10138 ESG	TET 10198 ESG	TET 10256 ESG	TET 10317 ESG	TET 10376 ESG
TET 10139 ESG	TET 10199 ESG	TET 10257 ESG	TET 10318 ESG	TET 10377 ESG
TET 10140 ESG	TET 10200 ESG	TET 10259 ESG	TET 10319 ESG	TET 10378 ESG
TET 10141 ESG	TET 10201 ESG	TET 10260 ESG	TET 10320 ESG	TET 10379 ESG
TET 10142 ESG	TET 10202 ESG	TET 10261 ESG	TET 10321 ESG	TET 10380 ESG
TET 10143 ESG	TET 10203 ESG	TET 10263 ESG	TET 10322 ESG	TET 10381 ESG
TET 10144 ESG	TET 10204 ESG	TET 10264 ESG	TET 10323 ESG	TET 10382 ESG
TET 10145 ESG	TET 10205 ESG	TET 10265 ESG	TET 10324 ESG	TET 10383 ESG
TET 10146 ESG	TET 10206 ESG	TET 10266 ESG	TET 10325 ESG	TET 10384 ESG

TET 10385 ESG	TET 10442 ESG	TET 10498 ESG	TET 10554 ESG	TFT 1757 ESW
TET 10386 ESG	TET 10443 ESG	TET 10499 ESG	TET 10555 ESG	TFT 1758 ESW
TET 10387 ESG	TET 10444 ESG	TET 10500 ESG	TET 10556 ESG	TFT 1759 ESW
TET 10388 ESG	TET 10445 ESG	TET 10501 ESG	TET 10557 ESG	TFT 1760 ESW
TET 10389 ESG	TET 10446 ESG	TET 10502 ESG	TET 10558 ESG	TFT 1761 ESW
TET 10390 ESG	TET 10447 ESG	TET 10503 ESG	TET 10559 ESG	TFT 1762 ESW
TET 10391 ESG	TET 10448 ESG	TET 10504 ESG	TET 10560 ESG	TFT 1763 ESW
TET 10392 ESG	TET 10449 ESG	TET 10505 ESG	TET 10561 ESG	TFT 1764 ESW
TET 10393 ESG	TET 10450 ESG	TET 10506 ESG	TET 10562 ESG	TFT 1765 ESW
TET 10394 ESG	TET 10451 ESG	TET 10507 ESG	TET 10563 ESG	TFT 1766 ESW
TET 10395 ESG	TET 10452 ESG	TET 10508 ESG	TET 10564 ESG	TFT 1767 ESW
TET 10396 ESG	TET 10453 ESG	TET 10509 ESG	TET 10565 ESG	TFT 1768 ESW
TET 10397 ESG	TET 10454 ESG	TET 10510 ESG	TET 10566 ESG	TFT 1769 ESW
TET 10398 ESG	TET 10455 ESG	TET 10511 ESG	TET 10567 ESG	TFT 1770 ESW
TET 10399 ESG	TET 10456 ESG	TET 10512 ESG	TET 10568 ESG	TFT 1771 ESW
TET 10400 ESG	TET 10457 ESG	TET 10513 ESG	TET 10569 ESG	TFT 1772 ESW
TET 10401 ESG	TET 10458 ESG	TET 10514 ESG	TET 10570 ESG	TFT 1773 ESW
TET 10402 ESG	TET 10459 ESG	TET 10515 ESG	TET 10571 ESG	TFT 1774 ESW
TET 10403 ESG	TET 10460 ESG	TET 10516 ESG	TET 10572 ESG	TFT 1775 ESW
TET 10404 ESG	TET 10461 ESG	TET 10517 ESG	TFT 1720 ESW	TFT 1776 ESW
TET 10405 ESG	TET 10462 ESG	TET 10518 ESG	TFT 1721 ESW	TFT 1777 ESW
TET 10406 ESG	TET 10463 ESG	TET 10519 ESG	TFT 1722 ESW	TFT 1778 ESW
TET 10407 ESG	TET 10464 ESG	TET 10520 ESG	TFT 1723 ESW	TFT 1779 ESW
TET 10408 ESG	TET 10465 ESG	TET 10521 ESG	TFT 1724 ESW	TK 0138 ESW
TET 10409 ESG	TET 10466 ESG	TET 10522 ESG	TFT 1725 ESW	TK 0139 ESW
TET 10410 ESG	TET 10467 ESG	TET 10523 ESG	TFT 1726 ESW	TK 0140 ESW
TET 10411 ESG	TET 10468 ESG	TET 10524 ESG	TFT 1727 ESW	TK 0141 ESW
TET 10412 ESG	TET 10469 ESG	TET 10525 ESG	TFT 1728 ESW	TK 0142 ESW
TET 10413 ESG	TET 10470 ESG	TET 10526 ESG	TFT 1729 ESW	TK 0143 ESW
TET 10414 ESG	TET 10471 ESG	TET 10527 ESG	TFT 1730 ESW	TK 0144 ESW
TET 10415 ESG	TET 10472 ESG	TET 10528 ESG	TFT 1731 ESW	TK 0145 ESW
TET 10416 ESG	TET 10473 ESG	TET 10529 ESG	TFT 1732 ESW	TK 0146 ESW
TET 10417 ESG	TET 10474 ESG	TET 10530 ESG	TFT 1733 ESW	TK 0147 ESW
TET 10418 ESG	TET 10475 ESG	TET 10531 ESG	TFT 1734 ESW	TK 0148 ESW
TET 10419 ESG	TET 10476 ESG	TET 10532 ESG	TFT 1735 ESW	TK 0149 ESW
TET 10420 ESG	TET 10477 ESG	TET 10533 ESG	TFT 1736 ESW	TK 0150 ESW
TET 10421 ESG	TET 10478 ESG	TET 10534 ESG	TFT 1737 ESW	TK 0151 ESW
TET 10422 ESG	TET 10479 ESG	TET 10535 ESG	TFT 1738 ESW	TK 0152 ESW
TET 10423 ESG	TET 10480 ESG	TET 10536 ESG	TFT 1739 ESW	TK 0153 ESW
TET 10425 ESG	TET 10481 ESG	TET 10537 ESG	TFT 1740 ESW	TK 0154 ESW
TET 10426 ESG	TET 10482 ESG	TET 10538 ESG	TFT 1741 ESW	TK 0155 ESW
TET 10427 ESG	TET 10483 ESG	TET 10539 ESG	TFT 1742 ESW	TK 0156 ESW
TET 10428 ESG	TET 10484 ESG	TET 10540 ESG	TFT 1743 ESW	TK 0157 ESW
TET 10429 ESG	TET 10485 ESG	TET 10541 ESG	TFT 1744 ESW	TK 0158 ESW
TET 10430 ESG	TET 10486 ESG	TET 10542 ESG	TFT 1745 ESW	TK 0180 ESW
TET 10431 ESG	TET 10487 ESG	TET 10543 ESG	TFT 1746 ESW	TK 0181 ESW
TET 10432 ESG	TET 10488 ESG	TET 10544 ESG	TFT 1747 ESW	TK 0182 ESW
TET 10433 ESG	TET 10489 ESG	TET 10545 ESG	TFT 1748 ESW	TK 0183 ESW
TET 10434 ESG	TET 10490 ESG	TET 10546 ESG	TFT 1749 ESW	TK 0184 ESW
TET 10435 ESG	TET 10491 ESG	TET 10547 ESG	TFT 1750 ESW	TK 0185 ESW
TET 10436 ESG	TET 10492 ESG	TET 10548 ESG	TFT 1751 ESW	ATK 0186 WHS
TET 10437 ESG	TET 10493 ESG	TET 10549 ESG	TFT 1752 ESW	ATK 0187 WHS
TET 10438 ESG	TET 10494 ESG	TET 10550 ESG	TFT 1753 ESW	ATK 0188 WHS
TET 10439 ESG	TET 10495 ESG	TET 10551 ESG	TFT 1754 ESW	ATK 0189 WHS
TET 10440 ESG	TET 10496 ESG	TET 10552 ESG	TFT 1755 ESW	ATK 0190 WHS
TET 10441 ESG	TET 10497 ESG	TET 10553 ESG	TFT 1756 ESW	UDD 1910 ESW

Eddie Stobart

UDD 1911 ESW	XET 15027 ESG	XET 15083 ESG	XET 15139 ESG	XET 15195 ESG
UFD 1912 ESW	XET 15028 ESG	XET 15084 ESG	XET 15140 ESG	XET 15196 ESG
WDD 1920 ESW	XET 15029 ESG	XET 15085 ESG	XET 15141 ESG	XET 15197 ESG
WDD 1921 ESW	XET 15030 ESG	XET 15086 ESG	XET 15142 ESG	XET 15198 ESG
WDD 1922 ESW	XET 15031 ESG	XET 15087 ESG	XET 15143 ESG	XET 15199 ESG
FDD 1923 ESW	XET 15032 ESG	XET 15088 ESG	XET 15144 ESG	XET 15200 ESG
WDD 1924 ESW	XET 15033 ESG	XET 15089 ESG	XET 15145 ESG	XET 15201 ESG
WDD 1925 ESW	XET 15034 ESG	XET 15090 ESG	XET 15146 ESG	XET 15202 ESG
WDD 1926 ESW	XET 15035 ESG	XET 15091 ESG	XET 15147 ESG	XET 15203 ESG
WDD 1927 ESW	XET 15036 ESG	XET 15092 ESG	XET 15148 ESG	XET 15204 ESG
WDD 1928 ESW	XET 15037 ESG	XET 15093 ESG	XET 15149 ESG	XET 15205 ESG
WDD 1929 ESW	XET 15038 ESG	XET 15094 ESG	XET 15150 ESG	XET 15206 ESG
WDD 1930 ESW	XET 15039 ESG	XET 15095 ESG	XET 15151 ESG	XET 15207 ESG
WDD 1931 ESW	XET 15040 ESG	XET 15096 ESG	XET 15152 ESG	XET 15208 ESG
WDD 1932 ESW	XET 15041 ESG	XET 15097 ESG	XET 15153 ESG	XET 15209 ESG
WDD 1933 ESW	XET 15042 ESG	XET 15098 ESG	XET 15154 ESG	XET 15210 ESG
WDD 1934 ESW	XET 15043 ESG	XET 15099 ESG	XET 15155 ESG	XET 15211 ESG
WDD 1935 ESW	XET 15044 ESG	XET 15100 ESG	XET 15156 ESG	XET 15212 ESG
WDD 1936 ESW	XET 15045 ESG	XET 15101 ESG	XET 15157 ESG	XET 15213 ESG
WDD 1937 ESW	XET 15046 ESG	XET 15102 ESG	XET 15158 ESG	XET 15214 ESG
WDD 1938 ESW	XET 15047 ESG	XET 15103 ESG	XET 15159 ESG	XET 15215 ESG
WDD 1939 ESW	XET 15048 ESG	XET 15104 ESG	XET 15160 ESG	XET 15216 ESG
WDD 1940 ESW	XET 15049 ESG	XET 15105 ESG	XET 15161 ESG	XET 15217 ESG
WDD 1941 ESW	XET 15050 ESG	XET 15106 ESG	XET 15162 ESG	XET 15218 ESG
WDD 1942 ESW	XET 15051 ESG	XET 15107 ESG	XET 15163 ESG	XET 15219 ESG
WDD 1943 ESW	XET 15052 ESG	XET 15108 ESG	XET 15164 ESG	XET 15220 ESG
WDD 1944 ESW	XET 15053 ESG	XET 15109 ESG	XET 15165 ESG	XET 15221 ESG
WDD 1945 ESW	XET 15054 ESG	XET 15110 ESG	XET 15166 ESG	XET 15222 ESG
WDD 1946 ESW	XET 15055 ESG	XET 15111 ESG	XET 15167 ESG	XET 15223 ESG
XET 15000 ESG	XET 15056 ESG	XET 15112 ESG	XET 15168 ESG	XET 15224 ESG
XET 15001 ESG	XET 15057 ESG	XET 15113 ESG	XET 15169 ESG	XET 15225 ESG
XET 15002 ESG	XET 15058 ESG	XET 15114 ESG	XET 15170 ESG	XET 15226 ESG
XET 15003 ESG	XET 15059 ESG	XET 15115 ESG	XET 15171 ESG	XET 15227 ESG
XET 15004 ESG	XET 15060 ESG	XET 15116 ESG	XET 15172 ESG	XET 15228 ESG
XET 15005 ESG	XET 15061 ESG	XET 15117 ESG	XET 15173 ESG	XET 15229 ESG
XET 15006 ESG	XET 15062 ESG	XET 15118 ESG	XET 15174 ESG	XET 15230 ESG
XET 15007 ESG	XET 15063 ESG	XET 15119 ESG	XET 15175 ESG	XET 15231 ESG
XET 15008 ESG	XET 15064 ESG	XET 15120 ESG	XET 15176 ESG	XET 15232 ESG
XET 15009 ESG	XET 15065 ESG	XET 15121 ESG	XET 15177 ESG	XET 15233 ESG
XET 15010 ESG	XET 15066 ESG	XET 15122 ESG	XET 15178 ESG	XET 15234 ESG
XET 15011 ESG	XET 15067 ESG	XET 15123 ESG	XET 15179 ESG	XET 15235 ESG
XET 15012 ESG	XET 15068 ESG	XET 15124 ESG	XET 15180 ESG	XET 15236 ESG
XET 15013 ESG	XET 15069 ESG	XET 15125 ESG	XET 15181 ESG	XET 15237 ESG
XET 15014 ESG	XET 15070 ESG	XET 15126 ESG	XET 15182 ESG	XET 15238 ESG
XET 15015 ESG	XET 15071 ESG	XET 15127 ESG	XET 15183 ESG	XET 15239 ESG
XET 15016 ESG	XET 15072 ESG	XET 15128 ESG	XET 15184 ESG	XET 15240 ESG
XET 15017 ESG	XET 15073 ESG	XET 15129 ESG	XET 15185 ESG	XET 15241 ESG
XET 15018 ESG	XET 15074 ESG	XET 15130 ESG	XET 15186 ESG	XET 15242 ESG
XET 15019 ESG	XET 15075 ESG	XET 15131 ESG	XET 15187 ESG	XET 15243 ESG
XET 15020 ESG	XET 15076 ESG	XET 15132 ESG	XET 15188 ESG	XET 15244 ESG
XET 15021 ESG	XET 15077 ESG	XET 15133 ESG	XET 15189 ESG	XET 15245 ESG
XET 15022 ESG	XET 15078 ESG	XET 15134 ESG	XET 15190 ESG	XET 15246 ESG
XET 15023 ESG	XET 15079 ESG	XET 15135 ESG	XET 15191 ESG	XET 15247 ESG
XET 15024 ESG	XET 15080 ESG	XET 15136 ESG	XET 15192 ESG	XET 15248 ESG
XET 15025 ESG	XET 15081 ESG	XET 15137 ESG	XET 15193 ESG	XET 15249 ESG
XET 15026 ESG	XET 15082 ESG	XET 15138 ESG	XET 15194 ESG	XET 15250 ESG

Eddie Stobart

XET 15251 ESG	XET 15307 ESG	XET 15363 ESG	XET 15420 ESG	XET 15476 ESG
XET 15252 ESG	XET 15308 ESG	XET 15364 ESG	XET 15421 ESG	XET 15477 ESG
XET 15253 ESG	XET 15309 ESG	XET 15365 ESG	XET 15422 ESG	XET 15478 ESG
XET 15254 ESG	XET 15310 ESG	XET 15366 ESG	XET 15423 ESG	XET 15479 ESG
XET 15255 ESG	XET 15311 ESG	XET 15367 ESG	XET 15424 ESG	XET 15480 ESG
XET 15256 ESG	XET 15312 ESG	XET 15368 ESG	XET 15425 ESG	XET 15481 ESG
XET 15257 ESG	XET 15313 ESG	XET 15369 ESG	XET 15426 ESG	XET 15482 ESG
XET 15258 ESG	XET 15314 ESG	XET 15370 ESG	XET 15427 ESG	XET 15483 ESG
XET 15259 ESG	XET 15315 ESG	XET 15371 ESG	XET 15428 ESG	XET 15484 ESG
XET 15260 ESG	XET 15316 ESG	XET 15372 ESG	XET 15429 ESG	XET 15485 ESG
XET 15261 ESG	XET 15317 ESG	XET 15373 ESG	XET 15430 ESG	XET 15486 ESG
XET 15262 ESG	XET 15318 ESG	XET 15374 ESG	XET 15431 ESG	XET 15487 ESG
XET 15263 ESG	XET 15319 ESG	XET 15375 ESG	XET 15432 ESG	XET 15488 ESG
XET 15264 ESG	XET 15320 ESG	XET 15376 ESG	XET 15433 ESG	XET 15489 ESG
XET 15265 ESG	XET 15321 ESG	XET 15377 ESG	XET 15434 ESG	XET 15490 ESG
XET 15266 ESG	XET 15322 ESG	XET 15378 ESG	XET 15435 ESG	XET 15491 ESG
XET 15267 ESG	XET 15323 ESG	XET 15379 ESG	XET 15436 ESG	XET 15492 ESG
XET 15268 ESG	XET 15324 ESG	XET 15380 ESG	XET 15437 ESG	XET 15493 ESG
XET 15269 ESG	XET 15325 ESG	XET 15381 ESG	XET 15438 ESG	XET 15494 ESG
XET 15270 ESG	XET 15326 ESG	XET 15382 ESG	XET 15439 ESG	XET 15495 ESG
XET 15271 ESG	XET 15327 ESG	XET 15383 ESG	XET 15440 ESG	XET 15496 ESG
XET 15272 ESG	XET 15328 ESG	XET 15384 ESG	XET 15441 ESG	XET 15497 ESG
XET 15273 ESG	XET 15329 ESG	XET 15385 ESG	XET 15442 ESG	XET 15498 ESG
XET 15274 ESG	XET 15330 ESG	XET 15386 ESG	XET 15443 ESG	XET 15499 ESG
XET 15275 ESG	XET 15331 ESG	XET 15387 ESG	XET 15444 ESG	XET 15500 ESG
XET 15276 ESG	XET 15332 ESG	XET 15388 ESG	XET 15445 ESG	XET 15501 ESG
XET 15277 ESG	XET 15333 ESG	XET 15389 ESG	XET 15446 ESG	XET 15502 ESG
XET 15278 ESG	XET 15334 ESG	XET 15390 ESG	XET 15447 ESG	XET 15503 ESG
XET 15279 ESG	XET 15335 ESG	XET 15391 ESG	XET 15448 ESG	XET 15504 ESG
XET 15280 ESG	XET 15336 ESG	XET 15392 ESG	XET 15449 ESG	XET 15505 ESG
XET 15281 ESG	XET 15337 ESG	XET 15393 ESG	XET 15450 ESG	XET 15506 ESG
XET 15282 ESG	XET 15338 ESG	XET 15394 ESG	XET 15451 ESG	XET 15507 ESG
XET 15283 ESG	XET 15339 ESG	XET 15395 ESG	XET 15452 ESG	XET 15508 ESG
XET 15284 ESG	XET 15340 ESG	XET 15396 ESG	XET 15453 ESG	XET 15509 ESG
XET 15285 ESG	XET 15341 ESG	XET 15397 ESG	XET 15454 ESG	XET 15510 ESG
XET 15286 ESG	XET 15342 ESG	XET 15398 ESG	XET 15455 ESG	XET 15511 ESG
XET 15287 ESG	XET 15343 ESG	XET 15399 ESG	XET 15456 ESG	XET 15512 ESG
XET 15288 ESG	XET 15344 ESG	XET 15400 ESG	XET 15457 ESG	XET 15513 ESG
XET 15289 ESG	XET 15345 ESG	XET 15401 ESG	XET 15458 ESG	XET 15514 ESG
XET 15290 ESG	XET 15346 ESG	XET 15402 ESG	XET 15459 ESG	XET 15515 ESG
XET 15291 ESG	XET 15347 ESG	XET 15403 ESG	XET 15460 ESG	XET 15516 ESG
XET 15292 ESG	XET 15348 ESG	XET 15404 ESG	XET 15461 ESG	XET 15517 ESG
XET 15293 ESG	XET 15349 ESG	XET 15405 ESG	XET 15462 ESG	XET 15518 ESG
XET 15294 ESG	XET 15350 ESG	XET 15406 ESG	XET 15463 ESG	XET 15519 ESG
XET 15295 ESG	XET 15351 ESG	XET 15407 ESG	XET 15464 ESG	XET 15520 ESG
XET 15296 ESG	XET 15352 ESG	XET 15408 ESG	XET 15465 ESG	XET 15521 ESG
XET 15297 ESG	XET 15353 ESG	XET 15409 ESG	XET 15466 ESG	XET 15522 ESG
XET 15298 ESG	XET 15354 ESG	XET 15410 ESG	XET 15467 ESG	XET 15523 ESG
XET 15299 ESG	XET 15355 ESG	XET 15411 ESG	XET 15468 ESG	XET 15524 ESG
XET 15300 ESG	XET 15356 ESG	XET 15412 ESG	XET 15469 ESG	XET 15525 ESG
XET 15301 ESG	XET 15357 ESG	XET 15413 ESG	XET 15470 ESG	XET 15526 ESG
XET 15302 ESG	XET 15358 ESG	XET 15414 ESG	XET 15471 ESG	XET 15527 ESG
XET 15303 ESG	XET 15359 ESG	XET 15415 ESG	XET 15472 ESG	XET 15528 ESG
XET 15304 ESG	XET 15360 ESG	XET 15416 ESG	XET 15473 ESG	XET 15529 ESG
XET 15305 ESG	XET 15361 ESG	XET 15418 ESG	XET 15474 ESG	XET 15530 ESG
XET 15306 ESG	XET 15362 ESG	XET 15419 ESG	XET 15475 ESG	XET 15531 ESG

Eddie Stobart

15578

XET 15532 ESG	XET 15546 ESG	XET 15560 ESG	XET 15574 ESG	XET 15588 ESG
XET 15533 ESG	XET 15547 ESG	XET 15561 ESG	XET 15575 ESG	XET 15589 ESG
XET 15534 ESG	XET 15548 ESG	XET 15562 ESG	XET 15576 ESG	XET 15590 ESG
XET 15535 ESG	XET 15549 ESG	XET 15563 ESG	XET 15577 ESG	XET 15591 ESG
XET 15536 ESG	XET 15550 ESG	XET 15564 ESG	XET 15579 ESG	XET 15592 ESG
XET 15537 ESG	XET 15551 ESG	XET 15565 ESG	XET 15580 ESG	XET 15593 ESG
XET 15538 ESG	XET 15552 ESG	XET 15566 ESG	XET 15581 ESG	YTK 0010 SIL
XET 15539 ESG	XET 15553 ESG	XET 15567 ESG	XET 15582 ESG	YTK 0011 SIL
XET 15540 ESG	XET 15554 ESG	XET 15568 ESG	XET 15583 ESG	YTK 0012 SIL
XET 15541 ESG	XET 15555 ESG	XET 15569 ESG	XET 15584 ESG	YTK 0013 SIL
XET 15542 ESG	XET 15556 ESG	XET 15570 ESG	XET 15585 ESG	YTK 0014 SIL
XET 15543 ESG	XET 15557 ESG	XET 15571 ESG	XET 15586 ESG	YTK 0015 SIL
XET 15544 ESG	XET 15558 ESG	XET 15572 ESG	XET 15587 ESG	YTK 0016 SIL
XET 15545 ESG	XET 15559 ESG	XET 15573 ESG		

Topaz

4100	CIK	4140	CIK	4148	CIK	4156	CIK	4166	CIK
4102	CIK	4142	CIK	4150	CIK	4160	CIK	4168	CIK
4104	CIK	4144	CIK	4152	CIK	4162	CIK	4170	CIK
4106	CIK	4146	CIK	4154	CIK	4164	CIK		
4172	CIK	4174	CIK	4178	CIK				

Walkers

LT 00112 WAL	LT 03312 WAL	TC 00117 WAL	TC 01207 WAL	TC 02016 WAL
LT 00212 WAL	LT 03412 WAL	TC 00210 WAL	TC 01210 WAL	TC 02017 WAL
LT 00312 WAL	LT 03512 WAL	TC 00216 WAL	TC 01216 WAL	TC 02110 WAL
LT 00412 WAL	LT 03612 WAL	TC 00217 WAL	TC 01217 WAL	TC 02116 WAL
LT 00512 WAL	LTB 00114 WAL	TC 00306 WAL	TC 01307 WAL	TC 02117 WAL
LT 00612 WAL	LTB 00214 WAL	TC 00310 WAL	TC 01310 WAL	TC 02210 WAL
LT 00712 WAL	LTB 00314 WAL	TC 00316 WAL	TC 01316 WAL	TC 02216 WAL
LT 00812 WAL	LTB 00414 WAL	TC 00317 WAL	TC 01317 WAL	TC 02217 WAL
LT 00912 WAL	LTB 00514 WAL	TC 00402 WAL	TC 01402 WAL	TC 02307 WAL
LT 01012 WAL	LTB 00614 WAL	TC 00410 WAL	TC 01410 WAL	TC 02310 WAL
LT 01112 WAL	LTB 00714 WAL	TC 00416 WAL	TC 01416 WAL	TC 02316 WAL
LT 01212 WAL	LTB 00814 WAL	TC 00417 WAL	TC 01417 WAL	TC 02317 WAL
LT 01312 WAL	LTB 00914 WAL	TC 00510 WAL	TC 01507 WAL	TC 02407 WAL
LT 01412 WAL	LTB 01014 WAL	TC 00516 WAL	TC 01510 WAL	TC 02410 WAL
LT 01512 WAL	LTB 01114 WAL	TC 00517 WAL	TC 01516 WAL	TC 02416 WAL
LT 01612 WAL	LTB 01214 WAL	TC 00610 WAL	TC 01517 WAL	TC 02417 WAL
LT 01712 WAL	LTB 01314 WAL	TC 00616 WAL	TC 01610 WAL	TC 02510 WAL
LT 01812 WAL	LTB 01414 WAL	TC 00707 WAL	TC 01616 WAL	TC 02516 WAL
LT 01912 WAL	LTB 01514 WAL	TC 00710 WAL	TC 01617 WAL	TC 02517 WAL
LT 02012 WAL	LTB 01614 WAL	TC 00716 WAL	TC 01707 WAL	TC 02610 WAL
LT 02112 WAL	LTB 01714 WAL	TC 00806 WAL	TC 01710 WAL	TC 02612 WAL
LT 02212 WAL	LTB 01814 WAL	TC 00807 WAL	TC 01716 WAL	TC 02616 WAL
LT 02312 WAL	LTB 01914 WAL	TC 00810 WAL	TC 01717 WAL	TC 02617 WAL
LT 02412 WAL	LTB 02014 WAL	TC 00816 WAL	TC 01810 WAL	TC 02702 WAL
LT 02512 WAL	LTB 02114 WAL	TC 00910 WAL	TC 01816 WAL	TC 02710 WAL
LT 02612 WAL	LTB 02214 WAL	TC 00916 WAL	TC 01817 WAL	TC 02716 WAL
LT 02712 WAL	LTB 02314 WAL	TC 01006 WAL	TC 01907 WAL	TC 02717 WAL
LT 02812 WAL	LTB 02414 WAL	TC 01010 WAL	TC 01910 WAL	TC 02810 WAL
LT 02912 WAL	LTB 02514 WAL	TC 01016 WAL	TC 01916 WAL	TC 02816 WAL
LT 03012 WAL	PT 03608 WAL	TC 01107 WAL	TC 01917 WAL	TC 02817 WAL
LT 03112 WAL	TC 00110 WAL	TC 01110 WAL	TC 02004 WAL	TC 02907 WAL
LT 03212 WAL	TC 00116 WAL	TC 01117 WAL	TC 02010 WAL	TC 02910 WAL

Walkers

TC 02916 WAL	TC 04010 WAL	TC 05016 WAL	TC 06216 WAL	TC 08116 WAL
TC 02917 WAL	TC 04016 WAL	TC 05017 WAL	TC 06217 WAL	TC 08216 WAL
TC 03010 WAL	TC 04017 WAL	TC 05104 WAL	TC 06307 WAL	TC 08316 WAL
TC 03016 WAL	TC 04107 WAL	TC 05110 WAL	TC 06310 WAL	TC 08404 WAL
TC 03017 WAL	TC 04110 WAL	TC 05116 WAL	TC 06316 WAL	TC 08416 WAL
TC 03110 WAL	TC 04116 WAL	TC 05117 WAL	TC 06317 WAL	TC 08516 WAL
TC 03116 WAL	TC 04117 WAL	TC 05207 WAL	TC 06410 WAL	TC 08616 WAL
TC 03117 WAL	TC 04204 WAL	TC 05210 WAL	TC 06416 WAL	TC 08704 WAL
TC 03204 WAL	TC 04207 WAL	TC 05216 WAL	TC 06417 WAL	TC 08716 WAL
TC 03210 WAL	TC 04210 WAL	TC 05217 WAL	TC 06502 WAL	TC 08816 WAL
TC 03216 WAL	TC 04216 WAL	TC 05310 WAL	TC 06510 WAL	TC 08916 WAL
TC 03217 WAL	TC 04217 WAL	TC 05316 WAL	TC 06516 WAL	TC 09004 WAL
TC 03310 WAL	TC 04304 WAL	TC 05317 WAL	TC 06517 WAL	TC 09016 WAL
TC 03316 WAL	TC 04310 WAL	TC 05410 WAL	TC 06610 WAL	TC 09116 WAL
TC 03317 WAL	TC 04316 WAL	TC 05416 WAL	TC 06616 WAL	TC 09216 WAL
TC 03410 WAL	TC 04317 WAL	TC 05417 WAL	TC 06710 WAL	TC 09316 WAL
TC 03412 WAL	TC 04404 WAL	TC 05510 WAL	TC 06716 WAL	TC 09404 WAL
TC 03416 WAL	TC 04407 WAL	TC 05516 WAL	TC 06810 WAL	TC 09416 WAL
TC 03417 WAL	TC 04410 WAL	TC 05517 WAL	TC 06816 WAL	TC 09516 WAL
TC 03507 WAL	TC 04416 WAL	TC 05610 WAL	TC 06904 WAL	TC 09616 WAL
TC 03510 WAL	TC 04417 WAL	TC 05616 WAL	TC 06910 WAL	TC 09704 WAL
TC 03516 WAL	TC 04507 WAL	TC 05617 WAL	TC 06916 WAL	TC 09715 WAL
TC 03517 WAL	TC 04510 WAL	TC 05710 WAL	TC 07010 WAL	TC 09716 WAL
TC 03604 WAL	TC 04516 WAL	TC 05716 WAL	TC 07016 WAL	TC 09804 WAL
TC 03610 WAL	TC 04517 WAL	TC 05717 WAL	TC 07106 WAL	TC 09816 WAL
TC 03616 WAL	TC 04607 WAL	TC 05810 WAL	TC 07110 WAL	TC 09904 WAL
TC 03617 WAL	TC 04610 WAL	TC 05816 WAL	TC 07204 WAL	TC 09916 WAL
TC 03702 WAL	TC 04616 WAL	TC 05817 WAL	TC 07216 WAL	TC 10104 WAL
TC 03704 WAL	TC 04617 WAL	TC 05907 WAL	TC 07304 WAL	TC 10204 WAL
TC 03707 WAL	TC 04710 WAL	TC 05910 WAL	TC 07316 WAL	TR 06603 WAL
TC 03710 WAL	TC 04716 WAL	TC 05916 WAL	TC 07416 WAL	TR 06702 WAL
TC 03716 WAL	TC 04717 WAL	TC 05917 WAL	TC 07516 WAL	TR 07108 WAL
TC 03717 WAL	TC 04804 WAL	TC 06010 WAL	TC 07604 WAL	TR 07308 WAL
TC 03810 WAL	TC 04810 WAL	TC 06016 WAL	TC 07616 WAL	TR 07702 WAL
TC 03816 WAL	TC 04816 WAL	TC 06017 WAL	TC 07716 WAL	TR 07902 WAL
TC 03817 WAL	TC 04817 WAL	TC 06107 WAL	TC 07804 WAL	TR 08202 WAL
TC 03904 WAL	TC 04907 WAL	TC 06110 WAL	TC 07816 WAL	TR 08302 WAL
TC 03910 WAL	TC 04910 WAL	TC 06116 WAL	TC 07916 WAL	TR 08502 WAL
TC 03916 WAL	TC 04916 WAL	TC 06117 WAL	TC 08004 WAL	TR 08802 WAL
TC 03917 WAL	TC 04917 WAL	TC 06210 WAL	TC 08016 WAL	TR 09002 WAL
TC 04004 WAL	TC 05010 WAL			

Warrens

WMT 006	CWW	WMT 352	CWW	WMT 402020029	CWW
WMT 111	White	WMT 363	CWW	WMT 402020030	CWW
WMT 176	White	WMT 374	CWW	WMT 402020031	CWW
WMT 196	White	WMT 378	CWW	WMT 402020032	CWW
WMT 216	White	WMT 379	CWW	WMT 402020033	CWW
WMT 218 DD	White	WMT 381	CWW	WMT 402020034	CWW
WMT 219	White	WMT 382	CWW	WMT 402020035	CWW
WMT 222	White	WMT 384 DD	CWW	WMT 402020036	CWW
WMT 226	White	WMT 386 DD	CWW	WMT 402020037	CWW
WMT 227	White	WMT 387 DD	CWW	WMT 402020038	CWW
WMT 229	White	WMT 388 DD	CWW	WMT 4021-056	CWW
WMT 232	White	WMT 390 DD	CWW	WMT 4021-064	CWW
WMT 237	White	WMT 402020001	CWW	WMT 4021-066	CWW
WMT 238	White	WMT 402020002	CWW	WMT 4021-068	CWW
WMT 239	White	WMT 402020003	CWW	WMT 4021-069	CWW
WMT 240	White	WMT 402020004	CWW	WMT 4021-070	CWW
WMT 244	White	WMT 402020005	CWW	WMT 4021-071	CWW
WMT 250 DD	White	WMT 402020006	CWW	WMT 4021-072	CWW
WMT 253 DD	White	WMT 402020007	CWW	WMT 4021-073	CWW
WMT 265	White	WMT 402020008	CWW	WMT 4021-079	CWW
WMT 272 C	Red	WMT 402020009	CWW	WMT 4021-082	CWW
WMT 274 C	Red	WMT 402020010	CWW	WMT 4021-084	CWW
WMT 278	White	WMT 402020011	CWW	WMT 4021-085	CIF
WMT 280 DD	White	WMT 402020012	CWW	WMT 4021-090	CIF
WMT 283	White	WMT 402020013	CWW	WMT 4021-093	CWW
WMT 292 DD	White	WMT 402020014	CWW	WMT 4021-095	CWW
WMT 293 DD	White	WMT 402020015	CWW	WMT 5022-093	CWW
WMT 298	White	WMT 402020016	CWW	WMT 5022-095	CWW
WMT 300	White	WMT 402020017	CWW	WMT 5022-096	CWW
WMT 306	White	WMT 402020018	CWW	WMT 5021040 DD	CWW
WMT 310	White	WMT 402020019	CWW	WMT 5021044 DD	CWW
WMT 312	White	WMT 402020020	CWW	WMT 5021045 DD	CWW
WMT 315	White	WMT 402020021	CWW	WMT 5021046 DD	CWW
WMT 316 DD	White	WMT 402020022	CWW	WMT 5022086 DD	CWW
WMT 336 DD	CWW	WMT 402020023	CWW	WMT 5022091 DD	CWW
WMT 337 DD	CWW	WMT 402020024	CWW	WMT 5022093DD	CWW
WMT 340 DD	CWW	WMT 402020025	CWW	WMT 5022095 DD	CIF
WMT 342 DD	CWW	WMT 402020026	CWW	WMT 5022096 DD	CIF
WMT 343	CWW	WMT 402020027	CWW	WMT 5022098 DD	CIF
WMT 351	CWW	WMT 402020028	CWW		

WS Transportation

Livery Codes

Code	Description	Code	Description	Code	Description
AFU	Aerial Filming Unit (Blue)	GRY	Graylaw	WSS	WS Sherburns LGV
ELD	Elite Dream	SEV	Severfield Blue	WST	WS Transportation
EXB	Explore Black	VEN	Venator Livery	WSW	WS Transportation White
EXP	Explore	WSB	WS Transportation Blue		

Code	Livery	Code	Livery	Code	Livery	Code	Livery	Code	Livery
ADR 01	Blue	BT 3-50-03	WSW	CT 655	WSB	CT 704	WSB	CT 753	WSB
ADR 02	Blue	BT 3-50-04	WSW	CT 656	WSB	CT 705	WSB	CT 754	WSB
BK 12	WSW	BT 3-50-05	Cream	CT 657	WSB	CT 706	WSB	CT 755	WSB
BT 200	WSW	BT 3-50-06	WSW	CT 658	WSB	CT 707	WSB	CT 756	WSB
BT 201	WSW	BT 3-50-07	WSW	CT 659	WSB	CT 708	WSB	CT 757	WSB
BT 202	WSW	BT 3-50-08	VEN	CT 660	WSB	CT 709	WSB	CT 758	WSB
BT 203	WSW	BT 3-50-09	WSW	CT 661	WSB	CT 710	WSB	CT 759	WSB
BT 204	WSW	BT 3-50-10	WSW	CT 662	WSB	CT 711	WSB	CT 760	WSB
BT 205	WSW	C 501	WSB	CT 663	WSB	CT 712	WSB	CT 761	WSB
BT 206	WSW	C 502	WSB	CT 664	WSB	CT 713	WSB	CT 762	WSB
BT 207	WSW	C 503	WSB	CT 665	WSB	CT 714	WSB	CT 763	WSB
BT 208	WSW	C 504	WSB	CT 666	WSB	CT 715	WSB	CT 764	WSB
BT 209	WSW	C 505	WSB	CT 667	WSB	CT 716	WSB	CT 765	WSB
BT 210	VEN	C 506	SEV	CT 668	WSB	CT 717	WSB	CT 766	WSB
BT 211	WSW	C 507	SEV	CT 669	WSB	CT 718	WSB	CT 767	WSB
BT 212	VEN	C 508	WSB	CT 670	WSB	CT 719	WSB	CT 768	WSB
BT 213	WSW	C 509	WSB	CT 671	WSB	CT 720	WSB	CT 769	WSB
BT 214	WSW	C 510	SEV	CT 672	WSB	CT 721	WSB	CT 770	WSB
BT 215	WSW	C 511	WSB	CT 673	WSB	CT 722	WSB	CT 771	WSB
BT 216	WSW	C 512	WSB	CT 674	WSB	CT 723	WSB	CT 772	WSB
BT 2-36-01	WSW	C 513	WSB	CT 675	WSB	CT 724	WSB	CT 773	WSB
BT 2-36-02	WSW	C 514	WSB	CT 676	WSB	CT 725	WSB	CT 774	WSB
BT 2-36-03	WSW	C 515	SEV	CT 677	WSB	CT 726	WSB	CT 775	WSB
BT 2-36-04	WSW	CL 100	Blue	CT 678	WSB	CT 727	WSB	CT 776	WSB
BT 2-36-05	WSW	CL 101	Blue	CT 679	WSB	CT 728	WSB	CT 777	WSB
BT 2-36-06	WSW	CL 102	Blue	CT 680	WSB	CT 729	WSB	CT 778	WSB
BT 2-36-07	WSW	CL 103	Blue	CT 681	WSB	CT 730	WSB	CT 779	WSB
BT 2-36-08	WSW	CL 104	Blue	CT 682	WSB	CT 731	WSB	CT 780	WSB
BT 2-36-09	WSW	CT 634	WSB	CT 683	WSB	CT 732	WSB	CT 781	WSB
BT 2-36-10	WSW	CT 635	WSB	CT 684	WSB	CT 733	WSB	CT 782	WSB
BT 2-36-11	WSW	CT 636	WSB	CT 685	WSB	CT 734	WSB	CT 783	WSB
BT 2-36-12	WSW	CT 637	WSB	CT 686	WSB	CT 735	WSB	CT 784	WSB
BT 2-36-13		CT 638	WSB	CT 687	WSB	CT 736	WSB	DD 01	WSB
BT 2-36-14		CT 639	WSB	CT 688	WSB	CT 737	WSB	DT101	WSB
BT 2-36-15D		CT 640	WSB	CT 689	WSB	CT 738	WSB	DT102	WSB
BT 2-36-16D		CT 641	WSB	CT 690	WSB	CT 739	WSB	DT103	WSB
BT 2-36-17D	WSW	CT 642	WSB	CT 691	WSB	CT 740	WSB	DT104	WSB
BT 2-36-18		CT 643	WSB	CT 692	WSB	CT 741	WSB	DT105	WSB
BT 2-36-19		CT 644	WSB	CT 693	WSB	CT 742	WSB	DT106	WSB
BT 2-36-20		CT 645	WSB	CT 694	WSB	CT 743	WSB	ED 1	ELD
BT 2-36-21		CT 646	WSB	CT 695	WSB	CT 744	WSB	ET 100	WSB
BT 2-36-22		CT 647	WSB	CT 696	WSB	CT 745	WSB	ET 101	WSB
BT 2-36-23		CT 648	WSB	CT 697	WSB	CT 746	WSB	ET 102	WSB
BT 2-36-24	WSW	CT 649	WSB	CT 698	WSB	CT 747	WSB	ET 103	WSB
BT 2-36-25	WSW	CT 650	WSB	CT 699	WSB	CT 748	WSB	ET 104	WSB
BT 2-36-26		CT 651	WSB	CT 700	WSB	CT 749	WSB	ET 105	WSB
BT 2-36-27	WSW	CT 652	WSB	CT 701	WSB	CT 750	WSB	ET 106	WSB
BT 3-50-01	WSW	CT 653	WSB	CT 702	WSB	CT 751	WSB	ET 107	WSB
BT 3-50-02	WSW	CT 654	WSB	CT 703	WSB	CT 752	WSB	ET 108	WSB

WS Transportation

ET 109	WSB	S 27	Blue	S 82	Blue	S 137	Blue	S 192	Blue
ET 110	WSB	S 28	Blue	S 83	Blue	S 138	Blue	S 193	Blue
ET 111	WSB	S 29	Blue	S 84	Blue	S 139	Blue	S 194	Blue
ET 112	WSB	S 30	Blue	S 85	Blue	S 140	Blue	S 195	Blue
ET 113	WSB	S 31	Blue	S 86	Blue	S 141	Blue	S 196	Blue
ET 114	WSB	S 32	Blue	S 87	Blue	S 142	Blue	S 197	Blue
ET 115	WSB	S 33	Blue	S 88	Blue	S 143	Blue	S 198	Blue
ET 116	WSB	S 34	Blue	S 89	Blue	S 144	Blue	S 199	Blue
ET 117	WSB	S 35	Blue	S 90	Blue	S 145	Blue	S 200	Blue
ET 118	WSB	S 36	Blue	S 91	Blue	S 146	Blue	S 201	Blue
ET 119	WSB	S 37	Blue	S 92	Blue	S 147	Blue	S 202	Blue
ET 120	WSB	S 38	Blue	S 93	Blue	S 148	Blue	S 203	Blue
ET 121	WSB	S 39	Blue	S 94	Blue	S 149	Blue	S 204	Blue
ET 122	WSB	S 40	Blue	S 95	Blue	S 150	Blue	S 205	Blue
ET 123	WSB	S 41	Blue	S 96	Blue	S 151	Blue	S 206	Blue
HEL 1	AFU	S 42	Blue	S 97	Blue	S 152	Blue	S 207	Blue
LT 01-30-01	Silver	S 43	Blue	S 98	Blue	S 153	Blue	S 208	Blue
MT 01	WSB	S 44	Blue	S 99	Blue	S 154	Blue	S 209	Blue
MT 02	WSB	S 45	Blue	S 100	Blue	S 155	Blue	S 210	Blue
NS 01	Black	S 46	Blue	S 101	Blue	S 156	Blue	S 211	Blue
NS 02	Black	S 47	Blue	S 102	Blue	S 157	Blue	S 212	Blue
NS 03	Black	S 48	Blue	S 103	Blue	S 158	Blue	S 213	Blue
NS 04	Black	S 49	Blue	S 104	Blue	S 159	Blue	S 214	Blue
NS 05	Black	S 50	Blue	S 105	Blue	S 160	Blue	S 215	Blue
NS 06	Black	S 51	Blue	S 106	Blue	S 161	Blue	S 216	Blue
NS 07	Black	S 52	Blue	S 107	Blue	S 162	Blue	S 217	Blue
NS 08	Black	S 53	Blue	S 108	Blue	S 163	Blue	S 218	Blue
RD 001	WSB	S 54	Blue	S 109	Blue	S 164	Blue	S 219	Blue
RD 002	WSB	S 55	Blue	S 110	Blue	S 165	Blue	S 220	Blue
S 1	Blue	S 56	Blue	S 111	Blue	S 166	Blue	S 221	Blue
S 2	Blue	S 57	Blue	S 112	Blue	S 167	Blue	S 222	Blue
S 3	Blue	S 58	Blue	S 113	Blue	S 168	Blue	S 223	Blue
S 4	Blue	S 59	Blue	S 114	Blue	S 169	Blue	S 224	Blue
S 5	Blue	S 60	Blue	S 115	Blue	S 170	Blue	S 225	Blue
S 6	Blue	S 61	Blue	S 116	Blue	S 171	Blue	S 226	Blue
S 7	Blue	S 62	Blue	S 117	Blue	S 172	Blue	S 227	Blue
S 8	Blue	S 63	Blue	S 118	Blue	S 173	Blue	S 228	Blue
S 9	Blue	S 64	Blue	S 119	Blue	S 174	Blue	S 229	Blue
S 10	Blue	S 65	Blue	S 120	Blue	S 175	Blue	S 230	Blue
S 11	Blue	S 66	Blue	S 121	Blue	S 176	Blue	S 231	Blue
S 12	Blue	S 67	Blue	S 122	Blue	S 177	Blue	S 232	Blue
S 13	Blue	S 68	Blue	S 123	Blue	S 178	Blue	S 233	Blue
S 14	Blue	S 69	Blue	S 124	Blue	S 179	Blue	S 234	Blue
S 15	Blue	S 70	Blue	S 125	Blue	S 180	Blue	S 235	Blue
S 16	Blue	S 71	Blue	S 126	Blue	S 181	Blue	S 236	Blue
S 17	Blue	S 72	Blue	S 127	Blue	S 182	Blue	S 237	Blue
S 18	Blue	S 73	Blue	S 128	Blue	S 183	Blue	S 238	Blue
S 10	Blue	S 74	Blue	S 129	Blue	S 184	Blue	S 239	Blue
S 20	Blue	S 75	Blue	S 130	Blue	S 185	Blue	S 240	Blue
S 21	Blue	S 76	Blue	S 131	Blue	S 186	Blue	S 241	Blue
S 22	Blue	S 77	Blue	S 132	Blue	S 187	Blue	S 242	Blue
S 23	Blue	S 78	Blue	S 133	Blue	S 188	Blue	S 243	Blue
S 24	Blue	S 79	Blue	S 134	Blue	S 189	Blue	S 244	Blue
S 25	Blue	S 80	Blue	S 135	Blue	S 190	Blue	S 245	Blue
S 26	Blue	S 81	Blue	S 136	Blue	S 191	Blue	S 246	Blue

WS Transportation

S 247	Blue	SB 02	Blue	T 235	Blue	T 290	Blue	T 345	Blue
S 248	Blue	SB 03	Blue	T 236	Blue	T 291	Blue	T 346	Blue
S 249	Blue	SB 04	Blue	T 237	Blue	T 292	Blue	T 347	Blue
S 250	Blue	SE 100	WST	T 238	Blue	T 293	Blue	T 348	Blue
S 251	Blue	SE 200	WST	T 239	Blue	T 294	Blue	T 349	Blue
S 252	Blue	SE 300	WST	T 240	Blue	T 295	Blue	T 350	Blue
S 253	Blue	SK 100	Blue	T 241	Blue	T 296	Blue	T 351	Blue
S 254	Blue	SK 300	Blue	T 242	Blue	T 297	Blue	T 352	Blue
S 255	Blue	SK 301	Blue	T 243	Blue	T 298	Blue	T 353	Blue
S 256	Blue	SK 302	Blue	T 244	Blue	T 299	Blue	T 354	Blue
S 257	Blue	SK 303	Blue	T 245	Blue	T 300	Blue	T 355	Blue
S 258	Blue	SDU 201	Blue	T 246	Blue	T 301	Blue	T 356	Blue
S 259	Blue	SDU 202	Blue	T 247	Blue	T 302	Blue	T 357	Blue
S 260	Blue	SDU 203	Blue	T 248	Blue	T 303	Blue	T 358	Blue
S 261	Blue	SDU 204	Blue	T 249	Blue	T 304	Blue	T 359	Blue
S 262	Blue	SDU 205	Blue	T 250	Blue	T 305	Blue	T 360	Blue
S 263	Blue	SDU 206	Blue	T 251	Blue	T 306	Blue	T 361	Blue
S 264	Blue	SDU 207	Blue	T 252	Blue	T 307	Blue	T 362	Blue
S 265	Blue	SDU 208	Blue	T 253	Blue	T 308	Blue	T 363	Blue
S 266	Blue	T 01	WSS	T 254	Blue	T 309	Blue	T 364	Blue
S 267	Blue	T 02	WSS	T 255	Blue	T 310	Blue	T 365	Blue
S 268	Blue	T 201	Blue	T 256	Blue	T 311	Blue	T 366	Blue
S 269	Blue	T 202	Blue	T 257	Blue	T 312	Blue	T 367	Blue
S 270	Blue	T 203	Blue	T 258	Blue	T 313	Blue	T 368	Blue
S 271	Blue	T 204	Blue	T 259	Blue	T 314	Blue	T 369	Blue
S 272	Blue	T 205	Blue	T 260	Blue	T 315	Blue	T 370	Blue
S 273	Blue	T 206	Blue	T 261	Blue	T 316	Blue	T 371	Blue
S 274	Blue	T 207	Blue	T 262	Blue	T 317	Blue	T 372	Blue
S 275	Blue	T 208	Blue	T 263	Blue	T 318	Blue	T 373	Blue
S 276	Blue	T 209	Blue	T 264	Blue	T 319	Blue	T 374	Blue
S 277	Blue	T 210	Blue	T 265	Blue	T 320	Blue	T 375	Blue
S 278	Blue	T 211	Blue	T 266	Blue	T 321	Blue	T 376	Blue
S 279	Blue	T 212	Blue	T 267	Blue	T 322	Blue	T 377	Blue
S 280	Blue	T 213	Blue	T 268	Blue	T 323	Blue	T 378	Blue
S 281	Blue	T 214	Blue	T 269	Blue	T 324	Blue	T 379	Blue
S 282	Blue	T 215	Blue	T 270	Blue	T 325	Blue	T 380	Blue
S 283	Blue	T 216	Blue	T 271	Blue	T 326	Blue	T 381	Blue
S 284	Blue	T 217	Blue	T 272	Blue	T 327	Blue	T 382	Blue
S 285	Blue	T 218	Blue	T 273	Blue	T 328	Blue	T 383	Blue
S 286	Blue	T 219	Blue	T 274	Blue	T 329	Blue	T 384	Blue
S 287	Blue	T 220	Blue	T 275	Blue	T 330	Blue	T 385	Blue
S 288	Blue	T 221	Blue	T 276	Blue	T 331	Blue	T 386	Blue
S 289	Blue	T 222	Blue	T 277	Blue	T 332	Blue	T 387	Blue
S 290	Blue	T 223	Blue	T 278	Blue	T 333	Blue	T 388	Blue
S 291	Blue	T 224	Blue	T 279	Blue	T 334	Blue	T 389	Blue
S 292	Blue	T 225	Blue	T 280	Blue	T 335	Blue	T 390	Blue
S 293	Blue	T 226	Blue	T 281	Blue	T 336	Blue	T 391	Blue
S 294	Blue	T 227	Blue	T 282	Blue	T 337	Blue	T 392	Blue
S 295	Blue	T 228	Blue	T 283	Blue	T 338	Blue	T 393	Blue
S 296	Blue	T 229	Blue	T 284	Blue	T 339	Blue	T 394	Blue
S 297	Blue	T 230	Blue	T 285	Blue	T 340	Blue	T 395	Blue
S 298	Blue	T 231	Blue	T 286	Blue	T 341	Blue	T 396	Blue
S 299	Blue	T 232	Blue	T 287	Blue	T 342	Blue	T 397	Blue
S 300	Blue	T 233	Blue	T 288	Blue	T 343	Blue	T 398	Blue
SB 01	Blue	T 234	Blue	T 289	Blue	T 344	Blue	T 399	Blue

WS Transportation

T 400	Blue	TT 21	WSW	TT 51	WSW	TT 80	WSW	TT 24	Blue
TSL 01	Blue	TT 22	WSW	TT 52	WSW	TT 81	WSW	TT 25	Blue
TSL 02	Blue	TT 23	WSW	TT 53	WSW	TT 82	WSW	TT 26	Blue
TSL 03	Blue	TT 24	WSW	TT 54	WSW	TT 101	WSW	TT 27	Blue
TSL 04	Blue	TT 25	WSW	TT 55	WSW	TT 4203	WSW	TT 28	Blue
TSL 05	Blue	TT 26	WSW	TT 56	WSW	TT 4208	WSW	UMFT 32	WSB
TSL 06	Blue	TT 27	WSW	TT 57	WSW	TT 01	Blue	UMFT 33	WSB
TSL 07	Blue	TT 28	WSW	TT 58	WSW	TT 02	Blue	UMFT 34	WSB
TSL 08	Blue	TT 29	WSW	TT 59	WSW	TT 03	Blue	USC 01	Blue
TSL 09	Blue	TT 30	WSW	TT 60	WSW	TT 04	Blue	USC 02	Blue
TT 01	WSW	TT 31	WSW	TT 61	WSW	TT 05	Blue	USC 03	Blue
TT 02	WSW	TT 32	WSW	TT 62	WSW	TT 06	Blue	USC 04	Blue
TT 03	WSW	TT 33	WSW	TT 63	WSW	TT 07	Blue	USC 05	Blue
TT 04	WSW	TT 34	WSW	TT 64	WSW	TT 08	Blue	USC 06	Blue
TT 05	WSW	TT 35	WSW	TT 65	WSW	TT 09	Blue	USC 07	Blue
TT 06	WSW	TT 36	WSW	TT 66	WSW	TT 10	Blue	USC 08	Blue
TT 07	WSW	TT 37	WSW	TT 67	WSW	TT 11	Blue	USC 09	Blue
TT 08	WSW	TT 38	WSW	TT 68	WSW	TT 12	Blue	USC 10	Blue
TT 09	WSW	TT 39	WSW	TT 69	WSW	TT 13	Blue	UT 01	Blue
TT 10	WSW	TT 40	WSW	TT 70	WSW	TT 14	Blue	UT 02	Blue
TT 11	WSW	TT 41	WSW	TT 71	WSW	TT 15	Blue	UT 03	Blue
TT 12	WSW	TT 42	WSW	TT 72	WSW	TT 16	Blue	UT 04	Blue
TT 13	WSW	TT 43	WSW	TT 73	WSW	TT 17	Blue	UT 05	Blue
TT 14	WSW	TT 44	WSW	TT 74	WSW	TT 18	Blue	UT 06	Blue
TT 15	WSW	TT 45	WSW	TT 75	WSW	TT 19	Blue	UT 07	Blue
TT 16	WSW	TT 46	WSW	TT 76	WSW	TT 20	Blue	UT 08	Blue
TT 17	WSW	TT 47	WSW	TT 77	WSW	TT 21	Blue	UT 09	Blue
TT 18	WSW	TT 48	WSW	TT 78	WSW	TT 22	Blue	UT 10	Blue
TT 19	WSW	TT 49	WSW	TT 79	WSW	TT 23	Blue	X 1	Blue
TT 20	WSW	TT 50	WSW						

Ken Mallinson / H E Payne / WMB Logistics / Middlebrook

CSTL 9	KMS / ITAB	FLA 309	Black	WMB 32 06	WMB Black
CS 11 M	KMS Green	FLP 405	KMS Green	WMB 33 06	WMB Black
CSTL 12	KMS Green	FLP 507	KMS Green	WMB 35 06	WMB Black
CS 67 M	KMS Green	FLP 531	KMS Green	WMB 36 06	WMB Black
SR 153	KMS Green	FLP 537	KMS Green	WMB 38 07	WMB Black
SR 180	KMS Green	LL 2 EX	KMS Green	WMB 40 07	WMB Black
SPE 01	KMS Green	HEP 205	HE Payne White	MT 219	Blue
SP 03	Black	HEP 209	HE Payne White	MT 266	Blue
SP 06	Black	HEP 210	HE Payne White	MT 293	Blue
SP 12	KMS Green	HEP R 12	HE Payne White	MT 369	Blue
SP 44	KMS Green				

CST 10

CMDT 001	EXP	FB 018	EXP	FB 099	EXP	FB 155	EXP	FBEXT 507	EXP
CMDT 002	EXP	FB 019	EXP	FB 100	EXP	FB 156	EXP	FBEXT 508	EXP
CMDT 003	EXP	FB 020	EXP	FB 101	EXP	FB 157	EXP	FBEXT 509	EXP
CORT 001	EXP	FB 021	EXP	FB 102	EXP	FB 158	EXP	FBEXT 510	EXP
CORT 002	EXP	FB 022	EXP	FB 103	EXP	FB 159	EXP	FBEXT 511	EXP
CST 01	EXP	FB 023	EXP	FB 104	EXP	FB 160	EXP	FBEXT 512	EXP
CST 02	EXP	FB 024	EXP	FB 105	EXP	FB 161	EXP	FBEXT 513	EXP
CST 03	EXP	FB 025	EXP	FB 106	EXP	FB 162	EXP	FBEXT 514	EXP
CST 04	EXP	FB 026	EXP	FB 107	EXP	FB 163	EXP	FBEXT 515	EXP
CST 05	EXP	FB 027	EXP	FB 108	EXP	FB 164	EXP	FBEXT 516	EXP
CSU 01	EXP	FB 028	EXP	FB 109	EXP	FB 165	EXP	FBEXT 517	EXP
CSU 02	EXP	FB 029	EXP	FB 110	EXP	FB 166	EXP	FBEXT 518	EXP
CSU 03	EXP	FB 030	EXP	FB 111	EXP	FB 167	EXP	FBEXT 519	EXP
CSU 04	EXP	FB 031	EXP	FB 112	EXP	FB 168	EXP	FBEXT 520	EXP
CSU 05	EXP	FB 032	EXP	FB 113	EXP	FB 169	EXP	FBEXT 521	EXP
CSU 06	EXP	FB 033	EXP	FB 114	EXP	FB 170	EXP	FBEXT 522	EXP
CSU 07	EXP	FB 034	EXP	FB 115	EXP	FB 171	EXP	FBEXT 523	EXP
CSU 08	EXP	FB 035	EXP	FB 116	EXP	FB 172	EXP	FBEXT 524	EXP
CSU 09	EXP	FB 036	EXP	FB 117	EXP	FB 173	EXP	FBEXT 525	EXP
CSU 10	EXP	FB 037	EXP	FB 118	EXP	FB 174	EXP	FBEXT 526	EXP
CSU 11	EXP	FB 038	EXP	FB 119	EXP	FB 175	EXP	FBTW 300	EXP
CSU 12	EXP	FB 039	EXP	FB 120	EXP	FB 176	EXP	FBTW 301	EXP
CSU 13	EXP	FB 040	EXP	FB 121	EXP	FB 177	EXP	FBTW 302	EXP
CSU 14	EXP	FB 041	EXP	FB 122	EXP	FB 178	EXP	FBTW 303	EXP
CSU 15	EXP	FB 042	EXP	FB 123	EXP	FB 179	EXP	FBTW 304	EXP
CSU 16	EXP	FB 043	EXP	FB 124	EXP	FB 180	EXP	FBTW 305	EXP
CSU 17	EXP	FB 044	EXP	FB 125	EXP	FB 181	EXP	FBTW 306	EXP
CSU 18	EXP	FB 045	EXP	FB 126	EXP	FB 182	EXP	FBTW 307	EXP
CSU 19	EXP	FB 046	EXP	FB 127	EXP	FB 183	EXP	FBTW 308	EXP
CSU 20	EXP	FB 047	EXP	FB 128	EXP	FB 184	EXP	FBTW 309	EXP
CSU 21	EXP	FB 048	EXP	FB 129	EXP	FB 185	EXP	FBTW 310	EXP
CSU 22	EXP	FB 049	EXP	FB 130	EXP	FB 186	EXP	FBTW 311	EXP
CSU 23	EXP	FB 050	EXP	FB 131	EXP	FB 187	EXP	FBTW 312	EXP
CSU 24	EXP	FB 051	EXP	FB 132	EXP	FB 188	EXP	FBTW 313	EXP
CSU 25	EXP	FB 052	EXP	FB 133	EXP	FB 189	EXP	FBTW 314	EXP
CSU 26	EXP	FB 053	EXP	FB 134	EXP	FB 190	EXP	FBTW 315	EXP
CSU 27	EXP	FB 054	EXP	FB 135	EXP	FB 191	EXP	FBTW 316	EXP
CSU 28	EXP	FB 055	EXP	FB 136	EXP	FB 192	EXP	FBTW 317	EXP
CSU 29	EXP	FB 056	EXP	FB 137	EXP	FB 193	EXP	FBTW 318	EXP
FB 001	EXP	FB 057	EXP	FB 138	EXP	FB 194	EXP	FBTW 319	EXP
FB 002	EXP	FB 058	EXP	FB 139	EXP	FB 195	EXP	FBTW 320	EXP
FB 003	EXP	FB 059	EXP	FB 140	EXP	FB 196	EXP	FBTW 321	EXP
FB 004	EXP	FB 085	EXP	FB 141	EXP	FB 197	EXP	FBTW 322	EXP
FB 005	EXP	FB 086	EXP	FB 142	EXP	FB 198	EXP	FBTW 323	EXP
FB 006	EXP	FB 087	EXP	FB 143	EXP	FB 199	EXP	FBTW 324	EXP
FB 007	EXP	FB 088	EXP	FB 144	EXP	FB 200	EXP	FBTW 325	EXP
FB 008	EXP	FB 089	EXP	FB 145	EXP	FB 201	EXP	FBTW 326	EXP
FB 009	EXP	FB 090	EXP	FB 146	EXP	FB 202	EXP	FBTW 327	EXP
FB 010	EXP	FB 091	EXP	FB 147	EXP	FB 203	EXP	FBTW 328	EXP
FB 011	EXP	FB 092	EXP	FB 148	EXP	FB 204	EXP	FBTW 329	EXP
FB 012	EXP	FB 093	EXP	FB 149	EXP	FBEXT 501	EXP	FBTW 330	EXP
FB 013	EXP	FB 094	EXP	FB 150	EXP	FBEXT 502	EXP	FBTW 331	EXP
FB 014	EXP	FB 095	EXP	FB 151	EXP	FBEXT 503	EXP	FBTW 332	EXP
FB 015	EXP	FB 096	EXP	FB 152	EXP	FBEXT 504	EXP	FBTW 333	EXP
FB 016	EXP	FB 097	EXP	FB 153	EXP	FBEXT 505	EXP	FBTW 334	EXP
FB 017	EXP	FB 098	EXP	FB 154	EXP	FBEXT 506	EXP	FBTW 335	EXP

Explore

FBTW 336	EXP	FBTW 384	EXP	FBTW 428	EXP	LL 813	EXP	SF 688	EXP
FBTW 337	EXP	FBTW 385	EXP	FBTW 429	EXP	LL 814	EXP	SF 689	EXP
FBTW 338	EXP	FBTW 386	EXP	FBTW 430	EXP	LL 815	EXP	SF 690	EXP
FBTW 339	EXP	FBTW 387	EXP	FBTW 431	EXP	LL 816	EXP	SF 691	EXP
FBTW 340	EXP	FBTW 388	EXP	FBTW 432	EXP	LL 817	EXP	SF 692	EXP
FBTW 341	EXP	FBTW 389	EXP	FBTW 433	EXP	SF 650	EXP	SF 693	EXP
FBTW 342	EXP	FBTW 390	EXP	FBTW 434	EXP	SF 651	EXP	SF 694	EXP
FBTW 343	EXP	FBTW 391	EXP	FBTW 435	EXP	SF 652	EXP	SF 695	EXP
FBTW 344	EXP	FBTW 392	EXP	FBTW 436	EXP	SF 653	EXP	SF 696	EXP
FBTW 345	EXP	FBTW 393	EXP	FBTW 437	EXP	SF 654	EXP	SF 697	EXP
FBTW 346	EXP	FBTW 394	EXP	FBTW 438	EXP	SF 655	EXP	SFEX 750	EXP
FBTW 347	EXP	FBTW 395	EXP	FBTW 439	EXP	SF 656	EXP	SFEX 751	EXP
FBTW 348	EXP	FBTW 396	EXP	FBTW 440	EXP	SF 657	EXP	SFEX 753	EXP
FBTW 349	EXP	FBTW 397	EXP	FBTW 441	EXP	SF 658	EXP	STUL 01	EXP
FBTW 350	EXP	FBTW 398	EXP	FBTW 442	EXP	SF 659	EXP	SU 600	EXP
FBTW 351	EXP	FBTW 399	EXP	FBTW 443	EXP	SF 660	EXP	SU 601	EXP
FBTW 352	EXP	FBTW 400	EXP	FBTW 444	EXP	SF 661	EXP	SU 602	EXP
FBTW 353	EXP	FBTW 401	EXP	FBTW 445	EXP	SF 662	EXP	SU 603	EXP
FBTW 354	EXP	FBTW 402	EXP	FBTW 446	EXP	SF 663	EXP	SU 604	EXP
FBTW 355	EXP	FBTW 403	EXP	FBTW 447	EXP	SF 664	EXP	SU 605	EXP
FBTW 356	EXP	FBTW 404	EXP	FBTW 448	EXP	SF 665	EXP	SU 606	EXP
FBTW 357	EXP	FBTW 405	EXP	FBTW 449	EXP	SF 666	EXP	SU 607	EXP
FBTW 358	EXP	FBTW 406	EXP	FBTW 507	EXB	SF 667	EXP	SU 608	EXP
FBTW 359	EXP	FBTW 407	EXP	FBTW 525	EXB	SF 668	EXP	SU 609	EXP
FBTW 362	EXP	FBTW 408	EXP	FBTW 567	EXB	SF 669	EXP	SU 610	EXP
FBTW 363	EXP	FBTW 409	EXP	FBTW 595	EXB	SF 670	EXP	SU 611	EXP
FBTW 364	EXP	FBTW 410	EXP	FBTW 607	EXB	SF 671	EXP	SU 612	EXP
FBTW 365	EXP	FBTW 411	EXP	FBTW 608	EXB	SF 672	EXP	SU 613	EXP
FBTW 366	EXP	FBTW 412	EXP	LL 09	EXP	SF 673	EXP	SU 614	EXP
FBTW 367	EXP	FBTW 413	EXP	LL 10	EXP	SF 674	EXP	SU 615	EXP
FBTW 368	EXP	FBTW 414	EXP	LL 12	EXP	SF 675	EXP	SU 616	EXP
FBTW 369	EXP	FBTW 415	EXP	LL 801	EXP	SF 676	EXP	SU 617	EXP
FBTW 370	EXP	FBTW 416	EXP	LL 802	EXP	SF 677	EXP	SU 618	EXP
FBTW 371	EXP	FBTW 417	EXP	LL 803	EXP	SF 678	EXP	SU 619	EXP
FBTW 373	EXP	FBTW 418	EXP	LL 804	EXP	SF 679	EXP	SU 620	EXP
FBTW 374	EXP	FBTW 419	EXP	LL 805	EXP	SF 680	EXP	SU 621	EXP
FBTW 375	EXP	FBTW 420	EXP	LL 806	EXP	SF 681	EXP	SU 622	EXP
FBTW 377	EXP	FBTW 421	EXP	LL 807	EXP	SF 682	EXP	SU 623	EXP
FBTW 378	EXP	FBTW 422	EXP	LL 808	EXP	SF 683	EXP	SU 624	EXP
FBTW 379	EXP	FBTW 423	EXP	LL 809	EXP	SF 684	EXP	SU 625	EXP
FBTW 380	EXP	FBTW 424	EXP	LL 810	EXP	SF 685	EXP	SU 626	EXP
FBTW 381	EXP	FBTW 425	EXP	LL 811	EXP	SF 686	EXP	SU 627	EXP
FBTW 382	EXP	FBTW 426	EXP	LL 812	EXP	SF 687	EXP	SU 628	EXP
FBTW 383	EXP	FBTW 427	EXP						

Graylaw

DD 501	GRY	DDT 305	GRY	DDT 312	GRY	FR 1002	GRY	TET 005	GRY
DD 502	GRY	DDT 306	GRY	DDT 313	GRY	FR 1003	GRY	TET 006	GRY
DD 503	GRY	DDT 307	GRY	DDT 314	GRY	HT 8531	GRY	TET 007	GRY
DDT 301	GRY	DDT 308	GRY	DDT 315	GRY	TET 001	GRY	TET 008	GRY
DDT 302	GRY	DDT 309	GRY	DDT 316	GRY	TET 002	GRY	TET 009	GRY
DDT 303	GRY	DDT 310	GRY	FR 1000	GRY	TET 003	GRY	TET 010	GRY
DDT 304	GRY	DDT 311	GRY	FR 1001	GRY	TET 004	GRY	TET 011	GRY

HT 8535

ACS002	M4A1016CS	M4A1076CS	M4A1136CS	M4A1196CS	M4M497CS
FS25	M4A1017CS	M4A1077CS	M4A1137CS	M4A1197CS	M4M498CS
FS26	M4A1018CS	M4A1078CS	M4A1138CS	M4A1198CS	M4M499CS
FS27	M4A1019CS	M4A1079CS	M4A1139CS	M4A1199CS	M4M500CS
FS28	M4A1020CS	M4A1080CS	M4A1140CS	M4A1200CS	M4M509CSTL
FS29	M4A1021CS	M4A1081CS	M4A1141CS	M4A1201CS	M4M511CS
FS30	M4A1022CS	M4A1082CS	M4A1142CS	M4A1202CS	M4M512CS
FS31	M4A1023CS	M4A1083CS	M4A1143CS	M4A1203CS	M4M513CS
FS32	M4A1024CS	M4A1084CS	M4A1144CS	M4A1204CS	M4M514CS
FS33	M4A1025CS	M4A1085CS	M4A1145CS	M4A1205CS	M4M515CS
FS34	M4A1026CS	M4A1086CS	M4A1146CS	M4M1206CS	M4M516CS
FS35	M4A1027CS	M4A1087CS	M4A1147CS	M4M446CS	M4M517CS
FS36	M4A1028CS	M4A1088CS	M4A1148CS	M4M447CS	M4M518CS
FS37	M4A1029CS	M4A1089CS	M4A1149CS	M4M448CS	M4M519CS
FS38	M4A1030CS	M4A1090CS	M4A1150CS	M4M449CS	M4M520CS
FS39	M4A1031CS	M4A1091CS	M4A1151CS	M4M450CS	M4M521CS
FS40	M4A1032CS	M4A1092CS	M4A1152CS	M4M451CS	M4M522CS
FS41	M4A1033CS	M4A1093CS	M4A1153CS	M4M452CS	M4M523CS
FS42	M4A1034CS	M4A1094CS	M4A1154CS	M4M453CS	M4M524CS
FS43	M4A1035CS	M4A1095CS	M4A1155CS	M4M454CS	M4M525CS
FS44	M4A1036CS	M4A1096CS	M4A1156CS	M4M455CS	M4M526CS
FS45	M4A1037CS	M4A1097CS	M4A1157CS	M4M456CS	M4M527CS
FS46	M4A1038CS	M4A1098CS	M4A1158CS	M4M457CS	M4M528CS
FS47	M4A1039CS	M4A1099CS	M4A1159CS	M4M458CS	M4M529CS
FS48	M4A1040CS	M4A1100CS	M4A1160CS	M4M459CS	M4M530CS
FS49	M4A1041CS	M4A1101CS	M4A1161CS	M4M460CS	M4M531CS
FS50	M4A1042CS	M4A1102CS	M4A1162CS	M4M461CS	M4M532CS
FS52	M4A1043CS	M4A1103CS	M4A1163CS	M4M462CS	M4M533CS
FS53	M4A1044CS	M4A1104CS	M4A1164CS	M4M464CS	M4M534CS
FS54	M4A1045CS	M4A1105CS	M4A1165CS	M4M465CS	M4M535CS
FS55	M4A1046CS	M4A1106CS	M4A1166CS	M4M466CS	M4M536CS
FS56	M4A1047CS	M4A1107CS	M4A1167CS	M4M467CS	M4M537CS
FS57	M4A1048CS	M4A1108CS	M4A1168CS	M4M468CS	M4M538CS
FS58	M4A1049CS	M4A1109CS	M4A1169CS	M4M469CS	M4M539CS
FS59	M4A1050CS	M4A1110CS	M4A1170CS	M4M470CS	M4M540CS
FS60	M4A1051CS	M4A1111CS	M4A1171CS	M4M471CS	M4M541CS
FS61	M4A1052CS	M4A1112CS	M4A1172CS	M4M472CS	M4M542CS
FS62	M4A1053CS	M4A1113CS	M4A1173CS	M4M473CS	M4M543CS
FS63	M4A1054CS	M4A1114CS	M4A1174CS	M4M474CS	M4M544CS
FS64	M4A1055CS	M4A1115CS	M4A1175CS	M4M475CS	M4M545CS
FS65	M4A1056CS	M4A1116CS	M4A1176CS	M4M476CS	M4M546CS
FS66	M4A1057CS	M4A1117CS	M4A1177CS	M4M477CS	M4M547CS
FS67	M4A1058CS	M4A1118CS	M4A1178CS	M4M478CS	M4M548CS
FS68	M4A1059CS	M4A1119CS	M4A1179CS	M4M479CS	M4M549CS
FS69	M4A1060CS	M4A1120CS	M4A1180CS	M4M480CS	M4M550CS
FS70	M4A1061CS	M4A1121CS	M4A1181CS	M4M481CS	M4M551CS
FS71	M4A1062CS	M4A1122CS	M4A1182CS	M4M482CS	M4M552CS
FS72	M4A1063CS	M4A1123CS	M4A1183CS	M4M483CS	M4M553CS
FS73	M4A1064CS	M4A1124CS	M4A1184CS	M4M484CS	M4M554CS
FS74	M4A1065CS	M4A1125CS	M4A1185CS	M4M485CS	M4M555CS
M4A1006CS	M4A1066CS	M4A1126CS	M4A1186CS	M4M486CS	M4M556CS
M4A1007CS	M4A1067CS	M4A1127CS	M4A1187CS	M4M487CS	M4M557CS
M4A1008CS	M4A1068CS	M4A1128CS	M4A1188CS	M4M488CS	M4M558CS
M4A1009CS	M4A1069CS	M4A1129CS	M4A1189CS	M4M489CS	M4M559CS
M4A1010CS	M4A1070CS	M4A1130CS	M4A1190CS	M4M491CS	M4M560CS
M4A1011CS	M4A1071CS	M4A1131CS	M4A1191CS	M4M492CS	M4M561CS
M4A1012CS	M4A1072CS	M4A1132CS	M4A1192CS	M4M493CS	M4M562CS
M4A1013CS	M4A1073CS	M4A1133CS	M4A1193CS	M4M494CS	M4M563CS
M4A1014CS	M4A1074CS	M4A1134CS	M4A1194CS	M4M495CS	M4M564CS
M4A1015CS	M4A1075CS	M4A1135CS	M4A1195CS	M4M496CS	M4M565CS

M4M566CS	M4M647CS	M4M709CS	MDA959CS	MDA1220CS	MDA1280CS
M4M567CS	M4M648CS	M4M710CS	MDA960CS	MDA1221CS	MDA1281CS
M4M568CS	M4M649CS	M4M711CS	MDA961CS	MDA1222CS	MDA1282CS
M4M569CS	M4M650CS	M4M712CS	MDA962CS	MDA1223CS	MDA1283CS
M4M570CS	M4M651CS	M4M713CS	MDA963CS	MDA1224CS	MDA1284CS
M4M571CS	M4M652CS	M4M714CS	MDA964CS	MDA1225CS	MDA1285CS
M4M572CS	M4M653CS	M4M715CS	MDA965CS	MDA1226CS	MDA1286CS
M4M573CS	M4M654CS	M4M716CS	MDA966CS	MDA1227CS	MDA1287CS
M4M574CS	M4M655CS	M4M717CS	MDA967CS	MDA1228CS	MDA1288CS
M4M575CS	M4M656CS	M4M718CS	MDA968CS	MDA1229CS	MDA1289CS
M4M576CS	M4M657CS	M4M719CS	MDA969CS	MDA1230CS	MDA1290CS
M4M577CS	M4M658CS	M4M720CS	MDA970CS	MDA1231CS	MDA1291CS
M4M578CS	M4M659CS	M4M721CS	MDA971CS	MDA1232CS	MDA1292CS
M4M579CS	M4M660CS	M4M722CS	MDA972CS	MDA1233CS	MDA1293CS
M4M580CS	M4M661CS	M4M723CS	MDA973CS	MDA1234CS	MDA1294CS
M4M581CS	M4M662CS	M4M724CS	MDA974CS	MDA1235CS	MDA1295CS
M4M582CS	M4M663CS	M4M725CS	MDA975CS	MDA1236CS	MDA1296CS
M4M583CS	M4M664CS	M4M726CS	MDA976CS	MDA1237CS	MDA1297CS
M4M584CS	M4M665CS	M4M727CS	MDA977CS	MDA1238CS	MDA1298CS
M4M585CS	M4M666CS	M4M728CS	MDA978CS	MDA1239CS	MDA1299CS
M4M586CS	M4M667CS	M4M729CS	MDA979CS	MDA1240CS	MDA1300CS
M4M587CS	M4M668CS	M4M730CS	MDA980CS	MDA1241CS	MDA1301CS
M4M588CS	M4M669CS	M4M731CS	MDA981CS	MDA1242CS	MDA1302CS
M4M589CS	M4M670CS	M4M732CS	MDA982CS	MDA1243CS	MDA1303CS
M4M590CS	M4M671CS	M4M733CS	MDA983CS	MDA1244CS	MDA1304CS
M4M591CS	M4M672CS	M4M734CS	MDA984CS	MDA1245CS	MDA1305CS
M4M592CS	M4M673CS	M4M735CS	MDA985CS	MDA1246CS	MDA1306CS
M4M593CS	M4M674CS	M4M776CS	MDA986CS	MDA1247CS	MDL001D
M4M594CS	M4M675CS	M4M777CS	MDA987CS	MDA1248CS	MDL201CS
M4M595CS	M4M676CS	M4M778CS	MDA988CS	MDA1249CS	MDL202CS
M4M596CS	M4M677CS	M4M779CS	MDA989CS	MDA1250CS	MDL203CS
M4M597CS	M4M678CS	M4M780CS	MDA990CS	MDA1251CS	MDL204CS
M4M598CS	M4M679CS	M4M781CS	MDA991CS	MDA1252CS	MDL205CS
M4M599CS	M4M680CS	M4M782CS	MDA992CS	MDA1253CS	MDL206CS
M4M600CS	M4M681CS	M4M783CS	MDA993CS	MDA1254CS	MDL207CS
M4M601CS	M4M682CS	M4M784CS	MDA994CS	MDA1255CS	MDL208CS
M4M602CS	M4M683CS	M4M785CS	MDA995CS	MDA1256CS	MDL209CS
M4M603CS	M4M686CS	M4M786CS	MDA996CS	MDA1257CS	MDL210CS
M4M604CS	M4M687CS	M4M787CS	MDA997CS	MDA1258CS	MDL211CS
M4M605CS	M4M688CS	M4M788CS	MDA998CS	MDA1259CS	MDL212CS
M4M626CS	M4M689CS	M4M789CS	MDA999CS	MDA1260CS	MDL213CS
M4M627CS	M4M690CS	M4M790CS	MDA1000CS	MDA1261CS	MDL214CS
M4M628CS	M4M691CS	M4M791CS	MDA1001CS	MDA1262CS	MDL215CS
M4M629CS	M4M692CS	M4M792CS	MDA1002CS	MDA1263CS	MDL217CS
M4M630CS	M4M693CS	M4M793CS	MDA1003CS	MDA1264CS	MDL218CS
M4M631CS	M4M694CS	M4M794CS	MDA1004CS	MDA1265CS	MDL220CS
M4M632CS	M4M695CS	M4M795CS	MDA1005CS	MDA1266CS	MDL222CS
M4M633CS	M4M696CS	M4M796CS	MDA1207CS	MDA1267CS	MDL223CS
M4M634CS	M4M697CS	M4M797CS	MDA1208CS	MDA1268CS	MDL224CS
M4M635CS	M4M698CS	M4M798CS	MDA1209CS	MDA1269CS	MDL225C3
M4M636CS	M4M699CS	M4M799CS	MDA1210CS	MDA1270CS	MDL226CS
M4M638CS	M4M700CS	M4M800CS	MDA1211CS	MDA1271CS	MDL227CS
M4M639CS	M4M701CS	M4M801CS	MDA1212CS	MDA1272CS	MDL228CS
M4M640CS	M4M702CS	M4M802CS	MDA1213CS	MDA1273CS	MDL229CS
M4M641CS	M4M703CS	M4M803CS	MDA1214CS	MDA1274CS	MDL230CS
M4M642CS	M4M704CS	M4M804CS	MDA1215CS	MDA1275CS	MDL231CS
M4M643CS	M4M705CS	M4M805CS	MDA1216CS	MDA1276CS	MDL232CS
M4M644CS	M4M706CS	MDA956CS	MDA1217CS	MDA1277CS	MDL233CS
M4M645CS	M4M707CS	MDA957CS	MDA1218CS	MDA1278CS	MDL235CS
M4M646CS	M4M708CS	MDA958CS	MDA1219CS	MDA1279CS	MDL236CS

Maritime Trailers

MDL237CS	MDL297CS	MDL357CS	MDL417CS	MDL760CS	MDL850CS
MDL238CS	MDL298CS	MDL358CS	MDL418CS	MDL761CS	MDL851CS
MDL239CS	MDL299CS	MDL359CS	MDL419CS	MDL762CS	MDL852CS
MDL240CS	MDL300CS	MDL360CS	MDL420CS	MDL763CS	MDL853CS
MDL241CS	MDL301CS	MDL361CS	MDL421CS	MDL764CS	MDL854CS
MDL242CS	MDL302CS	MDL362CS	MDL422CS	MDL765CS	MDL855CS
MDL243CS	MDL303CS	MDL363CS	MDL423CS	MDL766CS	MDL856CS
MDL244CS	MDL304CS	MDL364CS	MDL424CS	MDL767CS	MDL857CS
MDL245CS	MDL305CS	MDL365CS	MDL425CS	MDL768CS	MDL858CS
MDL246CS	MDL306CS	MDL366CS	MDL426CS	MDL769CS	MDL859CS
MDL247CS	MDL307CS	MDL367CS	MDL427CS	MDL770CS	MDL860CS
MDL248CS	MDL308CS	MDL368CS	MDL429CS	MDL771CS	MDL861CS
MDL249CS	MDL309CS	MDL369CS	MDL430CS	MDL772CS	MDL862CS
MDL250CS	MDL310CS	MDL370CS	MDL431CS	MDL773CS	MDL863CS
MDL251CS	MDL311CS	MDL371CS	MDL432CS	MDL774CS	MDL864CS
MDL252CS	MDL312CS	MDL372CS	MDL433CS	MDL775CS	MDL865CS
MDL253CS	MDL313CS	MDL373CS	MDL434CS	MDL806CS	MDL866CS
MDL254CS	MDL314CS	MDL374CS	MDL435CS	MDL807CS	MDL868CS
MDL255CS	MDL315CS	MDL375CS	MDL436CS	MDL808CS	MDL869CS
MDL256CS	MDL316CS	MDL376CS	MDL437CS	MDL809CS	MDL870CS
MDL257CS	MDL317CS	MDL377CS	MDL438CS	MDL810CS	MDL871CS
MDL258CS	MDL318CS	MDL378CS	MDL439CS	MDL811CS	MDL872CS
MDL259CS	MDL319CS	MDL379CS	MDL441CS	MDL812CS	MDL873CS
MDL260CS	MDL320CS	MDL380CS	MDL442CS	MDL813CS	MDL874CS
MDL261CS	MDL321CS	MDL381CS	MDL443CS	MDL814CS	MDL875CS
MDL262CS	MDL322CS	MDL382CS	MDL444CS	MDL815CS	MDL876CS
MDL263CS	MDL323CS	MDL383CS	MDL445CS	MDL816CS	MDL877CS
MDL264CS	MDL324CS	MDL384CS	MDL606CS	MDL817CS	MDL878CS
MDL265CS	MDL325CS	MDL385CS	MDL607CS	MDL818CS	MDL879CS
MDL266CS	MDL326CS	MDL386CS	MDL609CS	MDL819CS	MDL880CS
MDL267CS	MDL327CS	MDL387CS	MDL610CS	MDL820CS	MDL881CS
MDL268CS	MDL328CS	MDL388CS	MDL611CS	MDL821CS	MDL882CS
MDL269CS	MDL329CS	MDL389CS	MDL612CS	MDL822CS	MDL883CS
MDL270CS	MDL330CS	MDL390CS	MDL613CS	MDL823CS	MDL884CS
MDL271CS	MDL331CS	MDL391CS	MDL614CS	MDL824CS	MDL885CS
MDL272CS	MDL332CS	MDL392CS	MDL615CS	MDL825CS	MDL886CS
MDL273CS	MDL333CS	MDL393CS	MDL736CS	MDL826CS	MDL887CS
MDL274CS	MDL334CS	MDL394CS	MDL737CS	MDL827CS	MDL888CS
MDL275CS	MDL335CS	MDL395CS	MDL738CS	MDL828CS	MDL889CS
MDL276CS	MDL336CS	MDL396CS	MDL739CS	MDL829CS	MDL890CS
MDL277CS	MDL337CS	MDL397CS	MDL740CS	MDL830CS	MDL891CS
MDL278CS	MDL338CS	MDL398CS	MDL741CS	MDL831CS	MDL892CS
MDL279CS	MDL339CS	MDL399CS	MDL742CS	MDL832CS	MDL893CS
MDL280CS	MDL340CS	MDL400CS	MDL743CS	MDL833CS	MDL894CS
MDL281CS	MDL341CS	MDL401CS	MDL744CS	MDL834CS	MDL895CS
MDL282CS	MDL342CS	MDL402CS	MDL745CS	MDL835CS	MDL896CS
MDL283CS	MDL343CS	MDL403CS	MDL746CS	MDL836CS	MDL897CS
MDL284CS	MDL344CS	MDL404CS	MDL747CS	MDL837CS	MDL898CS
MDL285CS	MDL345CS	MDL405CS	MDL748CS	MDL838CS	MDL899CS
MDL286CS	MDL346CS	MDL406CS	MDL749CS	MDL839CS	MDL900CS
MDL287CS	MDL347CS	MDL407CS	MDL750CS	MDL840CS	MDL901CS
MDL288CS	MDL348CS	MDL408CS	MDL751CS	MDL841CS	MDL902CS
MDL289CS	MDL349CS	MDL409CS	MDL752CS	MDL842CS	MDL903CS
MDL290CS	MDL350CS	MDL410CS	MDL753CS	MDL843CS	MDL904CS
MDL291CS	MDL351CS	MDL411CS	MDL754CS	MDL844CS	MDL905CS
MDL292CS	MDL352CS	MDL412CS	MDL755CS	MDL845CS	MDL906CS
MDL293CS	MDL353CS	MDL413CS	MDL756CS	MDL846CS	MDL907CS
MDL294CS	MDL354CS	MDL414CS	MDL757CS	MDL847CS	MDL908CS
MDL295CS	MDL355CS	MDL415CS	MDL758CS	MDL848CS	MDL909CS
MDL296CS	MDL356CS	MDL416CS	MDL759CS	MDL849CS	MDL910CS

Maritime Trailers

MDL911CS	MGL1514GN	MGL1696	MGL1757	MGL1818	MGL1883
MDL912CS	MGL1515GN	MGL1697	MGL1758	MGL1819	MGL1884
MDL913CS	MGL1516GN	MGL1698	MGL1759	MGL1820	MGL1885
MDL914CS	MGL1518GN	MGL1699	MGL1760	MGL1821	MGL1886
MDL915CS	MGL1519GN	MGL1700	MGL1761	MGL1822	MGL1887
MDL916CS	MGL1546	MGL1701	MGL1762	MGL1823	MGL1888
MDL917CS	MGL1603	MGL1702	MGL1763	MGL1824	MGL1889
MDL918CS	MGL1612	MGL1703	MGL1764	MGL1825	MGL1890
MDL919CS	MGL1615	MGL1704	MGL1765	MGL1826	MGL1891
MDL920CS	MGL1620	MGL1705	MGL1766	MGL1827	MGL1892
MDL921CS	MGL1623	MGL1706	MGL1767	MGL1828	MGL1893
MDL922CS	MGL1631	MGL1707	MGL1768	MGL1829	MGL1894
MDL923CS	MGL1647	MGL1708	MGL1769	MGL1830	MGL1895
MDL924CS	MGL1648	MGL1709	MGL1770	MGL1831	MGL1896
MDL925CS	MGL1649	MGL1710	MGL1771	MGL1832	MGL1897
MDL926CS	MGL1650	MGL1711	MGL1772	MGL1833	MGL1898
MDL927CS	MGL1651	MGL1712	MGL1773	MGL1834	MGL1899
MDL928CS	MGL1652	MGL1713	MGL1774	MGL1835	MGL1900
MDL929CS	MGL1653	MGL1714	MGL1776	MGL1836	MGL1901
MDL930CS	MGL1654	MGL1715	MGL1777	MGL1837	MGL1902
MDL931CS	MGL1655	MGL1716	MGL1778	MGL1838	MGL1903
MDL932CS	MGL1656	MGL1717	MGL1779	MGL1839	MGL1904
MDL933CS	MGL1657	MGL1718	MGL1780	MGL1840	MGL1905
MDL934CS	MGL1658	MGL1719	MGL1781	MGL1841	MGL1906
MDL935CS	MGL1659	MGL1720	MGL1782	MGL1842	MGL1907
MDL936CS	MGL1660	MGL1721	MGL1783	MGL1843	MGL1908
MDL937CS	MGL1661	MGL1722	MGL1784	MGL1844	MGL1909
MDL938CS	MGL1662	MGL1723	MGL1785	MGL1845	MGL1910
MDL939CS	MGL1663	MGL1724	MGL1786	MGL1846	MGL1911
MDL940CS	MGL1664	MGL1725	MGL1787	MGL1847	MGL1912
MDL941CSX	MGL1665	MGL1726	MGL1788	MGL1849	MGL1913
MDL942CSX	MGL1666	MGL1727	MGL1789	MGL1850	MGL1914
MDL943CSX	MGL1667	MGL1728	MGL1790	MGL1852	MGL1915
MDL944CSX	MGL1668	MGL1730	MGL1791	MGL1853	MGL1916
MDL945CSX	MGL1670	MGL1731	MGL1792	MGL1854	MGL1917
MDL946CSX	MGL1671	MGL1732	MGL1793	MGL1855	MGL1918
MDL947CSX	MGL1672	MGL1733	MGL1794	MGL1856	MGL1919
MDL948CSX	MGL1673	MGL1734	MGL1795	MGL1857	MGL1920
MDL949CSX	MGL1674	MGL1735	MGL1796	MGL1858	MGL1921
MDL950CSX	MGL1675	MGL1736	MGL1797	MGL1859	MGL1922
MDL951CSX	MGL1676	MGL1737	MGL1798	MGL1860	MGL1923
MDL952CSX	MGL1677	MGL1738	MGL1799	MGL1861	MGL1924
MDL953CSX	MGL1678	MGL1739	MGL1800	MGL1863	MGL1925
MDL954CSX	MGL1679	MGL1740	MGL1801	MGL1864	MGL1926
MDL955CSX	MGL1680	MGL1741	MGL1802	MGL1865	MGL1927
MGL001TS	MGL1681	MGL1742	MGL1803	MGL1866	MGL1928
MGL002TS	MGL1682	MGL1743	MGL1804	MGL1867	MGL1929
MGL003TS	MGL1683	MGL1744	MGL1805	MGL1868	MGL1930
MGL004TS	MGL1684	MGL1745	MGL1806	MGL1869	MGL1931
MGL005TS	MGL1685	MGL1746	MGL1807	MGL1870	MCL1932
MGL006TS	MGL1686	MCL1747	MGL1808	MGL1871	MGL1933
MGL007TS	MGL1687	MGL1748	MGL1809	MGL1872	MGL1934
MGL008TS	MGL1688	MGL1749	MGL1810	MGL1873	MGL1935
MGL009TS	MGL1689	MGL1750	MGL1811	MGL1874	MGL1936
MGL010TS	MGL1690 -	MGL1751	MGL1812	MGL1875	MGL1938
MGL930SB	TESCO	MGL1752	MGL1813	MGL1877	MGL1939
MGL931SB	MGL1692	MGL1753	MGL1814	MGL1878	MGL1940
MGL933SB	MGL1693	MGL1754	MGL1815	MGL1879	MGL1941
MGL934SB	MGL1694	MGL1755	MGL1816	MGL1880	MGL1942
MGL1507GN	MGL1695	MGL1756	MGL1817	MGL1881	MGL1943

Maritime Trailers

MGL1944	MGL2005	MGL2066	MGL2126	MGL2189	MGL2259
MGL1945	MGL2006	MGL2067	MGL2127	MGL2190	MGL2260
MGL1946	MGL2007	MGL2068	MGL2129	MGL2191	MGL2261
MGL1947	MGL2008	MGL2069	MGL2130	MGL2192	MGL2262
MGL1948	MGL2009	MGL2070	MGL2131	MGL2193	MGL2263
MGL1949	MGL2011	MGL2071	MGL2132	MGL2194	MGL2264
MGL1950	MGL2012	MGL2072	MGL2133	MGL2195	MGL2265
MGL1951	MGL2013	MGL2073	MGL2134	MGL2196	MGL2266
MGL1952	MGL2014	MGL2074	MGL2135	MGL2197	MGL2267
MGL1953	MGL2015	MGL2075	MGL2136	MGL2198	MGL2268
MGL1954	MGL2016	MGL2076	MGL2137	MGL2199	MGL2269
MGL1955	MGL2017	MGL2077	MGL2138	MGL2200	MGL2270
MGL1956	MGL2018	MGL2078	MGL2139	MGL2201	MGL2271
MGL1957	MGL2019	MGL2079	MGL2140	MGL2210	MGL2272
MGL1958	MGL2020	MGL2080	MGL2141	MGL2211	MGL2273
MGL1959	MGL2021	MGL2081	MGL2142	MGL2212	MGL2274
MGL1960	MGL2022	MGL2082	MGL2144	MGL2213	MGL2275
MGL1961	MGL2023	MGL2083	MGL2145	MGL2214	MGL2276
MGL1962	MGL2024	MGL2084	MGL2146	MGL2215	MGL2277
MGL1963	MGL2025	MGL2085	MGL2147	MGL2216	MGL2278
MGL1965	MGL2026	MGL2086	MGL2148	MGL2217	MGL2279
MGL1966	MGL2027	MGL2087	MGL2149	MGL2218	MGL2280
MGL1967	MGL2028	MGL2088	MGL2150	MGL2219	MGL2281
MGL1968	MGL2029	MGL2089	MGL2151	MGL2220	MGL2282
MGL1969	MGL2030	MGL2090	MGL2152	MGL2221	MGL2283
MGL1970	MGL2031	MGL2091	MGL2153	MGL2222	MGL2284
MGL1971	MGL2032	MGL2092	MGL2154	MGL2223	MGL2285
MGL1972	MGL2033	MGL2093	MGL2155	MGL2224	MGL2286
MGL1973	MGL2034	MGL2094	MGL2156	MGL2225	MGL2287
MGL1974	MGL2035	MGL2095	MGL2157	MGL2226	MGL2288
MGL1975	MGL2036	MGL2096	MGL2158	MGL2227	MGL2289
MGL1976	MGL2037	MGL2097	MGL2159	MGL2228	MGL2291
MGL1977	MGL2038	MGL2098	MGL2160	MGL2229	MGL2292
MGL1978	MGL2039	MGL2099	MGL2161	MGL2230	MGL2293
MGL1979	MGL2040	MGL2100	MGL2162	MGL2231	MGL2294
MGL1980	MGL2041	MGL2101	MGL2163	MGL2232	MGL2295
MGL1981	MGL2042	MGL2102	MGL2164	MGL2234	MGL2296
MGL1982	MGL2043	MGL2103	MGL2165	MGL2235	MGL2297
MGL1983	MGL2044	MGL2104	MGL2166	MGL2236	MGL2298
MGL1984	MGL2045	MGL2105	MGL2167	MGL2237	MGL2299
MGL1985	MGL2046	MGL2106	MGL2168	MGL2238	MGL2300
MGL1986	MGL2047	MGL2107	MGL2169	MGL2239	MGL2301
MGL1987	MGL2048	MGL2108	MGL2170	MGL2240	MGL2302
MGL1988	MGL2049	MGL2109	MGL2171	MGL2241	MGL2303
MGL1989	MGL2050	MGL2110	MGL2172	MGL2243	MGL2304
MGL1990	MGL2051	MGL2111	MGL2173	MGL2244	MGL2305
MGL1991	MGL2052	MGL2112	MGL2175	MGL2245	MGL2306
MGL1992	MGL2053	MGL2113	MGL2176	MGL2246	MGL2307
MGL1993	MGL2054	MGL2114	MGL2177	MGL2247	MGL2308
MGL1994	MGL2055	MGL2115	MGL2178	MGL2248	MGL2309
MGL1995	MGL2056	MGL2116	MGL2179	MGL2249	MGL2310
MGL1996	MGL2057	MGL2117	MGL2180	MGL2250	MGL2311
MGL1997	MGL2058	MGL2118	MGL2181	MGL2251	MGL2312
MGL1998	MGL2059	MGL2119	MGL2182	MGL2252	MGL2313
MGL1999	MGL2060	MGL2120	MGL2183	MGL2253	MGL2314
MGL2000	MGL2061	MGL2121	MGL2184	MGL2254	MGL2315
MGL2001	MGL2062	MGL2122	MGL2185	MGL2255	MGL2316
MGL2002	MGL2063	MGL2123	MGL2186	MGL2256	MGL2317
MGL2003	MGL2064	MGL2124	MGL2187	MGL2257	MGL2318
MGL2004	MGL2065	MGL2125	MGL2188	MGL2258	MGL2319

Maritime Trailers

MGL2320	MGL2380	MGL2441	MGL2501	MGL2562	MGL2622
MGL2321	MGL2381	MGL2442	MGL2502	MGL2563	MGL2623
MGL2322	MGL2382	MGL2443	MGL2503	MGL2564	MGL2624
MGL2323	MGL2383	MGL2444	MGL2504	MGL2565	MGL2625
MGL2324	MGL2384	MGL2445	MGL2505	MGL2566	MGL2626
MGL2325	MGL2385	MGL2446	MGL2506	MGL2567	MGL2627
MGL2326	MGL2386	MGL2447	MGL2507	MGL2568	MGL2628
TESCO	MGL2387	MGL2448	MGL2508	MGL2569	MGL2629
MGL2327	MGL2388	MGL2449	MGL2509	MGL2570	MGL2630
MGL2328	MGL2389	MGL2450	MGL2510	MGL2571	MGL2631
MGL2329	MGL2390	MGL2451	MGL2511	MGL2572	MGL2632
MGL2330	MGL2391	MGL2452	MGL2512	MGL2573	MGL2633
MGL2331	MGL2392	MGL2453	MGL2513	MGL2574	MGL2634
MGL2332	MGL2393	MGL2454GS	MGL2514	MGL2575	MGL2635
MGL2333	MGL2394	MGL2455GS	MGL2515	MGL2576	MGL2636
MGL2334	MGL2395	MGL2456GS	MGL2516	MGL2577	MGL2637
MGL2335	MGL2396	MGL2457GS	MGL2517	MGL2578	MGL2638
MGL2336	MGL2397	MGL2458GS	MGL2518	MGL2579	MGL2639
MGL2337	MGL2398	MGL2459GS	MGL2519	MGL2580	MGL2640
MGL2338	MGL2399	MGL2460GS	MGL2520	MGL2581	MGL2641
MGL2339	MGL2400	MGL2461GS	MGL2521	MGL2582	MGL2642
MGL2340	MGL2401	MGL2462GS	MGL2522	MGL2583	MGL2643
MGL2341	MGL2402	MGL2463GS	MGL2523	MGL2584	MGL2644
MGL2342	MGL2403	MGL2464D	MGL2524	MGL2585	MGL2645
MGL2343	MGL2404	MGL2465-ST	MGL2525	MGL2586	MGL2646
MGL2344	MGL2405	MGL2466-ST	MGL2526	MGL2587	MGL2647
MGL2345	MGL2406	MGL2467-ST	MGL2527	MGL2588	MGL2648
MGL2346	MGL2407	MGL2468-ST	MGL2528	MGL2589	MGL2649
MGL2347	MGL2408	MGL2469-ST	MGL2529	MGL2590	MGL2650
MGL2348	MGL2409	MGL2470-ST	MGL2531	MGL2591	MGL2651
MGL2349	MGL2410	MGL2471-ST	MGL2532	MGL2592	MGL2652
MGL2350	MGL2411	MGL2472-ST	MGL2533	MGL2593	MGL2653
MGL2351	MGL2412	MGL2473-ST	MGL2534	MGL2594	MGL2654
MGL2352	MGL2413	MGL2474-ST	MGL2535	MGL2595	MGL2655
MGL2353	MGL2414	MGL2475-ST	MGL2536	MGL2596	MGL2656
MGL2354	MGL2415	MGL2476-ST	MGL2537	MGL2597	MGL2657
MGL2355	MGL2416	MGL2477-ST	MGL2538	MGL2598	MGL2658
MGL2356	MGL2417	MGL2478-ST	MGL2539	MGL2599	MGL2659
MGL2357	MGL2418	MGL2479-ST	MGL2540	MGL2600	MGL2660
MGL2358	MGL2419	MGL2480-ST	MGL2541	MGL2601	MGL2661
MGL2359	MGL2420	MGL2481-ST	MGL2542	MGL2602	MGL2662
MGL2360	MGL2421	MGL2482-ST	MGL2543	MGL2603	MGL2663
MGL2361	MGL2422	MGL2483-ST	MGL2544	MGL2604	MGL2664
MGL2362	MGL2423	MGL2484-ST	MGL2545	MGL2605	MGL2665
MGL2363	MGL2424	MGL2485-ST	MGL2546	MGL2606	MGL2666
MGL2364	MGL2425	MGL2486-ST	MGL2547	MGL2607	MGL2667
MGL2365	MGL2426	MGL2487-ST	MGL2548	MGL2608	MGL2668
MGL2367	MGL2427	MGL2488-ST	MGL2549	MGL2609	MGL2669
MGL2368	MGL2428	MGL2489-ST	MGL2550	MGL2610	MGL2670
MGL2369	MGL2429	MGL2490	MGL2551	MGL2611	MCL2071
MGL2370	MCL2430	MGL2491	MGL2552	MGL2612	MGL2672
MGL2371	MGL2431	MGL2492	MGL2553	MGL2613	MGL2673
MGL2372	MGL2433	MGL2493	MGL2554	MGL2614	MGL2674
MGL2373	MGL2434	MGL2494	MGL2555	MGL2615	MGL2675
MGL2374	MGL2435	MGL2495	MGL2556	MGL2616	MGL2676
MGL2375	MGL2436	MGL2496	MGL2557	MGL2617	MGL2677
MGL2376	MGL2437	MGL2497	MGL2558	MGL2618	MGL2678
MGL2377	MGL2438	MGL2498	MGL2559	MGL2619	MGL2679
MGL2378	MGL2439	MGL2499	MGL2560	MGL2620	MGL2680GS
MGL2379	MGL2440	MGL2500	MGL2561	MGL2621	MGL2681GS

MGL2682GS	MGL2761	MGL2821	MGL2881	MGL2941	MGL3001
MGL2683GS	MGL2762	MGL2822	MGL2882	MGL2942	MGL3002
MGL2684GS	MGL2763	MGL2823	MGL2883	MGL2943	MGL3003
MGL2685GS	MGL2764	MGL2824	MGL2884	MGL2944	MGL3004
MGL2686GS	MGL2765	MGL2825	MGL2885	MGL2945	MGL3005
MGL2687GS	MGL2766	MGL2826	MGL2886	MGL2946	MGL3006
MGL2688GS	MGL2767	MGL2827	MGL2887	MGL2947	MGL3007
MGL2689GS	MGL2768	MGL2828	MGL2888	MGL2948	MGL3008
MGL2700	MGL2769	MGL2829	MGL2889	MGL2949	MGL3009
MGL2706	MGL2770	MGL2830	MGL2890	MGL2950	MGL3010
MGL2710	MGL2771	MGL2831	MGL2891	MGL2951	MGL3011
MGL2711	MGL2772	MGL2832	MGL2892	MGL2952	MGL3012
MGL2712	MGL2773	MGL2833	MGL2893	MGL2953	MGL3013
MGL2713	MGL2774	MGL2834	MGL2894	MGL2954	MGL3014
MGL2714	MGL2775	MGL2835	MGL2895	MGL2955	MGL3015
MGL2715	MGL2776	MGL2836	MGL2896	MGL2956	MGL3016
MGL2716	MGL2777	MGL2837	MGL2897	MGL2957	MGL3017
MGL2717	MGL2778	MGL2838	MGL2898	MGL2958	MGL3018
MGL2718	MGL2779	MGL2839	MGL2899	MGL2959	MGL3019
MGL2720	MGL2780	MGL2840	MGL2900	MGL2960	MGL3020
MGL2721	MGL2781	MGL2841	MGL2901	MGL2961	MGL3021
MGL2722	MGL2782	MGL2842	MGL2902	MGL2962	MGL3022
MGL2723	MGL2783	MGL2843	MGL2903	MGL2963	MGL3023
MGL2724	MGL2784	MGL2844	MGL2904	MGL2964	MGL3024
MGL2725	MGL2785	MGL2845	MGL2905	MGL2965	MGL3025
MGL2726	MGL2786	MGL2846	MGL2906	MGL2966	MGL3026
MGL2727	MGL2787	MGL2847	MGL2907	MGL2967	MGL3027
MGL2728	MGL2788	MGL2848	MGL2908	MGL2968	MGL3028
MGL2729	MGL2789	MGL2849	MGL2909	MGL2969	MGL3029
MGL2730	MGL2790	MGL2850	MGL2910	MGL2970	MGL3030
MGL2731	MGL2791	MGL2851	MGL2911	MGL2971	MGL3031
MGL2732	MGL2792	MGL2852	MGL2912	MGL2972	MGL3032
MGL2733	MGL2793	MGL2853	MGL2913	MGL2973	MGL3033
MGL2734	MGL2794	MGL2854	MGL2914	MGL2974	MGL3034
MGL2735	MGL2795	MGL2855ONE	MGL2915	MGL2975	MGL3035
MGL2736	MGL2796	MGL2856ONE	MGL2916	MGL2976	MGL3036
MGL2737	MGL2797	MGL2857ONE	MGL2917	MGL2977	MGL3037
MGL2738	MGL2798	MGL2858ONE	MGL2918	MGL2978	MGL3038
MGL2739	MGL2799	MGL2859ONE	MGL2919	MGL2979	MGL3039
MGL2740	MGL2800	MGL2860GS	MGL2920	MGL2980	MGL3040
MGL2741	MGL2801	MGL2861GS	MGL2921	MGL2981	MGL3041
MGL2742	MGL2802	MGL2862GS	MGL2922	MGL2982	MGL3042
MGL2743	MGL2803	MGL2863GS	MGL2923	MGL2983	MGL3043
MGL2744	MGL2804	MGL2864GS	MGL2924	MGL2984	MGL3044
MGL2745	MGL2805	MGL2865GS	MGL2925	MGL2985	MGL3045
MGL2746	MGL2806	MGL2866GS	MGL2926	MGL2986	MGL3046
MGL2747	MGL2807	MGL2867GS	MGL2927	MGL2987	MGL3047
MGL2748	MGL2808	MGL2868GS	MGL2928	MGL2988	MGL3048
MGL2749	MGL2809	MGL2869GS	MGL2929	MGL2989	MGL3049
MGL2750	MGL2810	MGL2870	MGL2930	MGL2990	MGL3050
MGL2751	MGL2811	MGL2871	MGL2931	MGL2991	MGL3051
MGL2752	MGL2812	MGL2872	MGL2932	MGL2992	MGL3052
MGL2753	MGL2813	MGL2873	MGL2933	MGL2993	MGL3053
MGL2754	MGL2814	MGL2874	MGL2934	MGL2994	MGL3054
MGL2755	MGL2815	MGL2875	MGL2935	MGL2995	MGL3055
MGL2756	MGL2816	MGL2876	MGL2936	MGL2996	MGL3056
MGL2757	MGL2817	MGL2877	MGL2937	MGL2997	MGL3057
MGL2758	MGL2818	MGL2878	MGL2938	MGL2998	MGL3058
MGL2759	MGL2819	MGL2879	MGL2939	MGL2999	MGL3059
MGL2760	MGL2820	MGL2880	MGL2940	MGL3000	MGL3060

Maritime Trailers

MGL3061	MGL3121FS	MGL3181	MGL3241	MGL3301	MGL3361
MGL3062	MGL3122FS	MGL3182	MGL3242	MGL3302	MGL3362
MGL3063	MGL3123FS	MGL3183	MGL3243	MGL3303	MGL3363
MGL3064	MGL3124FS	MGL3184	MGL3244	MGL3304	MGL3364
MGL3065	MGL3125FS	MGL3185	MGL3245	MGL3305	MGL3365
MGL3066	MGL3126FS	MGL3186	MGL3246	MGL3306	MGL3366
MGL3067	MGL3127FS	MGL3187	MGL3247	MGL3307	MGL3367
MGL3068	MGL3128FS	MGL3188	MGL3248	MGL3308	MGL3368
MGL3069	MGL3129FS	MGL3189	MGL3249	MGL3309	MGL3369
MGL3070FOR	MGL3130FS	MGL3190	MGL3250	MGL3310	MGL3370
MGL3071FOR	MGL3131FS	MGL3191	MGL3251	MGL3311	MGL3371
MGL3072FOR	MGL3132FS	MGL3192	MGL3252	MGL3312	MGL3372
MGL3073FOR	MGL3133FS	MGL3193	MGL3253	MGL3313	MGL3373
MGL3074FOR	MGL3134FS	MGL3194	MGL3254	MGL3314	MGL3374
MGL3075FOR	MGL3135FS	MGL3195	MGL3255	MGL3315	MGL3375
MGL3076FOR	MGL3136FS	MGL3196	MGL3256	MGL3316	MGL3376
MGL3077FOR	MGL3137FS	MGL3197	MGL3257	MGL3317	MGL3377
MGL3078FOR	MGL3138FS	MGL3198	MGL3258	MGL3318	MGL3378
MGL3079FOR	MGL3139FS	MGL3199	MGL3259	MGL3319	MGL3379
MGL3080FS	MGL3140FS	MGL3200	MGL3260	MGL3320	MGL3380
MGL3081FS	MGL3141FS	MGL3201	MGL3261	MGL3321	MGL3381
MGL3082FS	MGL3142FS	MGL3202	MGL3262	MGL3322	MGL3382
MGL3083FS	MGL3143FS	MGL3203	MGL3263	MGL3323	MGL3383
MGL3084FS	MGL3144FS	MGL3204	MGL3264	MGL3324	MGL3384
MGL3085FS	MGL3145FS	MGL3205	MGL3265	MGL3325	MGL3385
MGL3086FS	MGL3146FS	MGL3206	MGL3266	MGL3326	MGL3386
MGL3087FS	MGL3147FS	MGL3207	MGL3267	MGL3327	MGL3387
MGL3088FS	MGL3148FS	MGL3208	MGL3268	MGL3328	MGL3388
MGL3089FS	MGL3149FS	MGL3209	MGL3269	MGL3329	MGL3389
MGL3090FS	MGL3150FS	MGL3210	MGL3270	MGL3330	MGL3390
MGL3091FS	MGL3151FS	MGL3211	MGL3271	MGL3331	MGL3391
MGL3092FS	MGL3152FS	MGL3212	MGL3272	MGL3332	MGL3392
MGL3093FS	MGL3153FS	MGL3213	MGL3273	MGL3333	MGL3393
MGL3094FS	MGL3154FS	MGL3214	MGL3274	MGL3334	MGL3394
MGL3095FS	MGL3155FS	MGL3215	MGL3275	MGL3335	MGL3395
MGL3096FS	MGL3156FS	MGL3216	MGL3276	MGL3336	MGL3396
MGL3097FS	MGL3157FS	MGL3217	MGL3277	MGL3337	MGL3397
MGL3098FS	MGL3158FS	MGL3218	MGL3278	MGL3338	MGL3398
MGL3099FS	MGL3159FS	MGL3219	MGL3279	MGL3339	MGL3399
MGL3100FS	MGL3160FS	MGL3220	MGL3280	MGL3340	MGL3400
MGL3101FS	MGL3161FS	MGL3221	MGL3281	MGL3341	MGL3401
MGL3102FS	MGL3162FS	MGL3222	MGL3282	MGL3342	MGL3402
MGL3103FS	MGL3163FS	MGL3223	MGL3283	MGL3343	MGL3403
MGL3104FS	MGL3164FS	MGL3224	MGL3284	MGL3344	MGL3404
MGL3105FS	MGL3165FS	MGL3225	MGL3285	MGL3345	MGL3405
MGL3106FS	MGL3166FS	MGL3226	MGL3286	MGL3346	MGL3406
MGL3107FS	MGL3167FS	MGL3227	MGL3287	MGL3347	MGL3407
MGL3108FS	MGL3168FS	MGL3228	MGL3288	MGL3348	MGL3408
MGL3109FS	MGL3169FS	MGL3229	MGL3289	MGL3349	MGL3409
MGL3110FS	MGL3170FS	MGL3230	MGL3290	MCL3350	MGL3410
MGL3111FS	MGL3171FS	MGL3231	MGL3291	MGL3351	MGL3411
MGL3112FS	MGL3172FS	MGL3232	MGL3292	MGL3352	MGL3412
MGL3113FS	MGL3173FS	MGL3233	MGL3293	MGL3353	MGL3413
MGL3114FS	MGL3174FS	MGL3234	MGL3294	MGL3354	MGL3414
MGL3115FS	MGL3175FS	MGL3235	MGL3295	MGL3355	MGL3415
MGL3116FS	MGL3176FS	MGL3236	MGL3296	MGL3356	MGL3416
MGL3117FS	MGL3177FS	MGL3237	MGL3297	MGL3357	MGL3417
MGL3118FS	MGL3178FS	MGL3238	MGL3298	MGL3358	MGL3418
MGL3119FS	MGL3179	MGL3239	MGL3299	MGL3359	MGL3419
MGL3120FS	MGL3180	MGL3240	MGL3300	MGL3360	MGL3420

Maritime Trailers

MGL3421	MGL3481FS	MGL3541	MGL3601	MGL3661	MGL3721
MGL3422	MGL3482FS	MGL3542	MGL3602	MGL3662	MGL3722
MGL3423	MGL3483FS	MGL3543	MGL3603	MGL3663	MGL3723
MGL3424	MGL3484FS	MGL3544	MGL3604	MGL3664	MGL3724
MGL3425	MGL3485FS	MGL3545	MGL3605	MGL3665	MGL3725
MGL3426	MGL3486FS	MGL3546	MGL3606	MGL3666	MGL3726
MGL3427	MGL3487FS	MGL3547	MGL3607	MGL3667	MGL3727
MGL3428	MGL3488FS	MGL3548	MGL3608	MGL3668	MGL3728
MGL3429FS	MGL3489FS	MGL3549	MGL3609	MGL3669	ORSAM632
MGL3430FS	MGL3490FS	MGL3550	MGL3610	MGL3670	ORSAM662
MGL3431FS	MGL3491FS	MGL3551	MGL3611	MGL3671	ORSAM2059
MGL3432FS	MGL3492FS	MGL3552	MGL3612	MGL3672	OT677
MGL3433FS	MGL3493FS	MGL3553	MGL3613	MGL3673	WCL715
MGL3434FS	MGL3494FS	MGL3554	MGL3614	MGL3674	WCL716
MGL3435FS	MGL3495FS	MGL3555	MGL3615	MGL3675	WCL717
MGL3436FS	MGL3496FS	MGL3556	MGL3616	MGL3676	WCL718
MGL3437FS	MGL3497FS	MGL3557	MGL3617	MGL3677	WCL719
MGL3438FS	MGL3498FS	MGL3558	MGL3618	MGL3678	WCL720
MGL3439FS	MGL3499FS	MGL3559	MGL3619	MGL3679	WCL721
MGL3440FS	MGL3500FS	MGL3560	MGL3620	MGL3680	WCL722
MGL3441FS	MGL3501FS	MGL3561	MGL3621	MGL3681	WCL723
MGL3442FS	MGL3502FS	MGL3562	MGL3622	MGL3682	WCL724
MGL3443FS	MGL3503FS	MGL3563	MGL3623	MGL3683	WCL725
MGL3444FS	MGL3504FS	MGL3564	MGL3624	MGL3684	WCL726
MGL3445FS	MGL3505FS	MGL3565	MGL3625	MGL3685	WCL727
MGL3446FS	MGL3506FS	MGL3566	MGL3626	MGL3686	WCL728
MGL3447FS	MGL3507FS	MGL3567	MGL3627	MGL3687	WCL729
MGL3448FS	MGL3508FS	MGL3568	MGL3628	MGL3688	WCL730
MGL3449FS	MGL3509FS	MGL3569	MGL3629	MGL3689	WCL731
MGL3450FS	MGL3510FS	MGL3570	MGL3630	MGL3690	WCL732
MGL3451FS	MGL3511FS	MGL3571	MGL3631	MGL3691	WCL733
MGL3452FS	MGL3512FS	MGL3572	MGL3632	MGL3692	WCL734
MGL3453FS	MGL3513FS	MGL3573	MGL3633	MGL3693	WCL735
MGL3454FS	MGL3514FS	MGL3574	MGL3634	MGL3694	WCL736
MGL3455FS	MGL3515FS	MGL3575	MGL3635	MGL3695	WCL737
MGL3456FS	MGL3516FS	MGL3576	MGL3636	MGL3696	WCL738
MGL3457FS	MGL3517FS	MGL3577	MGL3637	MGL3697	WCL739
MGL3458FS	MGL3518FS	MGL3578	MGL3638	MGL3698	WCL740
MGL3459FS	MGL3519FS	MGL3579	MGL3639	MGL3699	WCL741
MGL3460FS	MGL3520FS	MGL3580	MGL3640	MGL3700	WCL742
MGL3461FS	MGL3521FS	MGL3581	MGL3641	MGL3701	WCL743
MGL3462FS	MGL3522FS	MGL3582	MGL3642	MGL3702	WCL744
MGL3463FS	MGL3523FS	MGL3583	MGL3643	MGL3703	WCL745
MGL3464FS	MGL3524FS	MGL3584	MGL3644	MGL3704	WCL746
MGL3465FS	MGL3525FS	MGL3585	MGL3645	MGL3705	WCL747
MGL3466FS	MGL3526FS	MGL3586	MGL3646	MGL3706	WCL748
MGL3467FS	MGL3527FS	MGL3587	MGL3647	MGL3707	WCL750
MGL3468FS	MGL3528FS	MGL3588	MGL3648	MGL3708	WCL751
MGL3469FS	MGL3529	MGL3589	MGL3649	MGL3709	WCL752
MGL3470FS	MGL3530	MGL3590	MGL3650	MGL3710	WCL753
MGL3471FS	MGL3531	MGL3591	MGL3651	MGL3711	WCL754
MGL3472FS	MGL3532	MGL3592	MGL3652	MGL3712	WCL755
MGL3473FS	MGL3533	MGL3593	MGL3653	MGL3713	WCL756
MGL3474FS	MGL3534	MGL3594	MGL3654	MGL3714	WCL757
MGL3475FS	MGL3535	MGL3595	MGL3655	MGL3715	WCL758
MGL3476FS	MGL3536	MGL3596	MGL3656	MGL3716	WCL759
MGL3477FS	MGL3537	MGL3597	MGL3657	MGL3717	WCL760
MGL3478FS	MGL3538	MGL3598	MGL3658	MGL3718	WCL761
MGL3479FS	MGL3539	MGL3599	MGL3659	MGL3719	WCL762
MGL3480FS	MGL3540	MGL3600	MGL3660	MGL3720	WCL763

WCL764	WCL796	WCL824	WCL854	WCL884	WCL914
WCL765	WCL797	WCL825	WCL855	WCL885	WCL915
WCL766	WCL798	WCL826	WCL856	WCL886	WCL916
WCL767	WCL799	WCL827	WCL857	WCL887	WCL918
WCL768	WCL800	WCL828	WCL858	WCL888	WCL919
WCL769	WCL801	WCL829	WCL859	WCL889	WCL920
WCL771	WCL802	WCL830	WCL860	WCL890	WCL921
WCL772	WCL803	WCL831	WCL861	WCL891	WCL922
WCL773	WCL804	WCL832	WCL862	WCL893	WCL923
WCL774	WCL805	WCL833	WCL863	WCL894	WCL924
WCL775	WCL806	WCL834	WCL864	WCL895	WCL925
WCL776	WCL807	WCL836	WCL865	WCL896	WCL926
WCL777	WCL808	WCL837	WCL866	WCL897	WCL929
WCL778	WCL809	WCL838	WCL867	WCL898	WCL930
WCL779	WCL810	WCL839	WCL869	WCL899	WCL931
WCL781	WCL811	WCL841	WCL870	WCL900	WCL932
WCL782	WCL812	WCL842	WCL871	WCL901	WCL933
WCL784	WCL813	WCL843	WCL872	WCL902	WCL935
WCL785	WCL814	WCL844	WCL873	WCL903	WCL936
WCL786	WCL815	WCL845	WCL874	WCL904	WCL937
WCL787	WCL816	WCL846	WCL875	WCL906	WCL938
WCL788	WCL817	WCL847	WCL876	WCL907	WCL939
WCL789	WCL818	WCL848	WCL877	WCL908	WGS01
WCL790	WCL819	WCL849	WCL878	WCL909	WGS02
WCL791	WCL820	WCL850	WCL880	WCL910	WGS03
WCL792	WCL821	WCL851	WCL881	WCL911	WGS04
WCL793	WCL822	WCL852	WCL882	WCL912	WGS05
WCL795	WCL823	WCL853	WCL883	WCL913	

Notes

Handwritten notes:

FUML
3408

Column 1: 466, 1064, 1083, 1135, 1155, 3462, 1138, 3487, 1074, 1092, 1079, 1128, 1156, 1177, 1161, 1084, 1076, 1133, 1118, 1131, 1121, 1069, 1091, 1142, 1182

Column 2: 1138, 1064, 1083, 1060, 1075, 1078, 1070, 1066, 1074, 1062, 1069, 1065, 1123, 1166, 1143, 1081, 1062, 1090, 1077, 1088, 1071, 1179, 1191

YE67 USD TET
YL72 MBX TET

R28 BMT RED.
PX73 VNG AWS
PX73 VKN AWS
LS0? WHM
YY73 EKK Longs
PF73 KUA WS
RN24 DLT KMS
ET570 xplore
PN24 AVD WS
PN24 DVW XPl
PN24 DTW xPl
PN24 DVL XCl
PN24 DVX
PN24 APL KMS

ET550
6x 1285
6x 1282
6x 1253
6x 1242
6x 1234
6x 1239
6x 1303
x6 1300
6x 1276

ET543
ET547
ET576
HTT833
HTT834
ET542

SCT 0157
AVO 11136

232   16715   181 - 28650
1320   23208   162 33860
161   25193   34 NEO
232   10496   43 NEO
231   43513   49 NEO
232 236 23211   72 NEO
191   49852   50 NEO
                    39 NEO

Major UK HGV Fleets 2024